# LITERATURE

## ⟶ 150 ⟵
# MASTERPIECES OF FICTION, POETRY, AND DRAMA

*Edited by*
## BEVERLY LAWN
### ADELPHI UNIVERSITY

ST. MARTIN'S PRESS
New York

*Senior editor:* Mark Gallaher
*Managing editor:* Patricia Mansfield
*Development editor:* Julie Nord
*Project editor:* Erica Townsend
*Production associate:* Katherine Battiste
*Text and cover design:* Celine Brandes
*Cover photo:* Joel Meyerowitz © 1990


Library of Congress Catalog Card Number: 89-63914
Manufactured in the United States of America.
54321
fedcba

*For information, write:*
St. Martin's Press, Inc.
175 Fifth Avenue
New York, NY 10010

ISBN: 0-312-02357-X

## Acknowledgments

**Sherwood Anderson.** "Death in the Woods" reprinted by permission
of Harold Ober Associates Incorporated. Copyright 1926 by The American
Mercury, Inc. Copyright renewed 1953 by Eleanor Copenhaver Anderson.

**John Ashbery.** "Paradoxes and Oxymorons" from *Shadow Train* by
John Ashbery. Copyright © 1980, 1981 by John Ashbery. Reprinted by
permission of the publisher, Viking Penguin, a division of Penguin Books
USA Inc.

**Margaret Atwood.** "Book of Ancestors" from *Circe/Mud Poems* in
*Selected Poems, 1965–1975* by Margaret Atwood. Copyright © 1976 by
Margaret Atwood. Reprinted by permission of Houghton Mifflin Com-
pany. "Game after Supper" from *Procedures for Underground* in *Selected*

Acknowledgments and copyrights are continued at the back of the book
on pages 961–969, which constitute an extension of the copyright page.

# PREFACE

The only true introduction to literature lies in the reading of literary works of top quality, high interest, and great diversity. The aim in creating *Literature: 150 Masterpieces of Fiction, Poetry, and Drama* has been to maintain a constant focus in the minds of instructors and students on that one essential, invigorating experience. Therefore, the first and most important step in compiling this new anthology was to select a group of works that students would find engrossing, wonderfully varied, familiar at times, exotic at others, and generous in providing balanced samplings of the major periods, styles, genres, and elements of literature.

The forty short stories, one hundred poems, and ten plays collected in *Literature: 150 Masterpieces of Fiction, Poetry, and Drama* exemplify these qualities of excellence, excitement, and variety. Included are works that are widely considered indispensable to an appreciation of our literary inheritance. Writings by Nathaniel Hawthorne, D. H. Lawrence, James Joyce, Flannery O'Connor; the late medieval lyricists and balladeers, John Milton, William Blake, William Wordsworth, Walt Whitman, Emily Dickinson; Sophocles, William Shakespeare, Henrik Ibsen, and Anton Chekhov are just a part of the rich representation of literature's great traditions compiled here.

Although *Literature: 150 Masterpieces* is deliberately classical, reflecting and affirming the wealth of our literary history and tradition, it also stands for the view that history and tradition are ongoing processes that broaden and refocus even as anthologies such as this one are published and revised. A further purpose, therefore, was to show the true diversity of literary voices within the English-speaking nations—specifically, to include a fair representation of works by women and minority writers. The result is the inclusion of fifteen stories, twenty-five poems, and two plays by women, and five stories, eight poems, and one play by American minority writers—to our knowledge a better selection of such works than is achieved by any anthology of comparable length and price.

As communication and commerce among the many cultures of our world have expanded and quickened, readers have grown eager for exposure to the literature of other nations. The burgeoning discipline of comparative or world literature reflects this growing interest; an introductory literary anthology must do so as well. So this anthology includes superior translations of works by Gabriela Mistral, Pablo Neruda, Gabriel García Márquez, Guy de Maupassant, Eugène Ionesco, Feodor Dostoevsky, Leo Tolstoy, Anton Chekhov, Arcadii Averchenko, Franz Kafka, Isaac Bashevis Singer, and Tomasso Landolfi, in addition to Sophocles—thirteen works in all.

The selections included in *Literature: 150 Masterpieces* to address the need for broader representation of diverse literary voices are never marginal or obscure. Writers such as Langston Hughes, Ralph Ellison, Marianne Moore, Adrienne Rich, and Joyce Carol Oates are indisputably important literary figures; yet anthologists too often neglect them. This anthology seeks to claim places for such writers in our courses. It also seeks to open the door on a select group of recent writers whose works strike widely resonant chords in readers of many backgrounds, writers who have gained—or are quickly gaining—major stature: fiction writers Grace Paley, Raymond Carver, Jayne Anne Phillips, and Ann Beattie; poets Robert Hayden, David Ignatow, Louis Simpson, Robert Bly, Galway Kinnell, Lucille Clifton, Margaret Atwood, Seamus Heaney, Carolyn Forché, and Jimmy Santiago Baca; and dramatists Ed Bullins and Marsha Norman are some of these fresh, compelling voices that capture our own world and time so brilliantly. They have been all too infrequently anthologized up to now; this is unfortunate, since they provide all the evidence that any student needs to realize that literature is a vital voice in the world we inhabit.

This anthology also attempts to present works that have long been highly esteemed but less frequently taught. Because such works are likely to be new to students—and less overworked by instructors—both can perhaps come to their study with enthusiastic and open minds. The selections by Franz Kafka, Katherine Anne Porter, Isaac Bashevis Singer, Bernard Malamud, Peter Taylor, Flannery O'Connor, William Carlos Williams, D. H. Lawrence, Elizabeth Bishop, Randall Jarrell, Robert Lowell, and Sylvia Plath are examples of these alternatives to the usual, sometimes too familiar selections. Finally, to encourage comparative and in-depth study of individual writers, this book includes two poems by each of nineteen poets as well as works in two genres by Shakespeare, D. H. Lawrence, and Langston Hughes.

In keeping with the focus on the quality and diversity of the reading experience, *Literature: 150 Masterpieces* orders its selections in the most straightforward way possible—chronologically by author in each genre. Thus, students can experience the works first, and then reflect and perhaps comment and write on the changes in content, style, diction, and structure that literature has undergone through the centuries. Instructors are free to call attention to these developments as often as they like—or not at all.

*Literature: 150 Masterpieces* does not impose a historical focus on its users; nor does it impose a course structure based on thematic connections or on the study of literary styles, devices, or elements. Instructors using this book will have maximum flexibility in stressing these aspects of literature. And they will find this anthology, because of its selections, simplicity, conciseness, and low cost, adaptable to a wide variety of courses: yearlong as well as part-year courses in Introduction to Literature, Freshman Composition, Writing about Literature, and Humanities, for example.

This anthology offers what the classroom experiences of a great many colleagues have shown to be the really essential pedagogical tools: an introductory essay on the reading and study of literature, introductions to each of the three genres represented, and a further essay on the process of writing about literature. We have avoided a complex critical apparatus, choosing instead to annotate uncommon words and unfamiliar allusions and to provide a concluding glossary of literary terms with examples drawn solely from works in the anthology. All efforts have been made to create simple but truly useful aids in these features. However, at no point does the editorial or pedagogical content of *Literature: 150 Masterpieces* draw attention away from the anthology's true business: allowing the reader to discover, explore, and embrace the many intense realities that are the experience of literature.

A book's real life depends upon readers, who are its full partners in the creation of the literary experience. The imaginative role of active readers is too often taken for granted, minimized, or overlooked. The many instructors whose advice we have sought agree on the urgent need to engage students more completely in the adventure of reading. In its introductory essays and in every feature of its organization and presentation, *Literature: 150 Masterpieces of Fiction, Poetry, and Drama* seeks to remind its users—instructors and students alike—of the primacy of that role.

## ACKNOWLEDGMENTS

For the many incisive suggestions that brought this book to its celebration of the creative imagination of authors, instructors, and students, I thank especially Julie Nord, Mark Gallaher, and Erica Townsend of St. Martin's Press, and the many reviewers who contributed their wisdom and experience: Ellen Barker, West Georgia College; Kathleen Carroll, University of Maryland; Robert Davis, Richland College; Robert Gariepy, Eastern Washington University; Stanley Kozikowski, Bryant College; Ellen McManus, University of Illinois; Berwyn Moore, Gannon University; William Sheidley, University of Connecticut; Matthew Skulicz, Erie Community College; Judith Stanford, Rivier College; Alinda Sumers, Howard University; Bruce Taylor, University of Wisconsin at Eau Claire; and Cheryl Torsney, West Virginia University.

Beverly Lawn

# CONTENTS

# P O E T R Y  349

# INTRODUCTION TO POETRY  351

# D R A M A   475

## INTRODUCTION TO DRAMA    477

# INTRODUCTION TO LITERATURE

## THE EXPERIENCE OF LITERATURE

Literature begins with a writer and a reader. Without a reader, a story, poem, or play is only an object made of paper and ink. With a reader, it becomes an experience, an adventure, an imaginary world that may be colorful, exotic, fun, frightening—the reader makes all these things happen, in response to what the writer has written. This exchange between writer and reader must take place before we say anything at all about what a story, poem, or play means, or how to analyze it. So we begin our discussion with an exchange between the American poet Walt Whitman and us, the readers.

*A Noiseless Patient Spider*

A noiseless patient spider,
I mark'd where on a little promontory it stood isolated,
Mark'd how to explore the vacant vast surrounding,
It launch'd forth filament, filament, filament, out of itself,
Ever unreeling them, ever tirelessly speeding them.

And you O my soul where you stand,
Surrounded, detached, in measureless oceans of space,
Ceaselessly musing, venturing, throwing, seeking the spheres to
    connect them,
Till the bridge you will need be form'd, till the ductile anchor hold,
Till the gossamer thread you fling catch somewhere, O my soul.

The speaker (or the "I" of the poem who is speaking to us) suggests that there is a similarity between his soul and a spider spinning a web. He says that the spider stands "isolated," while his soul stands "Surrounded, detached." He says that both are absorbed in the process of sending out threads, of making connections: the spider "launch'd forth filament, filament, filament, out of itself," while the soul is decribed as "Ceaselessly musing, venturing, throwing . . . Till the gossamer thread [it] fling[s] catch somewhere. . . ."

The comparison is unusual and rather striking. In fact, it may explain why many of us find spiders and their webs fascinating— perhaps there is something in a spider's "noiseless patient" work that reminds us of ourselves. Aren't we all solitary beings who work most of our lives to build homes, find ways to get from place to place, and make connections between ourselves and others, just as Whitman's spider does? Having once read this poem, we realize that what Whitman's speaker has said of the spider, and of himself, we can also say of ourselves. This is only the first of the many threads of meaning we, as readers, can find in this one poem.

The spinning of the spider is very like the work we do as readers, as well. Each of us carries with us an enormous storehouse of memories, ideas, feelings, thoughts. When we read, some of those things come back to us as associations with whatever the writer has put down on paper. This active connecting of our own experience with what we are reading is a kind of web-making, too.

Notice how Whitman describes the actions of the spider and the soul: neither of them is moving, or going anywhere, yet their actions sound bold and courageous—he uses the words *explore, launch'd, venturing,* and *throwing* to describe them. Reading has similar qualities. You sit with a book, looking at the words printed in it, but in your mind you are venturing into unknown territories and trying to form connections between them and the world you have known so far. When you read great literature you will probably feel challenged and excited by it. Sometimes, too, you may feel a little frightened, a little unnerved. Perhaps you will feel, at other times, amused, reassured, relieved, or comforted.

If you don't feel much of anything, it may be that you're not making these vital connections between the work and what you already know. This happens to all readers from time to time. You may need to put the book aside for a few hours or even a day or two in order to return to it with a fresh, receptive mind. It usually helps enormously, however, to talk to someone about it. The best choice is to find someone else who has the same assigned reading. However, even talking to someone who has not read the work is often surprisingly useful.

Reading literature is not only a way out of the pressures and routines of life, but a way into and beyond ourselves that offers both pleasure and illumination. The pleasures of reading differ from the engrossing but passive ones of watching a movie, television show, football game, or an attractive, interesting person. The pleasures of reading come from our participation in it—like the fun of acting in a show, playing ball or a musical instrument, or caring for someone we love. Reading does not happen to us; we make it happen. A story, poem, or play may exist without our reading it, but it comes alive only when we read it. Because of this it may be best to think of literature as an event or experience, rather than as a collection of revered (but dusty!) books.

Not only do we make literature come alive each time we read it, we also give it a life that is a little different from any other life it has had. We read creatively. We fill in the blanks when the author leaves something unsaid. And the way we picture or respond to what an author describes is often colored by our individual feelings. If a character is described as wearing navy blue, one reader may think "conservative, repressed," another may think "classic, elegant," and a third may think "unoriginal, dowdy." Sometimes even the main ideas of a work can conjure up a great variety of responses in readers. This is why there is always room for further discussion of great literature. We can continue to read, talk, and write about works that have been studied for centuries past because each of us is capable of seeing these works in a new, slightly different way. And when we write about or explain our unique perspectives on a work, others will also be able to see something new in the work.

Besides pleasure, reading offers a particular kind of knowledge. Imaginative literature does not pretend to tell the "truth." It does not argue opinions the way a persuasive essay or political tract does, either. Nor does it present factual information, as a newspaper does. On the contrary, even when it is rooted in facts and actual events, literature is more apt to concentrate on all the things we imagine, feel, and think about those facts and events. Instead of simply describing a battle scene, for instance, literature will explore how we feel about a battle, how it affects or changes us, what our attitude toward it is. This exploration leads us to a different, but no less important, kind of "truth." This is the knowledge that literature can offer us.

Consider the Whitman poem we looked at earlier. The speaker of the poem remembers that he saw a spider flinging its silk into "the vacant vast surrounding." He then reports his soul, or imagination, doing the same thing. Readers see the connection between the spider, which is external to the writer, and the writer's feelings, which are internal. Whitman is implying a general connection between outer and inner realities. As the speaker internalizes the spider by proclaiming a kinship with it, so readers internalize the message of the poem. Some readers, inspired by Whitman's insights, go on to reflect on correspondences between themselves and the spider, the soul, the poet, the poem, other people, and other experiences. Whitman's poem makes sense to many readers at different times and in different places. For that reason, it may be said to express a particular kind of truth.

In their search for this elusive, internal kind of truth, writers often venture far beyond the boundaries of fact and established ways of thinking. Whitman, for example, does not concern himself with the fact that some spiders build webs, while others line their burrows, and that their habitats may be underground, above ground, or in the air. Nor does he mention the fact that all spiders are egg-laying predators. Instead, he focuses on two other characteristics: that spiders spin silk, and that they must spin out a dragline, or lifeline, to protect them from falling, and to enable them to ride for long distances. He draws our attention to these details because they are the ones that lead to his later description of the soul. To make a point about the ceaseless activity of the imagination, he takes another liberty with facts: he portrays the spider spinning endlessly without ever stopping—in fact, spiders do, and must, stop spinning on occasion.

In factual writing such as we might find in a natural history text, such gaps in information would be troubling. The writer could be quite fairly accused of presenting an incomplete and misleading picture of spiders. But in imaginative literature we do not have the same rules we have for factual writing. Imaginative literature serves a very different purpose. The purpose of literature is to create, represent, and clarify, rather than to reproduce, measure, or analyze scientifically the tangle of things and events in ordinary life. We read literature not so much for information as for insight and understanding. We do not generally read a poem such as Whitman's in order to learn about spiders, but to learn about ourselves: our feelings, compulsions, needs, and struggles.

The human desire to make sense of experience, identify connections among events, and discover some pattern and meaning in them, is perhaps the strongest force driving authors to write. These authors' visions can affect us, as readers, in deep and lasting ways, answering the same desire in us. Even if we remain fully aware that what we are reading is not "real," not a survey of daily life, we gradually accept the imagined world as true, and our experience of it becomes part of our memory storehouse. We have not literally seen Whitman's "noiseless patient spider," but through his poem we see it in our imagination and recognize its connection to ourselves. With this recognition, changes occur that could affect our consciousness of ourselves, others, the world. All imaginative literature—not only poems such as "A Noiseless Patient Spider," but also stories, novels, and plays—has this power.

## THE ELEMENTS OF LITERATURE

Literature has a common medium, *language;* a common mission, *to represent life imaginatively;* and a common method, *the portrayal of people in action.* Beyond these, its variations are practically infinite. This variety could make it difficult to discuss literature logically, or to make comparisons between one work and another. Therefore, there are some basic guidelines for analyzing and interpreting it that we try to follow. To begin reading and thinking about literature, we must learn some important, standard terms that identify its elements.

The major *genres* (types) of literature are fiction, poetry, and drama. Each of these genres has a separate section in this anthology, with an introduction. In these introductions, we define the features of the genre, discussing, for instance, what makes a poem a poem—and not a story. There are also features of literature that are present in all of the genres. These elements are character, plot, setting, point of view, tone, style, and theme.

*Characters* are the people of literature. *Characterization* is anything an author does to show us what those people are like. Characterization includes describing what characters look like;

what they think, say, and do (these are sometimes dissimilar); and how they are regarded by other characters. Often, the characterization is developed bit by bit, so that over the course of the work we get to know a character better and better. In the end, we become involved with the characters; we care about them and about what they do and what happens to them. Sometimes, on the other hand, we feel dislike or even hatred toward a character. All these responses are usually a result of both the author's characterization and the particular viewpoint each of us brings to the reading experience.

Literary characters, like living people, interact dynamically with the people and things around them. They come with histories, act within environments; through these things, we learn about them as well. Therefore, character and characterization depend in part on other literary elements such as plot and setting.

*Plot* is the sequence of major events, the things that happen in a literary work. Actions, both internal and external, make up a plot, but are not equivalent with it. A series of unrelated, pointless actions does not constitute a plot. In general, the actions in a plot have a cause-effect relationship with each other, so that if one action were removed or changed, the other would make less sense. The plot of Whitman's "A Noiseless Patient Spider" is simple and brief, but we can see that this is true. If, for instance, the spider were killing and wrapping up another insect for later consumption, instead of quietly spinning its web, the speaker's musings about his soul reaching out and building bridges would not make sense to us. Also, we would perceive the speaker quite differently if the poem were altered in this way; he might revolt or terrify us.

Of the three genres, fiction and drama rely more heavily on plot than poetry does. When you have read Nathaniel Hawthorne's "Young Goodman Brown," you will find that you remember it by its plot: Brown's journey into the forest and the profound changes it brings about in him. If it weren't for that journey, the story wouldn't exist. Susan Glaspell's play *Trifles* hinges on its five characters' attempts to solve a murder. Again, there wouldn't be a play at all without those small, separate attempts and the things that each reveals.

Poems vary in their reliance on plot. Some poems focus so much on plot that they seem almost like short stories in verse form. Robert Browning's "My Last Duchess" is one of these. Some, like Robert Frost's "The Road Not Taken," Emily Dickinson's "Because I could not stop for Death," and Denise Levertov's "The Dragonfly-Mother," have plots made up of concrete actions that express or symbolize something that is actually taking place in the speaker's mind. Others have plots that consist almost entirely of movements or shifts in the speaker's attitude or frame of mind. These poems often depict a sequence of events or thoughts that lead the speaker from a conflicted, troubled frame of mind to a resolved or satisfied one. Whitman's "A Noiseless Patient Spider" and Lucille Clifton's "Miss Rosie" are cases in point.

In the Whitman poem, the speaker begins by describing a creature very different and removed from himself. He recalls what he saw the spider doing and what it was about the spinning that attracted his interest. Then he moves into himself and begins describing the activities of his soul. One by one, he describes them so as to show a likeness with the activities of the spider. In this way, he builds the bridge between the spider and his soul and brings his own thoughts from a state of separation and aloneness to one of kinship and community with the spider.

In Clifton's "Miss Rosie," shifts in the speaker's *diction* (choice of words) mark the major steps in her evolving consciousness. She begins with images that express distaste at Miss Rosie's degradation. Then she moves to ones in which she contrasts, and reflects upon, Rosie's past and present circumstances. Finally, she arrives at a feeling of pride in the woman's endurance.

*Setting* is the context for the action: the time, place, culture, and atmosphere in which it occurs. A work may have several settings, and the relationships among them are often significant to the point of the work. The general setting for "Young Goodman Brown" is the village of seventeenth-century Puritan Salem, Massachusetts. Brown's mysterious nighttime journey is set in the forest, while the journey's prelude and its melancholy outcome are set in the village. Brown's forest experience takes him so far from the security he has known and affects him so deeply that we actually sense that the other setting—the village—is altered by it. Certainly we know that in Brown's eyes the promise of happiness and untroubled days that once characterized his life in the village has been forever replaced by fear and worry.

In Toni Cade Bambara's story "The Lesson," there are several settings that contrast and interact, telling us many things about Bambara's characters. Uptown and downtown New York City neighborhoods are the two main settings; the subway a third setting that connects the other two. Sylvia, Sugar, and the rest are poor uptown kids, originally from the South, who hate the dirt and deterioration of their block. Yet they really do not know much about life outside it, nor do they see how the way others live might apply to them. These observations already tell us a great deal about these characters. In addition, the contrasts between uptown and downtown, which Bambara, through Sylvia, shows by reporting details about streets, garbage, elevators, the subway, and F. A. O. Schwarz—a Fifth Avenue toy store—make setting a powerful element in this story.

Glaspell's *Trifles* is set in a rural area where farmers' wives can easily become isolated from each other. This setting is a critical factor in the unfolding mystery of how Mr. Wright met his end. The stage directions for Tennessee Williams's *Glass Menagerie* describe the Wingfields' St. Louis tenement apartment as "one of those vast hivelike conglomerations of cellular living-units that flower as warty growths in over-crowded centers of lower middle-class population." From this description, we understand immediately that setting will be very important in this play. Later we find that it has a major influence on Amanda's obsessive nostalgia, as well as on the sad and painful unfolding of events.

Almost all poems are presented as set in the mind of the *persona* (speaker) of the poem. But some poems, especially narrative ones, have instead specific, concrete settings, as does William Blake's "London" or Samuel Taylor Coleridge's "Kubla Khan," which takes place in the imaginary realm of Xanadu. In many other poems, we get a sense of what the setting is, though the poet may not spell this out. Clifton's "Miss Rosie," for instance, does not have a stated setting, but we conclude that it is set in the garbage-strewn street that appears to be Miss Rosie's home.

*Point of view* is the perspective or angle from which the speaker of a poem or the narrator of a story presents things to us. Point of view tells us things about the speaker or narrator, as well as about the things he or she is relating to us. We know early on in "The Lesson" that Sylvia disapproves of and dislikes Miss Moore. From Sylvia's descriptions of what she dislikes, we learn about both characters. However, the speaker's point of view should not be confused with the opinion or judgment of the author. The speaker or narrator and the attitude he or she takes toward setting, other characters, plot developments—all are a creation of the author and are there to create a certain effect, not to tell us what the author "thinks."

Point of view is a strong and obvious element in short stories, but often a subtler one in poems, which are usually presented by an anonymous speaker. Plays, however, normally do not have a central, explicit point of view because, in general, all characters in a play are allowed to speak for themselves. In some plays, there may be characters who never appear on stage; Mr. and Mrs. Wright in *Trifles* are examples of such characters. The other characters in *Trifles* present quite a range of points of view on the two of them, and show some changes in those attitudes as the play progresses. Other plays may have only one character, in which case the point of view would be very important.

In the strict sense, though, point of view depends on a central speaker or narrator, a device that is very rare in drama. The chorus of Greek tragedies, including the chorus in Sophocles' *Oedipus Rex*, presents society's view of the history and meaning of the action. Since the chorus functions as a narrator, it can be said to provide the point of view. In *The Glass Menagerie*, Tom, Laura's brother, introduces and narrates the dramatic action, which he himself participates in as a character. The play is therefore a stunning modern exception to the general rule, as Williams knew when he included the following statement in his stage directions: *"The narrator is an undisguised convention of the play. He takes whatever license with dramatic convention is convenient to his purposes."*

There are three basic points of view: first person ("I"), second person ("you")—which is rarely used—and third person ("he," "she," "it," and "they"). A third-person point of view can also be either *omniscient,* meaning "all-knowing," or *limited,* meaning "partially knowledgeable." All of these terms help us decide whether the speaker or narrator is objective or subjective, and to what degree he or she is either.

The third-person point of view is the most common in literature. With this point of view, all our information comes from someone who is not a character in the work. This position tends to make the speaker emotionally removed from the action and therefore, we presume, relatively objective. This apparent objectivity can achieve many things, encouraging readers to keep their minds open, and also maintaining a safe distance for readers if events become upsetting. However, sometimes authors want a different effect. Many authors work in the first-person point of view precisely because they want the subjectivity and the closeness to the story that this point of view brings. "The Lesson" would probably affect us differently if it were told in the third-person point of view. Subjectivity itself is an important issue in this story, which would be radically changed if Miss Moore, rather than Sylvia, were to provide the primary point of view.

When we refer to the *tone* of a literary work, we mean the attitude with which a speaker or narrator relates things to us. By *attitude*, we mean nearly the same thing as when we say that someone has taken a hostile "tone of voice" with us, or a friendly tone or a sarcastic tone. In literature, tone can vary considerably and change frequently. To study the tone of a work, it can be helpful to establish a systematic approach, perhaps asking yourself a standard set of questions each time: Is the tone of this work formal or informal? Is it emotional or intellectual? Is it straightforward or ironic? Does it convey any particular underlying feeling—excitement, frustration, anger, apathy? Does the tone change at any point?

Changes in a speaker's tone can tell us things about his or her attitudes and deeper feelings that aren't necessarily directly stated. Because of this, tone is also closely related to point of view. Tone becomes especially revealing with the first-person point of view because a narrator's character, personality, and experience are basic in our acceptance of a story's truth and persuasiveness. The casual, off-handed tone of Sylvia, the narrator of "The Lesson," for example, is a powerful factor in establishing the authenticity of her story.

*Style* in literature refers to the diction, *syntax* (sentence structure), and other linguistic features of a work. The style of any individual work is significant to our understanding of it. You may want to try and answer some standard questions when studying the style of a work: Are the sentences noticeably short or long, simple or complex? Are there particular words or expressions used throughout the work that are striking?

Style sets a writer's language apart from that of other writers. Just as no two people have identical fingerprints or voices, so no two writers use words in exactly the same way. An author's particular time and culture may influence his or her style, too. Certainly Hawthorne and Bambara, Glaspell and Williams, Whitman and Clifton, are all deliberate stylists with very different purposes and styles. And some of these differences are at least partly due to the times and cultures in which these writers worked. Consider the contrasting styles of Hawthorne and Bambara. Hawthorne, living and writing in nineteenth-century New England, was steeped in the power of Puritan history, myth, allegory, and religion. His style features formal diction, complex sentences, and many symbolic images and details that allude to other things. Bambara, living and writing in the present that we know, uses a colloquial (conversational) style and tone based on the street-talk an inner-city girl like Sylvia would actually use. Style generally tells us a great deal about an author's purposes.

*Theme* is the idea, point, or meaning of a story, poem, or play. Grasping the theme of a work could be considered the definitive or most important step in the process of understanding a work. If we think of theme as meaning, we can understand why theme directs and binds together all the other literary elements, revealing the roles they play. It is sometimes easy to confuse theme with *subject,* but they are not the same thing. We can say that the subject of Whitman's "A Noiseless Patient Spider" is the imagination, but this clearly does not tell us the idea or message of the poem. To identify the theme, we would need to say something more like "this poem explores the role of imagination in the speaker's life." Like style, theme is often a trait that sets one author apart from another. Whitman's themes, for instance, are apt to be quite distinct from Bambara's. "A Noiseless Patient Spider" seems to be an exploration of the relationships between nature and creativity, memory and imagination. "The Lesson," in contrast, can be said to explore the impact of experience on consciousness and opportunity, quite a different idea.

It takes careful analysis and reflection to come to an understanding of the theme of a work. Our first attempts to capture it are rarely just right. Most of us find we must begin with one idea, and test it out for a while by looking back at the work and considering whether all of it really focuses on this idea. We usually find that we must abandon or modify this first idea, sometimes repeatedly, before we arrive at an interpretation that really stands up to analysis. This process may require some patience, but it is an immensely important one, because it leads us from a hasty, incomplete understanding of what we have read to a full, complex, and carefully developed one.

Although a theme may sometimes be a *moral*, as in fairy tales or fables with flat one-dimensional characters and situations, normally it neither judges characters nor teaches readers how best to live. Even Nathaniel Hawthorne, who was deeply concerned with the moral dilemmas and predicaments we all face, did not conceive his chief aim to be the moral improvement of readers. So, to read the story "Young Goodman Brown" as instruction on how not to live would obscure and distort its meanings.

## THE EXPLORATION OF LITERATURE

As you read and discuss stories, poems, and plays with other people, be encouraged when you find a work that raises questions with no simple answers. The pleasure and illumination that literature brings comes from its complexity and open-endedness. Different analyses and interpretations based on evidence from a text, an author's life, or other pertinent contexts reflect the variety and richness of literature, and should be greeted with an open mind. Personal interpretations change, too, sometimes radically. We often find surprising new meanings in a work we thought we knew well. We may reenter the world of a literary work to find the same characters in the same situations doing the same things, but because of what we ourselves have experienced since the last reading, we contribute fresh associations and insights and respond more richly and deeply. We *know* what happens, and that very awareness prompts new pleasure and understanding.

Writers of literature welcome this interplay of permanence and change. Sophocles, who constructed tragedies from familiar myths, and Shakespeare, who often based his plays on historical materials, deliberately drew on their audiences' knowledge to heighten and deepen impact. Many writers make use of *allusions*— literary references that borrow the intellectual and emotional associations of history and of other literary works. Allusions can enhance the scope and power of the story, poem, or play in which they occur. In "Young Goodman Brown," Brown's sunset journey into the forest, for example, is heightened by readers' familiarity with the religiousness, moral strictness, and wariness toward nature of seventeenth-century New England Puritans. Just so, the satiric effect of Anton Chekhov's "A Marriage Proposal" relies on awareness of the importance of property in nineteenth-century Russian marriages. And the impact of Louis Simpson's "Walt Whitman at Bear Mountain" depends, in part, on an awareness of Whitman as a celebrant of democracy, the common life, nature, and the freedom of the open road.

A reader's life experience and knowledge of literature are assets in the literary experience. Perceptiveness, sensitivity, and common sense are strengths too. Primary, however, is what the nineteenth-century English poet Samuel Taylor Coleridge called "suspension of disbelief," the willingness to leave behind our skepticism about the "truth" of a poem, the will to enter and follow its lead. Coleridge's point applies equally to all imaginative literature. With a story, the idea typically means accepting a narrator's claims that certain people lived, behaved in certain ways, and had certain things happen to them. With a poem, it nearly always means two things at once: to "listen" to a poet's voice and to watch words and lines build meaning. With a play, it usually means to imagine in front of you characters confronting the conflicts that beset them.

Such creative collaboration of authors and readers is indispensable to literature. Yet just how we produce the illusion of life being lived remains mysterious. Imagination resists short cuts and formulas. In literature, as in life, characters are never fully known, stories never complete, insights and arguments never conclusive. The clarification and insight we derive from the experience will depend on how much we are willing to contribute. The more of ourselves we give, the more we gain. Literature invites us, then, to varied journeys of our making. In each of us, Whitman's "noiseless patient spider" is ready to spin on.

# FICTION

# INTRODUCTION TO FICTION

"Young Goodman Brown came forth at sunset into the street at Salem village; but put his head back, after crossing the threshold, to exchange a parting kiss with his young wife": so begins one of the most famous stories in nineteenth-century literature, Nathaniel Hawthorne's "Young Goodman Brown." More than a century later, "The Lesson," a story by Toni Cade Bambara, also begins with basic information, but to very different effect: "Back in the days when everyone was old and stupid or young and foolish and me and Sugar were the only ones just right, this lady moved on our block with nappy hair and proper speech and no makeup." Right from the start, both stories provide readers with essential facts about important characters and settings. The stories' main lines of action, and the reasons for them, become clearer as events unfold.

"Young Goodman Brown" and "The Lesson" conclude similarly, too, with indications of the impact of the characters' experiences. For Brown, his family, and his neighbors, the outcome has been devastating:

> And when he had lived long, and was borne to his grave a hoary corpse, followed by Faith, an aged woman, and children and grandchildren, a goodly procession, besides neighbors not a few, they carved no hopeful verse upon his tombstone, for his dying hour was gloom.

Sylvia's adventure in "The Lesson" causes her to look at herself and the world in a new way, too, but a way opposite to Brown's. As usual, her friend Sugar would just as soon go to Hascombs for cake and then on to the Sunset "for potato chips and ice cream sodas," but Sylvia wants to be alone for a change, go to the neighborhood bar, and then do some thinking. For the first time she sees herself as an unbeatable individual with some important catching up to do:

"Race you to Hascombs," she say.

We start down the block and she gets ahead which is O.K. by me cause I'm going to the West End and then over to the Drive to think this day through. She can run if she want to and even run faster. But ain't nobody gonna beat me at nuthin.

Not all stories conclude as powerfully as these, but most stories are based on actions that do change characters and events in some significant way. Ernest Hemingway's "A Clean, Well-Lighted Place" and Eudora Welty's "A Worn Path" are quiet stories revealing some people's weakness, selfishness, and unintentional cruelty, and others' strength, compassion, and tender generosity. These are stories, too, about a central character's capacity for hope and wonder, and about public and private happiness and unhappiness. In "A Worn Path," Old Phoenix's joy as she receives the nickel she plans to spend on a paper windmill to delight her lye-scarred grandson seems to pull together all we have learned about her brave and stoical character on the long, painful walk from the country to Natchez for the child's medicine: "He going to find it hard to believe there such a thing in the world. I'll march myself back where he waiting, holding it straight up in this hand." The older waiter in Hemingway's story, who defends an old customer's right to stay on after closing hour in the Spanish café because it is clean ("The light is very good and also, now, there are shadows of the leaves") admits that, unlike the young, married waiter, he is "With all those who do not want to go to bed. With all those who need a light for the night." But the story's conclusion shows the burden of the older waiter's inner disquiet, due, perhaps, to his own anxiety about growing old alone, and perhaps, also, to his guilt about not fighting hard enough for the old man's dignity and right to remain in a clean, safe place. After leaving the bar, the older waiter would go home and lie awake until dawn: "After all, he said to himself, it is probably only insomnia. Many must have it."

The human desire to make sense of experience, identify connections among events, and establish some pattern and meaning among them is answered in different ways by all literature. Compared with poetry and drama, fiction usually employs the elements of literature—(*character, plot, setting, point of view, tone, style,* and *theme*)—in a more straightforward manner, typically using a *narrator* to represent the action to readers. Sometimes the narrator is not identified; at other times he or she is a specific character in the story. The nature of the narrator, as we discussed in the Introduction to Literature, determines point of view and tone, which also enlarge a story's meaning.

The appeal of the *narrative form*, and of the narrator as the source of a story, may have roots in early childhood, when we listened to stories we could not read. Or it may derive from stories' general reliance on a sequence of events, usually in a cause-effect relationship to one another, that satisfies a basic human need for clarity and logic. In any case, the activities of telling, retelling, listening, and responding to stories go far back in history, long before the printed word became a conventional medium for narration. Tales were passed orally from person to person, group to group, society to society. Early narratives that were especially meaningful became common property; their narrators spoke with collective authority and purpose. Certain stories that shaped the consciousness and memory of entire peoples, such as Homer's *Iliad* and *Odyssey*, became known as *myths*.

The modern short story, in contrast, is likely a product of the solitary strivings of an individual, and the intentional expression of personal, not collective meaning. Even stories of allegorical suggestiveness such as Hawthorne's "Young Goodman Brown," and of fabulous dimensions such as Gabriel García Márquez's "A Very Old Man with Enormous Wings," do not presume to speak for everyone. Instead, modern short stories are usually presented as confidences between narrators and readers.

Since the nineteenth century, the short story has been an identifiable and popular literary form, distinguishable from its longer, more complex relative, the novel, by its smaller scope and simpler design. The short story's limitations are also its strengths: economy, intensity, and single focus enable readers to maintain their attention and engage their imaginations fully. Edgar Allan Poe noted these advantages in his 1842 review of Hawthorne's *Twice-Told Tales*. Poe argued that for maximum effect, stories should be short enough to read in "one sitting." He also claimed that "unity of effect," which distinguishes the tale from the novel, imposes certain obligations on a writer: "In the whole composition there should be no word written of which the tendency, direct or indirect, is not to the one pre-established design."

A short story's design, like that of a play or a poem, requires active participation to be deeply and vividly experienced. Such participation is needed not only for bringing out details of character and action, but for realizing the vitality of characters, the beginning, middle and end of the plot, and the significance of setting and language. Beyond these elements are the special contributions of the narrator's point of view, the lens through which we see the action, and of the narrator's tone, the voice through which we hear it. Finally, there is the matter of *time*, whose importance Poe recognized when he contended that effective tales are tightly plotted and readable in one sitting.

Like other forms of literature, short stories depend on time as a primary structural and psychological principle. Time is one of the elements in setting, for example, indicating when the action took place. Time is also the spine of plot, the sequence of events from beginning to end. The language of time indicates number or recurrence, as in *three characters, three paragraphs,* or *three pages.* Time also describes *duration,* the length or span between one moment and another. The verb *endure,* sometimes used as a synonym for *live through* or *experience,* suggests the physical and psychological dimensions of duration.

By framing a story's action, physical duration magnifies and intensifies the significance of events, and of the characters' responses to the action. We and the characters are pressed to look closely at the meaning of the events that occur. In stories, as in other literature and daily life, however, the meaning of duration is psychological as well as physical. An hour may resemble a minute, or a year. Contrasts in duration point up this *paradox,* or apparent contradiction. As fact or as dream, the forest-journey of Goodman Brown occurred in one night. Yet this single night overpowered his life, driving him from cheerful youth to dismal old age and death. Sylvia's adventure took place in a day, and ends with a recognition and seeming change of attitude that could have long-range implications.

Narrators, who normally report events after they have occurred, sometimes long after, serve to extend the duration of a story, and heighten its value by suggesting its current relevance. Although the events being narrated occurred in the past, they are significant enough to pertain in our present, the narrator seems to be saying.

In our imaginations, then, short stories take on the documentary credibility of history. Although we do not learn of Brown's death until the end of the story, "Young Goodman Brown" is related after Brown's death by a third-person, anonymous narrator in the past tense: "Young Goodman Brown set forth. . . ." Sylvia, the first-person narrator of "The Lesson," also tells her story in the past: "Back in the days when everyone was old. . . ," but we quickly forget that she is doing so because after her first paragraph she shifts to the present tense, which she sustains to the end, suggesting that the story is still going on, and raising significant questions about her subsequent life. Dramatic and poetic works borrowing the narrator of fiction frequently handle time as "The Lesson" does: they begin in the past, then shift to, and sustain, the present for the larger portion of the work. Williams's play *The Glass Menagerie* and Whitman's poem "A Noiseless Patient Spider" are pertinent examples.

The various faces of time, including duration, structure our imaginative experience. In the hour or less required to read a story, we can span cultures, continents, and centuries, and help shape a complete narrative of people in action. In the same hour, by shaping and feeling the characters' conflicts, recognitions, and resolutions as they are reported to us, we may, through our own imaginative venturing, come to know the essence of a man's, woman's, or child's life and perhaps along the way discover a truth about our own.

## NATHANIEL HAWTHORNE [1804–1864]

# Young Goodman Brown

Young Goodman Brown came forth at sunset into the street at Salem village; but put his head back, after crossing the threshold, to exchange a parting kiss with his young wife. And Faith, as the wife was aptly named, thrust her own pretty head into the street, letting the wind play with the pink ribbons of her cap while she called to Goodman Brown.

"Dearest heart," whispered she, softly and rather sadly, when her lips were close to his ear, "prithee put off your journey until sunrise and sleep in your own bed to-night. A lone woman is troubled with such dreams and such thoughts that she's afeared of herself sometimes. Pray tarry with me this night, dear husband, of all nights in the year."

"My love and my Faith," replied young Goodman Brown, "of all nights in the year, this one night must I tarry away from thee. My journey, as thou callest it, forth and back again, must needs be done 'twixt now and sunrise. What, my sweet, pretty wife, dost thou doubt me already, and we but three months married?"

"Then God bless you!" said Faith, with the pink ribbons; "and may you find all well when you come back."

"Amen!" cried Goodman Brown. "Say thy prayers, dear Faith, and go to bed at dusk, and no harm will come to thee."

So they parted; and the young man pursued his way until, being about to turn the corner by the meeting-house, he looked back and saw the head of Faith still peeping after him with a melancholy air, in spite of her pink ribbons.

"Poor little Faith!" thought he, for his heart smote him. "What a wretch am I to leave her on such an errand! She talks of dreams, too. Methought as she spoke there was trouble in her face, as if a dream had warned her what work is to be done to-night. But no, no; 't would kill her to think it. Well, she's a blessed angel on earth, and after this one night I'll cling to her skirts and follow her to heaven."

With this excellent resolve for the future, Goodman Brown felt himself justified in making more haste on his present evil purpose. He had taken a dreary road, darkened by all the gloomiest trees of the forest, which barely stood aside to let the narrow path creep through, and closed immediately behind. It was all as lonely as could be; and there is this peculiarity in such a solitude, that the traveller knows not who may be concealed by the innumerable trunks and the thick boughs overhead; so that with lonely footsteps he may yet be passing through an unseen multitude.

"There may be a devilish Indian behind every tree," said Goodman Brown to himself; and he glanced fearfully behind him as he added, "What if the devil himself should be at my very elbow!"

His head being turned back, he passed a crook of the road, and, looking forward again, beheld the figure of a man, in grave and decent attire, seated at the foot of an old tree. He arose at Goodman Brown's approach and walked onward side by side with him.

"You are late, Goodman Brown," said he. "The clock of the Old South was striking as I came through Boston, and that is full fifteen minutes agone."

"Faith kept me back a while," replied the young man, with a tremor in his voice, caused by the sudden appearance of his companion, though not wholly unexpected.

It was now deep dusk in the forest, and deepest in that part of it where these two were journeying. As nearly as could be discerned, the second traveller was about fifty years old, apparently in the same rank of life as Goodman Brown, and bearing a considerable resemblance to him, though perhaps more in expression than features. Still they might have been taken for father and son. And yet, though the elder person was as simply clad as the younger, and as simple in manner too, he had an indescribable air of one who knew the world, and who would not have felt abashed at the governor's dinner table or in King William's court,[1]

---

[1] The court of William III, king of England (1689–1702).

were it possible that his affairs should call him thither. But the only thing about him that could be fixed upon as remarkable was his staff, which bore the likeness of a great black snake, so curiously wrought that it might almost be seen to twist and wriggle itself like a living serpent. This, of course, must have been an ocular deception, assisted by the uncertain light.

"Come, Goodman Brown," cried his fellow-traveller, "this is a dull pace for the beginning of a journey. Take my staff, if you are so soon weary."

"Friend," said the other, exchanging his slow pace for a full stop, "having kept covenant by meeting thee here, it is my purpose now to return whence I came. I have scruples touching the matter thou wot'st of."

"Sayest thou so?" replied he of the serpent, smiling apart. "Let us walk on, nevertheless, reasoning as we go; and if I convince thee not thou shalt turn back. We are but a little way in the forest yet."

"Too far! too far!" exclaimed the goodman, unconsciously resuming his walk. "My father never went into the woods on such an errand, nor his father before him. We have been a race of honest men and good Christians since the days of the martyrs; and shall I be the first of the name of Brown that ever took this path and kept—"

"Such company, thou wouldst say," observed the elder person, interpreting his pause. "Well said, Goodman Brown! I have been as well acquainted with your family as with ever a one among the Puritans; and that's no trifle to say. I helped your grandfather, the constable, when he lashed the Quaker woman so smartly through the streets of Salem; and it was I that brought your father a pitch-pine knot, kindled at my own hearth, to set fire to an Indian village, in King Philip's war.[2] They were my good friends, both; and many a pleasant walk have we had along this path, and returned merrily after midnight. I would fain be friends with you for their sake."

"If it be as thou sayest," replied Goodman Brown, "I marvel they never spoke of these matters; or, verily, I marvel not, seeing

---

[2] The most important Indian uprising in colonial New England (1675–1676).

that the least rumor of the sort would have driven them from New England. We are a people of prayer, and good works to boot, and abide no such wickedness."

"Wickedness or not," said the traveller with the twisted staff, "I have a very general acquaintance here in New England. The deacons of many a church have drunk the communion wine with me; the selectmen of divers towns make me their chairman; and a majority of the Great and General Court are firm supporters of my interest. The governor and I, too—But these are state secrets."

"Can this be so?" cried Goodman Brown, with a stare of amazement at his undisturbed companion. "Howbeit, I have nothing to do with the governor and council; they have their own ways, and are no rule for a simple husbandman like me. But, were I to go on with thee, how should I meet the eye of that good old man, our minister, at Salem village? Oh, his voice would make me tremble both Sabbath day and lecture day."

Thus far the elder traveller had listened with due gravity; but now burst into a fit of irrepressible mirth, shaking himself so violently that his snake-like staff actually seemed to wriggle in sympathy.

"Ha! ha! ha!" shouted he again and again; then composing himself, "Well, go on, Goodman Brown, go on; but, prithee, don't kill me with laughing."

"Well, then, to end the matter at once," said Goodman Brown, considerably nettled, "there is my wife, Faith. It would break her dear little heart; and I'd rather break my own."

"Nay, if that be the case," answered the other, "e'en go thy ways, Goodman Brown. I would not for twenty old women like the one hobbling before us that Faith should come to any harm."

As he spoke he pointed his staff at a female figure on the path, in whom Goodman Brown recognized a very pious and exemplary dame, who had taught him his catechism in youth, and was still his moral and spiritual adviser, jointly with the minister and Deacon Gookin.

"A marvel, truly that Goody Cloyse should be so far in the wilderness at nightfall," said he. "But with your leave, friend, I shall take a cut through the woods until we have left this Christian woman behind. Being a stranger to you, she might ask whom I was consorting with and whither I was going."

"Be it so," said his fellow-traveller. "Betake you to the woods, and let me keep the path."

Accordingly the young man turned aside, but took care to watch his companion, who advanced softly along the road until he had come within a staff's length of the old dame. She, meanwhile, was making the best of her way, with singular speed for so aged a woman, and mumbling some indistinct words—a prayer, doubtless—as she went. The traveller put forth his staff and touched her withered neck with what seemed the serpent's tail.

"The devil!" screamed the pious old lady.

"Then Goody Cloyse knows her old friend?" observed the traveller, confronting her and leaning on his writhing stick.

"Ah, forsooth, and is it your worship indeed?" cried the good dame. "Yea, truly is it, and in the very image of my old gossip, Goodman Brown, the grandfather of the silly fellow that now is. But—would your worship believe it?—my broomstick hath strangely disappeared, stolen, as I suspect, by that unhanged witch, Goody Cory, and that, too, when I was all anointed with the juice of smallage, and cinquefoil, and wolf's bane—"

"Mingled with fine wheat and the fat of a new-born babe," said the shape of old Goodman Brown.

"Ah, your worship knows the recipe," cried the old lady, cackling aloud. "So, as I was saying, being all ready for the meeting, and no horse to ride on, I made up my mind to foot it; for they tell me there is a nice young man to be taken into communion to-night. But now your good worship will lend me your arm, and we shall be there in a twinkling."

"That can hardly be," answered her friend. "I may not spare you my arm, Goody Cloyse; but here is my staff, if you will."

So saying, he threw it down at her feet, where, perhaps, it assumed life, being one of the rods which its owner had formerly lent to the Egyptian magi. Of this fact, however, Goodman Brown could not take cognizance. He had cast up his eyes in astonishment, and, looking down again, beheld neither Goody Cloyse nor the serpentine staff, but his fellow-traveller alone, who waited for him as calmly as if nothing had happened.

"That old woman taught me my catechism," said the young man; and there was a world of meaning in this simple comment.

They continued to walk onward, while the elder traveller exhorted his companion to make good speed and persevere in the path, discoursing so aptly that his arguments seemed rather to spring up in the bosom of his auditor than to be suggested by himself. As they went, he plucked a branch of maple to serve for a walking stick, and began to strip it of the twigs and little boughs, which were wet with evening dew. The moment his fingers touched them they became strangely withered and dried up as with a week's sunshine. Thus the pair proceeded, at a good free pace, until suddenly, in a gloomy hollow of the road, Goodman Brown sat himself down on the stump of a tree and refused to go any farther.

"Friend," said he, stubbornly, "my mind is made up. Not another step will I budge on this errand. What if a wretched old woman do choose to go to the devil when I thought she was going to heaven: is that any reason why I should quit my dear Faith and go after her?"

"You will think better of this by and by," said his acquaintance, composedly. "Sit here and rest yourself a while; and when you feel like moving again, there is my staff to help you along."

Without more words, he threw his companion the maple stick, and was as speedily out of sight as if he had vanished into the deepening gloom. The young man sat a few moments by the roadside, applauding himself greatly, and thinking with how clear a conscience he should meet the minister in his morning walk, nor shrink from the eye of good old Deacon Gookin. And what calm sleep would be his that very night, which was to have been spent so wickedly, but so purely and sweetly now, in the arms of Faith! Amidst these pleasant and praiseworthy meditations, Goodman Brown heard the tramp of horses along the road, and deemed it advisable to conceal himself within the verge of the forest, conscious of the guilty purpose that had brought him thither, though now so happily turned from it.

On came the hoof tramps and the voices of the riders, two grave old voices, conversing soberly as they drew near. These mingled sounds appeared to pass along the road, within a few yards of the young man's hiding-place; but, owing doubtless to the depth of the gloom at that particular spot, neither the travellers nor their steeds were visible. Though their figures brushed the small boughs by the wayside, it could not be seen that they intercepted, even for a moment, the faint gleam from the strip of bright sky athwart which they must have passed. Goodman Brown alternately crouched and stood on tiptoe, pulling aside the branches and thrusting forth his head as far as he durst without discerning so much as a shadow. It vexed him the more, because he could have sworn, were such a thing possible, that he recognized the voices of the minister and Deacon Gookin, jogging along quietly, as they were wont to do, when bound to some ordination or ecclesiastical council. While yet within hearing, one of the riders stopped to pluck a switch.

"Of the two, reverend sir," said the voice like the deacon's, "I had rather miss an ordination dinner than to-night's meeting. They tell me that some of our community are to be here from Falmouth and beyond, and others from Connecticut and Rhode Island, besides several of the Indian powwows, who, after their fashion, know almost as much deviltry as the best of us. Moreover, there is a goodly young woman to be taken into communion."

"Mighty well, Deacon Gookin!" replied the solemn old tones of the minister. "Spur up, or we shall be late. Nothing can be done, you know, until I get on the ground."

The hoofs clattered again; and the voices, talking so strangely in the empty air, passed on through the forest, where no church had ever been gathered or solitary Christian prayed. Whither, then, could these holy men be journeying so deep into the heathen wilderness? Young Goodman Brown caught hold of a tree for support, being ready to sink down on the ground, faint and overburdened with the heavy sickness of his heart. He looked up to the sky, doubting whether there really was a heaven above him. Yet there was the blue arch, and the stars brightening in it.

"With heaven above and Faith below, I will yet stand firm against the devil!" cried Goodman Brown.

While he still gazed upward into the deep arch of the firmament and had lifted his hands to pray, a cloud, though no wind was stirring, hurried across the zenith and hid the brightening stars. The blue sky was still visible, except directly overhead, where this black mass of cloud was sweeping swiftly northward. Aloft in the air, as if from the depths of the cloud, came a confused and doubtful sound of voices. Once the listener fancied that he could distinguish the accents of townspeople of his own, men and women, both pious and ungodly, many of whom he had met at the communion table, and had seen others rioting at the tavern.

The next moment, so indistinct were the sounds, he doubted whether he had heard aught but the murmur of the old forest, whispering without a wind. Then came a stronger swell of those familiar tones, heard daily in the sunshine at Salem village, but never until now from a cloud of night. There was one voice, of a young woman, uttering lamentations, yet with an uncertain sorrow, and entreating for some favor, which, perhaps, it would grieve her to obtain; and all the unseen multitude, both saints and sinners, seemed to encourage her onward.

"Faith!" shouted Goodman Brown, in a voice of agony and desperation; and the echoes of the forest mocked him, crying, "Faith! Faith!" as if bewildered wretches were seeking her all through the wilderness.

The cry of grief, rage, and terror was yet piercing the night, when the unhappy husband held his breath for a response. There was a scream, drowned immediately in a louder murmur of voices, fading into far-off laughter, as the dark cloud swept away, leaving the clear and silent sky above Goodman Brown. But something fluttered lightly down through the air and caught on the branch of a tree. The young man seized it, and beheld a pink ribbon.

"My Faith is gone!" cried he after one stupefied moment. "There is no good on earth; and sin is but a name. Come, devil; for to thee is this world given."

And, maddened with despair, so that he laughed loud and long, did Goodman Brown grasp his staff and set forth again, at such a rate that he seemed to fly along the forest path rather than to walk or run. The road grew wilder and drearier and more faintly traced, and vanished at length, leaving him in the heart of the dark wilderness, still rushing onward with the instinct that guides mortal man to evil. The whole forest was peopled with frightful sounds—the creaking of the trees, the howling of wild beasts, and the yell of Indians; while sometimes the wind tolled like a distant church bell, and sometimes gave a broad roar around the traveller, as if all Nature were laughing him to scorn. But he was himself the chief horror of the scene, and shrank not from its other horrors.

"Ha! Ha! ha!" roared Goodman Brown when the wind laughed at him. "Let us hear which will laugh loudest. Think not to frighten me with your deviltry. Come witch, come wizard, come Indian powwow, come devil himself, and here comes Goodman Brown. You may as well fear him as he fear you."

In truth, all through the haunted forest there could be nothing more frightful than the figure of Goodman Brown. On he flew among the black pines, brandishing his staff with frenzied gestures, now giving vent to an inspiration of horrid blasphemy, and now shouting forth such laughter as set all the echoes of the forest laughing like demons around him. The fiend in his own shape is less hideous than when he rages in the breast of man. Thus sped the demoniac on his course, until, quivering among the trees, he saw a red light before him, as when the felled trunks and branches of a clearing have been set on fire, and throw up their lurid blaze against the sky, at the hour of midnight. He paused, in a lull of the tempest that had driven him onward, and heard the swell of what seemed a hymn, rolling solemnly from a distance with the weight of many voices. He knew the tune; it was a familiar one in the choir of the village meeting-house. The verse died heavily away, and was lengthened by a chorus, not of human voices, but of all the sounds of the benighted wilderness pealing in awful harmony together. Goodman Brown cried out, and his cry was lost to his own ear by its unison with the cry of the desert.

In the interval of silence he stole forward until the light glared full upon his eyes. At one extremity of an open space, hemmed in by the dark wall of the forest, arose a rock, bearing some rude, natural resemblance either to an alter or a pulpit, and surrounded by four blazing pines, their tops aflame, their stems untouched, like candles at an evening meeting. The mass of foliage that had overgrown the summit of the rock was all on fire, blazing high into the night and fitfully illuminating the whole field. Each pendent twig and leafy festoon was in a blaze. As the red light arose and fell, a numerous congregation alternately shone forth, then disappeared in shadow, and again grew, as it were, out of the darkness, peopling the heart of the solitary woods at once.

"A grave and dark-clad company," quoth Goodman Brown.

In truth they were such. Among them, quivering to and fro between gloom and splendor, appeared faces that would be seen next day at the council board of the province, and others which, Sabbath after Sabbath, looked devoutly heavenward, and benignantly over the crowded pews, from the holiest pulpits in the land. Some affirm that the lady of the governor was there. At least there were high dames well known to her, and wives of honored husbands, and widows, a great multitude, and ancient maidens, all of excellent repute, and fair young girls, who trembled lest their mothers should espy them. Either the sudden gleams of light flashing over the obscure field bedazzled Goodman Brown, or he recognized a score of the church members of Salem village famous for their especial sanctity. Good old Deacon Gookin had arrived, and waited at the skirts of that venerable saint, his revered pastor. But, irreverently consorting with these grave, reputable, and pious people, these elders of the church, these chaste dames and dewy virgins, there were men of dissolute lives and women of spotted fame, wretches given over to all mean and filthy vice, and suspected even of horrid crimes. It was strange to see that the good shrank not from the wicked, nor were the sinners abashed by the saints. Scattered also among their pale-faced enemies were the Indian priests, or powwows, who had often scared their native forest with more hideous incantations than any known to English witchcraft.

"But where is Faith?" thought Goodman Brown; and, as hope came into his heart, he trembled.

Another verse of the hymn arose, a slow and mournful strain, such as the pious love, but joined to words which expressed all that our nature can conceive of sin, and darkly hinted at far more. Unfathomable to mere mortals is the lore of fiends. Verse after verse was sung; and still the chorus of the desert swelled between like the deepest tone of a mighty organ; and with the final peal of that dreadful anthem there came a sound, as if the roaring wind, the rushing streams, the howling beasts, and every other voice of the unconcerted wilderness were mingling and according with the voice of guilty man in homage to the prince of all. The four blazing pines threw up a loftier flame, and obscurely discovered shapes and visages of horror on the smoke wreaths above the impious assembly. At the same moment the fire on the rock shot redly forth and formed a flowing arch above its base, where now appeared a figure. With reverence be it spoken, the figure bore no slight similitude, both in garb and manner, to some grave divine of the New England churches.

"Bring forth the converts!" cried a voice that echoed through the field and rolled into the forest.

At the word, Goodman Brown stepped forth from the shadow of the trees and approached the congregation, with whom he felt a loathful brotherhood by the sympathy of all that was wicked in his heart. He could have well-nigh sworn that the shape of his own dead father beckoned him to advance, looking downward from a smoke wreath, while a woman, with dim features of despair, threw out her hand to warn him back. Was it his mother? But he had no power to retreat one step, nor to resist, even in thought, when the minister and good old Deacon Gookin seized his arms and led him to the blazing rock. Thither came also the slender form of a veiled female, led between Goody Cloyse, that pious teacher of the catechism, and Martha Carrier, who had received the devil's promise to be queen of hell. A rampant hag was she. And there stood the proselytes[3] beneath the canopy of fire.

"Welcome, my children," said the dark figure, "to the communion of your race. Ye have found thus young your nature and your destiny. My children, look behind you!"

They turned; and flashing forth, as it were, in a sheet of flame, the fiend worshippers were seen; the smile of welcome gleamed darkly on every visage.

"There," resumed the sable form, "are all whom ye have reverenced from youth. Ye deemed them holier than yourselves and shrank from your own sin, contrasting it with their lives of righteousness and prayerful aspirations heavenward. Yet here are they all in my worshipping assembly. This night it shall be granted you to know their secret deeds: how hoary-bearded elders of the church have whispered wanton words to the young maids of their households; how many a woman, eager for widows' weeds, has given her husband a drink at bedtime and let him sleep his last sleep in her bosom; how beardless youths have made haste to inherit their fathers' wealth; and how fair damsels—blush not, sweet ones — have dug little graves in the garden, and bidden me, the sole guest, to an infant's funeral. By the sympathy of your human hearts for sin ye shall scent out all the places—whether in church, bed-chamber, street, field, or forest—where crime has been committed, and shall exult to behold the whole earth one stain of guilt, one mighty blood spot. Far more than this. It shall be yours to penetrate, in every bosom, the deep mystery of sin, the fountain of all wicked arts, and which inexhaustibly supplies

---

[3] Converts.

more evil impulses than human power—than my power at its utmost—can make manifest in deeds. And now, my children, look upon each other."

They did so; and, by the blaze of the hell-kindled torches, the wretched man beheld his Faith, and the wife her husband, trembling before that unhallowed altar.

"Lo, there ye stand, my children," said the figure, in a deep and solemn tone, almost sad with its despairing awfulness, as if his once angelic nature could yet mourn for our miserable race. "Depending upon one another's hearts, ye had still hoped that virtue were not all a dream. Now are ye undeceived. Evil is the nature of mankind. Evil must be your only happiness. Welcome again, my children, to the communion of your race."

"Welcome," repeated the fiend worshippers, in one cry of despair and triumph.

And there they stood, the only pair, as it seemed, who were yet hesitating on the verge of wickedness in this dark world. A basin was hallowed, naturally, in the rock. Did it contain water, reddened by the lurid light? or was it blood? or, perchance, a liquid flame? Herein did the shape of evil dip his hand and prepare to lay the mark of baptism upon their foreheads, that they might be partakers of the mystery of sin, more conscious of the secret guilt of others, both in deed and thought, than they could now be of their own. The husband cast one look at his pale wife, and Faith at him. What polluted wretches would the next glance show them to each other, shuddering alike at what they disclosed and what they saw!

"Faith! Faith!" cried the husband, "look up to heaven, and resist the wicked one."

Whether Faith obeyed he knew not. Hardly had he spoken when he found himself amid calm night and solitude, listening to a roar of the wind which died heavily away through the forest. He staggered against the rock, and felt it chill and damp; while a hanging twig, that had been all on fire, besprinkled his cheek with the coldest dew.

The next morning young Goodman Brown came slowly into the street of Salem village, staring around him like a bewildered man. The good old minister was taking a walk along the graveyard to get an appetite for breakfast and meditate his sermon, and bestowed a blessing, as he passed, on Goodman Brown. He shrank from the venerable saint as if to avoid an anathema. Old Deacon Gookin was at domestic worship, and the holy words of his prayer were heard through the open window. "What God doth the wizard pray to?" quoth Goodman Brown. Goody Cloyse, that excellent old Christian, stood in the early sunshine at her own lattice, catechizing a little girl who had brought her a pint of morning's milk. Goodman Brown snatched away the child as from the grasp of the fiend himself. Turning the corner by the meeting-house, he spied the head of Faith, with the pink ribbons, gazing anxiously forth, and bursting into such joy at sight of him that she skipped along the street and almost kissed her husband before the whole village. But Goodman Brown looked sternly and sadly into her face, and passed on without a greeting.

Had Goodman Brown fallen asleep in the forest and only dreamed a wild dream of a witch-meeting?

Be it so if you will; but, alas! it was a dream of evil omen for young Goodman Brown. A stern, a sad, a darkly meditative, a distrustful, if not a desperate man did he become from the night of that fearful dream. On the Sabbath day, when the congregation were singing a holy psalm, he could not listen because an anthem of sin rushed loudly upon his ear and drowned all the blessed strain. When the minister spoke from the pulpit with power and fervid eloquence, and, with his hand on the open Bible, of the sacred truths of our religion, and of saint-like lives and triumphant deaths, and of future bliss or misery unutterable, then did Goodman Brown turn pale, dreading lest the roof should thunder down upon the gray blasphemer and his hearers. Often, awaking suddenly at midnight, he shrank from the bosom of Faith; and at morning or eventide, when the family knelt down at prayer, he scowled and muttered to himself, and gazed sternly at his wife, and turned away. And when he had lived long, and was borne to his grave a hoary corpse, followed by Faith, an aged woman, and children and grandchildren, a goodly procession, besides neighbors not a few, they carved no hopeful verse upon his tombstone, for his dying hour was gloom.

# The Cask of Amontillado

The thousand injuries of Fortunato I had borne as I best could; but when he ventured upon insult, I vowed revenge. You, who so well know the nature of my soul, will not suppose, however, that I gave utterance to a threat. *At length* I would be avenged; this was a point definitely settled—but the very definitiveness with which it was resolved precluded the idea of risk. I must not only punish, but punish with impunity. A wrong is unredressed when retribution overtakes its redresser. It is equally unredressed when the avenger fails to make himself felt as such to him who has done the wrong.

It must be understood, that neither by word nor deed had I given Fortunato cause to doubt my good-will. I continued, as was my wont, to smile in his face, and he did not perceive that my smile *now* was at the thought of his immolation.

He had a weak point—this Fortunato—although in other regards he was a man to be respected and even feared. He prided himself on his connoisseurship in wine. Few Italians have the true virtuoso spirit. For the most part their enthusiasm is adopted to suit the time and opportunity to practice imposture upon the British and Austrian *millionaires.* In painting and gemmary Fortunato, like his countrymen, was a quack, but in the matter of old wines he was sincere. In this respect I did not differ from him materially; — I was skillful in the Italian vintages myself, and bought largely whenever I could.

It was about dusk, one evening during the supreme madness of the carnival season, that I encountered my friend. He accosted me with excessive warmth, for he had been drinking much. The man wore motley. He had on a tight-fitting parti-striped dress, and his head was surmounted by the conical cap and bells. I was so pleased to see him, that I thought I should never have done wringing his hand.

I said to him—"My dear Fortunato, you are luckily met. How remarkably well you are looking to-day! But I have received a pipe[1] of what passes for Amontillado,[2] and I have my doubts."

"How?" said he. "Amontillado? A pipe? Impossible! And in the middle of the carnival!"

"I have my doubts," I replied; "and I was silly enough to pay the full Amontillado price without consulting you in the matter. You were not to be found, and I was fearful of losing a bargain."

"Amontillado!"

"I have my doubts."

"Amontillado!"

"And I must satisfy them."

"Amontillado!"

"As you are engaged, I am on my way to Luchesi. If any one has a critical turn, it is he. He will tell me—"

"Luchesi cannot tell Amontillado from Sherry."

"And yet some fools will have it that his taste is a match for your own."

"Come, let us go."

"Whither?"

"To your vaults."

"My friend, no; I will not impose upon your good nature. I perceive you have an engagement. Luchesi—"

"I have no engagement; come."

"My friend, no. It is not the engagement, but the severe cold with which I perceive you are afflicted. The vaults are insufferably damp. They are encrusted with nitre."

"Let us go, nevertheless. The cold is merely nothing. Amontillado! You have been imposed upon. And as for Luchesi, he cannot distinguish Sherry from Amontillado."

Thus speaking, Fortunato possessed himself of my arm. Putting on a mask of black silk, and drawing a *roquelaure*[3] closely about my person, I suffered him to hurry me to my palazzo.

There were no attendants at home; they had absconded to make merry in honor of the time. I had told them that I should

---

[1] Wine cask.

[2] A prized Spanish sherry.

[3] Short cloak.

not return until the morning, and had given them explicit orders not to stir from the house. These orders were sufficient, I well knew, to insure their immediate disappearance, one and all, as soon as my back was turned.

I took from their sconces two flambeaux,[4] and giving one to Fortunato, bowed him through several suites of rooms to the archway that led into the vaults. I passed down a long and winding staircase, requesting him to be cautious as he followed. We came at length to the foot of the descent, and stood together on the damp ground of the catacombs of the Montresors.

The gait of my friend was unsteady, and the bells upon his cap jingled as he strode.

"The pipe," said he.

"It is farther on," said I; "but observe the white web-work which gleams from these cavern walls."

He turned towards me, and looked into my eyes with two filmy orbs that distilled the rheum of intoxication.

"Nitre?" he asked, at length.

"Nitre," I replied. "How long have you had that cough?"

"Ugh! ugh! ugh!—ugh! ugh! ugh!—ugh! ugh! ugh!—ugh! ugh! ugh!—ugh! ugh! ugh!"

My poor friend found it impossible to reply for many minutes.

"It is nothing," he said, at last.

"Come," I said, with decision, "we will go back; your health is precious. You are rich, respected, admired, beloved; you are happy, as once I was. You are a man to be missed. For me it is no matter. We will go back; you will be ill, and I cannot be responsible. Besides, there is Luchesi—"

"Enough," he said; "the cough is a mere nothing: it will not kill me. I shall not die of a cough."

"True—true," I replied; "and, indeed, I had no intention of alarming you unnecessarily—but you should use all proper caution. A draught of this Medoc will defend us from the damps."

Here I knocked off the neck of a bottle which I drew from a long row of its fellows that lay upon the mould.

"Drink," I said, presenting him the wine.

---

[4] Torches.

He raised it to his lips with a leer. He paused and nodded to me familiarly, while his bells jingled.

"I drink," he said, "to the buried that repose around us."

"And I to your long life."

He again took my arm, and we proceeded.

"These vaults," he said, "are extensive."

"The Montresors," I replied. "were a great and numerous family."

"I forget your arms."

"A huge human foot d'or, in a field azure; the foot crushes a serpent rampant whose fangs are imbedded in the heel."

"And the motto?"

"*Nemo me impune lacessit.*"[5]

"Good!" he said.

The wine sparkled in his eyes and the bells jingled. My own fancy grew warm with the Medoc. We had passed through walls of piled bones, with casks and puncheons intermingling into the inmost recesses of the catacombs. I paused again, and this time I made bold to seize Fortunato by an arm above the elbow.

"The nitre!" I said; "see, it increases. It hangs like moss upon the vaults. We are below the river's bed. The drops of moisture trickle among the bones. Come, we will go back ere it is too late. Your cough—"

"It is nothing," he said; "let us go on. But first, another draught of the Medoc."

I broke and reached him a flagon of De Grâve. He emptied it at a breath. His eyes flashed with a fierce light. He laughed and threw the bottle upwards with a gesticulation I did not understand.

I looked at him in surprise. He repeated the movement—a grotesque one.

"You do not comprehend?" he said.

"Not I," I replied.

"Then you are not of the brotherhood."

"How?"

"You are not of the masons."

---

[5] "No one dare attack me with impunity" (the motto of Scotland).

"Yes, yes," I said, "yes, yes."

"You? Impossible! A mason?"

"A mason," I replied.

"A sign," he said.

"It is this," I answered, producing a trowel from beneath the folds of my *roquelaure.*

"You jest," he exclaimed, recoiling a few paces. "But let us proceed to the Amontillado."

"Be it so," I said, replacing the tool beneath the cloak, and again offering him my arm. He leaned upon it heavily. We continued our route in search of the Amontillado. We passed through a range of low arches, descended, passed on, and descending again, arrived at a deep crypt, in which the foulness of the air caused our flambeaux rather to glow than flame.

At the most remote end of the crypt there appeared another less spacious. Its walls had been lined with human remains, piled to the vault overhead, in the fashion of the great catacombs of Paris. Three sides of this interior crypt were still ornamented in this manner. From the fourth the bones had been thrown down, and lay promiscuously upon the earth, forming at one point a mound of some size. Within the wall thus exposed by the displacing of the bones, we perceived a still interior recess, in depth about four feet, in width three, in height six or seven. It seemed to have been constructed for no especial use within itself, but formed merely the interval between two of the colossal supports of the roof of the catacombs, and was backed by one of their circumscribing walls of solid granite.

It was in vain that Fortunato, uplifting his dull torch, endeavored to pry into the depths of the recess. Its termination the feeble light did not enable us to see.

"Proceed," I said; "herein is the Amontillado. As for Luchesi—"

"He is an ignoramus," interrupted my friend, as he stepped unsteadily forward, while I followed immediately at his heels. In an instant he had reached the extremity of the niche, and finding his progress arrested by the rock, stood stupidly bewildered. A moment more and I had fettered him to the granite. In its surface were two iron staples, distant from each other about two feet, horizontally. From one of these depended a short chain, from the other a padlock. Throwing the links about his waist, it was but the work of a few seconds to secure it. He was too much astounded to resist. Withdrawing the key I stepped back from the recess.

"Pass your hand," I said, "over the wall; you cannot help feeling the nitre. Indeed it is *very* damp. Once more let me *implore* you to return. No? Then I must positively leave you. But I must first render you all the little attentions in my power."

"The Amontillado!" ejaculated my friend, not yet recovered from his astonishment.

"True," I replied; "the Amontillado."

As I said these words I busied myself among the pile of bones of which I have before spoken. Throwing them aside, I soon uncovered a quantity of building-stone and mortar. With these materials and with the aid of my trowel, I began vigorously to wall up the entrance of the niche.

I had scarcely laid the first tier of the masonry when I discovered that the intoxication of Fortunato had in a great measure worn off. The earliest indication I had of this was a low moaning cry from the depth of the recess. It was *not* the cry of a drunken man. There was then a long and obstinate silence. I laid the second tier, and the third, and the fourth; and then I heard the furious vibrations of the chain. The noise lasted for several minutes, during which, that I might hearken to it with the more satisfaction, I ceased my labors and sat down upon the bones. When at last the clanking subsided, I resumed the trowel, and finished without interruption the fifth, the sixth, and the seventh tier. The wall was now nearly upon a level with my breast. I again paused, and holding the flambeaux over the masonwork, threw a few feeble rays upon the figure within.

A succession of loud and shrill screams, bursting suddenly from the throat of the chained form, seemed to thrust me violently back. For a brief moment I hesitated—I trembled. Unsheathing my rapier, I began to grope with it about the recess; but the thought of an instant reassured me. I placed my hand upon the solid fabric of the catacombs, and felt satisfied. I reapproached the wall. I replied to the yells of him who clamored. I re-echoed—I aided—I surpassed them in volume and in strength. I did this, and the clamorer grew still.

It was now midnight, and my task was drawing to a close. I had completed the eighth, the ninth, and the tenth tier. I had finished a portion of the last and the eleventh; there remained but a single stone to be fitted and plastered in. I struggled with its weight; I placed it partially in its destined position. But now there came from out the niche a low laugh that erected the hairs upon my head. It was succeeded by a sad voice, which I had difficulty in recognizing as that of the noble Fortunato. The voice said—

"Ha! ha! ha!—he! he! he!—a very good joke indeed—an excellent jest. We will have many a rich laugh about it at the palazzo—he! he! he!—over our wine—he! he! he!"

"The Amontillado!" I said.

"He! he! he!—he! he! he!—yes, the Amontillado. But is it not getting late? Will not they be awaiting us at the palazzo, the Lady Fortunato and the rest? Let us be gone."

"Yes," I said, "let us be gone."

*"For the love of God, Montresor!"*

"Yes," I said, "for the love of God!"

But to these words I hearkened in vain for a reply. I grew impatient. I called aloud:

"Fortunato!"

No answer. I called again;

"Fortunato!"

No answer still, I thrust a torch through the remaining aperture and let it fall within. There came forth in return only a jingling of the bells. My heart grew sick—on account of the dampness of the catacombs. I hastened to make an end of my labor. I forced the last stone into its position; I plastered it up. Against the new masonry I re-erected the old rampart of bones. For the half of a century no mortal has disturbed them. *In pace requiescat!*[6]

---

[6] "May he rest in peace!"

FEODOR DOSTOEVSKY [1821–1881]

# A Christmas Tree
# and a Wedding

The other day I saw a wedding . . . but no! Better I tell you about the Christmas tree. The wedding was nice; I enjoyed it very much, but the other thing that happened was better. I do not know why, but while looking at the wedding, I thought about that Christmas tree. This was the way it happened.

On New Year's Eve, exactly five years ago, I was invited to a children's party. The host was a well-known businessman with many connections, friends and intrigues, so you might think the children's party was a pretext for the parents to meet each other and to talk things over in an innocent, casual and inadvertent manner.

I was an outsider. I did not have anything to contribute, and therefore I spent the evening on my own. There was another gentleman present who had no special family or position, but, like myself had dropped in on this family happiness. He was the first to catch my eye. He was a tall, lean man, very serious and very properly dressed. Actually he was not enjoying this family-type party in the least. If he withdrew into a corner, he immediately stopped smiling and knit his thick bushy black eyebrows. Except for our host, the man had not a single acquaintance at the whole party. Obviously, he was terribly bored, but he was making a gallant effort to play the role of a perfectly happy, contented man. Afterwards I learned he was a gentleman from the provinces, with important, puzzling business in the capital; he had brought our host a letter of introduction, from a person our host did not patronize, so this man was invited to this children's party only out of courtesy. He didn't even play cards. They offered him no cigars; no one engaged him in conversation. Perhaps we recognized the bird by its feathers from a distance; that is why my gentleman was compelled to sit out the whole evening and stroke

Translated by P. H. Porosky.

his whiskers merely to have something to do with his hands. His whiskers really were very fine, but he stroked them so diligently, you thought the whiskers came first, and were then fixed onto his face, the better to stroke them.

Besides this man—who had five well-fed boys—my attention was caught by a second gentleman. He was an important person. His name was Yulian Mastakovitch. With one glance, you saw he was a guest of honor. He looked down on the host much as the host looked down on the gentleman who stroked his whiskers. The host and hostess spoke to the important man from across a chasm of courtesy, waited on him, gave him drink, pampered him, and brought their guests to him for introductions. They did not take him to anyone.

When Yulian Mastakovitch commented, in regard to the evening, that he had seldom spent time in such a pleasant manner, I noticed tears sparkled in the host's eyes. In the presence of such a person, I was frightened, and, after admiring the children, I walked into a small deserted drawing-room and sat down beside an arbour of flowers which took up almost half of the room.

All the children were incredibly sweet. They absolutely refused to imitate their "elders," despite all the exhortations of their governesses and mothers. In an instant the children untwisted all the Christmas tree candy and broke half of the toys before they knew for whom they were intended. One small, black eyed, curly haired boy was especially nice. He kept wanting to shoot me with his wooden gun. But my attention was still more drawn to his sister, a girl of eleven, a quiet, pensive, pale little cupid with large thoughtful eyes. In some way, the children wounded her feelings, and so she came into the same room where I sat and busied herself in the corner—with her doll.

The guests respectfully pointed out one of the wealthy commissioned tax gatherers—her father. In a whisper someone said three hundred thousand roubles were already set aside for her dowry.

I swung around to look at those who were curious about such circumstances: my gaze fell on Yulian Mastakovitch. With his hands behind his back, with his head cocked a little to one side, he listened with extraordinary attention to the empty talk of the guests.

Later, I marveled at the wisdom of the host and hostess in the distribution of the children's gifts. The little girl—already the owner of three hundred thousand roubles—received the most expensive doll. Then followed presents lowering in value according to the class of the parents of these happy children. Finally, the last gift: a young boy, ten years-old, slender, small, freckled, red-haired, received only a book of stories about the marvels of nature and the tears of devotion—without pictures and even without engravings. He was the son of the governess of the hosts' children, a poor widow; he was a little boy, extremely oppressed and frightened. He wore a jacket made from a wretched nankeen.[1] After he received his book, he walked around the other toys for a long time; he wanted to play with the other children, but he did not dare; he already felt and understood his position.

I love to watch children. They are extraordinarily fascinating in their first independent interests in life. I noticed the red-haired boy was so tempted by the costly toys of the other children, especially a theater in which he certainly wanted to take some kind of part, that he decided to act differently. He smiled and began playing with the other children. He gave away his apple to a puffy little boy, who had bound up a full handkerchief of sweets. He even went as far as to carry another boy on his back, so they would not turn him away from the theater. But a minute later, a kind of mischievous child gave him a considerable beating. The boy did not dare to cry. Here the governess, his mother, appeared and ordered him not to disturb the play of the other children. Then the boy went to the same room where the little girl was. She allowed him to join her. Very eagerly they both began to dress the expensive doll.

I had been already sitting in the ivy-covered arbour for a half an hour. I was almost asleep, yet listening to the little conversations of the red-haired boy and the little beauty with the dowry of three hundred thousand fussing over her doll.

Suddenly Yulian Mastakovitch walked into the room. Under cover of the quarreling children, he had noiselessly left the drawing-room. A minute before I noticed he was talking very fervently with the father of the future heiress, with whom he had just become acquainted. He discussed the advantages of one branch

---

[1] A durable cotton fabric loomed in China.

of the service over another. Now he stood deep in thought, as if he were calculating something on his fingers.

"Three hundred . . . three hundred," he whispered. "Eleven, twelve, thirteen," and so forth. "Sixteen—five years! Let us assume it is at four per cent—five times twelve is sixty, yes, to that sixty . . . now let us assume what it will be in five years—four hundred. Yes! Well . . . oh, but he won't hold to four per cent, the swindler. Maybe he can get eight or ten. Well, five hundred, let us assume five hundred thousand, the final measure, that's certain. Well, say a little extra for frills. H'm . . ."

He ended his reflection. He blew his nose, and intended to leave the room. Suddenly he glanced at the little girl and stopped short. He did not see me behind the pots of greenery. It seemed to me that he was really disturbed. Either his calculations had affected him, or something else. He rubbed his hands and could not stand in one place. This nervousness increased to the utmost limit. And then he stopped and threw another resolute glance at the future heiress. He was about to advance, but first he looked around. On tiptoe, as if he felt guilty, he approached the children. With a half-smile, he drew near, stooped, and kissed the little girl on the head. Not expecting the attack, she cried out, frightened.

"And what are you doing here, sweet child?" he asked in a whisper, looking around a patting the girl on the cheek.

"We are playing."

"Ah, with him?" Yulian Mastakovitch looked to one side at the boy. "And you, my dear, go into the drawing-room."

The boy kept silent and stared at him with open eyes.

Yulian Mastakovitch again looked around him and again stooped to the little girl.

"And what is this you have," he asked, "A dolly, sweet child?"

"A dolly," the little girl answered, wrinkling her face, a trifle shy.

"A dolly . . . and do you know, my sweet child, from what your dolly is made?"

"I don't know . . ." answered the little girl in a whisper, hanging her head.

"From rags, darling. You'd better go into the drawing-room to your companions, little boy," said Yulian Mastakovitch, staring severely at the child. The little girl and boy made a wry face and held onto each other's hand. They did not want to be separated.

"And do you know why they gave you that doll?" asked Yulian Mastakovitch, lowering his voice more and more.

"I don't know."

"Because you have been a sweet, well-behaved child all week."

Here Yulian Mastakovitch, emotional as could be, looked around and lowered his voice more and more, and finally asked, inaudibly, almost standing completely still from excitement and with an impatient voice:

"And will you love me, sweet little girl? When I come to visit your parents?"

Having said this, Yulian Mastakovitch tried once again to kiss the sweet girl. The red-haired boy, seeing that she wanted to cry, gripped her hand and began to whimper from sheer sympathy for her. Yulian Mastakovitch became angry, and not in jest.

"Go away. Go away from here, go away!" he said to the little boy. "Go into the drawing-room! Go in there to your companions!"

"No, he doesn't have to, doesn't have to! You go away," said the little girl, almost crying, "Leave him alone, leave him alone!"

Someone made a noise at the door.

Yulian Mastakovitch immediately raised his majestic body and became frightened. But the red-haired boy was even more startled than Yulian Mastakovitch. He left the little girl and quietly, guided by the wall, passed from the drawing-room into the dining-room. To avoid arousing suspicion, Yulian Mastakovitch also went into the dining-room. He was red as a lobster. He glanced into the mirror, as if he were disconcerted. He was perhaps annoyed with himself for his fervor and his impatience. At first perhaps he was so struck by the calculations on his fingers, so enticed and inspired that in spite of all his dignity and importance, he decided to act like a little boy, and directly pursue the object of his attentions even though she could not possibly be *his* object for at least five more years.

I followed the respectable gentleman into the dining-room. I beheld a strange sight. All red from vexation and anger, Yulian Mastakovitch frightened the red-haired boy, who was walking farther and farther, and in his fear did not know where to run.

"Go away. What are you doing here? Go away, you scamp, go away! You're stealing the fruits here, ah? You're stealing the fruits here? Go away, you reprobate. Go away. You snot-nosed boy, go away. Go to your companions!"

The frightened boy tried to get under the table. Then his persecutor, flushed as could be, took out his large batiste handkerchief and began to lash under the table at the child, who remained absolutely quiet.

It must be noted that Yulian Mastakovitch was a little stout. He was a man, well-filled out, red-faced, sleek, with a paunch, with thick legs; in short, what is called a fine figure of a man, round as a nut. He was sweating, puffing and turning terribly red. Finally, he was almost in a frenzy, so great were his feelings of indignation and perhaps (who knows?) jealousy.

I burst out laughing at the top of my voice. Yulian Mastakovitch turned around, and despite all his manners, he was confounded into dust. From the opposite door at that moment came the host. The little boy climbed out from under the table and wiped his elbows and knees. Yulian Mastakovitch hurriedly blew his nose on a handkerchief, which he held in his hand by a corner.

Meanwhile, the host gave the three of us a puzzled look. But as with a man who knows life and looks at it with dead seriousness, he immediately availed himself of the chance to catch his guest in private.

"Here's the little boy," he said pointing to the red-haired boy, "for whom I was intending to intercede, your honor . . ."

"Ah?" answered Yulian Mastakovitch, still not fully put in order.

"The son of my children's governess," the host continued with a pleading tone. "A poor woman, a widow, wife of an honest official; and therefore . . . Yulian Mastakovitch if it were possible . . ."

"Oh, no, no," hurriedly answered Yulian Mastakovitch, "no, excuse me, Filip Alexyevitch, it's no way possible. I've asked, there are no vacancies. If there were, there are already ten candidates—all better qualified than he . . . I'm very sorry. Very sorry . . ."

"I am sorry," repeated the host. "The little boy is modest, quiet . . ."

"A very mischievous boy, as I've noticed," answered Yulian Mastakovitch, hysterically distorting his mouth. "Go away, little boy," he said addressing the child. "Why are you staying, go to your companions!"

It seemed he could not restrain himself. He glanced at me with one eye. In fun I could not restrain myself and burst out laughing directly in his face.

Yulian Mastakovitch immediately turned away, and clear enough for me to hear, he asked the host who was that strange young man. They whispered together and left the room. Afterwards, I saw Yulian Mastakovitch listening to the host, mistrustfully shaking his head.

After laughing to my heart's content, I returned to the drawing-room. Surrounded by the fathers and mothers of the families and the host and hostess, the great man was uttering a mating call with warmth, towards a lady to whom he had just been introduced.

The lady was holding by the hand the girl, with whom ten minutes ago Yulian Mastakovitch had had the scene in the drawing-room. Now, he was showering praise and delight about the beauty, talent, grace and good manners of the sweet child. He was fawning, obviously, over the mamma; the mother listened to him almost in tears from delight. The father's lips made a smile; the host rejoiced because of the general satisfaction. All the guests were the same, and even the children stopped playing in order not to disturb the conversation. The whole atmosphere was saturated with reverence.

Later, as if touched to the depth of her heart, I heard the mother of the interesting child beg Yulian Mastakovitch to do her the special honor of presenting them his precious acquaintanceship; and I heard, with his kind of unaffected delight, Yulian Mastakovitch accepting the invitation. Afterwards, the guests all dispersed in different directions, as decency demanded; they spilled out to each other touching words of praise upon the commissioned tax gatherer who worked farmers, his wife, their daughter, and especially Yulian Mastakovitch.

"Is that gentleman married?" I asked, almost aloud, of one of my acquaintances, who was standing closest to Yulian Mastakovitch.

Yulian Mastakovitch threw at me a searching, malicious glance.

"No!" my friend answered me, chagrined to the bottom of his heart at my awkwardness, which I had displayed deliberately.

Recently, I walked by a certain church. The crowd, the congress of people startled me. All around they talked about the wedding. The day was cloudy, and it was starting to drizzle; I made my way through the crowd around the church and saw the bridegroom.

He was a small, rotund, well-fed man with a slight paunch and highly dressed. He was running about, bustling, and giving orders. Finally, the voices of the crowd said that the bride was coming. I pushed my way through the crowd and saw a wonderful beauty, who had scarcely begun her first season. But the beauty was pale and sad. She looked distracted; it even seemed to me that her eyes were red from recent crying. The classical severity of every line of her face added a certain dignity and solemnity to her beauty. Through that severity and dignity, through that sadness, still appeared the first look of childish innocence—very naive, fluid, youthful, and yet neither asking nor entreating for mercy.

They were saying she was just sixteen years-old. Glancing carefully at the bridegroom, I suddenly recognized him as Yulian Mastakovitch, whom I had not seen for five years. I took a look at her. My God!

I began to push my way quickly out of the church. The voices of the crowd said the bride was rich: a dowry of five hundred thousand . . . and a trousseau with ever so much . . .

"It was a good calculation, though," I thought, and made my way out into the street.

## LEO TOLSTOY [1828–1910]

# How Much Land Does a Man Need?

### 1

An elder sister came to visit her younger sister in the country. The elder was married to a tradesman in town, the younger to a peasant in the village. As the sisters sat over their tea talking, the elder began to boast of the advantages of town life: saying how comfortably they lived there, how well they dressed, what fine clothes her children wore, what good things they ate and drank,

---

Translated by Alymer and Louise Maude.

and how she went to the theatre, promenades, and entertainments.

The younger sister was piqued, and in turn disparaged the life of a tradesman, and stood up for that of a peasant.

"I would not change my way of life for yours," said she. "We may live roughly, but at least we are free from anxiety. You live in better style than we do, but though you often earn more than you need, you are very likely to lose all you have. You know the proverb, 'Loss and gain are brothers twain.' It often happens that people who are wealthy one day are begging their bread the next. Our way is safer. Though a peasant's life is not a fat one, it is a long one. We shall never grow rich, but we shall always have enough to eat."

The elder sister said sneeringly:

"Enough? Yes, if you like to share with the pigs and the calves! What do you know of elegance or manners! However much your goodman may slave, you will die as you are living—on a dung heap—and your children the same."

"Well, what of that?" replied the younger. "Of course our work is rough and coarse. But, on the other hand, it is sure, and we need not bow down to anyone. But you, in your towns, are surrounded by temptations; to-day all may be right, but to-morrow the Evil One may tempt your husband with cards, wine, or women, and all will go to ruin. Don't such things happen often enough?"

Pahóm, the master of the house, was lying on the top of the stove and he listened to the women's chatter.

"It is perfectly true," thought he. "Busy as we are from childhood tilling mother earth, we peasants have no time to let any nonsense settle in our heads. Our only trouble is that we haven't land enough. If I had plenty of land, I shouldn't fear the Devil himself!"

The women finished their tea, chatted a while about dress, and then cleared away the tea-things and lay down to sleep.

But the Devil had been sitting behind the stove, and had heard all that was said. He was pleased that the peasant's wife had led her husband into boasting, and that he had said that if he had plenty of land he would not fear the Devil himself.

"All right," thought the Devil. "We will have a tussle. I'll give you land enough; and by means of that land I will get you into my power."

## 2

Close to the village there lived a lady, a small landowner who had an estate of about three hundred acres.[1] She had always lived on good terms with the peasants until she engaged as her steward an old soldier, who took to burdening the people with fines. However careful Pahóm tried to be, it happened again and again that now a horse of his got among the lady's oats, now a cow strayed into her garden, now his calves found their way into her meadows—and he always had to pay a fine.

Pahóm paid up, but grumbled and, going home in a temper, was rough with his family. All through that summer, Pahóm had much trouble because of this steward, and he was even glad when winter came and the cattle had to be stabled. Though he grudged the fodder when they could no longer graze on the pasture-land, at least he was free from anxiety about them.

In the winter the news got about that the lady was going to sell her land and that the keeper of the inn on the high road was bargaining for it. When the peasants heard this they were very much alarmed.

"Well," thought they, "if the innkeeper gets the land, he will worry us with fines worse than the lady's steward. We all depend on that estate."

So the peasants went on behalf of their Commune, and asked the lady not to sell the land to the innkeeper, offering her a better price for it themselves. The lady agreed to let them have it. Then the peasants tried to arrange for the Commune to buy the whole estate, so that it might be held by them all in common. They met twice to discuss it, but could not settle the matter; the Evil One sowed discord among them and they could not agree. So they decided to buy the land individually, each according to his means; and the lady agreed to this plan as she had to the other.

Presently Pahóm heard that a neighbor of his was buying fifty acres, and that the lady had consented to accept one half in cash and to wait a year for the other half. Pahóm felt envious.

---

[1] One hundred twenty desyatíns. The desyatína is properly 2.7 acres; but in this story round numbers are used [translators' note].

"Look at that," thought he, "the land is all being sold, and I shall get none of it." So he spoke to his wife.

"Other people are buying," said he, "and we must also buy twenty acres or so. Life is becoming impossible. That steward is simply crushing us with his fines."

So they put their heads together and considered how they could manage to buy it. They had one hundred rúbles laid by. They sold a colt and one half of their bees, hired out one of their sons as a laborer and took his wages in advance; borrowed the rest from a brother-in-law, and so scraped together half the purchase money.

Having done this, Pahóm chose out a farm of forty acres, some of it wooded, and went to the lady to bargain for it. They came to an agreement, and he shook hands with her upon it and paid her a deposit in advance. Then they went to town and signed the deeds; he paying half the price down, and undertaking to pay the remainder within two years.

So now Pahóm had land of his own. He borrowed seed, and sowed it on the land he had bought. The harvest was a good one, and within a year he had managed to pay off his debts both to the lady and to his brother-in-law. So he became a landowner, ploughing and sowing his own land, making hay on his own land, cutting his own trees, and feeding his cattle on his own pasture. When he went out to plough his fields, or to look at his growing corn, or at his grass-meadows, his heart would fill with joy. The grass that grew and the flowers that bloomed there seemed to him unlike any that grew elsewhere. Formerly, when he had passed by that land, it had appeared the same as any other land, but now it seemed quite different.

### 3

So Pahóm was well-contented, and everything would have been right if the neighboring peasants would only not have trespassed on his corn-fields and meadows. He appealed to them most civilly, but they still went on: now the Communal herdsmen would let the village cows stray into his meadows, then horses from the night pasture would get among his corn. Pahóm turned them out again and again, and forgave their owners, and for a long time he forbore to prosecute any one. But at last he lost patience and complained to the District Court. He knew it was the peasants' want of land, and no evil intent on their part, that caused the trouble, but he thought:

"I cannot go on overlooking it or they will destroy all I have. They must be taught a lesson."

So he had them up, gave them one lesson, and then another, and two or three of the peasants were fined. After a time Pahóm's neighbors began to bear him a grudge for this, and would now and then let their cattle on to his land on purpose. One peasant even got into Pahóm's wood at night and cut down five young lime trees for their bark. Pahóm passing through the wood one day noticed something white. He came nearer and saw the stripped trunks lying on the ground, and close by stood the stumps where the trees had been. Pahóm was furious.

"If he had only cut one here and there it would have been bad enough," thought Pahóm, "but the rascal has actually cut down a whole clump. If I could only find out who did this, I would pay him out."

He racked his brain as to who it could be. Finally he decided: "It must be Simon—no one else could have done it." So he went to Simon's homestead to have a look round, but he found nothing, and only had an angry scene. However, he now felt more certain than ever that Simon had done it, and he lodged a complaint. Simon was summoned. The case was tried, and retried, and at the end of it all Simon was acquitted, there being no evidence against him. Pahóm felt still more aggrieved, and let his anger loose upon the Elder and the Judges.

"You let thieves grease your palms," said he. "If you were honest folk yourselves you would not let a thief go free."

So Pahóm quarrelled with the Judges and with his neighbors. Threats to burn his building began to be uttered. So though Pahóm had more land, his place in the Commune was much worse than before.

About this time a rumor got about that many people were moving to new parts.

"There's no need for me to leave my land," thought Pahóm. "But some of the others might leave our village and then there would be more room for us. I would take over their land myself and make my estate a bit bigger. I could then live more at ease. As it is, I am still too cramped to be comfortable."

One day Pahóm was sitting at home when a peasant, passing through the village, happened to call in. He was allowed to stay the night, and supper was given him. Pahóm had a talk with this peasant and asked him where he came from. The stranger answered that he came from beyond the Vólga, where he had been working. One word led to another, and the man went on to say that many people were settling in those parts. He told how some people from his village had settled there. They had joined the Commune, and had had twenty-five acres per man granted them. The land was so good, he said, that the rye sown on it grew as high as a horse, and so thick that five cuts of a sickle made a sheaf. One peasant, he said, had brought nothing with him but his bare hands, and now he had six horses and two cows of his own.

Pahóm's heart kindled with desire. He thought:

"Why should I suffer in this narrow hole, if one can live so well elsewhere? I will sell my land and my homestead here, and with the money I will start afresh over there and get everything new. In this crowded place one is always having trouble. But I must first go and find out all about it myself."

Towards summer he got ready and started. He went down the Vólga on a steamer to Samára, then walked another three hundred miles on foot, and at last reached the place. It was just as the stranger had said. The peasants had plenty of land: every man had twenty-five acres of Communal land given him for his use, and any one who had money could buy, besides, at a rúble an acre as much good freehold land as he wanted.

Having found out all he wished to know, Pahóm returned home as autumn came on, and began selling off his belongings. He sold his land at a profit, sold his homestead and all his cattle, and withdrew from membership in the Commune. He only waited till the spring, and then started with his family for the new settlement.

### 4

As soon as Pahóm and his family reached their new abode, he applied for admission into the Commune of a large village. He stood treat to the Elders and obtained the necessary documents. Five shares of Communal land were given him for his own and his son's use: that is to say—125 acres (not all together, but in different fields) besides the use of the Communal pasture. Pahóm put up the buildings he needed, and bought cattle. Of the Communal land alone he had three times as much as at his former home, and the land was good corn-land. He was ten times better off than he had been. He had plenty of arable land and pasturage, and could keep as many head of cattle as he liked.

At first, in the bustle of building and settling down, Pahóm was pleased with it all, but when he got used to it he began to think that even here he had not enough land. The first year, he sowed wheat on his share of the Communal land and had a good crop. He wanted to go on sowing wheat, but had not enough Communal land for the purpose, and what he had already used was not available; for in those parts wheat is only sown on virgin soil or on fallow land. It is sown for one or two years, and then the land lies fallow till it is again overgrown with prairie grass. There were many who wanted such land and there was not enough for all; so that people quarreled about it. Those who were better off wanted it for growing wheat, and those who were poor wanted it to let to dealers, so that they might raise money to pay their taxes. Pahóm wanted to sow more wheat, so he rented land from a dealer for a year. He sowed much wheat and had a fine crop, but the land was too far from the village—the wheat had to be carted more than ten miles. After a time Pahóm noticed that some peasant-dealers were living on separate farms and were growing wealthy; and he thought:

"If I were to buy some freehold land and have a homestead on it, it would be a different thing altogether. Then it would all be nice and compact."

The question of buying freehold land recurred to him again and again.

He went on in the same way for three years, renting land and sowing wheat. The seasons turned out well and the crops were good, so that he began to lay money by. He might have gone on living contentedly, but he grew tired of having to rent other people's land every year, and having to scramble for it. Wherever there was good land to be had, the peasants would rush for it and it was taken up at once, so that unless you were sharp about it you got none. It happened in the third year that he and a dealer together rented a piece of pasture-land from some peasants; and they had already ploughed it up, when there was some dispute and the peasants went to law about it, and things fell out so that the labor was all lost.

"If it were my own land," thought Pahóm, "I should be independent, and there would not be all this unpleasantness."

So Pahóm began looking out for land which he could buy; and he came across a peasant who had bought thirteen hundred acres, but having got into difficulties was willing to sell again cheap. Pahóm bargained and haggled with him, and at last they settled the price at 1,500 rúbles, part in cash and part to be paid later. They had all but clinched the matter when a passing dealer happened to stop at Pahóm's one day to get a feed for his horses. He drank tea with Pahóm and they had a talk. The dealer said that he was just returning from the land of the Bashkírs, far away, where he had bought thirteen thousand acres of land, all for 1,000 rúbles. Pahóm questioned him further, and the tradesman said:

"All one need do is to make friends with the chiefs. I gave away about one hundred rúbles' worth of silk robes and carpets, besides a case of tea, and I gave wine to those who would drink it; and I got the land for less than a penny an acre."[2] And he showed Pahóm the title-deeds, saying:

"The land lies near a river, and the whole prairie is virgin soil."

Pahóm plied him with questions, and the tradesman said:

"There is more land there than you could cover if you walked a year, and it all belongs to the Bashkírs. They are as simple as sheep, and land can be got almost for nothing."

"There now," thought Pahóm, "with my one thousand rúbles, why should I get only thirteen hundred acres, and saddle myself with a debt besides? If I take it out there, I can get more than ten times as much for the money."

## 5

Pahóm inquired how to get to the place, and as soon as the tradesman had left him, he prepared to go there himself. He left his wife to look after the homestead, and started on his journey taking his man with him. They stopped at a town on their way

---

[2] Five kopéks for a desyatína [translators' note].

and bought a case of tea, some wine, and other presents, as the tradesman had advised. On and on they went until they had gone more than three hundred miles, and on the seventh day they came to a place where the Bashkírs had pitched their tents. It was all just as the tradesman had said. The people lived on the steppes, by a river, in felt-covered tents.[3] They neither tilled the ground, nor ate bread. Their cattle and horses grazed in herds on the steppe. The colts were tethered behind the tents, and the mares were driven to them twice a day. The mares were milked, and from the milk kumiss was made. It was the women who prepared kumiss, and they also made cheese. As far as the men were concerned, drinking kumiss and tea, eating mutton, and playing on their pipes, was all they cared about. They were all stout and merry, and all the summer long they never thought of doing any work. They were quite ignorant, and knew no Russian, but were good-natured enough.

As soon as they saw Pahóm, they came out of their tents and gathered round their visitor. An interpreter was found, and Pahóm told them he had come about some land. The Bashkírs seemed very glad; they took Pahóm and led him into one of the best tents, where they made him sit on some down cushions placed on a carpet, while they sat round him. They gave him some tea and kumiss, and had a sheep killed, and gave him mutton to eat. Pahóm took presents out of his cart and distributed them among the Bashkírs, and divided the tea amongst them. The Bashkírs were delighted. They talked a great deal among themselves, and then told the interpreter to translate.

"They wish to tell you," said the interpreter, "that they like you, and that it is our custom to do all we can to please a guest and to repay him for his gifts. You have given us presents, now tell us which of the things we possess please you best, that we may present them to you."

"What pleases me best here," answered Pahóm, "is your land. Our land is crowded and the soil is exhausted; but you have plenty of land and it is good land. I never saw the like of it."

The interpreter translated. The Bashkírs talked among them-

---

[3] A kibítka is a movable dwelling, made up of detachable wooden frames, forming a round, and covered over with felt [translators' note].

selves for a while. Pahóm could not understand what they were saying, but saw that they were much amused and that they shouted and laughed. Then they were silent and looked at Pahóm while the interpreter said:

"They wish me to tell you that in return for your presents they will gladly give you as much land as you want. You have only to point it out with your hand and it is yours."

The Bashkírs talked again for a while and began to dispute. Pahóm asked what they were disputing about, and the interpreter told him that some of them thought they ought to ask their Chief about the land and not act in his absence, while others thought there was no need to wait for his return.

## 6

**W**hile the Bashkírs were disputing, a man in a large fox-fur cap appeared on the scene. They all became silent and rose to their feet. The interpreter said, "This is our Chief himself."

Pahóm immediately fetched the best dressing-gown and five pounds of tea, and offered these to the Chief. The Chief accepted them, and seated himself in the place of honor. The Bashkírs at once began telling him something. The Chief listened for a while, then made a sign with his head for them to be silent, and addressing himself to Pahóm, said in Russian:

"Well, let it be so. Choose whatever piece of land you like; we have plenty of it."

"How can I take as much as I like?" thought Pahóm. "I must get a deed to make it secure, or else they may say, 'It is yours,' and afterwards may take it away again."

"Thank you for your kind words," he said aloud. "You have much land, and I only want a little. But I should like to be sure which bit is mine. Could it not be measured and made over to me? Life and death are in God's hands. You good people give it to me, but your children might wish to take it away again."

"You are quite right," said the Chief. "We will make it over to you."

"I heard that a dealer had been here," continued Pahóm, "and that you gave him a little land, too, and signed title-deeds to that effect. I should like to have it done in the same way."

The Chief understood.

"Yes," replied he, "that can be done quite easily. We have a scribe, and we will go to town with you and have the deed properly sealed."

"And what will be the price?" asked Pahóm.

"Our price is always the same: one thousand rúbles a day."

Pahóm did not understand.

"A day? What measure is that? How many acres would that be?"

"We do not know how to reckon it out," said the Chief. "We sell it by the day. As much as you can go round on your feet in a day is yours, and the price is one thousand rúbles a day."

Pahóm was surprised.

"But in a day you can get round a large tract of land," he said.

The Chief laughed.

"It will all be yours!" said he. "But there is one condition: If you don't return on the same day to the spot whence you started, your money is lost."

"But how am I to mark the way that I have gone?"

"Why, we shall go to any spot you like, and stay there. You must start from that spot and make your round, taking a spade with you. Wherever you think necessary, make a mark. At every turning, dig a hole and pile up the turf; then afterwards we will go round with a plough from hole to hole. You may make as large a circuit as you please, but before the sun sets you must return to the place you started from. All the land you cover will be yours."

Pahóm was delighted. It was decided to start early next morning. They talked a while, and after drinking some more kumiss and eating some more mutton, they had tea again, and then the night came on. They gave Pahóm a feather-bed to sleep on, and the Bashkírs dispersed for the night, promising to assemble the next morning at daybreak and ride out before sunrise to the appointed spot.

## 7

Pahóm lay on the feather-bed, but could not sleep. He kept thinking about the land.

"What a large tract I will mark off!" thought he. "I can easily do thirty-five miles in a day. The days are long now, and within a circuit of thirty-five miles what a lot of land there will be! I will sell the poorer land, or let it to peasants, but I'll pick out the best and farm it. I will buy two oxteams, and hire two more laborers. About a hundred and fifty acres shall be plough-land, and I will pasture cattle on the rest."

Pahóm lay awake all night, and dozed off only just before dawn. Hardly were his eyes closed when he had a dream. He thought he was lying in that same tent and heard somebody chuckling outside. He wondered who it could be, and rose and went out, and he saw the Bashkír Chief sitting in front of the tent holding his sides and rolling about with laughter. Going nearer to the Chief, Pahóm asked: "What are you laughing at?" But he saw that it was no longer the Chief, but the dealer who had recently stopped at his house and had told him about the land. Just as Pahóm was going to ask, "Have you been here long?" he saw that it was not the dealer, but the peasant who had come up from the Vólga, long ago, to Pahóm's old home. Then he saw that it was not the peasant either, but the Devil himself with hoofs and horns, sitting there and chuckling, and before him lay a man barefoot, prostrate on the ground, with only trousers and a shirt on. And Pahóm dreamt that he looked more attentively to see what sort of a man it was that was lying there, and he saw that the man was dead, and that it was himself! He awoke horror-struck.

"What things one does dream," thought he.

Looking round he saw through the open door that the dawn was breaking.

"It's time to wake them up," thought he. "We ought to be starting."

He got up, roused his man (who was sleeping in his cart), bade him harness; and went to call the Bashkírs.

"It's time to go to the steppe to measure the land," he said.

The Bashkírs rose and assembled, and the Chief came too. Then they began drinking kumiss again, and offered Pahóm some tea, but he would not wait.

"If we are to go, let us go. It is high time," said he.

## 8

The Bashkírs got ready and they all started: some mounted on horses, and some in carts. Pahóm drove in his own small cart with his servant and took a spade with him. When they reached the steppe, the morning red was beginning to kindle. They ascended a hillock (called by the Bashkírs a *shikhan*) and dismounting from their carts and their horses, gathered in one spot. The Chief came up to Pahóm and stretching out his arm towards the plain:

"See," said he, "all this, as far as your eye can reach, is ours. You may have any part of it you like."

Pahóm's eyes glistened: it was all virgin soil, as flat as the palm of your hand, as black as the seed of a poppy, and in the hollows different kinds of grasses grew breast high.

The Chief took off his fox-fur cap, placed it on the ground and said:

"This will be the mark. Start from here, and return here again. All the land you go round shall be yours."

Pahóm took out his money and put it on the cap. Then he took off his outer coat, remaining in his sleeveless under-coat. He unfastened his girdle and tied it tight below his stomach, put a little bag of bread into the breast of his coat, and tying a flask of water to his girdle, he drew up the tops of his boots, took the spade from his man, and stood ready to start. He considered for some moments which way he had better go—it was tempting everywhere.

"No matter," he concluded, "I will go towards the rising sun."

He turned his face to the east, stretched himself, and waited for the sun to appear above the rim.

"I must lose no time," he thought, "and it is easier walking while it is still cool."

The sun's rays had hardly flashed above the horizon, before Pahóm, carrying the spade over his shoulder, went down into the steppe.

Pahóm started walking neither slowly nor quickly. After having gone a thousand yards he stopped, dug a hole, and placed pieces of turf one on another to make it more visible. Then he went on; and now that he had walked off his stiffness he quickened his pace. After a while he dug another hole.

Pahóm looked back. The hillock could be distinctly seen in the sunlight, with the people on it, and the glittering tires of the cartwheels. At a rough guess Pahóm concluded that he had walked three miles. It was growing warmer; he took off his under-coat, flung it across his shoulder, and went on again. It had grown quite warm now; he looked at the sun, it was time to think of breakfast.

"The first shift is done, but there are four in a day, and it is too soon yet to turn. But I will just take off my boots," said he to himself.

He sat down, took off his boots, stuck them into his girdle, and went on. It was easy walking now.

"I will go on for another three miles," thought he, "and then turn to the left. This spot is so fine, that it would be a pity to lose it. The further one goes, the better the land seems."

He went straight on for a while, and when he looked round, the hillock was scarcely visible and the people on it looked like black ants, and he could just see something glistening there in the sun.

"Ah," thought Pahóm, "I have gone far enough in this direction, it is time to turn. Besides I am in a regular sweat, and very thirsty."

He stopped, dug a large hole, and heaped up pieces of turf. Next he untied his flask, had a drink, and then turned sharply to the left. He went on and on; the grass was high, and it was very hot.

Pahóm began to grow tired: he looked at the sun and saw that it was noon.

"Well," he thought, "I must have a rest."

He sat down, and ate some bread and drank some water; but he did not lie down, thinking that if he did he might fall asleep. After sitting a little while, he went on again. At first he walked easily: the food had strengthened him; but it had become terribly hot and he felt sleepy, still he went on, thinking: "An hour to suffer, a life-time to live."

He went a long way in this direction also, and was about to turn to the left again, when he perceived a damp hollow: "It would be a pity to leave that out," he thought. "Flax would do well there." So he went on past the hollow, and dug a hole on the other side of it before he turned the corner. Pahóm looked towards the hillock. The heat made the air hazy: it seemed to be quivering, and through the haze the people on the hillock could scarcely be seen.

"Ah!" thought Pahóm, "I have made the sides too long; I must take this one shorter." And he went along the third side, stepping faster. He looked at the sun: it was nearly half-way to the horizon, and he had not yet done two miles of the third side of the square. He was still ten miles from the goal.

"No," he thought, "though it will make my land lop-sided, I

must hurry back in a straight line now. I might go too far, and as
it is I have a great deal of land."

So Pahóm hurriedly dug a hole, and turned straight towards
the hillock.

## 9

Pahóm went straight towards the hillock, but he now walked
with difficulty. He was done up with the heat, his bare feet were
cut and bruised, and his legs began to fail. He longed to rest, but
it was impossible if he meant to get back before sunset. The sun
waits for no man, and it was sinking lower and lower.

"Oh dear," he thought, "if only I have not blundered trying
for too much! What if I am too late?"

He looked towards the hillock and at the sun. He was still far
from his goal, and the sun was already near the rim.

Pahóm walked on and on; it was very hard walking but he
went quicker and quicker. He pressed on, but was still far from
the place. He began running, threw away his coat, his boots, his
flask, and his cap, and kept only the spade which he used as a
support.

"What shall I do," he thought again. "I have grasped too much
and ruined the whole affair. I can't get there before the sun sets."

And his fear made him still more breathless. Pahóm went on
running, his soaking shirt and trousers stuck to him and his mouth
was parched. His breast was working like a blacksmith's bellows,
his heart was beating like a hammer, and his legs were giving way
as if they did not belong to him. Pahóm was seized with terror
lest he should die of the strain.

Though afraid of death, he could not stop. "After having run
all that way they will call me a fool if I stop now," thought he.
And he ran on and on, and drew near and heard the Bashkírs
yelling and shouting to him, and their cries inflamed his heart still
more. He gathered his last strength and ran on.

The sun was close to the rim, and cloaked in mist looked large,
and red as blood. Now, yes now, it was about to set! The sun was
quite low, but he was also quite near his aim. Pahóm could already
see the people on the hillock waving their arms to hurry him up.
He could see the fox-fur cap on the ground and the money on it,
and the Chief sitting on the ground holding his sides. And Pahóm
remembered his dream.

"There is plenty of land," thought he, "but will God let me live on it? I have lost my life. I have lost my life! I shall never reach that spot!"

Pahóm looked at the sun, which had reached the earth: one side of it had already disappeared. With all his remaining strength he rushed on, bending his body forward so that his legs could hardly follow fast enough to keep him from falling. Just as he reached the hillock it suddenly grew dark. He looked up—the sun had already set! He gave a cry: "All my labor has been in vain," thought he, and was about to stop, but he heard the Bashkírs still shouting, and remembered that though to him, from below, the sun seemed to have set, they on the hillock could still see it. He took a long breath and ran up the hillock. It was still light there. He reached the top and saw the cap. Before it sat the Chief laughing and holding his sides. Again Pahóm remembered his dream, and he uttered a cry: his legs gave way beneath him, he fell forward and reached the cap with his hands.

"Ah, that's a fine fellow!" exclaimed the Chief. "He has gained much land!"

Pahóm's servant came running up and tried to raise him, but he saw that blood was flowing from his mouth. Pahóm was dead!

The Bashkírs clicked their tongues to show their pity.

His servant picked up the spade and dug a grave long enough for Pahóm to lie in, and buried him in it. Six feet from his head to his heels was all he needed.

## SARAH ORNE JEWETT [1849–1909]

# A White Heron

### I

The woods were already filled with shadows one June evening, just before eight o'clock, though a bright sunset still glimmered faintly among the trunks of the trees. A little girl was driving home her cow, a plodding, dilatory, provoking creature in her behavior, but a valued companion for all that. They were going away from the western light, and striking deep into the dark woods, but their feet were familiar with the path, and it was no matter whether their eyes could see it or not.

There was hardly a night the summer through when the old cow could be found waiting at the pasture bars; on the contrary, it was her greatest pleasure to hide herself away among the high huckleberry bushes, and though she wore a loud bell she had made the discovery that if one stood perfectly still it would not ring. So Sylvia had to hunt for her until she found her and call Co'! Co'! with never an answering Moo, until her childish patience was quite spent. If the creature had not given good milk and plenty of it, the case would have seemed very different to her owners. Besides, Sylvia had all the time there was, and very little use to make of it. Sometimes in pleasant weather it was a consolation to look upon the cow's pranks as an intelligent attempt to play hide and seek, and as the child had no playmates she lent herself to this amusement with a good deal of zest. Though this chase had been so long that the wary animal herself had given an unusual signal of her whereabouts, Sylvia had only laughed when she came upon Mistress Moolly at the swamp-side, and urged her affectionately homeward with a twig of birch leaves. The old cow was not inclined to wander farther, she even turned in the right direction for once as they left the pasture, and stepped along the road at a good pace. She was quite ready to be milked now, and seldom stopped to browse. Sylvia wondered what her grandmother would say because they were so late. It was a great while since she had left home at half past five o'clock, but everybody knew the difficulty of making this errand a short one. Mrs. Tilley had chased the horned torment too many summer evenings herself to blame any one else for lingering, and was only thankful as she waited that she had Sylvia, nowadays, to give such valuable assistance. The good woman suspected that Sylvia loitered occasionally on her own account; there never was such a child for straying about out-of-doors since the world was made! Everybody said that it was a good change for a little maid who had tried to grow for eight years in a crowded manufacturing town, but, as for Sylvia herself, it seemed as if she never had been alive at all before she came to live at the farm. She thought often with wistful compassion of a wretched dry geranium that belonged to a town neighbor.

"'Afraid of folks,'" old Mrs. Tilley said to herself, with a smile, after she had made the unlikely choice of Sylvia from her daughter's houseful of children, and was returning to the farm. "'Afraid of folks,' they said! I guess she won't be troubled no great with 'em up to the old place!" When they reached the door of the lonely house and stopped to unlock it, and the cat came to purr loudly, and rub against them, a deserted pussy, indeed, but fat with young robins, Sylvia whispered that this was a beautiful place to live in, and she never should wish to go home.

The companions followed the shady wood-road, the cow taking slow steps, and the child very fast ones. The cow stopped long at the brook to drink, as if the pasture were not half a swamp, and Sylvia stood still and waited, letting her bare feet cool themselves in the shoal water, while the great twilight moths struck softly against her. She waded on through the brook as the cow moved away, and listened to the thrushes with a heart that beat fast with pleasure. There was a stirring in the great boughs overhead. They were full of little birds and beasts that seemed to be wide-awake, and going about their world, or else saying good-night to each other in sleepy twitters. Sylvia herself felt sleepy as she walked along. However, it was not much farther to the house, and the air was soft and sweet. She was not often in the woods so late as this, and it made her feel as if she were a part of the gray shadows and the moving leaves. She was just thinking how long it seemed since she first came to the farm a year ago, and wondering if every thing went on in the noisy town just the same as when she was there; the thought of the great red-faced boy who used to chase and frighten her made her hurry along the path to escape from the shadow of the trees.

Suddenly this little woods-girl is horror-stricken to hear a clear whistle not very far away. Not a bird's whistle, which would have a sort of friendliness, but a boy's whistle, determined, and some-what aggressive. Sylvia left the cow to whatever sad fate might await her, and stepped discreetly aside into the bushes, but she was just too late. The enemy had discovered her, and called out in a very cheerful and persuasive tone, "Halloa, little girl, how far is it to the road?" and trembling Sylvia answered almost inaudibly, "A good ways."

She did not dare to look boldly at the tall young man, who carried a gun over his shoulder, but she came out of her bush and again followed the cow, while he walked alongside.

"I have been hunting for some birds," the stranger said kindly, "and I have lost my way, and need a friend very much. Don't be afraid," he added gallantly. "Speak up and tell me what your name is, and whether you think I can spend the night at your house, and go out gunning early in the morning."

Sylvia was more alarmed than before. Would not her grandmother consider her much to blame? But who could have foreseen such an accident as this? It did not appear to be her fault, and she hung her head as if the stem of it were broken, but managed to answer, "Sylvy," with much effort when her companion again asked her name.

Mrs. Tilley was standing in the doorway when the trio came into view. The cow gave a loud moo by way of explanation.

"Yes, you'd better speak up for yourself, you old trial! Where'd she tucked herself away this time, Sylvy?" Sylvia kept an awed silence; she knew by instinct that her grandmother did not comprehend the gravity of the situation. She must be mistaking the stranger for one of the farmer-lads of the region.

The young man stood his gun beside the door, and dropped a heavy game-bag beside it; then he bade Mrs. Tilley good-evening, and repeated his wayfarer's story, and asked if he could have a night's lodging.

"Put me anywhere you like," he said. "I must be off early in the morning, before day; but I am very hungry, indeed. You can give me some milk at any rate, that's plain."

"Dear sakes, yes," responded the hostess, whose long slumbering hospitality seemed to be easily awakened. "You might fare better if you went out on the main road a mile or so, but you're welcome to what we've got. I'll milk right off, and you make yourself at home. You can sleep on husks or feathers," she proffered graciously. "I raised them all myself. There's good pasturing for geese just below here towards the ma'sh. Now step round and set a plate for the gentleman, Sylvy!" And Sylvia promptly stepped. She was glad to have something to do, and she was hungry herself.

It was a surprise to find so clean and comfortable a little dwelling in this New England wilderness. The young man had known the horrors of its most primitive housekeeping, and the dreary squalor of that level of society which does not rebel at the companionship of hens. This was the best thrift of an old-fashioned farmstead, though on such a small scale that it seemed like a hermitage. He listened eagerly to the old woman's quaint talk, he watched Sylvia's pale face and shining gray eyes with ever growing enthusiasm, and insisted that this was the best supper he had eaten for a month; then, afterward, the new-made friends sat down in the doorway together while the moon came up.

Soon it would be berry-time, and Sylvia was a great help at picking. The cow was a good milker, though a plaguy thing to keep track of, the hostess gossiped frankly, adding presently that she had buried four children, so that Sylvia's mother, and a son (who might be dead) in California were all the children she had left. "Dan, my boy, was a great hand to go gunning," she explained sadly. "I never wanted for pa'tridges or gray squer'ls while he was to home. He's been a great wand'rer, I expect, and he's no hand to write letters. There, I don't blame him, I'd ha' seen the world myself if it had been so I could.

"Sylvia takes after him," the grandmother continued affectionately, after a minute's pause. "There ain't a foot o' ground she don't know her way over, and the wild creatur's counts her one o' themselves. Squer'ls she'll tame to come an' feed right out o' her hands, and all sorts o' birds. Last winter she got the jay-birds to bangeing here, and I believe she'd 'a' scanted herself of her own meals to have plenty to throw out amongst 'em, if I hadn't kep' watch. Anything but crows, I tell her, I'm willin' to help support,—though Dan he went an' tamed one o' them that did seem to have reason same as folks. It was round here a good spell after he went away. Dan an' his father they didn't hitch,—but he never held up his head ag'in after Dan had dared him an' gone off."

The guest did not notice this hint of family sorrows in his eager interest in something else.

"So Sylvy knows all about birds, does she?" he exclaimed, as he looked round at the little girl who sat, very demure but increasingly sleepy, in the moonlight. "I am making a collection of birds myself. I have been at it ever since I was a boy." (Mrs. Tilley smiled.) "There are two or three very rare ones I have been hunting for these five years. I mean to get them on my own ground if they can be found."

"Do you cage 'em up?" asked Mrs. Tilley doubtfully, in response to this enthusiastic announcement.

"Oh, no, they're stuffed and preserved, dozens and dozens

of them," said the ornithologist, "and I have shot or snared every one myself. I caught a glimpse of a white heron three miles from here on Saturday, and I have followed it in this direction. They have never been found in this district at all. The little white heron, it is," and he turned again to look at Sylvia with the hope of discovering that the rare bird was one of her acquaintances.

But Sylvia was watching a hop-toad in the narrow footpath.

"You would know the heron if you saw it," the stranger continued eagerly. "A queer tall white bird with soft feathers and long thin legs. And it would have a nest perhaps in the top of a high tree, made of sticks, something like a hawk's nest."

Sylvia's heart gave a wild beat; she knew that strange white bird, and had once stolen softly near where it stood in some bright green swamp grass, away over at the other side of the woods. There was an open place where the sunshine always seemed strangely yellow and hot, where tall, nodding rushes grew, and her grandmother had warned her that she might sink in the soft black mud underneath and never be heard of more. Not far beyond were the salt marshes and beyond those was the sea, the sea which Sylvia wondered and dreamed about, but never had looked upon, though its great voice could often be heard above the noise of the woods on stormy nights.

"I can't think of anything I should like so much as to find that heron's nest," the handsome stranger was saying. "I would give ten dollars to anybody who could show it to me," he added desperately, "and I mean to spend my whole vacation hunting for it if need be. Perhaps it was only migrating, or had been chased out of its own region by some bird of prey."

Mrs. Tilley gave amazed attention to all this, but Sylvia still watched the toad, not divining, as she might have done at some calmer time, that the creature wished to get to its hole under the doorstep, and was much hindered by the unusual spectators at that hour of the evening. No amount of thought, that night, could decide how many wished-for treasures the ten dollars, so lightly spoken of, would buy.

The next day the young sportsman hovered about the woods, and Sylvia kept him company, having lost her first fear of the friendly lad, who proved to be most kind and sympathetic. He told her many things about the birds and what they knew and where they lived and what they did with themselves. And he gave her a jack-knife, which she thought as great a treasure as if she were a desert-islander. All day long he did not once make her troubled or afraid except when he brought down some unsuspecting singing creature from its bough. Sylvia would have liked him vastly better without his gun; she could not understand why he killed the very birds he seemed to like so much. But as the day waned, Sylvia still watched the young man with loving admiration. She had never seen anybody so charming and delightful; the woman's heart, asleep in the child, was vaguely thrilled by a dream of love. Some premonition of that great power stirred and swayed these young foresters who traversed the solemn woodlands with soft-footed silent care. They stopped to listen to a bird's song; they pressed forward again eagerly, parting the branches—speaking to each other rarely and in whispers; the young man going first and Sylvia following, fascinated, a few steps behind, with her gray eyes dark with excitement.

She grieved because the longed-for white heron was elusive, but she did not lead the guest, she only followed, and there was no such thing as speaking first. The sound of her own unquestioned voice would have terrified her—it was hard enough to answer yes or no when there was need of that. At last evening began to fall, and they drove the cow home together, and Sylvia smiled with pleasure when they came to the place where she heard the whistle and was afraid only the night before.

## II

Half a mile from home, at the farther edge of the woods, where the land was highest, a great pine-tree stood, the last of its generation. Whether it was left for a boundary mark, or for what reason, no one could say; the woodchoppers who had felled its mates were dead and gone long ago, and a whole forest of sturdy trees, pines and oaks and maples, had grown again. But the stately head of this old pine towered above them all and made a landmark for sea and shore miles and miles away. Sylvia knew it well. She had always believed that whoever climbed to the top of it could see the ocean; and the little girl had often laid her hand on the great rough trunk and looked up wistfully at those dark boughs that the wind always stirred, no matter how hot and still the air might be below. Now she thought of the tree with a new excitement, for why, if one climbed it at break of day, could not one see all the world, and easily discover whence the white heron flew, and mark the place, and find the hidden nest?

What a spirit of adventure, what wild ambition! What fancied triumph and delight and glory for the later morning when she could make known the secret! It was almost too real and too great for the childish heart to bear.

All night the door of the little house stood open, and the whippoorwills came and sang upon the very step. The young sportsman and his old hostess were sound asleep, but Sylvia's great design kept her broad awake and watching. She forgot to think of sleep. The short summer night seemed as long as the winter darkness, and at last when the whippoorwills ceased, and she was afraid the morning would after all come too soon, she stole out of the house and followed the pasture path through the woods, hastening toward the open ground beyond, listening with a sense of comfort and companionship to the drowsy twitter of a half-awakened bird, whose perch she had jarred in passing. Alas, if the great wave of human interest which flooded for the first time this dull little life should sweep away the satisfactions of an existence heart to heart with nature and the dumb life of the forest!

There was the huge tree asleep yet in the paling moonlight, and small and hopeful Sylvia began with utmost bravery to mount to the top of it, with tingling, eager blood coursing the channels of her whole frame, with her bare feet and fingers, that pinched and held like bird's claws to the monstrous ladder reaching up, up, almost to the sky itself. First she must mount the white oak tree that grew alongside, where she was almost lost among the dark branches and the green leaves heavy and wet with dew; a bird fluttered off its nest, and a red squirrel ran to and fro and scolded pettishly at the harmless housebreaker. Sylvia felt her way easily. She had often climbed there, and knew that higher still one of the oak's upper branches chafed against the pine trunk, just where its lower boughs were set close together. There, when she made the dangerous pass from one tree to the other, the great enterprise would really begin.

She crept out along the swaying oak limb at last, and took the daring step across into the old pine-tree. The way was harder than she thought; she must reach far and hold fast, the sharp dry twigs caught and held her and scratched her like angry talons, the pitch made her thin little fingers clumsy and stiff as she went round and round the tree's great stem, higher and higher upward. The sparrows and robins in the woods below were beginning to wake and twitter to the dawn, yet it seemed much lighter there aloft in the pine-tree, and the child knew that she must hurry if her project were to be of any use.

The tree seemed to lengthen itself out as she went up, and to reach farther and farther upward. It was like a great main-mast to the voyaging earth; it must truly have been amazed that morning through all its ponderous frame as it felt this determined spark of human spirit creeping and climbing from higher branch to branch. Who knows how steadily the least twigs held themselves to advantage this light, weak creature on her way! The old pine must have loved his new dependent. More than all the hawks, and bats, and moths, and even the sweet-voiced thrushes, was the brave, beating heart of the solitary gray-eyed child. And the tree stood still and held away the winds that June morning while the dawn grew bright in the east.

Sylvia's face was like a pale star, if one had seen it from the ground, when the last thorny bough was past, and she stood trembling and tired but wholly triumphant, high in the tree-top. Yes, there was the sea with the dawning sun making a golden dazzle over it, and toward that glorious east flew two hawks with slow-moving pinions. How low they looked in the air from that height when before one had only seen them far up, and dark against the blue sky. Their gray feathers were as soft as moths; they seemed only a little way from the tree, and Sylvia felt as if she too could go flying away among the clouds. Westward, the woodlands and farms reached miles and miles into the distance; here and there were church steeples, and white villages; truly it was a vast and awesome world.

The birds sang louder and louder. At last the sun came up bewilderingly bright. Sylvia could see the white sails of ships out at sea, and the clouds that were purple and rose-colored and yellow at first began to fade away. Where was the white heron's nest in the sea of green branches, and was this wonderful sight and pageant of the world the only reward for having climbed to such a giddy height? Now look down again, Sylvia, where the green marsh is set among the shining birches and dark hemlocks;

there where you saw the white heron once you will see him again; look, look! a white spot of him like a single floating feather comes up from the dead hemlock and grows larger, and rises, and comes close at last, and goes by the landmark pine with steady sweep of wing and outstretched slender neck and crested head. And wait! wait! do not move a foot or a finger, little girl, do not send an arrow of light and consciousness from your two eager eyes, for the heron has perched on a pine bough not far beyond yours, and cries back to his mate on the nest, and plumes his feathers for the new day!

The child gives a long sigh a minute later when a company of shouting cat-birds comes also to the tree, and vexed by their fluttering and lawlessness the solemn heron goes away. She knows his secret now, the wild, light, slender bird that floats and wavers, and goes back like an arrow presently to his home in the green world beneath. Then Sylvia, well satisfied, makes her perilous way down again, not daring to look far below the branch she stands on, ready to cry sometimes because her fingers ache and her lamed feet slip. Wondering over and over again what the stranger would say to her, and what he would think when she told him how to find his way straight to the heron's nest.

Sylvy, Sylvy! called the busy old grandmother again and again, but nobody answered, and the small husk bed was empty, and Sylvia had disappeared.

The guest waked from a dream, and remembering his day's pleasure hurried to dress himself that it might sooner begin. He was sure from the way the shy little girl looked once or twice yesterday that she had at least seen the white heron, and now she must really be persuaded to tell. Here she comes now, paler than ever, and her worn old frock is torn and tattered, and smeared with pine pitch. The grandmother and the sportsman stand in the door together and question her, and the splendid moment has come to speak of the dead hemlock-tree by the green marsh.

But Sylvia does not speak after all, though the old grandmother fretfully rebukes her, and the young man's kind appealing eyes are looking straight in her own. He can make them rich with money; he has promised it, and they are poor now. He is so well worth making happy, and he waits to hear the story she can tell.

No, she must keep silence! What is it that suddenly forbids

her and makes her dumb? Has she been nine years growing, and now, when the great world for the first time puts out a hand to her, must she thrust it aside for a bird's sake? The murmur of the pine's green branches is in her ears, she remembers how the white heron came flying through the golden air and how they watched the sea and the morning together, and Sylvia cannot speak; she cannot tell the heron's secret and give its life away.

Dear loyalty, that suffered a sharp pang as the guest went away disappointed later in the day, that could have served and followed him and loved him as a dog loves! Many a night Sylvia heard the echo of his whistle haunting the pasture path as she came home with the loitering cow. She forgot even her sorrow at the sharp report of his gun and the piteous sight of thrushes and sparrows dropping silent to the ground, their songs hushed and their pretty feathers stained and wet with blood. Were the birds better friends than their hunter might have been,—who can tell? Whatever treasures were lost to her, woodlands and summer-time, remember! Bring your gifts and graces and tell your secrets to this lonely country child!

## GUY DE MAUPASSANT [1850–1893]
# The Piece of String

It was market-day, and over all the roads round Goderville the peasants and their wives were coming towards the town. The men walked easily, lurching the whole body forward at every step. Their long legs were twisted and deformed by the slow, painful labors of the country:—by bending over to plough, which is what also makes their left shoulders too high and their figures crooked; and by reaping corn, which obliges them for steadiness' sake to

Translated by Jonathan Sturges.

spread their knees too wide. Their starched blue blouses, shining as though varnished, ornamented at collar and cuffs with little patterns of white stitch-work, and blown up big around their bony bodies, seemed exactly like balloons about to soar, but putting forth a head, two arms, and two feet.

Some of these fellows dragged a cow or a calf at the end of a rope. And just behind the animal, beating it over the back with a leaf-covered branch to hasten its pace, went their wives, carrying large baskets from which came forth the heads of chickens or the heads of ducks. These women walked with steps far shorter and quicker than the men; their figures, withered and upright, were adorned with scanty little shawls pinned over their flat bosoms; and they enveloped their heads each in a white cloth, close fastened round the hair and surmounted by a cap.

Now a char-à-banc[1] passed by, drawn by a jerky-paced nag. It shook up strangely the two men on the seat. And the woman at the bottom of the cart held fast to its sides to lessen the hard joltings.

In the market-place at Goderville was a great crowd, a mingled multitude of men and beasts. The horns of cattle, the high and long-napped hats of wealthy peasants, the head-dresses of the women, came to the surface of that sea. And voices clamorous, sharp, shrill, made a continuous and savage din. Above it a huge burst of laughter from the sturdy lungs of a merry yokel would sometimes sound, and sometimes a long bellow from a cow tied fast to the wall of a house.

It all smelled of the stable, of milk, of hay, and of perspiration, giving off that half-human, half-animal odor which is peculiar to the men of the fields.

Maître Hauchecorne, of Bréauté, had just arrived at Goderville, and was taking his way towards the square, when he perceived on the ground a little piece of string. Maître Hauchecorne, economical, like all true Normans, reflected that everything was worth picking up which could be of any use; and he stooped down—but painfully, because he suffered from rheumatism. He took the bit of thin cord from the ground, and was carefully preparing to roll it up when he saw Maître Malandain, the harness-

---

[1] A cart or wagon.

maker, on his door-step, looking at him. They had once had a quarrel about a halter, and they had remained angry, bearing malice on both sides. Maître Hauchecorne was overcome with a sort of shame at being seen by his enemy looking in the dirt so for a bit of string. He quickly hid his find beneath his blouse; then in the pocket of his breeches; then pretended to be still looking for something on the ground which he did not discover; and at last went off towards the market-place, with his head bent forward, and a body almost doubled in two by rheumatic pains.

He lost himself immediately in the crowd, which was clamorous, slow, and agitated by interminable bargains. The peasants examined the cows, went off, came back, always in great perplexity and fear of being cheated, never quite daring to decide, spying at the eye of the seller, trying ceaselessly to discover the tricks of the man and the defect in the beast.

The women, having placed their great baskets at their feet, had pulled out the poultry, which lay upon the ground, tied by the legs, with eyes scared, with combs scarlet.

They listened to propositions, maintaining the prices, with a dry manner, with an impassible face; or, suddenly, perhaps, deciding to take the lower price which was offered, they cried out to the customer, who was departing slowly:

"All right, I'll let you have them, Maît' Anthime."

Then, little by little, the square became empty, and when the *Angelus* struck midday those who lived at a distance poured into the inns.

At Jourdain's the great room was filled with eaters, just as the vast court was filled with vehicles of every sort—wagons, gigs, char-à-bancs, tilburys, tilt-carts which have no name, yellow with mud, misshapen, pieced together, raising their shafts to heaven like two arms, or it may be with their nose in the dirt and their rear in the air.

Just opposite to where the diners were at table the huge fireplace, full of clear flame, threw a lively heat on the backs of those who sat along the right. Three spits were turning, loaded with chickens, with pigeons, and with joints of mutton; and a delectable odor of roast meat, and of gravy gushing over crisp brown skin, took wing from the hearth, kindled merriment, caused mouths to water.

All the aristocracy of the plough were eating there, at Maît'

Jourdain's, the innkeeper's, a dealer in horses also, and a sharp fellow who had made a pretty penny in his day.

The dishes were passed around, were emptied, with jugs of yellow cider. Every one told of his affairs, of his purchases and his sales. They asked news about the crops. The weather was good for green stuffs, but a little wet for wheat.

All of a sudden the drum rolled in the court before the house. Every one, except some of the most indifferent, was on his feet at once, and ran to the door, to the windows, with his mouth still full and his napkin in his hand.

When the public crier had finished his tattoo he called forth in a jerky voice, making his pauses out of time:

"Be it known to the inhabitants of Goderville, and in general to all—persons present at the market, that there has been lost this morning, on the Beuzeville road between—nine and ten o'clock, a pocket-book of black leather, containing five hundred francs and business papers. You are requested to return it—to the mayor's office, at once, or to Maître Fortuné Houlbrèque, of Manneville. There will be twenty francs reward."

Then the man departed. They heard once more at a distance the dull beatings of the drum and the faint voice of the crier.

Then they began to talk of this event, reckoning up the chances which Maître Houlbrèque had of finding or of not finding his pocket-book again.

And the meal went on.

They were finishing their coffee when the corporal of gendarmes appeared on the threshold.

He asked:

"Is Maître Hauchecorne, of Bréauté, here?"

Maître Hauchecorne, seated at the other end of the table, answered: "Here I am."

And the corporal resumed:

"Maître Hauchecorne, will you have the kindness to come with me to the mayor's office? M. le Maire would like to speak to you."

The peasant, surprised and uneasy, gulped down his little glass of cognac, got up, and, even worse bent over than in the morning, since the first steps after a rest were always particularly difficult, started off, repeating:

"Here I am, here I am."

And he followed the corporal.

The mayor was waiting for him, seated in an arm-chair. He was the notary of the place, a tall, grave man of pompous speech.

"Maître Hauchecorne," said he, "this morning, on the Beuzeville road, you were seen to pick up the pocket-book lost by Maître Houlbréque, of Manneville."

The countryman, speechless, regarded the mayor, frightened already by this suspicion which rested on him he knew not why.

"I, I picked up that pocket-book?"

"Yes, you."

"I swear I didn't even know nothing about it at all."

"You were seen."

"They saw me, me? Who is that who saw me?"

M. Malandain, the harness-maker."

Then the old man remembered, understood, and, reddening with anger:

"Ah, he saw me, did he, the rascal? He saw me picking up this string here, M'sieu' le Maire."

And, fumbling at the bottom of his pocket, he pulled out of it the little end of string.

But the mayor incredulously shook his head:

"You will not make me believe, Maître Hauchecorne, that M. Malandain, who is a man worthy of credit, has mistaken this string for a pocket-book."

The peasant, furious, raised his hand and spit as if to attest his good faith, repeating:

"For all that, it is the truth of the good God, the blessed truth, M'sieu' le Maire. There! on my soul and my salvation I repeat it."

The mayor continued:

"After having picked up the thing in question, you even looked for some time in the mud to see if a piece of money had not dropped out of it."

The good man was suffocated with indignation and with fear:

"If they can say!—if they can say . . . such lies as that to slander an honest man! If they can say!—"

He might protest, he was not believed.

He was confronted with M. Malandain, who repeated and sustained his testimony. They abused one another for an hour. At his own request Maître Hauchecorne was searched. Nothing was found upon him.

At last, the mayor, much perplexed, sent him away, warning him that he would inform the public prosecutor, and ask for orders.

The news had spread. When he left the mayor's office, the old man was surrounded, interrogated with a curiosity which was serious or mocking as the case might be, but into which no indignation entered. And he began to tell the story of the string. They did not believe him. They laughed.

He passed on, button-holed by every one, himself button-holing his acquaintances, beginning over and over again his tale and his protestations, showing his pockets turned inside out to prove that he had nothing.

They said to him:

"You old rogue, *va!*"

And he grew angry, exasperated, feverish, in despair at not being believed, and always telling his story.

The night came. It was time to go home. He set out with three of his neighbors, to whom he pointed out the place where he had picked up the end of string; and all the way he talked of his adventure.

That evening he made the round in the village of Bréauté, so as to tell every one. He met only unbelievers.

He was ill of it all night long.

The next day, about one in the afternoon, Marius Paumelle, a farm hand of Maître Breton, the market-gardener at Ymauville, returned the pocket-book and its contents to Maître Houlbrèque, of Manneville.

This man said, indeed, that he had found it on the road; but not knowing how to read, he had carried it home and given it to his master.

The news spread to the environs. Maître Hauchecorne was informed. He put himself at once upon the go, and began to relate his story as completed by the *dénouement*. He triumphed.

"What grieved me," said he, "was not the thing itself, do you understand; but it was the lies. There's nothing does you so much harm as being in disgrace for lying."

All day he talked of his adventure, he told it on the roads to the people who passed; at the cabaret to the people who drank; and the next Sunday, when they came out of church. He even stopped strangers to tell them about it. He was easy, now, and yet something worried him without his knowing exactly what it was. People had a joking manner while they listened. They did not seem convinced. He seemed to feel their tittle-tattle behind his back.

On Tuesday of the next week he went to market at Goderville, prompted entirely by the need of telling his story.

Malandain, standing on his door-step, began to laugh as he saw him pass. Why?

He accosted a farmer of Criquetot, who did not let him finish, and, giving him a punch in the pit of his stomach, cried in his face: "Oh you great rogue, *va!*" Then turned his heel upon him.

Maître Hauchecorne remained speechless, and grew more and more uneasy. Why had they called him "great rogue"?

When seated at table in Jourdain's tavern he began again to explain the whole affair.

A horse-dealer at Montivilliers shouted at him:

"Get out, get out you old scamp; I know all about your string!"

Hauchecorne stammered:

"But since they found it again, the pocket-book!"

But the other continued:

"Hold your tongue, daddy; there's one who finds it and there's another who returns it. And no one the wiser."

The peasant was choked. He understood at last. They accused him of having had the pocket-book brought back by an accomplice, by a confederate.

He tried to protest. The whole table began to laugh.

He could not finish his dinner, and went away amid a chorus of jeers.

He went home, ashamed and indignant, choked with rage, with confusion, the more cast-down since from his Norman cunning, he was, perhaps, capable of having done what they accused him of, and even of boasting of it as a good trick. His innocence dimly seemed to him impossible to prove, his craftiness being so well known. And he felt himself struck to the heart by the injustice of the suspicion.

Then he began anew to tell of his adventure, lengthening his recital every day, each time adding new proofs, more energetic protestations, and more solemn oaths which he thought of, which he prepared in his hours of solitude, his mind being entirely occupied by the story of the string. The more complicated his defence, the more artful his arguments, the less he was believed.

"Those are liars' proofs," they said behind his back.

He felt this; it preyed upon his heart. He exhausted himself in useless efforts.

He was visibly wasting away.

The jokers now made him tell the story of "The Piece of String" to amuse them, just as you make a soldier who has been on a campaign tell his story of the battle. His mind, struck at the root, grew weak.

About the end of December he took to his bed.

He died early in January, and, in the delirium of the death-agony, he protested his innocence, repeating:

"A little bit of string—a little bit of string—see, here it is, M'sieu' le Maire."

### KATE CHOPIN [1851–1904]

# The Story of an Hour

Knowing that Mrs. Mallard was afflicted with a heart trouble, great care was taken to break to her as gently as possible the news of her husband's death.

It was her sister Josephine who told her, in broken sentences; veiled hints that revealed in half concealing. Her husband's friend Richards was there, too, near her. It was he who had been in the newspaper office when intelligence of the railroad disaster was received, with Brently Mallard's name leading the list of "killed." He had only taken the time to assure himself of its truth by a second telegram, and had hastened to forestall any less careful, less tender friend in bearing the sad message.

She did not hear the story as many women have heard the same, with a paralyzed inability to accept its significance. She wept at once, with sudden, wild abandonment, in her sister's arms.

When the storm of grief had spent itself she went away to her room alone. She would have no one follow her.

There stood, facing the open window, a comfortable, roomy armchair. Into this she sank, pressed down by a physical exhaustion that haunted her body and seemed to reach into her soul.

She could see in the open square before her house the tops of trees that were all aquiver with the new spring life. The delicious breath of rain was in the air. In the street below a peddler was crying his wares. The notes of a distant song which some one was singing reached her faintly, and countless sparrows were twittering in the eaves.

There were patches of blue sky showing here and there through the clouds that had met and piled one above the other in the west facing her window.

She sat with her head thrown back upon the cushion of the chair, quite motionless, except when a sob came up into her throat and shook her, as a child who had cried itself to sleep continues to sob in its dreams.

She was young, with a fair, calm face, whose lines bespoke repression and even a certain strength. But now there was a dull stare in her eyes, whose gaze was fixed away off yonder on one of those patches of blue sky. It was not a glance of reflection, but rather indicated a suspension of intelligent thought.

There was something coming to her and she was waiting for it, fearfully. What was it? She did not know; it was too subtle and elusive to name. But she felt it, creeping out of the sky, reaching toward her through the sounds, the scents, the color that filled the air.

Now her bosom rose and fell tumultuously. She was beginning to recognize this thing that was approaching to possess her, and she was striving to beat it back with her will—as powerless as her two white slender hands would have been.

When she abandoned herself a little whispered word escaped her slightly parted lips. She said it over and over under her breath: "free, free, free!" The vacant stare and the look of terror that had followed it went from her eyes. They stayed keen and bright. Her pulses beat fast, and the coursing blood warmed and relaxed every inch of her body.

She did not stop to ask if it were or were not a monstrous joy that held her. A clear and exalted perception enabled her to dismiss the suggestion as trivial.

She knew that she would weep again when she saw the kind, tender hands folded in death; the face that had never looked save with love upon her, fixed and gray and dead. But she saw beyond that bitter moment a long procession of years to come that would belong to her absolutely. And she opened and spread her arms out to them in welcome.

There would be no one to live for her during those coming years; she would live for herself. There would be no powerful will bending hers in that blind persistence with which men and women believe they have a right to impose a private will upon a fellow-creature. A kind intention or a cruel intention made the act seem no less a crime as she looked upon it in that brief moment of illumination.

And yet she had loved him—sometimes. Often she had not. What did it matter! What could love, the unsolved mystery, count for in face of this possession of self-assertion which she suddenly recognized as the strongest impulse of her being!

"Free! Body and soul free!" she kept whispering.

Josephine was kneeling before the closed door with her lips to the keyhole, imploring for admission. "Louise, open the door! I beg; open the door—you will make yourself ill. What are you doing, Louise? For heaven's sake open the door."

"Go away. I am not making myself ill." No; she was drinking in a very elixir of life through that open window.

Her fancy was running riot along those days ahead of her. Spring days, and summer days, and all sorts of days that would be her own. She breathed a quick prayer that life might be long. It was only yesterday she had thought with a shudder that life might be long.

She arose at length and opened the door to her sister's importunities. There was a feverish triumph in her eyes, and she carried herself unwittingly like a goddess of Victory. She clasped her sister's waist, and together they descended the stairs. Richards stood waiting for them at the bottom.

Some one was opening the front door with a latchkey. It was Brently Mallard who entered, a little travel-stained, composedly carrying his grip-sack and umbrella. He had been far from the scene of the accident, and did not even know there had been one. He stood amazed at Josephine's piercing cry; at Richards' quick motion to screen him from the view of his wife.

But Richards was too late.

When the doctors came they said she had died of heart disease—of joy that kills.

STEPHEN CRANE [1871–1900]

# The Bride Comes to Yellow Sky

*I*

The great Pullman was whirling onward with such dignity of motion that a glance from the window seemed simply to prove that the plains of Texas were pouring eastward. Vast flats of green grass, dull-hued spaces of mesquit[1] and cactus, little groups of frame houses, woods of light and tender trees, all were sweeping into the east, sweeping over the horizon, a precipice.

A newly married pair had boarded this coach at San Antonio. The man's face was reddened from many days in the wind and sun, and a direct result of his new black clothes was that his brick-colored hands were constantly performing in a most conscious fashion. From time to time he looked down respectfully at his attire. He sat with a hand on each knee, like a man waiting in a barber's shop. The glances he devoted to other passengers were furtive and shy.

The bride was not pretty, nor was she very young. She wore a dress of blue cashmere, with small reservations of velvet here and there, and with steel buttons abounding. She continually twisted her head to regard her puff sleeves, very stiff, straight, and high. They embarrassed her. It was quite apparent that she had cooked, and that she expected to cook, dutifully. The blushes caused by the careless scrutiny of some passengers as she had

---

[1] Trees and grass of the southwestern United States.

entered the car were strange to see upon this plain, under-class countenance, which was drawn in placid, almost emotionless lines.

They were evidently very happy. "Ever been in a parlor-car before?" he asked, smiling with delight.

"No," she answered; "I never was. It's fine, ain't it?"

"Great! And then after a while we'll go forward to the diner, and get a big lay-out. Finest meal in the world. Charge a dollar."

"Oh, do they?" cried the bride. "Charge a dollar? Why, that's too much—for us—ain't it, Jack?"

"Not this trip, anyhow," he answered bravely. "We're going to go the whole thing."

Later he explained to her about the trains. "You see, it's a thousand miles from one end of Texas to the other; and this train runs right across it, and never stops but four times." He had the pride of an owner. He pointed out to her the dazzling fittings of the coach; and in truth her eyes opened wider as she contemplated the sea-green figured velvet, the shining brass, silver, and glass, the wood that gleamed as darkly brilliant as the surface of a pool of oil. At one end a bronze figure sturdily held a support for a separated chamber, and at convenient places on the ceiling were frescos in olive and silver.

To the minds of the pair, their surroundings reflected the glory of their marriage that morning in San Antonio; this was the environment of their new estate; and the man's face in particular beamed with an elation that made him appear ridiculous to the negro porter. This individual at times surveyed them from afar with an amused and superior grin. On other occasions he bullied them with skill in ways that did not make it exactly plain to them that they were being bullied. He subtly used all the manners of the most unconquerable kind of snobbery. He oppressed them; but of this oppression they had small knowledge, and they speedily forgot that infrequently a number of travelers covered them with stares of derisive enjoyment. Historically there was supposed to be something infinitely humorous in their situation.

"We are due in Yellow Sky at 3:42," he said, looking tenderly into her eyes.

"Oh, are we?" she said, as if she had not been aware of it. To evince surprise at her husband's statement was part of her wifely amiability. She took from a pocket a little silver watch; and as she held it before her, and stared at it with a frown of attention, the new husband's face shone.

"I bought it in San Anton' from a friend of mine," he told her gleefully.

"It's seventeen minutes past twelve," she said, looking up at him with a kind of shy and clumsy coquetry. A passenger, noting this play, grew excessively sardonic, and winked at himself in one of the numerous mirrors.

At last they went to the dining-car. Two rows of negro waiters, in glowing white suits, surveyed their entrance with the interest, and also the equanimity, of men who had been forewarned. The pair fell to the lot of a waiter who happened to feel pleasure in steering them through their meal. He viewed them with the manner of a fatherly pilot, his countenance radiant with benevolence. The patronage, entwined with the ordinary deference, was not plain to them. And yet, as they returned to their coach, they showed in their faces a sense of escape.

To the left, miles down a long purple slope, was a little ribbon of mist where moved the keening Rio Grande. The train was approaching it at an angle, and the apex was Yellow Sky. Presently it was apparent that, as the distance from Yellow Sky grew shorter, the husband became commensurately restless. His brick-red hands were more insistent in their prominence. Occasionally he was even rather absent-minded and far-away when the bride leaned forward and addressed him.

As a matter of truth, Jack Potter was beginning to find the shadow of a deed weigh upon him like a leaden slab. He, the town marshal of Yellow Sky, a man known, liked, and feared in his corner, a prominent person, had gone to San Antonio to meet a girl he believed he loved, and there, after the usual prayers, had actually induced her to marry him, without consulting Yellow Sky for any part of the transaction. He was now bringing his bride before an innocent and unsuspecting community.

Of course people in Yellow Sky married as it pleased them, in accordance with a general custom; but such was Potter's thought of his duty to his friends, or of their idea of his duty, or of an unspoken form which does not control men in these matters, that he felt he was heinous. He had committed an extraordinary crime. Face to face with this girl in San Antonio, and spurred by his sharp impulse, he had gone headlong over all the social hedges.

At San Antonio he was like a man hidden in the dark. A knife to sever any friendly duty, any form, was easy to his hand in that remote city. But the hour of Yellow Sky—the hour of daylight—was approaching.

He knew full well that his marriage was an important thing to his town. It could only be exceeded by the burning of the new hotel. His friends could not forgive him. Frequently he had reflected on the advisability of telling them by telegraph, but a new cowardice had been upon him. He feared to do it. And now the train was hurrying him toward a scene of amazement, glee, and reproach. He glanced out of the window at the line of haze swinging slowly in toward the train.

Yellow Sky had a kind of brass band, which played painfully, to the delight of the populace. He laughed without heart as he thought of it. If the citizens could dream of his prospective arrival with his bride, they would parade the band at the station and escort them, amid cheers and laughing congratulations, to his adobe home.

He resolved that he would use all the devices of speed and plainscraft in making the journey from the station to his house. Once within that safe citadel, he could issue some sort of a vocal bulletin, and then not go among the citizens until they had time to wear off a little of their enthusiasm.

The bride looked anxiously at him. "What's worrying you, Jack?"

He laughed again. "I'm not worrying, girl; I'm only thinking of Yellow Sky."

She flushed in comprehension.

A sense of mutual guilt invaded their minds and developed a finer tenderness. They looked at each other with eyes softly aglow. But Potter often laughed the same nervous laugh; the flush upon the bride's face seemed quite permanent.

The traitor to the feelings of Yellow Sky narrowly watched the speeding landscape. "We're nearly there," he said.

Presently the porter came and announced the proximity of Potter's home. He held a brush in his hand, and, with all his airy superiority gone, he brushed Potter's new clothes as the latter slowly turned this way and that way. Potter fumbled out a coin and gave it to the porter, as he had seen others do. It was a heavy and muscle-bound business, as that of a man shoeing his first horse.

The porter took their bag, and as the train began to slow they moved forward to the hooded platform of the car. Presently the two engines and their long string of coaches rushed into the station of Yellow Sky.

"They have to take water here," said Potter, from a constricted throat and in mournful cadence, as one announcing death. Before the train stopped his eye had swept the length of the platform, and he was glad and astonished to see there was none upon it but the station-agent, who, with a slightly hurried and anxious air, was walking toward the water-tanks. When the train had halted, the porter alighted first, and placed in position a little temporary step.

"Come on, girl," said Potter, hoarsely. As he helped her down they each laughed on a false note. He took the bag from the negro, and bade his wife cling to his arm. As they slunk rapidly away, his hang-dog glance perceived that they were unloading the two trunks, and also that the station-agent, far ahead near the baggage-car, had turned and was running toward him, making gestures. He laughed, and groaned as he laughed, when he noted the first effect of his marital bliss upon Yellow Sky. He gripped his wife's arm firmly to his side, and they fled. Behind them the porter stood, chuckling fatuously.

## II

The California express on the Southern Railway was due at Yellow Sky in twenty-one minutes. There were six men at the bar of the Weary Gentleman Saloon. One was a drummer,[2] who talked a great deal and rapidly; three were Texans, who did not care to talk at that time; and two were Mexican sheep-herders, who did not talk as a general practice in the Weary Gentleman Saloon. The barkeeper's dog lay on the board walk that crossed in front of the door. His head was on his paws, and he glanced drowsily here and there with the constant vigilance of a dog that is kicked on occasion. Across the sandy street were some vivid green grass-

---

[2] A salesperson.

plots, so wonderful in appearance, amid the sands that burned near them in a blazing sun, that they caused a doubt in the mind. They exactly resembled the grass mats used to represent lawns on the stage. At the cooler end of the railway station, a man without a coat sat in a tilted chair and smoked his pipe. The fresh-cut bank of the Rio Grande circled near the town, and there could be seen beyond it a great plum-colored plain of mesquit.

Save for the busy drummer and his companions in the saloon, Yellow Sky was dozing. The new-comer leaned gracefully upon the bar, and recited many tales with the confidence of a bard who has come upon a new field.

"—and at the moment that the old man fell down-stairs with the bureau in his arms, the old woman was coming up with two scuttles of coal, and of course—"

The drummer's tale was interrupted by a young man who suddenly appeared in the open door. He cried: "Scratchy Wilson's drunk, and has turned loose with both hands." The two Mexicans at once set down their glasses and faded out of the rear entrance of the saloon.

The drummer, innocent and jocular, answered: "All right, old man. S'pose he has? Come in and have a drink, anyhow."

But the information had made such an obvious cleft in every skull in the room that the drummer was obliged to see its importance. All had become instantly solemn. "Say," said he, mystified, "what is this?" His three companions made the introductory gesture of eloquent speech; but the young man at the door forestalled them.

"It means, my friend," he answered, as he came into the saloon, "that for the next two hours this town won't be a health resort."

The barkeeper went to the door, and locked and barred it; reaching out of the window, he pulled in heavy wooden shutters, and barred them. Immediately a solemn, chapel-like gloom was upon the place. The drummer was looking from one to another.

"But say," he cried, "what is this, anyhow? You don't mean there is going to be a gun-fight?"

"Don't know whether there'll be a fight or not," answered one man, grimly; "but there'll be some shootin'—some good shootin'."

The young man who had warned them waved his hand. "Oh,

there'll be a fight fast enough, if any one wants it. Anybody can get a fight out there in the street. There's a fight just waiting."

The drummer seemed to be swayed between the interest of a foreigner and a perception of personal danger.

"What did you say his name was?" he asked.

"Scratchy Wilson," they answered in chorus.

"And will he kill anybody? What are you going to do? Does this happen often? Does he rampage around like this once a week or so? Can he break in that door?"

"No; he can't break down that door," replied the barkeeper. "He's tried it three times. But when he comes you'd better lay down on the floor, stranger. He's dead sure to shoot at it, and a bullet may come through."

Thereafter the drummer kept a strict eye upon the door. The time had not yet been called for him to hug the floor, but, as a minor precaution, he sidled near to the wall. "Will he kill anybody?" he said again.

The men laughed low and scornfully at the question.

"He's out to shoot, and he's out for trouble. Don't see any good in experimentin' with him."

"But what do you do in a case like this? What do you do?"

A man responded: "Why, he and Jack Potter—"

"But," in chorus the other men interrupted, "Jack Potter's in San Anton'."

"Well, who is he? What's he got to do with it?"

"Oh, he's the town marshal. He goes out and fights Scratchy when he gets on one of these tears."

"Wow!" said the drummer, mopping his brow. "Nice job he's got."

The voices had toned away to mere whisperings. The drummer wished to ask further questions, which were born of an increasing anxiety and bewilderment; but when he attempted them, the men merely looked at him in irritation and motioned him to remain silent. A tense waiting hush was upon them. In the deep shadows of the room their eyes shone as they listened for sounds from the street. One man made three gestures at the barkeeper; and the latter, moving like a ghost, handed him a glass and a bottle. The man poured a full glass of whisky, and set down the bottle noiselessly. He gulped the whisky in a swallow, and turned again toward the door in immovable silence. The drummer saw that the barkeeper, without a sound, had taken a Winchester from beneath the bar. Later he saw this individual beckoning to him, so he tiptoed across the room.

"You better come with me back of the bar."

"No, thanks," said the drummer, perspiring; "I'd rather be where I can make a break for the back door."

Whereupon the man of bottles made a kindly but peremptory gesture. The drummer obeyed it, and, finding himself seated on a box with his head below the level of the bar, balm was laid upon his soul at sight of various zinc and copper fittings that bore a resemblance to armor-plate. The barkeeper took a seat comfortably upon an adjacent box.

"You see," he whispered, "this here Scratchy Wilson is a wonder with a gun—a perfect wonder; and when he goes on the war-trail, we hunt our holes—naturally. He's about the last one of the old gang that used to hang out along the river here. He's a terror when he's drunk. When he's sober he's all right—kind of simple—wouldn't hurt a fly—nicest fellow in town. But when he's drunk—whoo!"

There were periods of stillness. "I wish Jack Potter was back from San Anton'," said the barkeeper. "He shot Wilson up once,—in the leg,—and he would sail in and pull out the kinks in this thing."

Presently they heard from a distance the sound of a shot, followed by three wild yowls. It instantly removed a bond from the men in the darkened saloon. There was a shuffling of feet. They looked at each other. "Here he comes," they said.

### III

A man in a maroon-colored flannel shirt, which had been purchased for purposes of decoration, and made principally by some Jewish women on the East Side of New York, rounded a corner and walked into the middle of the main street of Yellow Sky. In either hand the man held a long, heavy, blue-black revolver. Often he yelled, and these cries rang through a semblance of a deserted village, shrilly flying over the roofs in a volume that seemed to have no relation to the ordinary vocal strength of a man. It was as if the surrounding stillness formed the arch of a tomb over him.

These cries of ferocious challenge rang against walls of silence. And his boots had red tops with gilded imprints, of the kind beloved in winter by little sledding boys on the hillsides of New England.

The man's face flamed in a rage begot of whisky. His eyes, rolling, and yet keen for ambush, hunted the still doorways and windows. He walked with the creeping movement of the midnight cat. As it occurred to him, he roared menacing information. The long revolvers in his hands were as easy as straws; they were moved with an electric swiftness. The little fingers of each hand played sometimes in a musician's way. Plain from the low collar of the shirt, the cords of his neck straightened and sank, straightened and sank, as passion moved him. The only sounds were his terrible invitations. The calm adobes preserved their demeanor at the passing of this small thing in the middle of the street.

There was no offer of fight—no offer of fight. The man called to the sky. There were no attractions. He bellowed and fumed and swayed his revolvers here and everywhere.

The dog of the barkeeper of the Weary Gentleman Saloon had not appreciated the advance of events. He yet lay dozing in front of his master's door. At sight of the dog, the man paused and raised his revolver humorously. At sight of the man, the dog sprang up and walked diagonally away, with a sullen head, and growling. The man yelled, and the dog broke into a gallop. As it was about to enter an alley, there was a loud noise, a whistling, and something spat the ground directly before it. The dog screamed, and, wheeling in terror, galloped headlong in a new direction. Again there was a noise, a whistling, and sand was kicked viciously before it. Fear-stricken, the dog turned and flurried like an animal in a pen. The man stood laughing, his weapons at his hips.

Ultimately the man was attracted by the closed door of the Weary Gentleman Saloon. He went to it, and, hammering with a revolver, demanded drink.

The door remaining imperturbable, he picked a bit of paper from the walk, and nailed it to the framework with a knife. He then turned his back contemptuously upon this popular resort, and, walking to the opposite side of the street, and spinning there on his heel quickly and lithely, fired at the bit of paper. He missed it by a half-inch. He swore at himself, and went away. Later he comfortably fusilladed the windows of his most intimate friend. The man was playing with this town; it was a toy for him.

But still there was no offer of fight. The name of Jack Potter, his ancient antagonist, entered his mind, and he concluded that it would be a glad thing if he should go to Potter's house, and by bombardment induce him to come out and fight. He moved in the direction of his desire, chanting Apache scalp-music.

When he arrived at it, Potter's house presented the same still front as had the other adobes. Taking up a strategic position, the man howled a challenge. But this house regarded him as might a great stone god. It gave no sign. After a decent wait, the man howled further challenges, mingling with them wonderful epithets.

Presently there came the spectacle of a man churning himself into deepest rage over the immobility of a house. He fumed at it as the winter wind attacks a prairie cabin in the North. To the distance there should have gone the sound of a tumult like the fighting of two hundred Mexicans. As necessity bade him, he paused for breath or to reload his revolvers.

## IV

Potter and his bride walked sheepishly and with speed. Sometimes they laughed together shamefacedly and low.

"Next corner, dear," he said finally.

They put forth the efforts of a pair walking bowed against a strong wind. Potter was about to raise a finger to point the first appearance of the new home when, as they circled the corner, they came face to face with a man in a maroon-colored shirt, who was feverishly pushing cartridges into a large revolver. Upon the instant the man dropped his revolver to the ground, and, like lightning, whipped another from its holster. The second weapon was aimed at the bridegroom's chest.

There was a silence. Potter's mouth seemed to be merely a grave for his tongue. He exhibited an instinct to at once loosen his arm from the woman's grip, and he dropped the bag to the sand. As for the bride, her face had gone as yellow as old cloth. She was a slave to hideous rites, gazing at the apparitional snake.

The two men faced each other at a distance of three paces. He of the revolver smiled with a new and quiet ferocity.

"Tried to sneak up on me," he said. "Tried to sneak up on

me!" His eyes grew more baleful. As Potter made a slight movement, the man thrust his revolver venomously forward. "No; don't
you do it, Jack Potter. Don't you move a finger toward a gun just
yet. Don't you move an eyelash. The time has come for me to
settle with you, and I'm goin' to do it my own way, and loaf along
with no interferin'. So if you don't want a gun bent on you, just
mind what I tell you."

Potter looked at his enemy. "I ain't got a gun on me, Scratchy,"
he said. "Honest, I ain't." He was stiffening and steadying, but
yet somewhere at the back of his mind a vision of the Pullman
floated: the sea-green figured velvet, the shining brass, silver, and
glass, the wood that gleamed as darkly brilliant as the surface of
a pool of oil—all the glory of the marriage, the environment of the
new estate. "You know I fight when it comes to fighting, Scratchy
Wilson; but I ain't got a gun on me. You'll have to do all the
shootin' yourself."

His enemy's face went livid. He stepped forward, and lashed
his weapon to and fro before Potter's chest. "Don't you tell me
you ain't got no gun on you, you whelp. Don't tell me no lie like
that. There ain't a man in Texas ever seen you without no gun.
Don't take me for no kid." His eyes blazed with light, and his
throat worked like a pump.

"I ain't takin' you for no kid," answered Potter. His heels had
not moved an inch backward. "I'm takin' you for a damn fool. I
tell you I ain't got a gun, and I ain't. If you're goin' to shoot me
up, you better begin now; you'll never get a chance like this again."

So much enforced reasoning had told on Wilson's rage; he
was calmer. "If you ain't got a gun, why ain't you got a gun?" he
sneered. "Been to Sunday-school?"

"I ain't got a gun because I've just come from San Anton' with
my wife. I'm married," said Potter. "And if I'd thought there was
going to be any galoots like you prowling around when I brought
my wife home, I'd had a gun, and don't you forget it."

"Married!" said Scratchy, not at all comprehending.

"Yes, married. I'm married," said Potter, distinctly.

"Married?" said Scratchy. Seemingly for the first time, he saw
the drooping, drowning woman at the other man's side. "No!" he
said. He was like a creature allowed a glimpse of another world.
He moved a pace backward, and his arm, with the revolver,
dropped to his side. "Is this the lady?" he asked.

"Yes; this is the lady," answered Potter.

There was another period of silence.

"Well," said Wilson at last, slowly, "I s'pose it's all off now."

"It's all off if you say so, Scratchy. You know I did n't make the trouble." Potter lifted his valise.

"Well, I 'low it's off, Jack," said Wilson. He was looking at the ground. "Married!" He was not a student of chivalry; it was merely that in the presence of this foreign condition he was a simple child of the earlier plains. He picked up his starboard revolver, and, placing both weapons in their holsters, he went away. His feet made funnel-shaped tracks in the heavy sand.

## SHERWOOD ANDERSON [1876–1941]
# Death in the Woods

### 1

She was an old woman and lived on a farm near the town in which I lived. All country and small-town people have seen such old women, but no one knows much about them. Such an old woman comes into town driving an old worn-out horse or she comes afoot carrying a basket. She may own a few hens and have eggs to sell. She brings them in a basket and takes them to a grocer. There she trades them in. She gets some salt pork and some beans. Then she gets a pound or two of sugar and some flour.

Afterwards she goes to the butcher's and asks for some dog-meat. She may spend ten or fifteen cents, but when she does she asks for something. Formerly the butchers gave liver to any one who wanted to carry it away. In our family we were always having it. Once one of my brothers got a whole cow's liver at the slaughter-house near the fairgrounds in our town. We had it until we were sick of it. It never cost a cent. I have hated the thought of it ever since.

The old farm woman got some liver and a soup-bone. She never visited with any one, and as soon as she got what she wanted she lit out for home. It made quite a load for such an old body. No one gave her a lift. People drive right down a road and never notice an old woman like that.

There was such an old woman who used to come into town past our house one Summer and Fall when I was a young boy and was sick with what was called inflammatory rheumatism. She went home later carrying a heavy pack on her back. Two or three large gaunt-looking dogs followed at her heels.

The old woman was nothing special. She was one of the nameless ones that hardly any one knows, but she got into my thoughts. I have just suddenly now, after all these years, remembered her and what happened. It is a story. Her name was Grimes, and she lived with her husband and son in a small unpainted house on the bank of a small creek four miles from town.

The husband and son were a tough lot. Although the son was but twenty-one, he had already served a term in jail. It was whispered about that the woman's husband stole horses and ran them off to some other county. Now and then, when a horse turned up missing, the man had also disappeared. No one ever caught him. Once, when I was loafing at Tom Whitehead's livery-barn, the man came there and sat on the bench in front. Two or three other men were there, but no one spoke to him. He sat for a few minutes and then got up and went away. When he was leaving he turned around and stared at the men. There was a look of defiance in his eyes. "Well, I have tried to be friendly. You don't want to talk to me. It has been so wherever I have gone in this town. If, some day, one of your fine horses turns up missing, well, then what?" He did not say anything actually. "I'd like to bust one of you on the jaw," was about what his eyes said. I remember how the look in his eyes made me shiver.

The old man belonged to a family that had had money once. His name was Jake Grimes. It all comes back clearly now. His father, John Grimes, had owned a sawmill when the country was new, and had made money. Then he got to drinking and running after women. When he died there wasn't much left.

Jake blew in the rest. Pretty soon there wasn't any more lumber to cut and his land was nearly all gone.

He got his wife off a German farmer, for whom he went to work one June day in the wheat harvest. She was a young thing then and scared to death. You see, the farmer was up to something with the girl—she was, I think, a bound girl and his wife had her suspicions. She took it out on the girl when the man wasn't around. Then, when the wife had to go off to town for supplies, the farmer got after her. She told young Jake that nothing really ever happened, but he didn't know whether to believe it or not.

He got her pretty easy himself, the first time he was out with her. He wouldn't have married her if the German farmer hadn't tried to tell him where to get off. He got her to go riding with him in his buggy one night when he was threshing on the place, and then he came for her the next Sunday night.

She managed to get out of the house without her employer's seeing, but when she was getting into the buggy he showed up. It was almost dark, and he just popped up suddenly at the horse's head. He grabbed the horse by the bridle and Jake got out his buggy-whip.

They had it out all right! The German was a tough one. Maybe he didn't care whether his wife knew or not. Jake hit him over the face and shoulders with the buggy-whip, but the horse got to acting up and he had to get out.

Then the two men went for it. The girl didn't see it. The horse started to run away and went nearly a mile down the road before the girl got him stopped. Then she managed to tie him to a tree beside the road. (I wonder how I know all this. It must have stuck in my mind from small-town tales when I was a boy.) Jake found her there after he got through with the German. She was huddled up in the buggy seat, crying, scared to death. She told Jake a lot of stuff, how the German had tried to get her, how he chased her once into the barn, how another time, when they happened to be alone in the house together, he tore her dress open clear down the front. The German, she said, might have got her that time if he hadn't heard his old woman drive in at the gate. She had been off to town for supplies. Well, she would be putting the horse in the barn. The German managed to sneak off to the fields without his wife seeing. He told the girl he would kill her if she told. What could she do? She told a lie about ripping her dress in the barn when she was feeding the stock. I remember now that she was a bound girl and did not know where her father and mother were. Maybe she did not have any father. You know what I mean.

Such bound children were often enough cruelly treated. They

were children who had no parents, slaves really. There were very few orphan homes then. They were legally bound into some home. It was a matter of pure luck how it came out.

### 2

She married Jake and had a son and daughter, but the daughter died.

Then she settled down to feed stock. That was her job. At the German's place she had cooked the food for the German and his wife. The wife was a strong woman with big hips and worked most of the time in the fields with her husband. She fed them and fed the cows in the barn, fed the pigs, the horses and the chickens. Every moment of every day, as a young girl, was spent feeding something.

Then she married Jake Grimes and he had to be fed. She was a slight thing, and when she had been married for three or four years, and after the two children were born, her slender shoulders became stooped.

Jake always had a lot of big dogs around the house, that stood near the unused sawmill near the creek. He was always trading horses when he wasn't stealing something and had a lot of poor bony ones about. Also he kept three or four pigs and a cow. They were all pastured in the few acres left of the Grimes place and Jake did little enough work.

He went into debt for a threshing outfit and ran it for several years, but it did not pay. People did not trust him. They were afraid he would steal the grain at night. He had to go a long way off to get work and it cost too much to get there. In the Winter he hunted and cut a little firewood, to be sold in some nearby town. When the son grew up he was just like the father. They got drunk together. If there wasn't anything to eat in the house when they came home the old man gave his old woman a cut over the head. She had a few chickens of her own and had to kill one of them in a hurry. When they were all killed she wouldn't have any eggs to sell when she went to town, and then what would she do?

She had to scheme all her life about getting things fed, getting the pigs fed so they would grow fat and could be butchered in the Fall. When they were butchered her husband took most of the meat off to town and sold it. If he did not do it first the boy did. They fought sometimes and when they fought the old woman stood aside trembling.

She had got the habit of silence anyway—that was fixed. Sometimes, when she began to look old—she wasn't forty yet— and when the husband and son were both off, trading horses or drinking or hunting or stealing, she went around the house and the barnyard muttering to herself.

How was she going to get everything fed?—that was her problem. The dogs had to be fed. There wasn't enough hay in the barn for the horses and the cow. If she didn't feed the chickens how could they lay eggs? Without eggs to sell how could she get things in town, things she had to have to keep the life of the farm going? Thank heaven, she did not have to feed her husband—in a certain way. That hadn't lasted long after their marriage and after the babies came. Where he went on his long trips she did not know. Sometimes he was gone from home for weeks, and after the boy grew up they went off together.

They left everything at home for her to manage and she had no money. She knew no one. No one ever talked to her in town. When it was Winter she had to gather sticks of wood for her fire, had to try to keep the stock fed with very little grain.

The stock in the barn cried to her hungrily, the dogs followed her about. In the Winter the hens laid few enough eggs. They huddled in the corners of the barn and she kept watching them. If a hen lays an egg in the barn in the Winter and you do not find it, it freezes and breaks.

One day in Winter the old woman went off to town with a few eggs and the dogs followed her. She did not get started until nearly three o'clock and the snow was heavy. She hadn't been feeling very well for several days and so she went muttering along, scantily clad, her shoulders stooped. She had an old grain bag in which she carried her eggs, tucked away down in the bottom. There weren't many of them, but in Winter the price of eggs is up. She would get a little meat in exchange for the eggs, some salt pork, a little sugar, and some coffee perhaps. It might be the butcher would give her a piece of liver.

When she had got to town and was trading in her eggs the dogs lay by the door outside. She did pretty well, got the things she needed, more than she had hoped. Then she went to the butcher and he gave her some liver and some dog-meat.

It was the first time any one had spoken to her in a friendly way for a long time. The butcher was alone in his shop when she came in and was annoyed by the thought of such a sick-looking old woman out on such a day. It was bitter cold and the snow, that had let up during the afternoon, was falling again. The butcher said something about her husband and her son, swore at them, and the old woman stared at him, a look of mild surprise in her eyes as he talked. He said that if either the husband or the son were going to get any of the liver or the heavy bones with scraps of meat hanging to them that he had put into the grain bag, he'd see him starve first.

Starve, eh? Well, things had to be fed. Men had to be fed, and horses that weren't any good but maybe could be traded off, and the poor thin cow that hadn't given any milk for three months.

Horses, cows, pigs, dogs, men.

### 3

The old woman had to get back before darkness came if she could. The dogs followed at her heels, sniffing at the heavy grain bag she had fastened on her back. When she got to the edge of town she stopped by a fence and tied the bag on her back with a piece of rope she had carried in her dress-pocket for just that purpose. It was hard when she had to crawl over fences and once she fell over and landed in the snow. The dogs went frisking about. She had to struggle to get to her feet again, but she made it. The point of climbing over the fences was that there was a short cut over a hill and through a woods. She might have gone around by the road, but it was a mile farther that way. She was afraid she couldn't make it. And then, besides, the stock had to be fed. There was a little hay left and a little corn. Perhaps her husband and son would bring some home when they came. They had driven off in the only buggy the Grimes family had, a rickety thing, a rickety horse hitched to the buggy, two other rickety horses led by halters. They were going to trade horses, get a little money if they could. They might come home drunk. It would be well to have something in the house when they came back.

The son had an affair on with a woman at the county seat, fifteen miles away. She was a rough enough woman, a tough one. Once, in the Summer, the son had brought her to the house. Both she and the son had been drinking. Jake Grimes was away and the son and his woman ordered the old woman about like a servant. She didn't mind much; she was used to it. Whatever happened she never said anything. That was her way of getting along. She had managed that way when she was a young girl at the German's and ever since she had married Jake. That time her son brought his woman to the house they stayed all night, sleeping together just as though they were married. It hadn't shocked the old woman, not much. She had got past being shocked early in life.

With the pack on her back she went painfully along across an open field, wading in the deep snow, and got into the woods.

There was a path, but it was hard to follow. Just beyond the top of the hill, where the woods was thickest, there was a small clearing. Had some one once thought of building a house there? The clearing was as large as a building lot in town, large enough for a house and a garden. The path ran along the side of the clearing, and when she got there the old woman sat down to rest at the foot of a tree.

It was a foolish thing to do. When she got herself placed, the pack against the tree's trunk, it was nice, but what about getting up again? She worried about that for a moment and then quietly closed her eyes.

She must have slept for a time. When you are about so cold you can't get any colder. The afternoon grew a little warmer and the snow came thicker than ever. Then after a time the weather cleared. The moon even came out.

There were four Grimes dogs that had followed Mrs. Grimes into town, all tall gaunt fellows. Such men as Jake Grimes and his son always keep just such dogs. They kick and abuse them, but they stay. The Grimes dogs, in order to keep from starving, had to do a lot of foraging for themselves, and they had been at it while the old woman slept with her back to the tree at the side of the clearing. They had been chasing rabbits in the woods and in adjoining fields and in their ranging had picked up three other farm dogs.

After a time all the dogs came back to the clearing. They were excited about something. Such nights, cold and clear and with a moon, do things to dogs. It may be that some old instinct, come down from the time when they were wolves, and ranged the woods in packs on Winter nights, comes back to them.

The dogs in the clearing, before the old woman, had caught two or three rabbits and their immediate hunger had been satisfied. They began to play, running in circles in the clearing. Round and round they ran, each dog's nose at the tail of the next dog. In the clearing, under the snow-laden trees and under the wintry moon they made a strange picture, running thus silently, in a circle their running had beaten in the soft snow. The dogs made no sound. They ran around and around in the circle.

It may have been that the old woman saw them doing that before she died. She may have awakened once or twice and looked at the strange sight with dim old eyes.

She wouldn't be very cold now, just drowsy. Life hangs on a long time. Perhaps the old woman was out of her head. She may have dreamed of her girlhood at the German's, and before that, when she was a child and before her mother lit out and left her.

Her dreams couldn't have been very pleasant. Not many pleasant things had happened to her. Now and then one of the Grimes dogs left the running circle and came to stand before her. The dog thrust his face to her face. His red tongue was hanging out.

The running of the dogs may have been a kind of death ceremony. It may have been that the primitive instinct of the wolf, having been aroused in the dogs by the night and the running, made them somehow, afraid.

"Now we are no longer wolves. We are dogs, the servants of men. Keep alive, man! When man dies we become wolves again." When one of the dogs came to where the old woman sat with her back against the tree and thrust his nose close to her face he seemed satisfied and went back to run with the pack. All the Grimes dogs did it at some time during the evening, before she died. I knew all about it afterward, when I grew to be a man, because once in a woods in Illinois, on another Winter night, I saw a pack of dogs act just like that. The dogs were waiting for me to die as they had waited for the old woman that night when I was a child, but when it happened to me I was a young man and had no intention whatever of dying.

The old woman died softly and quietly. When she was dead

and when one of the Grimes dogs had come to her and had found her dead all the dogs stopped running.

They gathered about her.

Well, she was dead now. She had fed the Grimes dogs when she was alive, what about now?

There was the pack on her back, the grain bag containing the piece of salt pork, the liver the butcher had given her, the dog-meat, the soup-bones. The butcher in town, having been suddenly overcome with a feeling of pity, had loaded her grain bag heavily. It had been a big haul for the old woman.

It was a big haul for the dogs now.

### 4

One of the Grimes dogs sprang suddenly out from among the others and began worrying the pack on the old woman's back. Had the dogs really been wolves that one would have been the leader of the pack. What he did, all the others did.

All of them sank their teeth into the grain bag the old woman had fastened with ropes to her back.

They dragged the old woman's body out into the open clearing. The worn-out dress was quickly torn from her shoulders. When she was found, a day or two later, the dress had been torn from her body clear to the hips, but the dogs had not touched her body. They had got the meat out of the grain bag, that was all. Her body was frozen stiff when it was found, and the shoulders were so narrow and the body so slight that in death it looked like the body of some charming young girl.

Such things happened in towns of the Middle West, on farms near town, when I was a boy. A hunter out after rabbits found the old woman's body and did not touch it. Something, the beaten round path in the little snow-covered clearing, the silence of the place, the place where the dogs had worried the body trying to pull the grain bag away or tear it open — something startled the man and he hurried off to town.

I was in Main Street with one of my brothers who was town newsboy and who was taking the afternoon papers to the stores. It was almost night.

The hunter came into a grocery and told his story. Then he went into a hardware-shop and into a drugstore. Men began to gather on the sidewalks. Then they started out along the road to the place in the woods.

My brother should have gone on about his business of distributing papers but he didn't. Every one was going to the woods. The undertaker went and the town marshal. Several men got on a dray and rode out to where the path left the road and went into the woods, but the horses weren't very sharply shod and slid about on the slippery roads. They made no better time than those of us who walked.

The town marshal was a large man whose leg had been injured in the Civil War. He carried a heavy cane and limped rapidly along the road. My brother and I followed at his heels, and as we went other men and boys joined the crowd.

It had grown dark by the time we got to where the old woman had left the road but the moon had come out. The marshal was thinking there might have been a murder. He kept asking the hunter questions. The hunter went along with his gun across his shoulders, a dog following at his heels. It isn't often a rabbit hunter has a chance to be so conspicuous. He was taking full advantage of it, leading the procession with the town marshal. "I didn't see any wounds. She was a beautiful young girl. Her face was buried in the snow. No, I didn't know her." As a matter of fact, the hunter had not looked closely at the body. He had been frightened. She might have been murdered and some one might spring out from behind a tree and murder him. In a woods, in the late afternoon, when the trees are all bare and there is white snow on the ground, when all is silent, something creepy steals over the mind and body. If something strange or uncanny has happened in the neighborhood all you think about is getting away from there as fast as you can.

The crowd of men and boys had got to where the old woman had crossed the field and went, following the marshal and the hunter, up the slight incline and into the woods.

My brother and I were silent. He had his bundle of papers in a bag slung across his shoulder. When he got back to town he would have to go on distributing his papers before he went home to supper. If I went along, as he had no doubt already determined I should, we would both be late. Either mother or our older sister would have to warm our supper.

Well, we would have something to tell. A boy did not get such a chance very often. It was lucky we just happened to go into the grocery when the hunter came in. The hunter was a country fellow. Neither of us had ever seen him before.

Now the crowd of men and boys had got to the clearing. Darkness comes quickly on such Winter nights, but the full moon made everything clear. My brother and I stood near the tree, beneath which the old woman had died.

She did not look old, lying there in that light, frozen and still. One of the men turned her over in the snow and I saw everything. My body trembled with some strange mystical feeling and so did my brother's. It might have been the cold.

Neither of us had ever seen a woman's body before. It may have been the snow, clinging to the frozen flesh, that made it look so white and lovely, so like marble. No woman had come with the party from town; but one of the men, he was the town black-smith, took off his overcoat and spread it over her. Then he gathered her into his arms and started off to town, all the others following silently. At that time no one knew who she was.

## 5

I had seen everything, had seen the oval in the snow, like a miniature racetrack, where the dogs had run, had seen how the men were mystified, had seen the white bare young-looking shoulders, had heard the whispered comments of the men.

The men were simply mystified. They took the body to the undertaker's, and when the blacksmith, the hunter, the marshal and several others had got inside they closed the door. If father had been there perhaps he could have got in, but we boys couldn't.

I went with my brother to distribute the rest of his papers and when we got home it was my brother who told the story.

I kept silent and went to bed early. It may have been I was not satisfied with the way he told it.

Later, in the town, I must have heard other fragments of the old woman's story. She was recognized the next day and there was an investigation.

The husband and son were found somewhere and brought to town and there was an attempt to connect them with the woman's death, but it did not work. They had perfect enough alibis.

However, the town was against them. They had to get out. Where they went I never heard.

I remember only the picture there in the forest, the men standing about, the naked girlish-looking figure, face down in the snow, the tracks made by the running dogs and the clear cold Winter sky above. White fragments of clouds were drifting across the sky. They went racing across the little open space among the trees.

The scene in the forest had become for me, without my knowing it, the foundation for the real story I am now trying to tell. The fragments, you see, had to be picked up slowly, long afterwards.

Things happened. When I was a young man I worked on the farm of a German. The hired-girl was afraid of her employer. The farmer's wife hated her.

I saw things at that place. Once later, I had a half-uncanny, mystical adventure with dogs in an Illinois forest on a clear, moon-lit Winter night. When I was a schoolboy, and on a Summer day, I went with a boy friend out along a creek some miles from town and came to the house where the old woman had lived. No one had lived in the house since her death. The doors were broken from the hinges; the window lights were all broken. As the boy and I stood in the road outside, two dogs, just roving farm dogs no doubt, came running around the corner of the house. The dogs were tall, gaunt fellows and came down to the fence and glared through at us, standing in the road.

The whole thing, the story of the old woman's death, was to me as I grew older like music heard from far off. The notes had to be picked up slowly one at a time. Something had to be understood.

The woman who died was one destined to feed animal life. Anyway, that is all she ever did. She was feeding animal life before she was born, as a child, as a young woman working on the farm of the German, after she married, when she grew old and when she died. She fed animal life in cows, in chickens, in pigs, in horses, in dogs, in men. Her daughter had died in childhood and with her one son she had no articulate relations. On the night when she died she was hurrying homeward, bearing on her body food for animal life.

She died in the clearing in the woods and even after her death continued feeding animal life.

·You see it is likely that, when my brother told the story, that night when we got home and my mother and sister sat listening, I did not think he got the point. He was too young and so was I. A thing so complete has its own beauty.

I shall not try to emphasize the point. I am only explaining why I was dissatisfied then and have been ever since. I speak of that only that you may understand why I have been impelled to try to tell the simple story over again.

ARCADII AVERCHENKO [1881–1925]

# The Young Man Who Flew Past

## A Psycho-drama in the Life of Man

This sad and tragic history began thus:

Three persons, in three different poses, were carrying on an animated conversation on the sixth floor of a large stone house.

The woman, with plump, beautiful arms, was holding a bed sheet to her breast, forgetting that a bed sheet could not do double duty and cover her shapely bare knees at the same time. The woman was crying, and in the intervals between sobs she was saying:

"Oh, John! I swear to you I'm not guilty! He set my head in a whirl, he seduced me—and, I assure you, all against my will! I resisted—"

One of the men, still in his hat and overcoat, was gesticulating wildly and speaking reproachfully to the third person in the room:

"Scoundrel! I'm going to show you right now that you will perish like a cur and the law will be on my side! You shall pay for this meek victim! You reptile! You base seducer!"

Translated by Bernard Guilbert Guerney.

The third in this room was a young man who, although not dressed with the greatest meticulousness at the present moment, bore himself, nevertheless, with great dignity.

"I? Why, I have not done anything—I . . ." he protested, gazing sadly into an empty corner of the room.

"You haven't? Take this, then, you scoundrel!"

The powerful man in the overcoat flung open the window giving out upon the street, gathered the young man who was none too meticulously dressed into his arms, and heaved him out.

Finding himself flying through the air, the young man bashfully buttoned his vest, and whispered to himself in consolation:

"Never mind! Our failures merely serve to harden us!"

And he kept on flying downward.

He had not yet had time to reach the next floor (the fifth) in his flight, when a deep sigh issued from his breast.

A recollection of the woman whom he had just left poisoned with its bitterness all the delight in the sensation of flying.

"My God!" thought the young man. "Why, I loved her! And she could not find the courage even to confess everything to her husband! God be with her! Now I can feel that she is distant, and indifferent to me."

With this last thought, he had already reached the fifth floor and, as he flew past a window he peeked in, prompted by curiosity.

A young student was sitting reading a book at a lopsided table, his head propped up in his hands.

Seeing him, the young man who was flying past recalled his life; recalled that heretofore he had passed all his days in worldly distractions, forgetful of learning and books; and he felt drawn to the light of knowledge, to the discovery of nature's mysteries with a searching mind, drawn to admiration before the genius of the great masters of words.

"Dear, beloved student!" he wanted to cry out to the man reading, "you have awakened within me all my dormant aspirations, and cured me of the empty infatuation with the vanities of life, which have led me to such a grievous disenchantment on the sixth floor. . . ."

But, not wishing to distract the student from his studies, the young man refrained from calling out, flying down to the fourth floor instead, and here his thoughts took a different turn.

His heart contracted with a strange, sweet pain, while his head grew dizzy—from delight and admiration.

A young woman was sitting at the window of the fourth floor and, with a sewing machine before her, was at work upon something.

But her beautiful white hands had forgotten about work at the present moment, and her eyes—blue as cornflowers—were afar off, pensive and dreamy.

The young man could not take his eyes off this vision, and some new feeling, great and mighty, spread and grew within his heart.

And he understood that all his former encounters with women had been no more than empty infatuations, and that only now he understood that strange, mysterious word—Love.

And he was attracted to the quiet, domestic life; to the endearments of a being beloved beyond words; to a smiling existence, joyous and peaceful.

The next story, past which he was flying at the present moment, confirmed him still more in his inclination.

In the window of the third floor he saw a mother who, singing a quiet lullaby and laughing, was bouncing a plump, smiling baby; love, and a kind, motherly pride were sparkling in her eyes.

"I, too, want to marry the girl on the fourth floor, and have just such rosy, plump children as the one on the third floor," mused the young man, "and I would devote myself entirely to my family and find my happiness in this self-sacrifice."

But the second floor was now approaching. And the picture which the young man saw in a window of this floor forced his heart to contract again.

A man with disheveled hair and wandering gaze was seated at a luxurious writing table. He was gazing at a photograph in a frame before him; at the same time, he was writing with his right hand, and holding a revolver in his left, pressing its muzzle to his temple.

"Stop, madman!" the young man wanted to call out. "Life is so beautiful!" But some instinctive feeling restrained him.

The luxurious appointments of the room, its richness and comfort, led the young man to reflect that there is something else in life which could disrupt even all this comfort and contentment, as well as a whole family; something of the utmost force—mighty, terrific. . . .

"What can it be?" he wondered with a heavy heart. And, as if on purpose, Life gave him a harsh, unceremonious answer in a window of the first floor, which he had now reached.

Nearly concealed by the draperies, a young man was sitting at the window, sans coat and vest; a half-dressed woman was sitting on his knees, lovingly entwining the head of her beloved with her round, rosy arms, and passionately hugging him to her magnificent bosom. . . .

The young man who was flying past remembered that he had seen this woman (well-dressed) out walking with her husband— but this man was decidedly not her husband. Her husband was older, with curly black hair, half gray, while this man had beautiful fair hair.

And the young man recalled his former plans: of studying, after the student's example; of marrying the girl on the fourth floor; of a peaceful, domestic life, à la the third—and once more his heart was heavily oppressed.

He perceived all the ephemerality, all the uncertainty of the happiness of which he had dreamed; beheld, in the near future, a whole procession of young men with beautiful fair hair about his wife and himself; remembered the torments of the man on the second floor, and the measures which he had taken to free himself from these torments—and he understood.

"After all I have witnessed, living is not worth while! It is both foolish and tormenting," thought the young man, with a sickly, sardonic smile; and, contracting his eyebrows, he determinedly finished his flight to the very sidewalk.

Nor did his heart tremble when he touched the flagging of the pavement with his hands and, breaking these now useless members, he dashed out his brains against the hard, indifferent stone.

And, when the curious gathered around his motionless body, it never occurred to any of them what a complex drama the young man had lived through just a few moments before.

JAMES JOYCE [1882–1941]

# Araby

North Richmond Street,[1] being blind, was a quiet street except at the hour when the Christian Brothers' School set the boys free. An uninhabited house of two storeys stood at the blind end, detached from its neighbours in a square ground. The other houses of the street, conscious of decent lives within them, gazed at one another with brown imperturbable faces.

The former tenant of our house, a priest, had died in the back drawing-room. Air, musty from having been long enclosed, hung in all the rooms, and the waste room behind the kitchen was littered with old useless papers. Among these I found a few paper-covered books, the pages of which were curled and damp: *The Abbot*, by Walter Scott, *The Devout Communicant*, and *The Memoirs of Vidocq*.[2] I liked the last best because its leaves were yellow. The wild garden behind the house contained a central apple-tree and a few straggling bushes under one of which I found the late tenant's rusty bicycle-pump. He had been a very charitable priest; in his will he had left all his money to institutions and the furniture of his house to his sister.

When the short days of winter came dusk fell before we had well eaten our dinners. When we met in the street the houses had grown sombre. The space of sky above us was the colour of ever-changing violet and towards it the lamps of the street lifted their feeble lanterns. The cold air stung us and we played till our bodies glowed. Our shouts echoed in the silent street. The career of our play brought us through the dark muddy lanes behind the houses where we ran the gauntlet of the rough tribes from the cottages, to the back doors of the dark dripping gardens where odours arose from the ashpits, to the dark odorous stables where a coachman smoothed and combed the horse or shook music from the buckled

---

[1] A street in Dublin, Ireland.
[2] A romantic novel; an instructional manual for proper observance of the Eucharist; and autobiographical writings by Francois Eugène Vidocq (1775–1857), a French chief of detectives whose force consisted of ex-criminals.

harness. When we returned to the street light from the kitchen windows had filled the areas. If my uncle was seen turning the corner we hid in the shadow until we had seen him safely housed. Or if Mangan's sister came out on the doorstep to call her brother in to his tea we watched her from our shadow peer up and down the street. We waited to see whether she would remain or go in and, if she remained, we left our shadow and walked up to Mangan's steps resignedly. She was waiting for us, her figure defined by the light from the half-opened door. Her brother always teased her before he obeyed and I stood by the railings looking at her. Her dress swung as she moved her body and the soft rope of her hair tossed from side to side.

Every morning I lay on the floor in the front parlour watching her door. The blind was pulled down to within an inch of the sash so that I could not be seen. When she came out on the doorstep my heart leaped. I ran to the hall, seized my books, and followed her. I kept her brown figure always in my eye and, when we came near the point at which our ways diverged, I quickened my pace and passed her. This happened morning after morning. I had never spoken to her, except for a few casual words, and yet her name was like a summons to all my foolish blood.

Her image accompanied me even in places the most hostile to romance. On Saturday evenings when my aunt went marketing I had to go to carry some of the parcels. We walked through the flaring streets, jostled by drunken men and bargaining women, amid the curses of labourers, the shrill litanies of shop-boys who stood on guard by the barrel of pigs' cheeks, the nasal chanting of street-singers, who sang a *come-all-you* about O'Donovan Rossa, or a ballad about the troubles in our native land. These noises converged in a single sensation of life for me: I imagined that I bore my chalice safely through a throng of foes. Her name sprang to my lips at moments in strange prayers and praises which I myself did not understand. My eyes were often full of tears (I could not tell why) and at times a flood from my heart seemed to pour itself out into my bosom. I thought little of the future. I did not know whether I would ever speak to her or not or, if I spoke to her, how I could tell her of my confused adoration. But my body was like a harp and her words and gestures were like fingers running upon the wires.

One evening I went into the back drawing-room in which the

priest had died. It was a dark rainy evening and there was no sound in the house. Through one of the broken panes I heard the rain impinge upon the earth, the fine incessant needles of water playing in the sodden beds. Some distant lamp or lighted window gleamed below me. I was thankful that I could see so little. All my senses seemed to desire to veil themselves and, feeling that I was about to slip from them, I pressed the palms of my hands together until they trembled, murmuring: *O love! O love!* many times.

At last she spoke to me. When she addressed the first words to me I was so confused that I did not know what to answer. She asked me was I going to Araby. I forgot whether I answered yes or no. It would be a splendid bazaar, she said; she would love to go.

—And why can't you? I asked.

While she spoke she turned a silver bracelet round and round her wrist. She could not go, she said, because there would be a retreat that week in her convent. Her brother and two other boys were fighting for their caps and I was alone at the railings. She held one of the spikes, bowing her head towards me. The light from the lamp opposite our door caught the white curve of her neck, lit up her hair that rested there and, falling, lit up the hand upon the railing. It fell over one side of her dress and caught the white border of a petticoat, just visible as she stood at ease.

—It's well for you, she said.

—If I go, I said, I will bring you something.

What innumerable follies laid waste my waking and sleeping thoughts after that evening! I wished to annihilate the tedious intervening days. I chafed against the work of school. At night in my bedroom and by day in the classroom her image came between me and the page I strove to read. The syllables of the word *Araby* were called to me through the silence in which my soul luxuriated and cast an Eastern enchantment over me. I asked for leave to go to the bazaar on Saturday night. My aunt was surprised and hoped it was not some Freemason affair. I answered few questions in class. I watched my master's face pass from amiability to sternness; he hoped I was not beginning to idle. I could not call my wandering thoughts together. I had hardly any patience with the serious work of life which, now that it stood between me and my desire, seemed to me child's play, ugly monotonous child's play.

On Saturday morning I reminded my uncle that I wished to go to the bazaar in the evening. He was fussing at the hallstand, looking for the hat-brush, and answered me curtly:

—Yes, boy, I know.

As he was in the hall I could not go into the front parlour and lie at the window. I left the house in bad humour and walked slowly towards the school. The air was pitilessly raw and already my heart misgave me.

When I came home to dinner my uncle had not yet been home. Still it was early. I sat staring at the clock for some time and, when its ticking began to irritate me, I left the room. I mounted the staircase and gained the upper part of the house. The high cold empty gloomy rooms liberated me and I went from room to room singing. From the front window I saw my companions playing below in the street. Their cries reached me weakened and indistinct and, leaning my forehead against the cool glass, I looked over at the dark house where she lived. I may have stood there for an hour, seeing nothing but the brown-clad figure cast by my imagination, touched discreetly by the lamplight at the curved neck, at the hand upon the railings and at the border below the dress.

When I came downstairs again I found Mrs. Mercer sitting at the fire. She was an old garrulous woman, a pawnbroker's widow, who collected used stamps for some pious purpose. I had to endure the gossip of the tea-table. The meal was prolonged beyond an hour and still my uncle did not come. Mrs. Mercer stood up to go: she was sorry she couldn't wait any longer, but it was after eight o'clock and she did not like to be out late, as the night air was bad for her. When she had gone I began to walk up and down the room, clenching my fists. My aunt said:

I'm afraid you may put off your bazaar for this night of Our Lord.

At nine o'clock I heard my uncle's latchkey in the halldoor. I heard him talking to himself and heard the hallstand rocking when it had received the weight of his overcoat. I could interpret these signs. When he was midway through his dinner I asked him to give me the money to go to the bazaar. He had forgotten.

—The people are in bed and after their first sleep now, he said.

I did not smile. My aunt said to him energetically:

—Can't you give him the money and let him go? You've kept him late enough as it is.

My uncle said he was very sorry he had forgotten. He said he believed in the old saying: *All work and no play makes Jack a dull boy.* He asked me where I was going and, when I had told him a second time he asked me did I know *The Arab's Farewell to his Steed.* When I left the kitchen he was about to recite the opening lines of the piece to my aunt.

I held a florin tightly in my hand as I strode down Buckingham Street towards the station. The sight of the streets thronged with buyers and glaring with gas recalled to me the purpose of my journey. I took my seat in a third-class carriage of a deserted train. After an intolerable delay the train moved out of the station slowly. It crept onward among ruinous houses and over the twinkling river. At Westland Row Station a crowd of people pressed to the carriage doors; but the porters moved them back, saying that it was a special train for the bazaar. I remained alone in the bare carriage. In a few minutes the train drew up beside an improvised wooden platform. I passed out on to the road and saw by the lighted dial of a clock that it was ten minutes to ten. In front of me was a large building which displayed the magical name.

I could not find any sixpenny entrance and, fearing that the bazaar would be closed, I passed in quickly through a turnstile, handing a shilling to a weary-looking man. I found myself in a big hall girdled at half its height by a gallery. Nearly all the stalls were closed and the greater part of the hall was in darkness. I recognised a silence like that which pervades a church after a service. I walked into the centre of the bazaar timidly. A few people were gathered about the stalls which were still open. Before a curtain, over which the words *Café Chantant* were written in coloured lamps, two men were counting money on a salver. I listened to the fall of the coins.

Remembering with difficulty why I had come I went over to one of the stalls and examined porcelain vases and flowered tea-sets. At the door of the stall a young lady was talking and laughing with two young gentlemen. I remarked their English accents and listened vaguely to their conversation.

—O, I never said such a thing!

—O, but you did!

—O, but I didn't!

—Didn't she say that?

—Yes! I heard her.

—O, there's a . . . fib!

Observing me the young lady came over and asked me did I wish to buy anything. The tone of her voice was not encouraging; she seemed to have spoken to me out of a sense of duty. I looked humbly at the great jars that stood like eastern guards at either side of the dark entrance to the stall and murmured:

No, thank you.

The young lady changed the position of one of the vases and went back to the two young men. They began to talk of the same subject. Once or twice the young lady glanced at me over her shoulder.

I lingered before her stall, though I knew my stay was useless, to make my interest in her wares seem the more real. Then I turned away slowly and walked down the middle of the bazaar. I allowed the two pennies to fall against the sixpence in my pocket. I heard a voice call from one end of the gallery that the light was out. The upper part of the hall was now completely dark.

Gazing up into the darkness I saw myself as a creature driven and derided by vanity; and my eyes burned with anguish and anger.

# FRANZ KAFKA [1883–1924]

## The Judgment

It was a Sunday morning in the very height of spring. Georg Bendemann, a young merchant, was sitting in his own room on the first floor of one of a long row of small, ramshackle houses stretching beside the river which were scarcely distinguishable from each other except in height and coloring. He had just finished

Translated by Willa and Edwin Muir.

a letter to an old friend of his who was now living abroad, had put it into its envelope in a slow and dreamy fashion, and with his elbows propped on the writing table was gazing out of the window at the river, the bridge and the hills on the farther bank with their tender green.

He was thinking about his friend, who had actually run away to Russia some years before, being dissatisfied with his prospects at home. Now he was carrying on a business in St. Petersburg, which had flourished to begin with but had long been going downhill, as he always complained on his increasingly rare visits. So he was wearing himself out to no purpose in a foreign country, the unfamiliar full beard he wore did not quite conceal the face Georg had known so well since childhood, and his skin was growing so yellow as to indicate some latent disease. By his own account he had no regular connection with the colony of his fellow countrymen out there and almost no social intercourse with Russian families, so that he was resigning himself to becoming a permanent bachelor.

What could one write to such a man, who had obviously run off the rails, a man one could be sorry for but could not help. Should one advise him to come home, to transplant himself and take up his old friendships again—there was nothing to hinder him—and in general to rely on the help of his friends? But that was as good as telling him, and the more kindly the more offensively, that all his efforts hitherto had miscarried, that he should finally give up, come back home, and be gaped at by everyone as a returned prodigal, that only his friends knew what was what and that he himself was just a big child who should do what his successful and home-keeping friends prescribed. And was it certain, besides, that all the pain one would have to inflict on him would achieve its object? Perhaps it would not even be possible to get him to come home at all—he said himself that he was now out of touch with commerce in his native country—and then he would still be left an alien in a foreign land embittered by his friends' advice and more than ever estranged from them. But if he did follow their advice and then didn't fit in at home—not out of malice, of course, but through force of circumstances—couldn't get on with his friends or without them, felt humiliated, couldn't be said to have either friends or a country of his own any longer, wouldn't it have been better for him to stay abroad just as he was?

Taking all this into account, how could one be sure that he would make a success of life at home?

For such reasons, supposing one wanted to keep up correspondence with him, one could not send him any real news such as could frankly be told to the most distant acquaintance. It was more than three years since his last visit, and for this he offered the lame excuse that the political situation in Russia was too uncertain, which apparently would not permit even the briefest absence of a small business man while it allowed hundreds of thousands of Russians to travel peacefully abroad. But during these three years Georg's own position in life had changed a lot. Two years ago his mother had died, since when he and his father had shared the household together, and his friend had of course been informed of that and had expressed his sympathy in a letter phrased so dryly that the grief caused by such an event, one had to conclude, could not be realized in a distant country. Since that time, however, Georg had applied himself with greater determination to the business as well as to everything else.

Perhaps during his mother's lifetime his father's insistence on having everything his own way in the business had hindered him from developing any real activity of his own, perhaps since her death his father had become less aggressive, although he was still active in the business, perhaps it was mostly due to an accidental run of good fortune—which was very probable indeed—but at any rate during those two years the business had developed in a most unexpected way, the staff had had to be doubled, the turnover was five times as great, no doubt about it, farther progress lay just ahead.

But Georg's friend had no inkling of this improvement. In earlier years, perhaps for the last time in that letter of condolence, he had tried to persuade Georg to emigrate to Russia and had enlarged upon the prospects of success for precisely Georg's branch of trade. The figures quoted were microscopic by comparison with the range of Georg's present operations. Yet he shrank from letting his friend know about his business success, and if he were to do it now retrospectively that certainly would look peculiar.

So Georg confined himself to giving his friend unimportant items of gossip such as rise at random in the memory when one is idly thinking things over on a quiet Sunday. All he desired was to leave undisturbed the idea of the home town which his friend must have built up to his own content during the long interval. And so it happened to Georg that three times in three fairly widely separated letters he had told his friend about the engagement of an unimportant man to an equally unimportant girl, until indeed, quite contrary to his intentions, his friend began to show some interest in this notable event.

Yet Georg preferred to write about things like these rather than to confess that he himself had got engaged a month ago to a Fräulein Frieda Brandenfeld, a girl from a well-to-do family. He often discussed this friend of his with his fiancée and the peculiar relationship that had developed between them in their correspondence. "So he won't be coming to our wedding," said she, "and yet I have a right to get to know all your friends." "I don't want to trouble him," answered Georg, "don't misunderstand me, he would probably come, at least I think so, but he would feel that his hand had been forced and he would be hurt, perhaps he would envy me and certainly he'd be discontented and without being able to do anything about his discontent he'd have to go away again alone. Alone—do you know what that means?" "Yes, but may he not hear about our wedding in some other fashion?" "I can't prevent that, of course, but it's unlikely, considering the way he lives." "Since your friends are like that, Georg, you shouldn't ever have got engaged at all." "Well, we're both to blame for that; but I wouldn't have it any other way now." And when, breathing quickly under his kisses, she still brought out: "All the same, I do feel upset," he thought it could not really involve him in trouble were he to send the news to his friend. "That's the kind of man I am and he'll just have to take me as I am," he said to himself, "I can't cut myself to another pattern that might make a more suitable friend for him."

And in fact he did inform his friend, in the long letter he had been writing that Sunday morning, about his engagement, with these words: "I have saved my best news to the end. I have got engaged to a Fräulein Frieda Brandenfeld, a girl from a well-to-do family, who only came to live here a long time after you went away, so that you're hardly likely to know her. There will be time to tell you more about her later, for today let me just say that I am very happy and as between you and me the only difference in our relationship is that instead of a quite ordinary kind of friend you will now have in me a happy friend. Besides that, you will acquire in my fiancée, who sends her warm greetings and will soon write you herself, a genuine friend of the opposite sex, which is not without importance to a bachelor. I know that there are many reasons why you can't come to see us, but would not my wedding be precisely the right occasion for giving all obstacles the go-by? Still, however that may be, do just as seems good to you without regarding any interests but your own."

With this letter in his hand Georg had been sitting a long time at the writing table, his face turned towards the window. He had barely acknowledged, with an absent smile, a greeting waved to him from the street by a passing acquaintance.

At last he put the letter in his pocket and went out of his room across a small lobby into his father's room, which he had not entered for months. There was in fact no need for him to enter it, since he saw his father daily at business and they took their midday meal together at an eating house; in the evening, it was true, each did as he pleased, yet even then, unless Georg—as mostly happened—went out with friends or, more recently, visited his fiancée, they always sat for a while, each with his newspaper, in their common sitting room.

It surprised Georg how dark his father's room was even on this sunny morning. So it was overshadowed as much as that by the high wall on the other side of the narrow courtyard. His father was sitting by the window in a corner hung with various mementoes of Georg's dead mother, reading a newspaper which he held to one side before his eyes in an attempt to overcome a defect of vision. On the table stood the remains of his breakfast, not much of which seemed to have been eaten.

"Ah, Georg," said his father, rising at once to meet him. His heavy dressing gown swung open as he walked and the skirts of it fluttered around him.—"My father is still a giant of a man," said Georg to himself.

"It's unbearably dark here," he said aloud.

"Yes, it's dark enough," answered his father.

"And you've shut the window, too?"

"I prefer it like that."

"Well, it's quite warm outside," said Georg, as if continuing his previous remark, and sat down.

His father cleared away the breakfast dishes and set them on a chest.

"I really only wanted to tell you," went on Georg, who had

been vacantly following the old man's movements, "that I am now sending the news of my engagement to St. Petersburg." He drew the letter a little way from his pocket and let it drop back again.

"To St. Petersburg?" asked his father.

"To my friend there," said Georg, trying to meet his father's eye.—In business hours he's quite different, he was thinking, how solidly he sits here with his arms crossed.

"Oh yes. To your friend," said his father, with peculiar emphasis.

"Well, you know, Father, that I wanted not to tell him about my engagement at first. Out of consideration for him, that was the only reason. You know yourself he's a difficult man. I said to myself that someone else might tell him about my engagement, although he's such a solitary creature that that was hardly likely—I couldn't prevent that—but I wasn't ever going to tell him myself."

"And now you've changed your mind?" asked his father, laying his enormous newspaper on the window sill and on top of it his spectacles, which he covered with one hand.

"Yes, I've been thinking it over. If he's a good friend of mine, I said to myself, my being happily engaged should make him happy too. And so I wouldn't put off telling him any longer. But before I posted the letter I wanted to let you know."

"Georg," said his father, lengthening his toothless mouth, "listen to me! You've come to me about this business, to talk it over with me. No doubt that does you honor. But it's nothing, it's worse than nothing, if you don't tell me the whole truth. I don't want to stir up matters that shouldn't be mentioned here. Since the death of our dear mother certain things have been done that aren't right. Maybe the time will come for mentioning them, and maybe sooner than we think. There's many a thing in the business I'm not aware of, maybe it's not done behind my back—I'm not going to say that it's done behind my back—I'm not equal to things any longer, my memory's failing, I haven't an eye for so many things any longer. That's the course of nature in the first place, and in the second place the death of our dear mother hit me harder than it did you.—But since we're talking about it, about this letter, I beg you, Georg, don't deceive me. It's a trivial affair, it's hardly worth mentioning, so don't deceive me. Do you really have this friend in St. Petersburg?"

Georg rose in embarrassment. "Never mind my friends. A

thousand friends wouldn't make up to me for my father. Do you know what I think? You're not taking enough care of yourself. But old age must be taken care of. I can't do without you in the business, you know that very well, but if the business is going to undermine your health, I'm ready to close it down tomorrow forever. And that won't do. We'll have to make a change in your way of living. But a radical change. You sit here in the dark, and in the sitting room you would have plenty of light. You just take a bite of breakfast instead of properly keeping up your strength. You sit by a closed window, and the air would be so good for you. No, father! I'll get the doctor to come, and we'll follow his orders. We'll change your room, you can move into the front room and I'll move in here. You won't notice the change, all your things will be moved with you. But there's time for all that later, I'll put you to bed now for a little, I'm sure you need to rest. Come, I'll help you take off your things, you'll see I can do it. Or if you would rather go into the front room at once, you can lie down in my bed for the present. That would be the most sensible thing."

Georg stood close beside his father, who had let his head with its unkempt white hair sink on his chest.

"Georg," said his father in a low voice, without moving.

Georg knelt down at once beside his father, in the old man's weary face he saw the pupils, over-large, fixedly looking at him from the corners of the eyes.

"You have no friend in St. Petersburg. You've always been a leg-puller and you haven't even shrunk from pulling my leg. How could you have a friend out there! I can't believe it."

"Just think back a bit, Father," said Georg, lifting his father from the chair and slipping off his dressing gown as he stood feebly enough, "it'll soon be three years since my friend came to see us last. I remember that you used not to like him very much. At least twice I kept you from seeing him, although he was actually sitting with me in my room. I could quite well understand your dislike of him, my friend has his peculiarities. But then, later, you got on with him very well. I was proud because you listened to him and nodded and asked him questions. If you think back you're bound to remember. He used to tell us the most incredible stories of the Russian Revolution. For instance, when he was on a business trip to Kiev and ran into a riot, and saw a priest on a balcony who cut a broad cross in blood on the palm of his hand and held the hand up and appealed to the mob. You've told that story yourself once or twice since."

Meanwhile Georg had succeeded in lowering his father down again and carefully taking off the woollen drawers he wore over his linen underpants and his socks. The not particularly clean appearance of this underwear made him reproach himself for having been neglectful. It should have certainly been his duty to see that his father had clean changes of underwear. He had not yet explicitly discussed with his bride-to-be what arrangements should be made for his father in the future, for they had both of them silently taken it for granted that the old man would go on living alone in the old house. But now he made a quick, firm decision to take him into his own future establishment. It almost looked, on closer inspection, as if the care he meant to lavish there on his father might come too late.

He carried his father to bed in his arms. It gave him a dreadful feeling to notice that while he took the few steps towards the bed the old man on his breast was playing with his watch chain. He could not lay him down on the bed for a moment, so firmly did he hang on to the watch chain.

But as soon as he was laid in bed, all seemed well. He covered himself up and even drew the blankets farther than usual over his shoulders. He looked up at Georg with a not unfriendly eye.

"You begin to remember my friend, don't you?" asked Georg, giving him an encouraging nod.

"Am I well covered up now?" asked his father, as if he were not able to see whether his feet were properly tucked in or not.

"So you find it snug in bed already," said Georg, and tucked the blankets more closely around him.

"Am I well covered up?" asked the father once more, seeming to be strangely intent upon the answer.

"Don't worry, you're well covered up."

"No!" cried his father, cutting short the answer, threw the blankets off with a strength that sent them all flying in a moment and sprang erect in bed. Only one hand lightly touched the ceiling to steady him.

"You wanted to cover me up, I know, my young sprig, but I'm far from being covered up yet. And even if this is the last strength I have, it's enough for you, too much for you. Of course I know your friend. He would have been a son after my own heart. That's why you've been playing him false all these years. Why else? Do you think I haven't been sorry for him? And that's why you had to lock yourself up in your office—the Chief is busy, mustn't be disturbed—just so that you could write your lying letters to Russia. But thank goodness a father doesn't need to be taught how to see through his son. And now that you thought you'd got him down, so far down that you could set your bottom on him and sit on him and he wouldn't move, then my fine son makes up his mind to get married!"

Georg stared at the bogey conjured up by his father. His friend in St. Petersburg, whom his father suddenly knew too well, touched his imagination as never before. Lost in the vastness of Russia he saw him. At the door of an empty, plundered warehouse he saw him. Among the wreckage of his showcases, the slashed remnants of his wares, the falling gas brackets, he was just standing up. Why did he have to go so far away!

"But attend to me!" cried his father, and Georg, almost distracted, ran towards the bed to take everything in, yet came to a stop halfway.

"Because she lifted up her skirts," his father began to flute, "because she lifted her skirts like this, the nasty creature," and mimicking her he lifted his shirt so high that one could see the scar on this thigh from his war wound, "because she lifted her skirts like this and this you made up to her, and in order to make free with her undisturbed you have disgraced your mother's memory, betrayed your friend and stuck your father into bed so that he can't move. But he can move, or can't he?"

And he stood up quite unsupported and kicked his legs out. His insight made him radiant.

Georg shrank into a corner, as far away from his father as possible. A long time ago he had firmly made up his mind to watch closely every least movement so that he should not be surprised by any indirect attack, a pounce from behind or above. At this moment he recalled this long-forgotten resolve and forgot it again, like a man drawing a short thread through the eye of a needle.

"But your friend hasn't been betrayed after all!" cried his father, emphasizing the point with stabs of his forefinger. "I've been representing him here on the spot."

"You comedian!" Georg could not resist the retort, realized at once the harm done and, his eyes starting in his head, bit his tongue back, only too late, till the pain made his knees give.

"Yes, of course I've been playing a comedy! A comedy! That's a good expression! What other comfort was left to a poor old widower? Tell me—and while you're answering me be you still my living son—what else was left to me, in my back room, plagued by a disloyal staff, old to the marrow of my bones? And my son strutting through the world, finishing off deals that I had prepared for him, bursting with triumphant glee and stalking away from his father with the closed face of a respectable business man! Do you think I didn't love you, I, from whom you are sprung?"

Now he'll lean forward, thought Georg, what if he topples and smashes himself! These words went hissing through his mind.

His father leaned forward but did not topple. Since Georg did not come any nearer, as he had expected, he straightened himself again.

"Stay where you are, I don't need you! You think you have strength enough to come over here and that you're only hanging back of your own accord. Don't be too sure! I am still much the stronger of us two. All by myself I might have had to give way, but your mother has given me so much of her strength that I've established a fine connection with your friend and I have your customers here in my pocket!"

"He has pockets even in his shirt!" said Georg to himself, and believed that with this remark he could make him an impossible figure for all the world. Only for a moment did he think so, since he kept on forgetting everything.

"Just take your bride on your arm and try getting in my way! I'll sweep her from your very side, you don't know how!"

Georg made a grimace of disbelief. His father only nodded, confirming the truth of his words, towards Georg's corner.

"How you amused me today, coming to ask me if you should tell your friend about your engagement. He knows it already, you stupid boy, he knows it all! I've been writing to him, for you forgot to take my writing things away from me. That's why he hasn't been here for years, he knows everything a hundred times better than you do yourself, in his left hand he crumples your letters unopened while in his right hand he holds up my letters to read through!"

In his enthusiasm he waved his arm over his head. "He knows everything a thousand times better!" he cried.

"Ten thousand times!" said Georg, to make fun of his father, but in his very mouth the words turned into deadly earnest.

"For years I've been waiting for you to come with some such question! Do you think I concern myself with anything else? Do you think I read my newspapers? Look!" and he threw Georg a newspaper sheet which he had somehow taken to bed with him. An old newspaper, with a name entirely unknown to Georg.

"How long a time you've taken to grow up! Your mother had to die, she couldn't see the happy day, your friend is going to pieces in Russia, even three years ago he was yellow enough to be thrown away, and as for me, you see what condition I'm in. You have eyes in your head for that!"

"So you've been lying in wait for me!" cried Georg.

His father said pityingly, in an offhand manner: "I suppose you wanted to say that sooner. But now it doesn't matter." And in a louder voice: "So now you know what else there was in the world besides yourself, till now you've known only about yourself! An innocent child, yes, that you were, truly, but still more truly have you been a devilish human being!—And therefore take note: I sentence you now to death by drowning!"

Georg felt himself urged from the room, the crash with which his father fell on the bed behind him was still in his ears as he fled. On the staircase, which he rushed down as if its steps were an inclined plane, he ran into his charwoman on her way up to do the morning cleaning of the room. "Jesus!" she cried, and covered her face with her apron, but he was already gone. Out of the front door he rushed, across the roadway, driven towards the water. Already he was grasping at the railings as a starving man clutches food. He swung himself over, like the distinguished gymnast he had once been in his youth, to his parents' pride. With weakening grip he was still holding on when he spied between the railings a motor-bus coming which would easily cover the noise of his fall, called in a low voice: "Dear parents, I have always loved you, all the same," and let himself drop.

At this moment an unending stream of traffic was just going over the bridge.

## D. H. LAWRENCE [1885–1930]

# The Blind Man

Isabel Pervin was listening for two sounds—for the sound of wheels on the drive outside and for the noise of her husband's footsteps in the hall. Her dearest and oldest friend, a man who seemed almost indispensable to her living, would drive up in the rainy dusk of the closing November day. The trap had gone to fetch him from the station. And her husband, who had been blinded in Flanders, and who had a disfiguring mark on his brow, would be coming in from the outhouses.

He had been home for a year now. He was totally blind. Yet they had been very happy. The Grange was Maurice's own place. The back was a farmstead, and the Wernhams, who occupied the rear premises, acted as farmers. Isabel lived with her husband in the handsome rooms in front. She and he had been almost entirely alone together since he was wounded. They talked and sang and read together in a wonderful and unspeakable intimacy. Then she reviewed books for a Scottish newspaper, carrying on her old interest, and he occupied himself a good deal with the farm. Sightless, he could still discuss everything with Wernham, and he could also do a good deal of work about the place—menial work, it is true, but it gave him satisfaction. He milked the cows, carried in the pails, turned the separator, attended to the pigs and horses. Life was still very full and strangely serene for the blind man, peaceful with the almost incomprehensible peace of immediate contact in darkness. With his wife he had a whole world, rich and real and invisible.

They were newly and remotely happy. He did not even regret the loss of his sight in these times of dark, palpable joy. A certain exultance swelled his soul.

But as time wore on, sometimes the rich glamour would leave them. Sometimes, after months of this intensity, a sense of burden overcame Isabel, a weariness, a terrible *ennui,* in that silent house approached between a colonnade of tall-shafted pines. Then she felt she would go mad, for she could not bear it. And sometimes he had devastating fits of depression, which seemed to lay waste his whole being. It was worse than depression—a black misery, when his own life was a torture to him, and when his presence was unbearable to his wife. The dread went down to the roots of her soul as these black days recurred. In a kind of panic she tried to wrap herself up still further in her husband. She forced the old spontaneous cheerfulness and joy to continue. But the effort it cost her was almost too much. She knew she could not keep it up. She felt she would scream with the strain, and would give anything, anything, to escape. She longed to possess her husband utterly; it gave her inordinate joy to have him entirely to herself. And yet, when again he was gone in a black and massive misery, she could not bear him, she could not bear herself; she wished she could be snatched away off the earth altogether, anything rather than live at this cost.

Dazed, she schemed for a way out. She invited friends, she tried to give him some further connection with the outer world. But it was no good. After all their joy and suffering, after their dark, great year of blindness and solitude and unspeakable nearness, other people seemed to them both shallow, rattling, rather impertinent. Shallow prattle seemed presumptuous. He became impatient and irritated, she was wearied. And so they lapsed into their solitude again. For they preferred it.

But now, in a few weeks' time, her second baby would be born. The first had died, an infant, when her husband first went out to France. She looked with joy and relief to the coming of the second. It would be her salvation. But also she felt some anxiety. She was thirty years old, her husband was a year younger. They both wanted the child very much. Yet she could not help feeling afraid. She had her husband on her hands, a terrible joy to her, and a terrifying burden. The child would occupy her love and attention. And then, what of Maurice? What would he do? If only she could feel that he, too, would be at peace and happy when the child came! She did so want to luxuriate in a rich, physical satisfaction of maternity. But the man, what would he do? How could she provide for him, how avert those shattering black moods of his, which destroyed them both?

She sighed with fear. But at this time Bertie Reid wrote to Isabel. He was her old friend, a second or third cousin, a Scotchman, as she was a Scotchwoman. They had been brought up near to one another, and all her life he had been her friend, like a brother, but better than her own brothers. She loved him—though not in the marrying sense. There was a sort of kinship between them, an affinity. They understood one another instinctively. But Isabel would never have thought of marrying Bertie. It would have seemed like marrying in her own family.

Bertie was a barrister and a man of letters, a Scotchman of the intellectual type, quick, ironical, sentimental, and on his knees before the woman he adored but did not want to marry. Maurice Pervin was different. He came of a good old country family—the Grange was not a very great distance from Oxford. He was passionate, sensitive, perhaps over-sensitive, wincing—a big fellow with heavy limbs and a forehead that flushed painfully. For his mind was slow, as if drugged by the strong provincial blood that beat in his veins. He was very sensitive to his own mental slowness, his feelings being quick and acute. So that he was just the opposite to Bertie, whose mind was much quicker than his emotions, which were not so very fine.

From the first the two men did not like each other. Isabel felt that they *ought* to get on together. But they did not. She felt that if only each could have the clue to the other there would be such a rare understanding between them. It did not come off, however, Bertie adopted a slightly ironical attitude, very offensive to Maurice, who returned the Scotch irony with English resentment, a resentment which deepened sometimes into stupid hatred.

This was a little puzzling to Isabel. However, she accepted it in the course of things. Men were made freakish and unreasonable. Therefore, when Maurice was going out to France for the second time, she felt that, for her husband's sake, she must discontinue her friendship with Bertie. She wrote to the barrister to this effect. Bertram Reid simply replied that in this, as in all other matters, he must obey her wishes, if these were indeed her wishes.

For nearly two years nothing had passed between the two friends. Isabel rather gloried in the fact; she had no compunction. She had one great article of faith, which was, that husband and wife should be so important to one another, that the rest of the world simply did not count. She and Maurice were husband and wife. They loved one another. They would have children. Then let everybody and everything else fade into insignificance outside this connubial felicity. She professed herself quite happy and ready to receive Maurice's friends. She was happy and ready: the happy wife, the ready woman in possession. Without knowing why, the friends retired abashed, and came no more. Maurice, of course, took as much satisfaction in this connubial absorption as Isabel did.

He shared in Isabel's literary activities, she cultivated a real interest in agriculture and cattle-raising. For she, being at heart perhaps an emotional enthusiast, always cultivated the practical side of life and prided herself on her mastery of practical affairs. Thus the husband and wife had spent the five years of their married life. The last had been one of blindness and unspeakable intimacy. And now Isabel felt a great indifference coming over her, a sort of lethargy. She wanted to be allowed to bear her child in peace, to nod by the fire and drift vaguely, physically, from day to day. Maurice was like an ominous thunder-cloud. She had to keep waking up to remember him.

When a little note came from Bertie, asking if he were to put up a tombstone to their dead friendship, and speaking of the real pain he felt on account of her husband's loss of sight, she felt a pang, a fluttering agitation of re-awakening. And she read the letter to Maurice.

"Ask him to come down," he said.

"Ask Bertie to come here!" she re-echoed.

"Yes—if he wants to."

Isabel paused for a few moments.

"I know he wants to—he'd only be too glad," she replied. "But what about you, Maurice? How would you like it?"

"I should like it."

"Well—in that case—— But I thought you didn't care for him——"

"Oh, I don't know. I might think differently of him now," the blind man replied. It was rather abstruse to Isabel.

"Well, dear," she said, "if you're quite sure——"

"I'm sure enough. Let him come," said Maurice.

So Bertie was coming, coming this evening, in the November rain and darkness. Isabel was agitated, racked with her old restlessness and indecision. She had always suffered from this pain of doubt, just an agonizing sense of uncertainty. It had begun to pass off, in the lethargy of maternity. Now it returned, and she resented it. She struggled as usual to maintain her calm, composed, friendly bearing, a sort of mask she wore over all her body.

A woman had lighted a tall lamp beside the table and spread the cloth. The long dining-room was dim, with its elegant but rather severe pieces of old furniture. Only the round table glowed softly under the light. It had a rich, beautiful effect. The white cloth glistened and dropped its heavy, pointed lace corners almost to the carpet, the china was old and handsome, creamy-yellow, with a blotched pattern of harsh red and deep blue, the cups large and bell-shaped, the teapot gallant. Isabel looked at it with superficial appreciation.

Her nerves were hurting her. She looked automatically again at the high, uncurtained windows. In the last dusk she could just perceive outside a huge fir-tree swaying its boughs: it was as if she thought it rather than saw it. The rain came flying on the window panes. Ah, why had she no peace? These two men, why did they tear at her? Why did they not come—why was there this suspense?

She sat in a lassitude that was really suspense and irritation. Maurice, at least, might come in—there was nothing to keep him out. She rose to her feet. Catching sight of her reflection in a mirror, she glanced at herself with a slight smile of recognition, as if she were an old friend to herself. Her face was oval and calm, her nose a little arched. Her neck made a beautiful line down to her shoulder. With hair knotted loosely behind, she had something of a warm, maternal look. Thinking this of herself, she arched her eyebrows and her rather heavy eyelids, with a little flicker of a smile, and for a moment her grey eyes looked amused and wicked, a little sardonic, out of her transfigured Madonna face.

Then, resuming her air of womanly patience—she was really fatally self-determined—she went with a little jerk towards the door. Her eyes were slightly reddened.

She passed down the wide hall and through a door at the end. Then she was in the farm premises. The scent of dairy, and of farm-kitchen, and of farm-yard and of leather almost overcame her: but particularly the scent of dairy. They had been scalding out the pans. The flagged passage in front of her was dark, puddled, and wet. Light came out from the open kitchen door. She went forward and stood in the doorway. The farm-people were at tea, seated at a little distance from her, round a long, narrow table, in the centre of which stood a white lamp. Ruddy faces, ruddy hands holding food, red mouths working, heads bent over the tea-cups: men, land-girls, boys: it was tea-time, feeding-time. Some faces caught sight of her. Mrs. Wernham, going round behind the chairs with a large black teapot, halting slightly in her walk, was not aware of her for a moment. Then she turned suddenly.

"Oh, is it Madam!" she exclaimed. "Come in, then, come in! We're at tea." And she dragged forward a chair.

"No, I won't come in," said Isabel. "I'm afraid I interrupt your meal."

"No—no—not likely, Madam, not likely."

"Hasn't Mr. Pervin come in, do you know?"

"I'm sure I couldn't say! Missed him, have you, Madam?"

"No, I only wanted him to come in," laughed Isabel, as if shyly.

"Wanted him, did ye? Get up, boy—get up, now——"

Mrs. Wernham knocked one of the boys on the shoulder. He began to scrape his feet, chewing largely.

"I believe he's in top stable," said another face from the table.

"Ah! No, don't get up. I'm going myself," said Isabel.

"Don't you go out of a dirty night like this. Let the lad go. Get along wi' ye, boy," said Mrs. Wernham.

"No, no," said Isabel, with a decision that was always obeyed. "Go on with your tea, Tom. I'd like to go across to the stable, Mrs. Wernham."

"Did ever you hear tell!" exclaimed the woman.

"Isn't the trap late?" asked Isabel.

"Why, no," said Mrs. Wernham, peering into the distance at the tall, dim clock. "No, Madam—we can give it another quarter or twenty minutes yet, good—yes, every bit of a quarter."

"Ah! It seems late when darkness falls so early," said Isabel.

"It do, that it do. Bother the days, that they draw in so," answered Mrs. Wernham. "Proper miserable!"

"They are," said Isabel, withdrawing.

She pulled on her overshoes, wrapped a large tartan shawl around her, put on a man's felt hat, and ventured out along the causeways of the first yard. It was very dark. The wind was roaring in the great elms behind the outhouses. When she came to the second yard the darkness seemed deeper. She was unsure of her footing. She wished she had brought a lantern. Rain blew against her. Half she liked it, half she felt unwilling to battle.

She reached at last the just visible door of the stable. There was no sign of a light anywhere. Opening the upper half, she looked in: into a simple well of darkness. The smell of horses, and ammonia, and of warmth was startling to her, in that full night. She listened with all her ears but could hear nothing save the night, and the stirring of a horse.

"Maurice!" she called, softly and musically, though she was afraid. "Maurice—are you there?"

Nothing came from the darkness. She knew the rain and wind blew in upon the horses, the hot animal life. Feeling it wrong, she entered the stable and drew the lower half of the door shut, holding the upper part close. She did not stir, because she was aware of the presence of the dark hind-quarters of the horses, though she could not see them, and she was afraid. Something wild stirred in her heart.

She listened intensely. Then she heard a small noise in the distance—far away, it seemed—the chink of a pan, and a man's voice speaking a brief word. It would be Maurice, in the other part of the stable. She stood motionless, waiting for him to come through the partition door. The horses were so terrifyingly near to her, in the invisible.

The loud jarring of the inner door-latch made her start; the door was opened. She could hear and feel her husband entering and invisibly passing among the horses near to her, darkness as they were, actively intermingled. The rather low sound of his voice as he spoke to the horses came velvety to her nerves. How near he was, and how invisible! The darkness seemed to be in a strange swirl of violent life, just upon her. She turned giddy.

Her presence of mind made her call, quietly and musically:

"Maurice! Maurice—dea-ar!"

"Yes," he answered. "Isabel?"

She saw nothing, and the sound of his voice seemed to touch her.

"Hello!" she answered cheerfully, straining her eyes to see him. He was still busy, attending to the horses near her, but she saw only darkness. It made her almost desperate.

"Won't you come in, dear?" she said.

"Yes, I'm coming. Just half a minute. *Stand over—now!* Trap's not come, has it?"

"Not yet," said Isabel.

His voice was pleasant and ordinary, but it had a slight suggestion of the stable to her. She wished he would come away. Whilst he was so utterly invisible, she was afraid of him.

"How's the time?" he asked.

"Not yet six," she replied. She disliked to answer into the dark. Presently he came very near to her, and she retreated out of doors.

"The weather blows in here," he said, coming steadily forward, feeling for the doors. She shrank away. At last she could dimly see him.

"Bertie won't have much of a drive," he said, as he closed the doors.

"He won't indeed!" said Isabel calmly, watching the dark shape at the door.

"Give me your arm, dear," she said.

She pressed his arm close to her, as she went. But she longed to see him, to look at him. She was nervous. He walked erect, with face rather lifted, but with a curious tentative movement of his powerful, muscular legs. She could feel the clever, careful, strong contact of his feet with the earth, as she balanced against him. For a moment he was a tower of darkness to her, as if he rose out of the earth.

In the house-passage he wavered and went cautiously, with a curious look of silence about him as he felt for the bench. Then he sat down heavily. He was a man with rather sloping shoulders, but with heavy limbs, powerful legs that seemed to know the earth. His head was small, usually carried high and light. As he bent down to unfasten his gaiters and boots he did not look blind. His hair was brown and crisp, his hands were large, reddish, intelligent, the veins stood out in the wrists; and his thighs and knees seemed massive. When he stood up his face and neck were surcharged with blood, the veins stood out on his temples. She did not look at his blindness.

Isabel was always glad when they had passed through the dividing door into their own regions of repose and beauty. She was a little afraid of him, out there in the animal grossness of the back. His bearing also changed, as he smelt the familiar indefinable odour that pervaded his wife's surroundings, a delicate, refined scent, very faintly spicy. Perhaps it came from the potpourri bowls.

He stood at the foot of the stairs, arrested, listening. She watched him, and her heart sickened. He seemed to be listening to fate.

"He's not here yet," he said. "I'll go up and change."

"Maurice," she said, "you're not wishing he wouldn't come, are you?"

"I couldn't quite say," he answered. "I feel myself rather on the qui vive."

"I can see you are," she answered. And she reached up and kissed his cheek. She saw his mouth relax into a slow smile.

"What are you laughing at?" she said roguishly.

"You consoling me," he answered.

"Nay," she answered. "Why should I console you? You know we love each other—you know *how* married we are! What does anything else matter?"

"Nothing at all, my dear."

He felt for her face and touched it, smiling.

"*You're* all right, aren't you?" he asked anxiously.

"I'm wonderfully all right, love," she answered. "It's you I am a little troubled about, at times."

"Why me?" he said, touching her cheeks delicately with the tips of his fingers. The touch had an almost hypnotizing effect on her.

He went away upstairs. She saw him mount into the darkness, unseeing and unchanging. He did not know that the lamps on the upper corridor were unlighted. He went on into the darkness with unchanging step. She heard him in the bath-room.

Pervin moved about almost unconsciously in his familiar sur- roundings, dark though everything was. He seemed to know the presence of objects before he touched them. It was a pleasure to him to rock thus through a world of things, carried on the flood in a sort of blood-prescience.[1] He did not think much or trouble much. So long as he kept this sheer immediacy of blood-contact with the substantial world he was happy, he wanted no interven- tion of visual consciousness. In this state there was a certain rich positivity, bordering sometimes on rapture. Life seemed to move in him like a tide lapping, lapping, and advancing, enveloping all things darkly. It was a pleasure to stretch forth the hand and meet

---

[1] Blood-knowledge.

the unseen object, clasp it, and possess it in pure contact. He did not try to remember, to visualize. He did not want to. The new way of consciousness substituted itself in him.

The rich suffusion of this state generally kept him happy, reaching its culmination in the consuming passion for his wife. But at times the flow would seem to be checked and thrown back. Then it would beat inside him like a tangled sea, and he was tortured in the shattered chaos of his own blood. He grew to dread this arrest, this throw-back, this chaos inside himself, when he seemed merely at the mercy of his own powerful and conflicting elements. How to get some measure of control or surety, this was the question. And when the question rose maddening in him, he would clench his fists as if he would *compel* the whole universe to submit to him. But it was in vain. He could not even compel himself.

Tonight, however, he was still serene, though little tremors of unreasonable exasperation ran through him. He had to handle the razor very carefully, as he shaved, for it was not at one with him, he was afraid of it. His hearing also was too much sharpened. He heard the woman lighting the lamps on the corridor, and attending to the fire in the visitors' room. And then, as he went to his room, he heard the trap arrive. Then came Isabel's voice, lifted and calling, like a bell ringing:

"Is it you, Bertie? Have you come?"

And a man's voice answered out of the wind:

"Hello, Isabel! There you are."

"Have you had a miserable drive? I'm so sorry we couldn't send a closed carriage. I can't see you at all, you know."

"I'm coming. No, I liked the drive—it was like Perthshire. Well, how are you? You're looking fit as ever, as far as I can see."

"Oh, yes," said Isabel. "I'm wonderfully well. How are you? Rather thin, I think——"

"Worked to death—everybody's old cry. But I'm all right Ciss. How's Pervin?—isn't he here?"

"Oh, yes, he's upstairs changing. Yes, he's awfully well. Take off your wet things; I'll send them to be dried."

"And how are you both, in spirits? He doesn't fret?"

"No—no, not at all. No, on the contrary, really. We've been wonderfully happy, incredibly. It's more than I can understand—so wonderful: the nearness, and the peace——"

"Ah! Well, that's awfully good news——"

They moved away. Pervin heard no more. But a childish sense of desolation had come over him, as he heard their brisk voices. He seemed shut out—like a child that is left out. He was aimless and excluded, he did not know what to do with himself. The helpless desolation came over him. He fumbled nervously as he dressed himself, in a state almost of childishness. He disliked the Scotch accent in Bertie's speech, and the slight response it found on Isabel's tongue. He disliked the slight purr of complacency in the Scottish speech. He disliked intensely the glib way in which Isabel spoke of their happiness and nearness. It made him recoil. He was fretful and beside himself like a child, he had almost a childish nostalgia to be included in the life circle. And at the same time he was a man, dark and powerful and infuriated by his own weakness. By some fatal flaw, he could not be by himself, he had to depend on the support of another. And this very dependence enraged him. He hated Bertie Reid, and at the same time he knew the hatred was nonsense, he knew it was the outcome of his own weakness.

He went downstairs. Isabel was alone in the dining-room. She watched him enter, head erect, his feet tentative. He looked so strong-blooded and healthy and, at the same time, cancelled. Cancelled—that was the word that flew across her mind. Perhaps it was his scar suggested it.

"You heard Bertie come, Maurice?" she said.

"Yes—isn't he here?"

"He's in his room. He looks very thin and worn."

"I suppose he works himself to death."

A woman came in with a tray—and after a few minutes Bertie came down. He was a little dark man, with a very big forehead, thin, wispy hair, and sad, large eyes. His expression was inordinately sad—almost funny. He had odd, short legs.

Isabel watched him hesitate under the door, and glance nervously at her husband. Pervin heard him and turned.

"Here you are, now," said Isabel. "Come, let us eat."

Bertie went across to Maurice.

"How are you, Pervin?" he said, as he advanced.

The blind man stuck his hand out into space, and Bertie took it.

"Very fit. Glad you've come," said Maurice.

Isabel glanced at them, and glanced away, as if she could not bear to see them.

"Come," she said. "Come to table. Aren't you both awfully hungry? I am, tremendously."

"I'm afraid you waited for me," said Bertie, as they sat down.

Maurice had a curious monolithic way of sitting in a chair, erect and distant. Isabel's heart always beat when she caught sight of him thus.

"No," she replied to Bertie. "We're very little later than usual. We're having a sort of high tea, not dinner. Do you mind? It gives us such a nice long evening, uninterrupted."

"I like it," said Bertie.

Maurice was feeling, with curious little movements, almost like a cat kneading her bed, for his plate, his knife and fork, his napkin. He was getting the whole geography of his cover into his consciousness. He sat erect and inscrutable, remote-seeming. Bertie watched the static figure of the blind man, the delicate tactile discernment of the large, ruddy hands, and the curious mindless silence of the brow, above the scar. With difficulty he looked away, and without knowing what he did, picked up a little crystal bowl of violets from the table, and held them to his nose.

"They are sweet-scented," he said. "Where do they come from?"

"From the garden—under the windows," said Isabel.

"So late in the year—and so fragrant! Do you remember the violets under Aunt Bell's south wall?"

The two friends looked at each other and exchanged a smile, Isabel's eyes lighting up.

"Don't I?" she replied. "*Wasn't* she queer!"

"A curious old girl," laughed Bertie. "There's a streak of freak-ishness in the family, Isabel."

"Ah—but not in you and me, Bertie," said Isabel. "Give them to Maurice, will you?" she added, as Bertie was putting down the flowers. "Have you smelled the violets, dear? Do!—they are so scented."

Maurice held out his hand, and Bertie placed the tiny bowl against his large, warm-looking fingers. Maurice's hand closed over the thin white fingers of the barrister. Bertie carefully extri-cated himself. Then the two watched the blind man smelling the violets. He bent his head and seemed to be thinking. Isabel waited.

"Aren't they sweet, Maurice?" she said at last, anxiously.

"Very," he said. And he held out the bowl. Bertie took it. Both he and Isabel were a little afraid, and deeply disturbed.

The meal continued. Isabel and Bertie chatted spasmodically. The blind man was silent. He touched his food repeatedly, with quick, delicate touches of his knife-point, then cut irregular bits. He could not bear to be helped. Both Isabel and Bertie suffered: Isabel wondered why. She did not suffer when she was alone with Maurice. Bertie made her conscious of a strangeness.

After the meal the three drew their chairs to the fire, and sat down to talk. The decanters were put on a table near at hand. Isabel knocked the logs on the fire, and clouds of brilliant sparks went up the chimney. Bertie noticed a slight weariness in her bearing.

"You will be glad when your child comes now, Isabel?" he said.

She looked up to him with a quick wan smile.

"Yes, I shall be glad," she answered. "It begins to seem long. Yes, I shall be very glad. So will you, Maurice, won't you?" she added.

"Yes, I shall," replied her husband.

"We are both looking forward so much to having it," she said.

"Yes, of course," said Bertie.

He was a bachelor, three or four years older than Isabel. He lived in beautiful rooms overlooking the river, guarded by a faithful Scottish man-servant. And he had his friends among the fair sex—not lovers, friends. So long as he could avoid any danger of courtship or marriage, he adored a few good women with constant and unfailing homage, and he was chivalrously fond of quite a number. But if they seemed to encroach on him, he withdrew and detested them.

Isabel knew him very well, knew his beautiful constancy, and kindness, also his incurable weakness, which made him unable ever to enter into close contact of any sort. He was ashamed of himself because he could not marry, could not approach women physically. He wanted to do so. But he could not. At the centre of him he was afraid, helplessly and even brutally afraid. He had given up hope, had ceased to expect any more that he could escape his own weakness. Hence he was a brilliant and successful barrister, also a *littérateur*[2] of high repute, a rich man, and a great social success. At the centre he felt himself neuter, nothing.

Isabel knew him well. She despised him even while she admired him. She looked at his sad face, his little short legs, and felt contempt of him. She looked at his dark grey eyes, with their uncanny, almost childlike, intuition, and she loved him. He understood amazingly—but she had no fear of his understanding. As a man she patronized him.

And she turned to the impassive, silent figure of her husband. He sat leaning back, with folded arms, and face a little uptilted. His knees were straight and massive. She sighed, picked up the poker, and again began to prod the fire, to rouse the clouds of soft brilliant sparks.

"Isabel tells me," Bertie began suddenly, "that you have not suffered unbearably from the loss of sight."

Maurice straightened himself to attend but kept his arms folded.

"No," he said, "not unbearably. Now and again one struggles against it, you know. But there are compensations."

"They say it is much worse to be stone deaf," said Isabel.

"I believe it is," said Bertie. "Are there compensations?" he added, to Maurice.

"Yes. You cease to bother about a great many things." Again Maurice stretched his figure, stretched the strong muscles of his back, and leaned backwards, with uplifted face.

"And that is a relief," said Bertie. "But what is there in place of the bothering? What replaces the activity?"

There was a pause. At length the blind man replied, as out of a negligent, unattentive thinking:

"Oh, I don't know. There's a good deal when you're not active."

"Is there?" said Bertie. "What exactly? It always seems to me that when there is no thought and no action, there is nothing."

Again Maurice was slow in replying.

"There is something," he replied. "I couldn't tell you what it is."

---

[2] Literary person.

And the talk lapsed once more, Isabel and Bertie chatting gossip and reminiscence, the blind man silent.

At length Maurice rose restlessly, a big obtrusive figure. He felt tight and hampered. He wanted to go away.

"Do you mind," he said, "if I go and speak to Wernham?"

"No—go along, dear," said Isabel.

And he went out. A silence came over the two friends. At length Bertie said:

"Nevertheless, it is a great deprivation, Cissie."

"It is, Bertie. I know it is."

"Something lacking all the time," said Bertie.

"Yes, I know. And yet—and yet—Maurice is right. There is something else, something *there,* which you never knew was there, and which you can't express."

"What is there?" asked Bertie.

"I don't know—it's awfully hard to define it—but something strong and immediate. There's something strange in Maurice's presence—indefinable—but I couldn't do without it. I agree that it seems to put one's mind to sleep. But when we're alone I miss nothing, it seems awfully rich, almost splendid, you know."

"I'm afraid I don't follow," said Bertie.

They talked desultorily. The wind blew loudly outside, rain chattered on the window-panes, making a sharp drum-sound because of the closed, mellow-golden shutters inside. The logs burned slowly, with hot, almost invisible small flames. Bertie seemed uneasy, there were dark circles round his eyes. Isabel, rich with her approaching maternity, leaned looking into the fire. Her hair curled in odd, loose strands, very pleasing to the man. But she had a curious feeling of old woe in her heart, old, timeless night-woe.

"I suppose we're all deficient somewhere," said Bertie.

"I suppose so," said Isabel wearily.

"Damned, sooner or later."

"I don't know," she said, rousing herself. "I feel quite all right, you know. The child coming seems to make me indifferent to everything, just placid. I can't feel that there's anything to trouble about, you know."

"A good thing, I should say," he replied slowly.

"Well, there it is. I suppose it's just Nature. If only I felt I needn't trouble about Maurice, I should be perfectly content——"

"But you feel you must trouble about him?"

"Well—I don't know——" She even resented this much effort.

The night passed slowly. Isabel looked at the clock. "I say," she said. "It's nearly ten o'clock. Where can Maurice be? I'm sure they're all in bed at the back. Excuse me a moment."

She went out, returning almost immediately.

"It's all shut up and in darkness," she said. "I wonder where he is. He must have gone out to the farm——"

Bertie looked at her.

"I suppose he'll come in," he said.

"I suppose so," she said. "But it's unusual for him to be out now."

"Would you like me to go out and see?"

"Well—if you wouldn't mind. I'd go, but——" She did not want to make the physical effort.

Bertie put on an old overcoat and took a lantern. He went out from the side door. He shrank from the wet and roaring night. Such weather had a nervous effect on him: too much moisture everywhere made him feel almost imbecile. Unwilling, he went through it all. A dog barked violently at him. He peered in all the buildings. At last, as he opened the upper door of a sort of intermediate barn, he heard a grinding noise, and looking in, holding up his lantern, saw Maurice, in his shirt-sleeves, standing listening, holding the handle of a turnip-pulper. He had been pulping sweet roots, a pile of which lay dimly heaped in a corner behind him.

"That you, Wernham?" said Maurice, listening.

"No, it's me," said Bertie.

A large, half-wild grey cat was rubbing at Maurice's leg. The blind man stooped to rub its sides. Bertie watched the scene, then unconsciously entered and shut the door behind him. He was in a high sort of barn-place, from which, right and left, ran off the corridors in front of the stalled cattle. He watched the slow, stooping motion of the other man, as he caressed the great cat.

Maurice straightened himself.

"You came to look for me?" he said.

"Isabel was a little uneasy," said Bertie.

"I'll come in. I like messing about doing these jobs."

The cat had reared her sinister, feline length against his leg, clawing at his thigh affectionately. He lifted her claws out of his flesh.

"I hope I'm not in your way at all at the Grange here," said Bertie, rather shy and stiff.

"My way? No, not a bit. I'm glad Isabel has somebody to talk to. I'm afraid it's I who am in the way. I know I'm not very lively company. Isabel's all right, don't you think? She's not unhappy, is she?"

"I don't think so."

"What does she say?"

"She says she's very content—only a little troubled about you."

"Why me?"

"Perhaps afraid that you might brood," said Bertie, cautiously.

"She needn't be afraid of that." He continued to caress the flattened grey head of the cat with his fingers. "What I am a bit afraid of," he resumed, "is that she'll find me a dead weight, always alone with me down here."

"I don't think you need think that," said Bertie, though this was what he feared himself.

"I don't know," said Maurice. "Sometimes I feel it isn't fair that she's saddled with me." Then he dropped his voice curiously. "I say," he asked, secretly struggling, "is my face much disfigured? Do you mind telling me?"

"There is the scar," said Bertie, wondering. "Yes, it is a disfigurement. But more pitiable than shocking."

"A pretty bad scar, though," said Maurice.

"Oh, yes."

There was a pause.

"Sometimes I feel I am horrible," said Maurice, in a low voice, talking as if to himself. And Bertie actually felt a quiver of horror.

"That's nonsense," he said.

Maurice again straightened himself, leaving the cat.

"There's no telling," he said. Then again, in an odd tone, he added: "I don't really know you, do I?"

"Probably not," said Bertie.

"Do you mind if I touch you?"

The lawyer shrank away instinctively. And yet, out of very philanthropy, he said, in a small voice: "Not at all."

But he suffered as the blind man stretched out a strong, naked hand to him. Maurice accidentally knocked off Bertie's hat.

"I thought you were taller," he said, starting. Then he laid his hand on Bertie Reid's head, closing the dome of the skull in a soft, firm grasp, gathering it, as it were; then, shifting his grasp and softly closing again, with a fine, close pressure, till he had covered the skull and the face of the smaller man, tracing the brows, and touching the full, closed eyes, touching the small nose and the nostrils, the rough, short moustache, the mouth, the rather strong chin. The hand of the blind man grasped the shoulder, the arm, the hand of the other man. He seemed to take him, in the soft, travelling grasp.

"You seem young," he said quietly, at last.

The lawyer stood almost annihilated, unable to answer.

"Your head seems tender, as if you were young," Maurice repeated. "So do your hands. Touch my eyes, will you?—touch my scar."

Now Bertie quivered with revulsion. Yet he was under the power of the blind man, as if hypnotized. He lifted his hand, and laid the fingers on the scar, on the scarred eyes. Maurice suddenly covered them with his own hand, pressed the fingers of the other man upon his disfigured eye-sockets, trembling in every fibre, and rocking slightly, slowly, from side to side. He remained thus for a minute or more, whilst Bertie stood as if in a swoon, unconscious, imprisoned.

Then suddenly Maurice removed the hand of the other man from his brow, and stood holding it in his own.

"Oh, my God," he said, "we shall know each other now, shan't we? We shall know each other now."

Bertie could not answer. He gazed mute and terror-struck, overcome by his own weakness. He knew he could not answer. He had an unreasonable fear, lest the other man should suddenly destroy him. Whereas Maurice was actually filled with hot, poignant love, the passion of friendship. Perhaps it was this very passion of friendship which Bertie shrank from most.

"We're all right together now, aren't we?" said Maurice. "It's all right now, as long as we live, so far as we're concerned?"

"Yes," said Bertie, trying by any means to escape.

Maurice stood with head lifted, as if listening. The new delicate fulfilment of mortal friendship had come as a revelation and surprise to him, something exquisite and unhoped-for. He seemed to be listening to hear if it were real.

Then he turned for his coat.

"Come," he said, "we'll go to Isabel."

Bertie took the lantern and opened the door. The cat disappeared. The two men went in silence along the causeways. Isabel, as they came, thought their footsteps sounded strange. She looked up pathetically and anxiously for their entrance. There seemed a curious elation about Maurice. Bertie was haggard, with sunken eyes.

"What is it?" she asked.

"We've become friends," said Maurice, standing with his feet apart, like a strange colossus.

"Friends!" re-echoed Isabel. And she looked again at Bertie. He met her eyes with a furtive, haggard look; his eyes were as if glazed with misery.

"I'm so glad," she said, in sheer perplexity.

"Yes," said Maurice.

He was indeed so glad. Isabel took his hand with both hers, and held it fast.

"You'll be happier now, dear," she said.

But she was watching Bertie. She knew that he had one desire—to escape from this intimacy, this friendship, which had been thrust upon him. He could not bear it that he had been touched by the blind man, his insane reserve broken in. He was like a mollusc whose shell is broken.


## KATHERINE MANSFIELD [1888–1923]

# The Doll's House

When dear old Mrs. Hay went back to town after staying with the Burnells she sent the children a doll's house. It was so big that the carter and Pat carried it into the courtyard, and there it stayed, propped up on two wooden boxes beside the feed-room door. No harm could come of it; it was summer. And perhaps the smell of paint would have gone off by the time it had to be taken in. For, really, the smell of paint coming from that doll's house ("Sweet of old Mrs. Hay, of course; most sweet and generous!")—but the smell of paint was quite enough to make any one seriously ill, in Aunt Beryl's opinion. Even before the sacking was taken off. And when it was. . . .

There stood the doll's house, a dark, oily, spinach green, picked out with bright yellow. Its two solid little chimneys, glued on to the roof, were painted red and white, and the door, gleaming with yellow varnish, was like a little slab of toffee. Four windows, real windows, were divided into panes by a broad streak of green. There was actually a tiny porch, too, painted yellow, with big lumps of congealed paint hanging along the edge.

But perfect, perfect little house! Who could possibly mind the smell? It was part of the joy, part of the newness.

"Open it quickly, some one!"

The hook at the side was stuck fast. Pat pried it open with his penknife, and the whole house-front swung back, and—there you were, gazing at one and the same moment into the drawing-room and dining-room, the kitchen and two bedrooms. That is the way for a house to open! Why don't all houses open like that? How much more exciting than peering through the slit of a door into a mean little hall with a hatstand and two umbrellas! That is—isn't it?—what you long to know about a house when you put your hand on the knocker. Perhaps it is the way God opens houses at dead of night when He is taking a quiet turn with an angel. . . .

"O-oh!" The Burnell children sounded as though they were in despair. It was too marvellous; it was too much for them. They had never seen anything like it in their lives. All the rooms were papered. There were pictures on the walls, painted on the paper, with gold frames complete. Red carpet covered all the floors except the kitchen; red plush chairs in the drawing-room, green in the dining-room; tables, beds with real bedclothes, a cradle, a stove, a dresser with tiny plates and one big jug. But what Kezia liked more than anything, what she liked frightfully, was the lamp. It stood in the middle of the dining-room table, an exquisite little amber lamp with a white globe. It was even filled all ready for lighting, though, of course, you couldn't light it. But there was something inside that looked like oil, and that moved when you shook it.

The father and mother dolls, who sprawled very stiff as though they had fainted in the drawing-room, and their two little children asleep upstairs, were really too big for the doll's house. They didn't look as though they belonged. But the lamp was perfect. It seemed to smile at Kezia, to say, "I live here." The lamp was real.

The Burnell children could hardly walk to school fast enough the next morning. They burned to tell everybody, to describe, to— well—to boast about their doll's house before the school-bell rang.

"I'm to tell," said Isabel, "because I'm the eldest. And you two can join in after. But I'm to tell first."

There was nothing to answer. Isabel was bossy, but she was always right, and Lottie and Kezia knew too well the powers that went with being eldest. They brushed through the thick buttercups at the road edge and said nothing.

"And I'm to choose who's to come and see it first. Mother said I might."

For it had been arranged that while the doll's house stood in the courtyard they might ask the girls at school, two at a time, to come and look. Not to stay to tea, of course, or to come traipsing through the house. But just to stand quietly in the courtyard while Isabel pointed out the beauties, and Lottie and Kezia looked pleased. . . .

But hurry as they might, by the time they had reached the tarred palings of the boys' playground the bell had begun to jangle. They only just had time to whip off their hats and fall into line before the roll was called. Never mind. Isabel tried to make up for it by looking very important and mysterious and by whispering behind her hand to the girls near her, "Got something to tell you at playtime."

Playtime came and Isabel was surrounded. The girls of her class nearly fought to put their arms around her, to walk away with her, to beam flatteringly, to be her special friend. She held quite a court under the huge pine trees at the side of the playground. Nudging, giggling together, the little girls pressed up close. And the only two who stayed outside the ring were the two who were always outside, the little Kelveys. They knew better than to come anywhere near the Burnells.

For the fact was, the school the Burnell children went to was not at all the kind of place their parents would have chosen if there had been any choice. But there was none. It was the only school for miles. And the consequence was all the children in the neighbourhood, the Judge's little girls, the doctor's daughters, the store-keeper's children, the milkman's, were forced to mix together. Not to speak of there being an equal number of rude, rough little boys as well. But the line had to be drawn somewhere. It was drawn at the Kelveys. Many of the children, including the Burnells, were not allowed even to speak to them. They walked past the Kelveys with their heads in the air, and as they set the fashion in all matters of behaviour, the Kelveys were shunned by everybody. Even the teacher had a special voice for them, and a special smile for the other children when Lil Kelvey came up to her desk with a bunch of dreadfully common-looking flowers.

They were the daughters of a spry, hardworking little washer-woman, who went about from house to house by the day. This was awful enough. But where was Mr. Kelvey? Nobody knew for certain. But everybody said he was in prison. So they were the daughters of a washerwoman and a gaolbird.[1] Very nice company for other people's children! And they looked it. Why Mrs. Kelvey made them so conspicuous was hard to understand. The truth was they were dressed in "bits" given to her by the people for whom she worked. Lil, for instance, who was a stout, plain child, with big freckles, came to school in a dress made from a green art-serge table-cloth of the Burnells', with red plush sleeves from the Logans' curtains. Her hat, perched on top of her high forehead, was a grown-up woman's hat, once the property of Miss Lecky, the postmistress. It was turned up at the back and trimmed with a large scarlet quill. What a little guy she looked! It was impossible not to laugh. And her little sister, our Else, wore a long white dress, rather like a nightgown, and a pair of little boy's boots. But whatever our Else wore she would have looked strange. She was a tiny wishbone of a child, with cropped hair and enormous solemn eyes—a little white owl. Nobody had ever seen her smile; she scarcely ever spoke. She went through life holding on to Lil, with a piece of Lil's skirt screwed up in her hand. Where Lil went our Else followed. In the playground, on the road going to and from school, there was Lil marching in front and our Else holding on behind. Only when she wanted anything, or when she was out of breath, our Else gave Lil a tug, a twitch, and Lil stopped

---

[1] British spelling of *jailbird*.

and turned round. The Kelveys never failed to understand each other.

Now they hovered at the edge; you couldn't stop them listening. When the little girls turned round and sneered, Lil, as usual, gave her silly, shamefaced smile, but our Else only looked.

And Isabel's voice, so very proud, went on telling. The carpet made a great sensation, but so did the beds with real bedclothes, and the stove with an oven door.

When she finished Kezia broke in. "You've forgotten the lamp, Isabel."

"Oh, yes," said Isabel, "and there's a teeny little lamp, all made of yellow glass, with a white globe that stands on the dining-room table. You couldn't tell it from a real one."

"The lamp's best of all," cried Kezia. She thought Isabel wasn't making half enough of the little lamp. But nobody paid any attention. Isabel was choosing the two who were to come back with them that afternoon and see it. She chose Emmie Cole and Lena Logan. But when the others knew they were all to have a chance, they couldn't be nice enough to Isabel. One by one they put their arms round Isabel's waist and walked her off. They had something to whisper to her, a secret. "Isabel's *my* friend."

Only the little Kelveys moved away forgotten; there was nothing more for them to hear.

Days passed, and as more children saw the doll's house, the fame of it spread. It became the one subject, the rage. The one question was, "Have you seen Burnells' doll's house? Oh, ain't it lovely!" "Haven't you seen it? Oh, I say!"

Even the dinner hour was given up to talking about it. The little girls sat under the pines eating their thick mutton sandwiches and big slabs of johnny cake spread with butter. While always, as near as they could get, sat the Kelveys, our Else holding on to Lil, listening too, while they chewed their jam sandwiches out of a newspaper soaked with large red blobs. . . .

"Mother," said Kezia, "can't I ask the Kelveys just once?"

"Certainly not, Kezia."

"But why not?"

"Run away, Kezia; you know quite well why not."

At last everybody had seen it except them. On that day the subject rather flagged. It was the dinner hour. The children stood together under the pine trees, and suddenly, as they looked at the

Kelveys eating out of their paper, always by themselves, always listening, they wanted to be horrid to them. Emmie Cole started the whisper.

"Lil Kelvey's going to be a servant when she grows up."

"O-oh, how awful!" said Isabel Burnell, and she made eyes at Emmie.

Emmie swallowed in a very meaning way and nodded to Isabel as she'd seen her mother do on those occasions.

"It's true—it's true—it's true," she said.

Then Lena Logan's little eyes snapped. "Shall I ask her?" she whispered.

"Bet you don't," said Jessie May.

"Pooh, I'm not frightened," said Lena. Suddenly she gave a little squeal and danced in front of the other girls. "Watch! Watch me! Watch me now!" said Lena. And sliding, gliding, dragging one foot, giggling behind her hand, Lena went over to the Kelveys.

Lil looked up from her dinner. She wrapped the rest quickly away. Our Else stopped chewing. What was coming now?

"Is it true you're going to be a servant when you grow up, Lil Kelvey?" shrilled Lena.

Dead silence. But instead of answering, Lil only gave her silly, shamefaced smile. She didn't seem to mind the question at all. What a sell for Lena! The girls began to titter.

Lena couldn't stand that. She put her hands on her hips; she shot forward. "Yah, yer father's in prison!" she hissed, spitefully.

This was such a marvellous thing to have said that the little girls rushed away in a body, deeply, deeply excited, wild with joy. Some one found a long rope, and they began skipping. And never did they skip so high, run in and out so fast, or do such daring things as on that morning.

In the afternoon Pat called for the Burnell children with the buggy and they drove home. There were visitors. Isabel and Lottie, who liked visitors, went upstairs to change their pinafores. But Kezia thieved out at the back. Nobody was about; she began to swing on the big white gates of the courtyard. Presently, looking along the road, she saw two little dots. They grew bigger, they were coming towards her. Now she could see that one was in front and one close behind. Now she could see that they were the Kelveys. Kezia stopped swinging. She slipped off the gate as if she was going to run away. Then she hesitated. The Kelveys came nearer, and beside them walked their shadows, very long, stretching right across the road with their heads in the buttercups. Kezia clambered back on the gate; she had made up her mind; she swung out.

"Hullo," she said to the passing Kelveys.

They were so astounded that they stopped. Lil gave her silly smile. Our Else stared.

"You can come and see our doll's house if you want to," said Kezia, and she dragged one toe on the ground. But at that Lil turned red and shook her head quickly.

"Why not?" asked Kezia.

Lil gasped, then she said, "Your ma told our ma you wasn't to speak to us."

"Oh, well," said Kezia. She didn't know what to reply. "It doesn't matter. You can come and see our doll's house all the same. Come on. Nobody's looking."

But Lil shook her head still harder.

"Don't you want to?" asked Kezia.

Suddenly there was a twitch, a tug at Lil's skirt. She turned round. Our Else was looking at her with big, imploring eyes; she was frowning; she wanted to go. For a moment Lil looked at our Else very doubtfully. But then our Else twitched her skirt again. She started forward. Kezia led the way. Like two little stray cats they followed across the courtyard to where the doll's house stood.

"There it is," said Kezia.

There was a pause. Lil breathed loudly, almost snorted; our Else was still as a stone.

"I'll open it for you," said Kezia kindly. She undid the hook and they looked inside.

"There's the drawing-room and the dining-room, and that's the—"

"Kezia!"

Oh, what a start they gave!

"Kezia!"

It was Aunt Beryl's voice. They turned round. At the back door stood Aunt Beryl, staring as if she couldn't believe what she saw.

"How dare you ask the little Kelveys into the courtyard?" said her cold, furious voice. "You know as well as I do, you're not allowed to talk to them. Run away, children, run away at once. And don't come back again," said Aunt Beryl. And she stepped into the yard and shooed them out as if they were chickens.

"Off you go immediately!" she called, cold and proud.

They did not need telling twice. Burning with shame, shrinking together, Lil huddling along like her mother, our Else dazed, somehow they crossed the big courtyard and squeezed through the white gate.

"Wicked, disobedient little girl!" said Aunt Beryl bitterly to Kezia, and she slammed the doll's house to.

The afternoon had been awful. A letter had come from Willie Brent, a terrifying, threatening letter, saying if she did not meet him that evening in Pulman's Bush, he'd come to the front door and ask the reason why! But now that she had frightened those little rats of Kelveys and given Kezia a good scolding, her heart felt lighter. That ghastly pressure was gone. She went back to the house humming.

When the Kelveys were well out of sight of Burnells', they sat down to rest on a big red drain-pipe by the side of the road. Lil's cheeks were still burning; she took off the hat with the quill and held it on her knee. Dreamily they looked over the hay paddocks, past the creek, to the group of wattles where Logan's cows stood waiting to be milked. What were their thoughts?

Presently our Else nudged up close to her sister. But now she had forgotten the cross lady. She put out a finger and stroked her sister's quill; she smiled her rare smile.

"I seen the little lamp," she said, softly.

Then both were silent once more.


# KATHERINE ANNE PORTER [1890–1980]

# Rope

On the third day after they moved to the country he came walking back from the village carrying a basket of groceries and a twenty-four-yard coil of rope. She came out to meet him, wiping her hands on her green smock. Her hair was tumbled, her nose was scarlet with sunburn; he told her that already she looked like a born country woman. His gray flannel shirt stuck to him, his heavy shoes were dusty. She assured him he looked like a rural character in a play.

Had he brought the coffee? She had been waiting all day long for coffee. They had forgot it when they ordered at the store the first day.

Gosh, no, he hadn't. Lord, now he'd have to go back. Yes, he would if it killed him. He thought, though, he had everything else. She reminded him it was only because he didn't drink coffee himself. If he did he would remember it quick enough. Suppose they ran out of cigarettes? Then she saw the rope. What was that for? Well, he thought it might do to hang clothes on, or something. Naturally she asked him if he thought they were going to run a laundry? They already had a fifty-foot line hanging right before his eyes? Why, hadn't he noticed it, really? It was a blot on the landscape to her.

He thought there were a lot of things a rope might come in handy for. She wanted to know what, for instance. He thought a few seconds, but nothing occurred. They could wait and see, couldn't they? You need all sorts of strange odds and ends around a place in the country. She said, yes, that was so; but she thought just at that time when every penny counted, it seemed funny to buy more rope. That was all. She hadn't meant anything else. She hadn't just seen, not at first, why he felt it was necessary.

Well, thunder, he had bought it because he wanted to, and that was all there was to it. She thought that was reason enough, and couldn't understand why he hadn't said so, at first. Undoubtedly it would be useful, twenty-four yards of rope, there were hundreds of things, she couldn't think of any at the moment, but it would come in. Of course. As he had said, things always did in the country.

But she was a little disappointed about the coffee, and oh, look, look, look at the eggs! Oh, my, they're all running! What had he put on top of them? Hadn't he known eggs mustn't be squeezed? Squeezed, who had squeezed them, he wanted to know. What a silly thing to say. He had simply brought them along in the basket with the other things. If they got broke it was the grocer's fault. He should know better than to put heavy things on top of eggs.

She believed it was the rope. That was the heaviest thing in the pack, she saw him plainly when he came in from the road, the rope was a big package on top of everything. He desired the whole wide world to witness that this was not a fact. He had carried the rope in one hand and the basket in the other, and what was the use of her having eyes if that was the best they could do for her?

Well, anyhow, she could see one thing plain: no eggs for breakfast. They'd have to scramble them now, for supper. It was too damned bad. She had planned to have steak for supper. No ice, meat wouldn't keep. He wanted to know why she couldn't finish breaking the eggs in a bowl and set them in a cool place.

Cool place! If he could find one for her, she'd be glad to set them there. Well, then, it seemed to him they might very well cook the meat at the same time they cooked the eggs and then warm up the meat for tomorrow. The idea simply choked her. Warmed-over meat, when they might as well have had it fresh. Second best and scraps and makeshifts, even to the meat! He rubbed her shoulder a little. It doesn't really matter so much, does it, darling? Sometimes when they were playful, he would rub her shoulder and she would arch and purr. This time she hissed and almost clawed. He was getting ready to say that they could surely manage somehow when she turned on him and said, if he told her they could manage somehow she would certainly slap his face.

He swallowed the words red hot, his faced burned. He picked up the rope and started to put it on the top shelf. She would not have it on the top shelf, the jars and tins belonged there; positively she would not have the top shelf cluttered up with a lot of rope. She had borne all the clutter she meant to bear in the flat in town, there was space here at least and she meant to keep things in order.

Well, in that case, he wanted to know what the hammer and nails were doing up there? And why had she put them there when she knew very well he needed that hammer and those nails upstairs to fix the window sashes? She simply slowed down everything and made double work on the place with her insane habit of changing things around and hiding them.

She was sure she begged his pardon, and if she had had any reason to believe he was going to fix the sashes this summer she would have left the hammer and nails right where he put them; in the middle of the bedroom floor where they could step on them in the dark. And now if he didn't clear the whole mess out of there she would throw them down the well.

Oh, all right, all right—could he put them in the closet? Naturally not, there were brooms and mops and dustpans in the closet, and why couldn't he find a place for his rope outside her kitchen? Had he stopped to consider there were seven God-forsaken rooms in the house, and only one kitchen?

He wanted to know what of it? And did she realize she was making a complete fool of herself? And what did she take him for, a three-year-old idiot? The whole trouble with her was she needed something weaker than she was to heckle and tyrannize over. He wished to God now they had a couple of children she could take it out on. Maybe he'd get some rest.

Her face changed at this, she reminded him he had forgot the coffee and had bought a worthless piece of rope. And when she thought of all the things they actually needed to make the place even decently fit to live in, well, she could cry, that was all. She looked so forlorn, so lost and despairing he couldn't believe it was only a piece of rope that was causing all the racket. What *was* the matter, for God's sake?

Oh, would he please hush and go away, and *stay* away, if he could, for five minutes? By all means, yes, he would. He'd stay away indefinitely if she wished. Lord, yes, there was nothing he'd like better than to clear out and never come back. She couldn't for the life of her see what was holding him, then. It was a swell time. Here she was, stuck, miles from a railroad, with a half-empty house on her hands, and not a penny in her pocket, and everything on earth to do; it seemed the God-sent moment for him to get out from under. She was surprised he hadn't stayed in town as it was until she had come out and done the work and got things straightened out. It was his usual trick.

It appeared to him that this was going a little far. Just a touch out of bounds, if she didn't mind his saying so. Why the hell had he stayed in town the summer before? To do a half-dozen extra jobs to get the money he had sent her. That was it. She knew perfectly well they couldn't have done it otherwise. She had agreed with him at the time. And that was the only time so help him he had ever left her to do anything by herself.

Oh, he could tell that to his great-grandmother. She had her notion of what had kept him in town. Considerably more than a notion, if he wanted to know. So, she was going to bring all that up again, was she? Well, she could just think what she pleased. He was tired of explaining. It may have looked funny but he had simply got hooked in, and what could he do? It was impossible to believe that she was going to take it seriously. Yes, yes, she knew how it was with a man: if he was left by himself a minute, some woman was certain to kidnap him. And naturally he couldn't hurt her feelings by refusing!

Well, what was she raving about? Did she forget she had told him those two weeks alone in the country were the happiest she had known for four years? And how long had they been married when she said that? All right, shut up! If she thought that hadn't stuck in his craw.

She hadn't meant she was happy because she was away from him. She meant she was happy getting the devilish house nice and ready for him. That was what she had meant, and now look! Bringing up something she had said a year ago simply to justify himself for forgetting her coffee and breaking the eggs and buying a wretched piece of rope they couldn't afford. She really thought it was time to drop the subject, and now she wanted only two things in the world. She wanted him to get that rope from underfoot, and go back to the village and get her coffee, and if he could remember it, he might bring a metal mitt for the skillets, and two more curtain rods, and if there were any rubber gloves in the village, her hands were simply raw, and a bottle of milk of magnesia from the drugstore.

He looked out at the dark blue afternoon sweltering on the slopes, and mopped his forehead and sighed heavily and said, if only she could wait a minute for *anything,* he was going back. He had said so, hadn't he, the very instant they found he had overlooked it?

Oh, yes, well . . . run along. She was going to wash windows. The country was so beautiful! She doubted they'd have a moment to enjoy it. He meant to go, but he could not until he had said that if she wasn't such a hopeless melancholiac she might see that this was only for a few days. Couldn't she remember anything pleasant about the other summers? Hadn't they ever had any fun? She hadn't time to talk about it, and now would he please not leave that rope lying around for her to trip on? He picked it up, somehow it had toppled off the table, and walked out with it under his arm.

Was he going this minute? He certainly was. She thought so. Sometimes it seemed to her he had second sight about the precisely perfect moment to leave her ditched. She had meant to put the mattresses out to sun, if they put them out this minute they would get at least three hours, he must have heard her say that morning she meant to put them out. So of course he would walk off and leave her to it. She supposed he thought the exercise would do her good.

Well, he was merely going to get her coffee. A four-mile walk for two pounds of coffee was ridiculous, but he was perfectly willing to do it. The habit was making a wreck of her, but if she wanted to wreck herself there was nothing he could do about it. If he thought it was coffee that was making a wreck of her, she congratulated him: he must have a damned easy conscience.

Conscience or no conscience, he didn't see why the mattresses couldn't very well wait until tomorrow. And anyhow, for God's sake, were they living *in* the house, or were they going to let the house ride them to death? She paled at this, her face grew livid about the mouth, she looked quite dangerous, and reminded him that housekeeping was no more her work than it was his: she had other work to do as well, and when did he think she was going to find time to do it at this rate?

Was she going to start on that again? She knew as well as he did that his work brought in the regular money, hers was only occasional, if they depended on what *she* made—and she might as well get straight on this question once for all!

That was positively not the point. The question was, when both of them were working on their own time, was there going to be a division of the housework, or wasn't there? She merely wanted to know, she had to make her plans. Why, he thought that was all arranged. It was understood that he was to help. Hadn't he always, in summers?

Hadn't he, though? Oh, just hadn't he? And when, and where, and doing what? Lord, what an uproarious joke!

It was such a very uproarious joke that her face turned slightly purple, and she screamed with laughter. She laughed so hard she had to sit down, and finally a rush of tears spurted from her eyes and poured down into the lifted corners of her mouth. He dashed towards her and dragged her up to her feet and tried to pour water on her head. The dipper hung by a string on a nail and he broke it loose. Then he tried to pump water with one hand while she struggled in the other. So he gave it up and shook her instead.

She wrenched away, crying out for him to take his rope and go to hell, she had simply given him up: and ran. He heard her high-heeled bedroom slippers clattering and stumbling on the stairs.

He went out around the house and into the lane; he suddenly realized he had a blister on his heel and his shirt felt as if it were on fire. Things broke so suddenly you didn't know where you were. She could work herself into a fury about simply nothing. She was terrible, damn it: not an ounce of reason. You might as well talk to a sieve as that woman when she got going. Damned if he'd spend his life humoring her! Well, what to do now? He would take back the rope and exchange it for something else. Things accumulated, things were mountainous, you couldn't move them or sort them out or get rid of them. They just lay and rotted around. He'd take it back. Hell, why should he? He wanted it. What was it anyhow? A piece of rope. Imagine anybody caring more about a piece of rope than about a man's feelings. What earthly right had she to say a word about it? He remembered all the useless, meaningless things she bought for herself: Why? because I wanted it, that's why! He stopped and selected a large stone by the road. He would put the rope behind it. He would put it in the tool-box when he got back. He'd heard enough about it to last him a life-time.

When he came back she was leaning against the post box beside the road waiting. It was pretty late, the smell of broiled steak floated nose high in the cooling air. Her face was young and smooth and fresh-looking. Her unmanageable funny black hair was all on end. She waved to him from a distance, and he speeded up. She called out that supper was ready and waiting, was he starved?

You bet he was starved. Here was the coffee. He waved it at her. She looked at his other hand. What was that he had there?

Well, it was the rope again. He stopped short. He had meant to exchange it but forgot. She wanted to know why he should exchange it, if it was something he really wanted. Wasn't the air sweet now, and wasn't it fine to be here?

She walked beside him with one hand hooked into his leather belt. She pulled and jostled him a little as he walked, and leaned against him. He put his arm clear around her and patted her stomach. They exchanged wary smiles. Coffee, coffee for the Ootsum-Wootsums! He felt as if he were bringing her a beautiful present.

He was a love, she firmly believed, and if she had had her coffee in the morning, she wouldn't have behaved so funny . . . There was a whippoorwill still coming back, imagine, clear out of season, sitting in the crab-apple tree calling all by himself. Maybe his girl stood him up. Maybe she did. She hoped to hear him once more, she loved whippoorwills . . . He knew how she was, didn't he?

Sure, he knew how she was.

## WILLIAM FAULKNER [1897–1962]

# A Rose for Emily

### 1

When Miss Emily Grierson died, our whole town went to her funeral: the men through a sort of respectful affection for a fallen monument, the women mostly out of curiosity to see the inside of her house, which no one save an old man-servant—a combined gardener and cook—had seen in at least ten years.

It was a big, squarish frame house that had once been white, decorated with cupolas and spires and scrolled balconies in the heavily lightsome style of the seventies, set on what had once been our most select street. But garages and cotton gins had encroached and obliterated even the august names of that neighborhood; only Miss Emily's house was left, lifting its stubborn and coquettish decay above the cotton wagons and the gasoline pumps — an eyesore among eyesores. And now Miss Emily had gone to join the representatives of those august names where they lay in the cedar-bemused cemetery among the ranked and anonymous graves of Union and Confederate soldiers who fell at the battle of Jefferson.

Alive, Miss Emily had been a tradition, a duty, and a care; a sort of hereditary obligation upon the town, dating from that day in 1894 when Colonel Sartoris, the mayor—he who fathered the edict that no Negro woman should appear on the streets without an apron—remitted her taxes, the dispensation dating from the death of her father on into perpetuity. Not that Miss Emily would have accepted charity. Colonel Sartoris invented an involved tale to the effect that Miss Emily's father had loaned money to the town, which the town, as a matter of business, preferred this way of repaying. Only a man of Colonel Sartoris' generation and thought could have invented it, and only a woman could have believed it.

When the next generation, with its more modern ideas, became mayors and aldermen, this arrangement created some little dissatisfaction. On the first of the year they mailed her a tax notice. February came, and there was no reply. They wrote her a formal letter, asking her to call at the sheriff's office at her convenience. A week later the mayor wrote her himself, offering to call or to send his car for her, and received in reply a note on paper of an archaic shape, in a thin, flowing calligraphy in faded ink, to the effect that she no longer went out at all. The tax notice was also enclosed, without comment.

They called a special meeting of the Board of Aldermen. A deputation waited upon her, knocked at the door through which no visitor had passed since she ceased giving china-painting lessons eight or ten years earlier. They were admitted by the old Negro into a dim hall from which a stairway mounted into still more shadow. It smelled of dust and disuse—a close, dank smell. The Negro led them into the parlor. It was furnished in heavy, leather-covered furniture. When the Negro opened the blinds of one window, they could see that the leather was cracked; and when they sat down, a faint dust rose sluggishly about their thighs, spinning with slow motes in the single sun-ray. On a tarnished gilt easel before the fireplace stood a crayon portrait of Miss Emily's father.

They rose when she entered—a small, fat woman in black, with a thin gold chain descending to her waist and vanishing into her belt, leaning on an ebony cane with a tarnished gold head. Her skeleton was small and spare; perhaps that was why what would have been merely plumpness in another was obesity in her. She looked bloated, like a body long submerged in motionless water, and of that pallid hue. Her eyes, lost in the fatty ridges of her face, looked like two small pieces of coal pressed into a lump of dough as they moved from one face to another while the visitors stated their errand.

She did not ask them to sit. She just stood in the door and listened quietly until the spokesman came to a stumbling halt. Then they could hear the invisible watch ticking at the end of the gold chain.

Her voice was dry and cold. "I have no taxes in Jefferson. Colonel Sartoris explained it to me. Perhaps one of you can gain access to the city records and satisfy yourselves."

"But we have. We are the city authorities, Miss Emily. Didn't you get a notice from the sheriff, signed by him?"

"I received a paper, yes," Miss Emily said. "Perhaps he considers himself the sheriff. . . . I have no taxes in Jefferson."

"But there is nothing on the books to show that, you see. We must go by the — "

"See Colonel Sartoris. I have no taxes in Jefferson."

"But, Miss Emily—"

"See Colonel Sartoris." (Colonel Sartoris had been dead almost ten years.) "I have no taxes in Jefferson. Tobe!" The Negro appeared. "Show these gentlemen out."

## 2

So she vanquished them, horse and foot, just as she had vanquished their fathers thirty years before about the smell. That was two years after her father's death and a short time after her sweetheart—the one we believed would marry her—had deserted her. After her father's death she went out very little; after her sweetheart went away, people hardly saw her at all. A few of the ladies had the temerity to call, but were not received, and the only sign of life about the place was the Negro man—a young man then— going in and out with a market basket.

"Just as if a man—any man—could keep a kitchen properly," the ladies said; so they were not surprised when the smell developed. It was another link between the gross, teeming world and the high and mighty Griersons.

A neighbor, a woman, complained to the mayor, Judge Stevens, eighty years old.

"But what will you have me do about it, madam?" he said.

"Why, send her word to stop it," the woman said. "Isn't there a law?"

"I'm sure that won't be necessary," Judge Stevens said. "It's probably just a snake or a rat that nigger of hers killed in the yard. I'll speak to him about it."

The next day he received two more complaints, one from a man who came in diffident deprecation. "We really must do something about it, Judge. I'd be the last one in the world to bother Miss Emily, but we've got to do something." That night the Board of Aldermen met—three graybeards and one younger man, a member of the rising generation.

"It's simple enough," he said. "Send her word to have her place cleaned up. Give her a certain time to do it in, and if she don't. . . ."

"Dammit, sir," Judge Stevens said, "will you accuse a lady to her face of smelling bad?"

So the next night, after midnight, four men crossed Miss Emily's lawn and slunk about the house like burglars, sniffing along the base of the brickwork and at the cellar openings while one of them performed a regular sowing motion with his hand out of a sack slung from his shoulder. They broke open the cellar door and sprinkled lime there, and in all the outbuildings. As they recrossed the lawn, a window that had been dark was lighted and Miss Emily sat in it, the light behind her, and her upright torso motionless as that of an idol. They crept quietly across the lawn and into the shadow of the locusts that lined the street. After a week or two the smell went away.

That was when people had begun to feel really sorry for her. People in our town, remembering how old lady Wyatt, her great-aunt, had gone completely crazy at last, believed that the Griersons held themselves a little too high for what they really were. None of the young men were quite good enough for Miss Emily and such. We had long thought of them as a tableau, Miss Emily a slender figure in white in the background, her father a spraddled silhouette in the foreground, his back to her and clutching a horse-whip, the two of them framed by the back-flung front door. So when she got to be thirty and was still single, we were not pleased exactly, but vindicated; even with insanity in the family she wouldn't have turned down all of her chances if they had really materialized.

When her father died, it got about that the house was all that was left to her; and in a way, people were glad. At last they could pity Miss Emily. Being left alone, and a pauper, she had become humanized. Now she too would know the old thrill and the old despair of a penny more or less.

The day after his death all the ladies prepared to call at the house and offer condolence and aid, as is our custom. Miss Emily met them at the door, dressed as usual and with no trace of grief on her face. She told them that her father was not dead. She did that for three days, with the ministers calling on her, and the doctors, trying to persuade her to let them dispose of the body. Just as they were about to resort to law and force, she broke down, and they buried her father quickly.

We did not say she was crazy then. We believed she had to do that. We remembered all the young men her father had driven away, and we knew that with nothing left, she would have to cling to that which had robbed her, as people will.

3

She was sick for a long time. When we saw her again, her hair was cut short, making her look like a girl, with a vague resemblance to those angels in colored church windows—sort of tragic and serene.

The town had just let the contracts for paving the sidewalks, and in the summer after her father's death they began the work. The construction company came with niggers and mules and machinery, and a foreman named Homer Barron, a Yankee—a big, dark, ready man, with a big voice and eyes lighter than his face. The little boys would follow in groups to hear him cuss the niggers, and the niggers singing in time to the rise and fall of picks. Pretty soon he knew everybody in town. Whenever you heard a lot of laughing anywhere about the square, Homer Barron would be in the center of the group. Presently, we began to see him and Miss Emily on Sunday afternoons driving in the yellow-wheeled buggy and the matched team of bays from the livery stable.

At first we were glad that Miss Emily would have an interest, because the ladies all said, "Of course a Grierson would not think seriously of a Northerner, a day laborer." But there were still others, older people, who said that even grief could not cause a real lady to forget *noblesse oblige*—without calling it *noblesse oblige*. They just said, "Poor Emily. Her kinsfolk should come to her." She had some kin in Alabama; but years ago her father had fallen out with them over the estate of old lady Wyatt, the crazy woman, and there was no communication between the two families. They had not even been represented at the funeral.

And as soon as the old people said, "Poor Emily," the whispering began. "Do you suppose it's really so?" they said to one another. "Of course it is. What else could. . . ." This behind their hands; rustling of craned silk and satin behind jalousies closed upon the sun of Sunday afternoon as the thin, swift clop-clop-clop of the matched team passed: "Poor Emily."

She carried her head high enough—even when we believed that she was fallen. It was as if she demanded more than ever the recognition of her dignity as the last Grierson; as if it had wanted that touch of earthiness to reaffirm her imperviousness. Like when she bought the rat poison, the arsenic. That was over a year after they had begun to say "Poor Emily," and while the two female cousins were visiting her.

"I want some poison," she said to the druggist. She was over thirty then, still a slight woman, though thinner than usual, with cold, haughty black eyes in a face the flesh of which was strained across the temples and about the eye-sockets as you imagine a lighthouse-keeper's face ought to look. "I want some poison," she said.

"Yes, Miss Emily. What kind? For rats and such? I'd recom—"

"I want the best you have. I don't care what kind."

The druggist named several. "They'll kill anything up to an elephant. But what you want is—"

"Arsenic," Miss Emily said. "Is that a good one?"

"Is . . . arsenic? Yes, ma'am. But what you want—"

"I want arsenic."

The druggist looked down at her. She looked back at him, erect, her face like a strained flag. "Why, of course," the druggist said. "If that's what you want. But the law requires you to tell what you are going to use it for."

Miss Emily just stared at him, her head tilted back in order to look him eye for eye, until he looked away and went and got the arsenic and wrapped it up. The Negro delivery boy brought her the package; the druggist didn't come back. When she opened the package at home there was written on the box, under the skull and bones: "For rats."

4

So the next day we all said, "She will kill herself"; and we said it would be the best thing. When she had first begun to be seen with Homer Barron, we had said, "She will marry him." Then we said, "She will persuade him yet," because Homer himself had remarked—he liked men, and it was known that he drank with the younger men in the Elks' Club—that he was not a marrying man. Later we said, "Poor Emily" behind the jalousies as they passed on Sunday afternoon in the glittering buggy, Miss Emily with her head high and Homer Barron with his hat cocked and a cigar in his teeth, reins and whip in a yellow glove.

*[margin handwritten: drunk w/ the guys]*

Then some of the ladies began to say that it was a disgrace to the town and a bad example to the young people. The men did not want to interfere, but at last the ladies forced the Baptist minister—Miss Emily's people were Episcopal—to call upon her. He would never divulge what happened during that interview, but he refused to go back again. The next Sunday they again drove about the streets, and the following day the minister's wife wrote to Miss Emily's relations in Alabama.

So she had blood-kin under her roof again and we sat back to watch developments. At first nothing happened. Then we were sure that they were to be married. We learned that Miss Emily had been to the jeweler's and ordered a man's toilet set in silver, with the letters H.B. on each piece. Two days later we learned that she had bought a complete outfit of men's clothing, including a nightshirt, and we said, "They are married." We were really glad. We were glad because the two female cousins were even more Grierson than Miss Emily had ever been.

So we were not surprised when Homer Barron—the streets had been finished some time since—was gone. We were a little disappointed that there was not a public blowing-off, but we believed that he had gone on to prepare for Miss Emily's coming, or to give her a chance to get rid of the cousins. (By that time it was a cabal, and we were all Miss Emily's allies to help circumvent

*[margin handwritten: plot]*

the cousins.) Sure enough, after another week they departed. And, as we had expected all along, within three days Homer Barron was back in town. A neighbor saw the Negro man admit him at the kitchen door at dusk one evening.

And that was the last we saw of Homer Barron. And of Miss Emily for some time. The Negro man went in and out with the market basket, but the front door remained closed. Now and then we would see her at the window for a moment, as the men did that night when they sprinkled the lime, but for almost six months she did not appear on the streets. Then we knew that this was to be expected too; as if that quality of her father which had thwarted her woman's life so many times had been too virulent and too furious to die.

When we next saw Miss Emily, she had grown fat and her hair was turning gray. During the next few years it grew grayer and grayer until it attained an even pepper-and-salt iron-gray, when it ceased turning. Up to the day of her death at seventy-four it was still that vigorous iron-gray, like the hair of an active man.

From that time on her front door remained closed, save during a period of six or seven years, when she was about forty, during which she gave lessons in china-painting. She fitted up a studio in one of the downstairs rooms, where the daughters and grand-daughters of Colonel Sartoris' contemporaries were sent to her with the same regularity and in the same spirit that they were sent to church on Sundays with a twenty-five-cent piece for the collection plate. Meanwhile her taxes had been remitted.

Then the newer generation became the backbone and the spirit of the town, and the painting pupils grew up and fell away and did not send their children to her with boxes of color and tedious brushes and pictures cut from the ladies' magazines. The front door closed upon the last one and remained closed for good. When the town got free postal delivery, Miss Emily alone refused to let them fasten the metal numbers above her door and attach a mail-box to it. She would not listen to them.

Daily, monthly, yearly we watched the Negro grow grayer and more stooped, going in and out with the market basket. Each December we sent her a tax notice, which would be returned by the post office a week later, unclaimed. Now and then we would see her in one of the downstairs windows—she had evidently shut up the top floor of the house—like the carven torso of an idol in a niche, looking or not looking at us, we could never tell which. Thus she passed from generation to generation—dear, inescapable, impervious, tranquil, and perverse.

And so she died. Fell ill in the house filled with dust and shadows, with only a doddering Negro man to wait on her. We did not even know she was sick; we had long since given up trying to get any information from the Negro. He talked to no one, probably not even to her, for his voice had grown harsh and rusty, as if from disuse.

She died in one of the downstairs rooms, in a heavy walnut bed with a curtain, her gray head propped on a pillow yellow and moldy with age and lack of sunlight.

## 5

The Negro met the first of the ladies at the front door and let them in, with their hushed, sibilant voices and their quick, curious glances, and then he disappeared. He walked right through the house and out the back and was not seen again.

The two female cousins came at once. They held the funeral on the second day, with the town coming to look at Miss Emily beneath a mass of bought flowers, with the crayon face of her father musing profoundly above the bier and the ladies sibilant and macabre; and the very old men—some in their brushed Confederate uniforms—on the porch and the lawn, talking of Miss Emily as if she had been a contemporary of theirs, believing that they had danced with her and courted her perhaps, confusing time with its mathematical progression, as the old do, to whom all the past is not a diminishing road but, instead, a huge meadow which no winter ever quite touches, divided from them now by the narrow bottle-neck of the most recent decade of years.

Already we knew that there was one room in that region above stairs which no one had seen in forty years, and which would have to be forced. They waited until Miss Emily was decently in the ground before they opened it.

The violence of breaking down the door seemed to fill this room with pervading dust. A thin, acrid pall as of the tomb seemed to lie everywhere upon this room decked and furnished as for a bridal: upon the valance curtains of faded rose color, upon the rose-shaded lights, upon the dressing table, upon the delicate array of crystal and the man's toilet things backed with tarnished silver, silver so tarnished that the monogram was obscured. Among them lay a collar and tie, as if they had just been removed, which, lifted, left upon the surface a pale crescent in the dust. Upon a chair hung the suit, carefully folded; beneath it the two mute shoes and the discarded socks.

The man himself lay in the bed.

For a long while we just stood there, looking down at the profound and fleshless grin. The body had apparently once lain in the attitude of an embrace, but now the long sleep that outlasts love, that conquers even the grimace of love, had cuckolded him. What was left of him, rotted beneath what was left of the night-shirt, had become inextricable from the bed in which he lay; and upon him and upon the pillow beside him lay that even coating of the patient and biding dust.

Then we noticed that in the second pillow was the indentation of a head. One of us lifted something from it, and leaning forward, that faint and invisible dust dry and acrid in the nostrils, we saw a long strand of iron-gray hair.

## ERNEST HEMINGWAY [1899–1961]

# A Clean, Well-Lighted Place

It was late and every one had left the café except an old man who sat in the shadow the leaves of the tree made against the electric light. In the daytime the street was dusty, but at night the dew settled the dust and the old man liked to sit late because he was deaf and now at night it was quiet and he felt the difference. The two waiters inside the café knew that the old man was a little drunk, and while he was a good client they knew that if he became too drunk he would leave without paying, so they kept watch on him.

"Last week he tried to commit suicide," one waiter said.

"Why?"

"He was in despair."

"What about?"

"Nothing."

"How do you know it was nothing?"

"He has plenty of money."

They sat together at a table that was close against the wall near the door of the café and looked at the terrace where the tables were all empty except where the old man sat in the shadow of the leaves of the tree that moved slightly in the wind. A girl and a soldier went by in the street. The street light shone on the brass number of his collar. The girl wore no head covering and hurried beside him.

"The guard will pick him up," one waiter said.

"What does it matter if he gets what he's after?"

"He had better get off the street now. The guard will get him. They went by five minutes ago."

The old man sitting in the shadow rapped on his saucer with his glass. The younger waiter went over to him.

"What do you want?"

The old man looked at him. "Another brandy," he said.

"You'll be drunk," the waiter said. The old man looked at him. The waiter went away.

"He'll stay all night," he said to his colleague. "I'm sleepy now. I never get into bed before three o'clock. He should have killed himself last week."

The waiter took the brandy bottle and another saucer from the counter inside the café and marched out to the old man's table. He put down the saucer and poured the glass full of brandy.

"You should have killed yourself last week," he said to the deaf man. The old man motioned with his finger. "A little more," he said. The waiter poured on into the glass so that the brandy slopped over and ran down the stem into the top saucer of the pile. "Thank you," the old man said. The waiter took the bottle back inside the café. He sat down at the table with his colleague again.

"He's drunk now," he said.

"He's drunk every night."

"What did he want to kill himself for?"

"How should I know?"

"How did he do it?"

"He hung himself with a rope."

"Who cut him down?"

"His niece."

"Why did they do it?"

"Fear for his soul."

"How much money has he got?"

"He's got plenty."

"He must be eighty years old."

"Anyway I should say he was eighty."

"I wish he would go home. I never get to bed before three o'clock. What kind of hour is that to go to bed?"

"He stays up because he likes it."

"He's lonely. I'm not lonely. I have a wife waiting in bed for me."

"He had a wife once too."

"A wife would be no good to him now."

"You can't tell. He might be better with a wife."

"His niece looks after him."

"I know. You said she cut him down."

"I wouldn't want to be that old. An old man is a nasty thing."

"Not always. This old man is clean. He drinks without spilling. Even now, drunk. Look at him."

"I don't want to look at him. I wish he would go home. He has no regard for those who must work."

The old man looked from his glass across the square, then over at the waiters.

"Another brandy," he said, pointing to his glass. The waiter who was in a hurry came over.

"Finished," he said, speaking with that omission of syntax stupid people employ when talking to drunken people or foreigners. "No more tonight. Close now."

"Another," said the old man.

"No. Finished." The waiter wiped the edge of the table with a towel and shook his head.

The old man stood up, slowly counted the saucers, took a leather coin purse from his pocket and paid for the drinks, leaving half a peseta tip.

The waiter watched him go down the street, a very old man walking unsteadily but with dignity.

"Why didn't you let him stay and drink?" the unhurried waiter asked. They were putting up the shutters. "It is not half-past two."

"I want to go home to bed."

"What is an hour?"

"More to me than to him."

"An hour is the same."

"You talk like an old man yourself. He can buy a bottle and drink at home."

"It's not the same."

"No, it is not," agreed the waiter with a wife. He did not wish to be unjust. He was only in a hurry.

"And you? You have no fear of going home before your usual hour?"

"Are you trying to insult me?"

"No, hombre, only to make a joke."

"No," the waiter who was in a hurry said, rising from pulling down the metal shutters. "I have confidence. I am all confidence."

"You have youth, confidence, and a job," the older waiter said. "You have everything."

"And what do you lack?"

"Everything but work."

"You have everything I have."

"No. I have never had confidence and I am not young."

"Come on. Stop talking nonsense and lock up."

"I am of those who like to stay late at the café," the older waiter said. "With all those who do not want to go to bed. With all those who need a light for the night."

"I want to go home and into bed."

"We are of two different kinds," the older waiter said. He was now dressed to go home. "It is not only a question of youth and confidence although those things are very beautiful. Each night I am reluctant to close up because there may be some one who needs the café."

"Hombre, there are bodegas open all night long."

"You do not understand. This is a clean and pleasant café. It is well lighted. The light is very good and also, now, there are shadows of the leaves."

"Good night," said the younger waiter.

"Good night," the other said. Turning off the electric light he continued the conversation with himself. It is the light of course but it is necessary that the place be clean and pleasant. You do not want music. Certainly you do not want music. Nor can you stand before a bar with dignity although that is all that is provided for these hours. What did he fear? It was not fear or dread. It was a nothing that he knew too well. It was all a nothing and a man was nothing too. It was only that and light was all it needed and a certain cleanness and order. Some lived in it and never felt it but he knew it all was nada y pues nada y nada y pues nada.[1] Our nada who art in nada, nada be thy name thy kingdom nada thy will be nada in nada as it is in nada. Give us this nada our daily nada and nada us our nada as we nada our nadas and nada us not into nada but deliver us from nada; pues nada. Hail nothing full of nothing, nothing is with thee. He smiled and stood before a bar with a shining steam pressure coffee machine.

"What's yours?" asked the barman.

"Nada."

"Otro loco mas,"[2] said the barman and turned away.

"A little cup," said the waiter.

The barman poured it for him.

"The light is very bright and pleasant but the bar is unpolished," the waiter said.

The barman looked at him but did not answer. It was too late at night for conversation.

"You want another copita?" the barman asked.

"No, thank you," said the waiter and went out. He disliked bars and bodegas. A clean, well-lighted café was a very different thing. Now, without thinking further, he would go home to his room. He would lie in the bed and finally, with daylight, he would go to sleep. After all, he said to himself, it is probably only insomnia. Many must have it.

---

[1] ". . . nothing and then nothing and nothing and then nothing."

[2] "Another crazy one."

## LANGSTON HUGHES [1902–1967]

# Thank You, M'am

She was a large woman with a large purse that had everything in it but a hammer and nails. It had a long strap, and she carried it slung across her shoulder. It was about eleven o'clock at night, dark, and she was walking alone, when a boy ran up behind her and tried to snatch her purse. The strap broke with the sudden single tug the boy gave it from behind. But the boy's weight and the weight of the purse combined caused him to lose his balance. Instead of taking off full blast as he had hoped, the boy fell on his back on the sidewalk and his legs flew up. The large woman simply turned around and kicked him right square in his blue-jeaned sitter. Then she reached down, picked the boy up by his shirt front, and shook him until his teeth rattled.

⸱ After that the woman said, "Pick up my pocketbook, boy, and give it here."

She still held him tightly. But she bent down enough to permit him to stoop and pick up her purse. Then she said, "Now ain't you ashamed of yourself?"

Firmly gripped by his shirt front, the boy said, "Yes'm."

The woman said, "What did you want to do it for?"

The boy said, "I didn't aim to."

She said, "You a lie!"

By that time two or three people passed, stopped, turned to look, and some stood watching.

"If I turn you loose, will you run?" asked the woman.

"Yes'm," said the boy.

"Then I won't turn you loose," said the woman. She did not release him.

"Lady, I'm sorry," whispered the boy.

"Um-hum! Your face is dirty. I got a great mind to wash your face for you. Ain't you got nobody home to tell you to wash your face?"

"No'm," said the boy.

"Then it will get washed this evening," said the large woman, starting up the street, dragging the frightened boy behind her.

He looked as if he were fourteen or fifteen, frail and willow-wild, in tennis shoes and blue jeans.

The woman said, "You ought to be my son. I would teach you right from wrong. Least I can do right now is to wash your face. Are you hungry?"

"No'm," said the being-dragged boy. "I just want you to turn me loose."

"Was I bothering *you* when I turned that corner?" asked the woman.

"No'm."

"But you put yourself in contact with *me*," said the woman, "If you think that that contact is not going to last awhile, you got another thought coming. When I get through with you, sir, you are going to remember Mrs. Luella Bates Washington Jones."

Sweat popped out on the boy's face and he began to struggle. Mrs. Jones stopped, jerked him around in front of her, put a half nelson about his neck, and continued to drag him up the street. When she got to her door, she dragged the boy inside, down a hall, and into a large kitchenette-furnished room at the rear of the house. She switched on the light and left the door open. The boy could hear other roomers laughing and talking in the large house. Some of their doors were open, too, so he knew he and the woman were not alone. The woman still had him by the neck in the middle of her room.

She said, "What is your name?"

"Roger," answered the boy.

"Then, Roger, you go to that sink and wash your face," said the woman, whereupon she turned him loose—at last. Roger looked at the door—looked at the woman—looked at the door—*and went to the sink.*

"Let the water run until it gets warm," she said. "Here's a clean towel."

"You gonna take me to jail?" asked the boy, bending over the sink.

"Not with that face, I would not take you nowhere," said the woman. "Here I am trying to get home to cook me a bite to eat and you snatch my pocketbook! Maybe you ain't been to your supper either, late as it be. Have you?"

"There's nobody home at my house," said the boy.

"Then we'll eat," said the woman. "I believe you're hungry—or been hungry—to try to snatch my pocketbook!"

"I want a pair of blue suede shoes," said the boy.

"Well, you didn't have to snatch *my* pocketbook to get some suede shoes," said Mrs. Luella Bates Washington Jones. "You could of asked me."

"M'am?"

The water dripping from his face, the boy looked at her. There was a long pause. A very long pause. After he had dried his face, and not knowing what else to do, dried it again, the boy turned around, wondering what next. The door was open. He could make a dash for it down the hall. He could run, run, run, *run!*

The woman was sitting on the daybed. After a while she said, "I were young once and I wanted things I could not get."

There was another long pause. The boy's mouth opened. Then he frowned, not knowing he frowned.

The woman said, "Um-hum! You thought I was going to say *but,* didn't you? You thought I was going to say, *but I didn't snatch people's pocketbooks.* Well, I wasn't going to say that." Pause. Silence. "I have done things, too, which I would not tell you, son—neither tell God, if He didn't already know. Everybody's got something in common. So you set down while I fix us something to eat. You might run that comb through your hair so you will look presentable."

In another corner of the room behind a screen was a gas plate and an icebox. Mrs. Jones got up and went behind the screen. The woman did not watch the boy to see if he was going to run now, nor did she watch her purse, which she left behind her on the daybed. But the boy took care to sit on the far side of the room, away from the purse, where he thought she could easily see him out of the corner of her eye if she wanted to. He did not trust the woman *not* to trust him. And he did not want to be mistrusted now.

"Do you need somebody to go to the store," asked the boy, "maybe to get some milk or something?"

"Don't believe I do," said the woman, "unless you just want sweet milk yourself. I was going to make cocoa out of this canned milk I got here."

"That will be fine," said the boy.

She heated some lima beans and ham she had in the icebox,

made the cocoa, and set the table. The woman did not ask the boy anything about where he lived, or his folks, or anything else that would embarrass him. Instead, as they ate, she told him about her job in a hotel beauty shop that stayed open late, what the work was like, and how all kinds of women came in and out, blonds, redheads, and Spanish. Then she cut him a half of her ten-cent cake.

"Eat some more, son," she said.

When they were finished eating, she got up and said, "Now here, take this ten dollars and buy yourself some blue suede shoes. And next time, do not make the mistake of latching onto *my* pocketbook *nor nobody else's*—because shoes got by devilish ways will burn your feet. I got to get my rest now. But from here on in, son, I hope you will behave yourself."

She led him down the hall to the front door and opened it. "Good night! Behave yourself, boy!" she said, looking out into the street as he went down the steps.

The boy wanted to say something other than, "Thank you, M'am," to Mrs. Luella Bates Washington Jones, but although his lips moved, he couldn't even say that as he turned at the foot of the barren stoop and looked up at the large woman in the door. Then she shut the door.

## JAMES T. FARRELL [1904–1979]

# The Benefits of American Life

Takiss Tillios was a strong shepherd boy whose home land was located just at the hollow valley of two mountains in Arcadia, Greece, in the central section of the Peloponnesus.[1] He grew up on goat's milk and on pitch black bread whose cinders were not separated so as to produce more bread per pound. His hard-

---

[1] An idyllic pastoral region, rich in classical legend. See Keats, "Ode on a Grecian Urn" (l. 7).

working mother sold a piece of land, which produced enough wheat to pull the family through the whole year, in order to pay his steerage fare to America. For in America the streets were paved with gold; the buildings were taller than mountains; the women all dressed like princesses and the men had their pockets lined with money; every boy had a bicycle; and every man and woman owned an automobile. At the age of thirteen, Takiss, large for his age, arrived in a paradise known as Chicago.

He was met at the railroad station, a scared and bewildered boy, by a relative who took him to a home on South Halsted Street. With voluble beneficence, the relative immediately employed Takiss, offering him a salary of fifteen dollars a month and the privilege of sleeping on marble slabs in his candy kitchen. He told Takiss that all successful Greek men started that way, and he showed the boy Greek newspapers with pictures of stern, mustachioed Greek restaurant owners and candy store proprietors who recounted the story of their rise to fame and offered themselves as favorable candidates for marriage. And as a final word of advice, the relative told Takiss that his mother was getting old now, and that he should send her some of his wages to help her out.

Takiss quickly discovered what it meant to live in paradise. It meant working from six in the morning until six in the evening, and until even later on week-ends. It meant sweeping out the store, washing dishes and windows, polishing, arranging, mopping, running errands. It meant attending night school to learn English when he could scarcely keep his eyes open and where he was frequently laughed at for his blundering efforts. It meant walking along, living in the midst of dirty streets where coal dust, soot, smoke, and poisonous fumes of automobiles choked his nostrils and made him cough. It meant lonesome memories. For a long period, Takiss was a lonely boy remembering his homeland and his Grecian mountain, remembering the long, slow days with the sheep, remembering the smile and kiss of his old mother, remembering always.

And he was afraid of America, and of that tremendous paradise known as Chicago. He worked doggedly day after day, earning fifteen dollars a month, catching a cough from sleeping on marble slabs. He worked doggedly, and from his wages he saved a pittance which he deposited in an immigrant's savings bank. But he looked ahead to the day when he would be famous, with his picture in the Greek newspapers, a pride and an honor to his native Greece and to the great tradition of the great Socrates about whom his relative so frequently boasted. He dreamed of the time when he would become like Americans, talk like them, wear their clothes, ride in automobiles just as they did, walk along the streets with pretty American girls.

In time, Takiss learned things. He learned American words, but never how to speak them like an American. He learned that he was considered a dirty Greek greenhorn, and that many Americans would have been just as pleased if he and many of his countrymen had never come to their land. And he learned that American girls laughed sardonically at a young Greek greenhorn. Also, he learned of a place owned by a cousin of his, where for a little money he could go and find American girls who did not laugh at a Greek greenhorn, at least for five or ten minutes. He learned how to buy American clothes on installments, to wear a purple silk shirt, purple socks, and an orange tie. And he learned also, that in the store he could put some of the money received for sales into his pocket instead of into the cash register.

Eventually, the cousin employing him discharged him in anger, branding him a crook, a robber, a traitor. In the heated quarrel, Takiss asked him why, if he wanted honesty, he paid only six dollars a week wages, when he made so much money himself selling bad products and got his picture in the Greek newspapers as a successful pioneer in America.

Takiss was employed by other of his countrymen, in fruit stores, soda parlors, at hot-dog stands, and in restaurants. He acquired additional American knowledge, and more American words. And sometimes when he was dressed up, wearing his purple silk shirt, with socks to match, and the orange tie, he would walk in the parks or along Halsted Street, seeing American girls, wishing that he had one of his own, a blonde girl with a beautiful pink-white complexion.

Time slid from under Takiss, and he was a young man in his early twenties, with his first citizenship papers. He had worked like a dog, and he was still slaving at the same jobs, performing the same tasks and chores as he had always done since he had come to America. He earned eight dollars a week and was busy twelve hours a day in a candy store. He cleaned and mopped; he scrubbed; he polished; he washed; he waited on trade. And often when he was alone in the store he pocketed money from the cash register. Every week he deposited money in the bank, and almost nightly he looked in his bank book, proud of his savings, thinking of how he was going to achieve fame in America. But he was never able to save money, because he was always quitting or losing jobs and having to use savings to support himself between jobs, as well as to send money to his mother.

And he learned another thing . . . he learned how to dance like Americans. A Greek-American friend told him of a dancing school called a taxi-dance hall on West Madison Street, and showed him an advertisement from the Greek-American owner, Professor Christopolos, who stated in the ad that anyone could be as graceful as he if they learned dancing from his beautiful girls at only ten cents a dance. He paid a dollar and was given ten tickets and entered the dimly lighted dancing school of Professor Christopolos on the fourth flour of a dingy and decrepit building. Each ticket was good for one dance which lasted from a minute to a minute and a half. Any girl in the place would dance with him, because she received five cents for each dance. Takiss' tickets were quickly used up, and he bought more. It did not matter if he danced woodenly and clumsily, and the girls acted delighted to teach him. He went to this taxi-dance hall regularly, spending three, four, and five dollars every visit, and once in a while a girl would ask him if he wanted to take her home, and for a few more dollars he could get other favors, too. After he started going to the taxi-dance hall regularly he was able to save less money, and he sent little to his mother.

Takiss then spent some of his savings for a suit with bell-bottom trousers. He cultivated a mustache and long sideburns, greased his hair and parted it in the middle with meticulous attention. He began to look like a sheik, and listened to pick up all the words which the American-born sheiks used. He went to public dance halls where there was only an admission fee and longer dances. At these places, there were always swarms of girls, pretty American girls, some of them tall and beautiful blondes with milky skins and red lips like cherries. He would ask them to dance. Often they would dance with him, once. He would talk, and they would catch his accent, and when he asked them for a second dance they would thank him with great regret and exclaim that all their other dances were taken. So he would quickly be driven to dancing with the homely and ugly girls who were called wall-flowers. And then he would go back to Professor Christopolos' dancing school, where all the girls would dance with him for ten cents a dance.

One day, Takiss was twenty-five. His native Grecian mountains seemed to have receded in time and he saw them only in painful mists of memory, recalling their details and contours with lessening concreteness. Greece to him was a memory. He had been in America for twelve years, and he was working ten hours a day in a hot-dog stand for ten dollars a week, and able to graft from three to five dollars a week extra. He wanted to make money and to become famous like some of his Americanized countrymen. And when he was a rich man with a hot-dog stand or a restaurant of his own, he would return to Greece with an American wife and act like a millionaire. And he had thirty-five dollars in the bank as a start toward these riches. He wanted to get more money, but not by running a brothel as his fourth cousin George did, and not bootlegging as did George's friend, Mike. He remembered the things his mother, now dead, had told him, and he wanted to make his money and his fame in a way that his mother would have approved of. And then he would have his picture in a Greek-American newspaper.

And hard times came to America. Takiss was out of work in the winter, and again his savings melted. He was employed for ten dollars a week in a candy store, still working twelve hours a day, and in four months that job was gone. He worked for seven dollars a week washing dishes in a large restaurant, and then his pay was cut to five dollars, and he went home every night tired, with chafed hands and an aching back. He had less money, also, for taxi dances. And he lost that job.

He walked the streets looking for other work, and always he learned the same story . . . hard times. He ate very frugally, lived in a chilly, rat-infested room, and wished that he was back home again in his native Grecian mountains, or else that he was a rich and famous American-Greek. Every day he went out looking for a job, and sometimes he found work for a few days or a few weeks and was able to skim along while he tried again to find work.

One day he saw an advertisement with large letters at the top . . . DANCE MARATHON. The word Marathon struck him. Greek. He would win it and win another victory for his country as it had been done in ancient times. He would become a famous Greek athlete. He investigated, and learned that it was a contest in which everybody tried to dance longer than the others, and the winner received a five-hundred-dollar prize. And maybe if he won it, he would get a job in the moving pictures and become the idol of American girls, or go on the vaudeville stage, or be hired to dance in a cabaret. And while he was in the contest, he would be cared for, fed, and there would be no room rent to pay. He was strong and husky, even if he had been getting coughs in his chest for years ever since he had slept on those marble slabs. And he could dance. He was used to standing on his feet all day at work. And this was his chance to become rich. He would no longer have to tramp all over town to be told that there were no jobs because it was hard times. This was much better than saving up to own a candy store and grow fat like the American-Greeks for whom he had worked. And after he won this contest, and became famous, he would go back to Greece with a trunk full of clothes and money, and maybe a rich American girl whose skin was like milk.

Takiss entered the dance marathon, and when the rules were explained to him, he only understood that he was to stay out on the floor and dance, and if he was able to do that longer than anyone else, he would get five hundred dollars. A number was pinned on his back, and he was assigned a partner named Marie Glenn, a beautiful blonde American girl of the type he had always dreamed of as a possible wife. At first, when she met him, she shuddered, and her face broke into an expression of disgust. But then she saw that he was strong and husky with broad shoulders, and she smiled, offering him a limp hand and sweetly telling him that she knew they were sure going to be the winners.

The dance marathon was conducted in a public dance hall on the south side of Chicago. A ring was placed in the center with an orchestra dais at one end. Around the ring there were box seats, and behind them, rising rows of bleacher benches. The opening was described, in advertisements, as gala. An announcer talked through a microphone, and the promoters and judges wearing tuxedoes also addressed a full house. The contestants were introduced and some of them, but not Takiss, spoke to the crowd and the large radio audience all over America. It was all a new and promising, if confusing, world to Takiss, and he walked around the floor, feeling as lost and as out of place as he had on those first days in America. But it was leading at last to paradise.

The contest swung into action. They danced for three minutes out of every ten, and walked around and around the floor for the remaining time; and they were given fifteen minutes rest out of every hour. There was glamor in being watched by so many people, in eating sandwiches and drinking coffee before them, in receiving attention from doctors and nurses, and meeting all the others who, like himself, saw at the end of this contest five hundred dollars and fame. As the contestants got to talking to each other, Takiss heard them using one word over and over again . . . celebrity. A celebrity was somebody who was important, like Jack Dempsey and movie stars and Mr. Delphos, the famous American-Greek who was wealthy and owned a large dance hall known as the Bourbon Palace. They all wanted to be celebrities. And Takiss, too, he determined that he was going to be a celebrity.

Takiss had not imagined that anyone could dance for more than a week like this, and that maybe after a sleepless and tiring week he would be the winner. In less than twenty-four hours he learned that it was a grind more gruelling than he had calculated, and while he doggedly gritted his teeth, he determined that he would not let himself drop out. Still, he wished that he had not entered it. He wished he were back working in fruit stores and ice cream parlors the way he had been before hard times had come. He wished that he were a shepherd back in the Grecian mountains.

When his partner was tired, she put her arms around his neck or hips, laid her head against him, and fell asleep while he dragged her heavily around the floor, and when he fell asleep she did the same thing with him. Again and again their bodies were jolted, shoved, pushed against each other, and he began wanting her so that her very nearness became excruciating. And he noticed that she, particularly in the early dog hours of the mornings when there were scarcely any spectators in the hall, began brushing herself against him at every opportunity, looking feverishly into his eyes and telling him smutty jokes. And the other dancers became the same way, and the fellows used to tell him how much they wanted one of these girls, any girl.

Day after day the marathon grind went on. His eyes grew

heavy. His back ached. His feet became sore and raw, so that each step was pain and he felt often as if he were walking on fire. The hall was almost continuously stale with cigarette smoke and foul with body odors. He felt constantly dirty, sweaty, itchy. Dust got into his nostrils and his eyes. He began to cough again. His muscles knotted. He became like a person who was always only half awake, and everything took on the semblance of being a semi-dream. Marie, also, changed. She began to swell around the buttocks. Deep circles grew under her eyes. She became haggard and blowsy and looked like a worn-out prostitute. She used more and more cosmetics, and her face became like a ghastly caricature of the pretty girl who had entered the contest.

In the beginning, particularly because of his accent and Greek heritage, Takiss became the butt of many jokes. Constantly, he would be asked why he wasn't running a restaurant, and he would be given orders for a piece zapple pie kid. He was nicknamed Restaurant, Fruit Store, Socrates, and Zapple Pie Kid. In time, this wore down and failed to anger or disturb him. The grind settled into habitual misery and torture. He, like the other contestants, would long for fresh air, and during rest periods, when they were not so tired that they would be dragged like walking somnambulists to the rest cots, they would enter the vile and filthy dressing rooms or the equally unsavory lavatory and jam their heads out of the windows to breathe fresh air and to look yearningly down at the street where people walked free to do what they wished, not tired, able to breathe fresh air, even the fresh air of a city street that was saturated with carbon monoxide fumes and sootiness.

Day after day dragged on. Sometimes Takiss, Marie, or the other contestants would live in stupors of six, twelve hours a day, even longer. As the time passed, the contestants would switch from affected and over-stimulated good spirits to nasty, fighting nervousness, and then into that glaze-eyed stupor. Particularly in those dog hours of the early morning, they would be raw, if awake, and fight and curse. Sex, too, became a growing obsession, and in time was almost madness. Living so near to one another, their bodies touching so frequently, they told smuttier and smuttier jokes. Perversities and desires or propositions for perversities sprang up among them. It became a relentless process of both physical and mental torture. Constipation, diarrhea, sudden inabilities to control their kidneys so that now and then a contestant would be walking around the floor, drugged in sleep, with wet lines down his trousers, or if a girl, down her beach pyjamas which most of them wore regularly. Broken blood vessels and swollen veins in the legs. Headaches, eye troubles, sore throats, fevers, colds. Periods of sweatiness, followed by shivers and chills. And always that returning stupor, caused by sleeplessness and fatigue, and by the dreams and fantasies which they entertained as relief from that endless procession around and around the floor. And at the end of it all, money, the chance to become a celebrity, sex, and clean white bed sheets and a soft, fresh bed.

Ways of making money from day to day quickly developed and were used to the utmost so that all of the contestants started bank accounts. Every one of them developed some trick or act, a song, a dance, a stunt of some kind, and after putting it on, they would be showered with money from the crowd. One of the contestants, a raw country youth of Lithuanian origin with a nasal twang to his voice, chewed razor blades as his stunt. Takiss learned a dance. Stores, theatres, and politicians also paid them fees to wear signs or sweaters and jerseys with advertising printed on the front or back. Money was sent to them, mash notes, written in as ignorant and as bad English as that which Takiss used and wrote in. The various spectators picked favorites, cheered for them, shouted encouragement.

And still the days stretched out, past the first month, with contestant after contestant dropping out, and the field narrowing down. One day there would be a birthday party. Another day there was a floor wedding between two of the contestants who had been on the floor, and the wedding provided endless hours of raw jokes and humor about when they would have their wedding night, until, sex-crazed, both of the newlyweds went temporarily out of their heads and the girl screamed until she was dragged off the floor. Disqualified, they were out of the marathon, and a new note was introduced in the humor. Another day, a girl had an abscessed tooth extracted on the floor, and immediately afterward she rejoined the endless walking procession that tramped around in this ever dullening stupor. Another day, an Italian boy, who with his wife had entered the marathon because they were both unemployed and had been evicted, required crutches and ran a high fever. With his eyes intense from the fever, with suffering imprinted on his haggard face, he hobbled around and around. After twelve such hours he was forced out by the judges on the advice of a doctor.

Again and again Takiss wanted to quit and satisfy himself with the incidental money he had taken in, and as repeatedly he would go patiently on. Like the others, he would fall into that lumbrous sleep, and external means would be necessary to awaken him so that he might continue. The male nurses would slap him in the face with wet towels, put his shoes on the wrong feet, strap him into an electric vibrator machine, poke their fingers down his throat, tickle his calloused soles. During one period, his cough developed into a severe cold in the chest. For another period, he was not out of his stupor for three days. And Marie, his partner, experienced the same tortures. They went on. Days and nights, and days and nights, with the field narrowing to thirteen, ten, eight, five finally two couples. Then Marie collapsed and was carried off the floor and shipped to a hospital, and Takiss was disqualified. They each collected the two hundred and fifty dollars second place money.

After recuperation, Takiss entered other dance marathons, and became a professional. He secured a copy of *Yes, We Have No Bananas* with a Greek translation, and this, with his dance stunt, became very popular. He was able, with both attractions and with a growing audience of fans, to earn from ten to fifteen dollars a day in extra money. Even when he was forced to retire from marathons or was disqualified, he departed with added money. Again the desire to return to his homeland like a rich American grew upon him, and now his bank account, with foreign exchange rates, would make him very rich in Greece. He was something of a celebrity in this new world of his. His biography and picture appeared in Greek newspapers. A Greek merchant who sold a raisin beverage paid him and Marie each a hundred dollars to be photographed for a newspaper advertisement in which there was their signed testimony that they drank this beverage. He had a run of a week at a small theatre on South Halsted Street where there were many Greeks. Takiss became a famous American-Greek.

In all, Takiss participated in sixteen dance marathons. In eight of them, he collected money and was the winner of a thousand-dollar super-marathon in which only finalists from other marathons were permitted to enter and in which there were no rest

periods. He had money now, five thousand dollars. He returned
to Greece. But the strain of the marathons had ruined his lungs
and he had tuberculosis. Resorts for tuberculosis had been developed in his native mountains, and when he returned it was necessary for him to become a patient in one of them, and the money
he had earned was paid out while he lived there with his lungs
rotting away on him.

## ISAAC BASHEVIS SINGER [b. 1904]

# Joy

### I

Rabbi Bainish of Komarov, having buried Bunem, his third son,
stopped praying for his ailing children. Only one son and two
daughters remained, and all of them spat blood. His wife, frequently breaking into the solitude of his study would scream,
"Why are you so silent? Why don't you move heaven and earth?"
With clenched fists raised, she would wail, "What good are your
knowledge, your prayers, the merits of your ancestors, your prolonged fasts? What does He have against you—our Father in
Heaven? Why must all His anger be directed against you?" In her
despair she once snatched a sacred book and threw it on the floor.
Silently, Rabbi Bainish picked it up. His invariable answer was,
"Leave me alone!"

Though he was not yet fifty, the rabbi's beard, so thin that the
hairs could be numbered, had turned white as the beard of an old
man. His tall body stooped. His stern black eyes looked past
everyone. No longer did he comment on the Torah[1] nor preside
over meals. For weeks now he had not appeared at the house of
study. Though his followers came from other towns to visit him,
they had to return without being allowed even a greeting. Behind

Translated by Norbert Guterman and Elaine Gottlieb.
[1] The first five books of Moses, the Pentateuch.

his bolted door he sat, silent; it was a pregnant silence. The crowd, his "bread and butter" Hasidim,[2] gradually dispersed among other rabbis. Only his intimate circle, the old Hasidim, the wise ones, stayed. When Rebecca, his youngest daughter, died, the rabbi did not even follow her hearse. He gave orders to his sexton, Avigdor, to close the shutters, and they remained closed. Through a heart-shaped aperture in the shutters, came the meager light whereby the rabbi looked through books. He no longer recited the texts out loud; he merely thumbed the pages, opening a book at one place and then at another, and with one eye closed, stared vacantly beyond the pages and the walls. Dipping his pen in the inkwell, he would move a sheet of paper close to him, but he could not write. He would fill a pipe, but it remained unlit. There was no indication that he had touched the breakfast and supper that had been brought to his study. Weeks, months, went by like this.

One summer day the rabbi appeared at the house of study. Several boys and young men were studying there, while a couple of old men, hangers-on, were meditating. Since their rabbi had been absent for so long, all of them were frightened at the sight of him. Taking a step in one direction, and then a step back, the rabbi asked, "Where is Abraham Moshe of Borisov?"

"At the inn," said a young man who had not yet been struck dumb.

"Would you ask him to come to me, please?"

"I will, Rabbi."

The young man left immediately for the inn. Walking to the bookshelves, the rabbi drew out a book at random, glanced at a page, and then replaced the book. In his unbuttoned robe, his long fringed garment, his short trousers, white stockings, with hat pushed back on his head, his earlocks unkempt, his eyebrows contracted, he stood there. The house of study was so still that water could be heard dripping in the basin, and flies humming around the candlesticks. The grandfather clock, with its long chains and pomegranates on the dial, creaked and struck three. Through the open windows peeped the fruit trees in the orchard; one heard the chirping of birds. In the slanting pillars of dust, tiny particles vibrated, no longer matter, and not yet spirit, reflect-

---

[2] Community of devoutly pious Jewish mystics.

ing rainbow hues. The rabbi beckoned to a boy who had only recently left the Hebrew school and had begun to read the Talmud[3] on his own.

"What's your name, eh?"

"Moshe."

"What are you studying?"

"The first treatise."

"What chapter?"

"*Shur Shenagah ath haparah.*"

"How do you translate that?"

"A bull gored a cow."

The rabbi stamped his slippered foot. "Why did the bull gore the cow? What had the cow done to him?"

"A bull does not reason."

"But He who created the bull can reason."

The boy did not know the answer to that one. The rabbi pinched his check.

"Well, go study," he said, returning to his room.

Reb Abraham Moshe came to him shortly afterwards. He was a small, youthful-faced man, with white beard and earlocks, wearing a floor-length robe, a thick, moss-green sash, and carrying a long pipe that reached to his knees. Over his skullcap he wore a high cap. His eccentricities were well known. He would recite the morning prayer in the afternoon, and the afternoon prayer long after others had returned from the evening service. He chanted psalms at Purim,[4] and during the Kol Nidre prayer,[5] he slept. On Passover eve when everyone celebrated at the Passover feast, he would study a commentary of the Talmudic Treatises on Damages and Compensations. It was rumored that once, at the tavern, he had won a game of chess from a general, and that the general had rewarded him with a license to sell brandy. His wife ran the business; he himself spent more time at Komarov than at home. He would say that living at Komarov was like standing at the foot

---

[3] In general, the body of Jewish civil and ceremonial traditional law, commentary on the Pentateuch.

[4] Annual festival to commemorate the defeat of Haman's plot to murder Jews.

[5] Opening words of the Evening Service commencing on Yom Kippur, the Day of Atonement, declaring that all vows made rashly during the year shall be null and void.

of Mount Sinai; the air itself purified one. In a more jocular mood, he would comment that there was no need to study at Komarov; it was sufficient to loiter on a bench in the house of study and inhale the Torah as one breathed. The Hasidim knew that the rabbi held Reb Abraham Moshe in the highest esteem, discussed esoteric doctrine with him, and asked his advice. Reb Abraham Moshe was always seated at the head of the table. Nevertheless, each time he visited the rabbi, he spruced up like a young man. He would wash his hands, button his caftan, curl his earlocks, and comb his beard. He would enter with reverence, as one enters the house of a saint.

The rabbi had not sent for him since Rebecca's death; this in itself was an indication of the depth of the rabbi's grief. Reb Abraham Moshe did not shuffle now, as customarily, but walked briskly, almost running. When he had reached the rabbi's door he halted for a moment, touched his cap, his chest, wiped his brow with his handkerchief, and then walked in mincingly. The rabbi, having opened one of the shutters, sat smoking his pipe in the grandfather's chair with the ivory armrests. A half-full glass of tea stood on the table, a roll beside it. Apparently, the rabbi had recovered.

"Rabbi, I'm here," said Reb Abraham Moshe.

"So I see. Be seated."

"Thank you."

The rabbi remained silent a while. Placing his narrow hand on the table edge, he stared at the white nails of his long fingers. Then he said, "Abraham Moshe, it's bad."

"What's bad?"

"Abraham Moshe, it's worse than you think."

"What could be worse?" asked Abraham Moshe, ironically.

"Abraham Moshe, the atheists are right. There is no justice, no Judge."

Reb Abraham Moshe was accustomed to the rabbi's harsh words. At Komarov, even the Lord of the Universe would not be spared. But to be rebellious is one thing; to deny God, another. Reb Abraham Moshe turned pale. His knees shook.

"Then who rules the world, Rabbi?"

"It's not ruled."

"Who then?"

"A total lie!"

"Come, come . . ."

"A heap of dung . . ."

"Where did the dung come from?"

"In the beginning was the dung."

Reb Abraham Moshe froze. He wanted to speak, but his arguments caught in his throat. Well, it's his grief that talks, he thought. Nevertheless, he marveled. If Job could endure it, so should the rabbi.

"What should we do, then, Rabbi?" Reb Abraham Moshe asked hoarsely.

"We should worship idols."

To keep from falling, Reb Abraham Moshe gripped the table edge.

"What idols?" he asked. Everything inside him seemed to tighten.

The rabbi laughed briefly. "Don't be frightened; I won't send you to the priest. If the atheists are right, what's the difference between Terah and Abraham? Each served a different idol. Terah,[6] who was simpleminded, invented a clay god. Abraham invented a Creator. It is what one invents that matters. Even a lie must have some truth in it."

"You are merely being facetious," Reb Abraham Moshe stammered. His palate felt dry, his throat contracted.

"Well, stop trembling! Sit down!"

Reb Abraham Moshe sat down. The rabbi rose from his seat, walked to the window, and stood there a long time, staring into space. Then he walked to the book cabinet. The cabinet, which smelled of wine and snuffed-out valedictory candles, contained a spice box, and citron box, and a Hanukkah candelabra. The rabbi, taking out a Zohar,[7] opened it at random, stared at the page, nodded, and then, smacking his lips, exclaimed, "A nice invention, very nice!"

## II

More and more Hasidim departed. In the house of study, on Saturdays, scarcely a quorum remained. The sextons, all but Avigdor, had left. Finding her solitude unbearable, the rabbi's wife

---

[6] Abraham's father.

[7] A mystical commentary on the Bible.

went for a long visit to her brother, the rabbi of Biala. Reb Abraham Moshe stayed at Komarov. He spent one Sabbath each month with his family in his native town. If a man were not to be deserted when his body was sick, he reasoned, then he certainly should not be left alone during the sickness of his soul. If their rabbi were committing sins, God forbid, then one would be interdicted from associating with him, but actually, his piety was now greater than before. He prayed, studied, visited the ritual bathhouse. And he was so ardent in his charity, that he sold his dearest possessions— the silver candlesticks, the large Hanukkah candelabra, his gold watch, and Passover tray—and gave the proceeds to the poor. Reb Abraham Moshe told him reproachfully he was squandering his inheritance, but the rabbi replied, "Poor men *do* exist. That's one thing of which we can be certain."

The summer went by and the month of Elul came. On week days, Avigdor, the sexton, blew the ram's horn at the house of study. Komarov used to be crowded to capacity during the month of Elul; there were not enough beds at the inns, and young people would sleep in storerooms, barns, attics. But this year, it was quiet at Komarov. The shutters remained closed at the inns. Grass grew wild in the rabbi's courtyard; there was no one to trample it. Gossamer threads floated through the air. The apples, pears, and plums ripened on the trees in the orchard, because the boys who used to pick them were gone. The chirping of birds sounded louder than ever. Moles dug up numerous mounds of earth. Certain bushes sprouted berries of a poisonous sort. One day, the rabbi, on his way to the bathhouse, plucked one such berry. "If a thing like this can turn one into a corpse," he thought, "what is a corpse?" He sniffed it and threw it away. "If everything hinges on a berry, then all our affairs are berries." The rabbi entered the bathhouse. "Well, demons, where are you?" he said aloud, and his words were thrown back at him by the echo, "At least let there be devils." He sat on the bench, undressed, removed his fringed garment, and examined it. "Threads and knots and nothing else . . ."

The water was cold, but it made no difference to him. "Who is cold? And if one is cold, what of it?" The coldness cut his breath, and he clung to the railing. Then he plunged and stayed for a long while under the water. Something within him was laughing. "As long as you breathe, you must breathe." The rabbi dried himself and dressed. Returning to his study, he opened a Cabala[8] book, The Two Tablets of the Covenant. Here it was written that "the rigor of the law should be sweetened to deprive Satan of his nourishment." "Well, and what if it's a fairy tale?" The rabbi squinted one eye while the other kept staring. "The sun? Close your eyes and there is no sun. The birds? Stuff your ears and there are no birds. Pain? Swallow a wild berry, and the pain is gone. What is left, then? Nothing at all. The past no longer exists and the future has yet to come. The conclusion is that nothing exists beyond the moment. Well, if so, we really have nothing to worry about."

No more than thirty Hasidim gathered at Komarov for Rosh Hashanah. Although the rabbi appeared at the service in his cloak and shawl, one could not tell if he prayed, for he was silent. After the service the Hasidim sat at the table, but their rabbi's seat was vacant. An old man chanted a little song and the others gave him a rattling accompaniment. Reb Abraham Moshe repeated a comment the rabbi had made on the Torah twenty years ago. Thank God, the rabbi was alive, though for all practical purposes, he was dead.

Avigdor brought to the rabbi's room a decanter of wine, apples with honey, the head of a carp, two hallahs, a quarter of a chicken with stewed carrots, and a slice of pineapple for the blessing of the first fruit. But although it was already evening, the rabbi had touched nothing.

During the month of Elul he had fasted. His body felt as though it had been hollowed. Hunger still gnawed somewhere in his stomach, but it was a hunger unrelated to him. What had he, Bainish of Komarov, to do with food? Must one yield to the body's lusts? If one resists, what does it do—die? "Let it die, if that's what it wants. I am satisfied." A golden-green fly flew in through the open window from the other side of the curtain, and settled on the glazed eye of the carp. The rabbi murmured, "Well, what are you waiting for? Eat . . ."

As the rabbi sat half-awake, half-slumbering in his old chair, his arms on the arm rests, engrossed in thoughts he did not know he was thinking, divested of all external things, he suddenly

---

[8] The body of Jewish mystical teachings.

caught sight of his youngest daughter, Rebecca. Through the closed door she had entered and stood there, erect, pale, her hair plaited in two tresses, wearing her best gold-embroidered dress, a prayer book in one hand, a handkerchief in the other. Forgetting that she had died, the rabbi looked at her, half-surprised. "See, she's a grown girl, how come she's not a bride?" An extraordinary nobility spread over her features; she looked as though she had just recovered from an illness; the pearls of her necklace shone with an unearthly light, with the aura of the Days of Awe. With an expression of modesty and love she gazed at the rabbi.

"Happy holiday, Father."

"Happy holiday, happy new year," the rabbi said.

"Father, say grace."

"What? Of course, of course."

"Father, join the guests at table," she said, half-commanding, half-imploring.

An icy shudder ran through the rabbi's spine. "But she's dead!" At once his eyes were drenched with tears, and he jumped to his feet as though to rush toward her. Through the mist of tears Rebecca's form became distorted, grew longer and partly blurred, but she still loomed before him. The rabbi noticed the silver clasp of her prayer book and the lace of her handkerchief. Her left pigtail was tied with a white ribbon. But her face, as though veiled, dissolved into a blotch. The rabbi's voice broke.

"My daughter, are you here?"

"Yes, Father."

"Why have you come?"

"For you."

"When?"

"After the holidays."

She seemed to withdraw. In the whirling mist her form lost its substance, but her dress continued to drag on the floor in folds and waves like a golden train, and a glow arose from it. Soon this too dissolved, and nothing remained but a sense of wonder, a supernatural tang, a touch of heavenly joy. The rabbi did not weep, but luminous drops fell on his white silken robe embroidered with flowers and leaves. There was a fragrance of myrtle, cloves and saffron. He had a cloying sensation in his mouth, as if he had eaten marzipan.

The rabbi remembered what Rebecca had told him. He put on

his fur hat, stood up, and opened the door leading to the house of study. It was time for the evening prayer, but the old men had not yet left the table.

"Happy holiday, my friends," the rabbi said in a cheerful voice.

"Happy holiday, Rabbi."

"Avigdor, I want to say grace."

"I'm ready, Rabbi."

Avigdor brought the wine, and the rabbi, chanting a holiday tune, recited the prayer. He washed his hands with the appropriate blessing and said the prayer for bread. After taking some broth, the rabbi commented on the Torah, a thing he had not done in years. His voice was low, though audible. The rabbi took up the question of why the moon is obscured on Rosh Hashanah.[9] The answer is that on Rosh Hashanah one prays for life, and life means free choice, and freedom is Mystery. If one knew the truth how could there be freedom? If hell and paradise were in the middle of the marketplace, everyone would be a saint. Of all the blessings bestowed on man, the greatest lies in the fact that God's face is forever hidden from him. Men are the children of the Highest, and the Almighty plays hide and seek with them. He hides His face, and the children seek Him while they have faith that He exists. But what if, God forbid, one loses faith? The wicked live on denials; denials in themselves are also a faith, faith in evildoing, and from it one can draw strength for the body. But if the pious man loses his faith, the truth is shown to him, and he is recalled. This is the symbolic meaning of the words, "When a man dies in a tent": when the pious man falls from his rank, and becomes, like the wicked, without permanent shelter, then a light shines from above, and all doubts cease . . .

The rabbi's voice gradually grew weaker. The old men leaned toward him, intently listening. The house of study was so still that one could hear the candles flicker. Reb Abraham Moshe paled. He realized the meaning hidden behind all this. The moment Rosh Hashanah was over, he mailed some letters, having sat until daybreak writing them. The rabbi's wife returned from Biala, and for Yom Kippur[10] the Hasidim arrived in great number. The rabbi had

---

[9] Jewish New Year.

[10] The Day of Atonement, the holiest day in the Jewish calendar.

returned to his former self. During the Sukkoth holidays[11] he commented on the Torah in his arbor. On Hashanah Raba he prayed all through the night, until dawn, with his Hasidim. On Simchas Torah, he never wearied of dancing around the reading stand. His Hasidim said later that Komarov had not, even under the old rabbi, blessed be his memory, celebrated that holiday with such gusto. To each of his Hasidim the rabbi spoke personally, asking about his family, and carefully reading each petition. He helped the children decorate the arbor with lanterns, ribbons, bunches of grapes. With his own hands, he wove baskets of lulab leaves for the myrtles. He pinched the cheeks of boys who had come with their fathers, and gave them cookies. As a rule, the rabbi prayed late and alone, but on the day following Sukkoth, he prayed in the house of study with the first quorum. After the service he asked for a glass of coffee. Reb Abraham Moshe and a circle of young men stood watching the rabbi drink coffee. Between swallows, he puffed his pipe. He said, "I want you to know that the material world has no substance."

After breakfast, the rabbi said grace. Then he ordered his bed made ready and murmured something about his old prayer shawl. The moment he lay down he became moribund. His face grew as yellow as his fringed garment. His eyelids closed. Covered with wrinkles, his forehead assumed a strange aspect. Life could literally be seen departing from him; his body shrank and altered. The rabbi's wife wanted to call the doctor, but the rabbi signaled her not to do so. Opening his eyes, he looked toward the door. Between the door jambs, beside the mezuzah, all of them were standing—his four sons and two daughters, his father, blessed be his memory, and his grandfather. Reverently, they all looked in his direction, expectantly, with arms outstretched. Each of them emitted a different light. They bent forward as though restrained by an invisible fence. "So that's the way it is," the rabbi thought. "Well, now everything is clear." He heard his wife sob, and wanted to comfort her, but no strength remained in his throat and lips. Suddenly, Reb Abraham Moshe leaned over him, as though

---

[11] A time of rejoicing, a week-long Festival of the Tabernacles commemorating forty years of wandering in the wilderness. To celebrate, a circuit of the synagogue is made with plants waved. On Hashanah Raba, the seventh day, seven circuits are made. Outside Israel, a "ninth day," Simchas Torah, is also observed.

realizing that the rabbi wished to speak, and the rabbi murmured, "One should always be joyous."

Those were his final words.

TOMMASO LANDOLFI [1908–1979]

# Wedding Night

$A$t the end of the wedding banquet the chimney sweep was announced. The father, out of joviality, and because it seemed proper to him that a ceremony such as the cleaning of the chimney should be celebrated on just that day, gave the order to let him come in. But the man did not appear; he preferred to remain in the kitchen, where the great hearth was. Not all the toasts had yet been given, and this was why some of the guests, in their heart of hearts, criticized the interruption; nonetheless, due to the uproar made by the children, everyone rose from the table.

The bride had never seen a chimney sweep: she had been in boarding school when he used to come. Going into the kitchen she saw a tall, rather corpulent man, with serious gray beard and bent shoulders; he was dressed in a corduroy suit the color of linseed oil. His stoop was counterbalanced by the weight of two huge mountain boots which seemed to hold his entire body erect. Although he had just washed very carefully, the skin of his face was deeply tinted with black, as though many blackheads of varying dimensions had taken root there; a black deposit, gathered between the lines of his forehead and cheeks, conferred a quality of meditative wisdom on that physiognomy. But this impression quickly dissolved, and the man's great timidity became quite obvious, especially when his features broke into a sort of smile.

He nearly frightened the young bride, because he was standing behind the door, though he acted frightened himself; and, as

---

Translated by Raymond Rosenthal.

if he had been caught doing something reprehensible and had to justify his presence in that place, be began to repeat, speaking directly to the young bride, some sentences which she did not hear or did not understand. He stammered insistently and behaved as if he thought that what he said concerned her greatly and, all the while, he looked at her with the eyes of a beaten dog and yet significantly. From the very first moment the young bride was aware of his caterpillar nature.

He took off his jacket and began to unbutton his vest. She slipped out through the other door, but continued to follow what was going on in the kitchen; she had the feeling that something improper was about to happen and that her presence might make him uneasy in the performance of his rites. Somehow she almost felt ashamed for him. But there was no noise to feed her imagination and so she went back in again. The children had been sent away and he was alone. At that moment he was climbing a ladder set up inside the hood of the fireplace; his feet were bare and he was in his shirtsleeves, a brown shirt. Across his chest, fastened with leather straps, he had a tool which resembled the scraper for a kneading trough but whose use remained forever unknown to the young bride. And he had a kind of black gag, tied up behind his ears, which fitted over his mouth and nose. But she did not see him enter the flue of the chimney, because she ran away again.

When she came back the second time, the kitchen was empty and a strange smell, a terrible smell, had spread through it. Looking around her, the young bride connected it first with the man's large shoes set in a corner next to a bundle of clothes; it was, however, the death smell of the soot which was piling up on the hearthstone, falling in intermittent showers to the rhythm of a dull scraping which gnawed at the marrow of the house and which she felt echoing in her own entrails. In the intervals, a muffled rubbing revealed the man's laborious ascent.

An instant of absolute silence fell, an instant of lacerating suspense for the young bride. She continued to stare at the mouth of the flue, there under the hood at the end of the fireplace's black funnel; this mouth was not square but narrow, a dark slit.

Then a very high, guttural, inhuman cry sounded from some mysterious place, from the well, from the stones of the house, from the soul of the kitchen's pots and pans, from the very breast of the young bride, who was shaken by it through and through.

That bestial howl of agony soon proved to be a kind of joyous call: the man had burst through onto the roof. The muffled rubbings resumed more rapidly now; finally a black foot came down out of the slit searching for support—the foot of a hanged man. The foot found the first rung of the ladder and the young bride ran away.

In the courtyard, as the bride sat on a millstone, the old housekeeper, one of those women for whom everything is new, assumed the task of keeping her informed; she walked back and forth bringing her the news with a mysterious air. "Now he is doing his cleaning under the hood," and the young bride pictured him as he shook off the soot, standing upright on the pile like a gravedigger on a mound of earth. "But what does he put on his feet to claw into the wall?" And then she ran after him to ask him: "My good man, what do you put on your feet to claw into the wall?" A gay reply followed which could not be heard clearly. "Now he is eating breakfast," and the housekeeper remained inside. Then she reappeared with a few small edelweiss; she said that the man had taken them out of a very clean little box and had offered them for the young bride.

After some time he himself came out, dressed again and with a pack on his back. He crossed the courtyard to leave, but the father stopped him and began to question him benevolently about his life. The young bride approached, too. Here the man, in the weak sun of winter, his face darker, his beard flecked with black and his eyes puckered by the light, looked like a big moth, a nocturnal bird surprised by the day. Or rather he looked like a spider or crab louse; the fact is that the hood of the hearth, when seen from below and if there is enough light outside, is not completely black but leaks a gray and slimy sheen.

He said that for thirty-five years he had been traveling through those towns cleaning the chimneys, that next year he would take his young son along to teach him the trade, that picking edelweiss was now forbidden and he had been able to gather those few flowers on the sly, and other such inconsequential things. Yet, whether astute or halting, it was quite clear that he only wished to hide himself behind those words, that he let the curtain of words fall in the same way that the cuttlefish beclouds the water.

He knew about all the deaths in the family, yet none of them had ever seen him!

By now the young bride felt that she was no longer ashamed for him, but was actually ashamed of herself.

After the chimney sweep had gone, she placed the few edelweiss beneath the portraits of the dead.

## EUDORA WELTY [b. 1909]

# A Worn Path

It was December—a bright frozen day in the early morning. Far out in the country there was an old Negro woman with her head tied in a red rag, coming along a path through the pinewoods. Her name was Phoenix Jackson. She was very old and small and she walked slowly in the dark pine shadows, moving a little from side to side in her steps, with the balanced heaviness and lightness of a pendulum in a grandfather clock. She carried a thin, small cane made from an umbrella, and with this she kept tapping the frozen earth in front of her. This made a grave and persistent noise in the still air, that seemed meditative like the chirping of a solitary little bird.

She wore a dark striped dress reaching down to her shoe tops, and an equally long apron of bleached sugar sacks, with a full pocket: all neat and tidy, but every time she took a step she might have fallen over her shoelaces, which dragged from her unlaced shoes. She looked straight ahead. Her eyes were blue with age. Her skin had a pattern all its own of numberless branching wrinkles and, as though a whole little tree stood in the middle of her forehead, but a golden color ran underneath, and the two knobs of her cheeks were illumined by a yellow burning under the dark. Under the red rag her hair came down on her neck in the frailest of ringlets, still black, and with an odor like copper.

Now and then there was a quivering in the thicket. Old Phoenix said, "Out of my way, all you foxes, owls, beetles, jack rabbits, coons and wild animals! . . . Keep out from under these feet, little bobwhites. . . . Keep the big wild hogs out of my path. Don't let none of those come running my direction. I got a long way." Under her small black-freckled hand her cane, limber as a buggy whip, would switch at the brush as if to rouse up any hiding things.

On she went. The woods were deep and still. The sun made the pine needles almost too bright to look at, up where the wind rocked. The cones dropped as light as feathers. Down in the hollow was the mourning dove—it was not too late for him.

The path ran up a hill. "Seem like there is chains about my feet, time I get this far," she said, in the voice of argument old people keep to use with themselves. "Something always take a hold of me on this hill—pleads I should stay."

After she got to the top she turned and gave a full, severe look behind her where she had come. "Up through pines," she said at length. "Now down through oaks."

Her eyes opened their widest, and she started down gently. But before she got to the bottom of the hill a bush caught her dress.

Her fingers were busy and intent, but her skirts were full and long, so that before she could pull them free in one place they were caught in another. It was not possible to allow the dress to tear. "I in the thorny bush," she said. "Thorns, you doing your appointed work. Never want to let folks pass, no sir. Old eyes thought you was a pretty little *green* bush."

Finally, trembling all over, she stood free, and after a moment dared to stoop for her cane.

"Sun so high!" she cried, leaning back and looking, while the thick tears went over her eyes. "The time getting all gone here."

At the foot of this hill was a place where a log was laid across the creek.

"Now comes the trial," said Phoenix.

Putting her right foot out, she mounted the log and shut her eyes. Lifting her skirt, leveling her cane fiercely before her, like a festival figure in some parade, she began to march across. Then she opened her eyes and she was safe on the other side.

"I wasn't as old as I thought," she said.

But she sat down to rest. She spread her skirts on the bank around her and folded her hands over her knees. Up above her was a tree in a pearly cloud of mistletoe. She did not dare to close her eyes, and when a little boy brought her a plate with a slice of marble-cake on it she spoke to him. "That would be acceptable," she said. But when she went to take it there was just her own hand in the air.

So she left that tree, and had to go through a barbed-wire fence. There she had to creep and crawl, spreading her knees and stretching her fingers like a baby trying to climb the steps. But she talked loudly to herself: she could not let her dress be torn now, so late in the day, and she could not pay for having her arm or her leg sawed off if she got caught fast where she was.

At last she was safe through the fence and risen up out in the clearing. Big dead trees, like black men with one arm, were standing in the purple stalks of the withered cotton field. There sat a buzzard.

"Who you watching?"

In the furrow she made her way along.

"Glad this not the season for bulls," she said, looking sideways, "and the good Lord made his snakes to curl up and sleep in the winter. A pleasure I don't see no two-headed snake coming around that tree, where it come once. It took a while to get by him, back in the summer."

She passed through the old cotton and went into a field of dead corn. It whispered and shook and was taller than her head. "Through the maze now," she said, for there was no path.

Then there was something tall, black, and skinny there, moving before her.

At first she took it for a man. It could have been a man dancing in the field. But she stood still and listened, and it did not make a sound. It was as silent as a ghost.

"Ghost," she said sharply, "who be you the ghost of? For I have heard of nary death close by."

But there was no answer—only the ragged dancing in the wind.

She shut her eyes, reached out her hand, and touched a sleeve. She found a coat and inside that an emptiness, cold as ice.

"You scarecrow," she said. Her face lighted. "I ought to be shut up for good," she said with laughter. "My senses is gone. I too old. I the oldest people I ever know. Dance, old scarecrow," she said, "while I dancing with you."

She kicked her foot over the furrow, and with mouth drawn

down, shook her head once or twice in a little strutting way. Some husks blew down and whirled in streamers about her skirts.

Then she went on, parting her way from side to side with the cane, through the whispering field. At last she came to the end, to a wagon track where the silver grass blew between the red ruts. The quail were walking around like pullets, seeming all dainty and unseen.

"Walk pretty," she said. "This the easy place. This the easy going."

She followed the track, swaying through the quiet bare fields, through the little strings of trees silver in their dead leaves, past cabins silver from weather, with the doors and windows boarded shut, all like old women under a spell sitting there. "I walking in their sleep," she said, nodding her head vigorously.

In a ravine she went where a spring was silently flowing through a hollow log. Old Phoenix bent and drank. "Sweet-gum makes the water sweet," she said, and drank more. "Nobody know who made this well, for it was here when I was born."

The track crossed a swampy part where the moss hung as white as lace from every limb. "Sleep on, alligators, and blow your bubbles." Then the track went into the road.

Deep, deep the road went down between the high green-colored banks. Overhead the live-oaks met, and it was as dark as a cave.

A black dog with a lolling tongue came up out of the weeds by the ditch. She was meditating, and not ready, and when he came at her she only hit him a little with her cane. Over she went in the ditch, like a little puff of milkweed.

Down there, her senses drifted away. A dream visited her, and she reached her hand up, but nothing reached down and gave her a pull. So she lay there and presently went to talking. "Old woman," she said to herself, "that black dog come up out of the weeds to stall you off, and now there he sitting on his fine tail, smiling at you."

A white man finally came along and found her—a hunter, a young man, with his dog on a chain.

"Well, Granny!" he laughed. "What are you doing there?"

"Lying on my back like a June-bug waiting to be turned over, mister," she said, reaching up her hand.

He lifted her up, gave her a swing in the air, and set her down. "Anything broken, Granny?"

"No sir, them old dead weeds is springy enough," said Phoenix, when she had got her breath. "I thank you for your trouble."

"Where do you live, Granny?" he asked, while the two dogs were growling at each other.

"Away back yonder, sir, behind the ridge. You can't even see it from here."

"On your way home?"

"No sir, I going to town."

"Why, that's too far! That's as far as I walk when I come out myself, and I get something for my trouble." He patted the stuffed bag he carried, and there hung down a little closed claw. It was one of the bobwhites, with its beak hooked bitterly to show it was dead. "Now you go on home, Granny!"

"I bound to go to town, mister," said Phoenix. "The time come around."

He gave another laugh, filling the whole landscape. "I know you old colored people! Wouldn't miss going to town to see Santa Claus!"

But something held old Phoenix very still. The deep lines in her face went into a fierce and different radiation. Without warning, she had seen with her own eyes a flashing nickel fall out of the man's pocket onto the ground.

"How old are you, Granny?" he was saying.

"There is no telling, mister," she said, "no telling."

Then she gave a little cry and clapped her hands and said, "Git on away from here, dog! Look! Look at that dog!" She laughed as if in admiration. "He ain't scared of nobody. He a big black dog." She whispered, "Sic him!"

"Watch me get rid of that cur," said the man. "Sic him, Pete! Sic him!"

Phoenix heard the dogs fighting, and heard the man running and throwing sticks. She even heard a gunshot. But she was slowly bending forward by that time, further and further forward, the lid stretched down over her eyes, as if she were doing this in her sleep. Her chin was lowered almost to her knees. The yellow palm of her hand came out from the fold of her apron. Her fingers slid down and along the ground under the piece of money with the grace and care they would have in lifting an egg from under a setting hen. Then she slowly straightened up, she stood erect, and the nickel was in her apron pocket. A bird flew by. Her lips moved. "God watching me the whole time. I come to stealing."

The man came back, and his own dog panted about them. "Well, I scared him off that time," he said, and then he laughed and lifted his gun and pointed it at Phoenix.

She stood straight and faced him.

"Doesn't the gun scare you?" he said, still pointing it.

"No, sir, I seen plenty go off closer by, in my day, and for less than what I done," she said, holding utterly still.

He smiled, and shouldered the gun. "Well, Granny," he said, "you must be a hundred years old, and scared of nothing. I'd give you a dime if I had any money with me. But you take my advice and stay home, and nothing will happen to you."

"I bound to go on my way, mister," said Phoenix. She inclined her head in the red rag. Then they went in different directions, but she could hear the gun shooting again and again over the hill.

She walked on. The shadows hung from the oak trees to the road like curtains. Then she smelled wood-smoke, and smelled the river, and she saw a steeple and the cabins on their steep steps. Dozens of little black children whirled around her. There ahead was Natchez shining. Bells were ringing. She walked on.

In the paved city it was Christmas time. There were red and green electric lights strung and crisscrossed everywhere, and all turned on in the daytime. Old Phoenix would have been lost if she had not distrusted her eyesight and depended on her feet to know where to take her.

She paused quietly on the sidewalk where people were passing by. A lady came along in the crowd, carrying an armful of red-, green-, and silver-wrapped presents; she gave off perfume like the red roses in hot summer, and Phoenix stopped her.

"Please, missy, will you lace up my shoe?" She held up her foot.

"What do you want, Grandma?"

"See my shoe," said Phoenix. "Do all right for out in the country, but wouldn't look right to go in a big building."

"Stand still then, Grandma," said the lady. She put her packages down on the sidewalk beside her and laced and tied both shoes tightly.

"Can't lace 'em with a cane," said Phoenix. "Thank you, missy.

I doesn't mind asking a nice lady to tie up my shoe, when I gets out on the street."

Moving slowly and from side to side, she went into the big building, and into a tower of steps, where she walked up and around and around until her feet knew to stop.

She entered a door, and there she saw nailed up on the wall the document that had been stamped with the gold seal and framed in the gold frame, which matched the dream that was hung up in her head.

"Here I be," she said. There was a fixed and ceremonial stiffness over her body.

"A charity case, I suppose," said an attendant who sat at the desk before her.

But Phoenix only looked above her head. There was sweat on her face, the wrinkles in her skin shone like a bright net.

"Speak up, Grandma," the woman said. "What's your name? We must have your history, you know. Have you been here before? What seems to be the trouble with you?"

Old Phoenix only gave a twitch to her face as if a fly were bothering her.

"Are you deaf?" cried the attendant.

But then the nurse came in.

"Oh, that's just old Aunt Phoenix," she said. "She doesn't come for herself—she has a little grandson. She makes these trips just as regular as clockwork. She lives away back off the Old Natchez Trace." She bent down. "Well, Aunt Phoenix, why don't you just take a seat? We won't keep you standing after your long trip." She pointed.

The old woman sat down, bolt upright in the chair.

"Now, how is the boy?" asked the nurse.

Old Phoenix did not speak.

"I said, how is the boy?"

But Phoenix only waited and stared straight ahead, her face very solemn and withdrawn into rigidity.

"Is his throat any better?" asked the nurse. "Aunt Phoenix, don't you hear me? Is your grandson's throat any better since the last time you came for the medicine?"

With her hands on her knees, the old woman waited, silent, erect and motionless, just as if she were in armor.

"You mustn't take up our time this way, Aunt Phoenix," the

nurse said. "Tell us quickly about your grandson, and get it over. He isn't dead, is he?"

At last there came a flicker and then a flame of comprehension across her face, and she spoke.

"My grandson. It was my memory had left me. There I sat and forgot why I made my long trip."

"Forgot?" The nurse frowned. "After you came so far?"

Then Phoenix was ⎡like an old woman begging a dignified forgiveness for waking up frightened in the night.⎤ "I never did go to school, I was too old at the Surrender," she said in a soft voice. "I'm an old woman without an education. It was my memory fail me. My little grandson, he is just the same, and I forgot it in the coming."

"Throat never heals, does it?" said the nurse, speaking in a loud, sure voice to old Phoenix. By now she had a card with something written on it, a little list. "Yes. Swallowed lye. When was it?—January—two, three years ago—"

Phoenix spoke unasked now. "No, missy, he not dead, he just the same. Every little while his throat begin to close up again, and he not able to swallow. He not get his breath. He not able to help himself. So the time come around, and I go on another trip for the soothing medicine."

"All right. The doctor said as long as you came to get it, you could have it," said the nurse. "But it's an obstinate case."

"My little grandson, he sit up there in the house all wrapped up, waiting by himself," Phoenix went on. "We is the only two left in the world. He suffer and it don't seem to put him back at all. He got a sweet look. He going to last. He wear a little patch quilt and peep out holding his mouth open like a little bird. I remembers so plain now. I not going to forget him again, no, the whole enduring time. I could tell him from all the others in creation."

"All right." The nurse was trying to hush her now. She brought her a bottle of medicine. "Charity," she said, making a check mark in a book.

Old Phoenix held the bottle close to her eyes, and then carefully put it into her pocket.

"I thank you," she said.

"It's Christmas time, Grandma," said the attendant. "Could I give you a few pennies out of my purse?"

"Five pennies is a nickel," said Phoenix stiffly.

"Here's a nickel," said the attendant.

Phoenix rose carefully and held out her hand. She received the nickel and then fished the other nickel out of her pocket and laid it beside the new one. She stared at her palm closely, with her head on one side.

Then she gave a tap with her cane on the floor.

"This is what come to me to do," she said. "I going to the store and buy my child a little windmill they sells, made out of paper. He going to find it hard to believe there such a thing in the world. I'll march myself back where he waiting, holding it straight up in this hand."

She lifted her free hand, gave a little nod, turned around, and walked out of the doctor's office. Then her slow step began on the stairs, going down.

# John Cheever [1912–1982]

# The Swimmer

It was one of those midsummer Sundays when everyone sits around saying, "I *drank* too much last night." You might have heard it whispered by the parishioners leaving church, heard it from the lips of the priest himself, struggling with his cassock in the *vestiarium*,[1] heard it from the golf links and the tennis courts, heard it from the wild-life preserve where the leader of the Audubon group was suffering from a terrible hangover. "I *drank* too much," said Donald Westerhazy. "We all *drank* too much," said Lucinda Merrill. "It must have been the wine," said Helen Westerhazy. "I *drank* too much of that claret."

This was the edge of the Westerhazys' pool. The pool, fed by an artesian well with a high iron content, was a pale shade of

---

[1] Robing room.

green. It was a fine day. In the west there was a massive stand of cumulus cloud so like a city seen from a distance—from the bow of an approaching ship—that it might have had a name. Lisbon. Hackensack. The sun was hot. Neddy Merrill sat by the green water, one hand in it, one around a glass of gin. He was a slender man—he seemed to have the especial slenderness of youth—and while he was far from young he had slid down his banister that morning and given the bronze backside of Aphrodite[2] on the hall table a smack, as he jogged toward the smell of coffee in his dining room. He might have been compared to a summer's day, particularly the last hours of one, and while he lacked a tennis racket or a sail bag the impression was definitely one of youth, sport, and clement weather. He had been swimming and now he was breathing deeply, stertorously as if he could gulp into his lungs the components of that moment, the heat of the sun, the intenseness of his pleasure. It all seemed to flow into his chest. His own house stood in Bullet Park, eight miles to the south, where his four beautiful daughters would have had their lunch and might be playing tennis. Then it occurred to him that by taking a dogleg to the southwest he could reach his home by water.

His life was not confining and the delight he took in this observation could not be explained by its suggestion of escape. He seemed to see, with a cartographer's eye, that string of swimming pools, that quasi-subterranean stream that curved across the county. He had made a discovery, a contribution to modern geography; he would name the stream Lucinda after his wife. He was not a practical joker nor was he a fool but he was determinedly original and had a vague and modest idea of himself as a legendary figure. The day was beautiful and it seemed to him that a long swim might enlarge and celebrate its beauty.

He took off a sweater that was hung over his shoulders and dove in. He had an inexplicable contempt for men who did not hurl themselves into pools. He swam a choppy crawl, breathing either with every stroke or every fourth stroke and counting somewhere well in the back of his mind the one-two one-two of a flutter kick. It was not a serviceable stroke for long distances but the domestication of swimming had saddled the sport with some cus-

---

[2] The Greek goddess of love.

toms and in his part of the world a crawl was customary. To be embraced and sustained by the light green water was less a pleasure, it seemed, than the resumption of a natural condition, and he would have liked to swim without trunks, but this was not possible, considering his project. He hoisted himself up on the far curb—he never used the ladder—and started across the lawn. When Lucinda asked where he was going he said he was going to swim home.

The only maps and charts he had to go by were remembered or imaginary but these were clear enough. First there were the Grahams, the Hammers, the Lears, the Howlands, and the Crosscups. He would cross Ditmar Street to the Bunkers and come, after a short portage, to the Levys, the Welchers, and the public pool in Lancaster. Then there were the Hallorans, the Sachses, the Biswangers, Shirley Adams, the Gilmartins, and the Clydes. The day was lovely, and that he lived in a world so generously supplied with water seemed like a clemency, a beneficence. His heart was high and he ran across the grass. Making his way home by an uncommon route gave him the feeling that he was a pilgrim, an explorer, a man with a destiny, and he knew that he would find friends all along the way; friends would line the banks of the Lucinda River.

He went through a hedge that separated the Westerhazys' land from the Grahams', walked under some flowering apple trees, passed the shed that housed their pump and filter, and came out at the Grahams' pool. "Why, Neddy," Mrs. Graham said, "what a marvelous surprise. I've been trying to get you on the phone all morning. Here, let me get you a drink." He saw then, like any explorer, that the hospitable customs and traditions of the natives would have to be handled with diplomacy if he was ever going to reach his destination. He did not want to mystify or seem rude to the Grahams nor did he have the time to linger there. He swam the length of their pool and joined them in the sun and was rescued, a few minutes later, by the arrival of two carloads of friends from Connecticut. During the uproarious reunions he was able to slip away. He went down by the front of the Grahams' house, stepped over a thorny hedge, and crossed a vacant lot to the Hammers'. Mrs. Hammer, looking up from her roses, saw him swim by although she wasn't quite sure who it was. The Lears heard him splashing past the open windows of their living room.

The Howlands and the Crosscups were away. After leaving the Howlands' he crossed Ditmar Street and started for the Bunkers', where he could hear, even at that distance, the noise of a party.

The water refracted the sound of voices and laughter and seemed to suspend it in midair. The Bunkers' pool was on a rise and he climbed some stairs to a terrace where twenty-five or thirty men and women were drinking. The only person in the water was Rusty Towers, who floated there on a rubber raft. Oh, how bonny and lush were the banks of the Lucinda River! Prosperous men and women gathered by the sapphire-colored waters while caterer's men in white coats passed them cold gin. Overhead a red de Haviland trainer was circling around and around and around in the sky with something like the glee of a child in a swing. Ned felt a passing affection for the scene, a tenderness for the gathering, as if it was something he might touch. In the distance he heard thunder. As soon as Enid Bunker saw him she began to scream: "Oh, look who's here! What a marvelous surprise! When Lucinda said you couldn't come I thought I'd *die*." She made her way to him through the crowd, and when they had finished kissing she led him to the bar, a progress that was slowed by the fact that he stopped to kiss eight or ten other women and shake the hands of as many men. A smiling bartender he had seen at a hundred parties gave him a gin and tonic and he stood by the bar for a moment, anxious not to get stuck in any conversation that would delay his voyage. When he seemed about to be surrounded he dove in and swam close to the side to avoid colliding with Rusty's raft. At the far end of the pool he bypassed the Tomlinsons with a broad smile and jogged up the garden path. The gravel cut his feet but this was only unpleasantness. The party was confined to the pool, and as he went toward the house he heard the brilliant, watery sound of voices fade, heard the noise of a radio from the Bunkers' kitchen, where someone was listening to a ball game. Sunday afternoon. He made his way through the parked cars and down the grassy border of their driveway to Alewives Lane. He did not want to be seen on the road in his bathing trunks but there was no traffic and he made the short distance to the Levys' driveway, marked with a PRIVATE PROPERTY sign and a green tube for *The New York Times*. All the doors and windows of the big house were open but there were no signs of life; not even a dog barked. He went around the side of the house to the pool and saw that the Levys had only recently left. Glasses and bottles and dishes of nuts were on a table at the deep end, where there was a bathhouse or gazebo, hung with Japanese lanterns. After swimming the pool he got himself a glass and poured a drink. It was his fourth or fifth drink and he had swum nearly half the length of the Lucinda River. He felt tired, clean, and pleased at that moment to be alone; pleased with everything.

It would storm. The stand of cumulus cloud—that city—had risen and darkened, and while he sat there he heard the percussiveness of thunder again. The de Haviland trainer was still circling overhead and it seemed to Ned that he could almost hear the pilot laugh with pleasure in the afternoon; but when there was another peal of thunder he took off for home. A train whistle blew and he wondered what time it had gotten to be. Four? Five? He thought of the provincial station at that hour, where a waiter, his tuxedo concealed by a raincoat, a dwarf with some flowers wrapped in newspaper, and a woman who had been crying would be waiting for the local. It was suddenly growing dark; it was that moment when the pin-headed birds seemed to organize their song into some acute and knowledgeable recognition of the storm's approach. Then there was a fine noise of rushing water from the crown of an oak at his back, as if a spigot there had been turned. Then the noise of fountains came from the crowns of all the tall trees. Why did he love storms, what was the meaning of his excitement when the door sprang open and the rain wind fled rudely up the stairs, why had the simple task of shutting the windows of an old house seemed fitting and urgent, why did the first watery notes of a storm wind have for him the unmistakable sound of good news, cheer, glad tidings? Then there was an explosion, a smell of cordite, and rain lashed the Japanese lanterns that Mrs. Levy had bought in Kyoto the year before last, or was it the year before that?

He stayed in the Levys' gazebo until the storm had passed. The rain had cooled the air and he shivered. The force of the wind had stripped a maple of its red and yellow leaves and scattered them over the grass and the water. Since it was midsummer the tree must be blighted, and yet he felt a peculiar sadness at this sign of autumn. He braced his shoulders, emptied his glass, and started for the Welchers' pool. This meant crossing the Lindleys' riding ring and he was surprised to find it overgrown with grass and all the jumps dismantled. He wondered if the Lindleys had sold their horses or gone away for the summer and put them out to board. He seemed to remember having heard something about the Lindleys and their horses but the memory was unclear. On he went, barefoot through the wet grass, to the Welchers', where he found their pool was dry.

This breach in his chain of water disappointed him absurdly, and he felt like some explorer who seeks a torrential headwater and finds a dead stream. He was disappointed and mystified. It was common enough to go away for the summer but no one ever drained his pool. The Welchers had definitely gone away. The pool furniture was folded, stacked, and covered with a tarpaulin. The bathhouse was locked. All the windows of the house were shut, and when he went around to the driveway in front he saw a FOR SALE sign nailed to a tree. When had he last heard from the Welchers—when, that is, had he and Lucinda last regretted an invitation to dine with them? It seemed only a week or so ago. Was his memory failing or had he so disciplined it in the repression of unpleasant facts that he had damaged his sense of the truth? Then in the distance he heard the sound of a tennis game. This cheered him, cleared away all his apprehensions and let him regard the overcast sky and the cold air with indifference. This was the day that Neddy Merrill swam across the county. That was the day! He started off then for his most difficult portage.

Had you gone for a Sunday afternoon ride that day you might have seen him, close to naked, standing on the shoulders of Route 424, waiting for a chance to cross. You might have wondered if he was the victim of foul play, had his car broken down, or was he merely a fool. Standing barefoot in the deposits of the highway—beer cans, rags, and blowout patches—exposed to all kinds of ridicule, he seemed pitiful. He had known when he started that this was a part of his journey—it had been on his maps—but confronted with the lines of traffic, worming through the summery light, he found himself unprepared. He was laughed at, jeered at, a beer can was thrown at him, and he had no dignity or humor to bring to the situation. He could have gone back, back to the Westerhazys', where Lucinda would still be sitting in the sun. He had signed nothing, vowed nothing, pledged nothing, not even to himself. Why, believing as he did, that all human obduracy was susceptible to common sense, was he unable to turn back? Why was he determined to complete his journey even if it meant putting his life in danger? At what point had this prank, this joke, this piece of horseplay become serious? He could not go back, he could not even recall with any clearness the green water at the Wester-hazys', the sense of inhaling the day's components, the friendly and relaxed voices saying that they had *drunk* too much. In the space of an hour, more or less, he had covered a distance that made his return impossible.

An old man, tooling down the highway at fifteen miles an hour, let him get to the middle of the road, where there was a grass divider. Here he was exposed to the ridicule of the north-bound traffic, but after ten or fifteen minutes he was able to cross. From here he had only a short walk to the Recreation Center at the edge of the village of Lancaster, where there were some hand-ball courts and a public pool.

The effect of the water on voices, the illusion of brilliance and suspense, was the same here as it had been at the Bunkers' but the sounds here were louder, harsher, and more shrill, and as soon as he entered the crowded enclosure he was confronted with regimentation. "ALL SWIMMERS MUST TAKE A SHOWER BEFORE USING THE POOL. ALL SWIMMERS MUST USE THE FOOTBATH. ALL SWIMMERS MUST WEAR THEIR IDENTIFICATION DISKS." He took a shower, washed his feet in a cloudy and bitter solution, and made his way to the edge of the water. It stank of chlorine and looked to him like a sink. A pair of lifeguards in a pair of towers blew police whistles at what seemed to be regular intervals and abused the swimmers through a public address system. Neddy remembered the sapphire water at the Bunkers' with longing and thought that he might contaminate himself—damage his own prosperousness and charm—by swimming in this murk, but he reminded himself that he was an explorer, a pilgrim, and that this was merely a stagnant bend in the Lucinda River. He dove, scowling with dis-taste, into the chlorine and had to swim with his head above water to avoid collisions, but even so he was bumped into, splashed, and jostled. When he got to the shallow end both lifeguards were shouting at him: "Hey, you, you without the identification disk, get outa the water." He did, but they had no way of pursuing him and he went through the reek of suntan oil and chlorine out through the hurricane fence and passed the handball courts. By crossing the road he entered the wooded part of the Halloran estate. The woods were not cleared and the footing was treacherous and difficult until he reached the lawn and the clipped beech hedge that encircled their pool.

The Hallorans were friends, an elderly couple of enormous wealth who seemed to bask in the suspicion that they might be Communists. They were zealous reformers but they were not Communists, and yet when they were accused, as they sometimes were, of subversion, it seemed to gratify and excite them. Their beech hedge was yellow and he guessed this had been blighted like the Levys' maple. He called hullo, hullo, to warn the Hallorans of his approach, to palliate his invasion of their privacy. The Hallorans, for reasons that had never been explained to him, did not wear bathing suits. No explanations were in order, really. Their nakedness was a detail in their uncompromising zeal for reform and he stepped politely out of his trunks before he went through the opening in the hedge.

Mrs. Halloran, a stout woman with white hair and a serene face, was reading the *Times*. Mr. Halloran was taking beech leaves out of the water with a scoop. They seemed not surprised or displeased to see him. Their pool was perhaps the oldest in the country, a fieldstone rectangle, fed by a brook. It had no filter or pump and its waters were the opaque gold of the stream.

"I'm swimming across the county," Ned said.

"Why, I didn't know one could," exclaimed Mrs. Halloran.

"Well, I've made it from the Westerhazys'," Ned said. "That must be about four miles."

He left his trunks at the deep end, walked to the shallow end, and swam this stretch. As he was pulling himself out of the water he heard Mrs. Halloran say, "We've been *terribly* sorry to hear about all your misfortunes, Neddy."

"My misfortunes?" Ned asked. "I don't know what you mean."

"Why we heard that you'd sold the house and that your poor children. . . ."

"I don't recall having sold the house," Ned said, "and the girls are at home."

"Yes," Mrs. Halloran sighed. "Yes. . . ." Her voice filled the air with an unseasonable melancholy and Ned spoke briskly. "Thank you for the swim."

"Well, have a nice trip," said Mrs. Halloran.

Beyond the hedge he pulled on his trunks and fastened them. They were loose and he wondered if, during the space of an afternoon, he could have lost some weight. He was cold and he was tired and the naked Hallorans and their dark water had depressed him. The swim was too much for his strength but how could he have guessed this, sliding down the banister that morning and sitting in the Westerhazys' sun? His arms were lame. His legs felt rubbery and ached at the joints. The worst of it was the cold in his bones and the feeling that he might never be warm again. Leaves were falling down around him and he smelled wood smoke on the wind. Who would be burning wood at this time of the year?

He needed a drink. Whiskey would warm him, pick him up, carry him through the last of his journey, refresh his feeling that it was original and valorous to swim across the county. Channel swimmers took brandy. He needed a stimulant. He crossed the lawn in front of the Hallorans' house and went down a little path to where they had built a house for their only daughter, Helen, and her husband, Eric Sachs. The Sachses' pool was small and he found Helen and her husband there.

"Oh, *Neddy,*" Helen said. "Did you lunch at Mother's?"

"Not *really,*" Ned said. "I *did* stop to see your parents." This seemed to be explanation enough. "I'm terribly sorry to break in on you like this but I've taken a chill and I wonder if you'd give me a drink."

"Why, I'd *love* to," Helen said, "but there hasn't been anything in this house to drink since Eric's operation. That was three years ago."

Was he losing his memory, had his gift for concealing painful facts let him forget that he had sold his house, that his children were in trouble, and that his friend had been ill? His eyes slipped from Eric's face to his abdomen, where he saw three pale, sutured scars, two of them at least a foot long. Gone was his navel, and what, Neddy thought, would the roving hand, bed-checking one's gifts at 3 A.M., make of a belly with no navel, no link to birth, this breach in the succession?

"I'm sure you can get a drink at the Biswangers'," Helen said. "They're having an enormous do. You can hear it from here. Listen!"

She raised her head and from across the road, the lawns, the gardens, the woods, the fields, he heard again the brilliant noise of voices over water. "Well, I'll get wet," he said, still feeling that he had no freedom of choice about his means of travel. He dove into the Sachses' cold water, and gasping, close to drowning, made his way from one end of the pool to the other. "Lucinda and I want *terribly* to see you," he said over his shoulder, his face set toward the Biswangers'. "We're sorry it's been so long and we'll call you *very* soon."

He crossed some fields to the Biswangers' and the sounds of revelry there. They would be honored to give him a drink, they would be happy to give him a drink. The Biswangers invited him and Lucinda for dinner four times a year, six weeks in advance. They were always rebuffed and yet they continued to send out their invitations, unwilling to comprehend the rigid and undemocratic realities of their society. They were the sort of people who discussed the price of things at cocktails, exchanged market tips during dinner, and after dinner told dirty stories to mixed company. They did not belong to Neddy's set—they were not even on Lucinda's Christmas card list. He went toward their pool with feelings of indifference, charity, and some unease, since it seemed to be getting dark and these were the longest days of the year. The party when he joined it was noisy and large. Grace Biswanger was the kind of hostess who asked the optometrist, the veterinarian, the real-estate dealer, and the dentist. No one was swimming and the twilight, reflected on the water of the pool, had a wintry gleam. There was a bar and he started for this. When Grace Biswanger saw him she came toward him, not affectionately as he had every right to expect, but bellicosely.

"Why, this party has everything," she said loudly, "including a gate crasher."

She could not deal him a social blow—there was no question about this and he did not flinch. "As a gate crasher," he asked politely, "do I rate a drink?"

"Suit yourself," she said. "You don't seem to pay much attention to invitations."

She turned her back on him and joined some guests, and he went to the bar and ordered a whiskey. The bartender served him but he served him rudely. His was a world in which the caterer's men kept the social score, and to be rebuffed by a part-time barkeep meant that he had suffered some loss of social esteem. Or perhaps the man was new and uninformed. Then he heard Grace at his back say: "They went for broke overnight—nothing but income—and he showed up drunk one Sunday and asked us to loan him five thousand dollars. . . ." She was always talking about money. It was worse than eating your peas off a knife. He dove into the pool, swam its length, and went away.

The next pool on his list, the last but two, belonged to his old mistress, Shirley Adams. If he had suffered any injuries at the Biswangers' they would be cured here. Love—sexual roughhouse in fact—was the supreme elixir, the pain killer, the brightly colored pill that would put the spring back into his step, the joy of life in his heart. They had had an affair last week, last month, last year. He couldn't remember. It was he who had broken it off, his was the upper hand, and he stepped through the gate of the wall that surrounded her pool with nothing so considered as self-confidence. It seemed in a way to be his pool, as the lover, particularly the illicit lover, enjoys the possessions of his mistress with an authority unknown to holy matrimony. She was there, her hair the color of brass, but her figure, at the edge of the lighted, cerulean water, excited in him no profound memories. It had been, he thought, a lighthearted affair, although she had wept when he broke it off. She seemed confused to see him and he wondered if she was still wounded. Would she, God forbid, weep again?

"What do you want?" she asked.

"I'm swimming across the county."

"Good Christ. Will you ever grow up?"

"What's the matter?"

"If you've come here for money," she said, "I won't give you another cent."

"You could give me a drink."

"I could but I won't. I'm not alone."

"Well, I'm on my way."

He dove in and swam the pool, but when he tried to haul himself up onto the curb he found that the strength in his arms and shoulders had gone, and he paddled to the ladder and climbed out. Looking over his shoulder he saw, in the lighted bathhouse, a young man. Going out onto the dark lawn he smelled chrysanthemums or marigolds—some stubborn autumnal fragrance—on the night air, strong as gas. Looking overhead he saw that the stars had come out, but why should he seem to see Andromeda, Cepheus, and Cassiopeia? What had become of the constellations of midsummer? He began to cry.

It was probably the first time in his adult life that he had ever cried, certainly the first time in his life that he had ever felt so miserable, cold, tired, and bewildered. He could not understand the rudeness of the caterer's barkeep or the rudeness of a mistress who had come to him on her knees and showered his trousers with tears. He had swum too long, he had been immersed too long, and his nose and his throat were sore from the water. What he needed then was a drink, some company, and some clean, dry clothes, and while he could have cut directly across the road to his home he went on to the Gilmartins' pool. Here, for the first time in his life, he did not dive but went down the steps into the icy water and swam a hobbled sidestroke that he might have learned as a youth. He staggered with fatigue on his way to the Clydes' and paddled the length of their pool, stopping again and again with his hand on the curb to rest. He climbed up the ladder and wondered if he had the strength to get home. He had done what he wanted, he had swum the county, but he was so stupefied with exhaustion that his triumph seemed vague. Stooped, holding on to the gateposts for support, he turned up the driveway of his own house.

The place was dark. Was it so late that they had all gone to bed? Had Lucinda stayed at the Westerhazys' for supper? Had the girls joined her there or gone someplace else? Hadn't they agreed, as they usually did on Sunday, to regret all their invitations and stay at home? He tried the garage doors to see what cars were in but the doors were locked and rust came off the handles onto his hands. Going toward the house, he saw the force of the thunderstorm had knocked one of the rain gutters loose. It hung down over the front door like an umbrella rib, but it could be fixed in the morning. The house was locked, and he thought that the stupid cook or the stupid maid must have locked the place up until he remembered that it had been some time since they had employed a maid or a cook. He shouted, pounded on the door, tried to force it with his shoulder, and then, looking in at the windows, saw that the place was empty.

TILLIE OLSEN [b. 1913]

# I Stand Here Ironing

I stand here ironing, and what you asked me moves tormented back and forth with the iron.

"I wish you would manage the time to come in and talk with me about your daughter. I'm sure you can help me understand her. She's a youngster who needs help and whom I'm deeply interested in helping."

"Who needs help." . . . Even if I came, what good would it do? You think because I am her mother I have a key, or that in some way you could use me as a key? She has lived for nineteen years. There is all that life that has happened outside of me, beyond me.

And when is there time to remember, to sift, to weigh, to estimate, to total? I will start and there will be an interruption and I will have to gather it all together again. Or I will become engulfed with all I did or did not do, with what should have been and what cannot be helped.

She was a beautiful baby. The first and only one of our five that was beautiful at birth. You do not guess how new and uneasy her tenancy in her now-loveliness. You did not know her all those years she was thought homely, or see her poring over her baby pictures, making me tell her over and over how beautiful she had been—and would be, I would tell her—and was now, to the seeing eye. But the seeing eyes were few or non-existent. Including mine.

I nursed her. They feel that's important nowadays, I nursed all the children, but with her, with all the fierce rigidity of first motherhood, I did like the books then said. Though her cries battered me to trembling and my breasts ached with swollenness, I waited till the clock decreed.

Why do I put that first? I do not even know if it matters, or if it explains anything.

She was a beautiful baby. She blew shining bubbles of sound. She loved motion, loved light, loved color and music and textures. She would lie on the floor in her blue overalls patting the surface so hard in ecstasy her hands and feet would blur. She was a miracle

to me, but when she was eight months old I had to leave her
daytimes with the woman downstairs to whom she was no miracle
at all, for I worked or looked for work and for Emily's father, who
"could no longer endure" (he wrote in his good-bye note) "sharing
want with us."

I was nineteen. It was the pre-relief, pre-WPA world of the depression. I would start running as soon as I got off the streetcar,
running up the stairs, the place smelling sour, and awake or asleep
to startle awake, when she saw me she would break into a clogged
weeping that could not be comforted, a weeping I can hear yet.

After a while I found a job hashing at night so I could be with
her days, and it was better. But it came to where I had to bring
her to his family and leave her.

It took a long time to raise the money for her fare back. Then
she got chicken pox and I had to wait longer. When she finally
came, I hardly knew her, walking quick and nervous like her
father, looking like her father, thin, and dressed in a shoddy red
that yellowed her skin and glared at the pockmarks. All the baby
loveliness gone.

She was two. Old enough for nursery school they said, and I
did not know then what I know now—the fatigue of the long day,
and the lacerations of group life in the kinds of nurseries that are
only parking places for children.

Except that it would have made no difference if I had known.
It was the only place there was. It was the only way we could be
together, the only way I could hold a job.

And even without knowing, I knew. I knew the teacher that
was evil because all these years it has curdled into my memory,
the little boy hunched in the corner, her rasp, "why aren't you
outside, because Alvin hits you? that's no reason, go out, scaredy."
I knew Emily hated it even if she did not clutch and implore "don't
go Mommy" like the other children, mornings.

She always had a reason why we should stay home. Momma,
you look sick. Momma, I feel sick. Momma, the teachers aren't
there today, they're sick. Momma, we can't go, there was a
fire there last night. Momma, it's a holiday today, no school, they
told me.

But never a direct protest, never rebellion. I think of our others
in their three-, four-year-oldness—the explosions, the tempers,
the denunciations, the demands—and I feel suddenly ill. I put the

iron down. What in me demanded that goodness in her? And what was the cost, the cost to her of such goodness?

The old man living in the back once said in his gentle way: "You should smile at Emily more when you look at her." What *was* in my face when I looked at her? I loved her. There were all the acts of love.

It was only with the others I remembered what he said, and it was the face of joy, and not of care or tightness or worry I turned to them—too late for Emily. She does not smile easily, let alone almost always as her brothers and sisters do. Her face is closed and sombre, but when she wants, how fluid. You must have seen it in her pantomimes, you spoke of her rare gift for comedy on the stage that rouses a laughter out of the audience so dear they applaud and applaud and do not want to let her go.

Where does it come from, that comedy? There was none of it in her when she came back to me that second time, after I had to send her away again. She had a new daddy now to learn to love, and I think perhaps it was a better time.

Except when we left her alone nights, telling ourselves she was old enough.

"Can't you go some other time, Mommy, like tomorrow?" she would ask. "Will it be just a little while you'll be gone? Do you promise?"

The time we came back, the front door open, the clock on the floor in the hall. She rigid awake. "It wasn't just a little while. I didn't cry. Three times I called you, just three times, and then I ran downstairs to open the door so you could come faster. The clock talked loud. I threw it away, it scared me what it talked."

She said the clock talked loud again that night I went to the hospital to have Susan. She was delirious with the fever that comes before red measles, but she was fully conscious all the week I was gone and the week after we were home when she could not come near the new baby or me.

She did not get well. She stayed skeleton thin, not wanting to eat, and night after night she had nightmares. She would call for me, and I would rouse from exhaustion to sleepily call back: "You're all right, darling, go to sleep, it's just a dream," and if she still called, in a sterner voice, "now go to sleep, Emily, there's nothing to hurt you." Twice, only twice, when I had to get up for Susan anyhow, I went in to sit with her.

Now when it is too late (as if she would let me hold and

comfort her like I do the others) I get up and go to her at once at her moan or restless stirring. "Are you awake, Emily? Can I get you something?" And the answer is always the same: "No, I'm all right, go back to sleep, Mother."

They persuaded me at the clinic to send her away to a convalescent home in the country where "she can have the kind of food and care you can't manage for her, and you'll be free to concentrate on the new baby." They still send children to that place. I see pictures on the society page of sleek young women planning affairs to raise money for it, or dancing at the affairs, or decorating Easter eggs or filling Christmas stockings for the children.

They never have a picture of the children so I do not know if the girls still wear those gigantic red bows and the ravaged looks on the every other Sunday when parents can come to visit "unless otherwise notified"—as we were notified the first six weeks.

Oh it is a handsome place, green lawns and tall trees and fluted flower beds. High up on the balconies of each cottage the children stand, the girls in their red bows and white dresses, the boys in white suits and giant red ties. The parents stand below shrieking up to be heard and the children shriek down to be heard, and between them the invisible wall "Not To Be Contaminated by Parental Germs or Physical Affection."

There was a tiny girl who always stood hand in hand with Emily. Her parents never came. One visit she was gone. "They moved her to Rose Cottage," Emily shouted in explanation. "They don't like you to love anybody here."

She wrote once a week, the labored writing of a seven-year-old. "I am fine. How is the baby. If I write my leter nicly I will have a star. Love." There never was a star. We wrote every other day, letters she could never hold or keep but only hear read— once. "We simply do not have room for children to keep any personal possessions," they patiently explained when we pieced one Sunday's shrieking together to plead how much it would mean to Emily, who loved so to keep things, to be allowed to keep her letters and cards.

Each visit she looked frailer. "She isn't eating," they told us.

(They had runny eggs for breakfast or mush with lumps, Emily said later, I'd hold it in my mouth and not swallow. Nothing ever tasted good, just when they had chicken.)

It took us eight months to get her released home, and only

the fact that she gained back so little of her seven lost pounds convinced the social worker.

I used to try to hold and love her after she came back, but her body would stay stiff, and after a while she'd push away. She ate little. Food sickened her, and I think much of life too. Oh she had physical lightness and brightness, twinkling by on skates, bouncing like a ball up and down up and down over the jump rope, skimming over the hill; but these were momentary.

She fretted about her appearance, thin and dark and foreign-looking at a time when every little girl was supposed to look or thought she should look a chubby blonde replica of Shirley Temple. The doorbell sometimes rang for her, but no one seemed to come and play in the house or be a best friend. Maybe because we moved so much.

There was a boy she loved painfully through two school semesters. Months later she told me how she had taken pennies from my purse to buy him candy. "Licorice was his favorite and I brought him some every day, but he still liked Jennifer better'n me. Why, Mommy?" The kind of question for which there is no answer.

School was a worry to her. She was not glib or quick in a world where glibness and quickness were easily confused with ability to learn. To her overworked and exasperated teachers she was an overconscientious "slow learner" who kept trying to catch up and was absent entirely too often.

I let her be absent, though sometimes the illness was imaginary. How different from my now-strictness about attendance with the others. I wasn't working. We had a new baby. I was home anyhow. Sometimes, after Susan grew old enough, I would keep her home from school, too, to have them all together.

Mostly Emily had asthma, and her breathing, harsh and labored, would fill the house with a curiously tranquil sound. I would bring the two old dresser mirrors and her boxes of collections to her bed. She would select beads and single earrings, bottle tops and shells, dried flowers and pebbles, old postcards and scraps, all sorts of oddments; then she and Susan would play Kingdom, setting up landscapes and furniture, peopling them with action.

Those were the only times of peaceful companionship between her and Susan. I have edged away from it, that poisonous feeling between them, that terrible balancing of hurts and needs I had to do between the two, and did so badly, those earlier years.

Oh there are conflicts between the others too, each one human, needing, demanding, hurting, taking—but only between Emily and Susan, no, Emily toward Susan that corroding resentment. It seems so obvious on the surface, yet it is not obvious. Susan, the second child, Susan, golden- and curly-haired and chubby, quick and articulate and assured, everything in appearance and manner Emily was not; Susan, not able to resist Emily's precious things, losing or sometimes clumsily breaking them; Susan telling jokes and riddles to company for applause while Emily sat silent (to say to me later: that was *my* riddle, Mother, I told it to Susan); Susan, who for all the five years' difference in age was just a year behind Emily in developing physically.

I am glad for that slow physical development that widened the difference between her and her contemporaries, though she suffered over it. She was too vulnerable for that terrible world of youthful competition, of preening and parading, of constant measuring of yourself against every other, of envy, "If I had that copper hair," "If I had that skin. . . ." She tormented herself enough about not looking like the others, there was enough of unsureness, the having to be conscious of words before you speak, the constant caring—what are they thinking of me? without having it all magnified by the merciless physical drives.

Ronnie is calling. He is wet and I change him. It is rare there is such a cry now. That time of motherhood is almost behind me when the ear is not one's own but must always be racked and listening for the child cry, the child call. We sit for a while and I hold him, looking out over the city spread in charcoal with its soft aisles of light. *"Shoogily,"* he breathes and curls closer. I carry him back to bed, asleep. *Shoogily*. A funny word, a family word, inherited from Emily, invented by her to say: *comfort*.

In this and other ways she leaves her seal, I say aloud. And startle at my saying it. What do I mean? What did I start to gather together, to try and make coherent? I was at the terrible, growing years. War years. I do not remember them well. I was working, there were four smaller ones now, there was not time for her. She had to help be a mother, and housekeeper, and shopper. She had to set her seal. Mornings of crisis and near hysteria trying to get lunches packed, hair combed, coats and shoes found, everyone to school or Child Care on time, the baby ready for transportation. And always the paper scribbled on by a smaller one, the book looked at by Susan then mislaid, the homework not done. Running out to that huge school where she was one, she was lost, she was a drop; suffering over the unpreparedness, stammering and unsure in her classes.

There was so little time left at night after the kids were bedded down. She would struggle over books, always eating (it was in those years she developed her enormous appetite that is legendary in our family) and I would be ironing, or preparing food for the next day, or writing V-mail to Bill, or tending the baby. Sometimes, to make me laugh, or out of her despair, she would imitate happenings or types at school.

I think I said once: "Why don't you do something like this in the school amateur show?" One morning she phoned me at work, hardly understandable through the weeping: "Mother, I did it. I won, I won; they gave me first prize; they clapped and clapped and wouldn't let me go."

Now suddenly she was Somebody, and as imprisoned in her difference as she had been in anonymity.

She began to be asked to perform at other high schools, even in colleges, then at city and statewide affairs. The first one we went to, I only recognized her that first moment when thin, shy, she almost drowned herself into the curtains. Then: Was this Emily? The control, the command, the convulsing and deadly clowning, the spell, then the roaring, stamping audience, unwilling to let this rare and precious laughter out of their lives.

Afterwards: You ought to do something about her with a gift like that—but without money or knowing how, what does one do? We have left it all to her, and the gift has as often eddied inside, clogged and clotted, as been used and growing.

She is coming. She runs up the stairs two at a time with her light graceful step, and I know she is happy tonight. Whatever it was that occasioned your call did not happen today.

"Aren't you ever going to finish the ironing, Mother? Whistler painted his mother in a rocker. I'd have to paint mine standing over an ironing board." This is one of her communicative nights and she tells me everything and nothing as she fixes herself a plate of food out of the icebox.

She is so lovely. Why did you want me to come in at all? Why were you concerned? She will find her way.

She starts up the stairs to bed. "Don't get me up with the rest in the morning." "But I thought you were having midterms." "Oh, those," she comes back in, kisses me, and says quite lightly, "in a couple of years when we'll all be atom-dead they won't matter a bit."

She has said it before. She *believes* it. But because I have been dredging the past, and all that compounds a human being is so heavy and meaningful in me, I cannot endure it tonight.

I will never total it all. I will never come in to say: She was a child seldom smiled at. Her father left me before she was a year old. I had to work her first six years when there was work, or I sent her home and to his relatives. There were years she had care she hated. She was dark and thin and foreign-looking in a world where the prestige went to blondeness and curly hair and dimples, she was slow where glibness was prized. She was a child of anxious, not proud, love. We were poor and could not afford for her the soil of easy growth. I was a young mother, I was a distracted mother. There were other children pushing up, demanding. Her younger sister seemed all that she was not. There were years she did not want me to touch her. She kept too much in herself, her life was such she had to keep too much in herself. My wisdom came too late. She has much to her and probably little will come of it. She is a child of her age, of depression, of war, of fear.

Let her be. So all that is in her will not bloom—but in how many does it? There is still enough left to live by. Only help her to know—help make it so there is cause for her to know—that she is more than this dress on the ironing board, helpless before the iron.

## RALPH ELLISON [b. 1914]

# King of the Bingo Game

The woman in front of him was eating roasted peanuts that smelled so good that he could barely contain his hunger. He could not even sleep and wished they'd hurry and begin the bingo game. There, on his right, two fellows were drinking wine out of a bottle wrapped in a paper bag, and he could hear soft gurgling in the dark. His stomach gave a low, gnawing growl. "If this was down South," he thought, "all I'd have to do is lean over and say, 'Lady, gimme a few of those peanuts, please ma'm,' and she'd pass me the bag and never think nothing of it." Or he could ask the fellows for a drink in the same way. Folks down South stuck together that way; they didn't even have to know you. But up here it was different. Ask somebody for something, and they'd think you were crazy. Well, I ain't crazy. I'm just broke, 'cause I got no birth certificate to get a job, and Laura 'bout to die 'cause we got no money for a doctor. But I ain't crazy. And yet a pinpoint of doubt was focused in his mind as he glanced toward the screen and saw the hero stealthily entering a dark room and sending the beam of a flashlight along a wall of bookcases. This is where he finds the trapdoor, he remembered. The man would pass abruptly through the wall and find the girl tied to a bed, her legs and arms spread wide, and her clothing torn to rags. He laughed softly to himself. He had seen the picture three times, and this was one of the best scenes.

On his right the fellow whispered wide-eyed to his companion. "Man, look a-yonder!"

"Damn!"

"Wouldn't I like to have her tied up like that . . ."

"Hey! That fool's letting her loose!"

"Aw, man, he loves her."

"Love or no love!"

The man moved impatiently beside him, and he tried to involve himself in the scene. But Laura was on his mind. Tiring quickly of watching the picture he looked back to where the white beam filtered from the projection room above the balcony. It started small and grew large, specks of dust dancing in its white-ness as it reached the screen. It was strange how the beam always landed right on the screen and didn't mess up and fall somewhere else. But they had it all fixed. Everything was fixed. Now suppose when they showed that girl with her dress torn the girl started taking off the rest of her clothes, and when the guy came in he didn't untie her but kept her there and went to taking off his own clothes? *That* would be something to see. If a picture got out of hand like that those guys up there would go nuts. Yeah, and there'd be so many folks in here you couldn't find a seat for nine months! A strange sensation played over his skin. He shuddered. Yesterday he'd seen a bedbug on a woman's neck as they walked out into the bright street. But exploring his thigh through a hole in his pocket he found only goose pimples and old scars.

The bottle gurgled again. He closed his eyes. Now a dreamy music was accompanying the film and train whistles were sound-ing in the distance, and he was a boy again walking along a railroad trestle down South, and seeing the train coming, and running back as fast as he could go, and hearing the whistle blowing, and getting off the trestle to solid ground just in time, with the earth trembling beneath his feet, and feeling relieved as he ran down the cinder-strewn embankment onto the highway, and looking back and seeing with terror that the train had left the track and was following him right down the middle of the street, and all the white people laughing as he ran screaming . . .

"Wake up there, buddy! What the hell do you mean hollering like that! Can't you see we trying to enjoy this here picture?"

He stared at the man with gratitude.

"I'm sorry, old man," he said. "I musta been dreaming."

"Well, here, have a drink. And don't be making no noise like that, damn!"

His hands trembled as he tilted his head. It was not wine, but whiskey. Cold rye whiskey. He took a deep swoller, decided it was better not to take another, and handed the bottle back to its owner.

"Thanks, old man," he said.

Now he felt the cold whiskey breaking a warm path straight through the middle of him, growing hotter and sharper as it moved. He had not eaten all day, and it made him light-headed. The smell of the peanuts stabbed him like a knife, and he got up

and found a seat in the middle aisle. But no sooner did he sit than
he saw a row of intense-faced young girls, and got up again,
thinking, "You chicks musta been Lindy-hopping somewhere."
He found a seat several rows ahead as the lights came on, and he
saw the screen disappear behind a heavy red and gold curtain;
then the curtain rising, and the man with the microphone and a
uniformed attendant coming on the stage.

He felt for his bingo cards, smiling. The guy at the door
wouldn't like it if he knew about his having *five* cards. Well, not
everyone played the bingo game; and even with five cards he
didn't have much of a chance. For Laura, though, he had to have
faith. He studied the cards, each with its different numerals,
punching the free center hole in each and spreading them neatly
across his lap; and when the lights faded he sat slouched in his
seat so that he could look from his cards to the bingo wheel with
but a quick shifting of his eyes.

Ahead, at the end of the darkness, the man with the microphone was pressing a button attached to a long cord and spinning
the bingo wheel and calling out the number each time the wheel
came to rest. And each time the voice rang out his finger raced
over the cards for the number. With five cards he had to move
fast. He became nervous; there were too many cards, and the man
went too fast with his grating voice. Perhaps he should just select
one and throw the others away. But he was afraid. He became
warm. Wonder how much Laura's doctor would cost? Damn that,
watch the cards! And with despair he heard the man call three
in a row which he missed on all five cards. This way he'd never
win . . .

When he saw the row of holes punched across the third card,
he sat paralyzed and heard the man call three more numbers
before he stumbled forward, screaming.

"Bingo! Bingo!"

"Let that fool up there," someone called.

"Get up there, man!"

He stumbled down the aisle and up the steps to the stage into
a light so sharp and bright that for a moment it blinded him, and
he felt that he had moved into the spell of some strange, mysterious power. Yet it was as familiar as the sun, and he knew it was
the perfectly familiar bingo.

The man with the microphone was saying something to the

audience as he held out his card. A cold light flashed from the man's finger as the card left his hand. His knees trembled. The man stepped closer, checking the card against the numbers chalked on the board. Suppose he had made a mistake? The pomade on the man's hair made him feel faint, and he backed away. But the man was checking the card over the microphone now, and he had to stay. He stood tense, listening.

"Under the O, forty-four," the man chanted. "Under the I, seven. Under the G, three. Under the B, ninety-six. Under the N, thirteen!"

His breath came easier as the man smiled at the audience.

"Yessir, ladies and gentlemen, he's one of the chosen people!"

The audience rippled with laughter and applause.

"Step right up to the front of the stage."

He moved slowly forward, wishing that the light was not so bright.

"To win tonight's jackpot of $36.90 the wheel must stop between the double zero, understand?"

He nodded, knowing the ritual from the many days and nights he had watched the winners march across the stage to press the button that controlled the spinning wheel and receive the prizes. And now he followed the instructions as though he'd crossed the slippery stage a million prize-winning times.

The man was making some kind of a joke, and he nodded vacantly. So tense had he become that he felt a sudden desire to cry and shook it away. He felt vaguely that his whole life was determined by the bingo wheel; not only that which would happen now that he was at last before it, but all that had gone before, since his birth, and his mother's birth and the birth of his father. It had always been there, even though he had not been aware of it, handing out the unlucky cards and numbers of his days. The feeling persisted, and he started quickly away. I better get down from here before I make a fool of myself, he thought.

"Here, boy," the man called. "You haven't started yet."

Someone laughed as he went hesitantly back.

"Are you all reet?"

He grinned at the man's jive talk, but no words would come, and he knew it was not a convincing grin. For suddenly he knew that he stood on the slippery brink of some terrible embarrassment.

"Where are you from, boy?" the man asked.

"Down South."

"He's from down South, ladies and gentlemen," the man said. "Where from? Speak right into the mike."

"Rocky Mont," he said. "Rock' Mont, North Car'lina."

"So you decided to come down off that mountain to the U.S.," the man laughed. He felt that the man was making a fool of him, but then something cold was placed in his hand, and the lights were no longer behind him.

Standing before the wheel he felt alone, but that was somehow right, and he remembered his plan. He would give the wheel a short quick twirl. Just a touch of the button. He had watched it many times, and always it came close to double zero when it was short and quick. He steeled himself; the fear had left, and he felt a profound sense of promise, as though he were about to be repaid for all the things he'd suffered all his life. Trembling, he pressed the button. There was a whirl of lights, and in a second he realized with finality that though he wanted to, he could not stop. It was as though he held a high-powered line in his naked hand. His nerves tightened. As the wheel increased its speed it seemed to draw him more and more into its power, as though it held his fate; and with it came a deep need to submit, to whirl, to lose himself in its swirl of color. He could not stop it now, he knew. So let it be.

The button rested snugly in his palm where the man had placed it. And now he became aware of the man beside him, advising him through the microphone, while behind the shadowy audience hummed with noisy voices. He shifted his feet. There was still that feeling of helplessness within him, making part of him desire to turn back, even now that the jackpot was right in his hand. He squeezed the button until his fist ached. Then, like the sudden shriek of a subway whistle, a doubt tore through his head. Suppose he did not spin the wheel long enough? What could he do, and how could he tell? And then he knew, even as he wondered, that as long as he pressed the button, he could control the jackpot. He and only he could determine whether or not it was to be his. Not even the man with the microphone could do anything about it now. He felt drunk. Then, as though he had come down from a high hill into a valley of people, he heard the audience yelling.

"Come down from there, you jerk!"

"Let somebody else have a chance . . ."

"Ole Jack thinks he done found the end of the rainbow . . ."

The last voice was not unfriendly, and he turned and smiled dreamily into the yelling mouths. Then he turned his back squarely on them.

"Don't take too long, boy," a voice said.

He nodded. They were yelling behind him. Those folks did not understand what had happened to him. They had been playing the bingo game day in and night out for years, trying to win rent money or hamburger change. But not one of those wise guys had discovered this wonderful thing. He watched the wheel whirling past the numbers and experienced a burst of exaltation: This is God! This is the really truly God! He said it aloud, "This is God!"

He said it with such absolute conviction that he feared he would fall fainting into the footlights. But the crowd yelled so loud that they could not hear. Those fools, he thought. I'm here trying to tell them the most wonderful secret in the world, and they're yelling like they gone crazy. A hand fell upon his shoulder.

"You'll have to make a choice now, boy. You've taken too long."

He brushed the hand violently away.

"Leave me alone, man. I know what I'm doing!"

The man looked surprised and held on to the microphone for support. And because he did not wish to hurt the man's feelings he smiled, realizing with a sudden pang that there was no way of explaining to the man just why he had to stand there pressing the button forever.

"Come here," he called tiredly.

The man approached, rolling the heavy microphone across the stage.

"Anybody can play this bingo game, right?" he said.

"Sure, but . . ."

He smiled, feeling inclined to be patient with this slick looking white man with his blue sport shirt and his sharp gabardine suit.

"That's what I thought," he said. "Anybody can win the jackpot as long as they get the lucky number, right?"

"That's the rule, but after all . . ."

"That's what I thought," he said. "And the big prize goes to the man who knows how to win it?"

The man nodded speechlessly.

"Well then, go on over there and watch me win like I want to. I ain't going to hurt nobody," he said, "and I'll show you how to win. I mean to show the whole world how it's got to be done."

And because he understood, he smiled again to let the man know that he held nothing against him for being white and impatient. Then he refused to see the man any longer and stood pressing the button, the voices of the crowd reaching him like sounds in distant streets. Let them yell. All the Negroes down there were just ashamed because he was black like them. He smiled inwardly, knowing how it was. Most of the time he was ashamed of what Negroes did himself. Well, let them be ashamed for something this time. Like him. He was like a long thin black wire that was being stretched and wound upon the bingo wheel; wound until he wanted to scream; wound, but this time himself controlling the winding and the sadness and the shame, and because he did, Laura would be all right. Suddenly the lights flickered. He staggered backwards. Had something gone wrong? All this noise. Didn't they know that although he controlled the wheel, it also controlled him, and unless he pressed the button forever and forever and ever it would stop, leaving him high and dry, dry and high on this hard high slippery hill and Laura dead? There was only one chance; he had to do whatever the wheel demanded. And gripping the button in despair, he discovered with surprise that it imparted a nervous energy. His spine tingled. He felt a certain power.

Now he faced the raging crowd with defiance, its screams penetrating his eardrums like trumpets shrieking from a jukebox. The vague faces glowing in the bingo lights gave him a sense of himself that he had never known before. He was running the show, by God! They had to react to him, for he was their luck. This is *me*, he thought. Let the bastards yell. Then someone was laughing inside him, and he realized that somehow he had forgotten his own name. It was a sad, lost feeling to lose your name, and a crazy thing to do. That name had been given him by the white man who had owned his grandfather a long lost time ago down South. But maybe those wise guys knew his name.

"Who am I?" he screamed.

"Hurry up and bingo, you jerk!"

They didn't know either, he thought sadly. They didn't even know their own names, they were all poor nameless bastards.

Well, he didn't need that old name; he was reborn. For as long as he pressed the button he was The-man-who-pressed-the-button-who-held-the-prize-who-was-the-King-of-Bingo. That was the way it was, and he'd have to press the button even if nobody understood, even though Laura did not understand.

"Live!" he shouted.

The audience quieted like the dying of a huge fan.

"Live, Laura, baby. I got holt of it now, sugar. Live!"

He screamed it, tears streaming down his face. "I got nobody but YOU!"

The screams tore from his very guts. He felt as though the rush of blood to his head would burst out in baseball seams of small red droplets, like a head beaten by police clubs. Bending over he saw a trickle of blood splashing the toe of his shoe. With his free hand he searched his head. It was his nose. God, suppose something has gone wrong? He felt that the whole audience had somehow entered him and was stamping its feet in his stomach, and he was unable to throw them out. They wanted the prize, that was it. They wanted the secret for themselves. But they'd never get it; he would keep the bingo wheel whirling forever, and Laura would be safe in the wheel. But would she? It had to be, because if she were not safe the wheel would cease to turn; it could not go on. He had to get away, *vomit* all, and his mind formed an image of himself running with Laura in his arms down the tracks of the subway just ahead of an A train, running desperately *vomit* with people screaming for him to come out but knowing no way of leaving the tracks because to stop would bring the train crushing down upon him and to attempt to leave across the other tracks would mean to run into a hot third rail as high as his waist which threw blue sparks that blinded his eyes until he could hardly see.

He heard singing and the audience was clapping its hands.

> Shoot the liquor to him, Jim, boy!
> Clap-clap-clap
> Well a-calla the cop
> He's blowing his top!
> Shoot the liquor to him, Jim, boy!

Bitter anger grew within him at the singing. They think I'm crazy. Well let 'em laugh. I'll do what I got to do.

He was standing in an attitude of intense listening when he saw that they were watching something on the stage behind him. He felt weak. But when he turned he saw no one. If only his thumb did not ache so. Now they were applauding. And for a moment he thought that the wheel had stopped. But that was impossible, his thumb still pressed the button. Then he saw them. Two men in uniform beckoned from the end of the stage. They were coming toward him, walking in step, slowly, like a tap-dance team returning for a third encore. But their shoulders shot forward, and he backed away, looking wildly about. There was nothing to fight them with. He had only the long black cord which led to a plug somewhere back stage, and he couldn't use that because it operated the bingo wheel. He backed slowly, fixing the men with his eyes as his lips stretched over his teeth in a tight, fixed grin; moved toward the end of the stage and realizing that he couldn't go much further, for suddenly the cord became taut and he couldn't afford to break the cord. But he had to do something. The audience was howling. Suddenly he stopped dead, seeing the men halt, their legs lifted as in an interrupted step of a slow-motion dance. There was nothing to do but run in the other direction and he dashed forward, slipping and sliding. The men fell back, surprised. He struck out violently going past.

"Grab him!"

He ran, but all too quickly the cord tightened, resistingly, and he turned and ran back again. This time he slipped them, and discovered by running in a circle before the wheel he could keep the cord from tightening. But this way he had to flail his arms to keep the men away. Why couldn't they leave a man alone? He ran, circling.

"Ring down the curtain," someone yelled. But they couldn't do that. If they did the wheel flashing from the projection room would be cut off. But they had him before he could tell them so, trying to pry open his fist, and he was wrestling and trying to bring his knees into the fight and holding on the button, for it was his life. And now he was down, seeing a foot coming down, crushing his wrist cruelly, down, as he saw the wheel whirling serenely above.

"I can't give it up," he screamed. Then quietly, in a confidential tone, "Boys, I really can't give it up."

It landed hard against his head. And in the blank moment

they had it away from him, completely now. He fought them trying to pull him up from the stage as he watched the wheel spin slowly to a stop. Without surprise he saw it rest at double zero.

"You see," he pointed bitterly.

"Sure, boy, sure, it's O.K.," one of the men said smiling.

And seeing the man bow his head to someone he could not see, he felt very, very happy; he would receive what all the winners received.

But as he warmed in the justice of the man's tight smile he did not see the man's slow wink, nor see the bow-legged man behind him step clear of the swiftly descending curtain and set himself for a blow. He only felt the dull pain exploding in his skull, and he knew even as it slipped out of him that his luck had run out on the stage.

## BERNARD MALAMUD [1914–1986]

# The Jewbird

The window was open so the skinny bird flew in. Flappity-flap with its frazzled black wings. That's how it goes. It's open, you're in. Closed, you're out and that's your fate. The bird wearily flapped through the open kitchen window of Harry Cohen's top-floor apartment on First Avenue near the lower East River. On a rod on the wall hung an escaped canary cage, its door wide open, but this black-type longbeaked bird—its ruffled head and small dull eyes, crossed a little, making it look like a dissipated crow—landed if not smack on Cohen's thick lamb chop, at least on the table, close by. The frozen foods salesman was sitting at supper with his wife and young son on a hot August evening a year ago. Cohen, a heavy man with hairy chest and beefy shorts; Edie, in skinny yellow shorts and red halter; and their ten-year-old Morris (after her father)—Maurie, they called him, a nice kid though not overly bright—were all in the city after two weeks out, because Cohen's mother was dying. They had been enjoying Kingston,

238 BERNARD MALAMUD

New York, but drove back when Mama got sick in her flat in the Bronx.

"Right on the table," said Cohen, putting down his beer glass and swatting at the bird. "Son of a bitch."

"Harry, take care with your language," Edie said, looking at Maurie, who watched every move.

The bird cawed hoarsely and with a flap of its bedraggled wings—feathers tufted this way and that—rose heavily to the top of the open kitchen door, where it perched staring down.

"Gevalt, a pogrom!"[1]

"It's a talking bird," said Edie in astonishment.

"In Jewish," said Maurie.

"Wise guy," muttered Cohen. He gnawed on his chop, then put down the bone. "So if you can talk, say what's your business. What do you want here?"

"If you can't spare a lamb chop," said the bird, "I'll settle for a piece of herring with a crust of bread. You can't live on your nerve forever."

"This ain't a restaurant," Cohen replied. "All I'm asking is what brings you to this address?"

"The window was open," the bird sighed; adding after a moment, "I'm running. I'm flying but I'm also running."

"From whom?" asked Edie with interest.

"Anti-Semeets."

"Anti-Semites?" they all said.

"That's from who."

"What kind of anti-Semites bother a bird?" Edie asked.

"Any kind," said the bird, "also including eagles, vultures, and hawks. And once in a while some crows will take your eyes out."

"But aren't you a crow?"

"Me? I'm a Jewbird."

Cohen laughed heartily. "What do you mean by that?"

The bird began dovening.[2] He prayed without Book or tallith,[3] but with passion. Edie bowed her head though not Cohen. And

---

[1] An organized massacre of Jews.

[2] Praying.

[3] The scarf worn by Jews at prayer.

Maurie rocked back and forth with the prayer, looking up with one wide-open eye.

When the prayer was done Cohen remarked, "No hat, no phylacteries?"[4]

"I'm an old radical."

"You're sure you're not some kind of a ghost or dybbuk?"[5]

"Not a dybbuk," answered the bird, "though one of my relatives had such an experience once. It's all over now, thanks God. They freed her from a former lover, a crazy jealous man. She's now the mother of two wonderful children."

"Birds?" Cohen asked slyly.

"Why not?"

"What kind of birds?"

"Like me. Jewbirds."

Cohen tipped back in his chair and guffawed. "That's a big laugh. I've heard of a Jewfish but not a Jewbird."

"We're once removed." The bird rested on one skinny leg, then on the other. "Please, could you spare maybe a piece of herring with a small crust of bread?"

Edie got up from the table.

"What are you doing?" Cohen asked her.

"I'll clear the dishes."

Cohen turned to the bird. "So what's your name, if you don't mind saying?"

"Call me Schwartz."

"He might be an old Jew changed into a bird by somebody," said Edie, removing a plate.

"Are you?" asked Harry, lighting a cigar.

"Who knows?" answered Schwartz. "Does God tell us everything?"

Maurie got up on his chair. "What kind of herring?" he asked the bird in excitement.

"Get down, Maurie, or you'll fall," ordered Cohen.

"If you haven't got matjes, I'll take schmaltz,"[6] said Schwartz.

---

[4] Slips of parchment, containing passages from Exodus or Deuteronomy, encased by leather, and worn when praying on all days but the Sabbath.

[5] A clinging spirit, a demon or misplaced soul that enters a living body and speaks through its mouth.

[6] *Matjes*, expensive herring; *schmaltz*, cheap herring.

"All we have is marinated, with slices of onion—in a jar," said Edie.

"If you'll open for me the jar I'll eat marinated. Do you have also, if you don't mind, a piece of rye bread—the spitz?"[7]

Edie thought she had.

"Feed him out on the balcony," Cohen said. He spoke to the bird. "After that take off."

Schwartz closed both bird eyes. "I'm tired and it's a long way."

"Which direction are you headed, north or south?"

Schwartz, barely lifting his wings, shrugged.

"You don't know where you're going?"

"Where there's charity I'll go."

"Let him stay, papa," said Maurie. "He's only a bird."

"So stay the night," Cohen said, "but no longer."

In the morning Cohen ordered the bird out of the house but Maurie cried, so Schwartz stayed for a while. Maurie was still on vacation from school and his friends were away. He was lonely and Edie enjoyed the fun he had, playing with the bird.

"He's no trouble at all," she told Cohen, "and besides his appetite is very small."

"What'll you do when he makes dirty?"

"He flies across the street in a tree when he makes dirty, and if nobody passes below, who notices?"

"So all right," said Cohen, "but I'm dead set against it. I warn you he ain't gonna stay here long."

"What have you got against the poor bird?"

"Poor bird, my ass. He's a foxy bastard. He thinks he's a Jew."

"What difference does it make what he thinks?"

"A Jewbird, what a chuzpah. One false move and he's out on his drumsticks."

At Cohen's insistence Schwartz lived out on the balcony in a new wooden birdhouse Edie had bought him.

"With many thanks," said Schwartz, "though I would rather have a human roof over my head. You know how it is at my age. I like the warm, the windows, the smell of cooking. I would also be glad to see once in a while the *Jewish Morning Journal* and have

---

[7] The end of a loaf of bread.

now and then a schnapps because it helps my breathing, thanks
God. But whatever you give me, you won't hear complaints."

However, when Cohen brought home a bird feeder full of
dried corn, Schwartz said, "Impossible."

Cohen was annoyed. "What's the matter, crosseyes, is your
life getting too good for you? Are you forgetting what it means to
be migratory? I'll bet a helluva lot of crows you happen to be
acquainted with, Jews or otherwise, would give their eyeteeth to
eat this corn."

Schwartz did not answer. What can you say to a grubber
yung?[8]

"Not for my digestion," he later explained to Edie. "Cramps.
Herring is better even if it makes you thirsty. At least rainwater
don't cost anything." He laughed sadly in breathy caws.

And herring, thanks to Edie, who knew where to shop, was
what Schwartz got, with an occasional piece of potato pancake,
and even a bit of soupmeat when Cohen wasn't looking.

When school began in September, before Cohen would once
again suggest giving the bird the boot, Edie prevailed on him to
wait a little while until Maurie adjusted.

"To deprive him right now might hurt his school work, and
you know what trouble we had last year."

"So okay, but sooner or later the bird goes. That I promise
you."

Schwartz, though nobody had asked him, took on full responsibility for Maurie's performance in school. In return for favors
granted, when he was let in for an hour or two at night, he spent
most of his time overseeing the boy's lessons. He sat on top of
the dresser near Maurie's desk as he laboriously wrote out his
homework. Maurie was a restless type and Schwartz gently kept
him to his studies. He also listened to him practice his screechy
violin, taking a few minutes off now and then to rest his ears in
the bathroom. And they afterwards played dominoes. The boy
was an indifferent checker player and it was impossible to teach
him chess. When he was sick, Schwartz read him comic books
though he personally disliked them. But Maurie's work improved

---

[8] A vulgar, coarse young man.

in school and even his violin teacher admitted his playing was better. Edie gave Schwartz credit for these improvements though the bird pooh-poohed them.

Yet he was proud there was nothing lower than C minuses on Maurie's report card, and on Edie's insistence celebrated with a little schnapps.

"If he keeps up like this," Cohen said, "I'll get him in an Ivy League college for sure."

"Oh I hope so," sighed Edie.

But Schwartz shook his head. "He's a good boy—you don't have to worry. He won't be a shicker[9] or a wifebeater, God forbid, but a scholar he'll never be, if you know what I mean, although maybe a good mechanic. It's no disgrace in these times."

"If I were you," Cohen said, angered, "I'd keep my big snoot out of other people's private business."

"Harry, please," said Edie.

"My goddamn patience is wearing out. That crosseyes butts into everything."

Though he wasn't exactly a welcome guest in the house, Schwartz gained a few ounces although he did not improve in appearance. He looked bedraggled as ever, his feathers unkempt, as though he had just flown out of a snowstorm. He spent, he admitted, little time taking care of himself. Too much to think about. "Also outside plumbing," he told Edie. Still there was more glow to his eyes so that though Cohen went on calling him crosseyes he said it less emphatically.

Liking his situation, Schwartz tried tactfully to stay out of Cohen's way, but one night when Edie was at the movies and Maurie was taking a hot shower, the frozen foods salesman began a quarrel with the bird.

"For Christ sake, why don't you wash yourself sometimes? Why must you always stink like a dead fish?"

"Mr. Cohen, if you'll pardon me, if somebody eats garlic he will smell from garlic. I eat herring three times a day. Feed me flowers and I will smell like flowers."

"Who's obligated to feed you anything at all? You're lucky to get herring."

---

[9] A drunkard.

"Excuse me, I'm not complaining," said the bird. "You're complaining."

"What's more," said Cohen, "Even from out on the balcony I can hear you snoring away like a pig. It keeps me awake at night."

"Snoring," said Schwartz, "isn't a crime, thanks God."

"All in all you are a goddamn pest and free loader. Next thing you'll want to sleep in bed next to my wife."

"Mr. Cohen," said Schwartz, "on this rest assured. A bird is a bird."

"So you say, but how do I know you're a bird and not some kind of a goddamn devil?"

"If I was a devil you would know already. And I don't mean because your son's good marks."

"Shut up, you bastard bird," shouted Cohen.

"Grubber yung," cawed Schwartz, rising to the tips of his talons, his long wings outstretched.

Cohen was about to lunge for the bird's scrawny neck but Maurie came out of the bathroom, and for the rest of the evening until Schwartz's bedtime on the balcony, there was pretended peace.

But the quarrel had deeply disturbed Schwartz and he slept badly. His snoring woke him, and awake, he was fearful of what would become of him. Wanting to stay out of Cohen's way, he kept to the birdhouse as much as possible. Cramped by it, he paced back and forth on the balcony ledge, or sat on the birdhouse roof, staring into space. In evenings, while overseeing Maurie's lessons, he often fell asleep. Awakening, he nervously hopped around exploring the four corners of the room. He spent much time in Maurie's closet, and carefully examined his bureau drawers when they were left open. And once when he found a large paper bag on the floor, Schwartz poked his way into it to investigate what possibilities were. The boy was amused to see the bird in the paper bag.

"He wants to build a nest," he said to his mother.

Edie, sensing Schwartz's unhappiness, spoke to him quietly.

"Maybe if you did some of the things my husband wants you, you would get along better with him."

"Give me a for instance," Schwartz said.

"Like take a bath, for instance."

"I'm too old for baths," said the bird. "My feathers fall out without baths."

"He says you have a bad smell."

"Everybody smells. Some people smell because of their thoughts or because who they are. My bad smell comes from the food I eat. What does his come from?"

"I better not ask him or it might make him mad," said Edie.

In late November Schwartz froze on the balcony in the fog and cold, and especially on rainy days he woke with stiff joints and could barely move his wings. Already he felt twinges of rheumatism. He would have liked to spend more time in the warm house, particularly when Maurie was in school and Cohen at work. But though Edie was good-hearted and might have sneaked him in in the morning, just to thaw out, he was afraid to ask her. In the meantime Cohen, who had been reading articles about the migration of birds, came out on the balcony one night after work when Edie was in the kitchen preparing pot roast, and peeking into the birdhouse, warned Schwartz to be on his way soon if he knew what was good for him. "Time to hit the flyways."

"Mr. Cohen, why do you hate me so much?" asked the bird. "What did I do to you?"

"Because you're an A-number-one trouble maker, that's why. What's more, whoever heard of a Jewbird! Now scat or it's open war."

But Schwartz stubbornly refused to depart so Cohen embarked on a campaign of harassing him, meanwhile hiding it from Edie and Maurie. Maurie hated violence and Cohen didn't want to leave a bad impression. He thought maybe if he played dirty tricks on the bird he would fly off without being physically kicked out. The vacation was over, let him make his easy living off the fat of somebody else's land. Cohen worried about the effect of the bird's departure on Maurie's schooling but decided to take the chance, first, because the boy now seemed to have the knack of studying— give the black bird-bastard credit—and second, because Schwartz was driving him bats by being there always, even in his dreams.

The frozen foods salesman began his campaign against the bird by mixing watery cat food with the herring slices in Schwartz's dish. He also blew up and popped numerous paper bags outside the birdhouse as the bird slept, and when he got Schwartz good and nervous, though not enough to leave, he brought a full-grown cat into the house, supposedly a gift for little Maurie, who had always wanted a pussy. The cat never stopped springing up at Schwartz whenever he saw him, one day managing to claw out several of his tailfeathers. And even at lesson time, when the cat was usually excluded from Maurie's room, though somehow or other he quickly found his way in at the end of the lesson, Schwartz was desperately fearful of his life and flew from pinnacle to pinnacle—light fixture to clothestree to door-top—in order to elude the beast's wet jaws.

Once when the bird complained to Edie how hazardous his existence was, she said, "Be patient, Mr. Schwartz. When the cat gets to know you better he won't try to catch you any more."

"When he stops trying we will both be in Paradise," Schwartz answered. "Do me a favor and get rid of him. He makes my whole life worry. I'm losing feathers like a tree loses leaves."

"I'm awfully sorry but Maurie likes the pussy and sleeps with it."

What could Schwartz do? He worried but came to no decision, being afraid to leave. So he ate the herring garnished with cat food, tried hard not to hear the paper bags bursting like fire crackers outside the birdhouse at night, and lived terror-stricken closer to the ceiling than the floor, as the cat, his tail flicking, endlessly watched him.

Weeks went by. Then on the day after Cohen's mother had died in her flat in the Bronx, when Maurie came home with a zero on an arithmetic test, Cohen, enraged, waited until Edie had taken the boy to his violin lesson, then openly attacked the bird. He chased him with a broom on the balcony and Schwartz frantically flew back and forth, finally escaping into his birdhouse. Cohen triumphantly reached in, and grabbing both skinny legs, dragged the bird out, cawing loudly, his wings wildly beating. He whirled the bird around and around his head. But Schwartz, as he moved in circles, managed to swoop down and catch Cohen's nose in his beak, and hung on for dear life. Cohen cried out in great pain, punched the bird with his fist, and tugging at its legs with all his might, pulled his nose free. Again he swung the yawking Schwartz around until the bird grew dizzy, then with a furious heave, flung him into the night. Schwartz sank like stone into the street. Cohen then tossed the birdhouse and feeder after him, listening at the ledge until they crashed on the sidewalk below. For a full hour, broom in hand, his heart palpitating and nose throbbing with pain, Cohen waited for Schwartz to return but the broken-hearted bird didn't.

That's the end of that dirty bastard, the salesman thought and went in. Edie and Maurie had come home.

"Look," said Cohen, pointing to his bloody nose swollen three times its normal size, "what that sonofabitchy bird did. It's a permanent scar."

"Where is he now?" Edie asked, frightened.

"I threw him out and he flew away. Good riddance."

Nobody said no, though Edie touched a handkerchief to her eyes and Maurie rapidly tried the nine times table and found he knew approximately half.

In the spring when the winter's snow had melted, the boy, moved by a memory, wandered in the neighborhood, looking for Schwartz. He found a dead black bird in a small lot near the river, his two wings broken, neck twisted, and both bird-eyes plucked clean.

"Who did it to you, Mr. Schwartz?" Maurie wept.

"Anti-Semeets," Edie said later.

# PETER TAYLOR [b. 1917]

# A Walled Garden

No. Memphis in autumn has not the moss-hung oaks of Natchez. Nor, my dear young man, have we the exotic, the really exotic orange and yellow and rust foliage of the maples at Rye or Saratoga. When our five-month summer season burns itself out, the foliage is left a cheerless brown. Observe that Catawba tree beyond the wall, and the leaves under your feet here on the terrace are mustard and khaki colored; and the air, the atmosphere (who would dare to breathe a deep breath!) is virtually a sea of dust. But we do what we can. We've walled ourselves in here with these evergreens and box and jasmine. You must know, yourself, young man, that no beauty is native to us but the verdure of early summer. And it's as though I've had to take my finger, just so, and point out to Frances the lack of sympathy that there is in the climate and in the eroded countryside of this region. I have had to build this garden and say, "See, my child, how nice and sympathetic everything can be." But now she does see it my way, you understand. You understand, my daughter has finally made her life with me in this little garden plot, and year by year she has come to realize how little else there is hereabouts to compare with it.

And you, you know nothing of flowers? A young man who doesn't know the zinnia from the aster! How curious that you and my daughter should have made friends. I don't know under what circumstances you two may have met. In her League work, no doubt. She *throws* herself so into whatever work she undertakes. Oh? Why, of course, I should have guessed. She simply *spent* herself on the Chest Drive this year. . . . But my daughter has most of her permanent friends among the flower-minded people. She makes so few friends nowadays outside of our little circle, sees so few people outside our own garden here, really, that I find it quite strange for there to be someone who doesn't know flowers.

No, nothing, we've come to feel, is ever very lovely, really lovely, I mean, in this part of the nation, nothing *but* this garden; and you can well imagine what even this little bandbox of a garden once was. I created it out of a virtual chaos of a backyard—Franny's playground, I might say. For three years I nursed that little magnolia there, for one whole summer did nothing but water the ivy on the east wall of the house; if only you could have seen the scrubby hedge and the unsightly servants' quarters of our neighbors that are beyond my serpentine wall (I suppose, at least, they're still there). In those days it was all very different, you understand, and Frances's father was about the house, and Frances was a child. But now in the spring we have what is truly a sweet garden here, modeled on my mother's at Rye; for three weeks in March our hyacinths are an inspiration to Frances and to me and to all those who come to us regularly; the larkspur and marigold are heavenly in May over there beside the roses.

But you do not know the zinnia from the aster, young man? How curious that you two should have become friends. And now you are impatient with her, and you mustn't be; I don't mean to be too indulgent, but she'll be along presently. Only recently she's become incredibly painstaking in her toilet again. Whereas in the last few years she's not cared so much for the popular fads of dress. Gardens and floral design have occupied her—with what guidance I could give—have been pretty much her life, really. Now in the old days, I confess, before her father was taken from us—I lost Mr. Harris in the dreadfully hot summer of '48 (people don't generally realize what a dreadful year that was—the worst year for perennials and annuals, alike, since Terrible '30. Things died that year that I didn't think would *ever* die. A dreadful summer)—why, she used then to run here and there with people of every sort, it seemed. I put no restraint upon her, understand. How many times I've said to my Franny, "You must make your own life, my child, as you would have it." Yes, in those days she used to run here and there with people of every sort and variety, it seemed to me. Where was it you say you met, for she goes so few places that are really *out* anymore? But Mr. Harris would let me put no restraint upon her. I still remember the strongheadedness of her teens that had to be overcome and the testiness in her character when she was nearer to twenty than thirty. And you should have seen her as a tot of twelve when she would be somersaulting and rolling about on this very spot. Honestly, I see that child now, and mud on her middy blouse and her straight yellow hair in her eyes.

When I used to come back from visiting my people at Rye, she would grit her teeth at me and give her confidence to the black cook. I would find my own child become a mad little animal. It was through this door here from the sun room that I came one September afternoon—just such an afternoon as this, young man—still wearing my traveling suit, and called to my child across the yard for her to come and greet me. I had been away for the two miserable summer months, caring for my sick mother, but at the sight of me the little Indian turned, and with a whoop she ran to hide in the scraggly privet hedge that was at the far end of the yard. I called her twice to come from out that filthiest of shrubs. "Frances Ann!" We used to call her by her full name when her father was alive. But she didn't stir. She crouched at the roots of the hedge and spied at her travel-worn mother between the leaves.

I pleaded with her at first quite indulgently and good-naturedly and described the new ruffled dress and the paper cutouts

I had brought from her grandmother at Rye. (I wasn't to have Mother much longer, and I knew it, and it was hard to come home to this kind of scene.) At last I threatened to withhold my presents until Thanksgiving or Christmas. The cook in the kitchen may have heard some change in my tone, for she came to the kitchen door over beyond the latticework that we've since put up, and looked out first at me and then at the child. While I was threatening, my daughter crouched in the dirt and began to mumble things to herself that I could not hear, and the noises she made were like those of an angry little cat. It seems that it was a warmer afternoon than this one—but my garden does deceive—and I had been moving about in my heavy traveling suit. In my exasperation I stepped out into the rays of the sweltering sun, and into the yard which I so detested; and I uttered in a scream the child's full name, "Frances Ann Harris!" Just then the black cook stepped out onto the back porch, but I ordered her to return to the kitchen. I began to cross the yard toward Frances Ann—that scowling little creature who was *incredibly* the same Frances you've met—and simultaneously she began to crawl along the hedgerow toward the wire fence that divided my property from the neighbor's.

I believe it was the extreme heat that made me speak so very harshly and with such swiftness as to make my words incomprehensible. When I saw that the child had reached the fence and intended climbing it, I pulled off my hat, tearing my veil to pieces as I hurried my pace. I don't actually know what I was saying—I probably couldn't have told you even a moment later—and I didn't even feel any pain from the turn that I gave my ankle in the gully across the middle of the yard. But the child kept her nervous little eyes on me and her lips continued to move now and again. Each time her lips moved I believe I must have raised my voice in more intense rage and greater horror at her ugliness. And so, young man, striding straight through the hedge I reached her before she had climbed to the top of the wire fencing. I think I took her by the arm above the elbow, about here, and I said something like, "I shall have to punish you, Frances Ann." I did not jerk her. I didn't jerk her one bit, as she wished to make it appear, but rather, as soon as I touched her, she relaxed her hold on the wire and fell to the ground. But she lay there—in her canniness—only the briefest moment looking up and past me through the straight hair that hung over her face like an untrimmed mane. I had barely ordered her to rise when she sprang up and moved with such celerity that she soon was out of my reach again. I followed—running in those high heels—and this time I turned my other ankle in the gully, and I fell there on the ground in that yard, this garden. You won't believe it—pardon, I must sit down. . . . I hope you don't think it too odd, me telling you all this. . . . You won't believe it: I lay there in the ditch and she didn't come to aid me with childish apologies and such, but instead she deliberately climbed into her swing that hung from the dirty old poplar that was here formerly (I have had it cut down and the roots dug up) and she began to swing, not high and low, but only gently, and stared straight down at her mother through her long hair—which, you may be sure, young man, I had cut the very next day at my own beautician's and curled into a hundred ringlets.

### GRACE PALEY [b. 1922]

# A Conversation with My Father

---

**M**y father is eighty-six years old and in bed. His heart, that bloody motor, is equally old and will not do certain jobs any more. It still floods his head with brainy light. But it won't let his legs carry the weight of his body around the house. Despite my metaphors, this muscle failure is not due to his old heart, he says, but to a potassium shortage. Sitting on one pillow, leaning on three, he offers last-minute advice and makes a request.

"I would like you to write a simple story just once more," he says, "the kind de Maupassant wrote, or Chekhov, the kind you used to write. Just recognizable people and then write down what happened to them next."

I say, "Yes, why not? That's possible." I want to please him, though I don't remember writing that way. I *would* like to try to tell such a story, if he means the kind that begins: "There was a woman . . ." followed by plot, the absolute line between two points which I've always despised. Not for literary reasons, but because it takes all hope away. Everyone, real or invented, deserves the open destiny of life.

Finally I thought of a story that had been happening for a couple of years right across the street. I wrote it down, then read it aloud. "Pa," I said, "how about this? Do you mean something like this?"

> Once in my time there was a woman and she had a son.
> They lived nicely, in a small apartment in Manhattan. This boy
> at about fifteen became a junkie, which is not unusual in our
> neighborhood. In order to maintain her close friendship with
> him, she became a junkie too. She said it was part of the youth
> culture, with which she felt very much at home. After a while,
> for a number of reasons, the boy gave it all up and left the city
> and his mother in disgust. Hopeless and alone, she grieved. We
> all visit her.

"O.K., Pa, that's it," I said, "an unadorned and miserable tale."

"But that's not what I mean," my father said. "You misunderstood me on purpose. You know there's a lot more to it. You know that. You left everything out. Turgenev wouldn't do that. Chekhov wouldn't do that. There are in fact Russian writers you never heard of, you don't have an inkling of, as good as anyone, who can write a plain ordinary story, who would not leave out what you have left out. I object not to facts but to people sitting in trees talking senselessly, voices from who knows where. . . ."

"Forget that one, Pa, what have I left out now? In this one?"

"Her looks, for instance."

"Oh. Quite handsome, I think. Yes."

"Her hair?"

"Dark, with heavy braids, as though she were a girl or a foreigner."

"What were her parents like, her stock? That she became such a person. It's interesting, you know."

"From out of town. Professional people. The first to be divorced in their county. How's that? Enough?" I asked.

"With you, it's all a joke," he said. "What about the boy's father? Why didn't you mention him? Who was he? Or was the boy born out of wedlock?"

"Yes," I said. "He was born out of wedlock."

"For Godsakes, doesn't anyone in your stories get married? Doesn't anyone have the time to run down to City Hall before they jump into bed?"

"No," I said. "In real life, yes. But in my stories, no."

"Why do you answer me like that?"

"Oh, Pa, this is a simple story about a smart woman who came to N.Y.C. full of interest love trust excitement very up to date, and about her son, what a hard time she had in this world. Married or not, it's of small consequence."

"It is of great consequence," he said.

"O.K.," I said.

"O.K. O.K. yourself," he said, "but listen. I believe you that she's good-looking, but I don't think she was so smart."

"That's true," I said. "Actually that's the trouble with stories. People start out fantastic. You think they're extraordinary, but it turns out as the work goes along, they're just average with a good education. Sometimes the other way around, the person's a kind of dumb innocent, but he outwits you and you can't even think of an ending good enough."

"What do you do then?" he asked. He had been a doctor for a couple of decades and then an artist for a couple of decades and he's still interested in details, craft, technique.

"Well, you just have to let the story lie around till some agreement can be reached between you and the stubborn hero."

"Aren't you talking silly now?" he asked. "Start again," he said. "It so happens I'm not going out this evening. Tell the story again. See what you can do this time."

"O.K.," I said. "But it's not a five-minute job." Second attempt:

Once, across the street from us, there was a fine handsome woman, our neighbor. She had a son whom she loved because she'd known him since birth (in helpless chubby infancy, and in the wrestling, hugging ages, seven to ten, as well as earlier and later). This boy, when he fell into the fist of adolescence, became a junkie. He was not a hopeless one. He was in fact hopeful, an ideologue and successful converter. With his busy brilliance, he wrote persuasive articles for his high-school newspaper. Seeking a wider audience, using important connections, he drummed into Lower Manhattan newsstand distribution a periodical called *Oh! Golden Horse!*

In order to keep him from feeling guilty (because guilt is the stony heart of nine tenths of all clinically diagnosed cancers in America today, she said), and because she had always believed in giving bad habits room at home where one could keep an eye on them, she too became a junkie. Her kitchen was famous for a while—a center for intellectual addicts who knew what they were doing. A few felt artistic like Coleridge[1] and others were scientific and revolutionary like Leary.[2] Although she was often high herself, certain good mothering reflexes remained, and she saw to it that there was lots of orange juice around and honey and milk and vitamin pills. However, she never cooked anything but chili, and that no more than once a week. She explained, when we talked to her, seriously, with neighborly concern, that it was her part in the youth culture and she would rather be with the young, it was an honor, than with her own generation.

One week, while nodding through an Antonioni film, this boy was severely jabbed by the elbow of a stern and proselytizing girl, sitting beside him. She offered immediate apricots and nuts for his sugar level, spoke to him sharply, and took him home.

She had heard of him and his work and she herself published, edited, and wrote a competitive journal called *Man Does Live by Bread Alone*. In the organic heat of her continuous presence he could not help but become interested once more in his muscles, his arteries, and nerve connections. In fact he began to love them, treasure them, praise them with funny little songs in *Man Does Live.* . . .

> the fingers of my flesh transcend
> my transcendental soul
> the tightness in my shoulders end
> my teeth have made me whole

To the mouth of his head (that glory of will and determination) he brought hard apples, nuts, wheat germ, and soybean oil. He said to his old friends, From now on, I guess I'll keep my wits about me. I'm going on the natch. He said he was about to begin a spiritual deep-breathing journey. How about you too, Mom? he asked kindly.

His conversion was so radiant, splendid, that neighborhood

---

[1] Samuel Taylor Coleridge (1772–1834), English Romantic poet, who was an opium addict.
[2] Timothy Leary (b. 1920), sometime Harvard professor of psychology and early advocate of the use of LSD.

kids his age began to say that he had never been a real addict at all, only a journalist along for the smell of the story. The mother tried several times to give up what had become without her son and his friends a lonely habit. This effort only brought it to supportable levels. The boy and his girl took their electronic mimeograph and moved to the bushy edge of another borough. They were very strict. They said they would not see her again until she had been off drugs for sixty days.

At home alone in the evening, weeping, the mother read and reread the seven issues of *Oh! Golden Horse!* They seemed to her as truthful as ever. We often crossed the street to visit and console. But if we mentioned any of our children who were at college or in the hospital or dropouts at home, she would cry out, My baby! My baby! and burst into terrible, face-scarring, time-consuming tears. The End.

First my father was silent, then he said, "Number One: You have a nice sense of humor. Number Two: I see you can't tell a plain story. So don't waste time." Then he said sadly, "Number Three: I suppose that means she was alone, she was left like that, his mother. Alone. Probably sick?"

I said, "Yes."

"Poor woman. Poor girl, to be born in a time of fools, to live among fools. The end. The end. You were right to put that down. The end."

I didn't want to argue, but I had to say, "Well, it is not necessarily the end, Pa."

"Yes," he said, "what a tragedy. The end of a person."

"No, Pa," I begged him. "It doesn't have to be. She's only about forty. She could be a hundred different things in this world as time goes on. A teacher or a social worker. An ex-junkie! Sometimes it's better than having a master's in education."

"Jokes," he said. "As a writer that's your main trouble. You don't want to recognize it. Tragedy! Plain tragedy! Historical tragedy! No hope. The end."

"Oh, Pa," I said. "She could change."

"In your own life, too, you have to look it in the face." He took a couple of nitroglycerin. "Turn to five," he said, pointing to the dial on the oxygen tank. He inserted the tubes into his nostrils and breathed deep. He closed his eyes and said, "No."

I had promised the family to always let him have the last word when arguing, but in this case I had a different responsibility. That woman lives across the street. She's my knowledge and my invention. I'm sorry for her. I'm not going to leave her there in that house crying. (Actually neither would Life, which unlike me has no pity.)

Therefore: She did change. Of course her son never came home again. But right now, she's the receptionist in a storefront community clinic in the East Village. Most of the customers are young people, some old friends. The head doctor has said to her, "If we only had three people in this clinic with your experiences. . . ."

"The doctor said that?" My father took the oxygen tubes out of his nostrils and said, "Jokes. Jokes again."

"No, Pa, it could really happen that way, it's a funny world nowadays."

"No," he said. "Truth first. She will slide back. A person must have character. She does not."

"No, Pa," I said. "That's it. She's got a job. Forget it. She's in that storefront working."

"How long will it be?" he asked. "Tragedy! You too. When will you look it in the face?"

## NADINE GORDIMER [b. 1923]

# Town and Country Lovers

D<small>r.</small> Franz-Josef von Leinsdorf is a geologist absorbed in his work; wrapped up in it, as the saying goes—year after year the experience of this work enfolds him, swaddling him away from the landscapes, the cities, and the people, wherever he lives: Peru, New Zealand, the United States. He's always been like that, his mother could confirm from their native Austria. There, even as a handsome small boy he presented only his profile to her: turned away to his bits of rock and stone. His few relaxations have not changed much since then. An occasional skiing trip, listening to music, reading poetry—Rainer Maria Rilke[1] once stayed in his grandmother's hunting lodge in the forests of Styria and the boy was introduced to Rilke's poems while very young.

Layer upon layer, country after country, wherever his work takes him—and now he has been almost seven years in Africa. First the Côte d'Ivoire, and for the past five years, South Africa. The shortage of skilled manpower brought about his recruitment here. He has no interest in the politics of the countries he works in. His private preoccupation-within-the-preoccupation of his work has been research into underground watercourses, but the mining company that employs him in a senior though not executive capacity is interested only in mineral discovery. So he is much out in the field—which is the veld, here—seeking new gold, copper, platinum, and uranium deposits. When he is at home—on this particular job, in this particular country, this city—he lives in a two-roomed flat in a suburban block with a landscaped garden, and does his shopping at a supermarket conveniently across the street. He is not married—yet. That is how his colleagues, and the typists and secretaries at the mining company's head office, would define his situation. Both men and women would describe him as a good-looking man, in a foreign way, with the lower half of his face dark and middle-aged (his mouth is thin and curving, and no matter how close-shaven his beard shows like fine shot embedded in the skin round mouth and chin) and the upper half contradictorily young, with deep-set eyes (some would say grey, some black), thick eyelashes and brows. A tangled gaze: through which concentration and gleaming thoughtfulness perhaps appear as fire and languor. It is this that the women in the office mean when they remark he's not unattractive. Although the gaze seems to promise, he has never invited any one of them to go out with him. There is the general assumption he probably has a girl who's been picked for him, he's bespoken by one of his own kind, back home in Europe where he comes from. Many of these well-educated Europeans have no intention of becoming permanent immigrants; neither the remnant of white colonial life nor idealistic involvement with Black Africa appeals to them.

One advantage, at least, of living in underdeveloped or half-

---

[1] German poet [1875–1926], known for his lyric poetry.

developed countries is that flats are serviced. All Dr. von Leinsdorf
has to do for himself is buy his own supplies and cook an evening
meal if he doesn't want to go to a restaurant. It is simply a matter
of dropping in to the supermarket on his way from his car to his
flat after work in the afternoon. He wheels a trolley up and down
the shelves, and his simple needs are presented to him in the form
of tins, packages, plastic-wrapped meat, cheeses, fruit and vegetables, tubes, bottles . . . At the cashier's counters where customers must converge and queue there are racks of small items un-
categorized, for last-minute purchase. Here, as the coloured girl
cashier punches the adding machine, he picks up cigarettes and
perhaps a packet of salted nuts or a bar of nougat. Or razor-blades,
when he remembers he's running short. One evening in winter
he saw that the cardboard display was empty of the brand of
blades he preferred, and he drew the cashier's attention to this.
These young coloured girls are usually pretty unhelpful, taking
money and punching their machines in a manner that asserts with
the time-serving obstinacy of the half-literate the limit of any responsibility towards customers, but this one ran an alert glance
over the selection of razor-blades, apologized that she was not
allowed to leave her post, and said she would see that the stock
was replenished "next time." A day or two later she recognized
him, gravely, as he took his turn before her counter—"I ahssed
them, but it's out of stock. You can't get it. I did ahss about it."
He said this didn't matter. "When it comes in, I can keep a few
packets for you." He thanked her.

He was away with the prospectors the whole of the next week.
He arrived back in town just before nightfall on Friday, and was
on his way from car to flat with his arms full of briefcase, suitcase,
and canvas bags when someone stopped him by standing timidly
in his path. He was about to dodge round unseeingly on the
crowded pavement but she spoke. "We got the blades in now. I
didn't see you in the shop this week, but I kept some for when
you come. So . . ."

He recognized her. He had never seen her standing before,
and she was wearing a coat. She was rather small and finely-
made, for one of them. The coat was skimpy but no big backside
jutted. The cold brought an apricot-graining of warm colour to her
cheekbones, beneath which a very small face was quite delicately
hollowed, and the skin was smooth, the subdued satiny colour of

certain yellow wood. That crêpey hair, but worn drawn back flat and in a little knot pushed into one of the cheap wool chignons that (he recognized also) hung in the miscellany of small goods along with the razor-blades, at the supermarket. He said thanks, he was in a hurry, he'd only just got back from a trip—shifting the burdens he carried, to demonstrate. "Oh shame." She acknowledged his load. "But if you want I can run in and get it for you quickly. If you want."

He saw at once it was perfectly clear that all the girl meant was that she would go back to the supermarket, buy the blades, and bring the packet to him there where he stood, on the pavement. And it seemed that it was this certainty that made him say, in the kindly tone of assumption used for an obliging underling, "I live just across there—*Atlantis*—that flat building. Could you drop them by, for me—number seven-hundred-and-eighteen, seventh floor—"

She had not before been inside one of these big flat buildings near where she worked. She lived a bus- and train-ride away to the West of the city, but this side of the black townships, in a township for people of her tint. There was a pool with ferns, not plastic, and even a little waterfall pumped electrically over rocks, in the entrance of the building *Atlantis;* she didn't wait for the lift marked GOODS but took the one meant for whites and a white woman with one of those sausage-dogs on a lead got in with her but did not pay her any attention. The corridors leading to the flats were nicely glassed-in, not draughty.

He wondered if he should give her a twenty-cent piece for her trouble—ten cents would be right for a black; but she said, "Oh no—please, here—" standing outside his open door and awkwardly pushing back at his hand the change from the money he'd given her for the razor-blades. She was smiling, for the first time, in the dignity of refusing a tip. It was difficult to know how to treat these people, in this country; to know what they expected. In spite of her embarrassing refusal of the coin, she stood there, completely unassuming, fists thrust down the pockets of her cheap coat against the cold she'd come in from, rather pretty thin legs neatly aligned, knee to knee, ankle to ankle.

"Would you like a cup of coffee or something?"

He couldn't very well take her into his study-cum-living-room and offer her a drink. She followed him to his kitchen, but at the sight of her pulling out the single chair to drink her cup of coffee at the kitchen table, he said, "No—bring it in here—" and led the way into the big room where, among his books and his papers, his files of scientific correspondence (and the cigar boxes of stamps from the envelopes), his racks of records, his specimens of minerals and rocks, he lived alone.

It was no trouble to her; she saved him the trips to the supermarket and brought him his groceries two or three times a week. All he had to do was to leave a list and the key under the doormat, and she would come up in her lunch-hour to collect them, returning to put his supplies in the flat after work. Sometimes he was home and sometimes not. He bought a box of chocolates and left it, with a note, for her to find; and that was acceptable, apparently, as a gratuity.

Her eyes went over everything in the flat although her body tried to conceal its sense of being out of place by remaining as still as possible, holding its contours in the chair offered her as a stranger's coat is set aside and remains exactly as left until the owner takes it up to go. "You collect?"

"Well, these are specimens—connected with my work."

"My brother used to collect. Miniatures. With brandy and whisky and that, in them. From all over. Different countries."

The second time she watched him grinding coffee for the cup he had offered her she said, "You always do that? Always when you make coffee?"

"But of course. It is no good, for you. Do I make it too strong?"

"Oh it's just I'm not used to it. We buy it ready—you know, it's in a bottle, you just add a bit to the milk or water."

He laughed, instructive: "That's not coffee, that's a synthetic flavouring. In my country we drink only real coffee, fresh, from the beans—you smell how good it is as it's being ground?"

She was stopped by the caretaker and asked what she wanted in the building? Heavy with the *bona fides* of groceries clutched to her body, she said she was working at number 718, on the seventh floor. The caretaker did not tell her not to use the whites' lift; after all, she was not black; her family was very light-skinned.

There was the item "grey button for trousers" on one of his shopping lists. She said as she unpacked the supermarket carrier, "Give me the pants, so long, then," and sat on his sofa that was always gritty with fragments of pipe tobacco, sewing in and out through the four holes of the button with firm, fluent movements of the right hand, gestures supplying the articulacy missing from her talk. She had a little yokel's, peasant's (he thought of it) gap between her two front teeth when she smiled that he didn't much like, but, face ellipsed to three-quarter angle, eyes cast down in concentration with soft lips almost closed, this didn't matter. He said, watching her sew, "You're a good girl"; and touched her.

She remade the bed every late afternoon when they left it and she dressed again before she went home. After a week there was a day when late afternoon became evening, and they were still in the bed.

"Can't you stay the night?"

"My mother," she said.

"Phone her. Make an excuse." He was a foreigner. He had been in the country five years, but he didn't understand that people don't usually have telephones in their houses, where she lived. She got up to dress. He didn't want that tender body to go out in the night cold and kept hindering her with the interruption of his hands; saying nothing. Before she put on her coat, when the body had already disappeared, he spoke, "But you must make some arrangement."

"Oh my mother!" Her face opened to fear and vacancy he could not read.

He was not entirely convinced the woman would think of her daughter as some pure and unsullied virgin . . . "Why?"

The girl said, "S'e'll be scared. S'e'll be scared we get caught."

"Don't tell her anything. Say I'm employing you." In this country he was working in now there were generally rooms on the roofs of flat buildings for tenants' servants.

She said: "That's what I told the caretaker."

She ground fresh coffee beans every time he wanted a cup while he was working at night. She never attempted to cook anything until she had watched in silence while he did it the way he liked, and she learned to reproduce exactly the simple dishes he preferred. She handled his pieces of rock and stone, at first admiring the colours—"It'd make a beautiful ring or necklace, ay." Then he showed her the striations, the formation of each piece, and explained what each was, and how, in the long life of the earth, it had been formed. He named the mineral it yielded, and what that was used for. He worked at his papers, writing, writing, every night, so it did not matter that they could not go out together to public places. On Sundays she got into his car in the basement garage and they drove to the country and picnicked away up in the Magaliesberg, where there was no one. He read or poked about among the rocks; they climbed together, to the mountain pools. He taught her to swim. She had never seen the sea. She squealed and shrieked in the water, showing the gap between her teeth, as—it crossed his mind—she must do when among her own people. Occasionally he had to go out to dinner at the houses of colleagues from the mining company; she sewed and listened to the radio in the flat and he found her in the bed, warm and already asleep, by the time he came in. He made his way into her body without speaking; she made him welcome without a word. Once he put on evening dress for a dinner at his country's consulate; watching him brush one or two fallen hairs from the shoulders of the dark jacket that sat so well on him, she saw a huge room, all chandeliers and people dancing some dance from a costume film— stately, hand-to-hand. She supposed he was going to fetch, in her place in the car, a partner for the evening. They never kissed when either left the flat; he said, suddenly, kindly, pausing as he picked up cigarettes and keys, "Don't be lonely." And added, "Wouldn't you like to visit your family sometimes, when I have to go out?"

He had told her he was going home to his mother in the forests and mountains of his country near the Italian border (he showed her on the map) after Christmas. She had not told him how her mother, not knowing there was any other variety, assumed he was a medical doctor, so she had talked to her about the doctor's children and the doctor's wife who was a very kind lady, glad to have someone who could help out in the surgery as well as the flat.

She remarked wonderingly on his ability to work until midnight or later, after a day at work. She was so tired when she came home from her cash register at the supermarket that once dinner was eaten she could scarcely keep awake. He explained in a way she could understand that while the work she did was repetitive, undemanding of any real response from her intelligence, requiring little mental or physical effort and therefore unrewarding, his work was his greatest interest, it taxed his mental capacities to their limit, exercised all his concentration, and rewarded him constantly as much with the excitement of a problem presented as with the satisfaction of a problem solved. He said later, putting away his papers, speaking out of a silence: "Have you done other kinds of work?" She said, "I was in a clothing factory before. Sportbeau shirts; you know? But the pay's better in the shop."

Of course. Being a conscientious newspaper-reader in every country he lived in, he was aware that it was only recently that the retail consumer trade in this one had been allowed to employ coloureds as shop assistants; even punching a cash register represented advancement. With the continuing shortage of semi-skilled whites a girl like this might be able to edge a little farther into the white-collar category. He began to teach her to type. He was aware that her English was poor, even though, as a foreigner, in his ears her pronunciation did not offend, nor categorize her as it would in those of someone of his education whose mother tongue was English. He corrected her grammatical mistakes but missed the less obvious ones because of his own sometimes exotic English usage—she continued to use the singular pronoun "it" when what was required was the plural "they." Because he was a foreigner (although so clever, as she saw) she was less inhibited than she might have been by the words she knew she misspelled in her typing. While she sat at the typewriter she thought how one day she would type notes for him, as well as making coffee the way he liked it, and taking him inside her body without saying anything, and sitting (even if only through the empty streets of quiet Sundays) beside him in his car, like a wife.

On a summer night near Christmas—he had already bought and hidden a slightly showy but nevertheless good watch he thought she would like—there was a knocking at the door that brought her out of the bathroom and him to his feet, at his work-table. No one ever came to the flat at night; he had no friends intimate enough to drop in without warning. The summons was an imperious banging that did not pause and clearly would not stop until the door was opened.

She stood in the open bathroom doorway gazing at him across the passage into the living-room; her bare feet and shoulders were

free of a big bath-towel. She said nothing, did not even whisper.
The flat seemed to shake with the strong unhurried blows.

He made as if to go to the door, at last, but now she ran and
clutched him by both arms. She shook her head wildly; her lips
drew back but her teeth were clenched, she didn't speak. She
pulled him into the bedroom, snatched some clothes from the
clean laundry laid out on the bed, and got into the wall-cupboard,
thrusting the key at his hand. Although his arms and calves felt
weakly cold he was horrified, distastefully embarrassed at the sight
of her pressed back crouching there under his suits and coat; it
was horrible and ridiculous. *Come out!* he whispered. *No! Come
out!* She hissed: *Where? Where can I go?*

*Never mind! Get out of there!*

He put out his hand to grasp her. At bay, she said with all
the force of her terrible whisper, baring the gap in her teeth: *I'll
throw myself out the window.*

She forced the key into his hand like the handle of a knife.
He closed the door on her face and drove the key home in the
lock, then dropped it among coins in his trouser pocket.

He unslotted the chain that was looped across the flat door.
He turned the serrated knob of the Yale lock. The three policemen,
two in plain clothes, stood there without impatience although they
had been banging on the door for several minutes. The big dark
one with an elaborate moustache held out in a hand wearing a
plaited gilt ring some sort of identity card.

Dr. von Leinsdorf said quietly, the blood coming strangely
back to legs and arms, "What is it?"

The sergeant told him they knew there was a coloured girl in
the flat. They had had information; "I been watching this flat three
months, I know."

"I am alone here." Dr. von Leinsdorf did not raise his voice.

"I know, I know who is here. Come—" And the sergeant and
his two assistants went into the living-room, the kitchen, the
bathroom (the sergeant picked up a bottle of after-shave cologne,
seemed to study the French label), and the bedroom. The assistants removed the clean laundry that was laid upon the bed and
then turned back the bedding, carrying the sheets over to be
examined by the sergeant under the lamp. They talked to one
another in Afrikaans, which the Doctor did not understand. The

sergeant himself looked under the bed, and lifted the long curtains at the window. The wall-cupboard was of the kind that has no knobs; he saw that it was locked and began to ask in Afrikaans, then politely changed to English, "Give us the key."

Dr. von Leinsdorf said, "I'm sorry, I left it at my office—I always lock and take my keys with me in the mornings."

"It's no good, man, you better give me the key."

He smiled a little, reasonably. "It's on my office desk."

The assistants produced a screwdriver and he watched while they inserted it where the cupboard doors met, gave it quick, firm but not forceful leverage. He heard the lock give.

She had been naked, it was true, when they knocked. But now she was wearing a long-sleeved T-shirt with an appliquéd butterfly motif on one breast, and a pair of jeans. Her feet were still bare; she had managed, by feel, in the dark, to get into some of the clothing she had snatched from the bed, but she had no shoes. She had perhaps been weeping behind the cupboard door (her cheeks looked stained) but now her face was sullen and she was breathing heavily, her diaphragm contracting and expanding exaggeratedly and her breasts pushing against the cloth. It made her appear angry; it might simply have been that she was half-suffocated in the cupboard and needed oxygen. She did not look at Dr. von Leinsdorf. She would not reply to the sergeant's questions.

They were taken to the police station where they were at once separated and in turn led for examination by the district surgeon. The man's underwear was taken away and examined, as the sheets had been, for signs of his seed. When the girl was undressed, it was discovered that beneath her jeans she was wearing a pair of men's briefs with his name on the neatly-sewn laundry tag; in her haste, she had taken the wrong garment to her hiding-place.

Now she cried, standing there before the district surgeon in a man's underwear.

He courteously pretended not to notice. He handed briefs, jeans, and T-shirt round the door, and motioned her to lie on a white-sheeted high table where he placed her legs apart, resting in stirrups, and put into her where the other had made his way so warmly a cold hard instrument that expanded wider and wider. Her thighs and knees trembled uncontrollably while the doctor looked into her and touched her deep inside with more hard instruments, carrying wafers of gauze.

When she came out of the examining room back to the charge office, Dr. von Leinsdorf was not there; they must have taken him somewhere else. She spent what was left of the night in a cell, as he must be doing; but early in the morning she was released and taken home to her mother's house in the coloured township by a white man who explained he was the clerk of the lawyer who had been engaged for her by Dr. von Leinsdorf. Dr. von Leinsdorf, the clerk said, had also been bailed out that morning. He did not say when, or if she would see him again.

A statement made by the girl to the police was handed in to Court when she and the man appeared to meet charges of contravening the Immorality Act in a Johannesburg flat on the night of — December, 19—. *I lived with the white man in his flat. He had intercourse with me sometimes. He gave me tablets to take to prevent me becoming pregnant.*

Interviewed by the Sunday papers, the girl said, "I'm sorry for the sadness brought to my mother." She said she was one of nine children of a female laundry worker. She had left school in Standard Three because there was no money at home for gym clothes or a school blazer. She had worked as a machinist in a factory and a cashier in a supermarket. Dr. von Leinsdorf taught her to type his notes.

Dr. Franz-Josef von Leinsdorf, described as the grandson of a baroness, a cultured man engaged in international mineralogical research, said he accepted social distinctions between people but didn't think they should be legally imposed. "Even in my own country it's difficult for a person from a higher class to marry one from a lower class."

The two accused gave no evidence. They did not greet or speak to each other in Court. The Defence argued that the sergeant's evidence that they had been living together as man and wife was heresay. (The woman with the dachshund, the caretaker?) The magistrate acquitted them because the State failed to prove carnal intercourse had taken place on the night of — December, 19—.

The girl's mother was quoted, with photograph, in the Sunday papers: "I won't let my daughter work as a servant for a white man again."

## II

The farm children play together when they are small; but once the white children go away to school they soon don't play together any more, even in the holidays. Although most of the black children get some sort of schooling, they drop every year farther behind the grades passed by the white children; the childish vocabulary, the child's exploration of the adventurous possibilities of dam, koppies, mealie lands, and veld—there comes a time when the white children have surpassed these with the vocabulary of boarding-school and the possibilities of inter-school sports matches and the kind of adventures seen at the cinema. This usefully coincides with the age of twelve or thirteen; so that by the time early adolescence is reached, the black children are making, along with the bodily changes common to all, an easy transition to adult forms of address, beginning to call their old playmates *missus* and *baasie*—little master.

The trouble was Paulus Eysendyck did not seem to realize that Thebedi was now simply one of the crowd of farm children down at the kraal, recognizable in his sisters' old clothes. The first Christmas holidays after he had gone to boarding-school he brought home for Thebedi a painted box he had made in his wood-work class. He had to give it to her secretly because he had nothing for the other children at the kraal.[2] And she gave him, before he went back to school, a bracelet she had made of thin brass wire and the grey-and-white beans of the castor-oil crop his father cultivated. (When they used to play together, she was the one who had taught Paulus how to make clay oxen for their toy spans.[3]) There was a craze, even in the *platteland* towns like the one where he was at school, for boys to wear elephant-hair and other bracelets beside their watch-straps; his was admired, friends asked him to get similar ones for them. He said the natives made them on his father's farm and he would try.

---

[2] An enclosed native living area.
[3] A pair of animals driven as a team.

When he was fifteen, six feet tall, and tramping round at school dances with the girls from the "sister" school in the same town; when he had learnt how to tease and flirt and fondle quite intimately these girls who were the daughters of prosperous farmers like his father; when he had even met one who, at a wedding he had attended with his parents on a nearby farm, had let him do with her in a locked storeroom what people did when they made love—when he was as far from his childhood as all this, he still brought home from a shop in town a red plastic belt and gilt hoop ear-rings for the black girl, Thebedi. She told her father the missus had given these to her as a reward for some work she had done—it was true she sometimes was called to help out in the farmhouse. She told the girls in the kraal that she had a sweetheart nobody knew about, far away, away on another farm, and they giggled, and teased, and admired her. There was a boy in the kraal called Njabulo who said he wished he could have brought her a belt and ear-rings.

When the farmer's son was home for the holidays she wandered far from the kraal and her companions. He went for walks alone. They had not arranged this; it was an urge each followed independently. He knew it was she, from a long way off. She knew that his dog would not bark at her. Down at the dried-up river-bed where five or six years ago the children had caught a leguaan one great day—a creature that combined ideally the size and ferocious aspect of the crocodile with the harmlessness of the lizard—they squatted side by side on the earth bank. He told her traveller's tales: about school, about the punishments at school, particularly, exaggerating both their nature and his indifference to them. He told her about the town of Middleburg, which she had never seen. She had nothing to tell but she prompted with many questions, like any good listener. While he talked he twisted and tugged at the roots of white stinkwood and Cape willow trees that looped out of the eroded earth around them. It had always been a good spot for children's games, down there hidden by the mesh of old, ant-eaten trees held in place by vigorous ones, wild asparagus bushing up between the trunks, and here and there prickly-pear cactus sunken-skinned and bristly, like an old man's face, keeping alive sapless until the next rainy season. She punctured the dry hide of a prickly-pear again and again with a sharp stick while she listened. She laughed a lot at what he told her, sometimes dropping her face on her knees, sharing amusement with the cool shady earth beneath her bare feet. She put on her pair of shoes—white sandals, thickly Blanco-ed against the farm dust— when he was on the farm, but these were taken off and laid aside, at the river-bed.

One summer afternoon when there was water flowing there and it was very hot she waded in as they used to do when they were children, her dress bunched modestly and tucked into the legs of her pants. The schoolgirls he went swimming with at dams or pools on neighbouring farms wore bikinis but the sight of their dazzling bellies and thighs in the sunlight had never made him feel what he felt now, when the girl came up the bank and sat beside him, the drops of water beading off her dark legs the only points of light in the earth-smelling, deep shade. They were not afraid of one another, they had known one another always; he did with her what he had done that time in the storeroom at the wedding, and this time it was so lovely, so lovely, he was surprised . . . and she was surprised by it, too—he could see in her dark face that was part of the shade, with her big dark eyes, shiny as soft water, watching him attentively: as she had when they used to huddle over their teams of mud oxen, as she had when he told her about detention weekends at school.

They went to the river-bed often through those summer hol- idays. They met just before the light went, as it does quite quickly, and each returned home with the dark—she to her mother's hut, he to the farmhouse—in time for the evening meal. He did not tell her about school or town any more. She did not ask questions any longer. He told her, each time, when they would meet again. Once or twice it was very early in the morning; the lowing of the cows being driven to graze came to them where they lay, dividing them with unspoken recognition of the sound read in their two pairs of eyes, opening so close to each other.

He was a popular boy at school. He was in the second, then the first soccer team. The head girl of the "sister" school was said to have a crush on him; he didn't particularly like her, but there was a pretty blonde who put up her long hair into a kind of doughnut with a black ribbon round it, whom he took to see films when the schoolboys and girls had a free Saturday afternoon. He had been driving tractors and other farm vehicles since he was ten years old, and as soon as he was eighteen he got a driver's licence and in the holidays, this last year of his school life, he took neighbours' daughters to dances and to the drive-in cinema that had just opened twenty kilometers from the farm. His sisters were married, by then; his parents often left him in charge of the farm over the weekend while they visited the young wives and grand-children.

When Thebedi saw the farmer and his wife drive away on a Saturday afternoon, the boot of their Mercedes filled with fresh-killed poultry and vegetables from the garden that it was part of her father's work to tend, she knew that she must come not to the river-bed but up to the house. The house was an old one, thick-walled, dark against the heat. The kitchen was its lively thoroughfare, with servants, food supplies, begging cats and dogs, pots boiling over, washing being damped for ironing, and the big deep-freezer the missus had ordered from town, bearing a cro-cheted mat and a vase of plastic irises. But the dining-room with the bulging-legged heavy table was shut up in its rich, old smell of soup and tomato sauce. The sitting-room curtains were drawn and the T.V. set silent. The door of the parents' bedroom was locked and the empty rooms where the girls had slept had sheets of plastic spread over the beds. It was in one of these that she and the farmer's son stayed together whole nights—almost: she had to get away before the house servants, who knew her, came in at dawn. There was a risk someone would discover her or traces of her presence if he took her to his own bedroom, although she had looked into it many times when she was helping out in the house and knew well, there, the row of silver cups he had won at school.

When she was eighteen and the farmer's son nineteen and working with his father on the farm before entering a veterinary college, the young man Njabulo asked her father for her. Njabulo's parents met with hers and the money he was to pay in place of the cows it is customary to give a prospective bride's parents was settled upon. He had no cows to offer; he was a labourer on the Eysendyck farm, like her father. A bright youngster; old Eysen-dyck had taught him brick-laying and was using him for odd jobs in construction, around the place. She did not tell the farmer's son that her parents had arranged for her to marry. She did not tell him, either, before he left for his first term at the veterinary college, that she thought she was going to have a baby. Two months after her marriage to Njabulo, she gave birth to a daughter.

There was no disgrace in that; among her people it is customary for a young man to make sure, before marriage, that the chosen girl is not barren, and Njabulo made love to her then. But the infant was very light and did not quickly grow darker as most African babies do. Already at birth there was on its head a quantity of straight, fine floss, like that which carries the seeds of certain weeds in the veld. The unfocused eyes it opened were grey flecked with yellow. Njabulo was the matt, opaque coffee-grounds colour that has always been called black; the colour of Thebedi's legs on which beaded water looked oyster-shell blue, the same colour as Thebedi's face, where the black eyes, with their interested gaze and clear whites, were so dominant.

Njabulo made no complaint. Out of his farm labourer's earnings he bought from the Indian store a cellophane-windowed pack containing a pink plastic bath, six napkins, a card of safety pins, a knitted jacket, cap and bootees, a dress, and a tin of Johnson's Baby Powder, for Thebedi's baby.

When it was two weeks old Paulus Eysendyck arrived home from the veterinary college for the holidays. He drank a glass of fresh, still-warm milk in the childhood familiarity of his mother's kitchen and heard her discussing with the old house-servant where they could get a reliable substitute to help out now that the girl Thebedi had had a baby. For the first time since he was a small boy he came right into the kraal. It was eleven o'clock in the morning. The men were at work in the lands. He looked about him, urgently; the women turned away, each not wanting to be the one approached to point out where Thebedi lived. Thebedi appeared, coming slowly from the hut Njabulo had built in white man's style, with a tin chimney, and a proper window with glass panes set in straight as walls made of unfired bricks would allow. She greeted him with hands brought together and a token movement representing the respectful bob with which she was accustomed to acknowledge she was in the presence of his father or mother. He lowered his head under the doorway of her home and went in. He said, "I want to see. Show me."

She had taken the bundle off her back before she came out into the light to face him. She moved between the iron bedstead made up with Njabulo's checked blankets and the small wooden table where the pink plastic bath stood among food and kitchen pots, and picked up the bundle from the snugly-blanketed grocer's

box where it lay. The infant was asleep; she revealed the closed, pale, plump tiny face, with a bubble of spit at the corner of the mouth, the spidery pink hands stirring. She took off the woollen cap and the straight fine hair flew up after it in static electricity, showing gilded strands here and there. He said nothing. She was watching him as she had done when they were little, and the gang of children had trodden down a crop in their games or transgressed in some other way for which he, as the farmer's son, the white one among them, must intercede with the farmer. She disturbed the sleeping face by scratching or tickling gently at a cheek with one finger, and slowly the eyes opened, saw nothing, were still asleep, and then, awake, no longer narrowed, looked out at them, grey with yellowish flecks, his own hazel eyes.

He struggled for a moment with a grimace of tears, anger, and self-pity. She could not put out her hand to him. He said, "You haven't been near the house with it?"

She shook her head.

"Never?"

Again she shook her head.

"Don't take it out. Stay inside. Can't you take it away somewhere. You must give it to someone—"

She moved to the door with him.

He said, "I'll see what I will do. I don't know." And then he said: "I feel like killing myself."

Her eyes began to glow, to thicken with tears. For a moment there was the feeling between them that used to come when they were alone down at the river-bed.

He walked out.

Two days later, when his mother and father had left the farm for the day, he appeared again. The women were away on the lands, weeding, as they were employed to do as casual labour in the summer; only the very old remained, propped up on the ground outside the huts in the flies and the sun. Thebedi did not ask him in. The child had not been well; it had diarrhoea. He asked where its food was. She said, "The milk comes from me." He went into Njabulo's house, where the child lay; she did not follow but stayed outside the door and watched without seeing an old crone who had lost her mind, talking to herself, talking to the fowls who ignored her.

She thought she heard small grunts from the hut, the kind of infant grunt that indicates a full stomach, a deep sleep. After a time, long or short she did not know, he came out and walked away with plodding stride (his father's gait) out of sight, towards his father's house.

The baby was not fed during the night and although she kept telling Njabulo it was sleeping, he saw for himself in the morning that it was dead. He comforted her with words and caresses. She did not cry but simply sat, staring at the door. Her hands were cold as dead chickens' feet to his touch.

Njabulo buried the little baby where farm workers were buried, in the place in the veld the farmer had given them. Some of the mounds had been left to weather away unmarked, others were covered with stones and a few had fallen wooden crosses. He was going to make a cross but before it was finished the police came and dug up the grave and took away the dead baby: someone— one of the other labourers? their women?—had reported that the baby was almost white, that, strong and healthy, it had died suddenly after a visit by the farmer's son. Pathological tests on the infant corpse showed intestinal damage not always consistent with death by natural causes.

Thebedi went for the first time to the country town where Paulus had been to school, to give evidence at the preparatory examination into the charge of murder brought against him. She cried hysterically in the witness box, saying yes, yes (the gilt hoop ear-rings swung in her ears), she saw the accused pouring liquid into the baby's mouth. She said he had threatened to shoot her if she told anyone.

More than a year went by before, in that same town, the case was brought to trial. She came to Court with a new-born baby on her back. She wore gilt hoop ear-rings; she was calm; she said she had not seen what the white man did in the house.

Paulus Eysendyck said he had visited the hut but had not poisoned the child.

The Defence did not contest that there had been a love relationship between the accused and the girl, or that intercourse had taken place, but submitted there was no proof that the child was the accused's.

The judge told the accused there was strong suspicion against him but not enough proof that he had committed the crime. The Court could not accept the girl's evidence because it was clear she had committed perjury either at this trial or at the preparatory examination. There was the suggestion in the mind of the Court that she might be an accomplice in the crime; but, again, insufficient proof.

The judge commended the honourable behaviour of the husband (sitting in court in a brown-and-yellow-quartered golf cap bought for Sundays) who had not rejected his wife and had "even provided clothes for the unfortunate infant out of his slender means."

The verdict on the accused was "not guilty."

The young white man refused to accept the congratulations of press and public and left the Court with his mother's raincoat shielding his face from photographers. His father said to the press, "I will try and carry on as best I can to hold up my head in the district."

Interviewed by the Sunday papers, who spelled her name in a variety of ways, the black girl, speaking in her own language, was quoted beneath her photograph: "It was a thing of our childhood, we don't see each other anymore."

# FLANNERY O'CONNOR [1925–1964]

## A Temple of the Holy Ghost

All weekend the two girls were calling each other Temple One and Temple Two, shaking with laughter and getting so red and hot that they were positively ugly, particularly Joanne who had spots on her face anyway. They came in the brown convent uniforms they had to wear to Mount St. Scholastica but as soon as they opened their suitcases, they took off the uniforms and put on red skirts and loud blouses. They put on lipstick and their Sunday shoes and walked around in the high heels all over the house, always passing the long mirror in the hall slowly to get a look at their legs. None of their ways were lost on the child. If only one of them had come, that one would have played with her, but since there were two of them, she was out of it and watched them suspiciously from a distance.

They were fourteen—two years older than she was—but neither of them was bright, which was why they had been sent to the convent. If they had gone to a regular school, they wouldn't have done anything but think about boys; at the convent the sisters, her mother said, would keep a grip on their necks. The child decided, after observing them for a few hours, that they were practically morons and she was glad to think that they were only second cousins and she couldn't have inherited any of their stupidity. Susan called herself Su-zan. She was very skinny but she had a pretty pointed face and red hair. Joanne had yellow hair that was naturally curly but she talked through her nose and when she laughed, she turned purple in patches. Neither one of them could say an intelligent thing and all their sentences began, "You know this boy I know well one time he . . ."

They were to stay all weekend and her mother said she didn't see how she would entertain them since she didn't know any boys their age. At this, the child, struck suddenly with genius, shouted, "There's Cheat! Get Cheat to come! Ask Miss Kirby to get Cheat to come show them around!" and she nearly choked on the food she had in her mouth. She doubled over laughing and hit the table with her fist and looked at the two bewildered girls while water started in her eyes and rolled down her fat cheeks and the braces she had in her mouth glared like tin. She had never thought of anything so funny before.

Her mother laughed in a guarded way and Miss Kirby blushed and carried her fork delicately to her mouth with one pea on it. She was a long-faced blonde schoolteacher who boarded with them and Mr. Cheatam was her admirer, a rich old farmer who arrived every Saturday afternoon in a fifteen-year-old baby-blue Pontiac powdered with red clay dust and black inside with Negroes that he charged ten cents apiece to bring into town on Saturday afternoons. After he dumped them he came to see Miss Kirby, always bringing a little gift—a bag of boiled peanuts or a watermelon or a stalk of sugar cane and once a wholesale box of Baby Ruth candy bars. He was bald-headed except for a little fringe of rust-colored hair and his face was nearly the same color as the unpaved roads and washed like them with ruts and gulleys. He wore a pale green shirt with a thin black stripe in it and blue galluses and his trousers cut across a protruding stomach that he pressed tenderly from time to time with his big flat thumb. All his teeth were backed with gold and he would roll his eyes at Miss Kirby in an impish way and say, "Haw haw," sitting in their porch swing with his legs spread apart and his hightopped shoes pointing in opposite directions on the floor.

"I don't think Cheat is going to be in town this weekend," Miss Kirby said, not in the least understanding that this was a joke, and the child was convulsed afresh, threw herself backward in her chair, fell out of it, rolled on the floor, and lay there heaving. Her mother told her if she didn't stop this foolishness she would have to leave the table.

Yesterday her mother had arranged with Alonzo Myers to drive them the forty-five miles to Mayville, where the convent was, to get the girls for the weekend and Sunday afternoon he was hired to drive them back again. He was an eighteen-year-old boy who weighed two hundred and fifty pounds and worked for the taxi company and he was all you could get to drive you anywhere. He smoked or rather chewed a short black cigar and he had a round sweaty chest that showed through the yellow nylon shirt he wore. When he drove all the windows of the car had to be open.

"Well there's Alonzo!" the child roared from the floor. "Get Alonzo to show em around! Get Alonzo!"

The two girls, who had seen Alonzo, began to scream their indignation.

Her mother thought this was funny too but she said, "That'll be about enough out of you," and changed the subject. She asked them why they called each other Temple One and Temple Two and this sent them off into gales of giggles. Finally they managed to explain. Sister Perpetua, the oldest nun at the Sisters of Mercy in Mayville, had given them a lecture on what to do if a young man should—here they laughed so hard they were not able to go on without going back to the beginning—on what to do if a young man should—they put their heads in their laps—on what to do if—they finally managed to shout it out—if he should "behave in an ungentlemanly manner with them in the back of an automobile." Sister Perpetua said they were to say, "Stop sir! I am a Temple of the Holy Ghost!" and that would put an end to it. The child sat up off the floor with a blank face. She didn't see anything so funny in this. What was really funny was the idea of Mr. Cheatam or Alonzo Myers beauing them around. That killed her.

Her mother didn't laugh at what they had said. "I think you girls are pretty silly," she said. "After all, that's what you are— Temples of the Holy Ghost."

The two of them looked up at her, politely concealing their giggles, but with astonished faces as if they were beginning to realize that she was made of the same stuff as Sister Perpetua.

Miss Kirby preserved her set expression and the child thought, it's all over her head anyhow. I am a Temple of the Holy Ghost, she said to herself, and was pleased with the phrase. It made her feel as if somebody had given her a present.

After dinner, her mother collapsed on the bed and said, "Those girls are going to drive me crazy if I don't get some entertainment for them. They're awful."

"I bet I know who you could get," the child started.

"Now listen. I don't want to hear any more about Mr. Cheatam," her mother said. "You embarrass Miss Kirby. He's her only friend. Oh my Lord," and she sat up and looked mournfully out the window, "that poor soul is so lonesome she'll even ride in that car that smells like the last circle in hell."

And she's a Temple of the Holy Ghost too, the child reflected. "I wasn't thinking of him," she said. "I was thinking of those two Wilkinses, Wendell and Cory, that visit old lady Buchell out on her farm. They're her grandsons. They work for her."

"Now that's an idea," her mother murmured and gave her an appreciative look. But then she slumped again. "They're only farm boys. These girls would turn up their noses at them."

"Huh," the child said. "They wear pants. They're sixteen and they got a car. Somebody said they were both going to be Church of God preachers because you don't have to know nothing to be one."

"They would be perfectly safe with those boys all right," her mother said and in a minute she got up and called their grandmother on the telephone and after she had talked to the old woman a half an hour, it was arranged that Wendell and Cory would come to supper and afterwards take the girls to the fair.

Susan and Joanne were so pleased that they washed their hair and rolled it up on aluminum curlers. Hah, thought the child, sitting cross-legged on the bed to watch them undo the curlers, wait'll you get a load of Wendell and Cory! "You'll like these boys," she said. "Wendell is six feet tall ands got red hair. Cory is six feet six inches talls got black hair and wears a sport jacket and they gottem this car with a squirrel tail on the front."

"How does a child like you know so much about these men?" Susan asked and pushed her face up close to the mirror to watch the pupils in her eyes dilate.

The child lay back on the bed and began to count the narrow boards in the ceiling until she lost her place. I know them all right, she said to someone. We fought in the world war together. They were under me and I saved them five times from Japanese suicide divers and Wendell said I am going to marry that kid and the other said oh no you ain't I am and I said neither one of you is because I will court marshall you all before you can bat an eye. "I've seen them around is all," she said.

When they came the girls stared at them a second and then began to giggle and talk to each other about the convent. They sat in the swing together and Wendell and Cory sat on the banisters together. They sat like monkeys, their knees on a level with their shoulders and their arms hanging down between. They were short thin boys with red faces and high cheekbones and pale seed-like eyes. They had brought a harmonica and a guitar. One of them began to blow softly on the mouth organ, watching the girls over it, and the other started strumming the guitar and then began to sing, not watching them but keeping his head tilted upward as if he were only interested in hearing himself. He was singing a hillbilly song that sounded half like a love song and half like a hymn.

The child was standing on a barrel pushed into some bushes at the side of the house, her face on a level with the porch floor. The sun was going down and the sky was turning a bruised violet color that seemed to be connected with the sweet mournful sound of the music. Wendell began to smile as he sang and to look at the girls. He looked at Susan with a dog-like loving look and sang,

> "I've found a friend in Jesus,
> He's everything to me,
> He's the lily of the valley,
> He's the One who's set me free!"

Then he turned the same look on Joanne and sang,

> "A wall of fire about me,
> I've nothing now to fear,

> He's the lily of the valley,
> And I'll always have Him near!"

The girls looked at each other and held their lips stiff so as not to giggle but Susan let out one anyway and clapped her hand on her mouth. The singer frowned and for a few seconds only strummed the guitar. Then he began "The Old Rugged Cross" and they listened politely but when he had finished they said, "Let us sing one!" and before he could start another, they began to sing with their convent-trained voices.

> "Tantum-ergo Sacramentum
> Veneremur Cernui:
> Et antiquum documentum
> Novo cedat ritui:"

The child watched the boys' solemn faces turn with perplexed frowning stares at each other as if they were uncertain whether they were being made fun of.

> "Praestet fides supplementum
> Sensuum defectui.
> Genitori, Genitoque
> Laus et jubilatio
>
> Salus, honor, virtus quoque . . ."

The boys' faces were dark red in the gray-purple light. They looked fierce and startled.

> "Sit et benedictio;
> Procedenti ab utroque
> Compar sit laudatio.
> Amen."

The girls dragged out the Amen and then there was a silence.

"That must be Jew singing," Wendell said and began to tune the guitar.

The girls giggled idiotically but the child stamped her foot on the barrel. "You big dumb ox!" she shouted. "You big dumb Church of God ox!" she roared and fell off the barrel and scrambled up and shot around the corner of the house as they jumped from the banister to see who was shouting.

Her mother had arranged for them to have supper in the back yard and she had a table laid out there under some Japanese lanterns that she pulled out for garden parties. "I ain't eating with them," the child said and snatched her plate off the table and carried it to the kitchen and sat down with the thin blue-gummed cook and ate her supper.

"Howcome you be so ugly sometime?" the cook asked.

"Those stupid idiots," the child said.

The lanterns gilded the leaves of the trees orange on the level where they hung and above them was black-green and below them were different dim muted colors that made the girls sitting at the table look prettier than they were. From time to time, the child turned her head and glared out the kitchen window at the scene below.

"God could strike you deaf dumb and blind," the cook said, "and then you wouldn't be as smart as you is."

"I would still be smarter than some," the child said.

After supper they left for the fair. She wanted to go to the fair but not with them so even if they had asked her she wouldn't have gone. She went upstairs and paced the long bedroom with her hands locked together behind her back and her head thrust forward and an expression, fierce and dreamy both, on her face. She didn't turn on the electric light but let the darkness collect and make the room smaller and more private. At regular intervals a light crossed the open window and threw shadows on the wall. She stopped and stood looking out over the dark slopes, past where the pond glinted silver, past the wall of woods to the speckled sky where a long finger of light was revolving up and around and away, searching the air as if it were hunting for the lost sun. It was the beacon light from the fair.

She could hear the distant sound of the calliope and she saw in her head all the tents raised up in a kind of gold sawdust light and the diamond ring of the ferris wheel going around and around up in the air and down again and the screeking merry-go-round going around and around on the ground. A fair lasted five or six days and there was a special afternoon for school children and a special night for niggers. She had gone last year on the afternoon for school children and had seen the monkeys and the fat man and had ridden on the ferris wheel. Certain tents were closed then because they contained things that would be known only to grown people but she had looked with interest at the advertising on the closed tents, at the faded-looking pictures on the canvas of people in tights, with stiff stretched composed faces like the faces of the martyrs waiting to have their tongues cut out by the Roman soldier. She had imagined that what was inside these tents concerned medicine and she had made up her mind to be a doctor when she grew up.

She had since changed and decided to be an engineer but as she looked out the window and followed the revolving searchlight as it widened and shortened and wheeled in its arc, she felt that she would have to be much more than just a doctor or an engineer. She would have to be a saint because that was the occupation that included everything you could know; and yet she knew she would never be a saint. She did not steal or murder but she was a born liar and slothful and she sassed her mother and was deliberately ugly to almost everybody. She was eaten up also with the sin of Pride, the worst one. She made fun of the Baptist preacher who came to the school at commencement to give the devotional. She would pull down her mouth and hold her forehead as if she were in agony and groan, "Fawther, we thank Thee," exactly the way he did and she had been told many times not to do it. She could never be a saint, but she thought she could be a martyr if they killed her quick.

She could stand to be shot but not to be burned in oil. She didn't know if she could stand to be torn to pieces by lions or not. She began to prepare her martyrdom, seeing herself in a pair of tights in a great arena, lit by the early Christians hanging in cages of fire, making a gold dusty light that fell on her and the lions. The first lion charged forward and fell at her feet converted. A whole series of lions did the same. The lions liked her so much she even slept with them and finally the Romans were obliged to burn her but to their astonishment she would not burn down and finding she was so hard to kill, they finally cut off her head very quickly with a sword and she went immediately to heaven. She rehearsed this several times, returning each time at the entrance of Paradise to the lions.

Finally she got up from the window and got ready for bed and got in without saying her prayers. There were two heavy double beds in the room. The girls were occupying the other one and she tried to think of something cold and clammy that she could hide in their bed but her thought was fruitless. She didn't have anything she could think of, like a chicken carcass or a piece of beef liver. The sound of the calliope coming through the window kept her awake and she remembered that she hadn't said her prayers and got up and knelt down and began them. She took a running start and went through to the other side of the Apostle's Creed and then hung by her chin on the side of the bed, empty-minded. Her prayers, when she remembered to say them, were usually perfunctory but sometimes when she had done something wrong or heard music or lost something, or sometimes for no reason at all, she would be moved to fervor and would think of Christ on the long journey to Calvary, crushed three times on the rough cross. Her mind would stay on this a while and then get empty and when something roused her, she would find that she was thinking of a different thing entirely, of some dog or some girl or something she was going to do some day. Tonight, remembering Wendell and Cory, she was filled with thanksgiving and almost weeping with delight, she said, "Lord, Lord, thank You that I'm not in the Church of God, thank You Lord, thank You!" and got back in bed and kept repeating it until she went to sleep.

The girls came in at a quarter to twelve and waked her up with their giggling. They turned on the small blue-shaded lamp to see to get undressed by and their skinny shadows climbed up the wall and broke and continued moving about softly on the ceiling. The child sat up to hear what all they had seen at the fair. Susan had a plastic pistol full of cheap candy and Joanne a pasteboard cat with red polka dots on it. "Did you see the monkeys dance?" the child asked. "Did you see that fat man and those midgets?"

"All kinds of freaks," Joanne said. And then she said to Susan, "I enjoyed it all but the you-know-what," and her face assumed a peculiar expression as if she had bit into something that she didn't know if she liked or not.

The other stood still and shook her head once and nodded slightly at the child. "Little pitchers,"[1] she said in a low voice but the child heard it and her heart began to beat very fast.

She got out of bed and climbed onto the footboard of theirs. They turned off the light and got in but she didn't move. She sat there, looking hard at them until their faces were well defined in the dark. "I'm not as old as you all," she said, "but I'm about a million times smarter."

---

[1] "Little pitchers have big ears."

"There are some things," Susan said, "that a child of your age doesn't know," and they both began to giggle.

"Go back to your own bed," Joanne said.

The child didn't move. "One time," she said, her voice hollow-sounding in the dark, "I saw this rabbit have rabbits."

There was a silence. Then Susan said, "How?" in an indifferent tone and she knew that she had them. She said she wouldn't tell until they told about the you-know-what. Actually she had never seen a rabbit have rabbits but she forgot this as they began to tell what they had seen in the tent.

It had been a freak with a particular name but they couldn't remember the name. The tent where it was had been divided into two parts by a black curtain, one side for men and one for women. The freak went from one side to the other, talking first to the men and then to the women, but everyone could hear. The stage ran all the way across the front. The girls heard the freak say to the men, "I'm going to show you this and if you laugh, God may strike you the same way." The freak had a country voice, slow and nasal and neither high nor low, just flat. "God made me thisaway and if you laugh He may strike you the same way. This is the way He wanted me to be and I ain't disputing His way. I'm showing you because I got to make the best of it. I expect you to act like ladies and gentlemen. I never done it to myself nor had a thing to do with it but I'm making the best of it. I don't dispute hit." Then there was a long silence on the other side of the tent and finally the freak left the men and came over onto the women's side and said the same thing.

The child felt every muscle strained as if she were hearing the answer to a riddle that was more puzzling than the riddle itself. "You mean it had two heads?" she said.

"No," Susan said, "it was a man and woman both. It pulled up its dress and showed us. It had on a blue dress."

The child wanted to ask how it could be a man and woman both without two heads but she did not. She wanted to get back into her own bed and think it out and she began to climb down off the footboard.

"What about the rabbit?" Joanne asked.

The child stopped and only her face appeared over the footboard, abstracted, absent. "It spit them out of its mouth," she said, "six of them."

She lay in bed trying to picture the tent with the freak walking from side to side but she was too sleepy to figure it out. She was better able to see the faces of the country people watching, the men more solemn than they were in church, and the women stern and polite, with painted-looking eyes, standing as if they were waiting for the first note of the piano to begin the hymn. She could hear the freak saying, "God made me thisaway and I don't dispute hit," and the people saying, "Amen. Amen."

"God done this to me and I praise Him."

"Amen. Amen."

"He could strike you thisaway."

"Amen. Amen."

"But he has not."

"Amen."

"Raise yourself up. A temple of the Holy Ghost. You! You are God's temple, don't you know? Don't you know? God's Spirit has a dwelling in you, don't you know?"

"Amen. Amen."

"If anybody desecrates the temple of God, God will bring him to ruin and if you laugh, He may strike you thisaway. A temple of God is a holy thing. Amen. Amen."

"I am a temple of the Holy Ghost."

"Amen."

The people began to slap their hands without making a loud noise and with a regular beat between the Amens, more and more softly, as if they knew there was a child near, half asleep.

T he next afternoon the girls put on their brown convent uniforms again and the child and her mother took them back to Mount St. Scholastica. "Oh glory, oh Pete!" they said. "Back to the salt mines." Alonzo Myers drove them and the child sat in front with him and her mother sat in back between the two girls, telling them such things as how pleased she was to have had them and how they must come back again and then about the good times she and their mothers had had when they were girls at the convent. The child didn't listen to any of this twaddle but kept as close to the locked door as she could get and held her head out the window. They had thought Alonzo would smell better on Sunday but he did not. With her hair blowing over her face she could look directly into the ivory sun which was framed in the middle of the blue afternoon but when she pulled it away from her eyes she had to squint.

Mount St. Scholastica was a red brick house set back in a garden in the center of town. There was a filling station on one side of it and a firehouse on the other. It had a high black grille-work fence around it and narrow bricked walks between old trees and japonica bushes that were heavy with blooms. A big moon-faced nun came bustling to the door to let them in and embraced her mother and would have done the same to her but she stuck out her hand and preserved a frigid frown, looking just past the sister's shoes at the wainscoting. They had a tendency to kiss even homely children, but the nun shook her hand vigorously and even cracked her knuckles a little and said they must come to the chapel, that benediction was just beginning. You put your foot in their door and they got you praying, the child thought as they hurried down the polished corridor.

You'd think she had to catch a train, she continued in the same ugly vein as they entered the chapel where the sisters were kneeling on one side and the girls, all in brown uniforms, on the other. The chapel smelled of incense. It was light green and gold, a series of springing arches that ended with the one over the altar where the priest was kneeling in front of the monstrance,[2] bowed low. A small boy in a surplice was standing behind him, swinging the censer. The child knelt down between her mother and the nun and they were well into the *"Tantum Ergo"* before her ugly thoughts stopped and she began to realize that she was in the presence of God. Hep me not to be so mean, she began mechanically. Hep me not to give her so much sass. Hep me not to talk like I do. Her mind began to get quiet and then empty but when the priest raised the monstrance with the Host shining ivory-colored in the center of it, she was thinking of the tent at the fair that had the freak in it. The freak was saying, "I don't dispute hit. This is the way He wanted me to be."

As they were leaving the convent door, the big nun swooped down on her mischievously and nearly smothered her in the black habit, mashing the side of her face into the crucifix hitched onto

---

[2] An open or transparent vessel of gold or silver in which the Host, or conse-crated bread of the Eucharist, is exposed at Mass.

her belt and then holding her off and looking at her with little periwinkle eyes.

On the way home she and her mother sat in the back and Alonzo drove by himself in the front. The child observed three folds of fat in the back of his neck and noted that his ears were pointed almost like a pig's. Her mother, making conversation, asked him if he had gone to the fair.

"Gone," he said, "and never missed a thing and it was good I gone when I did because they ain't going to have it next week like they said they was."

"Why?" asked her mother.

"They shut it on down," he said. "Some of the preachers from town gone out and inspected it and got the police to shut it on down."

Her mother let the conversation drop and the child's round face was lost in thought. She turned it toward the window and looked out over a stretch of pasture land that rose and fell with a gathering greenness until it touched the dark woods. The sun was a huge red ball like an elevated Host drenched in blood and when it sank out of sight, it left a line in the sky like a red clay road hanging over the trees.


## GABRIEL GARCÍA MÁRQUEZ [b. 1928]

# A Very Old Man with Enormous Wings

On the third day of rain they had killed so many crabs inside the house that Pelayo had to cross his drenched courtyard and throw them into the sea, because the newborn child had a temperature all night and they thought it was due to the stench. The world had been sad since Tuesday. Sea and sky were a single ash-gray thing and the sands of the beach, which on March nights

---

Translated by Gabriel García Márquez.

glimmered like powdered light, had become a stew of mud and rotten shellfish. The light was so weak at noon that when Pelayo was coming back to the house after throwing away the crabs, it was hard for him to see what it was that was moving and groaning in the rear of the courtyard. He had to go very close to see that it was an old man, a very old man, lying face down in the mud, who, in spite of his tremendous efforts, couldn't get up, impeded by his enormous wings.

Frightened by that nightmare, Pelayo ran to get Elisenda, his wife, who was putting compresses on the sick child, and he took her to the rear of the courtyard. They both looked at the fallen body with mute stupor. He was dressed like a ragpicker. There were only a few faded hairs left on his bald skull and very few teeth in his mouth, and his pitiful condition of a drenched great-grandfather had taken away any sense of grandeur he might have had. His huge buzzard wings, dirty and half-plucked, were forever entangled in the mud. They looked at him so long and so closely that Pelayo and Elisenda very soon overcame their surprise and in the end found him familiar. Then they dared speak to him, and he answered in an incomprehensible dialect with a strong sailor's voice. That was how they skipped over the inconvenience of the wings and quite intelligently concluded that he was a lonely cast-away from some foreign ship wrecked by the storm. And yet, they called in a neighbor woman who knew everything about life and death to see him, and all she needed was one look to show them their mistake.

"He's an angel," she told them. "He must have been coming for the child, but the poor fellow is so old that the rain knocked him down."

On the following day everyone knew that a flesh-and-blood angel was held captive in Pelayo's house. Against the judgment of the wise neighbor woman, for whom angels in those times were the fugitive survivors of a celestial conspiracy, they did not have the heart to club him to death. Pelayo watched over him all after-noon from the kitchen, armed with his bailiff's club, and before going to bed he dragged him out of the mud and locked him up with the hens in the wire chicken coop. In the middle of the night, when the rain stopped, Pelayo and Elisenda were still killing crabs. A short time afterward the child woke up without a fever and with a desire to eat. Then they felt magnanimous and decided to put the angel on a raft with fresh water and provisions for three days and leave him to his fate on the high seas. But when they went out into the courtyard with the first light of dawn, they found the whole neighborhood in front of the chicken coop having fun with the angel, without the slightest reverence, tossing him things to eat through the openings in the wire as if he weren't a supernatural creature but a circus animal.

Father Gonzaga arrived before seven o'clock, alarmed at the strange news. By that time onlookers less frivolous than those at dawn had already arrived and they were making all kinds of conjectures concerning the captive's future. The simplest among them thought that he should be named mayor of the world. Others of sterner mind felt that he should be promoted to the rank of five-star general in order to win all wars. Some visionaries hoped that he could be put to stud in order to implant on earth a race of winged wise men who could take charge of the universe. But Father Gonzaga, before becoming a priest, had been a robust woodcutter. Standing by the wire, he reviewed his catechism in an instant and asked them to open the door so that he could take a close look at that pitiful man who looked more like a huge decrepit hen among the fascinated chickens. He was lying in a corner drying his open wings in the sunlight among the fruit peels and breakfast leftovers that the early risers had thrown him. Alien to the impertinences of the world, he only lifted his antiquarian eyes and murmured something in his dialect when Father Gonzaga went into the chicken coop and said good morning to him in Latin. The parish priest had his first suspicion of an impostor when he saw that he did not understand the language of God or know how to greet His ministers. Then he noticed that seen close up he was much too human: he had an unbearable smell of the outdoors, the back side of his wings was strewn with parasites and his main feathers had been mistreated by terrestrial winds, and nothing about him measured up to the proud dignity of angels. Then he came out of the chicken coop and in a brief sermon warned the curious against the risks of being ingenuous. He reminded them that the devil had the bad habit of making use of carnival tricks in order to confuse the unwary. He argued that if wings were not the essential element in determining the difference between a hawk and an airplane, they were even less so in the recognition of angels. Nevertheless, he promised to write a letter to his bishop so that the latter would write to his primate so that the latter would write to the Supreme Pontiff in order to get the final verdict from the highest courts.

His prudence fell on sterile hearts. The news of the captive angel spread with such rapidity that after a few hours the court-yard had the bustle of a marketplace and they had to call in troops with fixed bayonets to disperse the mob that was about to knock the house down. Elisenda, her spine all twisted from sweeping up so much marketplace trash, then got the idea of fencing in the yard and charging five cents admission to see the angel.

The curious came from far away. A traveling carnival arrived with a flying acrobat who buzzed over the crowd several times, but no one paid any attention to him because his wings were not those of an angel but, rather, those of a sidereal bat. The most unfortunate invalids on earth came in search of health: a poor woman who since childhood had been counting her heartbeats and had run out of numbers; a Portuguese man who couldn't sleep because the noise of the stars disturbed him; a sleep-walker who got up at night to undo the things he had done while awake; and many others with less serious ailments. In the midst of that shipwreck disorder that made the earth tremble, Pelayo and Eli-senda were happy with fatigue, for in less than a week they had crammed their rooms with money and the line of pilgrims waiting their turn to enter still reached beyond the horizon.

The angel was the only one who took no part in his own act. He spent his time trying to get comfortable in his borrowed nest, befuddled by the hellish heat of the oil lamps and sacramental candles that had been placed along the wire. At first they tried to make him eat some mothballs, which, according to the wisdom of the wise neighbor woman, were the food prescribed for angels. But he turned them down, just as he turned down the papal lunches that the penitents brought him, and they never found out whether it was because he was an angel or because he was an old man that in the end he ate nothing but eggplant mush. His only supernatural virtue seemed to be patience. Especially during the first days, when the hens pecked at him, searching for the stellar parasites that proliferated in his wings, and the cripples pulled out feathers to touch their defective parts with, and even the most merciful threw stones at him, trying to get him to rise so they could see him standing. The only time they succeeded in arousing him was when they burned his side with an iron for branding steers, for he had been motionless for so many hours that they thought he was dead. He awoke with a start, ranting in his hermetic language and with tears in his eyes, and he flapped his wings a couple of times, which brought on a whirlwind of chicken dung and lunar dust and a gale of panic that did not seem to be of this world. Although many thought that his reaction had been one not of rage but of pain, from then on they were careful not to annoy him, because the majority understood that his passivity was not that of a hero taking his ease but that of a cataclysm in repose.

Father Gonzaga held back the crowd's frivolity with formulas of maidservant inspiration while awaiting the arrival of a final judgment on the nature of the captive. But the mail from Rome showed no sense of urgency. They spent their time finding out if the prisoner had a navel, if his dialect had any connection with Aramaic, how many times he could fit on the head of a pin, or whether he wasn't just a Norwegian with wings. Those meager letters might have come and gone until the end of time if a providential event had not put an end to the priest's tribulations.

It so happened that during those days, among so many other carnival attractions, there arrived in town the traveling show of the woman who had been changed into a spider for having disobeyed her parents. The admission to see her was not only less than the admission to see the angel, but people were permitted to ask her all manner of questions about her absurd state and to examine her up and down so that no one would ever doubt the truth of her horror. She was a frightful tarantula the size of a ram and with the head of a sad maiden. What was most heart-rending, however, was not her outlandish shape but the sincere affliction with which she recounted the details of her misfortune. While still practically a child she had sneaked out of her parents' house to go to a dance, and while she was coming back through the woods after having danced all night without permission, a fearful thunderclap rent the sky in two and through the crack came the lightning bolt of brimstone that changed her into a spider. Her only nourishment came from the meatballs that charitable souls chose to toss into her mouth. A spectacle like that, full of so much human truth and with such a fearful lesson, was bound to defeat without even trying that of a haughty angel who scarcely deigned to look at mortals. Besides, the few miracles attributed to the angel showed a certain mental disorder, like the blind man who didn't recover his sight but grew three new teeth, or the paralytic who didn't get to walk but almost won the lottery, and the leper whose sores sprouted sunflowers. Those consolation miracles, which were more like mocking fun, had already ruined the angel's reputation when the woman who had been changed into a spider finally crushed him completely. That was how Father Gonzaga was cured forever of his insomnia and Pelayo's courtyard went back to being as empty as during the time it had rained for three days and crabs walked through the bedrooms.

The owners of the house had no reason to lament. With the money they saved they built a two-story mansion with balconies and gardens and high netting so that crabs wouldn't get in during the winter, and with iron bars on the windows so that angels wouldn't get in. Pelayo also set up a rabbit warren close to town and gave up his job as bailiff for good, and Elisenda bought some satin pumps with high heels and many dresses of iridescent silk, the kind worn on Sunday by the most desirable women in those times. The chicken coop was the only thing that didn't receive any attention. If they washed it down with creolin and burned tears of myrrh inside it every so often, it was not in homage to the angel but to drive away the dungheap stench that still hung everywhere like a ghost and was turning the new house into an old one. At first, when the child learned to walk, they were careful that he not get too close to the chicken coop. But then they began to lose their fears and got used to the smell, and before the child got his second teeth he'd gone inside the chicken coop to play, where the wires were falling apart. The angel was no less standoffish with him than with other mortals, but he tolerated the most ingenious infamies with the patience of a dog who had no illusions. They both came down with chicken pox at the same time. The doctor who took care of the child couldn't resist the temptation to listen to the angel's heart, and he found so much whistling in the heart and so many sounds in his kidneys that it seemed impossible for him to be alive. What surprised him most, however, was the logic of his wings. They seemed so natural on that completely human organism that he couldn't understand why other men didn't have them too.

When the child began school it had been some time since the

sun and rain had caused the collapse of the chicken coop. The
angel went dragging himself about here and there like a stray
dying man. They would drive him out of the bedroom with a
broom and a moment later find him in the kitchen. He seemed to
be in so many places at the same time that they grew to think that
he'd been duplicated, that he was reproducing himself all through
the house, and the exasperated and unhinged Elisenda shouted
that it was awful living in that hell full of angels. He could scarcely
eat and his antiquarian eyes had also become so foggy that he
went about bumping into posts. All he had left were the bare
cannulae[1] of his last feathers. Pelayo threw a blanket over him and
extended him the charity of letting him sleep in the shed, and
only then did they notice that he had a temperature at night, and
was delirious with the tongue twisters of an old Norwegian. That
was one of the few times they became alarmed, for they thought
he was going to die and not even the wise neighbor woman had
been able to tell them what to do with dead angels.

And yet he not only survived his worst winter, but seemed
improved with the first sunny days. He remained motionless for
several days in the farthest corner of the courtyard, where no one
would see him, and at the beginning of December some large, stiff
feathers began to grow on his wings, the feathers of a scarecrow,
which looked more like another misfortune of decrepitude. But he
must have known the reason for those changes, for he was quite
careful that no one should notice them, that no one should hear
the sea chanteys that he sometimes sang under the stars. One
morning Elisenda was cutting some bunches of onions for lunch
when a wind that seemed to come from the high seas blew into
the kitchen. Then she went to the window and caught the angel
in his first attempts at flight. They were so clumsy that his fingernails opened a furrow in the vegetable patch and he was on the
point of knocking the shed down with the ungainly flapping that
slipped on the light and couldn't get a grip on the air. But he did
manage to gain altitude. Elisenda let out a sigh of relief, for herself
and for him, when she saw him pass over the last houses, holding
himself up in some way with the risky flapping of a senile vulture.
She kept watching him even when she was through cutting the

---

[1] Tubular shafts.

onions and she kept on watching until it was no longer possible for her to see him, because then he was no longer an annoyance in her life but an imaginary dot on the horizon of the sea.

## DONALD BARTHELME [1931–1989]
# The King of Jazz

**W**ell I'm the king of jazz now, thought Hokie Mokie to himself as he oiled the slide on his trombone. Hasn't been a 'bone man been king of jazz for many years. But now that Spicy Mac-Lammermoor, the old king, is dead, I guess I'm it. Maybe I better play a few notes out of this window here, to reassure myself.

"Wow!" said somebody standing on the sidewalk. "Did you hear that?"

"I did," said his companion.

"Can you distinguish our great homemade American jazz performers, each from the other?"

"Used to could."

"Then who was that playing?"

"Sounds like Hokie Mokie to me. Those few but perfectly selected notes have the real epiphanic glow."

"The what?"

"The real epiphanic glow, such as is obtained only by artists of the caliber of Hokie Mokie, who's from Pass Christian, Mississippi. He's the king of jazz, now that Spicy MacLammermoor is gone."

**H**okie Mokie put his trombone in its trombone case and went to a gig. At the gig everyone fell back before him, bowing.

"Hi Bucky! Hi Zoot! Hi Freddie! Hi George! Hi Thad! Hi Roy! Hi Dexter! Hi Jo! Hi Willie! Hi Greens!"

"What we gonna play, Hokie? You the king of jazz now, you gotta decide."

"How 'bout 'Smoke'?"

"Wow!" everybody said. "Did you hear that? Hokie Mokie can just knock a fella out, just the way he pronounces a word. What a intonation on that boy! God Almighty!"

"I don't want to play 'Smoke,'" somebody said.

"Would you repeat that stranger?"

"I don't want to play 'Smoke.' 'Smoke' is dull. I don't like the changes. I refuse to play 'Smoke.'"

"He refuses to play 'Smoke'! But Hokie Mokie is the king of jazz and he says 'Smoke'!"

"Man, you from outa town or something? What do you mean you refuse to play 'Smoke'? How'd you get on this gig anyhow? Who hired you?"

"I am Hideo Yamaguchi, from Tokyo, Japan."

"Oh, you're one of those Japanese cats, eh?"

"Yes, I'm the top trombone man in all of Japan."

"Well you're welcome here until we hear you play. Tell me, is the Tennessee Tea Room still the top jazz place in Tokyo?"

"No, the top jazz place in Tokyo is the Square Box now."

"That's nice. OK, now we gonna play 'Smoke' just like Hokie said. You ready, Hokie? OK, give you four for nothin'. One! Two! Three! Four!"

The two men who had been standing under Hokie's window had followed him into the club. Now they said:

"Good God!"

"Yes, that's Hokie's famous 'English sunrise' way of playing. Playing with lots of rays coming out of it, some red rays, some blue rays, some green rays, some green stemming from a violet center, some olive stemming from a tan center—"

"That young Japanese fellow is pretty good, too."

"Yes, he is pretty good. And he holds his horn in a peculiar way. That's frequently the mark of a superior player."

"Bent over like that with his head between his knees—good God, he's sensational!"

He's sensational, Hokie thought. Maybe I ought to kill him.

But at that moment somebody came in the door pushing in front of him a four-and-one-half-octave marimba. Yes, it was Fat Man Jones, and he began to play even before he was fully in the door.

"What're we playing?"

"'Billie's Bounce.'"

"That's what I thought it was. What're we in?"

"F."

"That's what I thought we were in. Didn't you use to play with Maynard?"

"Yeah I was in that band for a while until I was in the hospital."

"What for?"

"I was tired."

"What can we add to Hokie's fantastic playing?"

"How 'bout some rain or stars?"

"Maybe that's presumptuous?"

"Ask him if he'd mind."

"You ask him, I'm scared. You don't fool around with the king of jazz. That young Japanese guy's pretty good, too."

"He's sensational."

"You think he's playing in Japanese?"

"Well I don't think it's English."

This trombone's been makin' my neck green for thirty-five years, Hokie thought. How come I got to stand up to yet another challenge, this late in life?

"Well, Hideo—"

"Yes, Mr. Mokie?"

"You did well on both 'Smoke' and 'Billie's Bounce.' You're just about as good as me, I regret to say. In fact, I've decided you're *better* than me. It's a hideous thing to contemplate, but there it is. I have only been the king of jazz for twenty-four hours, but the unforgiving logic of this art demands we bow to Truth, when we hear it."

"Maybe you're mistaken?"

"No, I got ears. I'm not mistaken. Hideo Yamaguchi is the new king of jazz."

"You want to be king emeritus?"

"No, I'm just going to fold up my horn and steal away. This gig is yours, Hideo. You can pick the next tune."

"How 'bout 'Cream'?"

"OK, you heard what Hideo said, it's 'Cream.' You ready, Hideo?"

"Hokie, you don't have to leave. You can play too. Just move a little over to the side there—"

"Thank you, Hideo, that's very gracious of you. I guess I will play a little, since I'm still here. Sotto voce, of course."

"Hideo is wonderful on 'Cream'!"

"Yes, I imagine it's his best tune."

"What's that sound coming in from the side there?"

"Which side?"

"The left."

"You mean that sound that sounds like the cutting edge of life? That sounds like polar bears crossing Arctic ice pans? That sounds like a herd of musk ox in full flight? That sounds like male walruses diving to the bottom of the sea? That sounds like fumaroles[1] smoking on the slopes of Mt. Katmai? That sounds like the wild turkey walking through the deep, soft forest? That sounds like beavers chewing trees in an Appalachian marsh? That sounds like an oyster fungus growing on an aspen trunk? That sounds like a mule deer wandering a montane of the Sierra Nevada? That sounds like prairie dogs kissing? That sounds like witch grass tumbling or a river meandering? That sounds like manatees munching seaweed at Cape Sable? That sounds like coatimundis moving in packs across the face of Arkansas? That sounds like—"

"Good God, it's Hokie! Even with a cup mute on, he's blowing Hideo right off the stand!"

"Hideo's playing on his knees now! Good God, he's reaching into his belt for a large steel sword—Stop him!"

"Wow! That was the most exciting 'Cream' ever played! Is Hideo all right?"

"Yes, somebody is getting him a glass of water."

"You're my man, Hokie! That was the dadblangedest thing I ever saw!"

"You're the king of jazz once again!"

"Hokie Mokie is the most happening thing there is!"

"Yes, Mr. Hokie sir, I have to admit it, you blew me right off the stand. I see I have many years of work and study before me still."

"That's OK, son. Don't think a thing about it. It happens to the best of us. Or it almost happens to the best of us. Now I want everybody to have a good time because we're gonna play 'Flats.' 'Flats' is next."

"With your permission, sir, I will return to my hotel and pack. I am most grateful for everything I have learned here."

"That's OK, Hideo. Have a nice day. He-he. Now, 'Flats.'"

---

[1] Holes in volcanic regions that emit hot gases.

# JOHN UPDIKE [b. 1932]

# Pygmalion

What he liked about his first wife was her gift of mimicry; after a party, theirs or another couple's, she would vivify for him what they had seen, the faces, the voices, twisting her pretty mouth into small contortions that brought back, for a dazzling instant, the presence of an absent acquaintance. "Well, if I reawy—how does Gwen talk?—if I *re*-awwy cared about conserwation—" And he, the husband, would laugh and laugh, even though Gwen was secretly his mistress and would become his second wife. What he liked about *her* was her liveliness in bed, and what he disliked about his first wife was the way she would ask to have her back rubbed and then, under his laboring hands, night after night, fall asleep.

For the first years of the new marriage, after he and Gwen had returned from a party he would wait, unconsciously, for the imitations, the recapitulation, to begin. He would even prompt, "What did you make of our hostess's brother?"

"Oh," Gwen would simply say, "he seemed very pleasant." Sensing with feminine intuition that he expected more, she might add, "Harmless. Maybe a little stuffy." Her eyes flashed as she heard in his expectant silence an unvoiced demand, and with that touching, childlike impediment of hers she blurted out, "What are you reawy after?"

"Oh, nothing. Nothing. It's just—Marguerite met him once a few years ago and she was struck by what a pompous nitwit he was. That way he has of sucking his pipestem and ending every statement with 'Do you follow me?'"

"I thought he was perfectly pleasant," Gwen said frostily, and turned her back to remove her silvery, snug party dress. As she wriggled it down over her hips she turned her head and defiantly added, "He had a *lot* to say about tax shelters."

"I bet he did," Pygmalion scoffed feebly, numbed by the sight of his wife frontally advancing, nude, toward him and their marital bed. "It's awfully late," he warned her.

"Oh, come on," she said, the lights out.

The first imitation Gwen did was of Marguerite's second husband, Ed; they had all unexpectedly met at a Save the Whales benefit ball, to which invitations had been sent out indiscriminately. "Oh-ho-*ho*," she boomed in the privacy of their bedroom afterward, "so you're my noble predecessor!" In aside she added, "Noble, my ass. He hates you so much you turned him on."

"I did?" he said. "I thought he was perfectly pleasant, in what could have been an awkward encounter."

"Yes, in*dee*dy," she agreed, imitating hearty Ed, and for a dazzling second allowing the man's slightly glassy and slack expression of forced benignity to invade her own usually petite and rounded features. "Nothing awkward about *us*, ho ho," she went on, encouraged. "And tell me, old chap, why *is* it your child-support check is never on time anymore?"

He laughed and laughed, entranced to see his bride arrive at what he conceived to be proper womanliness—a plastic, alert sensitivity to the human environment, a susceptible responsiveness tugged this way and that by the currents of Nature herself. He could not know the world, was his fear, unless a woman translated it for him. Now, when they returned from a gathering, and he asked what she had made of so-and-so, Gwen would stand in her underwear and consider, as if onstage. "We-hell, my dear," she would announce in sudden, fluting parody, "if it wasn't for Portugal there *rally* wouldn't be a country left in Europe!"

"Oh, come on," he would protest, delighted to see her pretty features distort themselves into an uncanny, snobbish horsiness.

"How did she do it?" Gwen would ask, as if professionally intent. "Something with the chin, sort of rolling it from side to side without unclenching the teeth."

"You've got it!" he applauded.

"Of course you *knoaow*," she went on in the assumed voice, "there *used* to be Greece, but now all these dreadful *A*rabs. . . ."

"Oh, yes, yes," he said, his face smarting from laughing so hard, so proudly. She had become perfect for him.

In bed she pointed out. "It's awfully late."

"Want a back rub?"

"Mmmm. That would be reawy nice." As his left hand labored on the smooth, warm, pliable surface, his wife—that small something in her that was all her own—sank out of reach; night after night, she fell asleep.

# ESTELA PORTILLO TRAMBLEY [b. 1936]

# The Burning

The women of the barrio, the ones pock-marked by life, sat in council. Existence in dark cubicles of wounds had withered the spirit. Now, all as one, had found a heart. One tired soul stood up to speak. "Many times I see the light she makes of darkness, and that light is a greater blackness, still."

There was some skepticism from the timid. "Are you sure?"

"In those caves outside the town, she lives for days away from everybody. At night, when she is in the caves, small blinking lights appear, like fireflies. Where do they come from? I say, the blackness of her drowns the life in me."

Another woman with a strange wildness in her eyes nodded her head in affirmation. "Yes, she drinks the bitterness of good and swallows, like the devil-wolf, the red honey milk of evil."

A cadaverous one looked up into a darkened sky. "I hear thunder; lightning is not far." In unison they agreed, "We could use some rain."

The oldest one among them, one with dirty claws, stood up with arms outstretched and stood menacingly against the first lightning bolt that cleaved the darkness. Her voice was harsh and came from ages past. "She must burn!"

The finality was a cloud, black and tortured. Each looked into another's eyes to find assent or protest. There was only frenzy, tight and straining. The thunder was riding the lightning now, directly over their heads. It was a blazing canopy that urged them on to deeds of fear. There was still no rain. They found blistering words to justify the deed to come. One woman, heavy with anger, crouched to pour out further accusations. "She is the devil's pawn. On nights like this, when the air is heavy like thick blood, she sings among the dead, preferring them to the living. You know why she does it . . . eh? I'll tell you! She chases the dead back to their graves."

"Yes, yes. She stays and stays when death comes. Never a whimper, nor a tear, but I sense she feels the death as life like

one possessed. They say she catches the flitting souls of the
dead and turns them into flies. That way the soul never finds
heaven."

"Flies! Flies! She is a plague!"

A clap of thunder reaffirmed. The old one with nervous,
clutching claws made the most grievous charge, the cause for this
meeting of the judgment. She shaped with bony gestures the anger
of the heart. "She is the enemy of God! She put obscenities on
our doorsteps to make us her accomplices. Sacrilege against the
holy church!"

There was a fervor now, rising like a tide. They were for her
burning now. All the council howled that Lela must burn that
night. The sentence belonged to night alone. The hurricane could
feed in darkness. Fear could be disguised as outrage at night.
There were currents now that wanted sacrifice. Sacrifice is the
umbilical cord of superstition. It would devastate before finding a
calm. Lela was the eye of the storm, the artery that must flow to
make them whole when the earth turned to light. To catch an evil
when it bounced as shadow in their lives, to find it trapped in
human body, this was an effective stimulant to some; to others it
was a natural depressant to cut the fear, the dam of frustration.
This would be their method of revelation. The doubt of themselves
would dissolve.

But women know mercy! Mercy? It was swallowed whole by
chasms of desire and fear of the unknown. Tempests grow in
narrow margins that want a freedom they don't understand.
Slaves always punish the free.

But who was Lela? She had come across the mountain to
their pueblo many years before. She had crossed la Barranca del
Cobre alone. She had walked into the pueblo one day, a bloody,
ragged, half-starved young girl. In an apron she carried some
shining sand. She stood there, like a frightened fawn, at the
edge of the village. As the people of the pueblo gathered
around her strangeness, she smiled, putting out her hand
for touch. They drew back and she fell to the ground in
exhaustion.

They took her in, but she remained a stranger the rest of her
life in the pueblo upon which she had stumbled. At the beginning,
she seemed but a harmless child. But, as time passed and she
resisted their pattern of life, she was left alone. The people knew

she was a Tarahumara from Batopilas.[1] Part of her strangeness
was the rooted depth of her own religion. She did not convert to
Christianity. People grew hostile and suspicious of her.

But she had also brought with her the miracle sand. It had
strange curative powers. In no time, she began to cure those in
the pueblo who suffered from skin disease, from sores, or open
wounds.

"Is it the magic of her devil gods?" the people asked themselves. Still, they came for the miracle cure that was swift and
clean. She became their *curandera*[2] outside their Christian faith.

The people in her new home needed her, and she loved them
in silence and from a distance. She forgave them for not accepting
her strangeness and learned to find adventure in the Oneness of
herself.

Many times she wanted to go back to Batopilas, but too many
people needed her here. She learned the use of medicinal herbs
and learned to set broken bones. This was what she was meant
to do in life. This purpose would not let her return to Batopilas.
Still, she did not convert to Christianity. The people, begrudgingly,
believed in her curative powers, but did not believe in her. Many
years had passed and Lela was now an old woman, and the council
of women this night of impending storm had decided her fate.

Lela lay dying in her one room hut. There was a fire with
teeth that consumed her body. She only knew that her time was
near an end as she lay in her small cot. Above the bed was a long
shelf she had built herself that held rows of clay figurines. These
were painted in gay colors and the expression of the tiny faces
measured the seasons of the heart. They were live little faces
showing the full circle of human joy and pain, doubt and fear,
humor and sobriety. In all expressions there was a fierceness for
life.

Lela had molded them through the years, and now they stood
over her head like guardians over their maker. . . . Clay figurines,
an act of love learned early in her childhood of long ago. In

---

[1] An area in the high, pine country of the Sierra Madre Mountains in the south
of Chihuahua Province, Mexico.
[2] A healer.

Batopilas, each home had its own rural god. He was a friend and a comforter. The little rural gods were like any other people. They did not rule or demand allegiance. The little rural gods of river, sky, fire, seed, birds, all were chosen members of each family. Because they sanctified all human acts, they were the actions of the living, like an aura. They were a shrine to creation.

Lela's mother had taught the little girl to mold the clay figures that represented the rural gods. This was her work and that of Lela's in the village, to provide clay little gods for each home and for festive occasions. This is why Lela never gave them up in her new home. She had molded them with her hands, but they dwelled boundless in the center of her being. The little gods had always been very real, very important, in her reverence for life.

There had been in Batopilas a stone image of the greater god, Tecuat.[3] He was an impressive god of power that commanded silence and obedience. People did not get close to Tecuat except in ritual. As a girl, Lela would tiptoe respectfully around the figure of Tecuat, then she would breathe a sigh of relief and run off to find the little gods.

This was her game, god-hunting. One day, she had walked too far towards the pines, too far towards a roar that spoke of rushing life. She followed a yellow butterfly that also heard a command of dreams. She followed the butterfly that flitted towards a lake. As she followed, she looked for little gods in the glint of the sun, and in the open branches that pierced the absoluteness of the sky. The soft breath of wind was the breath of little gods, and the crystal shine of rocks close to the lake was a winking language that spoke of peace and the wildness of all joy.

When she had reached the lake, she stepped into the water without hesitation. She felt the cool wet mud against her open toes. She walked into the water, touching the ripple of its broken surface with her finger tips. After a while, there was no more bottom. She began to cut the water with smooth, clean strokes, swimming out towards the pearl-green rocks that hid the roar. She floated for a while looking up at the light filtering through eternal trees. The silence spoke of something other than itself. It

---

[3] A derivative of the Toltec sun god.

spoke in colors born of water and sun. She began to swim more rapidly towards the turn that led to the cradle of the roar, the waterfall. . . .

This is what Lela, the old Lela dying on her bed, was remembering . . . the waterfall. It helped to ease the pain that came in waves that broke against her soul and blackened the world. Then, there was the calm, the calm into which the experience machine brought back the yesterdays that were now soft, kind memories. She opened her eyes and looked up at the row of clay figures. She was not alone. "The waterfall . . ." she whispered to herself. She remembered the grotto behind the waterfall. It had been her hermitage of dreams, of wonder. Here her Oneness had knitted all the little gods unto herself until she felt the whole of earth—things within her being. Suddenly, the pain cut her body in two. She gripped the edge of the cot. There were blurs of throbbing white that whirled into black, and all her body trembled until another interval of peace returned for a little while.

There was no thought; there was no dream in the quiet body. She was a simple calm that would not last. The calm was a gift from the little gods. She slept. It was a fitful, brief sleep that ended with the next crash of pain. The pain found gradual absorption. She could feel the bed sheet clinging to her body, wet with perspiration. She asked herself in a half-moan, "When will the body give way?" Give way . . . give way, for so long, Lela had given way and had found ways to open herself and the world she understood. It had been a vital force in her. She could have been content in Batopilas. The simple truths of Nature might have fulfilled her to the end of her days if she had remained in Batopilas. But there was always that reach in her for a larger self. Nature was a greatness, but she felt a different hunger and a different thirst.

There was a world beyond Batopilas; there were people beyond Batopilas. She was no longer a child. It was easy to find little gods in Nature, but as she grew older, it became a child's game. There was time to be a child, but there was now time for something more. That is why, one day, she had walked away from Batopilas.

Beyond the desert, she would find another pueblo. She knew there were many pueblos and many deserts. There was nothing to fear because her little gods were with her. On the first day of her journey, she walked all day. The piercing sun beat down on her and the world, as she scanned the horizon for signs of a way. Something at a distance would be a hope, would be a way to something new, a way to the larger self. At dusk, she felt great hunger and great thirst. Her body ached and her skin felt parched and dry. The night wind felt cold, so she looked for a shelter against the wind. She found a clump of mesquite[4] behind some giant sahuaros.[5] This was not the greenness she knew so well, but a garden of stars in the night sky comforted her until she fell asleep.

At first light she awakened refreshed and quickly resumed her journey. She knew she must make the best out of the early hours before the sun rose. By late morning, the desert yielded a mountain at a distance. She reached the mountain in time to rest from the sun and the physical effort of her journey. When the sun began to fall, she started up a path made narrow by a blanket of desert brush. It tore the flesh of her feet and legs as she made her way up the path. In a little while, it was hard to find sure footing. The path had lost itself in a cleavage of rocks. Night had fallen. She was not afraid, for the night sky, again, was full of blinking little gods.

Then it happened. She lost her footing and fell down, down over a crevice between two huge boulders. As she fell, her lungs filled with air. Her body hit soft sand, but the edge of her foot felt the sharpness of a stone. She lay there stunned for a few minutes until she felt a sharp pain at the side of her foot. Somewhat dizzy, she sat up and noticed that the side of her foot was bleeding profusely. She sat there and watched the blood-flow that found its way into the soft sand. She looked up at the boulders that silently rebuked her helplessness; then she began to cry softly. She had to stanch the blood. She wiped away her tears with the side of her sleeve and tore off a piece of skirt to use as a bandage. As she looked down at the wound again, she noticed that the sand where she had fallen was extremely crystalline and loose. It shone against a rising moon. She scooped up a handful and looked at it with fascination. "The sand of little gods," she whispered to

---

[4] Trees or grass of the southwestern United States.
[5] Cactuses.

herself. She took some sand and rubbed it on the wound before
she applied the bandage. By now, she felt a burning fever. She
wrapped the strip of skirt around the wound now covered with
the fine, shining sand. Then she slept. But it was a fitful sleep,
for her body burned with fever. Half awake and half in a dream,
she saw the sands take the shapes of happy, little gods. Then, at
other times, the pain told her she was going to die. After a long
time, her exhausted body slept until the dawn passed over her
head.

When she finally awakened, she felt extremely well. Her body
was rested and her temperature, to her great surprise, was normal.
She looked down at the wound. The blood was caked on the
bandage. She took it off to look at the wound. She could hardly
believe her eyes. There was no longer any open wound. There
was a healthy scab, and the area around the wound had no infection. It was a healing that normally would have taken weeks. She
stood on her foot and felt no pain. "My little gods!" she thought.
She fell down on her knees and kissed the shining sand. After a
while, she removed her apron and filled it with the shining sand.
She secured it carefully before she set off on her climb. As she
made her way out of the crevice, she marked the path leading to
the shining sand to find her way to it again. It was hard making
marks with a sharp stone, and it seemed to take forever. At last,
she reached the top of the crevice and noticed, to her great joy,
that it led down to a pueblo at a distance. She made her way to
strangers that day. Now, at the end of a lifetime, Lela felt the pain
roll, roll, roll, roll itself into a blindness. She struggled through
the blackness until she gasped back the beginning of the calm.
With the new calm came a ringing memory from her childhood.
She saw the kindly face of the goddess, Ta Te. She who was born
of the union of clean rock, she who was eternal. Yes, Ta Te
understood all the verdant things . . . the verdant things.

And who were these women who sat in council? They were one
full sweep of hate; they were one full wave of fear. Now these
village women were outlined against a greyish sky where a storm
refused to break. Spiderlike, apelike, toadlike was the ferocity
of their deadness. These were creatures of the earth who mingled with mankind. But they were minions to torture because
the twist of littleness bound them to condemn all things un-

known, all things untried. The infernal army could not be stopped now. The scurrying creatures began to gather firewood in the gloom. With antlike obedience they hurried back and forth carrying wood to Lela's hut. They piled it in a circle around her little house. The rhythm of their feet sang, "We'll do! We'll do!"

"The circle of fire will drain her powers!" claimed the old one with claws.

"Show me! Show me! Show me!" Voices lost as one.

As the old one with claws ordered more wood, the parish priest came running from his church. With raised arms he shouted as he ran, "Stop! Do you hear? Stop this madness!"

It can be argued that evil is not the reversal of good, but the vacuum of good. Thus, the emptiness is a standing still, a being dead, an infinite pain . . . like dead wood. No one listened to him.

"Burn! Burn! Burn!"

Life? The wood? The emptiness? The labor pains were that of something already lost, something left to the indefinite in life. The priest went from one woman to another begging, pleading, taking the wood from their hands.

"Burn! Burn! Burn!"

The old priest reasoned. "All is forgiven, my children. She only made some figurines of clay!"

There was a hush. The one woman with the claws approached the priest and spit out the condemnation, "She took our holy saints, Mary, Joseph, and many others and made them obscene. How can you defend the right hand of the devil? Drinking saints! Winking saints! Who can forgive the hideous suggestions of her clay devils? Who?"

The priest said simply, "You."

But if there is only darkness in a narrow belief, who can believe beyond the belief, or even understand the belief itself? The women could not forgive because they did not believe beyond a belief that did not go beyond symbol and law. Somehow, symbol and law, without love, leaves no opening. The clay figures in the church with sweet, painted faces lifted to heaven were much more than figures of clay to these women. Their still postures with praying hands were a security. Now, the priest who had blessed them with holy water said they were not a sanctuary of God. Why did he contradict himself?

The old one with the claws felt triumphant. "She has made our saints into pagan gods!"

The priest shook his head sadly. "It is not a sin, what she did!"

No one listened. The piling of wood continued until the match was lit. Happy . . . Happy fire . . . it would burn the sin and the sinner.

Something in Lela told her this was the last struggle now. She looked up at her clay figurines one last time. Her eyes had lost their focus. The little gods had melted into one another; all colors were mixed. They grew into silver strands of light that crossed and mingled and found new forms that pulled away from one center. In half consciousness, she whispered, "Yes, yes, pull away. Find other ways, other selves, grow. . . ."

She smiled; the last calm had taken her back to the caves outside the pueblo. The caves were not like the grotto behind the waterfall, but they were a place for Oneness, where one could look for the larger self. Here the solitude of the heart was a bird in space. Here, in the silence of aloneness, she had looked for the little gods in the townspeople. In her mind, she had molded their smiles, their tears, their embraces, their seeking, their *just being*. Her larger self told her that the miracle of the living act was supreme, the giving, the receiving, the stumbling, and the getting up.

In the caves she had sadly thought of how she had failed to reach them as a friend. Her silences and her strangeness had kept them apart. But, she would find a way of communicating, a way of letting them know that she loved them. "If I give shape and form to their beauty," she thought. "If I cannot tell them I love them with words. . . ."

The light of the moving, mixing little gods was becoming a darkness. Her body would give in now. Yet, she still wished for Batopilas and the old ways with her last breath, "If only . . . if only I could be buried in the tradition of my fathers . . . a clean burning for new life . . . but here, here, there is a dark hole for the dead body. . . . Oh, little gods, take me back to my fathers. . . ."

The little gods were racing to the waterfall.

## JOYCE CAROL OATES [b. 1938]

# The Girl

### I  Background Material

Came by with a truck, The Director and Roybay and a boy I
didn't know. Roybay leaned out the window, very friendly. I got
in and we drove around for a while. The Director telling us about
his movie-vision, all speeded-up because his friend, his contact,
had lent him the equipment from an educational film company in
town, and it had to be back Sunday P.M. The Director said: "It's
all a matter of art and compromise." He was very excited. I knew
him from before, a few days before; his name was DePinto or
DeLino, something strange, but he was called The Director. He
was in the third person most of the time.

Roybay, two hundred fifty pounds, very cheerful and easy
and my closest friend of all of them, was The Motorcyclist. They
used his motorcycle for an authentic detail. It didn't work; it was
broken down. But they propped it up in the sand and it looked
very real.

A boy with a scruffy face, like an explorer's face, was The
Cop.

I was The Girl.

The Director said: "Oh Jesus honey your tan, your tanned
legs, your feet, my God even your feet your toes, are tan, tanned,
you're so lovely. . . ." And he stared at me, he stared. When we
met before, he had not stared like this. His voice was hoarse, his
eyebrows ragged. It was all music with him, his voice and his way
of moving, the life inside him. "I mean, look at her! Isn't she—?
Isn't it?"

"Perfect," Roybay said.

The boy with the scruffy face, wedged in between Roybay the
driver and The Director, with me on The Director's lap and my
legs sort of on his lap, stared at me and turned out to be a kid my
age. I caught a look of his but rejected it. I never found out his
name.

Later they said to me: "What were their names? Don't you
know? Can't you remember? Can't you—?"

They were angry. They said: "Describe them."
But.
The Director. The Motorcyclist. The Cop. The Girl.

I thought there were more, more than that. If you eliminate
The Girl. If you try to remember. More? More than two? Oh, I
believe a dozen or two, fifty, any large reasonable number tramping down the sand. There was the motorcycle, broken. They
hauled it out in the back of the truck with the film equipment and
other stuff. I could describe the Santa Monica Freeway if I wanted
to. But not them. I think there were more than three but I don't
know. Where did they come from? Who were they? The reason I
could describe the Freeway is that I knew it already, not memorized but in pieces, the way you know your environment.

I was The Girl. No need to describe. Anyone studying me,
face to face, would be in my presence and would not need a
description. I looked different. The costume didn't matter, the
bright red and green shapes—cats and kittens—wouldn't show
anyway. The film was black-and-white. It was a short-skirted
dress, a top that tied in back, looped around and tied in back like
a halter, the material just cotton or anything, bright shapes of red
and green distortions in the material. It came from a Miss Chelsea
shop in Van Nuys. I wasn't wearing anything else, anything underneath.

Someone real said to me later, a real policeman: ". . . need
your cooperation. . . ."

The Director explained that he needed everyone's cooperation.
He had assisted someone making a film once, or he had watched
it happen, he said how crucial it is to cooperate; he wouldn't have
the footage for re-takes and all the equipment had to be returned
in eighteen hours. Had a sharkish skinny glamourish face, a wide-
brimmed hat perched on his head. Wore sunglasses. We all did.
The beach was very bright at three in the afternoon. I had yellow-
lensed glasses with white plastic wrap-around frames, like goggles. It wasn't very warm. The wind came in from the ocean,
chilly.

The way up, I got hypnotized by the expressway signs and
all the names of the towns and beaches and the arrows pointing
up off to the right, always up off to the right and off the highway
and off the map.

"Which stretch of beach? Where? How far up the coast? Can't

you identify it, can't you remember? We need your cooperation, can't you cooperate?"

On film, any stretch of beach resembles any stretch of beach. They called it The Beach.

## II   *The Rehearsal*

The Director moved us around, walked with us; put his hands on me and turned me, stepped on my bare feet, scratched his head up beneath the straw-colored hat, made noises with his mouth, very excited, saying to himself little words: "Here—yeah— like this—this—this way—" The Motorcyclist, who was Roybay, straddled the motorcycle to wait. Had a sunny broad face with red-blond-brown hair frizzy all around it. Even his beard was frizzy. It wasn't hot but he looked hot. Was six foot three or four, taller than my father, who is or was six foot exactly. That is my way of telling if a man is tall: taller than my father, then he's *tall*; shorter than my father, *not tall*. The world could be divided that way.

No, I haven't seen my father for a while. But the world is still there.

The Director complained about the setting. The beach was beautiful but empty. "Got to imagine people crowding in, people in the place of boulders and rocks and scrubby damn flowers and sand dunes and eucalyptus and all this crap, it's hobbling to the eye," he said. He had wanted a city movie. He had wanted the movie to take place in the real world. "Really wanted Venice Beach on a Sunday, packed, but room for the motorcycle, and the whole world crowded in . . . a miscellaneous flood of people, souls, to represent the entire world . . . and the coming-together of the world in my story. In The Girl. Oh look at her," he said dreamily, looking at me, "couldn't the world come together in her? It could. But this place is so empty . . . it's wild here, a wild innocent natural setting, it's too beautiful, it could be a travelogue. . . ."

The Cop asked about splicing things together. Couldn't you—?

The Director waved him away. It was hard to concentrate.

The Cop giggled and whispered to me: "Jeeze, these guys are something, huh? How'd you meet them? I met them this morning. Where do you go to school? You go to school? Around here?"

I snubbed him, eye-to-eye.

He blushed. He was about sixteen, behind his bushy hair and sunglasses and policeman's hat. It had a tin badge on it. The Director had bought it at a costume store. The Cop had only a hat. The rest of him was a T-shirt and jeans. A club two feet long and maybe an inch and a half in diameter, but no gun. The Director had found the club in a garbage can, he said, months ago. He carried it everywhere with him. It had generated his need for a film, he said; he kept taking it from The Cop and using it to make lines in the sand.

The Director's mind was always going. It was white-hot. His body never stopped, his knees jerked as if keeping time to something. I felt the energy in him, even when he wasn't touching me. Only when he held the camera in his hands, between his hands, was he calmed down.

After a while, Roybay said, sounding nervous: "What do we do? What do I do? Somebody might come along here, huh?—we better hurry it up, huh?"

"This can't be hurried," The Director said.

The Motorcyclist was the only one of them I knew. His name was *Roybay*. Or *Robbie*. Or maybe it was *Roy Bean* (?) . . . sometimes just *Roy* or *Ray*. Said he came over from Trinidad, Colorado—I think. Or someone else his size said that, some other day. Had a big worried forehead tanned pink-red. You don't tan dark, with a complexion like that. He wore a crash helmet and goggles and a leather jacket, the sleeves a little short for his arms. The night I met him, he was explaining the fact that vegetables are not meek and passive, as people think, but exert great pressure in forcing themselves up through the soil . . . and think about vines, twisting tendrils, feelers that could choke large animals to death or pull them down into quicksand. . . . He was a vegetarian, but he scorned meekness. Believed in strength. Up at 7 A.M. for two hours of weight-lifting, very slow, Yoga-slow, and a careful diet of vegetables and vegetable juices. Said fruit was too acid, too sharp. Explained that an ox's muscles were extremely powerful and that the carnivores of the world could learn from the ox.

Or his name could have been something like *Roy baby, Roy, baby* if someone called out and slurred the words together.

The Director placed rocks on the sand. Kicked dents in the sand. He cleared debris out of the way, tossing things hand over hand, then he found a child's toy—a fire truck—and stood with it, spinning the little wheels, thinking, then he moved one of the rocks a few inches and said to me: "You walk to this point. Try it."

They watched.

The Director said that I was a sweet girl. He said that now I should practice running, from the rock out to the water. He followed alongside me. He told me when to stop. He kissed my forehead and said I was very sweet, this was part of the tragedy. He tossed the toy fire truck off to the side. Rubbed his hands together, excited. I could smell it on him, the excitement.

"I'm an orphan," he said suddenly. "I'm from a Methodist orphanage up in Seattle."

The Motorcyclist laughed. The Cop grinned stupidly; he was still standing where The Director had placed him.

"You don't get many chances in life," The Director said, "so I would hate to mess this up. It would make me very angry if something went wrong . . . if one of you went wrong . . . But you're not going to, huh, are you? Not even you?" he said, looking at me. As if I was special. He had a sharkish look caused by one tooth, I think—a side tooth that was a little longer than the rest of his teeth. If you glanced at him you wouldn't notice that tooth, not really; but somehow you would start to think of a shark a few seconds later.

In a magical presence. I knew. I knew but I was outside, not on film. The Director walked with me along the beach, his feet in ankle-high boots and mine bare, talking to me, stroking my arms, saying . . . saying . . . *What did he say? Don't remember?* No, the noise was too much. The waves. Gulls. Birds. Words come this way and that, I don't catch them all, try to ease with the feeling, the music behind them. I took music lessons once. Piano lessons with Miss Dorsey, three blocks from my grandmother's house; from ten until thirteen. Could memorize. Could count out a beat one two three, *one* two three, one *two* three, a habit to retain throughout life. When The Director told me what to do I listened to the beat of his voice. I knew I was in a magical presence, he was not an ordinary man, but I was outside him, outside waiting. I was not yet The Girl. I was The Girl later.

*It was a movie, a movie-making!* I screamed. When I woke for the half-dozenth time, snatching at someone's wrist. I clawed, had to make contact. I didn't want to sink back again. I said: *It was real, it was a movie, there was film in the camera!*

*You mean someone filmed it? Filmed that? Someone had a camera?*

The Director carried it in his hands. Had to adjust it, squinted down into it, made noises with his mouth; he took a long time. The Cop, licking his lips, said to me: "Hey, I thought the movie cameras were real big. Pushed around on wheels. With some moving parts, like a crane or something . . . ? Where are you from?"

"You couldn't push wheels in the sand," I told him.

The Director looked over at us. "What are you two talking about? Be quiet. You," he said to The Cop, "you, you're not in the script yet, you're off-camera, go stand on the other side of that hill. Don't clutter my mind."

He walked out to the surf, stood there, was very agitated. I looked at Roybay, who was looking at me. Our eyes didn't come together; he was looking at me like on film. The Girl. Over there, straddling the broken-down rusty-handle-barred motorcycle, was The Motorcyclist. He was not from Trinidad, Colorado, or from anywhere. I saw The Cop's cap disappear over a hill behind some spiky weeds and ridges of sand.

The Director came back. He said to The Motorcyclist, "What this is, maybe, it's a poem centered in the head of The Cop, but I had it off-center; I was imagining it in The Girl. But . . . but . . . it wasn't working. It's a test of The Cop. I don't know him. Do you? I don't know who the hell he is. It will be an experiment. He rushes in to the rescue . . . and sees the scene and . . . the test is upon him. The audience will see it too. I've been dreaming this for so long, this tiny eight-minute poem," he said, putting his arm around my shoulder now, excited, "I can't miss my chance. It's not just that it's crowding my head, but people are going to be very interested in this; I know certain people who are going to pay a lot to see it. Look, it's a poem, honey. The parts must cooperate. Nothing unripe or resisting. All parts in a poem . . . in a work of art. . . . Please, do you understand, do you?"

So sensitive. It was a sensitive moment. Staring eye-to-eye with me, dark green lenses and yellow lenses, shatter-proof.

I told him yes. I had to say yes. And it was almost true; some of his words caught in me, snagged, like the rough edge of a fingernail in your clothing.

The Director said softly: "What it is . . . is . . . it's a vision, it can't be resisted. Why resist? Resist? Resist anything? If a vision comes up from the inside of the earth, it must be sacred, or down out of the sky—even, equal—because the way up is the same as the way down, the sky is a mirror and vice versa. Right? I wanted The Girl to resist The Motorcyclist and I wanted The Cop to use the club like a Zen master's stick but now I see it differently, with the scene all set. It goes the way it must. You can't control a vision. It's like going down a stairway and you're cautious and frightened and then the stairway breaks, the last step gives way, and you fall and yet you're not afraid, you're not afraid after all, you're saved. You don't understand me, I know, but you'll feel it, you'll understand in a while. Don't resist," he said to me. "If you deny the way things must operate, you turn yourself and everyone else into a phantom. We'll all be here together. One thing. We'll be sacred. Don't doubt. Now I'll talk to The Cop, the Savior . . . he's the Savior. . . . I wonder can he bear the weight of the testing?"

### III   *The Performance*

Space around me. Hair blowing, back toward shore an arrow out of sight. The air is cold. Nervous, but doing O.K.

The Director says in a whisper-shout: "Okay. Okay. No, slow down . . . slow . . . slow down. . . . Look over here. . . . The other way. . . ." It is very easy now that the camera is working. It is very easy. I am The Girl watching the film of The Girl walking on a beach watching the water. Now The Girl watching The Girl turning The Girl in black-and-white approached by a shape, a dark thing, out of the corner of the eye. The eye must be the camera. The dark thing must be a shape with legs, with arms, with a white-helmeted head.

Now the film speeds up.

A surprise, how light you become on film! You are very graceful. It's a suspension of gravity. The Director calls to me, yells to me: *Run. Run.* But I can't. I am too light, and then too heavy; the hand on my shoulder weighs me down. I think I am giggling. *Hurry up! Hurry up!*

The marker is a real rock.

*Scream!* cries The Director.

But I can't, I can't get breath. They are at me. I scramble up onto my feet. But. But I have lost hold. I can't see. The Director is very close to us, right beside us. *Turn her around, make her scream—hurry up—do it like this, like this, do it fast like this—come on—*

The film is speeded up. Too fast. I have lost hold of it, can't see. I am being driven backwards, downwards, burrowed-into, like a hammer being hammered being hammered against all at once. Do I see noseholes, eyeholes, mouthholes?

Something being pounded into flesh like meat.

### IV   A Sequel

I was babbling, hanging onto someone's wrist. Not the doctor, who was in a hurry on his rounds, but a nurse. I said: "Did they find them? The police? Did it get in the newspapers? Was the movie shown? Was it—?"

What? What? At the important instant I lost sight of her, one adult face like another. Then it contracted into someone's regular-sized face. The ceiling above him seemed to open behind his face and to glow, fluorescent lighting as if for a stage, a studio. Why, this must be someone who knows me! He is looking at me without disgust. I don't know him. But I pretend. I ask him if they were caught, if—He says not to think about it right now. He says not to think about it. He says: "The police, they won't find them anyway . . . they don't give a damn about you . . . don't torture yourself."

But, but.

Raw reddened meat, scraped raw, hair yanked out in hand-fuls. A scalp bleeding and sandy. Sandy grit in my mouth. It was a jelly, a transformation. But I wanted to know. Wanted. I reached for his wrist but couldn't get it.

You can be real, but you can be stronger than real; speeded-up, lighted-up. It does take a camera. The Director helped them drag me back saying *Oh it was beautiful . . . it was beautiful . . .* and there were tears in the creases around his mouth. I strained to get free, to break the shape out of my head and into his. Strained, twisted. But there was too much noise. The back of my head was hurt and emptied out. Too much battered into me, I couldn't tell them apart, there were two of them but maybe two hundred or two thousand, I couldn't know.

But I couldn't talk right. The man tried to listen politely but here is what I said: ". . . rockhand, two of them, bird-burrow, truck, toy, wheel, the arrow, the exit, the way out. . . ." Another man, also in the room, tried to interrupt. Kept asking "Who were they? How many? Five, six, a dozen? Twenty? Where did it happen? Where did you meet them? Who are you?" but I kept on talking, babbling, now I was saying saints' names that got into my head somehow . . . the names of saints like beads on a rosary, but I didn't know them, the saints had terrible names to twist my head out of shape: ". . . Saint Camarillo, Saint Oxnard, Saint . . . Saint Ventura . . . Saint Ynez . . . Saint Goleta . . . Saint Gaviota . . . Saint Jalama . . . Saint Casmalia . . . Saint Saint Saint. . . ."

### V   *The Vision*

A rainy wintry day, and I crossed Carpenter Street and my eye drifted right onto someone. The Director. I stared at him and started to run after him. He turned around, staring. Didn't recognize me. Didn't know. Behind him a laundromat, some kids playing in the doorway, yelling. Too much confusion. The Director walked sideways, sideways staring at me, trying to remember. He hadn't any sunglasses now. His skin was sour-looking.

I ran up to him. I said: "Don't you remember? Don't you—?" I laughed.

I forgave him, he looked so sick. He was about twenty-eight, thirty years old. Edgy, cautious. Creases down both sides of his mouth.

He stared at me.

Except for the rain and a bad cold, my eyes reddened, I was pretty again and recovered. I laughed but started to remember something out of the corner of my eye. Didn't want to remember. So I smiled, grinned at him, and he tried to match the way I looked.

"I'm new here, I just came here . . . I'm from. . . . I'm from up the coast, from Seattle. . . . I don't know you. . . ."

A kind of shutter clicked in his head. Showing in his eyes. He was walking sideways and I reached out for his wrist, a bony wrist, and he shook me loose. His lips were thin and chalk-colored, chalky cheesy sour-colored. One of his nostrils was bigger than the other and looked sore. That single shark tooth was greenish. he said: ". . . just in for a day, overnight, down from Seattle and . . . uh . . . I don't know you. . . . Don't remember. I'm confused. I'm not well, my feet are wet, I'm from out of town."

"What happened to the movie?" I asked.

He watched me. A long time passed. Someone walked by him on the pavement, in the rain, the way passersby walk in a movie, behind the main actors. They are not in focus and that person was not in focus either.

"Was it a real movie? Did it have film, the camera?" I asked. Beginning to be afraid. Beginning. But I kept it back, the taste in my mouth. Kept smiling to show him no harm. "Oh hey look," I said, "look, it had film, didn't it? I mean it had film? I mean you made a real movie, didn't you? I mean—"

Finally he began to see me. The creases around his mouth turned into a smile. It was like a crucial scene now; he put his hand on my shoulder and kissed my forehead, in the rain. He said: "Honey oh yeah. Yeah.

Don't you ever doubt that. I mean, did you doubt that? All these months? You should never have doubted that. I mean, that's the whole thing. That's it. That's the purpose, the center, the reason behind it, all of it, the focus, the. . . . You know what I mean? The Vision?"

I knew what he meant.

So I was saved.

## TONI CADE BAMBARA [b. 1939]

# The Lesson

Back in the days when everyone was old and stupid or young and foolish and me and Sugar were the only ones just right, this lady moved on our block with nappy hair and proper speech and no makeup. And quite naturally we laughed at her, laughed the way we did at the junk man who went about his business like he was some big-time president and his sorry-ass horse his secretary. And we kinda hated her too, hated the way we did the winos who cluttered up our parks and pissed on our handball walls and stank up our hallways and stairs so you couldn't halfway play hide-and-seek without a goddamn gas mask. Miss Moore was her name. The only woman on the block with no first name. And she was black as hell, cept for her feet, which were fish-white and spooky. And she was always planning these boring-ass things for us to do, us being my cousin, mostly, who lived on the block cause we all moved North the same time and to the same apartment then spread out gradual to breathe. And our parents would yank our heads into some kinda shape and crisp up our clothes so we'd be presentable for travel with Miss Moore, who always looked like she was going to church, though she never did. Which is just one of the things the grownups talked about when they talked behind her back like a dog. But when she came calling with some sachet she'd sewed up or some gingerbread she'd made or some book, why then they'd all be too embarrassed to turn her down and we'd get handed over all spruced up. She'd been to college and said it was only right that she should take responsibility for the young ones' education, and she not even related by marriage or blood. So they'd go for it. Specially Aunt Gretchen. She was the main gofer in the family. You got some ole dumb shit foolishness you want somebody to go for, you send for Aunt Gretchen. She been screwed into the go-along for so long, it's a blood-deep natural thing with her. Which is how she got saddled with me and Sugar and Junior in the first place while our mothers were in a la-de-da apartment up the block having a good ole time.

So this one day Miss Moore rounds us all up at the mailbox

*317*

and it's puredee hot and she's knockin herself out about arithmetic. And school suppose to let up in summer I heard, but she don't never let up. And the starch in my pinafore scratching the shit outta me and I'm really hating this nappy-head bitch and her goddamn college degree. I'd much rather go to the pool or to the show where it's cool. So me and Sugar leaning on the mailbox being surly, which is a Miss Moore word. And Flyboy checking out what everybody brought for lunch. And Fat Butt already wasting his peanut-butter-and-jelly sandwich like the pig he is. And Junebug punchin on Q.T.'s arm for potato chips. And Rosie Giraffe shifting from one hip to the other waiting for somebody to step on her foot or ask her if she from Georgia so she can kick ass, preferably Mercedes'. And Miss Moore asking us do we know what money is, like we a bunch of retards. I mean real money, she say, like it's only poker chips or monopoly papers we lay on the grocer. So right away I'm tired of this and say so. And would much rather snatch Sugar and go to the Sunset and terrorize the West Indian kids and take their hair ribbons and their money too. And Miss Moore files that remark away for next week's lesson on brotherhood, I can tell. And finally I say we oughta get to the subway cause it's cooler and besides we might meet some cute boys. Sugar done swiped her mama's lipstick, so we ready.

So we heading down the street and she's boring us silly about what things cost and what our parents make and how much goes for rent and how money ain't divided up right in this country. And then she gets to the part about we all poor and live in the slums, which I don't feature. And I'm ready to speak on that, but she steps out in the street and hails two cabs just like that. Then she hustles half the crew in with her and hands me a five-dollar bill and tells me to calculate 10 percent tip for the driver. And we're off. Me and Sugar and Junebug and Flyboy hangin out the window and hollering to everybody, putting lipstick on each other cause Flyboy a faggot anyway, and making farts with our sweaty armpits. But I'm mostly trying to figure how to spend this money. But they all fascinated with the meter ticking and Junebug starts laying bets as to how much it'll read when Flyboy can't hold his breath no more. Then Sugar lays bets as to how much it'll be when we get there. So I'm stuck. Don't nobody want to go for my plan, which is to jump out at the next light and run off the first bar-b-

que we can find. Then the driver tells us to get the hell out cause
we there already. And the meter reads eighty-five cents. And I'm
stalling to figure out the tip and Sugar say give him a dime. And
I decide he don't need it bad as I do, so later for him. But then he
tries to take off with Junebug foot still in the door so we talk about
his mama something ferocious. Then we check out that we on
Fifth Avenue and everybody dressed up in stockings. One lady in
a fur coat, hot as it is. White folks crazy.

"This is the place," Miss Moore say, presenting it to us in the
voice she uses at the museum. "Let's look in the windows before
we go in."

"Can we steal?" Sugar asks very serious like she's getting the
ground rules squared away before she plays. "I beg your pardon,"
say Miss Moore, and we fall out. So she leads us around the
windows of the toy store and me and Sugar screamin, "This is
mine, that's mine, I gotta have that, that was made for me, I was
born for that," till Big Butt drowns us out.

"Hey, I'm goin to buy that there."

"That there? You don't even know what it is, stupid."

"I do so," he say punchin on Rosie Giraffe. "It's a microscope."

"Whatcha gonna do with a microscope, fool?"

"Look at things."

"Like what, Ronald?" ask Miss Moore. And Big Butt ain't got
the first notion. So here go Miss Moore gabbing about the thousands of bacteria in a drop of water and the somethinorother in a
speck of blood and the million and one living things in the air
around us is invisible to the naked eye. And what she say that
for? Junebug go to town on that "naked" and we rolling. Then
Miss Moore ask what it cost. So we all jam into the window
smudgin it up and the price tag say $300. So then she ask how
long'd take for Big Butt and Junebug to save up their allowances.
"Too long," I say. "Yeh," adds Sugar, "outgrown it by that time."
And Miss Moore say no, you never outgrow learning instruments.
"Why, even medical students and interns and," blah, blah, blah.
And we ready to choke Big Butt for bringing it up in the first
damn place.

"This here costs four hundred eighty dollars," say Rosie Giraffe. So we pile up all over her to see what she pointin out. My
eyes tell me it's a chunk of glass cracked with something heavy,

and different-color inks dripped into the splits, then the whole thing put into a oven or something. But for $480 it don't make sense.

"That's a paperweight made of semi-precious stones fused together under tremendous pressure," she explains slowly, with her hands doing the mining and all the factory work.

"So what's a paperweight?" asks Rosie Giraffe.

"To weigh paper with, dumbbell," say Flyboy, the wise man from the East.

"Not exactly," say Miss Moore, which is what she say when you warm or way off too. "It's to weigh paper down so it won't scatter and make your desk untidy." So right away me and Sugar curtsy to each other and then to Mercedes who is more the tidy type.

"We don't keep paper on top of the desk in my class," say Junebug, figuring Miss Moore crazy or lyin one.

"At home, then," she say. "Don't you have a calendar and a pencil case and a blotter and a letter-opener on your desk at home where you do your homework?" And she know damn well what our homes look like cause she nosys around in them every chance she gets.

"I don't even have a desk," say Junebug. "Do we?"

"No. And I don't get no homework neither," says Big Butt.

"And I don't even have a home," say Flyboy like he do at school to keep the white folks off his back and sorry for him. Send this poor kid to camp posters, is his specialty.

"I do," says Mercedes. "I have a box of stationery on my desk and a picture of my cat. My godmother bought the stationery and the desk. There's a big rose on each sheet and the envelopes smell like roses."

"Who wants to know about your smelly-ass stationery," say Rosie Giraffe fore I can get my two cents in.

"It's important to have a work area all your own so that . . ."

"Will you look at this sailboat, please," say Flyboy, cuttin her off and pointin to the thing like it was his. So once again we tumble all over each other to gaze at this magnificent thing in the toy store which is just big enough to maybe sail two kittens across the pond if you strap them to the posts tight. We all start reciting the price tag like we in assembly. "Handcrafted sailboat of fiberglass at one thousand one hundred ninety-five dollars."

"Unbelievable," I hear myself say and am really stunned. I read it again for myself just in case the group recitation put me in a trance. Same thing. For some reason this pisses me off. We look at Miss Moore and she lookin at us, waiting for I dunno what.

"Who'd pay all that when you can buy a sailboat set for a quarter at Pop's, a tube of glue for a dime, and a ball of string for eight cents? It must have a motor and a whole lot else besides," I say. "My sailboat cost me about fifty cents."

"But will it take water?" say Mercedes with her smart ass.

"Took mine to Alley Pond Park once," say Flyboy. "String broke. Lost it. Pity."

"Sailed mine in Central Park and it keeled over and sank. Had to ask my father for another dollar."

"And you got the strap," laugh Big Butt. "The jerk didn't even have a string on it. My old man wailed on his behind."

Little Q.T. was staring hard at the sailboat and you could see he wanted it bad. But he too little and somebody'd just take it from him. So what the hell. "This boat for kids, Miss Moore?"

"Parents silly to buy something like that just to get all broke up," say Rosie Giraffe.

"That much money it should last forever," I figure.

"My father'd buy it for me if I wanted it."

"Your father, my ass," say Rosie Giraffe getting a chance to finally push Mercedes.

"Must be rich people shop here," say Q.T.

"You are a very bright boy," say Flyboy. "What was your first clue?" And he rap him on the head with the back of his knuckles, since Q.T. the only one he could get away with. Though Q.T. liable to come up behind you years later and get his licks in when you half expect it.

"What I want to know is," I says to Miss Moore though I never talk to her, I wouldn't give the bitch that satisfaction, "is how much a real boat costs? I figure a thousand'd get you a yacht any day."

"Why don't you check that out," she says, "and report back to the group?" Which really pains my ass. If you gonna mess up a perfectly good swim day least you could do is have some answers. "Let's go in," she say like she got something up her sleeve. only she don't lead the way. So me and Sugar turn the corner to where the entrance is, but when we get there I kinda hang back.

Not that I'm scared, what's there to be afraid of, just a toy store. But I feel funny, shame. But what I got to be shamed about? Got as much right to go in as anybody. But somehow I can't seem to get hold of the door, so I step away for Sugar to lead. But she hangs back too. And I look at her and she looks at me and this is ridiculous. I mean, damn, I have never ever been shy about doing nothing or going nowhere. But then Mercedes steps up and then Rosie Giraffe and Big Butt crowd in behind and shove, and next thing we all stuffed into the doorway with only Mercedes squeezing past us, smoothing out her jumper and walking right down the aisle. Then the rest of us tumble in like a glued-together jigsaw done all wrong. And people lookin at us. And it's like the time me and Sugar crashed into the Catholic church on a dare. But once we got in there and everything so hushed and holy and the candles and the bowin and the handkerchiefs on all the drooping heads, I just couldn't go through with the plan. Which was for me to run up to the altar and do a tap dance while Sugar played the nose flute and messed around in the holy water. And Sugar kept givin me the elbow. Then later teased me so bad I tied her up in the shower and turned it on and locked her in. And she'd be there till this day if Aunt Gretchen hadn't finally figured I was lyin about the boarder takin a shower.

Same thing in the store. We all walkin on tiptoe and hardly touchin the games and puzzles and things. And I watched Miss Moore who is steady watchin us like she waitin for a sign. Like Mama Drewery watches the sky and sniffs the air and takes note of just how much slant is in the bird formation. Then me and Sugar bump smack into each other, so busy gazing at the toys, 'specially the sailboat. But we don't laugh and go into our fat-lady bump-stomach routine. We just stare at that price tag. Then Sugar run a finger over the whole boat. And I'm jealous and want to hit her. Maybe not her, but I sure want to punch somebody in the mouth.

"Watcha bring us here for, Miss Moore?"

"You sound angry, Sylvia. Are you mad about something?" Givin me one of them grins like she tellin a grown-up joke that never turns out to be funny. And she's lookin very closely at me like maybe she plannin to do my portrait from memory. I'm mad, but I won't give her that satisfaction. So I slouch around the store bein very bored and say, "Let's go."

Me and Sugar at the back of the train watchin the tracks

whizzin by large then small then gettin gobbled up in the dark. I'm thinkin about this tricky toy I saw in the store. A clown that somersaults on a bar then does chin-ups just cause you yank lightly at his leg. Cost $35. I could see me askin my mother for a $35 birthday clown. "You wanna who that costs what?" she'd say, cocking her head to the side to get a better view of the hole in my head. Thirty-five dollars could buy new bunk beds for Junior and Gretchen's boy. Thirty-five dollars and the whole household could go visit Granddaddy Nelson in the country. Thirty-five dollars would pay for the rent and the piano bill too. Who are these people that spend that much for performing clowns and $1000 for toy sailboats? What kinda work they do and how they live and how come we ain't in on it? Where we are is who we are, Miss Moore always pointin out. But it don't necessarily have to be that way, she always adds then waits for somebody to say that poor people have to wake up and demand their share of the pie and don't none of us know what kind of pie she talkin about in the first damn place. But she ain't so smart cause I still got her four dollars from the taxi and she sure ain't gettin it. Messin up my day with this shit. Sugar nudges me in my pocket and winks.

Miss Moore lines us up in front of the mailbox where we started from, seem like years ago, and I got a headache for thinkin so hard. And we lean all over each other so we can hold up under the draggy-ass lecture she always finishes us off with at the end before we thank her for borin us to tears. But she just looks at us like she readin tea leaves. Finally she say, "Well, what did you think of F. A. O. Schwarz?"[1]

Rosie Giraffe mumbles, "White folks crazy."

"I'd like to go there again when I get my birthday money," says Mercedes, and we shove her out the pack so she has to lean on the mailbox by herself.

"I'd like a shower. Tiring day," say Flyboy.

Then Sugar surprises me by saying, "You know, Miss Moore, I don't think all of us here put together eat in a year what that sailboat costs." And Miss Moore lights up like somebody goosed her. "And?" she say, urging Sugar on. Only I'm standin on her foot so she don't continue.

"Imagine for a minute what kind of society it is in which some

---

[1] A famous New York City toy store.

people can spend on a toy what it would cost to feed a family of six or seven. What do you think?"

"I think," say Sugar pushing me off her feet like she never done before, cause I whip her ass in a minute, "that this is not much of a democracy if you ask me. Equal chance to pursue happiness means an equal crack at the dough, don't it?" Miss Moore is besides herself and I am disgusted with Sugar's treachery. So I stand on her foot one more time to see if she'll shove me. She shuts up, and Miss Moore looks at me, sorrowfully I'm thinkin. And somethin weird is going on, I can feel it in my chest.

"Anybody else learn anything today?" lookin dead at me. I walk away and Sugar has to run to catch up and don't even seem to notice when I shrug her arm off my shoulder.

"Well, we got four dollars anyway," she says.

"Uh hunh."

"We could go to Hascombs and get half a chocolate layer and then go to the Sunset and still have plenty money for potato chips and ice cream sodas."

"Uh hunh."

"Race you to Hascombs," she say.

We start down the block and she gets ahead which is O.K. by me cause I'm going to the West End[2] and then over to the Drive[3] to think this day through. She can run if she want to and even run faster. But ain't nobody gonna beat me at nuthin.

---

[2] A bar near Columbia University, in upper Manhattan.
[3] Riverside Drive.

RAYMOND CARVER [1939–1988]

# The Third Thing That Killed My Father Off

I'll tell you what did my father in. The third thing was Dummy, that Dummy died. The first thing was Pearl Harbor. And the second thing was moving to my grandfather's farm near We-natchee.[1] That's where my father finished out his days, except they were probably finished before that.

My father blamed Dummy's death on Dummy's wife. Then he blamed it on the fish. And finally he blamed himself—because he was the one that showed Dummy the ad in the back of *Field and Stream* for live black bass shipped anywhere in the U.S.

It was after he got the fish that Dummy started acting peculiar. The fish changed Dummy's whole personality. That's what my father said.

I never knew Dummy's real name. If anyone did, I never heard it. Dummy it was then, and it's Dummy I remember him by now. He was a little wrinkled man, bald-headed, short but very pow-erful in the arms and legs. If he grinned, which was seldom, his lips folded back over brown, broken teeth. It gave him a crafty expression. His watery eyes stayed fastened on your mouth when you were talking—and if you weren't, they'd go to someplace queer on your body.

I don't think he was really deaf. At least not as deaf as he made out. But he sure couldn't talk. That was for certain.

Deaf or no, Dummy'd been on as a common laborer out at the sawmill since the 1920s. This was the Cascade Lumber Company in Yakima, Washington. The years I knew him, Dummy was work-ing as a cleanup man. And all those years I never saw him with anything different on. Meaning a felt hat, a khaki workshirt, a denim jacket over a pair of coveralls. In his top pockets he carried rolls of toilet paper, as one of his jobs was to clean and supply the

---

[1] Town in the state of Washington.

toilets. It kept him busy, seeing as how the men on nights used to walk off after their tours with a roll or two in their lunchboxes.

Dummy carried a flashlight, even though he worked days. He also carried wrenches, pliers, screwdrivers, friction tape, all the same things the millwrights carried. Well, it made them kid Dummy, the way he was, always carrying everything. Carl Lowe, Ted Slade, Johnny Wait, they were the worst kidders of the ones that kidded Dummy. But Dummy took it all in stride. I think he'd gotten used to it.

My father never kidded Dummy. Not to my knowledge, anyway. Dad was a big, heavy-shouldered man with a crew-haircut, double chin, and a belly of real size. Dummy was always staring at that belly. He'd come to the filing room where my father worked, and he'd sit on a stool and watch my dad's belly while he used the big emery wheels on the saws.

**D**ummy had a house as good as anyone's.

It was a tarpaper-covered affair near the river, five or six miles from town. Half a mile behind the house, at the end of a pasture, there lay a big gravel pit that the state had dug when they were paving the roads around there. Three good-sized holes had been scooped out, and over the years they'd filled with water. By and by, the three ponds came together to make one.

It was deep. It had a darkish look to it.

Dummy had a wife as well as a house. She was a woman years younger and said to go around with Mexicans. Father said it was busybodies that said that, men like Lowe and Wait and Slade.

She was a small stout woman with glittery little eyes. The first time I saw her, I saw those eyes. It was when I was with Pete Jensen and we were on our bicycles and we stopped at Dummy's to get a glass of water.

When she opened the door, I told her I was Del Fraser's son. I said, "He works with—" And then I realized. "You know, your husband. We were on our bicycles and thought we could get a drink."

"Wait here," she said.

She came back with a little tin cup of water in each hand. I downed mine in a single gulp.

But she didn't offer us more. She watched us without saying

anything. When we started to get on our bicycles, she came over
to the edge of the porch.

"You little fellas had a car now, I might catch a ride with you."
She grinned. Her teeth looked too big for her mouth.

"Let's go," Pete said, and we went.

There weren't many places you could fish for bass in our part of
the state. There was rainbow mostly, a few brook and Dolly Var-
den in some of the high mountain streams, and silvers in Blue
Lake and Lake Rimrock. That was mostly it, except for the runs
of steelhead and salmon in some of the freshwater rivers in late
fall. But if you were a fisherman, it was enough to keep you busy.
No one fished for bass. A lot of people I knew had never seen a
bass except for pictures. But my father had seen plenty of them
when he was growing up in Arkansas and Georgia, and he had
high hopes to do with Dummy's bass, Dummy being a friend.

The day the fish arrived, I'd gone swimming at the city pool.
I remember coming home and going out again to get them since
Dad was going to give Dummy a hand—three tanks Parcel Post
from Baton Rouge, Louisiana.

We went in Dummy's pickup, Dad and Dummy and me.

These tanks turned out to be barrels, really, the three of them
crated in pine lath. They were standing in the shade out back of
the train depot, and it took my dad and Dummy both to lift each
crate into the truck.

Dummy drove very carefully through town and just as carefully all the way to his house. He went right through his yard
without stopping. He went on down to within feet of the pond.
By that time it was nearly dark, so he kept his headlights on and
took out a hammer and a tire iron from under the seat, and then
the two of them lugged the crates up close to the water and started
tearing open the first one.

The barrel inside was wrapped in burlap, and there were these
nickel-sized holes in the lid. They raised it off and Dummy aimed
his flashlight in.

It looked like a million bass fingerlings were finning inside. It
was the strangest sight, all those live things busy in there, like a
little ocean that had come on the train.

Dummy scooted the barrel to the edge of the water and poured
it out. He took his flashlight and shined it into the pond. But there

was nothing to be seen anymore. You could hear the frogs going, but you could hear them going anytime it newly got dark.

"Let me get the other crates," my father said, and he reached over as if to take the hammer from Dummy's coveralls. But Dummy pulled back and shook his head.

He undid the other two crates himself, leaving dark drops of blood on the lath where he ripped his hand doing it.

From that night on, Dummy was different.

Dummy wouldn't let anyone come around now anymore. He put up fencing all around the pasture, and then he fenced off the pond with electrical barbed wire. They said it cost him all his savings for that fence.

Of course, my father wouldn't have anything to do with Dummy after that. Not since Dummy ran him off. Not from fishing, mind you, because the bass were just babies still. But even from trying to get a look.

One evening two years after, when Dad was working late and I took him his food and a jar of iced tea, I found him standing talking with Syd Glover, the millwright. Just as I came in, I heard Dad saying, "You'd reckon the fool was married to them fish, the way he acts."

"From what I hear," Syd said, "he'd do better to put that fence round his house."

My father saw me then, and I saw him signal Syd Glover with his eyes.

But a month later my dad finally made Dummy do it. What he did was, he told Dummy how you had to thin out the weak ones on account of keeping things fit for the rest of them. Dummy stood there pulling at his ear and staring at the floor. Dad said, Yeah, he'd be down to do it tomorrow because it had to be done. Dummy never said yes, actually. He just never said no, is all. All he did was pull on his ear some more.

When Dad got home that day, I was ready and waiting. I had his old bass plugs out and was testing the treble hooks with my finger.

"You set?" he called to me, jumping out of the car. "I'll go to the toilet, you put the stuff in. You can drive us out there if you want."

I'd stowed everything in the back seat and was trying out the wheel when he came back out wearing his fishing hat and eating a wedge of cake with both hands.

Mother was standing in the door watching. She was a fair-skinned woman, her blonde hair pulled back in a tight bun and fastened down with a rhinestone clip. I wonder if she ever went around back in those happy days, or what she ever really did.

I let out the handbrake. Mother watched until I'd shifted gears, and then, still unsmiling, she went back inside.

It was a fine afternoon. We had all the windows down to let the air in. We crossed the Moxee Bridge and swung west onto Slater Road. Alfalfa fields stood off to either side, and farther on it was corn fields.

Dad had his hand out the window. He was letting the wind carry it back. He was restless, I could see.

It wasn't long before we pulled up at Dummy's. He came out of the house wearing his hat. His wife was looking out the window.

"You got your frying pan ready?" Dad hollered out to Dummy, but Dummy just stood there eyeing the car. "Hey, Dummy!" Dad yelled. "Hey, Dummy, where's your pole, Dummy?"

Dummy jerked his head back and forth. He moved his weight from one leg to the other and looked at the ground and then at us. His tongue rested on his lower lip, and he began working his foot into the dirt.

I shouldered the creel. I handed Dad his pole and picked up my own.

"We set to go?" Dad said. "Hey, Dummy, we set to go?"

Dummy took off his hat and, with the same hand, he wiped his wrist over his head. He turned abruptly, and we followed him across the spongy pasture. Every twenty feet or so a snipe sprang up from the clumps of grass at the edge of the old furrows.

At the end of the pasture, the ground sloped gently and became dry and rocky, nettle bushes and scrub oaks scattered here and there. We cut to the right, following an old set of car tracks, going through a field of milkweed that came up to our waists, the dry pods at the tops of the stalks rattling angrily as we pushed through. Presently, I saw the sheen of water over Dummy's shoulder, and I heard Dad shout, "Oh, Lord, look at that!"

But Dummy slowed down and kept bringing his hand up and

moving his hat back and forth over his head, and then he just stopped flat.

Dad said, "Well, what do you think Dummy? One place good as another? Where do you say we should come onto it?"

Dummy wet his lower lip.

"What's the matter with you, Dummy?" Dad said. "This your pond, ain't it?"

Dummy looked down and picked an ant off his coveralls.

"Well, hell," Dad said, letting out his breath. He took out his watch. "If it's still all right with you, we'll get to it before it gets too dark."

Dummy stuck his hands in his pockets and turned back to the pond. He started walking again. We trailed along behind. We could see the whole pond now, the water dimpled with rising fish. Every so often a bass would leap clear and come down in a splash.

"Great God," I heard my father say.

We came up to the pond at an open place, a gravel beach kind of.

Dad motioned to me and dropped into a crouch. I dropped too. He was peering into the water in front of us, and when I looked, I saw what had taken him so.

"Honest to God," he whispered.

A school of bass was cruising, twenty, thirty, not one of them under two pounds. They veered off, and then they shifted and came back, so densely spaced they looked like they were bumping up against each other. I could see their big, heavy-lidded eyes watching us as they went by. They flashed away again, and again they came back.

They were asking for it. It didn't make any difference if we stayed squatted or stood up. The fish just didn't think a thing about us. I tell you, it was a sight to behold.

We sat there for quite a while, watching that school of bass go so innocently about their business, Dummy the whole time pulling at his fingers and looking around as if he expected someone to show up. All over the pond the bass were coming up to nuzzle the water, or jumping clear and falling back, or coming up to the surface to swim along with their dorsals sticking out.

Dad signaled, and we got up to cast. I tell you, I was shaky with excitement. I could hardly get the plug loose from the cork handle of my pole. It was while I was trying to get the hooks out that I felt Dummy seize my shoulder with his big fingers. I looked, and in answer Dummy worked his chin in Dad's direction. What he wanted was clear enough, no more than one pole.

Dad took off his hat and then put it back on and then he moved over to where I stood.

"You go on, Jack," he said. "That's all right, son—you do it now."

I looked at Dummy just before I laid out my cast. His face had gone rigid, and there was a thin line of drool on his chin.

"Come back stout on the sucker when he strikes," Dad said. "Sons of bitches got mouths hard as doorknobs."

I flipped off the drag lever and threw back my arm. I sent her out a good forty feet. The water was boiling even before I had time to take up the slack.

"Hit him!" Dad yelled. "Hit the son of a bitch! Hit him good!"

I came back hard, twice. I had him, all right. The rod bowed over and jerked back and forth. Dad kept yelling what to do.

"Let him go, let him go! Let him run! Give him more line! Now wind in! Wind in! No, let him run! Woo-ee! Will you look at that!"

The bass danced around the pond. Every time it came up out of the water, it shook its head so hard you could hear the plug rattle. And then he'd take off again. But by and by I wore him out and had him in up close. He looked enormous, six or seven pounds maybe. He lay on his side, whipped, mouth open, gills working. My knees felt so weak I could hardly stand. But I held the rod up, the line tight.

Dad waded out over his shoes. But when he reached for the fish, Dummy started sputtering, shaking his head, waving his arms.

"Now what the hell's the matter with you, Dummy? The boy's got hold of the biggest bass I ever seen, and he ain't going to throw him back, by God!"

Dummy kept carrying on and gesturing toward the pond.

"I ain't about to let this boy's fish go. You hear me, Dummy? You got another think coming if you think I'm going to do that."

Dummy reached for my line. Meanwhile, the bass had gained some strength back. He turned himself over and started swimming again. I yelled and then I lost my head and slammed down the brake on the reel and started winding. The bass made a last, furious run.

That was that. The line broke. I almost fell over on my back.

"Come on, Jack," Dad said, and I saw him grabbing up his pole. "Come on, goddamn the fool, before I knock the man down."

That February the river flooded.

It had snowed pretty heavy the first weeks of December, and turned real cold before Christmas. The ground froze. The snow stayed where it was. But toward the end of January, the Chinook wind struck. I woke up one morning to hear the house getting buffeted and the steady drizzle of water running off the roof.

It blew for five days, and on the third day the river began to rise.

"She's up to fifteen feet," my father said one evening, looking over his newspaper. "Which is three feet over what you need to flood. Old Dummy going to lose his darlings."

I wanted to go down to the Moxee Bridge to see how high the water was running. But my dad wouldn't let me. He said a flood was nothing to see.

Two days later the river crested, and after that the water began to subside.

Orin Marshall and Danny Owens and I bicycled out to Dummy's one morning a week after. We parked our bicycles and walked across the pasture that bordered Dummy's property.

It was a wet, blustery day, the clouds dark and broken, moving fast across the sky. The ground was soppy wet and we kept coming to puddles in the thick grass. Danny was just learning how to cuss, and he filled the air with the best he had every time he stepped in over his shoes. We could see the swollen river at the end of the pasture. The water was still high and out of its channel, surging around the trunks of trees and eating away at the edge of the land. Out toward the middle, the current moved heavy and swift, and now and then a bush floated by, or a tree with its branches sticking up.

We came to Dummy's fence and found a cow wedged in up against the wire. She was bloated and her skin was shiny-looking and gray. It was the first dead thing of any size I'd ever seen. I remember Orin took a stick and touched the open eyes.

We moved on down the fence, toward the river. We were afraid to go near the wire because we thought it might still have electricity in it. But at the edge of what looked like a deep canal, the fence came to an end. The ground had simply dropped into the water here, and the fence along with it.

We crossed over and followed the new channel that cut directly into Dummy's land and headed straight for his pond, going into it lengthwise and forcing an outlet for itself at the other end, then twisting off until it joined up with the river farther on.

You didn't doubt that most of Dummy's fish had been carried off. But those that hadn't been were free to come and go.

Then I caught sight of Dummy. It scared me, seeing him. I motioned to the other fellows, and we all got down.

Dummy was standing at the far side of the pond near where the water was rushing out. He was just standing there, the saddest man I ever saw.

"I sure do feel sorry for old Dummy, though," my father said at supper a few weeks after. "Mind, the poor devil brought it on himself. But you can't help but be troubled for him."

Dad went on to say George Laycock saw Dummy's wife sitting in the Sportsman's Club with a big Mexican fellow.

"And that ain't the half of it—"

Mother looked up at him sharply and then at me. But I just went on eating like I hadn't heard a thing.

Dad said, "Damn it to hell, Bea, the boy's old enough!"

He'd changed a lot, Dummy had. He was never around any of the men anymore, not if he could help it. No one felt like joking with him either, not since he'd chased Carl Lowe with a two-by-four stud after Carl tipped Dummy's hat off. But the worst of it was that Dummy was missing from work a day or two a week on the average now, and there was some talk of his being laid off.

"The man's going off the deep end," Dad said. "Clear crazy if he don't watch out."

Then on a Sunday afternoon just before my birthday, Dad and

I were cleaning the garage. It was a warm, drifty day. You could see the dust hanging in the air. Mother came to the back door and said, "Del, it's for you. I think it's Vern."

I followed Dad in to wash up. When he was through talking, he put the phone down and turned to us.

"It's Dummy," he said. "Did in his wife with a hammer and drowned himself. Vern just heard it in town."

When we got out there, cars were parked all around. The gate to the pasture stood open, and I could see tire marks that led on to the pond.

The screen door was propped ajar with a box, and there was this lean, pock-faced man in slacks and sports shirt and wearing a shoulder holster. He watched Dad and me get out of the car.

"I was his friend," Dad said to the man.

The man shook his head. "Don't care who you are. Clear off unless you got business here."

"Did they find him?" Dad said.

"They're dragging," the man said, and adjusted the fit of his gun.

"All right if we walk down? I knew him pretty well."

The man said, "Take your chances. They chase you off, don't say you wasn't warned.

We went on across the pasture, taking pretty much the same route we had the day we tried fishing. There were motorboats going on the pond, dirty fluffs of exhaust hanging over it. You could see where the high water had cut away the ground and carried off trees and rocks. The two boats had uniformed men in them, and they were going back and forth, one man steering and the other man handling the rope and hooks.

An ambulance waited on the gravel beach where we'd set ourselves to cast for Dummy's bass. Two men in white lounged against the back, smoking cigarettes.

One of the motorboats cut off. We all looked up. The man in back stood up and started heaving on his rope. After a time, an arm came out of the water. It looked like the hooks had gotten Dummy in the side. The arm went back down and then it came out again, along with a bundle of something.

It's not him, I thought. It's something else that has been in there for years.

The man in the front of the boat moved to the back, and together the two men hauled the dripping thing over the side.

I looked at Dad. His face was funny the way it was set.

"Women," he said. He said, "That's what the wrong kind of woman can do to you, Jack."

**B**ut I don't think Dad really believed it. I think he just didn't know who to blame or what to say.

It seemed to me everything took a bad turn for my father after that. Just like Dummy, he wasn't the same man anymore. That arm coming up and going back down in the water, it was like so long to good times and hello to bad. Because it was nothing but that all the years after Dummy drowned himself in that dark water.

Is that what happens when a friend dies? Bad luck for the pals he left behind?

But as I said, Pearl Harbor and having to move back to his dad's place didn't do my dad one bit of good, either.

## ALICE WALKER [b. 1944]

# Roselily

---

*Dearly Beloved,*

She dreams; dragging herself across the world. A small girl in her mother's white robe and veil, knee raised waist high through a bowl of quicksand soup. The man who stands beside her is against this standing on the front porch of her house, being married to the sound of cars whizzing by on highway 61.

*we are gathered here*

Like cotton to be weighed. Her fingers at the last minute busily removing dry leaves and twigs. Aware it is a superficial sweep. She knows he blames Mississippi for the respectful way the men turn their heads up in the yard, the women stand waiting and knowledgeable, their children held from mischief by teachings from the wrong God. He glares beyond them to the occupants of the cars, white faces glued to promises beyond a country wedding, noses thrust forward like dogs on a track. For him they usurp the wedding.

*in the sight of God*

Yes, open house. That is what country black folks like. She dreams she does not already have three children. A squeeze around the flowers in her hands chokes off three and four and five years of breath. Instantly she is ashamed and frightened in her superstition. She looks for the first time at the preacher, forces humility into her eyes, as if she believes he is, in fact, a man of God. She can imagine God, a small black boy, timidly pulling the preacher's coattail.

*to join this man and this woman*

She thinks of ropes, chains, handcuffs, his religion. His place of worship. Where she will be required to sit apart with covered head. In Chicago, a word she hears when thinking of smoke, from his description of what a cinder was, which they never had in Panther Burn. She sees hovering over the heads of the clean neighbors in her front yard black specks falling, clinging, from the sky. But in Chicago. Respect, a chance to build. Her children at last from underneath the detrimental wheel. A chance to be on top. What a relief, she thinks. What a vision, a view, from up so high.

*in holy matrimony.*

Her fourth child she gave away to the child's father who had some money. Certainly a good job. Had gone to Harvard. Was a good man but weak because good language meant so much to him he could not live with Roselily. Could not abide TV in the living room, five beds in three rooms, no Bach except from four to six on Sunday afternoons. No chess at all. She does not forget to worry about her son among his father's people. She wonders if the New England climate will agree with him. If he will ever come down to Mississippi, as his father did, to try to right the country's wrongs. She wonders if he will be stronger than his father. His father cried off and on throughout her pregnancy. Went to skin and bones. Suffered nightmares, retching and falling out of bed. Tried to kill himself. Later told his wife he found the right baby through friends. Vouched for, the sterling qualities that would make up his character.

It is not her nature to blame. Still, she is not entirely thankful. She supposes New England, the North, to be quite different from what she knows. It seems right somehow to her that people who move there to live return home completely changed. She thinks of the air, the smoke, the cinders. Imagines cinders big as hailstones; heavy, weighing on the people. Wonders how this pressure finds it way into the veins, roping the springs of laughter.

*If there's anybody here that knows a reason why*

But of course they know no reason why beyond what they daily have come to know. She thinks of the man who will be her husband, feels shut away from him because of the stiff severity of his plain black suit. His religion. A lifetime of black and white. Of veils. Covered head. It is as if her children are already gone from her. Not dead, but exalted on a pedestal, a stalk that has no roots. She wonders how to make new roots. It is beyond her. She wonders what one does with memories in a brand-new life. This had seemed easy, until she thought of it. "The reasons why . . . the people who" . . . she thinks, and does not wonder where the thought is from.

*these two should not be joined*

She thinks of her mother, who is dead. Dead, but still her mother. Joined. This is confusing. Of her father. A gray old man who sold wild mink, rabbit, fox skins to Sears, Roebuck. He stands in the yard, like a man waiting for a train. Her young sisters stand behind her in smooth green dresses, with flowers in their hands and hair. They giggle, she feels, at the absurdity of the wedding. They are ready for something new. She thinks the man beside her should marry one of them. She feels old. Yoked. An arm seems to reach

out from behind her and snatch her backward. She thinks of
cemeteries and the long sleep of grandparents mingling in the dirt.
She believes that she believes in ghosts. In the soil giving back
what it takes.

*together,*

In the city. He sees her in a new way. This she knows, and is
grateful. But is it new enough? She cannot always be a bride and
virgin, wearing robes and veil. Even now her body itches to be
free of satin and voile, organdy and lily of the valley. Memories
crash against her. Memories of being bare to the sun. She wonders
what it will be like. Not to have to go to a job. Not to work in a
sewing plant. Not to worry about learning to sew straight seams
in workingmen's overalls, jeans, and dress pants. Her place will
be in the home, he has said, repeatedly, promising her rest she
had prayed for. But now she wonders. When she is rested, what
will she do? They will make babies — she thinks practically about
her fine brown body, his strong black one. They will be inevitable.
Her hands will be full. Full of what? Babies. She is not comforted.

*let him speak*

She wishes she had asked him to explain more of what he meant.
But she was impatient. Impatient to be done with sewing. With
doing everything for three children, alone. Impatient to leave the
girls she had known since childhood, their children growing up,
their husbands hanging around her, already old, seedy. Nothing
about them that she wanted, or needed. The fathers of her children
driving by, waving, not waving; reminders of times she would
just as soon forget. Impatient to see the South Side, where they
would live and build and be respectable and respected and free.
Her husband would free her. A romantic hush. Proposal. Promises. A new life! Respectable, reclaimed, renewed. Free! In robe
and veil.

*or forever hold*

She does not even know if she loves him. She loves his sobriety.
His refusal to sing just because he knows the tune. She loves his

pride. His blackness and his gray car. She loves his understanding of her *condition.* She thinks she loves the effort he will make to redo her into what he truly wants. His love of her makes her completely conscious of how unloved she was before. This is something; though it makes her unbearably sad. Melancholy. She blinks her eyes. Remembers she is finally being married, like other girls. Like other girls, women? Something strains upward behind her eyes. She thinks of the something as a rat trapped, concerned, scurrying to and fro in her head, peering through the windows of her eyes. She wants to live for once. But doesn't know quite what that means. Wonders if she has ever done it. If she ever will. The preacher is odious to her. She wants to strike him out of the way, out of her light, with the back of her hand. It seems to her he has always been standing in front of her, barring her way.

*his peace.*

The rest she does not hear. She feels a kiss, passionate, rousing, within the general pandemonium. Cars drive up blowing their horns. Firecrackers go off. Dogs come from under the house and begin to yelp and bark. Her husband's hand is like the clasp of an iron gate. People congratulate. Her children press against her. They look with awe and distaste mixed with hope at their new father. He stands curiously apart, in spite of the people crowding about to grasp his free hand. He smiles at them all but his eyes are as if turned inward. He knows they cannot understand that he is not a Christian. He will not explain himself. He feels different, he looks it. The old women thought he was like one of their sons except that he had somehow got away from them. Still a son, not a son. Changed.

She thinks how it will be later in the night in the silvery gray car. How they will spin through the darkness of Mississippi and in the morning be in Chicago, Illinois. She thinks of Lincoln, the president. That is all she knows about the place. She feels ignorant, *wrong*, backward. She presses her worried fingers into his palm. He is standing in front of her. In the crush of well-wishing people, he does not look back.

# ANN BEATTIE [b. 1947]

# Tuesday Night

Henry was supposed to bring the child home at six o'clock, but they usually did not arrive until eight or eight-thirty, with Joanna overtired and complaining that she did not want to go to bed the minute she came through the door. Henry had taught her that phrase. "The minute she comes through the door" was something I had said once, and he mocked me with it in defending her. "Let the poor child have a minute before she goes to bed. She *did* just come through the door." The poor child is, of course, crazy about Henry. He allows her to call him that, instead of "Daddy." And now he takes her to dinner at a French restaurant that she adores, which doesn't open until five-thirty. That means that she gets home close to eight. I am a beast if I refuse to let her eat her escargots. And it would be cruel to tell her that her father's support payments fluctuate wildly, while the French dining remains a constant. Forget the money—Henry has been a good father. He visits every Tuesday night, carefully twirls her crayons in the pencil sharpener, and takes her every other weekend. The only bad thing he has done to her—and even Henry agreed about that— was to introduce her to the sleepie he had living with him right after the divorce: an obnoxious woman, who taught Joanna to sing "I'm a Woman." Fortunately, she did not remember many of the words, but I thought I'd lose my mind when she went around the house singing "Doubleyou oh oh em ay en" for two weeks. Sometimes the sleepie tucked a fresh flower in Joanna's hair—like Maria Muldaur, she explained. The child had the good sense to be embarrassed.

The men I know are very friendly with one another. When Henry was at the house last week, he helped Dan, who lives with me, carry a bookcase up the steep, narrow steps to the second floor. Henry and Dan talk about nutrition—Dan's current interest. My brother Bobby, the only person I know who is seriously interested in hallucinogens at the age of twenty-six, gladly makes a fool of himself in front of Henry by bringing out his green yoyo, which glows by the miracle of two internal batteries. Dan tells

Bobby that if he's going to take drugs he should try dosing his body with vitamins before and after. The three of them Christmas-shop for me. Last year they had dinner at an Italian restaurant downtown. I asked Dan what they ordered, and he said, "Oh, we all had manicotti."

I have been subsisting on red zinger tea and watermelon, trying to lose weight. Dan and Henry and Bobby are all thin. Joanna takes after her father in her build. She is long and graceful, with chiselled features that would shame Marisa Berenson. She is ten years old. When I was at the laundry to pick up the clothes yesterday, a woman mistook me, from the back, for her cousin Addie.

In Joanna's class at school they are having a discussion of problems with the environment. She wants to take our big avocado plant in to school. I have tried patiently to explain that the plant does not have anything to do with environmental problems. She says that they are discussing nature, too. "What's the harm?" Dan says. So he goes to work and leaves it to me to fit the towering avocado into the Audi. I also get roped into baking cookies, so Joanna can take them to school and pass them around to celebrate her birthday. She tells me that it is the custom to put the cookies in a box wrapped in birthday paper. We select a paper with yellow bears standing in concentric circles. Dan dumps bran into the chocolate-chip-cookie dough. He forbids me to use a dot of red food coloring in the sugar-cookie hearts.

My best friend, Dianne, comes over in the mornings and turns her nose up at my red zinger. Sometimes she takes a shower here, because she loves our shower head. "How come you're not in there all the time?" she says. My brother is sweet on her. He finds her extremely attractive. He asked me if I had noticed the little droplets of water from the shower on her forehead, just at the hairline. Bobby lends her money, because her husband doesn't give her enough. I know for a fact that Dianne is thinking of having an affair with him.

Dan has to work late at his office on Tuesday nights, and a while ago I decided that I wanted that one night to myself each week—a night without any of them. Dianne said, "I know what you mean," but Bobby took great offense and didn't come to visit that night, or any other night, for two weeks. Joanna was delighted that she could be picked up after school by Dianne, in Dianne's 1966 Mustang convertible, and that the two of them could visit until Henry came by Dianne's to pick her up. Dan, who keeps saying that our relationship is going sour—although it isn't—pursed his lips and nodded when I told him about Tuesday nights, but he said nothing. The first night alone I read a dirty magazine that had been lying around the house for some time. Then I took off all my clothes and looked in the hall mirror and decided to go on a diet, so I skipped dinner. I made a long-distance call to a friend in California who had just had a baby. We talked about the spidery little veins in her thighs, and I swore to her over and over again that they would go away. Then I took one of each kind of vitamin pill we have in the house.

The next week, I had prepared for my spare time better. I had bought whole-wheat flour and clover honey, and I made four loaves of whole-wheat bread, I made a piecrust, putting dough in the sink and rolling it out there, which made a lot of sense but which I would never let anybody see me doing. Then I read *Vogue*. Later on, I took out the yoga book I had bought that afternoon and put it in my plastic cookbook-holder and put that down on the floor and stared at it as I tried to get into the postures. I overcooked the piecrust and it burned. I got depressed and drank a Drambuie. The week after that, I ventured out. I went to a movie and bought myself a chocolate milkshake afterward. I sat at the drugstore counter and drank it. I was going to get my birth-control-pill prescription refilled while I was there, but I decided that would be depressing.

Joanna sleeps at her father's apartment now on Tuesday nights. Since he considers her too old to be read a fairy tale before bed, Henry waltzes with her. She wears a long nightgown and a pair of high-heeled shoes that some woman left there. She says that he usually plays "The Blue Danube" but sometimes he kids around and puts on "Idiot Wind" or "Forever Young" and they dip and twirl to it. She has hinted that she would like to take dancing lessons. Last week, she danced through the living room at our house on her pogo stick. Dan had given it to her, saying that now she had a partner, and it would save him money not having to pay for dancing lessons. He told her that if she had any questions she could ask him. He said she could call him "Mr. Daniel." She was disgusted with him. If she were Dan's child, I am sure he would still be reading her fairy tales.

Another Tuesday night, I went out and bought plants. I used my American Express card and got seventy dollars' worth of plants and some plant-hangers. The woman in the store helped me carry the boxes out to the car. I went home and drove nails into the top of the window frames and hung the plants. They did not need to be watered yet, but I held the plastic plant-waterer up to them, to see what it would be like to water them. I squeezed the plastic bottle, and stared at the curved plastic tube coming out of it. Later, I gave myself a facial with egg whites.

There is a mouse. I first saw it in the kitchen—a small gray mouse, moseying along, taking its time in getting from under the counter to the back of the stove. I had Dan seal off the little mouse hole in the back of the stove. Then I saw the mouse again, under the chest in the living room.

"It's a mouse. It's one little mouse," Dan said. "Let it be."

"Everybody knows that if there's one mouse there are more," I said. "We've got to get rid of them."

Dan, the humanist, was secretly glad the mouse had resurfaced—that he hadn't done any damage in sealing off its home.

"It looked like the same mouse to me," Henry said.

"They all look that way," I said. "That doesn't mean—"

"Poor thing," Dan said.

"Are either of you going to set traps, or do I have to do it?"

"You have to do it," Dan said. "I can't stand it. I don't want to kill a mouse."

"I think there's only one mouse," Henry said.

Glaring at them, I went into the kitchen and took the mouse-traps out of their cellophane packages. I stared at them with tears in my eyes. I didn't know how to set them. Dan and Henry had made me seem like a cold-blooded killer.

"Maybe it will just leave," Dan said.

"Don't be ridiculous, Dan," I said. "If you aren't going to help, at least don't sit around snickering with Henry."

"We're not snickering," Henry said.

"You two certainly are buddy-buddy."

"What's the matter now? You want us to hate each other?" Henry said.

"I don't know how to set a mousetrap," I said. "I can't do it myself."

"Poor Mommy," Joanna said. She was in the hallway outside the living room, listening. I almost turned on her to tell her not to be sarcastic, when I realized that she was serious. She felt sorry for me. With someone on my side, I felt new courage about going back into the kitchen and tackling the problem of traps.

Dianne called and said she had asked her husband if he could go out one night a week, so she could go out with friends or stay home by herself. He said no, but agreed to take stained-glass lessons with her.

One Tuesday, it rained. I stayed home and daydreamed, and remembered the past. I thought about the boy I dated my last year in high school, who used to take me out to the country on weekends, to where some cousins of his lived. I wondered why he always went there, because we never got near the house. He would drive partway up their long driveway in the woods and then pull off onto a narrow little road that trucks sometimes used when they were logging the property. We parked on the little road and necked. Sometimes the boy would drive slowly along on the country roads looking for rabbits, and whenever he saw one, which was pretty often—sometimes even two or three rabbits at once—he floored it, trying to run the rabbit down. There was no radio in the car. He had a portable radio that got only two stations (soul music and classical) and I held it on my lap. He liked the volume turned up very loud.

Joanna comes to my bedroom and announces that Uncle Bobby is on the phone.

"I got a dog," he says.

"What kind?"

"Aren't you even surprised?"

"Yes. Where did you get the dog?"

"A guy I knew a little bit in college is going to jail, and he persuaded me to take the dog."

"What is he going to jail for?"

"Burglary."

"Joanna," I say, "don't stand there staring at me when I'm talking on the phone."

"He robbed a house," Bobby says.

"What kind of a dog is it?" I ask.

"Malamute and German shepherd. It's in heat."

"Well," I say, "you always wanted a dog."

"I call you all the time, and you never call me," Bobby says.

"I never have interesting news."

"You could call and tell me what you do on Tuesday nights."

"Nothing very interesting," I say.

"You could go to a bar and have rum drinks and weep," Bobby says. He chuckles.

"Are you stoned?" I ask.

"Sure I am. Been home from work for an hour and a half. Ate a Celeste pizza, had a little smoke."

"Do you really have a dog?" I ask.

"If you were a male dog, you wouldn't have any doubt of it."

"You're always much more clever than I am. It's hard to talk to you on the phone, Bobby."

"It's hard to be me," Bobby says. A silence. "I'm not sure the dog likes me."

"Bring it over. Joanna will love it."

"I'll be around with it Tuesday night," he says.

"Why is it so interesting to you that I have one night a week to myself?"

"Whatever you do," Bobby says, "don't rob a house."

We hang up, and I go tell Joanna the news.

"You yelled at me," she says.

"I did not. I asked you not to stand there staring at me while I was on the phone."

"You raised your voice," she says.

Soon it will be Tuesday night.

Joanna asks me suspiciously what I do on Tuesday nights.

"What does your father say I do?" I ask.

"He says he doesn't know."

"Does he seem curious?"

"It's hard to tell with him," she says.

Having got my answer, I've forgotten about her question.

"So what things do you do?" she says.

"Sometimes you like to play in your tent," I say defensively.

"Well, I like some time to just do what I want to do, too, Joanna."

"That's O.K.," she says. She sounds like an adult placating a child.

I have to face the fact that I don't do much of anything on Tuesdays, and that one night alone each week isn't making me any less edgy or more agreeable to live with. I tell Dan this, as if it's his fault.

"I don't think you ever wanted to divorce Henry," Dan says.

"Oh, Dan, I *did*."

"You two seem to get along fine."

"But we fought. We didn't get along."

He looks at me. "Oh," he says. He is being inordinately nice to me, because of the scene I threw when a mouse got caught in one of the traps. The trap didn't kill it. It just got it by the paw, and Dan had to beat it to death with a screwdriver.

"Maybe you'd rather the two of us did something regularly on Tuesday nights," he says now. "Maybe I could get the night of my meetings changed."

"Thank you," I say. "Maybe I should give it a little longer."

"That's up to you," he says. "There hasn't been enough time to judge by, I guess."

Inordinately kind. Deferential. He has been saying for a long time that our relationship is turning sour, and now it must have turned so sour for him that he doesn't even want to fight. What does he want?

"Maybe you'd like a night—" I begin.

"The hell with that," he says. "If there has to be so much time alone, I can't see the point of living together."

I hate fights. The day after this one, I get weepy and go over to Dianne's. She ends up subtly suggesting that I take stained-glass lessons. We drink some sherry and I drive home. The last thing I want is to run into her husband, who calls me "the squirrel" behind my back. Dianne says that when I call and he answers, he lets her know it's me on the phone by puffing up his cheeks to make himself look like a squirrel.

Tonight, Dan and I each sit on a side of Joanna's tester bed to say good night to her. The canopy above the bed is white nylon, with small, puckered stars. She is ready for sleep. As soon as she goes to sleep, Dan will be ready to talk to me. Dan has clicked off the light next to Joanna's bed. Going out of the bedroom before him, I grope for the hall light. I remember Henry saying to me, as a way of leading up to talking about divorce, that going to work one morning he had driven over a hill and had been astonished when at the top he saw a huge yellow tree, and realized for the first time that it was autumn.

## JAYNE ANNE PHILLIPS [b. 1952]

# Cheers

The sewing woman lived across the tracks, down past Arey's Feed Store. Row of skinny houses on a mud alley. Her rooms smelled of salted grease and old newspaper. Behind the ironing board she was thin, scooping up papers that shuffled open in her hands. Her eyebrows were arched sharp and painted on.

She made cheerleading suits for ten-year-olds. Threading the machine, she clicked her red nails on the needle and pulled my shirt over my head. In the other room the kids watched *Queen for a Day.* She bent over me. I saw each eyelash painted black and hard and separate. Honey, she said. Turn around this way. And on the wall there was a postcard of orange trees in Florida. A man in a straw hat reached up with his hand all curled. Beautiful Bounty said the card in wavy red letters.

I got part of it made up, she said, fitting the red vest. You girls are bout the same size as mine. All you girls are bout the same. She pursed her red lips and pinched the cloth together. Tell me somethin Honey. How'd I manage all these kids an no man. On television there was loud applause for the queen, whose roses were sharp and real. Her machine buzzed like an animal beside the round clock. She frowned as she pressed the button with her foot, then furled the red cloth out and pulled me to her. Her pointed white face was smudged around the eyes. I watched the pale strand of scalp in her hair. There, she said.

When I left she tucked the money in her sweater. She had pins between her teeth and lipstick gone grainy in the cracks of her mouth. I had a red swing skirt and a bumpy *A* on my chest. Lord, she said. You do look pretty.

# POETRY

# INTRODUCTION TO POETRY

Poetry occurs any time, anywhere that people combine words and sound together in unusual and arresting ways. It happens in songs, hymns, opera; in the nursery rhymes we never quite forget; in striking phrases that say so much. The songs "Michael Row the Boat Ashore," Bob Dylan's "Blowin' in the Wind," Lennon and McCartney's "Eleanor Rigby," Harry Chapin's "Cat's in the Cradle," Paul Simon's "Graceland," Tracy Chapman's "Revolution," and Phil Collins's "Paradise" all have poetry in common. So, too, do the hymn "Amazing Grace," Puccini's opera "Madam Butterfly," the rhyme "Three Blind Mice," and Ezra Pound's "In a Station of the Metro," with its famous image of faces in a subway crowd as "Petals on a wet, black bough."

If the imagination spoke one language, many people believe it would speak poetry. For poets use language in extraordinary and exciting ways. Often they combine two very different words or phrases, or jump from idea to idea or line to line, leaving readers to fill in, or forget, the gaps. *Poetic imagery* concretely expresses such mental leaping. The foundation of all poetic imagery, *metaphor* (the implied comparison of dissimilar things), actually abolishes the space we conventionally use to separate two ideas. In T. S. Eliot's "The Love Song of J. Alfred Prufrock," for example, Prufrock, the speaker, compares city smog to a cat. He makes this leap by concentrating on the qualities they share when they are in motion. So, the smog is said to rub "its back upon the windowpanes," lick "its tongue into the corners of the evening," curl "once about the house" and sleep.

Metaphors always serve the general meaning of a poem, even when they appear only once. Local, or specific, metaphors, as they are sometimes called, occur in stanza two of Walt Whitman's "A Noiseless Patient Spider." Whitman's speaker compares his soul to an astronomer or navigator, seeking to connect with a landmass; to a bridge-builder laying down a temporary line on which to construct a permanent bridge; and to a sailor throwing out an anchor. An extended metaphor may run for several lines, or even encompass an entire poem, as it does in the speaker's comparison of his creative soul to a "noiseless patient spider" spinning out its silk.

The *simile* is a metaphor that uses *like* or *as* to link explicitly two different ideas. In Sylvia Plath's "Morning Song," for example, the vowel sounds of a newborn infant's cries "rise like balloons." Other kinds of poetic imagery, also based on metaphor, are *personification* (attribution of human qualities and powers to an abstraction) and *apostrophe* (direct address to someone or something not literally listening). Whitman's speaker uses apostrophe when he addresses his soul as "O my soul," and personification when he invests it with human properties.

But while the unusual combinations of words, ideas, and feelings we find in poetry may lift us out of ordinary life and language, they come from the things and experiences of daily life. Poetry is made of concrete words and the things they stand for: spiders, people, hair, roads; recognizable emotions like hate and love; shared experiences like birth and death. The commonalities become springboards for poets' and readers' imaginations.

Most poets further strengthen the framework of shared understandings by drawing on the customary literary elements of *character, plot, setting, point of view, tone, style,* and *theme* to give substance and form to their ideas and feelings; they set their poems within specific situations, much as storytellers and playwrights do; and they use a *persona* (speaker). Whether poems are written from first-person, second-person, or third-person point of view, they are always spoken by a particular imaginary or real person in a particular place and time. An absent lover longing to return home is the speaker of the anonymous ballad "Western Wind." A loving friend, grieving the death of an innocent country girl, is the speaker of William Wordsworth's "A Slumber Did My Spirit Seal." Because the persona may not represent the poet, it is important to separate the two. In some poems, the distance between poet and persona seems obvious: certainly Robert Browning is not the Duke of Ferrara in "My Last Duchess," nor Gwendolyn Brooks the seven kids at the Golden Shovel pool hall in "We Real Cool." In other poems, especially when a speaker expresses ideas known to be the poet's own, the distance between poet and persona may seem less great.

Still, for all the help poems provide, relative to their size they often require more intense and intimate collaboration between writers and readers, and consequently greater time and attention, than stories and plays do. Because poems are compact and condensed, because they do communicate on several levels at once, they challenge our imaginations in unaccustomed ways. We need to think about the *denotative* (literal) and *connotative* (suggestive) meanings of words, about the nature and contributions of a poem's *rhythm and sound effects,* and about its visual shape and progress line by line, stanza by stanza. Looking, listening, and watching a poem develop as we read it may seem a tall order. But poets, like the rest of us, yearn to be understood and appreciated. Before sharing a new poem, they revise until they feel that it is ready to be shared.

Allowing a poem to speak for itself is a useful way to begin. Since the *line,* rather than the sentence, is a poem's basic unit of meaning, letting a poem explain itself, line after line, gradually brings out its larger meanings. In the first stanza of "A Noiseless Patient Spider," for example, the narrator, "I," declares that he "mark'd," or noticed, "a noiseless patient spider" "isolated," "on a little promontory," launching its silken filaments "out of itself" into "the vacant vast surrounding . . . Ever unreeling them, ever tirelessly speeding them." In the second stanza, the narrator applies the spinning imagery to the activities of his soul, who he addresses reverently and directly: "O my soul." Like the spider, the speaker's soul stands alone, "Surrounded, detach'd," having no resources beyond itself. Yet as the spider continues to spin, so the soul continues, striving to catch hold, to find an "anchor" somewhere. The connection between these two events is expressed by the poem's structure and wording: the two stanzas are versions of the creative act occurring at different times. By association and implication, then, we realize that the speaker sees the "noiseless patient spider" as a twin of his creative soul, which also strives to build a "bridge" across "measureless oceans of space."

"A Noiseless Patient Spider" communicates visually and aurally, as well as metaphorically. Its varying line-lengths and rhythms, its repeated *s* sounds and frequent present participles, suggest the persistent creativity of both the spider and the speaker's soul. In doing so they heighten, and perhaps extend, the poem's verbal meanings. They make the poem a kind of model of creative imagination the speaker talks about. So this poem, like many others, can be said to enact what it describes.

Lucille Clifton's "Miss Rosie" develops the speaker's recognition in a similar way. Each line adds a new image or idea to the one before it; each two lines express a further idea or image; all lines in succession produce the poem's meaning. Readers recreate the scene perception by perception, much as the poet originally did. First, Miss Rosie is addressed as a passive thing, "wrapped up like garbage" and enveloped by smells; next as a crazy lady in an "old man's shoes / with the little toe cut out / . . . waiting for [her] mind"; next as a "wet brown bag of a woman / who . . . used to be called Georgia Rose," thus identifying her origin and race; finally, as a person deserving respect and honor. Verbs, carefully selected and ordered, physically express the speaker's changing attitudes: watching gives way to speaking ("I say") and standing up ("I stand up / through your destruction / I stand up").

In the minute or less needed to read these fourteen lines, we gain three memorable pictures of Miss Rosie, each of them true as far as it goes, each of them indicative of a different kind of degradation, and each revealing a deeper understanding on the speaker's part. The speaker, addressing Miss Rosie throughout, actually sees the woman with greater and greater detail and depth until, near the poem's end, the speaker is able to honor Miss Rosie's history, tragic though it may be. The shape of the poem reinforces this meaning by organizing the evolving perceptions into small units, each ending with the speaker's own physical response. The sound of the poem, too, enhances its overall meanings. The cadences of the speaker's lines fall like the sounds of soul music, which has deep roots in the music and religious experience of African-American culture.

Clifton's "Miss Rosie" is a reminder that the sense, sound, and shape of poems reinforce each other and together create meaning and value. The concreteness, order, and appropriateness of a poem's words; its evolution line by line; its sounds and rhythms; and its shape on the page all contribute to its value and power. Although all work together dynamically in a poem, each makes an individual contribution as well.

The first dynamic element, *sense,* is largely the product of the nature and sequence of a poem's words. Samuel Taylor Coleridge, the nineteenth-century English poet and critic, wrote that prose is words in their best order, poetry the best words in the best order. While people might disagree about what words and order are best, they would agree that the *diction* (selection of words) of poetry, and the *syntax* (word order and sentence-structure) of poetry, generally do distinguish poetry from prose. The diction of poetry tends to be more concrete, specific, sensuous, and suggestive than that of prose. Similarly, the syntax of poetry tends to be more compressed, lacking many of the qualifying and transitional words and phrases that prose employs to move logically from point to point.

What a poet puts in and leaves out, both equally important, give poetry its distinctive density and power. Similarly, what a poem literally says and what it suggests, both equally important, enrich its meanings. A word or phrase may be deliberately *ambiguous* or *ironic*; or a statement may be *paradoxical* (apparently self-contradictory, but on a deeper level true), as is the final line of William Blake's "London": "And blights with plagues the Marriage hearse." Or one word or phrase used suggestively, prominently, and usually repeatedly, may become a *symbol*, or a stylized and sustained pattern of symbols may become an *allegory*. Depending on how widely they are recognized, symbols can be personal (Yeats's Byzantium), social (the American or the Canadian flag), or mythic (a cross, the sea, a dove).

A second dynamic element is *sound*. The sounds of certain words suggest the meaning of the thing they describe; examples of such *onomatopoeia* are *buzz* and *hum*. Other sound effects depend on repetition: *alliteration* (repetition of initial consonant sounds), consonance (repetition of internal consonant sounds), and *assonance* (repetition of internal vowel sounds). Often these sound effects occur together in one line. While most poets use alliteration, consonance, and assonance within a particular line, traditional poets often employ *end-rhyme* (close repetition of sounds at the ends of lines) throughout an entire poem, changing specific rhyme sounds with each new stanza. The overall pattern of end-rhymes is called a *rhyme scheme*.

Just as diction, syntax, and line-by-line development together produce the sense of a poem, so individual sounds and rhythmic (recurring) patterns produce the overall sound of a poem. In poetry, the organization of sounds is as important as the organization of words. All poetry has rhythms that emphasize certain sounds and create patterns. In free verse, these patterns are irregular, and referred to as *cadences*. While most modern poets do not favor consistent patterns, most traditional pre-modern poets honor regular patterns, referred to as *meter,* and break with them only for important reasons. It is therefore wise to expect regular rhythmic patterns in pre-modern poetry and to consider why one pattern has been selected over another.

The metrical units of traditional poetry, *feet,* are made of sets of two or three syllables, each set having one syllable that is stressed more heavily than the other or others. The five most common feet are *iamb, trochee, anapest, dactyl,* and *spondee.* The *iamb* and the *anapest* are known as "rising feet" because they end with a stressed syllable; the *trochee* and the *dactyl* as "falling feet" because they end with an unstressed syllable. The *spondee* is a metrical foot of two stressed syllables. A clever little poem by Coleridge offers an easy way of remembering the major metrical feet:

> Trochee trips from long to short.
> From long to long in solemn sort
> Slow Spondee stalks; strong foot! yet ill able
> Ever to come up with Dactyl trisyllable.
> Iambics march from short to long
> With a leap and a bound the swift Anapests throng.

The meter of a traditional poem is detected by counting the number of feet in a line. A poem is said to have a certain meter when most lines follow the same pattern. The Coleridge poem above is written in tetrameter—four feet to a line.

Line groupings, called *stanzas,* enable poets to establish close relationships among lines. In traditional poetry, stanzas have recognizable patterns of end-rhymes, which give the poem its rhyme scheme. Common stanzas are the *couplet* (two-line stanza), *tercet* (three-line stanza), and *quatrain* (four-line stanza). Stylized line-groupings such as the *sonnet, ode,* and *terza rima* follow established rhyme schemes; examples of the forms can be found in the glossary. Modern and contemporary poets often deviate from these traditional patterns and vary the shape and length of stanzas (and lines) to further individualize meanings. Thus, the original designs that emerge are called *free verse.*

Poets, like storytellers and playwrights, build on tradition even as they break with it. William Wordsworth, an English poet who wrote in the late eighteenth and early nineteenth centuries, began his poetic career with a revolutionary volume called *Lyrical Ballads,* which included poems by his friend Samuel Taylor Coleridge as well. Wordsworth sought to restore the sound of common speech to poetry which, in his opinion, had become too stiff and artificial. With humble country people as his subject, and the ancient ballad form as his influence, he created poems that stood out for their moving simplicity and directness. A group of these, the "Lucy poems," celebrates a rural child who died too young. "A Slumber Did My Spirit Seal," a tribute to this child, follows the traditional *ballad stanza,* which is comprised of quatrains with an *abab* rhyme scheme (that is, alternate lines rhyme) of alternating lines of tetrameter and trimeter.

The third dynamic element in poetry is *shape,* or visual design. Poets, including writers of prose poems, deliberately choose shapes that suit their meanings. Shape is created by number of stanzas, length of lines, and margins. A vivid example of the power of shape is George Herbert's "Easter Wings," often called a *concrete,* or *shaped, poem.* The poem calls attention to itself visually, and its shape suggests the poem's subject. While the shapes of most poems do not advertise themselves so boldly, it is fair to say that the visual appearance of any poem is a significant factor in its total meaning.

Sense, sound, and shape are essential considerations of poetry of any period. The Bible contains some splendid poetry in the Song of Solomon, the Psalms, and Ecclesiastes, for example. Poetry also provided a vehicle for most narrative and drama before the seventeenth century. Homer's *Iliad,* the ancient Greek epic of the Trojan Wars, and his *Odyssey,* the famous account of the adventures of the hero Odysseus, were sung in verse. Shakespeare's comedies, tragedies, and history plays are all *dramatic poetry.*

The three early uses of poetry in narrative, drama, and song have continued into the present. *Narrative, dramatic,* and *lyric poetry* appear in popular songs and in powerful modern and contemporary poems. James Wright's "A Blessing," Elizabeth Bishop's "In the Waiting Room," and Carolyn Forché's "The Colonel" are examples of modern narratives. Langston Hughes's "Night Funeral in Harlem," a poem in three voices, is essentially dramatic. Lucille Clifton's "Miss Rosie," David Ignatow's prose-poem "Did you know that hair is flying around in the universe?" and Garrett Kaoru Hongo's "Who among You Knows the Essence of Garlic?" are essentially lyric poems, poems that evoke emotion. Pablo Neruda's "The Clock Fallen into the Sea" and Jimmy Santiago Baca's "Cloudy Day" combine narrative and lyric voices, as do many other modern and contemporary poems, and as does Walt Whitman's "A Noiseless Patient Spider." These, too, evoke strong emotion.

While the names of these primary types of poetry have remained the same throughout the centuries, poetic purposes and styles have changed significantly. Before the printing press made poetry widely available in relatively permanent form, oral poetry recorded myths and major events. The chanters and speakers of these significant poems relied on repeated sounds and rhythms as memory aids. In most modern cultures, rich oral traditions persist. The impulse and style of early ballads are very much alive in today's songs and street music, including Rap. While some of today's poets do use traditional rhyme and meter, many since Walt Whitman, and most since William Carlos Williams, H. D., and Ezra Pound, have favored free verse based on cadences, the rhythms created by the phrases of speech.

The fundamental point is that poetry, like language itself, stands in dynamic relation to its time, and changes with the values of its time. Whatever style we personally may favor, there is no one right way for all poetry. The root meanings of the words *poet* and *poem* support this view. Ancient Greek in origin, the words *poetry* and *poem* literally mean "a thing made or created," and the word *poet* means "maker." In its classical sense, *poetry* has been, and can be, used to include all kinds of imaginative literature. In the same metaphorical way, the word *poet* can be said to pertain to us, the readers, for we make poems happen. Without us, poems would remain words and spaces on a page, or sounds in the air. With us, they do become poems: compact, compressed, energetic visions that radiate new meanings the more deeply we experience them.

ANONYMOUS

# Western Wind

Western wind, when will thou blow,
The small rain down can rain?
Christ, if my love were in my arms,
And I in my bed again!

ANONYMOUS

# Edward

"Why does your brand sae drap wi' bluid,[1]
    Edward, Edward?
Why does your brand sae drap wi' bluid,
    And why sae sad gang° ye, O?"—          °*go*
"O I ha'e kill'd my hawk sae guid,                          5
    Mither, mither;
O I ha'e kill'd my hawk sae guid,
    And had nae mair° but he, O."          °*more*

"Your hawkes bluid was never sae reid,
    Edward, Edward;                          10
Your hawkes bluid was never sae reid,
    My dear son, I tell thee, O."—
"O I ha'e kill'd my red-roan° steed,          °*chestnut*
    Mither, mither;
O I ha'e kill'd my red-roan steed,                          15
    That earst° was sae fair and free, O."          °*once*

---

[1] "Why does your sword so drip with blood, . . .?"

"Your steed was auld, and ye ha'e gat mair,°          °more
    Edward, Edward;
Your steed was auld, and ye ha'e gat mair:
    Some other dule° ye dree,° O."          °grief/suffer
"O I ha'e kill'd my fader dear,          21
    Mither, mither;
O I ha'e kill'd my fader dear,
    Alas, and wae° is me, O!"          °woe

"And whatten penance wul ye dree° for that,          °undergo
    Edward, Edward?          26
Whatten penance wul ye dree for that,
    My dear son, now tell me, O?"—
"I'll set my feet in yonder boat,
    Mither, mither;          30
I'll set my feet in yonder boat,
    And I'll fare over the sea, O."

"And what wul ye do wi' your towers and your ha',°          °hall
    Edward, Edward?
And what will ye do wi' your towers and your ha',          35
    That were sae fair to see, O?"
"I'll let thame stand til they down fa',°          °fall
    Mither, mither;
I'll let thame stand til they down fa',          39
    For here never mair maun° I be, O."          °must

"And what wul ye leave to your bairns° and your wife,          °children
    Edward, Edward?
And what wul ye leave to your bairns and your wife,
    When ye gang over the sea, O?"—
"The warldes room: late them beg thrae life;          45
    Mither, mither;
The warldes room: late them beg thrae life;
    For thame never mair wul I see, O."

"And what wul ye leave to your ain° mither dear,          °own
    Edward, Edward?          50
And what wul ye leave to your ain mither dear,
    My dear son, now tell me, O?"—

"The curse of hell frae° me sal° ye bear,        °*from/shall*
    Mither, mither;
The curse of hell frae me sal ye bear:        55
    Sic° counseils ye gave to me, O!"        °*such*


# SIR WALTER RALEGH [ca. 1552–1618]

## The Nymph's Reply to the Shepherd

If all the world and love were young,
And truth in every shepherd's tongue,
These pretty pleasures might me move
To live with thee and be thy love.

Time drives the flocks from field to fold        5
When rivers rage and rocks grow cold,
And Philomel° becometh dumb;        °*nightingale*
The rest complains of cares to come.

The flowers do fade, and wanton fields
To wayward winter reckoning yields;        10
A honey tongue, a heart of gall,
Is fancy's spring but sorrow's fall.

Thy gowns, thy shoes, thy beds of roses,
Thy cap, thy kirtle,° and thy posies        °*skirt*
Soon break, soon wither, soon forgotten,        15
In folly ripe, in reason rotten.

Thy belt of straw and ivy buds,
Thy coral clasps and amber studs,
All these in me no means can move
To come to thee and be thy love.        20

But could youth last and love still breed,
Had joys no date, nor age no need,
Then these delights my mind might move
To live with thee and be thy love.

## SIR PHILIP SIDNEY [1554–1586]

# With how sad steps, Oh Moon, thou climb'st the skies[1]

With how sad steps, Oh Moon, thou climb'st the skies!
How silently, and with how wan a face!
What, may it be that even in heavenly place
That busy archer° his sharp arrows tries?      °Cupid
Sure, if that long-with-love-acquainted eyes      5
Can judge of love, thou feel'st a lover's case,
I read it in thy looks; thy languished grace,
To me, that feel the like, thy state descries.
Then, even of fellowship, Oh Moon, tell me,
Is constant love deemed there but want of wit?      10
Are beauties there as proud as here they be?
Do they above love to be loved, and yet
Those lovers scorn whom that love doth possess?
Do they call virtue there ungratefulness?

## CHRISTOPHER MARLOWE [1564–1593]

# The Passionate Shepherd to His Love

Come live with me, and be my love,
And we will all the pleasures prove,°      °test, experience

---

[1] Number 31 from the sonnet sequence *Astrophel and Stella*.

That valleys, groves, hills and fields,
Woods, or steepy mountains yields.

And we will sit upon the rocks,                              5
Seeing the shepherds feed their flocks,
By shallow rivers, to whose falls,
Melodious birds sing madrigals.

And I will make thee beds of roses,
And a thousand fragrant posies,                            10
A cap of flowers, and a kirtle°                          °skirt
Embroidered all with leaves of myrtle;

A gown made of the finest wool,
Which from our pretty lambs we pull,
Fair-linéd slippers for the cold,                         15
With buckles of the purest gold;

A belt of straw and ivy buds
With coral clasps and amber studs:
And if these pleasures may thee move,
Come live with me, and be my love.                        20

The shepherd swains shall dance and sing,
For thy delight each May morning:
If these delights thy mind may move,
Then live with me, and be my love.


# WILLIAM SHAKESPEARE [1564–1616]
## Sonnets

### 18

Shall I compare thee to a summer's day?
Thou art more lovely and more temperate.
Rough winds do shake the darling buds of May,
And summer's lease hath all too short a date.

Sometimes too hot the eye of heaven shines,                                          5
And often is his gold complexion dimmed;
And every fair from fair sometime declines,
By chance, or nature's changing course, untrimmed:°          °unadorned
But thy eternal summer shall not fade
Nor lose possession of that fair° thou ow'st,°               °beauty/own
Nor shall Death brag thou wand'rest in his shade            11
When in eternal lines to time thou grow'st.
    So long as men can breathe or eyes can see,
    So long lives this, and this gives life to thee.

### 130

My mistress' eyes are nothing like the sun,
Coral is far more red, than her lips red,
If snow be white, why then her breasts are dun:°              °gray
If hairs be wires, black wires grow on her head:
I have seen roses damasked,° red and white,                  °variegated
But no such roses see I in her cheeks,                       6
And in some perfumes is there more delight,
Than in the breath that from my mistress reeks,°             °is exhaled
I love to hear her speak, yet well I know,
That music hath a far more pleasing sound:                   10
I grant I never saw a goddess go,°                           °walk
My mistress when she walks treads on the ground.
    And yet by heaven I think my love as rare,
    As any she belied° with false compare.                °misrepresented

## JOHN DONNE [1572–1631]

# The Bait

Come live with me, and be my love,[1]
And we will some new pleasures prove

---

[1] Compare Marlowe's "The Passionate Shepherd to His Love."

Of golden sands, and crystal brooks, *creeks*
With silken lines, and silver hooks.

There will the river whispering run                          5
Warm'd by thy eyes, more than the Sun. *inflame w/ love*
And there th' enamour'd fish will stay,
Begging themselves they may betray.

When thou wilt swim in that live bath, *become limp*
Each fish, which every channel hath,                         10
Will amorously to thee swim,                *enamour*
Gladder to catch thee, than thou him.

If thou, to be so seen, be'st loth,
By Sun, or Moon, thou dark'nest both,
And if myself have leave to see,                             15
I need not their light, having thee.

Let others freeze with angling reeds,
And cut their legs, with shells and weeds,
Or treacherously poor fish beset,
With strangling snare, or windowy net:                       20

Let coarse bold hands, from slimy nest
The bedded fish in banks out-wrest,°              °drag out
Or curious traitors,° sleeve-silk² flies            °lures
Bewitch poor fishes' wand'ring eyes. *Appeal,*
*Attraction*

For thee, thou need'st no such deceit,                       25
For thou thyself art thine own bait;
That fish, that is not catch'd thereby,
Alas, is wiser far than I.

---

² A kind of silk that can be divided into fine filaments.

# Batter my heart,
# three-person'd God[1]

Batter my heart, three-person'd God; for you
As yet but knock, breathe, shine, and seek to mend;
That I may rise, and stand, o'erthrow me, and bend
Your force, to break, blow, burn, and make me new.
I, like an usurp'd town, to another due,                    5
Labour to admit you, but Oh, to no end,
Reason your viceroy in me, me should defend,
But is captiv'd, and proves weak or untrue.
Yet dearly I love you, and would be loved fain,
But am betroth'd unto your enemy:                          10
Divorce me, untie, or break that knot again,
Take me to you, imprison me, for I
Except you enthral me, never shall be free,
Nor ever chaste, except you ravish me.

## ROBERT HERRICK [1591–1674]

# Delight in Disorder

A sweet disorder in the dress
Kindles in clothes a wantonness.
A lawn° about the shoulders thrown          °scarf of fine linen
Into a fine distraction:                                    4
An erring° lace, which here and there         °wandering
Enthrals the crimson stomacher:°              °lower bodice

[1] Number 14 from *Holy Sonnets*.

A cuff neglectful, and thereby
Ribbands to flow confusedly:
A winning wave (deserving note)
In the tempestuous petticoat:                    10
A careless shoe-string, in whose tie
I see a wild civility:
Do more bewitch me than when art
Is too precise in every part.

# To the Virgins, to Make Much of Time

Gather ye rosebuds while ye may:
    Old Time is still a-flying,
And this same flower that smiles today
    Tomorrow will be dying.

The glorious lamp of heaven, the sun,        5
    The higher he's a-getting,
The sooner will his race be run,
    And nearer he's to setting.

That age is best which is the first,
    When youth and blood are warmer;        10
But, being spent, the worse, and worst
    Times, still succeed the former.

Then be not coy, but use your time,
    And while ye may, go marry:
For having lost but once your prime,        15
    You may for ever tarry.

## GEORGE HERBERT [1593–1633]

# Easter Wings

Lord, who createdst man in wealth and store,° °*abundance*
Though foolishly he lost the same,
Decaying  more  and  more,
Till  he  became
Most poor;                                                         5
With  Thee
O  let  me  rise
As    larks,    harmoniously,
And  sing  this  day  Thy  victories:
Then  shall  the  fall  further  the  flight  in  me.[1]      10

My    tender   age   in   sorrow   did   begin:
And still with sicknesses and shame
Thou  did'st  so  punish  sin,
That   I   became
Most  thin.                                                       15
With  Thee
Let  me  combine
And feel this day Thy victory;
For,  if  I  imp[2]  my  wing  on  Thine,
Affliction  shall  advance  the  flight  in  me.              20

## JOHN MILTON [1608–1674]

# When I consider how
# my light is spent

When I consider how my light is spent
Ere half my days in this dark world and wide,

---

[1] A reference to the doctrine of *felix culpa*, ("happy fault") in which Adam's fall was thought of as "happy," for had there not been a fall, there would not have been the promise of redemption.   [2] Engraft feathers on a damaged wing to restore the ability to fly.

And that one Talent[1] which is death to hide
Lodged with me useless, though my Soul more bent
To serve therewith my Maker, and present                                    5
    My true account, lest He returning chide) *scold*
    "Doth God exact day-labor, light denied?"
    I fondly° ask. But Patience, to prevent                °*foolishly*
That murmur, soon replies, "God doth not need
    Either man's work or his own gifts. Who best                10
    Bear His mild yoke, they serve Him best. His state *Bondage, link*
Is Kingly: Thousands at his bidding speed,
    And post o'er Land and Ocean without rest;
    They also serve who only stand and wait." *famous line*

## RICHARD LOVELACE [1618–1657]

# To Lucasta,
# Going to the Wars

Tell me not, Sweet, I am unkind
    That from the nunnery
Of thy chaste breast and quiet mind
    To war and arms I fly.

True, a new mistress now I chase,                                           5
    The first foe in the field;
And with a stronger faith embrace
    A sword, a horse, a shield.

Yet this inconstancy is such
    As you too shall adore;                                         10
I could not love thee, Dear, so much,
    Loved I not Honor more.

---

[1] A reference to the parable of the servants to whom various talents (weights of gold) were entrusted. The man who received only one talent neglected it and deserved the reproach of his master (Matt. 25:14–30).

## ANDREW MARVELL [1621–1678]

# To His Coy Mistress

Had we but world enough, and time,
This coyness, lady, were no crime.
We would sit down, and think which way
To walk, and pass our long love's day.
Thou by the Indian Ganges' side                    5
Should'st rubies find: I by the tide
Of Humber[1] would complain. I would
Love you ten years before the Flood,
And you should, if you please, refuse
Till the conversion of the Jews.                    10
My vegetable love should grow
Vaster than empires, and more slow.
An hundred years should go to praise
Thine eyes, and on thy forehead gaze:
Two hundred to adore each breast:                   15
But thirty thousand to the rest;
An age at least to every part,
And the last age should show your heart.
For, lady, you deserve this state,°        °dignity
Nor would I love at lower rate.                      20
　　But at my back I always hear
Time's wingéd chariot hurrying near:
And yonder all before us lie
Deserts of vast eternity.
Thy beauty shall no more be found;                  25
Nor, in thy marble vault, shall sound
My echoing song: then worms shall try
That long-preserved virginity,
And your quaint honor turn to dust,
And into ashes all my lust.                         30
The grave's a fine and private place,
But none, I think, do there embrace.

---

[1] River flowing by Hull, England, where Marvell lived.

Now, therefore, while the youthful hue
Sits on thy skin like morning dew,
And while thy willing soul transpires                    35
At every pore with instant fires,
Now let us sport us while we may;
And now, like amorous birds of prey,
Rather at once our Time devour,
Than languish in his slow-chapt° power.        °*slow-devouring*
Let us roll all our strength and all                         41
Our sweetness up into one ball,
And tear our pleasures with rough strife
Thorough the iron gates of life.
Thus, though we cannot make our sun                45
Stand still, yet we will make him run.


## HENRY VAUGHAN [c. 1621–1695]

# The Retreat

Happy those early days! when I
Shined in my angel-infancy.
Before I understood this place
Appointed for my second race,[1]
Or taught my soul to fancy aught                            5
But a white, celestial thought;
When yet I had not walked above
A mile or two from my first love,
And looking back, at that short space
Could see a glimpse of his bright face;                   10
When on some gilded cloud or flower
My gazing soul would dwell an hour,
And in those weaker glories spy
Some shadows of eternity;

---

[1] A phrase suggesting the doctrine of preexistence.

Before I taught my tongue to wound                    15
My conscience with a sinful sound,
Or had the black art to dispense
A several° sin to every sense,                        °*different*
But felt through all this fleshly dress
Bright shoots of everlastingness.                     20
    Oh, how I long to travel back,
And tread again that ancient track!
That I might once more reach that plain,
Where first I left my glorious train;
From whence the enlightened spirit sees               25
That shady city of palm trees;[2]
But ah! my soul with too much stay
Is drunk, and staggers in the way.
Some men a forward motion love,
But I by backward steps would move;                   30
And when this dust falls to the urn,
In that state I came, return.


## JOHN DRYDEN [1631–1700]

# A Song for St. Cecilia's Day[1]

### 1

From harmony, from heavenly harmony
   This universal frame began:
  When Nature underneath a heap
    Of jarring atoms lay,
   And could not heave her head,    *elevate / lift, raise,*   5
The tuneful voice was heard from high:   *throw, push, pull*
    "Arise, ye more than dead."

---

[2] As Moses was permitted a vision of the Promised Land, "the valley of Jericho, the city of palm trees" (Deut. 34:3).

[1] St. Cecilia is the patron saint of music.

Then cold, and hot, and moist, and dry,
In order to their stations leap,
    And Music's power obey.          10
From harmony, from heavenly harmony
    This universal frame began:
    From harmony to harmony
Through all the compass of the notes it ran,
The diapason[2] closing full in man.        15

### 2

What passion cannot Music raise and quell!  *quiet*
    When Jubal[3] struck the corded shell,  *formal adresses*
    His listening brethren stood around, *(referring to mem.*
    And, wondering, on their faces fell  *of a profession, etc.*
    To worship that celestial sound        20
*reflecting* Less than a god they thought there could not dwell
*heaven or* Within the hollow of that shell
*Chinese* That spoke so sweetly and so well.
*(mythical being)* What passion cannot Music raise and quell!

### 3

       *resounding melody of*
The trumpet's loud clangor *(clangs/ringing* 25
    Excites us to arms,     *sound)*
With shrill notes of anger,
    And mortal alarms.
The double double double beat
    Of the thundering drum        30
Cries: "Hark! the foes come;
Charge, charge, 'tis too late to retreat."

### 4

The soft complaining flute
In dying notes discovers *(sorrow)*
The woes of hopeless lovers, 
Whose dirge is whispered by the warbling lute.   35 *trilling*
*song of griefs*    *(instrument w/ thi*
*manner w/ many turns*

---

[2] The complete compass of notes in the musical scale. [3] Referred to in Gen. 4:21
as the creator of the lyre and the pipe.  *+ variations*

### 5

Sharp violins proclaim *~piercing pain*
Their jealous pangs, and desperation,
Fury, frantic indignation, *Anger*
Depth of pains, and height of passion,                    40
 For the fair, disdainful dame.

### 6

But O! what art can teach,
What human voice can reach,
The sacred organ's praise?
 Notes inspiring holy love,                          45
Notes that wing their heavenly ways
 To mend the choirs above.

### 7

Orpheus[4] could lead the savage race; *untamed*
And trees unrooted left their place,
 Sequacious of the lyre; *intellectually servile*   50
But bright Cecilia raised the wonder higher:
When to her organ vocal breath was given,
An angel heard, and straight appeared,
 Mistaking earth for heaven.

GRAND CHORUS

*As from the power of sacred lays*                        55
 *The spheres began to move,*
*And sung the great Creator's praise*
 *To all the blest above;*
*So, when the last and dreadful hour* *use up or destroy*
*This crumbling pageant shall devour,* *as if by eating*  60
*The trumpet shall be heard on high,*
*The dead shall live, the living die,*
*And Music shall untune the sky.*

---

[4] A legendary poet, son of Apollo and one of the Muses, who played his lyre so
wonderfully that he tamed savage beasts.

## JONATHAN SWIFT [1667–1745]

# A Description of the Morning

Now hardly here and there an hackney coach
Appearing, showed the ruddy morn's approach.
Now Betty from her master's bed had flown,
And softly stole to discompose her own;
The slipshod 'prentice from his master's door          5
Had pared the dirt, and sprinkled round the floor.
Now Moll had whirled her mop with dextrous airs,
Prepared to scrub the entry and the stairs.
The youth with broomy stumps began to trace
The kennel's° edge, where wheels had worn the place.          °gutter's
The small-coal man was heard with cadence deep,          11
Till drowned in shriller notes of chimney sweep:
Duns at his lordship's gate began to meet;
And brickdust Moll had screamed through half the street.
The turnkey now his flock returning sees,          15
Duly let out a-nights to steal for fees:
The watchful bailiffs take their silent stands,
And schoolboys lag with satchels in their hands.

## WILLIAM BLAKE [1757–1827]

# London

I wander thro' each charter'd[1] street,
Near where the charter'd Thames does flow,
And mark in every face I meet
Marks of weakness, marks of woe.

---

[1] Given liberty, but also, ironically, preempted as private property and rented out.

In every cry of every Man,                                              5
In every Infant's cry of fear,
In every voice, in every ban,[2]
The mind-forg'd manacles I hear.   *Handcuffs*

How the Chimney-sweeper's cry
Every blackening Church appalls;                                        10
And the hapless Soldier's sigh
Runs in blood down Palace walls.

But most through midnight streets I hear
How the youthful Harlot's curse
Blasts the new born Infant's tear,[3]                                   15
And blights with plagues the Marriage hearse.[4]

*deteriorate*                                                 *coffin*

# The Garden of Love

I went to the Garden of Love,
And saw what I never had seen:
A Chapel was built in the midst,
Where I used to play on the green.

And the gates of this Chapel were shut,                                 5
And "Thou shalt not" writ over the door;
So I turned to the Garden of Love
That so many sweet flowers bore.

And I saw it was filled with graves,
And tombstones where flowers should be;                                 10
And priests in black gowns were walking their rounds,
And binding with briars my joys & desires.

*Strictly plant*

---

[2] Political and legal prohibition, but also a proclamation of a marriage.   [3] Implying prenatal blindness resulting from venereal disease.   [4] Funeral bier or coach.

## WILLIAM WORDSWORTH [1770–1850]
# A Slumber Did My Spirit Seal

A slumber did my spirit seal;
    I had no human fears;
She seemed a thing that could not feel
    The touch of earthly years.

No motion has she now, no force;             5
    She neither hears nor sees;
Rolled round in earth's diurnal° course,      °*daily*
    With rocks, and stones, and trees.

## SAMUEL TAYLOR COLERIDGE [1772–1834]
# Kubla Khan

In Xanadu did Kubla Khan[1]
    A stately pleasure dome decree:
Where Alph, the sacred river, ran
Through caverns measureless to man
    Down to a sunless sea.          5
So twice five miles of fertile ground
With walls and towers were girdled round:
And here were gardens bright with sinuous rills,
Where blossomed many an incense-bearing tree,
And here were forests ancient as the hills,     10
Enfolding sunny spots of greenery.

[handwritten annotations: "exotic"; "an order usu. having the force of law."; "encircled"; "winding small brook"; "pleasing scent"; "containing"]

---

[1] Kubla Khan founded the Mongol empire in the thirteenth century. Xanadu, Alph, and Mount Abora are modifications of exotic geographical names that Coleridge read of in books of travel and exploration.

But oh! that deep romantic chasm which slanted
Down the green hill athwart a cedarn cover!
A savage place; as holy and enchanted
As e'er beneath a waning moon was haunted                    15
By woman wailing for her demon lover!
And from this chasm, with ceaseless turmoil seething,
As if this earth in fast thick pants were breathing,
A mighty fountain momently was forced,
Amid whose swift half-intermitted burst                       20
Huge fragments vaulted like rebounding hail,
Or chaffy grain beneath the thresher's flail;
And 'mid these dancing rocks at once and ever
It flung up momently the sacred river.
Five miles meandering with a mazy motion                      25
Through wood and dale the sacred river ran,
Then reached the caverns measureless to man,
And sank in tumult to a lifeless ocean:
And 'mid this tumult Kubla heard from far
Ancestral voices prophesying war!                             30

    The shadow of the dome of pleasure
    Floated midway on the waves;
    Where was heard the mingled measure
    From the fountain and the caves.
It was a miracle of rare device,                              35
A sunny pleasure dome with caves of ice!

    A damsel with a dulcimer
    In a vision once I saw:
    It was an Abyssinian maid,
    And on her dulcimer she played,                           40
    Singing of Mount Abora.²
    Could I revive within me
    Her symphony and song,
    To such a deep delight 'twould win me,
That with music loud and long,                                45
I would build that dome in air,
That sunny dome! those caves of ice!

---

² Apparent reference to Milton's *Paradise Lost* (4.280–82).

And all who heard should see them there,
And all should cry, Beware! Beware!
His flashing eyes, his floating hair!                                    50
Weave a circle round him thrice,[3]
And close your eyes with holy dread,
For he on honey-dew hath fed,
And drunk the milk of Paradise.[4]


## GEORGE GORDON, LORD BYRON [1788–1824]

# She Walks in Beauty

She walks in Beauty, like the night
    Of cloudless climes and starry skies; *climate*
And all that's best of dark and bright
    Meet in her aspect and her eyes:
Thus mellowed to that tender light                                       5
    Which Heaven to gaudy day denies. *flashy*

One shade the more, one ray the less,
    Had half impaired the nameless grace *drunk*
Which waves in every raven tress, *Shiny, Braid*
    Or softly lightens o'er her face;        *black* 10
Where thoughts serenely sweet express, *calm*
    How pure, how dear their dwelling-place.

And on that cheek, and o'er that brow,
    So soft, so calm, yet eloquent,
The smiles that win, the tints that glow,                                15
    But tell of days in goodness spent,
A mind at peace with all below,
    A heart whose love is innocent!

---

[3] A magic ritual to protect the poet from intrusions.    [4] Apparent reference to
Plato's comparison of inspired poets to "Bacchic maidens who draw milk and
honey from the rivers" (*Ion* 533–34).

## PERCY BYSSHE SHELLEY [1792–1822]

# Ode to the West Wind

### 1

O wild West Wind, thou breath of Autumn's being,
Thou, from whose unseen presence the leaves dead
Are driven, like ghosts from an enchanter fleeing, *sorcerer*

*destructive* Yellow, and black, and pale, and hectic red,
Pestilence-stricken multitudes: O thou,                     5
Who chariotest to their dark wintry bed

The wingéd seeds, where they lie cold and low,
Each like a corpse within its grave, until     *blue colored*
Thine azure sister of the Spring shall blow      *the sky*

Her clarion o'er the dreaming earth, and fill              10
(Driving sweet buds like flocks to feed in air)
With living hues and odors plain and hill: *color*

Wild Spirit, which art moving everywhere;
Destroyer and preserver; hear, oh, hear!

### 2

*branchs of tree* Thou on whose stream, mid the steep sky's commotion,  15
Loose clouds like earth's decaying leaves are shed,
Shook from the tangled boughs of Heaven and Ocean,

*occuring in air* Angels of rain and lightning: there are spread  *straight up*
On the blue surface of thine aery surge  *to go*
Like the bright hair uplifted from the head  *rise*       20

Of some fierce Maenad,[1] even from the dim verge
Of the horizon to the zenith's height, *highest pt. reached in heavens*
The locks of the approaching storm. Thou dirge  *by a celestial body.*

---

[1] A female attendant of Bacchus, the god of wine.

*a song of grief*

Of the dying year, to which this closing night
Will be the dome of a vast sepulcher,                    25
Vaulted with all thy congregated might

Of vapors, from whose solid atmosphere
Black rain, and fire, and hail will burst: oh, hear!

### 3

Thou who didst waken from his summer dreams
The blue Mediterranean, where he lay,                    30
Lulled by the coil of his crystálline streams,

Beside a pumice isle in Baiae's bay,[2]
And saw in sleep old palaces and towers
Quivering within the wave's intenser day,

All overgrown with azure moss and flowers              35
So sweet, the sense faints picturing them! Thou
For whose path the Atlantic's level powers

Cleave themselves into chasms, while far below
The sea-blooms and the oozy woods which wear
The sapless foliage of the ocean, know                  40

Thy voice, and suddenly grow gray with fear,
And tremble and despoil themselves: oh, hear!

### 4

If I were a dead leaf thou mightest bear;
If I were a swift cloud to fly with thee;
A wave to pant beneath thy power, and share            45

The impulse of thy strength, only less free
Than thou, O uncontrollable! If even
I were as in my boyhood, and could be

---

[2] Near Naples, the site of the palaces of Julius Caesar, Pompey, and Nero.

The comrade of thy wanderings over Heaven
As then, when to outstrip thy skiey speed          50
Scarce seemed a vision; I would ne'er have striven

As thus with thee in prayer in my sore need.
Oh, lift me as a wave, a leaf, a cloud!
I fall upon the thorns of life! I bleed!

A heavy weight of hours has chained and bowed      55
One too like thee; tameless, and swift, and proud.

5

Make me thy lyre, even as the forest is:
What if my leaves are falling like its own!
The tumult of thy mighty harmonies

Will take from both a deep, autumnal tone,         60
Sweet though in sadness. Be thou, Spirit fierce,
My spirit! Be thou me, impetuous one!

Drive my dead thoughts over the universe
Like withered leaves to quicken a new birth!
And, by the incantation of this verse,             65

Scatter, as from an unextinguished hearth
Ashes and sparks, my words among mankind!
Be through my lips to unawakened earth

The trumpet of a prophecy! O, Wind,
If Winter comes, can Spring be far behind?         70

# Ozymandias[1]

 

I met a traveler from an antique land
Who said: Two vast and trunkless legs of stone

---

[1] Greek name for Ramses II of Egypt, who reigned in the thirteenth century B.C.

Stand in the desert . . . Near them, on the sand,
Half sunk, a shattered visage lies, whose frown,
And wrinkled lip, and sneer of cold command,
Tell that its sculptor well those passions read
Which yet survive, stamped on these lifeless things,
The hand that mocked them, and the heart that fed:
And on the pedestal these words appear:
"My name is Ozymandias, king of kings:                    10
Look on my works, ye Mighty, and despair!"
Nothing beside remains. Round the decay
Of that colossal wreck, boundless and bare
The lone and level sands stretch far away.

## JOHN KEATS [1795–1821]

# Ode on a Grecian Urn

### 1

Thou still unravished bride of quietness,
    Thou foster child of silence and slow time,
Sylvan° historian, who canst thus express                    °rustic
    A flowery tale more sweetly than our rhyme:
What leaf-fringed legend haunts about thy shape              5
    Of deities or mortals, or of both,
        In Tempe or the dales of Arcady?[1]
    What men or gods are these? What maidens loth?
What mad pursuit? What struggle to escape?
        What pipes and timbrels? What wild ecstasy?          10

### 2

Heard melodies are sweet, but those unheard
    Are sweeter; therefore, ye soft pipes, play on;
Not to the sensual ear, but, more endeared,
    Pipe to the spirit ditties of no tone:

---

[1] Tempe is a valley sacred to Apollo, god of music and poetry. Arcady is a region
in Greece frequently presented as an idyllic pastoral scene.

Fair youth, beneath the trees, thou canst not leave                    15
    Thy song, nor ever can those trees be bare;
        Bold Lover, never, never canst thou kiss,
Though winning near the goal—yet, do not grieve;
    She cannot fade, though thou has not thy bliss,
        For ever wilt thou love, and she be fair!                    20

### 3

Ah, happy, happy boughs! that cannot shed
    Your leaves, nor ever bid the Spring adieu;
And, happy melodist, unwearied,
    For ever piping songs for ever new;
More happy love! more happy, happy love.                    25
    For ever warm and still to be enjoyed,
        For ever panting, and for ever young,
All breathing human passion far above,
    That leaves a heart high-sorrowful and cloyed,
        A burning forehead, and a parching tongue.                    30

### 4

Who are these coming to the sacrifice?
    To what green altar, O mysterious priest,
Lead'st thou that heifer lowing at the skies,
    And all her silken flanks with garlands drest?
What little town by river or sea shore,                    35
    Or mountain-built with peaceful citadel,
        Is emptied of this folk, this pious morn?
And, little town, thy streets for evermore
    Will silent be; and not a soul to tell
        Why thou art desolate, can e'er return.                    40

### 5

O Attic² shape! Fair attitude! with brede³
    Of marble men and maidens overwrought,
With forest branches and the trodden weed;

---

² Belonging to Attica, or ancient Athens, and connoting elegance.    ³ Embroidery.

Thou, silent form, dost tease us out of thought
As doth eternity: Cold Pastoral!                                    45
    When old age shall this generation waste,
        Thou shalt remain, in midst of other woe
Than ours, a friend to man, to whom thou say'st,
    "Beauty is truth, truth beauty,"—that is all
        Ye know on earth, and all ye need to know.          50

# To Autumn

Season of mists and mellow fruitfulness,
    Close bosom-friend of the maturing sun;
Conspiring with him how to load and bless
    With fruit the vines that round the thatch-eaves run;
To bend with apples the mossed cottage-trees,                    5
    And fill all fruit with ripeness to the core;
        To swell the gourd, and plump the hazel shells
    With a sweet kernel; to set budding more,
And still more, later flowers for the bees,
Until they think warm days will never cease,                    10
        For Summer has o'er-brimmed their clammy cells.

Who hath not seen thee oft amid thy store?
    Sometimes whoever seeks abroad may find
Thee sitting careless on a granary floor,
    Thy hair soft-lifted by the winnowing wind;               15
Or on a half-reaped furrow sound asleep,
    Drowsed with the fume of poppies, while thy hook
        Spares the next swath and all its twinéd flowers:
And sometimes like a gleaner thou dost keep
    Steady thy laden head across a brook;                     20
    Or by a cider-press, with patient look,
        Thou watchest the last oozings hours by hours.

Where are the songs of Spring? Aye, where are they?
    Think not of them, thou hast thy music too—

While barréd° clouds bloom the soft-dying day,                    °banded
   And touch the stubble-plains with rosy hue;        26
Then in a wailful choir the small gnats mourn
   Among the river sallows,° borne aloft               °willows
   Or sinking as the light wind lives or dies;
And full-grown lambs loud bleat from hilly bourn;°               °region
   Hedge crickets sing, and now with treble soft       31
   The redbreast whistles from a garden-croft;°        °enclosed plot
   And gathering swallows twitter in the skies.

## ELIZABETH BARRETT BROWNING [1806–1861]

# If thou must love me, let it be for nought[1]

If thou must love me, let it be for nought
Except for love's sake only. Do not say
"I love her for her smile—her look—her way
Of speaking gently,—for a trick of thought
That falls in well with mine, and certes° brought            °surely
A sense of pleasant ease on such a day"—                        6
For these things in themselves, Belovèd, may
Be changed, or change for thee,—and love, so wrought,
May be unwrought so. Neither love me for
Thine own dear pity's wiping my cheeks dry,—                    10
A creature might forget to weep, who bore
Thy comfort long, and lose thy love thereby!
But love me for love's sake, that evermore
Thou mayst love on, through love's eternity.

---

[1] Number 14 from *Sonnets from the Portuguese.*

## ALFRED, LORD TENNYSON [1809–1892]
# The Splendor Falls
# on Castle Walls[1]

The splendor falls on castle walls
   And snowy summits old in story:
The long light shakes across the lakes,
   And the wild cataract leaps in glory.
Blow, bugle, blow, set the wild echoes flying,     5
Blow, bugle; answer, echoes, dying, dying, dying.

O hark, O hear! how thin and clear,
   And thinner, clearer, farther going!
O sweet and far from cliff and scar
   The horns of Elfland faintly blowing!     10
Blow, let us hear the purple glens replying:
Blow, bugle; answer, echoes, dying, dying, dying.

O love, they die in yon rich sky,
   They faint on hill or field or river;
Our echoes roll from soul to soul,     15
   And grow for ever and for ever.
Blow, bugle, blow, set the wild echoes flying,
And answer, echoes, answer, dying, dying, dying.

## ROBERT BROWNING [1812–1889]
# My Last Duchess[1]
### FERRARA

That's my last Duchess painted on the wall,
Looking as if she were alive. I call   

---

*The Splendor Falls . . . :* [1] Song, from *The Princess.*
*My Last Duchess:* [1] The poem is based on incidents from the life of Alfonso II,
Duke of Ferrara, whose first wife, a young woman, died in 1561.

That piece a wonder, now: Frà Pandolf's[2] hands
Worked busily a day, and there she stands.
Will't please you sit and look at her? I said          5
"Frà Pandolf" by design, for never read
Strangers like you that pictured countenance,
The depth and passion of its earnest glance,
But to myself they turned (since none puts by
The curtain I have drawn for you, but I)               10
And seemed as they would ask me, if they durst,
How such a glance came there; so, not the first
Are you to turn and ask thus. Sir, 'twas not
Her husband's presence only, called that spot
Of joy into the Duchess' cheek; perhaps               15
Frà Pandolf chanced to say, "Her mantle laps
Over my lady's wrist too much," or "Paint
Must never hope to reproduce the faint
Half-flush that dies along her throat": such stuff
Was courtesy, she thought, and cause enough           20
For calling up that spot of joy. She had
A heart—how shall I say?—too soon made glad,
Too easily impressed: she liked whate'er
She looked on, and her looks went everywhere.
Sir, 'twas all one! My favor at her breast,           25
The dropping of the daylight in the West,
The bough of cherries some officious fool
Broke in the orchard for her, the white mule
She rode with round the terrace—all and each
Would draw from her alike the approving speech,       30
Or blush, at least. She thanked men,—good! but
    thanked
Somehow—I know not how—as if she ranked
My gift of a nine-hundred-years-old name
With anybody's gift. Who'd stoop to blame
This sort of trifling? Even had you skill             35
In speech—(which I have not)—to make your will
Quite clear to such an one, and say, "Just this
Or that in you disgusts me; here you miss,

---

[2] An imaginary painter.

Or there exceed the mark"—and if she let
Herself be lessoned so, nor plainly set                                40
Her wits to yours, forsooth, and made excuse,
—E'en then would be some stooping; and I choose
Never to stoop. Oh sir, she smiled, no doubt,
Whene'er I passed her; but who passed without
Much the same smile? This grew; I gave commands;       45
Then all smiles stopped together. There she stands
As if alive. Will't please you rise? We'll meet
The company below, then. I repeat,
The Count your master's known munificence
Is ample warrant that no just pretence                            50
Of mine for dowry will be disallowed;
Though his fair daughter's self, as I avowed
At starting, is my object. Nay, we'll go
Together down, sir. Notice Neptune, though,
Taming a sea-horse, thought a rarity,                              55
Which Claus of Innsbruck[3] cast in bronze for me!

# WALT WHITMAN [1819–1892]

# A Noiseless Patient Spider

A noiseless patient spider,
I mark'd where on a little promontory it stood isolated,
Mark'd how to explore the vacant vast surrounding,
It launch'd forth filament, filament, filament, out of itself,
Ever unreeling them, ever tirelessly speeding them.          5

And you O my soul where you stand,
Surrounded, detached, in measureless oceans of space,
Ceaselessly musing, venturing, throwing, seeking the spheres
    to connect them,

---

[3] An unidentified or imaginary sculptor. The count of Tyrol had his capital at
Innsbruck.

Till the bridge you will need be form'd, till the ductile anchor
    hold,
Till the gossamer thread you fling catch somewhere, O my
    soul.                                                          10


# There Was a Child Went Forth


There was a child went forth every day,
And the first object he look'd upon, that object he became,
And that object became part of him for the day or a certain part
    of the day,
Or for many years or stretching cycles of years.

The early lilacs became part of this child,                       5
And grass and white and red morning-glories, and white and red
    clover, and the song of the phœbe-bird,
And the Third-month lambs and the sow's pink-faint litter, and
    the mare's foal and the cow's calf,
And the noisy brood of the barnyard or by the mire of the pond-
    side,
And the fish suspending themselves so curiously below there, and
    the beautiful curious liquid,
And the water-plants with their graceful flat heads, all became
    part of him.                                                  10

The field-sprouts of Fourth-month and Fifth-month became part
    of him,
Winter-grain sprouts and those of the light-yellow corn, and the
    esculent roots of the garden,
And the apple-trees cover'd with blossoms and the fruit afterward,
    and wood-berries, and the commonest weeds by the road,
And the old drunkard staggering home from the outhouse of the
    tavern whence he had lately risen,
And the schoolmistress that pass'd on her way to the school,     15
And the friendly boys that pass'd, and the quarrelsome boys,
And the tidy and fresh-cheek'd girls, and the barefoot negro boy
    and girl,

And all the changes of city and country wherever he went.

His own parents, he that had father'd him and she that had
    conceiv'd him in her womb and birth'd him,
They gave this child more of themselves than that,          20
They gave him afterward every day, they became part of him.

The mother at home quietly placing the dishes on the supper-
    table,
The mother with mild words, clean her cap and gown, a whole-
    some odor falling off her person and clothes as she walks by,
The father, strong, self-sufficient, manly, mean, anger'd, unjust,
The blow, the quick loud word, the tight bargain, the crafty
    lure,          25
The family usages, the language, the company, the furniture, the
    yearning and swelling heart,
Affection that will not be gainsay'd, the sense of what is real, the
    thought if after all it should prove unreal,
The doubts of day-time and the doubts of night-time, the curious
    whether and how,
Whether that which appears so is so, or is it all flashes and specks?
Men and women crowding fast in the streets, if they are not flashes
    and specks what are they?          30
The streets themselves and the façades of houses, and goods in
    the windows,
Vehicles, teams, the heavy-plank'd wharves, the huge crossing at
    the ferries,
The village on the highland seen from afar at sunset, the river
    between,
Shadows, aureola and mist, the light falling on roofs and gables
    of white or brown two miles off,
The schooner near by sleepily dropping down the tide, the little
    boat slack-tow'd astern,          35
The hurrying tumbling waves, quick-broken crests, slapping,
The strata of color'd clouds, the long bar of maroon-tint away
    solitary by itself, the spread of purity it lies motionless in,
The horizon's edge, the flying sea-crow, the fragrance of salt marsh
    and shore mud,
These became part of that child who went forth every day, and
    who now goes, and will always go forth every day.

## MATTHEW ARNOLD [1822–1888]

# Dover Beach

The sea is calm tonight,
The tide is full, the moon lies fair
Upon the straights;—on the French coast the light
Gleams and is gone; the cliffs of England stand,
Glimmering and vast out in the tranquil bay.      5
Come to the window, sweet is the night-air!

Only, from the long line of spray
Where the sea meets the moon-blanched land,
Listen! you hear the grating roar
Of pebbles which the waves draw back, and fling,      10
At their return, up the high strand,
Begin, and cease, and then again begin,
With tremulous cadence slow, and bring
The eternal note of sadness in.

Sophocles long ago      15
Heard it on the Aegean, and it brought
Into his mind the turbid ebb and flow
Of human misery; we
Find also in the sound a thought,
Hearing it by this distant northern sea.      20

The Sea of Faith
Was once, too, at the full, and round earth's shore
Lay like the folds of a bright girdle furled.
But now I only hear
Its melancholy, long, withdrawing roar,      25
Retreating, to the breath
Of the night-wind, down the vast edges drear
And naked shingles of the world.

Ah, love, let us be true
To one another! for the world, which seems      30

To lie before us like a land of dreams,
So various so beautiful, so new,
Hath really neither joy, nor love, nor light,
Nor certitude, nor peace, nor help for pain;
And we are here as on a darkling plain                    35
Swept with confused alarms of struggle and flight,
Where ignorant armies clash by night.

## EMILY DICKINSON [1830–1886]

# After great pain, a formal feeling comes[1]

After great pain, a formal feeling comes—
The Nerves sit ceremonious, like Tombs—
The stiff Heart questions was it He, that bore,
And Yesterday, or Centuries before?

The Feet, mechanical, go round—                            5
Of Ground, or Air, or Ought—
A Wooden way
Regardless grown,
A Quartz contentment, like a stone—

This is the Hour of Lead—                                 10
Remembered, if outlived,
As Freezing persons, recollect the Snow—
First—Chill—then Stupor—then the letting go—

---

[1] Also known as J. 341, according to Thomas Johnson's chronology of composition. Dickinson did not use titles.

# Because I could not
# stop for Death[1]

Because I could not stop for Death—
He kindly stopped for me—
The Carriage held but just Ourselves—
And Immortality.

We slowly drove—He knew no haste                    5
And I had put away
My labor and my leisure too,
For His Civility—

We passed the School, where Children strove
At Recess—in the Ring—                              10
We passed the Fields of Gazing Grain—
We passed the Setting Sun—

Or rather—He passed Us—
The Dews drew quivering and chill—
For only Gossamer, my Gown—                         15
My Tippet°—only Tulle—            °scarf or stole

We paused before a House that seemed
A Swelling of the Ground—
The Roof was scarcely visible—
The Cornice—in the Ground—                          20

Since then—'tis Centuries—and yet
Feels shorter than the Day
I first surmised the Horses' Heads
Were toward Eternity—

---

[1] Also known as J. 712.

# I heard a Fly buzz
# —when I died[1]

I heard a Fly buzz—when I died—
The Stillness in the Room
Was like the Stillness in the Air—
Between the Heaves of Storm—

The Eyes around—had wrung them dry—          5
And Breaths were gathering firm
For that last Onset—when the King
Be witnessed—in the Room—

I willed my Keepsakes—Signed away
What portion of me be                        10
Assignable—and then it was
There interposed a Fly—

With Blue—uncertain stumbling Buzz—
Between the light—and me—
And then the Windows failed—and then         15
I could not see to see—

## CHRISTINA ROSSETTI [1830–1894]

# Song

When I am dead, my dearest,
    Sing no sad songs for me;
Plant thou no roses at my head,
    Nor shady cypress tree:

---

[1] Also known as J. 465.

Be the green grass above me                    5
    With showers and dewdrops wet;
And if thou wilt, remember,
    And if thou wilt, forget,

I shall not see the shadows,
    I shall not feel the rain;                  10
I shall not hear the nightingale
    Sing on, as if in pain:
And dreaming through the twilight
    That doth not rise nor set,
Haply I may remember,                          15
    And haply may forget.


## THOMAS HARDY [1840–1928]

# Neutral Tones

We stood by a pond that winter day,
And the sun was white, as though chidden of God,
And a few leaves lay on the starving sod;
    —They had fallen from an ash, and were gray.

Your eyes on me were as eyes that rove          5
Over tedious riddles of years ago;
And some words played between us to and fro
    On which lost the more by our love.

The smile on your mouth was the deadest thing
Alive enough to have strength to die;           10
And a grin of bitterness swept thereby
    Like an ominous bird a-wing. . . .

Since then, keen lessons that love deceives,
And wrings with wrong, have shaped to me
Your face, and the God-curst sun, and a tree,   15
    And a pond edged with grayish leaves.

# The Darkling[1] Thrush

I leant upon a coppice° gate     °*gate to a small wood*
 When Frost was specter-gray,
And Winter's dregs made desolate
 The weakening eye of day.
The tangled bine-stems° scored the sky    °*twining stems*
 Like strings of broken lyres,       6
And all mankind that haunted nigh
 Had sought their household fires.

The land's sharp features seemed to be
 The Century's corpse[2] outleant,     10
His crypt the cloudy canopy,
 The wind his death-lament.
The ancient pulse of germ and birth
 Was shrunken hard and dry,
And every spirit upon earth       15
 Seemed fervorless as I.

At once a voice arose among
 The bleak twigs overhead
In a full-hearted evensong
 Of joy illimited;         20
An aged thrush, frail, gaunt, and small,
 In blast-beruffled plume,
Had chosen thus to fling his soul
 Upon the growing gloom.

So little cause for carolings       25
 Of such ecstatic sound
Was written on terrestrial things
 Afar or nigh around,
That I could think there trembled through
 His happy good-night air      30
Some blessed Hope, whereof he knew
 And I was unaware.

---

[1] Of the dark. [2] This poem was written on December 31, 1900.

## GERARD MANLEY HOPKINS [1844–1889]

# Pied Beauty

Glory be to God for dappled things—
    For skies of couple-color as a brinded° cow;        °streaked
      For rose-moles all in stipple° upon trout that swim;   °spots
Fresh-firecoal chestnut-falls;° finches' wings;      °husked chestnuts
    Landscape plotted and pieced—fold, fallow, and plow;    5
    And all trades, their gear and tackle and trim.

All things counter,° original, spare, strange;        °contrary
    Whatever is fickle, freckled (who knows how?)
      With swift, slow; sweet, sour; adazzle, dim;
He fathers-forth whose beauty is past change:        10
                Praise Him.

# God's Grandeur

The world is charged with the grandeur of God.
    It will flame out, like shining from shook foil;°   °shaken gold-foil
    It gathers to a greatness, like the ooze of oil
Crushed.° Why do men then now not reck° his rod? °from olives/heed
Generations have trod, have trod, have trod;      5
    And all is seared with trade; bleared, smeared with toil;
    And wears man's smudge and shares man's smell: the soil
Is bare now, nor can foot feel, being shod.

And for all this, nature is never spent;
    There lives the dearest freshness deep down things;   10
And though the last lights off the black West went
    Oh, morning, at the brown brink eastward, springs—
Because the Holy Ghost over the bent
    World broods with warm breast and with ah! bright wings.

## A. E. HOUSMAN [1859–1936]

# Loveliest of Trees, the Cherry Now

Loveliest of trees, the cherry now
Is hung with bloom along the bough,
And stands about the woodland ride
Wearing white for Eastertide

Now, of my threescore years and ten,                5
Twenty will not come again,
And take from seventy springs a score,
It only leaves me fifty more.

And since to look at things in bloom
Fifty springs are little room,                       10
About the woodlands I will go
To see the cherry hung with snow.

## WILLIAM BUTLER YEATS [1865–1939]

# Sailing to Byzantium[1]

### 1

That is no country for old men. The young
In one another's arms, birds in the trees
—Those dying generations—at their song,
The salmon-falls, the mackerel-crowded seas,

---

[1] Ancient Greek city, renamed Constantinople by the Roman emperor Constantine I, which became the capital of the Eastern Roman or Byzantine Empire after the fall of Rome in 476 A.D. The city, now modern Istanbul, Turkey, is famous for its mosques, mosaics, and other works of art.

Fish, flesh, or fowl, commend all summer long          5
Whatever is begotten, born, and dies.
Caught in that sensual music all neglect
Monuments of unageing intellect.


### 2

An aged man is but a paltry thing,
A tattered coat upon a stick, unless                   10
Soul clap its hands and sing, and louder sing
For every tatter in its mortal dress,
Nor is there singing school but studying
Monuments of its own magnificence;
And therefore I have sailed the seas and come          15
To the holy city of Byzantium.


### 3

O sages standing in God's holy fire
As in the gold mosaic of a wall,
Come from the holy fire, perne° in a gyre,°        °spin/spiral
And be the singing-masters of my soul.                 20
Consume my heart away; sick with desire
And fastened to a dying animal
It knows not what it is; and gather me
Into the artifice of eternity.


### 4

Once out of nature I shall never take                  25
My bodily form from any natural thing,
But such a form as Grecian goldsmiths make
Of hammered gold and gold enameling
To keep a drowsy Emperor awake;
Or set upon a golden bough to sing                     30
To lords and ladies of Byzantium
Of what is past, or passing, or to come.

# The Second Coming

Turning and turning in the widening gyre[1]
The falcon cannot hear the falconer;
Things fall apart; the centre cannot hold;
Mere anarchy is loosed upon the world,
The blood-dimmed tide is loosed, and everywhere   5
The ceremony of innocence is drowned;
The best lack all conviction, while the worst
Are full of passionate intensity.

Surely some revelation is at hand;
Surely the Second Coming is at hand           10
The Second Coming! Hardly are those words out
When a vast image out of *Spiritus Mundi*[2]
Troubles my sight: somewhere in sands of the desert
A shape with lion body and the head of a man,
A gaze blank and pitiless as the sun,          15
Is moving its slow thighs, while all about it
Reel shadows of the indignant desert birds.
The darkness drops again; but now I know
That twenty centuries of stony sleep
Were vexed to nightmare by a rocking cradle,    20
And what rough beast, its hour come round at last,
Slouches towards Bethlehem to be born?

---

[1] A circling, spiraling motion, representing for Yeats a cycle of history.   [2] The
spirit or soul of the universe.

## ROBERT FROST [1874–1963]

# Birches

---

When I see birches bend to left and right
Across the lines of straighter darker trees,
I like to think some boy's been swinging them.
But swinging doesn't bend them down to stay
As ice-storms do. Often you must have seen them          5
Loaded with ice a sunny winter morning
After a rain. They click upon themselves
As the breeze rises, and turn many-colored
As the stir cracks and crazes their enamel.
Soon the sun's warmth makes them shed crystal shells     10
Shattering and avalanching on the snow-crust—
Such heaps of broken glass to sweep away
You'd think the inner dome of heaven had fallen.
They are dragged to the withered bracken by the load,
And they seem not to break; though once they are bowed 15
So low for long, they never right themselves:
You may see their trunks arching in the woods
Years afterwards, trailing their leaves on the ground
Like girls on hands and knees that throw their hair
Before them over their heads to dry in the sun.          20
But I was going to say when Truth broke in
With all her matter-of-fact about the ice-storm,
I should prefer to have some boy bend them
As he went out and in to fetch the cows—
Some boy too far from town to learn baseball,           25
Whose only play was what he found himself,
Summer or winter, and could play alone.
One by one he subdued his father's trees
By riding them down over and over again
Until he took the stiffness out of them,                 30
And not one but hung limp, not one was left
For him to conquer. He learned all there was
To learn about not launching out too soon
And so not carrying the tree away
Clear to the ground. He always kept his poise           35

To the top branches, climbing carefully
With the same pains you use to fill a cup
Up to the brim, and even above the brim.
Then he flung outward, feet first, with a swish,
Kicking his way down through the air to the ground.    40
So was I once myself a swinger of birches.
And so I dream of going back to be.
It's when I'm weary of considerations,
And life is too much like a pathless wood
Where your face burns and tickles with the cobwebs    45
Broken across it, and one eye is weeping
From a twig's having lashed across it open.
I'd like to get away from earth awhile
And then come back to it and begin over.
May no fate willfully misunderstand me    50
And half grant what I wish and snatch me away
Not to return. Earth's the right place for love:
I don't know where it's likely to go better.
I'd like to go by climbing a birch tree,
And climb black branches up a snow-white trunk    55
*Toward* heaven, till the tree could bear no more,
But dipped its top and set me down again.
That would be good both going and coming back.
One could do worse than be a swinger of birches.

# The Road Not Taken

Two roads diverged in a yellow wood,
And sorry I could not travel both
And be one traveler, long I stood
And looked down one as far as I could
To where it bent in the undergrowth;    5

Then took the other, as just as fair,
And having perhaps the better claim,

Because it was grassy and wanted wear;
Though as for that, the passing there
Had worn them really about the same,          10

And both that morning equally lay
In leaves no step had trodden black.
Oh, I kept the first for another day!
Yet knowing how way leads on to way,
I doubted if I should ever come back.          15

I shall be telling this with a sigh
Somewhere ages and ages hence:
Two roads diverged in a wood, and I—
I took the one less traveled by,
And that has made all the difference.          20

## Amy Lowell [1874–1925]

# The Taxi

When I go away from you
The world beats dead
Like a slackened drum.
I call out for you against the jutted stars
And shout into the ridges of the wind.          5
Streets coming fast,
One after the other,
Wedge you away from me,
And the lamps of the city prick my eyes
So that I can no longer see your face.          10
Why should I leave you,
To wound myself upon the sharp edges
    of the night?

WALLACE STEVENS [1879–1955]

# Thirteen Ways of Looking at a Blackbird

### 1

Among twenty snowy mountains,
The only moving thing
Was the eye of the blackbird.

### 2

I was of three minds,
Like a tree                                                              5
In which there are three blackbirds.

### 3

The blackbird whirled in the autumn winds.
It was a small part of the pantomime.

### 4

A man and a woman
Are one.                                                                10
A man and a woman and a blackbird
Are one.

### 5

I do not know which to prefer,
The beauty of inflections
Or the beauty of innuendoes,                                            15
The blackbird whistling
Or just after.

### 6

Icicles filled the long window
With barbaric glass.
The shadow of the blackbird                                             20

Crossed it, to and fro.
The mood
Traced in the shadow
An indecipherable cause.

### 7

O thin men of Haddam,[1]         25
Why do you imagine golden birds?
Do you not see how the blackbird
Walks around the feet
Of the women about you?

### 8

I know noble accents         30
And lucid, inescapable rhythms;
But I know, too,
That the blackbird is involved
In what I know.

### 9

When the blackbird flew out of sight,     35
It marked the edge
Of one of many circles.

### 10

At the sight of blackbirds
Flying in a green light,
Even the bawds of euphony      40
Would cry out sharply.

### 11

He rode over Connecticut
In a glass coach.
Once, a fear pierced him,
In that he mistook      45
The shadow of his equipage
For blackbirds.

---

[1] A town in Connecticut.

### 12

The river is moving.
The blackbird must be flying.

### 13

It was evening all afternoon.                                50
It was snowing
And it was going to snow.
The blackbird sat
In the cedar-limbs.

## WILLIAM CARLOS WILLIAMS [1883–1963]
# To Elsie

The pure products of America
go crazy—
mountain folk from Kentucky

or the ribbed north end of
Jersey                                                        5
with its isolate lakes and

valleys, its deaf-mutes, thieves
old names
and promiscuity between

devil-may-care men who have taken                             10
to railroading
out of sheer lust of adventure—

and young slatterns, bathed
in filth
from Monday to Saturday                                       15

to be tricked out that night
with gauds
from imaginations which have no

peasant traditions to give them
character                                    20
but flutter and flaunt

sheer rags—succumbing without
emotion
save numbed terror

under some hedge of choke-cherry            25
or viburnum—
which they cannot express—

Unless it be that marriage
perhaps
with a dash of Indian blood                  30

will throw up a girl so desolate
so hemmed round
with disease or murder

that she'll be rescued by an
agent—                                       35
reared by the state and

sent out at fifteen to work in
some hard pressed
house in the suburbs—

some doctor's family, some Elsie—            40
voluptuous water
expressing with broken

brain the truth about us—
her great
ungainly hips and flopping breasts           45

addressed to cheap
jewelry
and rich young men with fine eyes

as if the earth under our feet
were                                                    *50*
an excrement of some sky

and we degraded prisoners
destined
to hunger until we eat filth

while the imagination strains            *55*
after deer
going by fields of goldenrod in

the stifling heat of September
Somehow
it seems to destroy us                        *60*

It is only in isolate flecks that
something
is given off

No one
to witness                                            *65*
and adjust, no one to drive the car

# D. H. LAWRENCE [1885–1930]

# Kangaroo

In the northern hemisphere
Life seems to leap at the air, or skim under the wind
Like stags on rocky ground, or pawing horses, or springy scut-
    tailed rabbits.

Or else rush horizontal to charge at the sky's horizon,
Like bulls or bisons or wild pigs.                                    5

Or slip like water slippery towards its ends,
As foxes, stoats, and wolves, and prairie dogs.

Only mice, and moles, and rats, and badgers, and beavers, and
    perhaps bears
Seem belly-plumbed to the earth's mid-navel.
Or frogs that when they leap come flop, and flop to the center of
    the earth.                                                        10

But the yellow antipodal Kangaroo, when she sits up,
Who can unseat her, like a liquid drop that is heavy, and just
    touches earth.

The downward drip
The down-urge.
So much denser than cold-blooded frogs.                              15

Delicate mother Kangaroo
Sitting up there rabbit-wise, but huge, plumb-weighted,
And lifting her beautiful slender face, oh! so much more gently
    and finely lined than a rabbit's, or than a hare's,
Lifting her face to nibble at a round white peppermint drop which
    she loves, sensitive mother Kangaroo.

Her sensitive, long, pure-bred face.                                 20
Her full antipodal eyes, so dark,
So big and quiet and remote, having watched so many empty
    dawns in silent Australia.

Her little loose hands, and drooping Victorian shoulders.
And then her great weight below the waist, her vast pale belly
With a thin young yellow little paw hanging out, and straggle of
    a long thin ear, like ribbon,                                    25
Like a funny trimming to the middle of her belly, thin little dangle
    of an immature paw, and one thin ear.

Her belly, her big haunches
And, in addition, the great muscular python-stretch of her tail.

There, she shan't have any more peppermint drops.
So she wistfully, sensitively sniffs the air, and then turns, goes off
    in slow sad leaps                                                30

On the long flat skis of her legs,
Steered and propelled by that steel-strong snake of a tail.

Stops again, half turns, inquisitive to look back.
While something stirs quickly in her belly, and a lean little face
    comes out, as from a window,
Peaked and a bit dismayed.                                            35
Only to disappear again quickly away from the sight of the world,
    to snuggle down in the warmth,
Leaving the trail of a different paw hanging out.

Still she watches with eternal, cocked wistfulness!
How full her eyes are, like the full, fathomless, shining eyes of an
    Australian black-boy
Who has been lost so many centuries on the margins of
    existence!                                                      40

She watches with insatiable wistfulness.
Untold centuries of watching for something to come,
For a new signal from life, in that silent lost land of the South.

Where nothing bites but insects and snakes and the sun, small
    life.
Where no bull roared, no cow ever lowed, no stag cried, no
    leopard screeched, no lion coughed, no dog barked,            45
But all was silent save for parrots occasionally, in the haunted blue
    bush.

Wistfully watching, with wonderful liquid eyes.
And all her weight, all her blood, dripping sack-wise down to-
    wards the earth's center,
And the live little-one taking in its paw at the door of her belly.

Leap then, and come down on the line that draws to the earth's
    deep, heavy center.                                            50

## EZRA POUND [1885–1972]
# In a Station of the Metro[1]

The apparition of these faces in the crowd;
Petals on a wet, black bough.

# The River-Merchant's Wife: a Letter

While my hair was still cut straight across my forehead
I played about the front gate, pulling flowers.
You came by on bamboo stilts, playing horse,
You walked about my seat, playing with blue plums.
And we went on living in the village of Chōkan:      5
Two small people, without dislike or suspicion.

At fourteen I married My Lord you.
I never laughed, being bashful.
Lowering my head, I looked at the wall.
Called to, a thousand times, I never looked back.      10

At fifteen I stopped scowling,
I desired my dust to be mingled with yours
Forever and forever and forever.
Why should I climb the look out?

At sixteen you departed,      15
You went into far Ku-tō-en, by the river of swirling eddies,

---

[1] Paris subway.

And you have been gone five months.
The monkeys make sorrowful noise overhead.

You dragged your feet when you went out.
By the gate now, the moss is grown, the different mosses,     20
Too deep to clear them away!
The leaves fall early this autumn, in wind.
The paired butterflies are already yellow with August
Over the grass in the West garden;
They hurt me. I grow older.                                   25
If you are coming down through the narrows of the river Kiang,
Please let me know beforehand,
And I will come out to meet you
                    As far as Chō-fū-Sa.
                                        *By Rihaku (Li T'ai Po)*[1]

# H. D. (HILDA DOOLITTLE) [1886–1961]
## Oread[1]

Whirl up, sea—
whirl your pointed pines,
splash your great pines
on our rocks,
hurl your green over us,
cover us with your pools of fir.

---

*The River-Merchant's Wife:*   [1] Adapted from the Chinese of Li T'ai Po, an eighth-century poet whose name in Japanese is Rihaku. Pound worked from transliterations of Chinese ideograms in the papers of American Orientalist Ernest Fenollosa.
*Oread:*   [1] Mountain nymph.

## MARIANNE MOORE [1887–1972]
# The Steeple-Jack

### REVISED, 1961

Dürer[1] would have seen a reason for living
    in a town like this, with eight stranded whales
to look at; with the sweet sea air coming into your house
on a fine day, from water etched
    with waves as formal as the scales         5
on a fish.

One by one in two's and three's, the seagulls keep
    flying back and forth over the town clock,
or sailing around the lighthouse without moving their wings
rising steadily with a slight         10
    quiver of the body—or flock
mewing where

a sea the purple of the peacock's neck is
    paled to greenish azure as Dürer changed
the pine green of the Tyrol to peacock blue and guinea    15
gray. You can see a twenty-five-
    pound lobster; and fish nets arranged
to dry. The

whirlwind fife-and-drum of the storm bends the salt
    marsh grass, disturbs stars in the sky and the    20
star on the steeple; it is a privilege to see so
much confusion. Disguised by what
    might seem the opposite, the sea-
side flowers and

trees are favored by the fog so that you have    25
    the tropics at first hand: the trumpet vine,
foxglove, giant snapdragon, a salpiglossis that has

---

[1] Albrecht Dürer, fifteenth-century German painter and engraver.

spots and stripes; morning-glories, gourds,
     or moon-vines trained on fishing twine
at the back door:                                                    30

cattails, flags, blueberries and spiderwort,
     striped grass, lichens, sunflowers, asters, daisies—,
yellow and crab-claw ragged sailors with green bracts—
     toad-plant,
petunias, ferns; pink lilies, blue
     ones, tigers; poppies; black sweet-peas.                       35
The climate

is not right for the banyan, frangipani, or
     jack-fruit trees; or for exotic serpent
life. Ring lizard and snakeskin for the foot, if you see fit;
but here they've cats, not cobras, to                               40
     keep down the rats. The diffident
little newt

with white pin-dots on black horizontal spaced-
     out bands lives here: yet there is nothing that
ambition can buy or take away. The college student                  45
named Ambrose sits on the hillside
     with his not-native books and hat
and sees boats

at sea progress white and rigid as if in
     a groove. Liking an elegance of which                          50
the source is not bravado, he knows by heart the antique
sugar-bowl shaped summerhouse of
     interlacing slats, and the pitch
of the church

spire, not true, from which a man in scarlet lets                   55
     down a rope as a spider spins a thread;
he might be part of a novel, but on the sidewalk a
sign says C. J. Poole, Steeple Jack,
     in black and white; and one in red
and white says                                                      60

Danger. The church portico has four fluted
    columns, each a single piece of stone, made
modester by whitewash. This would be a fit haven for
waifs, children, animals, prisoners,
    and presidents who have repaid        65
sin-driven

senators by not thinking about them. The
    place has a schoolhouse, a post-office in a
store, fish-houses, hen-houses, a three-masted
    schooner on        70
the stocks. The hero, the student,
    the steeple jack, each in his way,
is at home.

It could not be dangerous to be living
    in a town like this, of simple people,        75

who have a steeple-jack placing danger signs by the church
while he is gilding the solid-
    pointed star, which on a steeple
stands for hope.

# T. S. ELIOT [1888–1965]

# The Love Song of J. Alfred Prufrock

*S'io credesse che mia riposta fosse*
*A persona che mai tornasse al mondo,*
*Questa fiamma staria senza piu scosse.*
*Ma perciocche giammai di questo fondo*
*Non torno vivo alcun, s'i'odo il vero,*
*Senza tema d'infamia ti rispondo.*[1]

---

[1] "If I believed that my answer would be to one who would ever return to the world, this flame would shake no more; but since no one ever returns alive from this depth, if what I hear is true, I answer you without fear of infamy." This is Guido da Montefeltro's answer to Dante when asked why he is being punished in hell (*Inferno* 27.61–66).

Let us go then, you and I,
When the evening is spread out against the sky
Like a patient etherized upon a table;
Let us go, through certain half-deserted streets,
The muttering retreats                                          5
Of restless nights in one-night cheap hotels
And sawdust restaurants with oyster-shells:
Streets that follow like a tedious argument
Of insidious intent
To lead you to an overwhelming question . . .                  10
Oh, do not ask, "What is it?"
Let us go and make our visit.

In the room the women come and go
Talking of Michelangelo.

The yellow fog that rubs its back upon the window-panes,        15
The yellow smoke that rubs its muzzle on the window-panes
Licked its tongue into the corners of the evening,
Lingered upon the pools that stand in drains,
Let fall upon its back the soot that falls from chimneys,
Slipped by the terrace, made a sudden leap,                     20
And seeing that it was a soft October night,
Curled once about the house, and fell asleep.

And indeed there will be time
For the yellow smoke that slides along the street,
Rubbing its back upon the window-panes;                         25
There will be time, there will be time
To prepare a face to meet the faces that you meet;
There will be time to murder and create,
And time for all the works and days[2] of hands
That lift and drop a question on your plate;                   30
Time for you and time for me,
And time yet for a hundred indecisions,
And for a hundred visions and revisions,
Before the taking of a toast and tea.

---

[2] An allusion to Hesiod's *Works and Days*, a poem praising hard work in the fields. Hesiod (eighth century B.C.) was known as the father of Greek didactic poetry.

In the room the women come and go                                    35
Talking of Michelangelo.


And indeed there will be time
To wonder, "Do I dare?" and, "Do I dare?"
Time to turn back and descend the stair,
With a bald spot in the middle of my hair—                          40
[They will say: "How his hair is growing thin!"]
My morning coat, my collar mounting firmly to the chin,
My necktie rich and modest, but asserted by a simple pin—
[They will say: "But how his arms and legs are thin!"]
Do I dare
Disturb the universe?                                                45
In a minute there is time
For decisions and revisions which a minute will reverse.


For I have known them all already, known them all:—
Have known the evenings, mornings, afternoons,
I have measured out my life with coffee spoons;                     50
I know the voices dying with a dying fall
Beneath the music from a farther room.
        So how should I presume?


And I have known the eyes already, known them all—                  55
The eyes that fix you in a formulated phrase,
And when I am formulated, sprawling on a pin,
When I am pinned and wriggling on the wall,
Then how should I begin
To spit out all the butt-ends of my days and ways?                  60
        And how should I presume?


And I have known the arms already, known them all—
Arms that are braceleted and white and bare
[But in the lamplight, downed with light brown hair!]
Is it perfume from a dress                                           65
That makes me so digress?
Arms that lie along a table, or wrap about a shawl.
        And should I then presume?
        And how should I begin?


                    ·      ·      ·      ·      ·

Shall I say, I have gone at dusk through narrow streets    70
And watched the smoke that rises from the pipes
Of lonely men in shirt-sleeves, leaning out of windows? . . .

I should have been a pair of ragged claws
Scuttling across the floors of silent seas.


      .    .    .    .    .

And the afternoon, the evening, sleeps so peacefully!    75
Smoothed by long fingers,
Asleep . . . tired . . . or it malingers,
Stretched on the floor, here beside you and me.
Should I, after tea and cakes and ices,
Have the strength to force the moment to its crisis?    80
But though I have wept and fasted, wept and prayed,
Though I have seen my head [grown slightly bald] brought in
    upon a platter,[3]
I am no prophet—and here's no great matter;
I have seen the moment of my greatness flicker,
And I have seen the eternal Footman hold my coat, and
    snicker,    85
And in short, I was afraid.

And would it have been worth it, after all,
After the cups, the marmalade, the tea,
Among the porcelain, among some talk of you and me,
Would it have been worth while,    90
To have bitten off the matter with a smile,
To have squeezed the universe into a ball
To roll it toward some overwhelming question,
To say: "I am Lazarus, come from the dead,[4]
Come back to tell you all, I shall tell you all"—    95
If one, settling a pillow by her head,
     Should say: "That is not what I meant at all.
     That is not it, at all."

---

[3] The head of John the Baptist who, at the request of Salome, was executed. His head was then brought in to Herodias on a charger.    [4] The brother of Mary and Martha, who was raised from death by Christ (John 11:1–44).

And would it have been worth it, after all,
Would it have been worth while                                          100
After the sunsets and the dooryards and the sprinkled streets,
After the novels, after the teacups, after the skirts that trail along
    the floor—
And this, and so much more?—
It is impossible to say just what I mean!
But as if a magic lantern threw the nerves in patterns on a
    screen:                                                                  105
Would it have been worth while,
If one, settling a pillow or throwing off a shawl,
And turning toward the window, should say:
    "That is not it at all,
    That is not what I meant, at all."                                    110


       .     .     .     .     .

No! I am not Prince Hamlet, nor was meant to be;
Am an attendant lord, one that will do
To swell a progress, start a scene or two,
Advise the prince; no doubt, an easy tool,
Deferential, glad to be of use,                                          115
Politic, cautious, and meticulous;
Full of high sentence, but a bit obtuse;
At times, indeed, almost ridiculous—
Almost, at times, the Fool.

I grow old . . . I grow old . . .                                        120
I shall wear the bottoms of my trousers rolled.[5]

Shall I part my hair behind? Do I dare to eat a peach?
I shall wear white flannel trousers, and walk upon the beach.
I have heard the mermaids singing, each to each.

I do not think that they will sing to me.                                125

I have seen them riding seaward on the waves
Combing the white hair of the waves blown back
When the wind blows the water white and black.

---

[5] Cuffed, a new fashion when the poem was written.

We have lingered in the chambers of the sea
By sea-girls wreathed with seaweed red and brown        *130*
Till human voices wake us, and we drown.


## GABRIELA MISTRAL [1889–1957]

# Land of Absence[1]

Land of absence,
strange land,
lighter than angel
or subtle sign,
color of dead algae,                                     *5*
color of falcon,
with the age of all time,
with no age content.

It bears no pomegranate
nor grows jasmin,                                        *10*
and has no skies
nor indigo seas.
Its name, a name
that has never been heard,
*and in a land without name*                             *15*
*I shall die.*

Neither bridge nor boat
brought me here.
No one told me
it was island or shore.                                  *20*
A land I did not search for
and did not discover.

---

[1] Translated by Doris Dana.

Like a fable
that I learned,
a dream of taking                                    25
and letting go,
and it is my land
where I live and I die

It was born to me of things
that are not of land,                                30
of kingdoms and kingdoms
that I had and I lost,
of all things living
that I have seen die,
of all that was mine                                 35
and went from me.

I lost ranges of mountains
wherein I could sleep.
I lost orchards of gold
that were sweet to live.                              40
I lost islands of indigo
and sugar cane,
and the shadows of these
I saw circling me,
and together and loving                              45
become a land.

I saw manes of fog
without back or nape,
saw sleeping breaths
pursue me,                                           50
and in years of wandering
become a land,
*and in a land without name*
*I shall die.*

## EDNA ST. VINCENT MILLAY [1892–1950]
# Spring

To what purpose, April, do you return again?
Beauty is not enough.
You can no longer quiet me with the redness
Of little leaves opening stickily.
I know what I know.                                              5
The sun is hot on my neck as I observe
The spikes of the crocus.
The smell of the earth is good.
It is apparent that there is no death.
But what does that signify?                                     10
Not only under ground are the brains of men
Eaten by maggots.
Life in itself
Is nothing,
An empty cup, a flight of uncarpeted stairs.                    15
It is not enough that yearly, down this hill,
April
Comes like an idiot, babbling and strewing flowers.

## E. E. CUMMINGS [1894–1962]
# Buffalo Bill 's

Buffalo Bill 's
defunct
            who used to
            ride a watersmooth-silver
                                    stallion                     5
and break onetwothreefourfive pigeonsjustlikethat

                                                        Jesus
he was a handsome man
                        and what i want to know is
how do you like your blueeyed boy                    *10*
Mister Death


# my sweet old etcetera

my sweet old etcetera
aunt lucy during the recent

war could and what
is more did tell you just
what everybody was fighting                          *5*

for,
my sister

isabel created hundreds
(and
hundreds) of socks not to                            *10*
mention shirts fleaproof earwarmers

etcetera wristers etcetera, my
mother hoped that

i would die etcetera
bravely of course my father used                     *15*
to become hoarse talking about how it was
a privilege and if only he
could meanwhile my

self etcetera lay quietly
in the deep mud et                                   *20*

cetera
(dreaming,
et
    cetera, of
Your smile                                                   25
eyes knees and of your Etcetera)

## LANGSTON HUGHES [1902–1967]

# Harlem

What happens to a dream deferred?

Does it dry up
like a raisin in the sun?
Or fester like a sore—
And then run?                                              5
Does it stink like rotten meat?
Or crust and sugar over—
like a syrupy sweet?

Maybe it just sags
like a heavy load.                                         10

*Or does it explode?*

# Night Funeral in Harlem

Night funeral
in Harlem:

*Where did they get
Them two fine cars?*

Insurance man, he did not pay—                          5
His insurance lapsed the other day—
Yet they got a satin box
For his head to lay.

    Night funeral
    in Harlem:                          10

    *Who was it sent*
    *That wreath of flowers?*

Them flowers came
from that poor boy's friends—
They'll want flowers, too,                          15
When they meet their ends.

    Night funeral
    in Harlem:

    *Who preached that*
    *Black boy to his grave?*                          20

Old preacher-man
Preached that boy away—
Charged Five Dollars
His girl friend had to pay.

    Night funeral                          25
    in Harlem.

When it was all over
And the lid shut on his head
and the organ had done played
and the last prayers been said                          30
and six pallbearers
Carried him out for dead
And off down Lenox Avenue
That long black hearse sped,
    The street light                          35
    At his corner
    Shined just like a tear—

That boy that they was mournin'
Was so dear, so dear
To them folks that brought the flowers,                    40
To that girl who paid the preacher-man—
It was all their tears that made
    That poor boy's
    Funeral grand.

    Night funeral                                      45
    in Harlem.


## PABLO NERUDA [1904–1973]

# The Clock Fallen into the Sea

There is so much dark light in space
and so many dimensions suddenly yellow
because the wind does not fall
and the leaves do not breathe.

It is a Sunday day arrested in the sea,                        5
a day like a submerged ship,
a drop of time assaulted by scales
that are fiercely dressed in transparent dampness.

There are months seriously accumulated in a vestment
that we wish to smell weeping with closed eyes,               10
and there are years in a single blind sign of water
deposited and green,
there is the age that neither fingers nor light captured,
much more praiseworthy than a broken fan,
much more silent than a disinterred foot,                     15

---

Translated by Donald D. Walsh.

there is the nuptial age of the days dissolved
in a sad tomb traversed by fish.

The petals of time fall immensely
like vague umbrellas looking like the sky,
growing around, it is scarcely                                    20
a bell never seen,
a flooded rose, a jellyfish, a long
shattered throbbing:
but it's not that, it's something that scarcely touches and spends,
a confused trace without sound or birds,                         25
a dissipation of perfumes and races.

The clock that in the field stretched out upon the moss
and struck a hip with its electric form
runs rickety and wounded beneath the fearful water
that ripples palpitating with central currents.                  30

# W. H. Auden [1907–1973]

# Musée des Beaux Arts[1]

About suffering they were never wrong,
The Old Masters: how well they understood
Its human position; how it takes place
While someone else is eating or opening a window or just walking
    dully along;
How, when the aged are reverently, passionately waiting          5
For the miraculous birth, there always must be
Children who did not specially want it to happen, skating
On a pond at the edge of the wood:
They never forgot
That even the dreadful martyrdom must run its course             10

---

[1] Museum of Fine Arts.

Anyhow in a corner, some untidy spot
Where the dogs go on with their doggy life and the torturer's
 horse
Scratches its innocent behind on a tree.

In Brueghel's *Icarus*,[2] for instance: how everything turns away
Quite leisurely from the disaster; the ploughman may          15
Have heard the splash, the forsaken cry,
But for him it was not an important failure; the sun shone
As it had to on the white legs disappearing into the green
Water; and the expensive delicate ship that must have seen
Something amazing, a boy falling out of the sky,          20
Had somewhere to get to and sailed calmly on.


## THEODORE ROETHKE [1908–1963]

# I Knew a Woman

I knew a woman, lovely in her bones,
When small birds sighed, she would sigh back at them;
Ah, when she moved, she moved more ways than one:
The shapes a bright container can contain!
Of her choice virtues only gods should speak,          5
Or English poets who grew up on Greek
(I'd have them sing in chorus, cheek to cheek).

How well her wishes went! She stroked my chin,
She taught me Turn, and Counter-turn, and Stand;[1]
She taught me Touch, that undulant white skin;          10
I nibbled meekly from her proffered hand;
She was the sickle; I, poor I, the rake,

---

*Musée des Beaux Arts:* ² *Landscape with the Fall of Icarus*, a sixteenth-century painting by Pieter Brueghel the Elder. Daedalus constructed wings of wax. His son,
Icarus, flew too near the sun, the wax melted, and he fell into the sea and
drowned.
*I Knew a Woman:* ¹ Terms used to identify the three parts of a Pindaric ode, a
verse form attributed to Pindar, a Greek poet of the fifth century B.C.

Coming behind her for her pretty sake
(But what prodigious mowing we did make).

Love likes a gander, and adores a goose:                    15
Her full lips pursed, the errant note to seize;
She played it quick, she played it light and loose;
My eyes, they dazzled at her flowing knees;
Her several parts could keep a pure repose,
Or one hip quiver with a mobile nose                        20
(She moved in circles, and those circles moved).

Let seed be grass, and grass turn into hay:
I'm martyr to a motion not my own;
What's freedom for? To know eternity.
I swear she cast a shadow white as stone.                   25
But who would count eternity in days?
These old bones live to learn her wanton ways:
(I measure time by how a body sways).

# ELIZABETH BISHOP [1911–1979]

# In the Waiting Room

In Worcester, Massachusetts,
I went with Aunt Consuelo
to keep her dentist's appointment
and sat and waited for her
in the dentist's waiting room.                              5
It was winter. It got dark
early. The waiting room
was full of grown-up people,
arctics and overcoats,
lamps and magazines.                                        10
My aunt was inside
what seemed like a long time
and while I waited I read
the *National Geographic*

(I could read) and carefully                                    15
studied the photographs:
the inside of a volcano,
black, and full of ashes;
then it was spilling over
in rivulets of fire.                                            20
Osa and Martin Johnson[1]
dressed in riding breeches,
laced boots, and pith helmets.
A dead man slung on a pole
—"Long Pig," the caption said.                                 25
Babies with pointed heads
wound round and round with string;
black, naked women with necks
wound round and round with wire
like the necks of light bulbs.                                 30
Their breasts were horrifying.
I read it right straight through.
I was too shy to stop.
And then I looked at the cover:
the yellow margins, the date.                                  35

Suddenly, from inside,
came an *oh!* of pain
—Aunt Consuelo's voice—
not very loud or long.
I wasn't at all surprised;                                      40
even then I knew she was
a foolish, timid woman.
I might have been embarrassed,
but wasn't. What took me
completely by surprise                                          45
was that it was *me:*
my voice, in my mouth.
Without thinking at all
I was my foolish aunt,

---

[1] Martin and Osa Johnson were explorers, writers, and film producers. They produced and appeared in numerous travelogues.

I—we—were falling, falling,                    50
our eyes glued to the cover
of the *National Geographic,*
February, 1918.

I said to myself: three days
and you'll be seven years old.                 55
I was saying it to stop
the sensation of falling off
the round, turning world
into cold, blue-black space.
But I felt: you are an *I,*                     60
you are an *Elizabeth,*
you are one of *them.*
*Why* should you be one, too?
I scarcely dared to look
to see what it was I was.                       65
I gave a sidelong glance
—I couldn't look any higher—
at shadowy gray knees,
trousers and skirts and boots
and different pairs of hands                    70
lying under the lamps.
I knew that nothing stranger
had ever happened, that nothing
stranger could ever happen.
Why should I be my aunt,                        75
or me, or anyone?
What similarities—
boots, hands, the family voice
I felt in my throat, or even
the *National Geographic*                       80
and those awful hanging breasts—
held us all together
or made us all just one?
How—I didn't know any
word for it—how "unlikely". . .                 85
How had I come to be here,
like them, and overhear

a cry of pain that could have
got loud and worse but hadn't?

The waiting room was bright                                      90
and too hot. It was sliding
beneath a big black wave,
another, and another.

Then I was back in it.
The War was on. Outside,                                          95
in Worcester, Massachusetts,
were night and slush and cold.
and it was still the fifth
of February, 1918.


## ROBERT HAYDEN [1913–1980]

# Those Winter Sundays

Sundays too my father got up early
and put his clothes on in the blueblack cold,
then with cracked hands that ached
from labor in the weekday weather made
banked fires blaze. No one ever thanked him.                      5

I'd wake and hear the cold splintering, breaking.
When the rooms were warm, he'd call,
and slowly I would rise and dress,
fearing the chronic angers of that house,

Speaking indifferently to him,                                    10
who had driven out the cold
and polished my good shoes as well.
What did I know, what did I know
of love's austere and lonely offices?

DAVID IGNATOW [b. 1914]

# Did you know that hair is
# flying around in the universe?

Did you know that hair is flying around in the universe? Hair
trimmed from beards in barbershops, from mustaches at the mirror, from underarms, from crotches, legs and chests—human hair.
It all gets dumped into a fill-in space and then the wind gets at it
and sails it back into the cities and towns and villages, right   5
through your open windows during summer and even during
winter down your chimney. Hair, brown, black, red, white, grey
and yellow. They get all mixed up and you find them on your
pullover sweater and wonder who did you come up against with
yellow hair which you happen to like and you dream of its actually   10
having happened that you were in touch with a person with yellow
hair.

That's not the whole of it. Think of walking through the street on
a windy day or even on a calm, balmy day. The hair is floating all
around you and you are walking through perhaps an invisible or   15
fine mist of cut hairs. Black, brown, red that you would not have
cared to touch in a million years because you associate them with
certain kinds of faces and behavior but there are the hairs of these
people touching and clinging to you, as if trying to tell you that
hair is everywhere and everybody has it and that it's hopeless to   20
try to pick black or brown or red off your sleeves but not yellow
hair.

It would be an act of insanity. You need to pick them all off or
none and let yourself be covered by them all, like a new kind of
fur coat or perhaps a new hairy skin to protect you from the
weather. Hair of all colors. What a pretty sight that would make,   25
wouldn't it, and you would have a coat of many colors, and I bet
you would be proud of it, especially if you saw everyone else
wearing a coat of many colors. How about that? Because people
cut their hair and let it fly out over the world where it lands on
everyone and everyone is sharing in the coat of many colors.   30

RANDALL JARRELL [1914–1965]

# The Woman at the Washington Zoo

The saris go by me from the embassies.

Cloth from the moon. Cloth from another planet.
They look back at the leopard like the leopard.

And I. . . .
             this print of mine, that has kept its color    5
Alive through so many cleanings; this dull null
Navy I wear to work, and wear from work, and so
To my bed, so to my grave, with no
Complaints, no comment: neither from my chief,
The Deputy Chief Assistant, nor his chief—    10
Only I complain. . . . this serviceable
Body that no sunlight dyes, no hand suffuses
But, dome-shadowed, withering among columns,
Wavy beneath fountains—small, far-off, shining
In the eyes of animals, these beings trapped    15
As I am trapped but not, themselves, the trap,
Aging, but without knowledge of their age,
Kept safe here, knowing not of death, for death—
Oh, bars of my own body, open, open!

The world goes by my cage and never sees me.    20
And there come not to me, as come to these,
The wild beasts, sparrows pecking the llamas' grain,
Pigeons settling on the bears' bread, buzzards
Tearing the meat the flies have clouded. . . .
                                  Vulture,    25
When you come for the white rat that the foxes left,
Take off the red helmet of your head, the black
Wings that have shadowed me, and step to me as man:
The wild brother at whose feet the white wolves fawn,
To whose hand of power the great lioness    30

Stalks, purring. . . .
　　　　　　　　You know what I was,
You see what I am: change me, change me!

## DYLAN THOMAS [1914–1953]

# Do Not Go Gentle
# into That Good Night

Do not go gentle into that good night,
Old age should burn and rave at close of day;
Rage, rage against the dying of the light.

Though wise men at their end know dark is right,
Because their words have forked no lightning they　　　5
Do not go gentle into that good night.

Good men, the last wave by, crying how bright
Their frail deeds might have danced in a green bay,
Rage, rage against the dying of the light.

Wild men who caught and sang the sun in flight,　　　10
And learn, too late, they grieved it on its way,
Do not go gentle into that good night.

Grave men, near death, who see with blinding sight
Blind eyes could blaze like meteors and be gay,
Rage, rage against the dying of the light.　　　15

And you, my father, there on the sad height,
Curse, bless, me now with your fierce tears, I pray.
Do not go gentle into that good night.
Rage, rage against the dying of the light.

## GWENDOLYN BROOKS [b. 1917]

# The Mother

Abortions will not let you forget.
You remember the children you got that you did not get,
The damp small pulps with a little or with no hair,
The singers and workers that never handled the air.
You will never neglect or beat                                          5
Them, or silence or buy with a sweet.
You will never wind up the sucking-thumb
Or scuttle off ghosts that come.
You will never leave them, controlling your luscious sigh,
Return for a snack of them, with gobbling mother-eye.          10

I have heard in the voices of the wind the voices of my dim killed
    children.
I have contracted. I have eased
My dim dears at the breasts they could never suck.
I have said, Sweets, if I sinned, if I seized
Your luck                                                               15
And your lives from your unfinished reach,
If I stole your births and your names,
Your straight baby tears and your games,
Your stilted or lovely loves, your tumults, your marriages, aches,
    and your deaths,
If I poisoned the beginnings of your breaths,                    20
Believe that even in my deliberateness I was not deliberate.
Though why should I whine,
Whine that the crime was other than mine?—
Since anyhow you are dead.
Or rather, or instead,                                                  25
You were never made.
But that too, I am afraid,
Is faulty: oh, what shall I say, how is the truth to be said?
You were born, you had body, you died.
It is just that you never giggled or planned or cried.           30

Believe me, I loved you all.
Believe me, I knew you, though faintly, and I loved, I loved you
All.

# We Real Cool

The Pool Players.
Seven at the Golden Shovel.

We real cool. We
Left school. We

Lurk late. We                                                    5
Strike straight. We

Sing sin. We
Thin gin. We

Jazz June. We
Die soon.                                                       10

## ROBERT LOWELL [1917–1977]

# The Picture

### (FOR ELIZABETH)[1]

This might be nature—twenty stories high,
two water tanks, tobacco shingle, girdled
by stapled pasture wire, while bed to bed,

---

[1] Elizabeth Hardwick, Lowell's second wife.

we lie gazing into the ether's crystal ball,
sky and a sky and sky and sky, till death—  5
my heart stops, this might be heaven. Twenty years
ago, we shot for less, could settle for
a picture, out of style then and now in,
of seven daffodils. We watched them blow:
buttercup yellow were the flowers, and green  10
the stems as fresh paint, over them the wind,
the blowzy wooden branches of the elms,
the sack of hornets sopping up the flame—
still over us, still in parenthesis.

# Water

It was a Maine lobster town—
each morning boatloads of hands
pushed off for granite
quarries on the islands,

and left dozens of bleak  5
white frame houses stuck
like oyster shells
on a hill of rock,

and below us, the sea lapped
the raw little match-stick  10
mazes of a weir,[1]
where the fish for bait were trapped.

Remember? We sat on a slab of rock.
From this distance in time,
it seems the color  15
of iris, rotting and turning purpler,

---

[1] An enclosure set in the water to catch fish.

but it was only
the usual gray rock
turning the usual green
when drenched by the sea.                                   20

The sea drenched the rock
at our feet all day,
and kept tearing away
flake after flake.

One night you dreamed                                        25
you were a mermaid clinging to a wharf-pile,
and trying to pull
off the barnacles with your hands.

We wished our two souls
might return like gulls                                      30
to the rock. In the end,
the water was too cold for us.

## RICHARD WILBUR [b. 1921]

# Love Calls Us to the Things of This World

The eyes open to a cry of pulleys,
And spirited from sleep, the astounded soul
Hangs for a moment bodiless and simple
As false dawn.
                    Outside the open window                 5
The morning air is all awash with angels.

Some are in bed-sheets, some are in blouses,
Some are in smocks: but truly there they are.
Now they are rising together in calm swells
Of halcyon feeling, filling whatever they wear             10
With the deep joy of their impersonal breathing;

Now they are flying in place, conveying
The terrible speed of their omnipresence, moving
And staying like white water; and now of a sudden
They swoon down into so rapt a quiet            15
That nobody seems to be there.
                     The soul shrinks


From all that it is about to remember,
From the punctual rape of every bléssed day,
And cries,                                       20
         "Oh, let there be nothing on earth but laundry,
Nothing but rosy hands in the rising steam
And clear dances done in the sight of heaven."


Yet, as the sun acknowledges
With a warm look the world's hunks and colors,   25
The soul descends once more in bitter love
To accept the waking body, saying now
In a changed voice as the man yawns and rises,


"Bring them down from their ruddy gallows;
Let there be clean linen for the backs of thieves;  30
Let lovers go fresh and sweet to be undone,
And the heaviest nuns walk in a pure floating
Of dark habits,
              keeping their difficult balance."


## JAMES DICKEY [b. 1923]

# The Lifeguard

In a stable of boats I lie still,
From all sleeping children hidden.
The leap of a fish from its shadow
Makes the whole lake instantly tremble.
With my foot on the water, I feel               5
The moon outside

Take on the utmost of its power.
I rise and go out through the boats.
I set my broad sole upon silver,
On the skin of the sky, on the moonlight,                    10
Stepping outward from earth onto water
In quest of the miracle

This village of children believed
That I could perform as I dived
For one who had sunk from my sight.                          15
I saw his cropped haircut go under.
I leapt, and my steep body flashed
Once, in the sun.

Dark drew all the light from my eyes.
Like a man who explores his death                            20
By the pull of his slow-moving shoulders,
I hung head down in the cold,
Wide-eyed, contained, and alone
Among the weeds,

And my fingertips turned into stone                          25
From clutching immovable blackness.
Time after time I leapt upward
Exploding in breath, and fell back
From the change in the children's faces
At my defeat.                                                30

Beneath them, I swam to the boathouse
With only my life in my arms
To wait for the lake to shine back
At the risen moon with such power
That my steps on the light of the ripples                    35
Might be sustained.

Beneath me is nothing but brightness
Like the ghost of a snowfield in summer.
As I move toward the center of the lake,
Which is also the center of the moon,                        40
I am thinking of how I may be
The savior of one

Who has already died in my care.
The dark trees fade from around me.
The moon's dust hovers together.                               45
I call softly out, and the child's
Voice answers through blinding water.
Patiently, slowly,

He rises, dilating to break
The surface of stone with his forehead.                        50
He is one I do not remember
Having ever seen in his life.
The ground I stand on is trembling
Upon his smile.

I wash the black mud from my hands.                            55
On a light given off by the grave.
I kneel in the quick of the moon
At the heart of a distant forest
And hold in my arms a child
Of water, water, water.                                        60

## DENISE LEVERTOV [b. 1923]

# The Dragonfly-Mother[1]

I was setting out from my house
to keep my promise

but the Dragonfly-Mother stopped me.

I was to speak to a multitude
for a good cause, but at home                                   5

---

[1] Readers may be interested to read "The Earthwoman and the Waterwoman"
(*Collected Earlier Poems*, p. 31), a poem written in 1957, to which this 1979 poem
makes some allusions [author's note].

the Dragonfly-Mother was listening
not to a speech but to the creak of
                    stretching tissue,
tense hum of leaves unfurling.

Who is the Dragonfly-Mother?                           10
What does she do?

She is the one who hovers
on stairways of air,
                    sometimes almost
grazing your cheekbone,                                15
she is the one who darts unforeseeably
into unsuspected dimensions,

who sees in water
her own blue fire zigzag, and lifts
her self in laughter                                   20
into the tearful pale sky

that sails blurred clouds in the stream.

◆

She sat at my round table,
we told one another dreams,
I stayed home breaking my promise.                     25

When she left I slept
three hours, and arose

and wrote. I remember the cold
Waterwoman, in dragonfly dresses

and blue shoes, long ago.                              30
She is the same,

whose children were thin,
left at home when she went out dancing.
She is the Dragonfly-Mother,

that cold                                                                      *35*
is only the rush of air

swiftness brings.
There is a summer
over the water, over

the river mirrors                                                              *40*
where she hovers, a summer
fertile, abundant, where dreams
grow into acts and journeys.

Her children
are swimmers, nymphs and newts, metamorphic.        *45*
                                        When she tells
her stories she listens; when she listens
she tells you the story you utter.

                                ◆

When I broke my promise,
and slept, and later                                                           *50*

cooked and ate the food she had bought
and left in my kitchen,

I kept a tryst with myself,
a long promise that can be fulfilled
only poem by poem,                                                             *55*
broken over and over.

                        I too,
a creature, grow among reeds,
        in mud, in air,
in sunbright cold, in fever                                                    *60*
of blue-gold zenith, winds
of passage.

                Dragonfly-Mother's
a messenger,
if I don't trust her                                                           *65*
I can't keep faith.

> There is a summer
in the sleep
of broken promises, fertile dreams,
acts of passage, hovering                                    70
journeys over the fathomless waters.

**LOUIS SIMPSON** [b. 1923]

# Walt Whitman
# at Bear Mountain

> . . . life which does not give the preference to
> any other life, of any previous period, which
> therefore prefers its own existence . . .
> —*Ortega y Gasset*

Neither on horseback nor seated,
But like himself, squarely on two feet,
The poet of death and lilacs
Loafs by the footpath. Even the bronze looks alive
Where it is folded like cloth. And he seems friendly.    5

"Where is the Mississippi panorama
And the girl who played the piano?
Where are you, Walt?
The Open Road goes to the used-car lot.

"Where is the nation you promised?                       10
These houses built of wood sustain
Colossal snows,
And the light above the street is sick to death.

"As for the people—see how they neglect you!
Only a poet pauses to read the inscription."        15

"I am here," he answered.
"It seems you have found me out.
Yet, did I not warn you that it was Myself
I advertised? Were my words not sufficiently plain?

"I gave no prescriptions,                           20
And those who have taken my moods for prophecies
Mistake the matter."
Then, vastly amused—"Why do you reproach me?
I freely confess I am wholly disreputable.
Yet I am happy, because you have found me out."     25

A crocodile in wrinkled metal loafing . . .

Then all the realtors,
Pickpockets, salesmen, and the actors performing
Official scenarios,
Turned a deaf ear, for they had contracted          30
American dreams.

But the man who keeps a store on a lonely road,
And the housewife who knows she's dumb,
And the earth, are relieved.

All that grave weight of America                    35
Cancelled! Like Greece and Rome.
The future in ruins!
The castles, the prisons, the cathedrals
Unbuilding, and roses
Blossoming from the stones that are not there . . . 40

The clouds are lifting from the high Sierras,
The Bay mists clearing.
And the angel in the gate, the flowering plum,
Dances like Italy, imagining red.

# ROBERT BLY [b. 1926]

## For My Son Noah, Ten Years Old

Night and day arrive, and day after day goes by,
and what is old remains old, and what is young
   remains young, and grows old.
The lumber pile does not grow younger, nor the
   two-by-fours lose their darkness,         5
but the old tree goes on, the barn stands without help
   so many years;
the advocate of darkness and night is not lost.

The horse steps up, swings on one leg, turns its body,
the chicken flapping claws onto the roost, its wings   10
   whelping and walloping,
but what is primitive is not to be shot out into the
   night and the dark.
And slowly the kind man comes closer, loses his rage,
   sits down at table.         15

# ALLEN GINSBERG [b. 1926]

## A Supermarket in California

What thoughts I have of you tonight, Walt Whitman, for I
walked down the sidestreets under the trees with a headache self-
conscious looking at the full moon.

In my hungry fatigue, and shopping for images, I went into
the neon fruit supermarket, dreaming of your enumerations!

What peaches and what penumbras![1] Whole families shopping at night! Aisles full of husbands! Wives in the avocados, babies in the tomatoes!—and you, Garcia Lorca,[2] what were you doing down by the watermelons?

I saw you, Walt Whitman, childless, lonely old grubber, poking among the meats in the refrigerator and eyeing the grocery boys.

I heard you asking questions of each: Who killed the pork chops? What price bananas? Are you my Angel?                              5

I wandered in and out of the brilliant stacks of cans following you, and followed in my imagination by the store detective.

We strode down the open corridors together in our solitary fancy tasting artichokes, possessing every frozen delicacy, and never passing the cashier.

Where are we going, Walt Whitman? The doors close in an hour. Which way does your beard point tonight?

(I touch your book and dream of our odyssey[3] in the supermarket and feel absurd.)

Will we walk all night through solitary streets? The trees add shade to shade, lights out in the houses, we'll both be lonely.    10

Will we stroll dreaming of the lost America of love past blue automobiles in driveways, home to our silent cottage?

Ah, dear father, graybeard, lonely old courage-teacher, what America did you have when Charon quit poling his ferry and you got out on a smoking bank and stood watching the boat disappear on the black waters of Lethe?[4]

Berkeley 1955

---

[1] Spaces of partial illumination (as in an eclipse) between the shadow and the light.   [2] Spanish poet and playwright.   [3] Wandering journey—from the *Odyssey* of Homer, an epic poem that describes the wanderings of Odysseus.   [4] In Greek mythology, Charon is the ferryman who brings souls across the river Styx in the underworld. The waters of Lethe, a second of the five rivers of the underworld, were said to cause forgetfulness. Dead souls were required to taste its water, to forget everything that was said or done when they were alive.

## JOHN ASHBERY [b. 1927]

# Paradoxes and Oxymorons

This poem is concerned with language on a very plain level.
Look at it talking to you. You look out a window
Or pretend to fidget. You have it but you don't have it.
You miss it, it misses you. You miss each other.

The poem is sad because it wants to be yours, and cannot be.      5
What's a plain level? It is that and other things,
Bringing a system of them into play. Play?
Well, actually, yes, but I consider play to be

A deeper outside thing, a dreamed role-pattern,
As in the division of grace these long August days            10
Without proof. Open-ended. And before you know it
It gets lost in the steam and chatter of typewriters.

It has been played once more. I think you exist only
To tease me into doing it, on your level, and then you aren't there
Or have adopted a different attitude. And the poem              15
Has set me softly down beside you. The poem is you.


## GALWAY KINNELL [b. 1927]

# Vapor Trail Reflected
# in the Frog Pond

### *1*

The old watch: their
thick eyes
puff and foreclosure by the moon. The young, heads
trailed by the beginnings of necks,

shiver,                                                                  5
in the guarantee they shall be bodies.

In the frog pond
the vapor trail of a SAC[1] bomber creeps,

I hear its drone, drifting, high up
in immaculate ozone.                                                    10

2

And I hear,
coming over the hills, America singing,
her varied carols I hear:
crack of deputies' rifles practicing their aim on stray dogs at night,
sput of cattleprod,                                                     15
TV groaning at the smells of the human body,
curses of the soldier as he poisons, burns, grinds, and stabs
the rice of the world,
with open mouth, crying strong, hysterical curses.

3

And by rice paddies in Asia                                             20
bones
wearing a few shadows
walk down a dirt road, smashed
bloodsuckers on their heel, knowing
the flesh a man throws down in the sunshine                             25
dogs shall eat
and the flesh that is upthrown in the air
shall be seized by birds,
shoulder blades smooth, unmarked by old feather-holes,
hands rivered                                                           30
by blue, erratic wanderings of the blood,
eyes crinkled up
as they gaze up at the drifting sun that gives us our lives,
seed dazzled over the footbattered blaze of the earth.

---

[1] Strategic Air Command.

## W. S. MERWIN [b. 1927]
# A Door

This is a place where a door might be
here where I am standing
in the light outside all the walls

there would be a shadow here
all day long                                          5
and a door into it
where now there is me

and somebody would come and knock
on this air
long after I have gone                                10
and there in front of me a life
would open

## JAMES WRIGHT [1927–1980]
# A Blessing

Just off the highway to Rochester, Minnesota,
Twilight bounds softly forth on the grass.
And the eyes of those two Indian ponies
Darken with kindness.
They have come gladly out of the willows            5
To welcome my friend and me.
We step over the barbed wire into the pasture
Where they have been grazing all day, alone.
They ripple tensely, they can hardly contain their happiness
That we have come.                                  10
They bow shyly as wet swans. They love each other.

There is no loneliness like theirs.
At home once more,
They begin munching the young tufts of spring in the
    darkness.
I would like to hold the slenderer one in my arms,                          15
For she has walked over to me
And nuzzled my left hand.
She is black and white,
Her mane falls wild on her forehead,
And the light breeze moves me to caress her long ear       20
That is delicate as the skin over a girl's wrist.
Suddenly I realize
That if I stepped out of my body I would break
Into blossom.

## PHILIP LEVINE [b. 1928]

# Starlight

My father stands in the warm evening
on the porch of my first house.
I am four years old and growing tired.
I see his head among the stars,
the glow of his cigarette, redder                                    5
than the summer moon riding
low over the old neighborhood. We
are alone, and he asks me if I am happy.
"Are you happy?" I cannot answer.
I do not really understand the word,                                10
and the voice, my father's voice, is not
his voice, but somehow thick and choked,
a voice I have not heard before, but
heard often since. He bends and passes
a thumb beneath each of my eyes.                                    15
The cigarette is gone, but I can smell
the tiredness that hangs on his breath.
He has found nothing, and he smiles

and holds my head with both his hands.
Then he lifts me to his shoulder,                               20
and now I too am there among the stars,
as tall as he. Are you happy? I say.
He nods in answer, Yes! oh yes! oh yes!
And in that new voice he says nothing,
holding my head tight against his head,                         25
his eyes closed up against the starlight,
as though those tiny blinking eyes
of light might find a tall, gaunt child
holding his child against the promises
of autumn, until the boy slept                                  30
never to waken in that world again.


## ANNE SEXTON [1928–1974]

# Two Hands

From the sea came a hand,
ignorant as a penny,
troubled with the salt of its mother,
mute with the silence of the fishes,
quick with the altars of the tides,                             5
and God reached out of His mouth
and called it man.
Up came the other hand
and God called it woman.
The hands applauded.                                            10
And this was no sin.
It was as it was meant to be.

I see them roaming the streets:
Levi complaining about his mattress,
Sarah studying a beetle,                                        15
Mandrake holding his coffee mug,
Sally playing the drum at a football game,
John closing the eyes of the dying woman,

and some who are in prison,
even the prison of their bodies,                                    20
as Christ was prisoned in His body
until the triumph came.

Unwind, hands,
you angel webs,
unwind like the coil of a jumping jack,                             25
cup together and let yourselves fill up with sun
and applaud, world,
applaud.

## ADRIENNE RICH [b. 1929]

# Diving into the Wreck

First having read the book of myths,
and loaded the camera,
and checked the edge of the knife-blade,
I put on
the body-armor of black rubber                                     5
the absurd flippers
the grave and awkward mask.
I am having to do this
not like Cousteau with his
assiduous team                                                     10
aboard the sun-flooded schooner
but here alone.

There is a ladder.
The ladder is always there
hanging innocently                                                 15
close to the side of the schooner.
We know what it is for,
we who have used it.
Otherwise
it's a piece of maritime floss                                     20
some sundry equipment.

I go down.
Rung after rung and still
the oxygen immerses me
the blue light                                              25
the clear atoms
of our human air.
I go down.
My flippers cripple me,
I crawl like an insect down the ladder              30
and there is no one
to tell me when the ocean
will begin.

First the air is blue and then
it is bluer and then green and then               35
black I am blacking out and yet
my mask is powerful
it pumps my blood with power
the sea is another story
the sea is not a question of power                40
I have to learn alone
to turn my body without force
in the deep element.

And now: it is easy to forget
what I came for                                           45
among so many who have always
lived here
swaying their crenellated fans
between the reefs
and besides                                               50
you breathe differently down here.

I came to explore the wreck.
The words are purposes.
The words are maps.
I came to see the damage that was done        55
and the treasures that prevail.
I stroke the beam of my lamp
slowly along the flank

of something more permanent
than fish or weed                                            60

the thing I came for:
the wreck and not the story of the wreck
the thing itself and not the myth
the drowned face always staring
toward the sun                                               65
the evidence of damage
worn by salt and sway into this threadbare beauty
the ribs of the disaster
curving their assertion
among the tentative haunters.                                70

This is the place.
And I am here, the mermaid whose dark hair
streams black, the merman in his armored body
We circle silently
about the wreck                                              75
we dive into the hold.
I am she: I am he

whose drowned face sleeps with open eyes
whose breasts still bear the stress
whose silver, copper, vermeil cargo lies                     80
obscurely inside barrels
half-wedged and left to rot
we are the half-destroyed instruments
that once held to a course
the water-eaten log                                          85
the fouled compass

We are, I am, you are
by cowardice or courage
the one who find our way
back to this scene                                           90
carrying a knife, a camera
a book of myths
in which
our names do not appear.

# TED HUGHES [b. 1930]

## The Thought-Fox

---

I imagine this midnight moment's forest:
Something else is alive
Beside the clock's loneliness
And this blank page where my fingers move.

Through the window I see no star:                        5
Something more near
Though deeper within darkness
Is entering the loneliness:

Cold, delicately as the dark snow
A fox's nose touches twig, leaf;                         10
Two eyes serve a movement, that now
And again now, and now, and now

Sets neat prints into the snow
Between trees, and warily a lame
Shadow lags by stump and in hollow                       15
Of a body that is bold to come

Across clearings, an eye,
A widening deepening greenness,
Brilliantly, concentratedly,
Coming about its own business                            20

Till, with a sudden sharp hot stink of fox,
It enters the dark hole of the head.
The window is starless still; the clock ticks,
The page is printed.

# SYLVIA PLATH [1932–1963]

## Morning Song

Love set you going like a fat gold watch.
The midwife slapped your footsoles, and your bald cry
Took its place among the elements.

Our voices echo, magnifying your arrival. New statue.
In a drafty museum, your nakedness                                5
Shadows our safety. We stand round blankly as walls.

I'm no more your mother
Than the cloud that distils a mirror to reflect its own slow
Effacement at the wind's hand.

All night your moth-breath                                       10
Flickers among the flat pink roses. I wake to listen:
A far sea moves in my ear.

One cry, and I stumble from bed, cow-heavy and floral
In my Victorian nightgown.
Your mouth opens clean as a cat's. The window square  15

Whitens and swallows its dull stars. And now you try
Your handful of notes;
The clear vowels rise like balloons.


## Mary's Song

The Sunday lamb cracks in its fat.
The fat
Sacrifices its opacity. . . .

A window, holy gold.
The fire makes it precious,                                    5
The same fire

Melting the tallow heretics,
Ousting the Jews.
Their thick palls float

Over the cicatrix of Poland, burnt-out                         10
Germany.
They do not die.

Grey birds obsess my heart,
Mouth-ash, ash of eye.
They settle. On the high                                       15

Precipice
That emptied one man into space
The ovens glowed like heavens, incandescent,

It is a heart,
This holocaust I walk in,                                      20
O golden child the world will kill and eat.

## MARY OLIVER [b. 1935]

# Poem for My Father's Ghost

Now is my father
A traveler, like all the bold men
He talked of, endlessly
And with boundless admiration,
Over the supper table,                                         5
Or gazing up from his white pillow—
Book on his lap always, until
Even that grew too heavy to hold.

Now is my father free of all binding fevers.
Now is my father                                                  10
Traveling where there is no road.

Finally, he could not lift a hand
To cover his eyes.
Now he climbs to the eye of the river,
He strides through the Dakotas.                                  15
He disappears into the mountains. And though he looks
Cold and hungry as any man
At the end of a questing season,

He is one of *them* now:
He cannot be stopped.                                            20

Now is my father
Walking the wind,
Sniffing the deep Pacific
That begins at the end of the world.

Vanished from us utterly,                                        25
Now is my father circling the deepest forest—
Then turning in to the last red campfire burning
In the final hills.

Where chieftains, warriors and heroes
Rise and make him welcome,                                       30
Recognizing, under the shambles of his body,
A brother who has walked his thousand miles.

## LUCILLE CLIFTON [b. 1936]

# Miss Rosie

When I watch you
wrapped up like garbage
sitting, surrounded by the smell

of too old potato peels
or                                                    5
when I watch you
in your old man's shoes
with the little toe cut out
sitting, waiting for your mind
like next week's grocery                             10
I say
when I watch you
you wet brown bag of a woman
who used to be the best looking gal in Georgia
used to be called the Georgia Rose                   15
I stand up
through your destruction
I stand up

## MARGARET ATWOOD [b. 1939]

# Book of Ancestors

### *i*

Book of Ancestors: these brutal, with curled
beards and bulls' heads . these flattened,
slender with ritual . these contorted
by ecstacy or pain . these bearing
knife, leaf, snake                                    5

    and these, closer to us,
copper hawkman arched on the squat rock
pyramid, and plumed and beak-
nosed priests pressing his arms and feet
down, heart slashed from his opened                   10
flesh, lifted to where
the sun, red and dilated
with his blood, glows in the still hungry sky

Whether he thinks this is
an act of will:                                                    15

   the life set free
by him alone, offered, ribs expanding
by themselves, bone petals,
the heart released and flickering in the
taloned hand, handful of liquid                                   20
fire joined to that other fire
an instant before the sacrificed eyes
burst like feathered stars in the darkness

of the painted border.

### ii

So much for the gods and their                                    25
static demands . our demands, former
demands, death patterns
obscure as fragments of an
archeology, these frescoes
on a crumbling temple                                             30
wall we look at now and can scarcely
piece together

   History
is over, we take place
in a season, an undivided                                         35
space, no necessities

hold us closed, distort
us. I lean behind you, mouth touching
your spine, my arms around
you, palm above the heart,                                        40
your blood insistent under
my hand, quick and mortal

### iii

Midwinter, the window
is luminous with blown snow, the fire
burns inside its bars                                             45

On the floor your body curves
like that: the ancient pose, neck slackened, arms
thrown above the head, vital
throat and belly lying
undefended. light slides over you,                          50
this is not an altar, they are not
acting or watching

You are intact, you turn
towards me, your eyes opening, the eyes
intricate and easily bruised, you open          55

yourself to me gently, what
they tried, we
tried but could never do
before . without blood, the killed
heart . to take                                               60
that risk, to offer life and remain

alive, open yourself like this and become whole

## Game after Supper

This is before electricity,
it is when there were porches.

On the sagging porch an old man
is rocking. The porch is wooden,

the house is wooden and grey;                    5
in the living room which smells of
smoke and mildew, soon
the woman will light the kerosene lamp.

There is a barn but I am not in the barn;
there is an orchard too, gone bad,              10

its apples like soft cork
but I am not there either.

I am hiding in the long grass
with my two dead cousins,
the membrane grown already                    15
across their throats.

We hear crickets and our own hearts
close to our ears;
though we giggle, we are afraid.

From the shadows around                        20
the corner of the house
a tall man is coming to find us:

He will be an uncle,
if we are lucky.

## Seamus Heaney [b. 1939]

# Digging

Between my finger and my thumb
The squat pen rests; snug as a gun.

Under my window, a clean rasping sound
When the spade sinks into gravelly ground:
My father, digging. I look down                 5

Till his straining rump among the flowerbeds
Bends low, comes up twenty years away
Stooping in rhythm through potato drills
Where he was digging.

The coarse boot nestled on the lug, the shaft   10
Against the inside knee was levered firmly.

He rooted out tall tops, buried the bright edge deep
To scatter new potatoes that we picked
Loving their cool hardness in our hands.

By God, the old man could handle a spade.        15
Just like his old man.

My grandfather cut more turf in a day
Than any other man on Toner's bog.
Once I carried him milk in a bottle
Corked sloppily with paper. He straightened up        20
To drink it, then fell to right away

Nicking and slicing neatly, heaving sods
Over his shoulder, going down and down
For the good turf. Digging.

The cold smell of potato mould, the squelch and slap        25
Of soggy peat, the curt cuts of an edge
Through living roots awaken in my head.
But I've no spade to follow men like them.

Between my finger and my thumb
The squat pen rests.        30
I'll dig with it.


## SHARON OLDS [b. 1942]

# The Victims

When Mother divorced you, we were glad. She took it and
took it, in silence, all those years and then
kicked you out, suddenly, and her
kids loved it. Then you were fired, and we
grinned inside, the way people grinned when        5

Nixon's helicopter lifted off the South
Lawn for the last time. We were tickled
to think of your office taken away,
your secretaries taken away,
your lunches with three double bourbons,                    10
your pencils, your reams of paper. Would they take your
suits back, too, those dark
carcasses hung in your closet, and the black
noses of your shoes with their large pores?
She had taught us to take it, to hate you and take it      15
until we pricked with her for your
annihilation, Father. Now I
pass the bums in doorways, the white
slugs of their bodies gleaming through slits in their
suits of compressed silt, the stained                      20
flippers of their hands, the underwater
fire of their eyes, ships gone down with the
lanterns lit, and I wonder who took it and
took it from them in silence until they had
given it all away and had nothing                          25
left but this.

## TESS GALLAGHER [b. 1943]

# The Sky behind It

When it rains you remember snow.
Always there is a tree
behind it and the slant roofs thickening,
piling on sleep so the bed drifts
and you fall again into the best saving shape.             5

Today you noticed yourself at a distance
and the others
in the foreground, just appearances, walking

so out of harm and hope
they rose as after a dying                               10
you saw happening to yourself alone
in a far room.

This knowing that whatever you do
it means more
than could possibly happen, that thought      15
and the satisfaction of music
through and around the house. If
the air could empty, you would be there
as a listening
that would move with the rooms.               20

To stay apart is to dream
of the house no one lives in.
You notice the snow so includes each
momentary conclusion, each
breath taking entry, that something           25
lasts. For once
you don't discuss it with anyone.

You go in. You
look out the window and see yourself
coming up beside the house                     30
to knock at the window.
You let yourself in. You do
and the house shows through, dissolving
behind-the-scenes to the harmony
of a set table, space for a sigh, the vine,   35
the sky behind it.

So the happy ending arrives
like a membership you suspected all along.
The house is empty. You
let yourself in. You do.                       40
You go in.

PHILIP SCHULTZ [b. 1945]

# My Guardian Angel Stein

In our house every floor was a wailing wall
& each sideward glance a history of insult.
Nightly Grandma bolted the doors believing God

had a personal grievance to settle on our heads.
Not Atreus[1] exactly but we had furies (Uncle Jake                    5
banged the tables demanding respect from fate) & enough

outrage to impress Aristotle[2] with the prophetic unity
of our misfortune. No wonder I hid behind the sofa sketching
demons to identify the faces in my dreams & stayed under

bath water until my lungs split like pomegranate seeds.        10
Stein arrived one New Year's Eve fresh from a salvation in Buda-
pest.
Nothing in his 6,000 years prepared him for our nightly
bacchanal°
                                                                    °*revel*

of immigrant indignity except his stint in the Hundred Years' War
where he lost his eyesight & faith both. This myopic angel knew
everything about calamity (he taught King David the art of
hubris                                                                 15

& Moses the price of fame) & quoted Dante to prove others
had it worse. On winter nights we memorized the Dead Sea Scrolls
until I could sleep without a night light & he explained why

the stars appear only at night ("Insomniacs, they study the Torah[3]
all day"). Once I asked him outright, "Stein, why is our house  20

---

[1] In Greek legend, king of Mycenae and father of Agamemnon and Menelaus.
The story of the house of Atreus is filled with murder, incest, and revenge.
[2] Greek philosopher, 384–322 B.C.  [3] The body of wisdom and law contained in
Jewish Scripture and other sacred literature and oral tradition.

so unhappy?" Adjusting his rimless glasses, he said: "Boychick,

life is a comedy salted with despair. All humans are disappointed.
Laugh yourself to sleep each night & with luck, pluck & credit
    cards
you'll beat them at their own game. Catharsis is necessary in this
    house!"

Ah, Stein, bless your outsized wings & balding pate & while I'm
    at it                                                          25
why not bless the imagination's lonely fray with time, which, yes,
like love & family romance, has neither beginning, middle nor
    end.

## CAROLYN FORCHÉ [b. 1950]

# The Colonel

What you have heard is true. I was in his house. His wife carried
a tray of coffee and sugar. His daughter filed her nails, his son
went out for the night. There were daily papers, pet dogs, a pistol
on the cushion beside him. The moon swung bare on its black
cord over the house. On the television was a cop show. It was in   5
English. Broken bottles were embedded in the walls around the
house to scoop the kneecaps from a man's legs or cut his hands
to lace. On the windows there were gratings like those in liquor
stores. We had dinner, rack of lamb, good wine, a gold bell was
on the table for calling the maid. The maid brought green man-   10
goes, salt, a type of bread. I was asked how I enjoyed the country.
There was a brief commercial in Spanish. His wife took everything
away. There was some talk then of how difficult it had become to
govern. The parrot said hello on the terrace. The colonel told it to
shut up, and pushed himself from the table. My friend said to me   15
with his eyes: say nothing. The colonel returned with a sack used
to bring groceries home. He spilled many human ears on the table.
They were like dried peach halves. There is no other way to say
this. He took one of them in his hands, shook it in our faces,

dropped it into a water glass. It came alive there. I am tired of   20
fooling around he said. As for the rights of anyone, tell your
people they can go fuck themselves. He swept the ears to the floor
with his arm and held the last of his wine in the air. Something
for your poetry, no? he said. Some of the ears on the floor caught
this scrap of his voice. Some of the ears on the floor were pressed   25
to the ground.

May 1978

### GARRETT KAORU HONGO [b. 1951]

# Who among You Knows
# the Essence of Garlic?

Can your foreigner's nose smell mullets
roasting in a glaze of brown bean paste
and sprinkled with novas of sea salt?

Can you hear my grandmother
chant the mushroom's sutra?[1]                                        5

Can you hear the papayas crying
as they bleed in porcelain plates?

I'm telling you that the bamboo
slips the long pliant shoots
of its myriad soft tongues                                           10
into your mouth that is full of oranges.

I'm saying that the silver waterfalls
of bean threads will burst in hot oil
and stain your lips like zinc.

---

[1] A precept summarizing Vedic teaching; a discourse of the Buddha.

The marbled skin of the blue mackerel          15
works good for men. The purple oils
from its flesh perfume the tongues of women.

If you swallow them whole, the rice cakes
soaking in a broth of coconut milk and brown sugar
will never leave the bottom of your stomach.   .    20

Flukes of giant black mushrooms
leap from their murky tubs
and strangle the toes of young carrots.

Broiling chickens ooze grease,
yellow tears of fat collect                     25
and spatter in the smoking pot.

Soft ripe pears, blushing
on the kitchen window sill,
kneel like plump women
taking a long, luxurious shampoo,              30
and invite you to bite their hips.

Why not grab basketfuls of steaming noodles,
lush and slick as the hair of a fine lady,
and squeeze?      .

The shrimps, big as Portuguese thumbs,          35
stew among cut guavas, red onions,
ginger root, and rosemary in lemon juice,
the palm oil bubbling to the top,
breaking through layers and layers
of shredded coconut and sliced cashews.         40

Who among you knows the essence
of garlic and black lotus root,
of red and green peppers sizzling
among squads of oysters in the skillet,
of crushed ginger, fresh green onions,          45
and pale-blue rice wine simmering
in the stomach of a big red fish?

## JIMMY SANTIAGO BACA [b. 1952]

# Cloudy Day

It is windy today. A wall of wind crashes against,
windows clunk against, iron frames
as wind swings past broken glass
and seethes, like a frightened cat
in empty spaces of the cellblock.                                    5

In the exercise yard
we sat huddled in our prison jackets,
on our haunches against the fence,
and the wind carried our words
over the fence,                                                      10
while the vigilant guard on the tower
held his cap at the sudden gust.

I could see the main tower from where I sat,
and the wind in my face
gave me the feeling I could grasp                                    15
the tower like a cornstalk,
and snap it from its roots of rock.
The wind plays it like a flute,
this hollow shoot of rock.
The brim girded with barbwire                                        20
with a guard sitting there also,
listening intently to the sounds
as clouds cover the sun.

I thought of the day I was coming to prison,
in the back seat of a police car,                                    25
hands and ankles chained, the policeman pointed,
    "See that big water tank? The big
    silver one out there, sticking up?
    That's the prison."

And here I am, I cannot believe it.                          *30*
Sometimes it is such a dream, a dream,
where I stand up in the face of the wind,
like now, it blows at my jacket,
and my eyelids flick a little bit.
while I stare disbelieving. . . .                            *35*

The third day of spring,
and four years later, I can tell you,
how a man can endure, how a man
can become so cruel, how he can die
or become so cold. I can tell you this,                      *40*
I have seen it every day, every day,
and still I am strong enough to love you,
love myself and feel good;
even as the earth shakes and trembles,
and I have not a thing to my name,                           *45*
I feel as if I have everything, everything.

# DRAMA

# INTRODUCTION TO DRAMA

For most of us, there are moments in life when events seem to coalesce and yield important insights into ourselves or someone else that have important consequences. Particular words, gestures, or sequences of actions fall into a pattern that sheds sudden light on many things beyond themselves. At such moments, we seem to see more clearly, to understand more deeply why things have happened as they have. Sometimes these recognitions inspire significant shifts in the directions of our lives. Plays, whether large or small, achieve much of their power in just this way.

In Susan Glaspell's *Trifles,* a one-act play in which five characters attempt to solve a murder, Mrs. Hale and Mrs. Peters are left in the kitchen to attend to what their husbands call "trifles," small, unimportant matters. Mrs. Hale breaks through the polite talk to express her view that the murdered man may have been a solid citizen, but he was "hard," and cold:

> Mrs. Hale: Yes—good; he didn't drink, and kept his word as well as most, I guess, and paid his debts. But he was a hard man, Mrs. Peters. Just to pass the time of day with him. *(Shivers.)* Like a raw wind that gets to the bone. . . .

Mrs. Hale's realization prompts a series of insights about the husband's destructiveness and the wife's long suffering that brings the originally unsympathetic Mrs. Peters to her own recognitions, and both Mrs. Hale and Mrs. Peters to the decision to cover up the "trifle" that would offer the wife's motive and conclusively convict her. The recognitions of Mrs. Hale and Mrs. Peters mark turning points in the action of *Trifles,* illuminating both past and future. But they do not happen by themselves; playwrights and readers make them happen.

As readers of plays, we have a deep stake in the sequence and meaning of characters and events, not only because we are informed and moved by them, but because it is we who "produce" the plays we read. Lacking production teams of actors, directors, producers, set designers, lighting technicians, costume designers, and makeup artists, we must rely exclusively on the text and the resources of our imaginations.

Although most plays are written for the stage, it is important to keep in mind that most plays are written to be read as well as acted. In fact, silent reading, reflection, and memorization are essential to an actor's preparation of a role for the stage. Playwrights, actors, and readers have much the same imaginative challenge: to create the illusion of real people in action—speaking, gesturing, moving about on stage, moving toward some important truth. To succeed in this challenge, when we read a play we collaborate with the playwright in creating the *illusion of life being lived* on an imaginary stage, or in the setting specified in the play itself.

"But I am the opposite of a stage magician," says Tom Wingfield, poet-narrator of Tennessee Williams's *The Glass Menagerie.* "He gives you illusion that has the appearance of truth. I give you truth in the pleasant disguise of illusion." This strange wedding of truth and illusion does occur in *The Glass Menagerie* and in most plays we read. It occurs through action, which provides the substance and form for all imaginative literature. But the *action of drama* is the most immediate. Unlike fiction, which relies on a narrator, or poetry, which relies on a speaker or persona, to relate the actions of the characters, drama normally represents characters in action directly. Drama is not *about* action. Drama *is* action, purposefully structured and heightened by all the devices language and staging can muster.

The spine that structures, supports, and motivates dramatic action is *plot*. Although a plot does not include every small action, it should, if well thought-out and constructed, "justify" every action. Events occur; because they have occurred, new ones occur. In *Oedipus Rex* by Sophocles, King Oedipus summons the Shepherd to learn the terrible truth about Oedipus's own past because he must, because preceding events compel him to do so. Similarly, in Shakespeare's *Hamlet,* the prince needs to expose Claudius as his father's murderer because, among other reasons, Prince Hamlet has heard the ghost's revelation and been disturbed by his mother's quick remarriage to Claudius.

A plot's relentless causality propels the action from its *conflict* to its *climax* and *resolution*. Yet to succeed, playwrights must engage us early in the central problem of their plots. *Oedipus Rex* begins with the king himself questioning a group of his subjects sitting "in various attitudes of despair." Why, Oedipus asks, "Why have you strewn yourselves before these altars / In supplication, with your boughs and garlands?" The real answer to this ironic question is discovered through the action of the play: the progressive unfolding of the truth behind the mysterious plague, the ominous prophesies of the Oracle, and the forebodings of the blind Teiresias, for example. *Hamlet* opens with the changing of the guard at Elsinore Castle. The earlier watch is said to have been "quiet," yet the soldiers quickly come to an unsettling subject, the appearance of the ghost of the dead king, Hamlet's father. The eerie atmosphere of the midnight watch and the sentries' nervousness about the ghost establish, in the lines before the ghost appears, a strong sense that something unnatural and terrible is about to happen.

The opening scenes of modern plays that depend on the representation of more ordinary people, events, and circumstances also engage audiences as quickly as possible in the central conflict or problem. Henrik Ibsen's *A Doll's House*, for example, cues us to the theme of the interrelationships of truth, power, and money in Nora's first lines: "Be sure to hide the Christmas tree, Helene. The children mustn't see it before tonight when we've trimmed it. *(Opens her purse; to the Porter.)* How much?" Eugène Ionesco's *The Lesson*, a chilling one-act play about complicitous and fatal abuses of power, starts with the maid calling out "Yes. I'm coming" on her way to answer the doorbell. After the student enters, the maid asks simply, "Have you come for the lesson?" immediately identifying the play's subject and major line of action.

The primacy of *unity of action* is an idea shared by successful playwrights across the centuries. In about 330 B.C., the Greek philosopher Aristotle, using *Oedipus Rex* to define and analyze tragedy as a dramatic form, emphasized, among other points, the necessity of unity of action. A play like *Oedipus Rex*, Aristotle argued in his *Poetics*, succeeds because all elements relate to the central action, or plot. In its turn, the plot must have completeness, with a beginning, middle, and end; unity; and a certain magnitude. These strong underpinnings help to produce *catharsis*, the purgation of the tragic emotions, pity and fear.

Many of Aristotle's insights into drama have had lasting influence. Traditionally, for example, *dramatic action* unfolds in five successive stages: *exposition* of the background events that created the present situation, *rising action* that complicates it, *climax* or turning point that reverses the action, *dénouement,* or *falling action,* that unravels the predicament, and *resolution* that brings new balance and stability.

In order to achieve a sustained, coherent illusion of living action, most playwrights keep stage directions and exposition to a minimum, unless their purpose requires a break with convention. By focusing attention on *dialogue* and *gestures,* they advance dramatic action concretely, fulfilling the distinctive purposes of drama as a recognizable literary form. Other conventions, such as *flashback,* allow them to move the action backward in time believably. The *play-within-a-play* and *subplots,* dramatic conventions used by many playwrights including Shakespeare, are ways of achieving further dramatic complexity. Lighting, sets, makeup and costuming, and the stage itself serve to enhance the illusion necessary to effective drama. Such conventions place plays within a long tradition, and invest them with historical resonance.

Some conventions have proved to be rooted in the values and fashions of the periods in which they were written, especially those having to do with politics, morality, and religion. Modern plays, for instance, written within a different political context, typically do not abide by classical Greek dramatic conventions that tragic heroes must have high social standing, that characters should be listed in order of rank and speak in order of rank, and that violence should be excluded from the stage.

Premodern plays require of audiences an act of faith in regard to historical matters, because audiences are likely to be unfamiliar with the facts of earlier periods and must rely on the playwright's presentation of people, language, dress, and mores. Yet the more a reader seeks to know about the period in which a play was written and about the period in which it is supposed to occur, the deeper the experience. We understand Greek tragedy more deeply when we know that it originated in myths and rituals of authority and power, suffering and sacrifice, and recognition and rebirth; and that, to win the audience's respect and identification, and achieve catharsis, playwrights typically chose a hero of high station and superior virtues marred by a *tragic flaw,* a critical weakness.

We can also heighten our appreciation by knowing that plays were produced in ancient Greece as major community events akin to primitive tribal gatherings or today's concerts and stadium games, with one essential difference. These competitive theatrical spectacles, often witnessed in open-air amphitheaters by hundreds and thousands at a time, presumed to speak for all men and women for all time.

The roots of drama in religious ritual, attended by citizens as a civic duty at the time of such festivals as those of Dionysus, the god of wine, over five centuries before Christ, ensured that plays, tragic or farcical, would be taken as more than entertainment. About fifteen hundred years later, in the Middle Ages, miracle and morality plays infused this tradition with medieval Christian doctrine and practice. Instead of honoring the gods or demigods through dramatic interpretation of ancient myths, medieval playwrights portrayed the life of Christ and the treacherous journeys of ordinary mortals toward salvation.

In the fifteenth and sixteenth centuries, a period generally known as the Renaissance, politics, history, myth, and individual personality collaborated in new and complex ways. Shakespeare's histories and tragedies, for example, written in the late sixteenth century during the reign of the childless Queen Elizabeth when civil tensions were mounting, explore, among other things, the issue of orderly succession of power from a variety of social and psychological perspectives.

By the time of Henrik Ibsen and Anton Chekhov—the late nineteenth century—social roles and behavior had become a chief topic of debate. Ibsen offers a provocative critique of conventional attitudes toward gender in *A Doll's House*, and Chekhov a clever satire of the interrelationship of marriage and property in *A Marriage Proposal*. In the twentieth century, Eugène Ionesco analyzes language and power in *The Lesson*; Tennessee Williams explores the tyranny of a mother's fantasies about the past over herself and her children in *The Glass Menagerie*; in *A Son, Come Home*, Ed Bullins shows a loving mother and son struggling to overcome the physical and cultural distances that have grown between them; and in *'night, Mother*, Marsha Norman reveals the weakening of a young woman's will to live as she faces the apparent meaningless of her existence.

Although the theme and subjects and characters of most modern plays are secular rather than religious, something remains of drama's religious inheritance, particularly for theater audiences. Since religion is concerned with two orders of experience, the worldly and the sacred, many religious rituals seek to transform the worldly into the sacred in the hearts of believers; theatrical illusion works in a similar way. The symbolic act of leaving ordinary life behind, of joining a group and entering a room that turns dark and then brightens to reveal another order of experience, effectively creates the characters and actions before our eyes. The mystery and magic are then sustained for the duration of the action when, as though to return us to the reality of daily life, the lights go on.

The plays we remember and cherish are usually those that significantly expand our awareness of ourselves and other people. In this respect, Walt Whitman's spider metaphor in his poem "A Noiseless Patient Spider" pertains not just to the speaker of the poem, nor to the poet, but to all of us seeking new worlds on "the gossamer thread" of imagination. Although traditions and conventions can serve to enrich a play's meanings and deepen its impact, they can also constrain playwrights and audiences looking for a new kind of drama.

Tennessee Williams was such a playwright, and *The Glass Menagerie* is such a play. First produced in New York in 1945, before the end of World War II, *The Glass Menagerie* seeks to demonstrate the dominance of the irrational in human life by taking a respected idea and rational system, history, and showing its potential to destroy as well as to illuminate. In doing so, Williams not only departs from many long-standing dramatic traditions and popular theatrical conventions, but deliberately blurs generic distinctions among drama, fiction, and poetry. *The Glass Menagerie* is a play with strong narrative and poetic elements. It is also a play about the tyranny of memory in the lives of an abandoned mother, her poet-son and crippled daughter, and the "gentleman caller" whose visit shatters the fragile illusions that held the family together.

Few well-known playwrights, present or past, are quite so explicit about intentions as Williams is in this play. The imagery he uses to describe his cast of characters—for example, the crippled young woman, Laura, ". . . like a piece of her own glass collection, too exquisitely fragile to move from the shelf"—immediately suggests the play's poetic approach. But his poetic purposes are definitively confirmed as early as the stage directions to Scene I, when he announces his subject, theme, and method:

> The scene is memory and is therefore nonrealistic. Memory takes a lot of poetic license. It omits some details; others are exaggerated, according to the emotional value of the articles it touches, for memory is seated predominantly in the heart. The interior is therefore rather dim and poetic.

To magnify further the role of memory in human consciousness and behavior, Williams resorts to a device conscientiously avoided by most playwrights: the narrator of fiction, whose memory tells the tale, whose memory *is* the tale. After the playwright has introduced the setting, a depressed and depressing St. Louis tenement, Tom, the poet-narrator, announces the truth of his illusion, and the liberties he will take to reveal the truth: "To begin with, I turn back time. . . . The play is memory. Being a memory play, it is dimly lighted, it is sentimental, it is not realistic." The scene, characters, and action are memory. The theme of the play is memory, too, in its many contrary forms: memory as an instrument of consolation, hope, and imagination; or of cruelty, despair, and desolation.

The persistence of memory, Tom seems to be saying, is the mind's one certain quality. So long as there is consciousness, memory endures. At the play's conclusion, the end of Scene VII, Tom describes his life after leaving his mother, Amanda, and his sister, Laura. He recalls strange cities where he walked late at night past lighted stores, when suddenly the memory of Laura overwhelmed him: "The window is filled with pieces of colored glass, tiny transparent bottles in delicate colors, like bits of a shattered rainbow. Then all at once my sister touches my shoulder. I turn around and look into her eyes. . . ." He then addresses the Laura of memory: "Oh, Laura, Laura, I tried to leave you behind me, but I am more faithful than I intended to be!" Tom closes the play with an allusion to the candles of the past, and a plea to Laura to blow them out. As though in answer, the Laura of memory does blow them out, effectively obliterating Tom's painful vision of her and the illusion of life he, and we, created with words. Yet for many of us, after a reading or performance, *The Glass Menagerie* shimmers on in afterlife as a memory that just will not let go.

# Oedipus Rex

### List of Characters

OEDIPUS
A PRIEST
CREON
TEIRESIAS
IOCASTÊ
MESSENGER
SHEPHERD OF LAÏOS
SECOND MESSENGER
CHORUS OF THEBAN ELDERS

S C E N E.   *Before the palace of Oedipus, King of Thebes. A central door and two lateral doors open onto a platform which runs the length of the façade. On the platform, right and left, are altars; and three steps lead down into the "orchestra," or chorus-ground. At the beginning of the action these steps are crowded by Suppliants who have brought branches and chaplets of olive leaves and who lie in various attitudes of despair. Oedipus enters.*

---

## PROLOGUE

OEDIPUS:   My children, generations of the living
In the line of Kadmos,° nursed at his ancient hearth,
Why have you strewn yourselves before these altars
In supplication, with your boughs and garlands?
The breath of incense rises from the city
With a sound of prayer and lamentation.
                                    Children,
I would not have you speak through messengers,

---

An English version by Dudley Fitts and Robert Fitzgerald.
Prologue.   2 *Kadmos* mythical founder of Thebes

And therefore I have come myself to hear you—
I, Oedipus, who bear the famous name.
*(To a Priest.)* You, there, since you are eldest
    in the company,                                          10
Speak for them all, tell me what preys upon you,
Whether you come in dread, or crave some blessing:
Tell me, and never doubt that I will help you
In every way I can; I should be heartless
Were I not moved to find you suppliant here.        15
PRIEST:   Great Oedipus, O powerful King of Thebes!
You see how all the ages of our people
Cling to your altar steps: here are boys
Who can barely stand alone, and here are priests
By weight of age, as I am a priest of God,           20
And young men chosen from those yet unmarried;
As for the others, all that multitude,
They wait with olive chaplets in the squares,
At the two shrines of Pallas,° and where Apollo°
Speaks in the glowing embers.
                      Your own eyes            25
Must tell you: Thebes is in her extremity
And cannot lift her head from the surge of death.
A rust consumes the buds and fruits of the earth;
The herds are sick; children die unborn,
And labor is vain. The god of plague and pyre       30
Raids like detestable lightning through the city,
And all the house of Kadmos is laid waste,
All emptied, and all darkened: Death alone
Battens upon the misery of Thebes.

You are not one of the immortal gods, we know;      35
Yet we have come to you to make our prayer
As to the man of all men best in adversity
And wisest in the ways of God. You saved us
From the Sphinx,° that flinty singer, and the tribute

---

²⁴ ***Pallas*** Athena, goddess of wisdom, protectress of Athens   ²⁴ ***Apollo*** god of
light and healing   ³⁹ ***Sphinx*** a monster (body of a lion, wings of a bird, face of a
woman) who asked the riddle, "What goes on four legs in the morning, two at
(continued on p. 486)

We paid to her so long; yet you were never                    40
Better informed than we, nor could we teach you:
It was some god breathed in you to set us free.

Therefore, O mighty King, we turn to you:
Find us our safety, find us a remedy,
Whether by counsel of the gods or the men.                    45
A king of wisdom tested in the past
Can act in a time of troubles, and act well.
Noblest of men, restore
Life to your city! Think how all men call you
Liberator for your triumph long ago;                          50
Ah, when your years of kingship are remembered,
Let them not say *We rose, but later fell*—
Keep the State from going down in the storm!
Once, years ago, with happy augury,
You brought us fortune; be the same again!                    55
No man questions your power to rule the land:
But rule over men, not over a dead city!
Ships are only hulls, citadels are nothing,
When no life moves in the empty passageways.

OEDIPUS:   Poor children! You may be sure I know               60
All that you longed for in your coming here.
I know that you are deathly sick; and yet,
Sick as you are, not one is as sick as I.
Each of you suffers in himself alone
His anguish, not another's; but my spirit                     65
Groans for the city, for myself, for you.

I was not sleeping, you are not waking me.
No, I have been in tears for a long while
And in my restless thought walked many ways.
In all my search, I found one helpful course,                 70
And that I have taken: I have sent Creon,
Son of Menoikeus, brother of the Queen,

---

noon, and three in the evening?" and who killed those who could not answer.
When Oedipus responded correctly that man crawls on all fours in infancy,
walks upright in maturity, and uses a staff in old age, the Sphinx destroyed
herself.

To Delphi, Apollo's place of revelation,
To learn there, if he can,
What act or pledge of mine may save the city.          75
I have counted the days, and now, this very day,
I am troubled, for he has overstayed his time.
What is he doing? He has been gone too long.
Yet whenever he comes back, I should do ill
To scant whatever hint the god may give.               80
PRIEST:   It is a timely promise. At this instant
They tell me Creon is here.
OEDIPUS:                        O Lord Apollo!
May his news be fair as his face is radiant!
PRIEST:   It could not be otherwise: he is crowned with bay,
The chaplet is thick with berries.
OEDIPUS:                          We shall soon know;    85
He is near enough to hear us now.


*Enter Creon.*


                            O Prince:
Brother: son of Menoikeus:
What answer do you bring us from the god?
CREON:   It is favorable. I can tell you, great afflictions
Will turn out well, if they are taken well.            90
OEDIPUS:   What was the oracle? These vague words
Leave me still hanging between hope and fear.
CREON:   Is it your pleasure to hear me with all these
Gathered around us? I am prepared to speak,
But should we not go in?
OEDIPUS:                        Let them all hear it.     95
It is for them I suffer, more than myself.
CREON:   Then I will tell you what I heard at Delphi.

In plain words
The god commands us to expel from the land of Thebes
An old defilement that it seems we shelter.            100
It is a deathly thing, beyond expiation.
We must not let it feed upon us longer.
OEDIPUS:   What defilement? How shall we rid ourselves of it?

CREON:   By exile or death, blood for blood. It was
   Murder that brought the plague-wind on the city.    105
OEDIPUS:   Murder of whom? Surely the god has named him?
CREON:   My lord: long ago Laïos was our king,
   Before you came to govern us.
OEDIPUS:                  I know;
   I learned of him from others; I never saw him.
CREON:   He was murdered; and Apollo commands us now    110
   To take revenge upon whoever killed him.
OEDIPUS:   Upon whom? Where are they? Where shall we find a
   clue
   To solve that crime, after so many years?
CREON:   Here in this land, he said.
                           If we make enquiry,
   We may touch things that otherwise escape us.    115
OEDIPUS:   Tell me: Was Laïos murdered in his house,
   Or in the fields, or in some foreign country?
CREON:   He said he planned to make a pilgrimage.
   He did not come home again.
OEDIPUS:                And was there no one,
   No witness, no companion, to tell what happened?    120
CREON:   They were all killed but one, and he got away
   So frightened that he could remember one thing only.
OEDIPUS:   What was that one thing? One may be the key
   To everything, if we resolve to use it.
CREON:   He said that a band of highwaymen attacked them,   125
   Outnumbered them, and overwhelmed the King.
OEDIPUS:   Strange, that a highwayman should be so daring—
   Unless some faction here bribed him to do it.
CREON:   We thought of that. But after Laïos' death
   New troubles arose and we had no avenger.    130
OEDIPUS:   What troubles could prevent your hunting down the
   killers?
CREON:   The riddling Sphinx's song
   Made us deaf to all mysteries but her own.
OEDIPUS:   Then once more I must bring what is dark to light.
   It is most fitting that Apollo shows,    135
   As you do, this compunction for the dead.
   You shall see how I stand by you, as I should,
   To avenge the city and the city's god,

And not as though it were for some distant friend,
But for my own sake, to be rid of evil.                    *140*
Whoever killed King Laïos might—who knows?—
Decide at any moment to kill me as well.
By avenging the murdered king I protect myself.
Come, then, my children: leave the altar steps,
Lift up your olive boughs!
                            One of you go                    *145*
And summon the people of Kadmos to gather here.
I will do all that I can; you may tell them that.

                                     *(Exit a Page.)*

So, with the help of God,
We shall be saved—or else indeed we are lost.
PRIEST:   Let us rise, children. It was for this we came,                    *150*
And now the King has promised it himself.
Phoibos° has sent us an oracle; may he descend
Himself to save us and drive out the plague.

*Exeunt Oedipus and Creon into the palace by the central door. The
Priest and the Suppliants disperse right and left. After a short
pause the Chorus enters the orchestra.*

# PÁRODOS

CHORUS:   What is God singing in his profound                    *Strophe 1*
   Delphi of gold and shadow?
What oracle for Thebes, the sunwhipped city?
Fear unjoints me, the roots of my heart tremble.
Now I remember, O Healer, your power, and wonder;                    *5*
Will you send doom like a sudden cloud, or weave it
Like nightfall of the past?
Speak, speak to us, issue of holy sound:
Dearest to our expectancy: be tender!

---

[152] **Phoibos** Phoebus Apollo, the sun god

Let me pray to Athenê, the immortal daughter *Antistrophe 1*
   of Zeus,                                            *10*
And to Artemis her sister
Who keeps her famous throne in the market ring,
And to Apollo, bowman at the far butts of heaven—

O gods, descend! Like three streams leap against
The fires of our grief, the fires of darkness;        *15*
Be swift to bring us rest!

As in the old time from the brilliant house
Of air you stepped to save us, come again!

Now our afflictions have no end,        *Strophe 2*
Now all our stricken host lies down        *20*
And no man fights off death with his mind;

The noble plowland bears no grain,
And groaning mothers cannot bear—
See, how our lives like birds take wing,
Like sparks that fly when a fire soars,        *25*
To the shore of the god of evening.

The plague burns on, it is pitiless        *Antistrophe 2*
Though pallid children laden with death
Lie unwept in the stony ways,
And old gray women by every path        *30*
Flock to the strand about the altars

There to strike their breasts and cry
Worship of Phoibos in wailing prayers:
Be kind, God's golden child!

There are no swords in this attack by fire,        *Strophe 3  35*
No shields, but we are ringed with cries.
Send the besieger plunging from our homes
Into the vast sea-room of the Atlantic
Or into the waves that foam eastward of Thrace—
For the day ravages what the night spares—        *40*

Destroy our enemy, lord of thunder!
Let him be riven by lightning from heaven!

Phoibos Apollo, stretch the sun's bowstring,          *Antistrophe 3*
That golden cord, until it sing for us,
Flashing arrows in heaven!
                          Artemis, Huntress,          45
Race with flaring lights upon our mountains!
O scarlet god, O golden-banded brow,
O Theban Bacchos° in a storm of Maenads,°

*Enter Oedipus, center.*

Whirl upon Death, that all the Undying hate!
Come with blinding cressets, come in joy!          50

---

# SCENE I

OEDIPUS:   Is this your prayer? It may be answered. Come,
    Listen to me, act as the crisis demands,
    And you shall have relief from all these evils.

Until now I was a stranger to this tale,
As I had been a stranger to the crime.          5
Could I track down the murderer without a clue?
But now, friends,
As one who became a citizen after the murder,
I make this proclamation to all Thebans:
If any man knows by whose hand Laïos, son of Labdakos,   10
Met his death, I direct that man to tell me everything,
No matter what he fears for having so long withheld it.
Let it stand as promised that no further trouble
Will come to him, but he may leave the land in safety.

---

Párodos.   **⁴⁸ Bacchos** Dionysos, god of wine, thus scarlet-faced   **⁴⁸ Maenads**
Dionysos's female attendants

Moreover: If anyone knows the murderer to be foreign,    15
Let him not keep silent: he shall have his reward from me.
However, if he does conceal it; if any man
Fearing for his friend or for himself disobeys this edict,
Hear what I propose to do:

I solemnly forbid the people of this country,    20
Where power and throne are mine, ever to receive that man
Or speak to him, no matter who he is, or let him
Join in sacrifice, lustration, or in prayer.
I decree that he be driven from every house,

Being, as he is, corruption itself to us: the Delphic    25
Voice of Zeus has pronounced this revelation.
Thus I associate myself with the oracle
And take the side of the murdered king.

As for the criminal, I pray to God—
Whether it be a lurking thief, or one of a number—    30
I pray that that man's life be consumed in evil and
    wretchedness.
And as for me, this curse applies no less
If it should turn out that the culprit is my guest here,
Sharing my hearth.
               You have heard the penalty.
I lay it on you now to attend to this    35
For my sake, for Apollo's, for the sick
Sterile city that heaven has abandoned.
Suppose the oracle had given you no command:
Should this defilement go uncleansed for ever?
You should have found the murderer: your king,    40
A noble king, had been destroyed!
                  Now I,
Having the power that he held before me,
Having his bed, begetting children there
Upon his wife, as he would have, had he lived—
Their son would have been my children's brother,    45
If Laïos had had luck in fatherhood!
(But surely ill luck rushed upon his reign)—
I say I take the son's part, just as though

I were his son, to press the fight for him
And see it won! I'll find the hand that brought          50
Death to Labdakos' and Polydoros' child,
Heir of Kadmos' and Agenor's line.
And as for those who fail me,
May the gods deny them the fruit of the earth,
Fruit of the womb, and may they rot utterly!           55
Let them be wretched as we are wretched, and worse!

For you, for loyal Thebans, and for all
Who find my actions right, I pray the favor
Of justice, and of all the immortal gods.
CHORAGOS:° Since I am under oath, my lord I swear      60
    I did not do the murder, I cannot name
    The murderer. Might not the oracle
    That has ordained the search tell where to find him?
OEDIPUS:   An honest question. But no man in the world
    Can make the gods do more than the gods will.       65
CHORAGOS:   There is one last expedient—
OEDIPUS:                              Tell me what it is.
    Though it seem slight, you must not hold it back.
CHORAGOS:   A lord clairvoyant to the lord Apollo,
    As we all know, is the skilled Teiresias.
    One might learn much about this from him, Oedipus.   70
OEDIPUS:   I am not wasting time:
    Creon spoke of this, and I have sent for him—
    Twice, in fact; it is strange that he is not here.
CHORAGOS:   The other matter—that old report—seems useless.
OEDIPUS:   Tell me. I am interested in all reports.      75
CHORAGOS:   The King was said to have been killed by
        highwaymen.
OEDIPUS:   I know. But we have no witnesses to that.
CHORAGOS:   If the killer can feel a particle of dread,
    Your curse will bring him out of hiding!
OEDIPUS:                              No.
    The man who dared that act will fear no curse.       80

*Enter the blind seer Teiresias, led by a Page.*

———————————

Scene I.   **⁶⁰ Choragos** leader of the chorus

CHORAGOS:   But there is one man who may detect the criminal.
This is Teiresias, this is the holy prophet
In whom, alone of all men, truth was born.
OEDIPUS:   Teiresias: seer: student of mysteries,
Of all that's taught and all that no man tells,                    85
Secrets of Heaven and secrets of the earth:
Blind though you are, you know the city lies
Sick with plague; and from this plague, my lord,
We find that you alone can guard or save us.

Possibly you did not hear the messengers?                         90
Apollo, when we sent to him,
Sent us back word that this great pestilence
Would lift, but only if we established clearly
The identity of those who murdered Laïos.
They must be killed or exiled.
                                          Can you use          95
Birdflight or any art of divination
To purify yourself, and Thebes, and me
From this contagion? We are in your hands.
There is no fairer duty
Than that of helping others in distress.                          100
TEIRESIAS:   How dreadful knowledge of the truth can be
When there's no help in truth! I knew this well,
But did not act on it: else I should not have come.
OEDIPUS:   What is troubling you? Why are your eyes so cold?
TEIRESIAS:   Let me go home. Bear your own fate, and I'll          105
Bear mine. It is better so: trust what I say.
OEDIPUS:   What you say is ungracious and unhelpful
To your native country. Do not refuse to speak.
TEIRESIAS:   When it comes to speech, your own is neither
temperate
Nor opportune. I wish to be more prudent.                         110
OEDIPUS:   In God's name, we all beg you—
TEIRESIAS:                                     You are all ignorant.
No; I will never tell you what I know.
Now it is my misery; then, it would be yours.
OEDIPUS:   What! You do know something, and will not tell us?
You would betray us all and wreck the State?                      115

TEIRESIAS:   I do not intend to torture myself, or you.
  Why persist in asking? You will not persuade me.
OEDIPUS:   What a wicked old man you are! You'd try a stone's
  Patience! Out with it! Have you no feeling at all?
TEIRESIAS.:   You call me unfeeling. If you could only see          120
  The nature of your own feelings . . .
OEDIPUS:                                            Why,
  Who would not feel as I do? Who could endure
  Your arrogance toward the city?
TEIRESIAS:                                  What does it matter!
  Whether I speak or not, it is bound to come.
OEDIPUS:   Then, if "it" is bound to come, you are bound
  to tell me.                                                          125
TEIRESIAS:   No, I will not go on. Rage as you please.
OEDIPUS:   Rage? Why not!
                                  And I'll tell you what I think:
  You planned it, you had it done, you all but
  Killed him with your own hands: if you had eyes,
  I'd say the crime was yours, and yours alone.                      130
TEIRESIAS:   So? I charge you, then,
  Abide by the proclamation you have made:
  From this day forth
  Never speak again to these men or to me;
  You yourself are the pollution of this country.                   135
OEDIPUS:   You dare say that! Can you possibly think you have
  Some way of going free, after such insolence?
TEIRESIAS:   I have gone free. It is the truth sustains me.
OEDIPUS:   Who taught you shamelessness? It was not your
  craft.
TEIRESIAS:   You did. You made me speak. I did not want to.    140
OEDIPUS:   Speak what? Let me hear it again more clearly.
TEIRESIAS:   Was it not clear before? Are you tempting me?
OEDIPUS:   I did not understand it. Say it again.
TEIRESIAS:   I say that you are the murderer whom you seek.
OEDIPUS:   Now twice you have spat out infamy. You'll pay
  for it!                                                             145
TEIRESIAS:   Would you care for more? Do you wish to be really
  angry?
OEDIPUS:   Say what you will. Whatever you say is worthless.

TEIRESIAS:   I say you live in hideous shame with those
   Most dear to you. You cannot see the evil.
OEDIPUS:   It seems you can go on mounting like this for ever. *150*
TEIRESIAS:   I can, if there is power in truth.
OEDIPUS:                            There is:
   But not for you, not for you,
   You sightless, witless, senseless, mad old man!
TEIRESIAS:   You are the madman. There is no one here
   Who will not curse you soon, as you curse me. *155*
OEDIPUS:   You child of endless night! You cannot hurt me
   Or any other man who sees the sun.
TEIRESIAS:   True: it is not from me your fate will come.
   That lies within Apollo's competence,
   As it is his concern.
OEDIPUS:           Tell me: *160*
   Are you speaking for Creon, or for yourself?
TEIRESIAS:   Creon is no threat. You weave your own doom.
OEDIPUS:   Wealth, power, craft of statesmanship!
   Kingly position, everywhere admired!
   What savage envy is stored up against these, *165*
   If Creon, whom I trusted, Creon my friend,
   For this great office which the city once
   Put in my hands unsought—if for this power
   Creon desires in secret to destroy me!

   He has brought this decrepit fortune-teller, this *170*
   Collector of dirty pennies, this prophet fraud—
   Why, he is no more clairvoyant than I am!
                     Tell us:
   Has your mystic mummery ever approached the truth?
   When that hellcat the Sphinx was performing here,
   What help were you to these people? *175*
   Her magic was not for the first man who came along:
   It demanded a real exorcist. Your birds—
   What good were they? or the gods, for the matter of that?
   But I came by,
   Oedipus, the simple man, who knows nothing— *180*
   I thought it out for myself, no birds helped me!
   And this is the man you think you can destroy,
   That you may be close to Creon when he's king!
   Well, you and your friend Creon, it seems to me,

Will suffer most. If you were not an old man,                    185
You would have paid already for your plot.
CHORAGOS:   We cannot see that his words or yours
Have been spoken except in anger, Oedipus,
And of anger we have no need. How can God's will
Be accomplished best? That is what most concerns us.    190
TEIRESIAS:   You are a king. But where argument's concerned
I am your man, as much a king as you.
I am not your servant, but Apollo's.
I have no need of Creon to speak for me.

Listen to me. You mock my blindness, do you?           195
But I say that you, with both your eyes, are blind:
You cannot see the wretchedness of your life,
Nor in whose house you live, no, nor with whom.
Who are your father and mother? Can you tell me?
You do not even know the blind wrongs                   200
That you have done them, on earth and in the world below.
But the double lash of your parents' curse will whip you
Out of this land some day, with only night
Upon your precious eyes.
Your cries then—where will they not be heard?          205
What fastness of Kithairon° will not echo them?
And that bridal-descant of yours—you'll know it then,
The song they sang when you came here to Thebes
And found your misguided berthing.
All this, and more, that you cannot guess at now,      210
Will bring you to yourself among your children.
Be angry, then. Curse Creon. Curse my words.
I tell you, no man that walks upon the earth
Shall be rooted out more horribly than you.
OEDIPUS:   Am I to bear this from him?—Damnation         215
Take you! Out of this place! Out of my sight!
TEIRESIAS:   I would not have come at all if you had not asked
me.
OEDIPUS:   Could I have told that you'd talk nonsense, that
You'd come here to make a fool of yourself, and of me?

---

Scene I.   ²⁰⁶ *fastness of Kithairon* stronghold in a mountain near Thebes

TEIRESIAS:   A fool? Your parents thought me sane enough.    *220*
OEDIPUS:   My parents again!—Wait: who were my parents?
TEIRESIAS:   This day will give you a father, and break your
heart.
OEDIPUS:   Your infantile riddles! Your damned abracadabra!
TEIRESIAS:   You were a great man once at solving riddles.
OEDIPUS:   Mock me with that if you like; you will find
it true.    *225*
TEIRESIAS:   It was true enough. It brought about your ruin.
OEDIPUS:   But if it saved this town?
TEIRESIAS *(to the Page)*:              Boy, give me your hand.
OEDIPUS:   Yes, boy; lead him away.
                          —While you are here
We can do nothing. Go; leave us in peace.
TEIRESIAS:   I will go when I have said what I have to say.    *230*
How can you hurt me? And I tell you again:
The man you have been looking for all this time,
The damned man, the murderer of Laïos,
That man is in Thebes. To your mind he is foreignborn,
But it will soon be shown that he is a Theban,    *235*
A revelation that will fail to please.
                          A blind man,
Who has his eyes now; a penniless man, who is rich now;
And he will go tapping the strange earth with his staff;
To the children with whom he lives now he will be
Brother and father—the very same; to her    *240*
Who bore him, son and husband—the very same
Who came to his father's bed, wet with his father's blood.

Enough. Go think that over.
If later you find error in what I have said.
You may say that I have no skill in prophecy.    *245*

*Exit Teiresias, led by his Page. Oedipus goes into the palace.*

## ODE I

CHORUS:   The Delphic stone of prophecies              *Strophe 1*
   Remembers ancient regicide

And a still bloody hand.
That killer's hour of flight has come.
He must be stronger than riderless                                         5
Coursers of untiring wind,
For the son of Zeus° armed with his father's thunder
Leaps in lightning after him;
And the Furies° follow him, the sad Furies.
Holy Parnossos' peak of snow                        *Antistrophe 1*    10
Flashes and blinds that secret man,
That all shall hunt him down:
Though he may roam the forest shade
Like a bull gone wild from pasture
To rage through glooms of stone.                                          15
Doom comes down on him; flight will not avail him;
For the world's heart calls him desolate,
And the immortal Furies follow, for ever follow.

But now a wilder thing is heard                         *Strophe 2*
From the old man skilled at hearing Fate in the wingbeat of
    a bird.                                                              20
Bewildered as a blown bird, my soul hovers and cannot find
Foothold in this debate, or any reason or rest of mind.
But no man ever brought—none can bring
Proof of strife between Thebes' royal house,
Labdakos' line,° and the son of Polybos;°                                25
And never until now has any man brought word
Of Laïos' dark death staining Oedipus the King.

Divine Zeus and Apollo hold                         *Antistrophe 2*
Perfect intelligence alone of all tales ever told;
And well though this diviner works, he works in his
    own night;                                                          30
No man can judge that rough unknown or trust in second
    sight,
For wisdom changes hands among the wise.
Shall I believe my great lord criminal
At a raging word that a blind old man let fall?

---

Ode I.   ⁷ *son of Zeus* Apollo   ⁹ *Furies* avenging deities   ²⁵ *Labdakos' line* family
of Laïos   ²⁵ *son of Polybos* Oedipus (so the Chorus believes)

I saw him, when the carrion woman faced him of old,   35
Prove his heroic mind! These evil words are lies.

---

## SCENE II

CREON:   Men of Thebes:
I am told that heavy accusations
Have been brought against me by King Oedipus.
I am not the kind of man to bear this tamely.

If in these present difficulties   5
He holds me accountable for any harm to him
Through anything I have said or done—why, then,
I do not value life in this dishonor.
It is not as though this rumor touched upon
Some private indiscretion. The matter is grave.   10
The fact is that I am being called disloyal
To the State, to my fellow citizens, to my friends.
CHORAGOS:   He may have spoken in anger, not from his mind.
CREON:   But did you not hear him say I was the one
Who seduced the old prophet into lying?   15
CHORAGOS:   The thing was said; I do not know how seriously.
CREON:   But you were watching him! Were his eyes steady?
Did he look like a man in his right mind?
CHORAGOS:                                I do not know.
I cannot judge the behavior of great men.
But here is the King himself.

*Enter Oedipus.*

OEDIPUS:                          So you dared come back.   20
Why? How brazen of you to come to my house,
You murderer!
            Do you think I do not know
That you plotted to kill me, plotted to steal my throne?
Tell me, in God's name: am I coward, a fool,
That you should dream you could accomplish this?   25
A fool who could not see your slippery game?
A coward, not to fight back when I saw it?

You are the fool, Creon, are you not? hoping
Without support or friends to get a throne?
Thrones may be won or bought: you could do neither.    30
CREON:   Now listen to me. You have talked; let me talk, too.
You cannot judge unless you know the facts.
OEDIPUS:   You speak well: there is one fact; but I find it hard
To learn from the deadliest enemy I have.
CREON:   That above all I must dispute with you.    35
OEDIPUS:   That above all I will not hear you deny.
CREON:   If you think there is anything good in being stubborn
Against all reason, then I say you are wrong.
OEDIPUS:   If you think a man can sin against his own kind
And not be punished for it, I say you are mad.    40
CREON:   I agree. But tell me: what have I done to you?
OEDIPUS:   You advised me to send for that wizard, did you not?
CREON:   I did. I should do it again.
OEDIPUS:                            Very well. Now tell me:
How long has it been since Laïos—
CREON:                            What of Laïos?
OEDIPUS:   Since he vanished in that onset by the road?    45
CREON:   It was long ago, a long time.
OEDIPUS:                            And this prophet,
Was he practicing here then?
CREON:                            He was; and with honor, as now.
   OEDIPUS:   Did he speak of me at that time?
CREON:                            He never did;
At least, not when I was present.
OEDIPUS:                            But . . . the enquiry?
I suppose you held one?
CREON:                            We did, but we learned nothing.    50
OEDIPUS:   Why did the prophet not speak against me then?
CREON:   I do not know; and I am the kind of man
Who holds his tongue when he has no facts to go on.
OEDIPUS:   There's one fact that you know, and you could tell it.
CREON:   What fact is that? If I know it, you shall have it.    55
OEDIPUS:   If he were not involved with you, he could not say
That it was I who murdered Laïos.
CREON:   If he says that, you are the one that knows it!—
But now it is my turn to question you.
OEDIPUS:   Put your questions. I am no murderer.    60

CREON:   First, then: You married my sister?
OEDIPUS:                                    I married your sister.
CREON:   And you rule the kingdom equally with her?
OEDIPUS:   Everything that she wants she has from me.
CREON:   And I am the third, equal to both of you?
OEDIPUS:   That is why I call you a bad friend.                65
CREON:   No. Reason it out, as I have done.

   Think of this first. Would any sane man prefer
Power, with all a king's anxieties,
To that same power and the grace of sleep?
Certainly not I.                                              70
I have never longed for the king's power—only his rights.
Would any wise man differ from me in this?
As matters stand, I have my way in everything
With your consent, and no responsibilities.
If I were king, I should be a slave to policy.               75
How could I desire a scepter more
Than what is now mine—untroubled influence?
No, I have not gone mad; I need no honors,
Except those with the perquisites I have now.
I am welcome everywhere; every man salutes me,              80
And those who want your favor seek my ear,
Since I know how to manage what they ask.
Should I exchange this ease for that anxiety?
Besides, no sober mind is treasonable.
I hate anarchy                                               85
And never would deal with any man who likes it.

   Test what I have said. Go to the priestess
At Delphi, ask if I quoted her correctly.
And as for this other thing: if I am found
Guilty of treason with Teiresias,                           90
Then sentence me to death! You have my word
It is a sentence I should cast my vote for—
But not without evidence!
                 You do wrong
When you take good men for bad, bad men for good.
A true friend thrown aside—why, life itself                 95
Is not more precious!
              In time you will know this well:

For time, and time alone, will show just the man,
Though scoundrels are discovered in a day.
CHORAGOS:   This is well said, and a prudent man would ponder
    it.
Judgments too quickly formed are dangerous.                    *100*
OEDIPUS:   But is he not quick in his duplicity?
    And shall I not be quick to parry him?
    Would you have me stand still, hold my peace, and let
    This man win everything, through my inaction?
CREON:   And you want—what is it, then? To banish me?          *105*
OEDIPUS:   No, not exile. It is your death I want,
    So that all the world may see what treason means.
CREON:   You will persist then? You will not believe me?
OEDIPUS:   How can I believe you?
CREON:                               Then you are a fool.
OEDIPUS:   To save myself?
CREON:                               In justice, think of me.    *110*
OEDIPUS:   You are evil incarnate.
CREON:                               But suppose that you are wrong?
OEDIPUS:   Still I must rule.
CREON:                               But not if you rule badly.
OEDIPUS:   O city, city!
CREON:                       It is my city, too!
CHORAGOS:   Now, my lords, be still. I see the Queen,
    Iocastê, coming from her palace chambers;                   *115*
    And it is time she came, for the sake of you both.
    This dreadful quarrel can be resolved through her.


*Enter Iocastê.*


IOCASTÊ:   Poor foolish men, what wicked din is this?
    With Thebes sick to death, is it not shameful
    That you should rake some private quarrel up?               *120*
    (*To Oedipus.*) Come into the house.
                               —And you, Creon, go now:
    Let us have no more of this tumult over nothing.
CREON:   Nothing? No, sister: what your husband plans for me
    Is one of two great evils: exile or death.
OEDIPUS:   He is right.

          Why, woman, I have caught him squarely    125
Plotting against my life.

CREON:                     No! Let me die
  Accurst if ever I have wished you harm!

IOCASTÉ:   Ah, believe it, Oedipus!
  In the name of the gods, respect this oath of his
  For my sake, for the sake of these people here!        130

CHORAGOS:   Open your mind to her, my lord. Be ruled    *Strophe 1*
  by her, I beg you!

OEDIPUS:   What would you have me do?

CHORAGOS:   Respect Creon's word. He has never spoken like a
  fool,
  And now he has sworn an oath.

OEDIPUS:                  You know what you ask?

CHORAGOS:                      I do.

OEDIPUS:                  Speak on, then.

CHORAGOS:   A friend so sworn should not be baited so,       135
  In blind malice, and without final proof.

OEDIPUS:   You are aware, I hope, that what you say
  Means death for me, or exile at the least.

CHORAGOS:   No, I swear by Helios,° first in Heaven!     *Strophe 2*
  May I die friendless and accurst,                140
  The worst of deaths, if ever I meant that!
     It is the withering fields
        That hurt my sick heart:
    Must we bear all these ills,
       And now your bad blood as well?         145

OEDIPUS:   Then let him go. And let me die, if I must,
  Or be driven by him in shame from the land of Thebes.
  It is your unhappiness, and not his talk,
  That touches me.
              As for him—
  Wherever he is, I will hate him as long as I live.      150

CREON:   Ugly in yielding, as you were ugly in rage!
  Natures like yours chiefly torment themselves.

---

Scene II.   ¹³⁹ *Helios* sun god

OEDIPUS:   Can you not go? Can you not leave me?
CREON:                                                I can.
   You do not know me; but the city knows me,
   And in its eyes I am just, if not in yours. (*Exit Creon.*)        155

CHORAGOS:   Lady Iocastê, did you not ask the King to go to his
       chambers?                                            *Antistrophe 1*
IOCASTÊ:   First tell me what has happened.
CHORAGOS:   There was suspicion without evidence; yet it
   rankled
   As even false charges will.
IOCASTÊ:                         On both sides?
CHORAGOS:                                    On both.
IOCASTÊ:                                    But what was said?
CHORAGOS:   Oh let it rest, let it be done with!                 160
   Have we not suffered enough?
OEDIPUS:   You see to what your decency has brought you:
   You have made difficulties where my heart saw none.

CHORAGOS:   Oedipus, it is not once only I have          *Antistrophe 2*
       told you—
   You must know I should count myself unwise              165
   To the point of madness, should I now forsake you—
       You, under whose hand,
           In the storm of another time,
       Our dear land sailed out free.
           But now stand fast at the helm!                 170
IOCASTÊ:   In God's name, Oedipus, inform your wife as well:
   Why are you so set in this hard anger?
OEDIPUS:   I will tell you, for none of these men deserves
   My confidence as you do. It is Creon's work,
   His treachery, his plotting against me.                 175
IOCASTÊ:   Go on, if you can make this clear to me.
OEDIPUS:   He charges me with the murder of Laïos.
IOCASTÊ:   Has he some knowledge? Or does he speak from
       hearsay?
OEDIPUS:   He would not commit himself to such a charge,
   But he has brought in that damnable soothsayer          180
   To tell his story.
IOCASTÊ:                    Set your mind at rest.

If it is a question of soothsayers, I tell you
That you will find no man whose craft gives knowledge
Of the unknowable.
                              Here is my proof.

An oracle was reported to Laïos once                         185
(I will not say from Phoibos himself, but from
His appointed ministers, at any rate)
That his doom would be death at the hands of his own
    son—
His son, born of his flesh and of mine!

Now, you remember the story: Laïos was killed              190
By marauding strangers where three highways meet;
But his child had not been three days in this world
Before the King had pierced the baby's ankles
And left him to die on a lonely mountainside.

Thus, Apollo never caused that child                        195
To kill his father, and it was not Laïos' fate
To die at the hands of his son, as he had feared.
This is what prophets and prophecies are worth!
Have no dread of them.
                              It is God himself
Who can show us what he wills, in his own way.             200
OEDIPUS:   How strange a shadowy memory crossed my mind,
    Just now while you were speaking; it chilled my heart.
IOCASTÊ:   What do you mean? What memory do you speak of?
OEDIPUS:   If I understand you, Laïos was killed
    At a place where three roads meet.
IOCASTÊ:                              So it was said;        205
    We have no later story.
OEDIPUS:                    Where did it happen?
IOCASTÊ:   Phokis, it is called: at a place where the Theban Way
    Divides into the roads towards Delphi and Daulia.
OEDIPUS:   When?
IOCASTÊ:           We had the news not long before you came
    And proved the right to your succession here.          210
OEDIPUS:   Ah, what net has God been weaving for me?

IOCASTÊ:   Oedipus! Why does this trouble you?

OEDIPUS:                                    Do not ask me yet.
First, tell me how Laïos looked, and tell me
How old he was.

IOCASTÊ:                 He was tall, his hair just touched
With white; his form was not unlike your own.          215

OEDIPUS:   I think that I myself may be accurst
By my own ignorant edict.

IOCASTÊ:                           You speak strangely.
It makes me tremble to look at you, my King.

OEDIPUS:   I am not sure that the blind man cannot see.
But I should know better if you were to tell me—       220

IOCASTÊ:   Anything—though I dread to hear you ask it.

OEDIPUS:   Was the King lightly escorted, or did he ride
With a large company, as a ruler should?

IOCASTÊ:   There were five men with him in all: one was a
herald;
And a single chariot, which he was driving.            225

OEDIPUS:   Alas, that makes it plain enough!
                                        But who—
Who told you how it happened?

IOCASTÊ:                              A household servant,
The only one to escape.

OEDIPUS:                   And is he still
A servant of ours?

IOCASTÊ:              No; for when he came back at last
And found you enthroned in the place of the dead
   king,                                               230
He came to me, touched my hand with his, and begged
That I would send him away to the frontier district
Where only the shepherds go—
As far away from the city as I could send him.
I granted his prayer; for although the man was a slave,  235
He had earned more than this favor at my hands.

OEDIPUS:   Can he be called back quickly?

IOCASTÊ:                                    Easily.
But why?

OEDIPUS:     I have taken too much upon myself
Without enquiry; therefore I wish to consult him.

IOCASTÊ:   Then he shall come.

                                 But am I not one also         240
   To whom you might confide these fears of yours!
OEDIPUS:   That is your right; it will not be denied you,
   Now least of all; for I have reached a pitch
   Of wild foreboding. Is there anyone
   To whom I should sooner speak?                  245
   Polybos of Corinth is my father.
   My mother is a Dorian: Meropê.
   I grew up chief among the men of Corinth
   Until a strange thing happened—
   Not worth my passion, it may be, but strange.     250

   At a feast, a drunken man maundering in his cups
   Cries out that I am not my father's son!

   I contained myself that night, though I felt anger
   And a sinking heart. The next day I visited
   My father and mother, and questioned them.
      They stormed,                      255
   Calling it all the slanderous rant of a fool;
   And this relieved me. Yet the suspicion
   Remained always aching in my mind;
   I knew there was talk; I could not rest;
   And finally, saying nothing to my parents,     260
   I went to the shrine at Delphi.
   The god dismissed my question without reply;
   He spoke of other things.
                     Some were clear,
   Full of wretchedness, dreadful, unbearable:
   As, that I should lie with my own mother, breed     265
   Children from whom all men would turn their eyes;
   And that I should be my father's murderer.

   I heard all this, and fled. And from that day
   Corinth to me was only in the stars
   Descending in that quarter of the sky,     270
   As I wandered farther and farther on my way
   To a land where I should never see the evil
   Sung by the oracle. And I came to this country

Where, so you say, King Laïos was killed.

I will tell you all that happened there, my lady.          *275*

There were three highways
Coming together at a place I passed;
And there a herald came towards me, and a chariot
Drawn by horses, with a man such as you describe
Seated in it. The groom leading the horses          *280*
Forced me off the road at his lord's command;
But as this charioteer lurched over towards me
I struck him in my rage. The old man saw me
And brought his double goad down upon my head
As I came abreast.
                              He was paid back, and more!          *285*
Swinging my club in this right hand I knocked him
Out of his car, and he rolled on the ground.
                                                    I killed him.

I killed them all.
Now if that stranger and Laïos were—kin,
Where is a man more miserable than I?          *290*
More hated by the gods? Citizen and alien alike
Must never shelter me or speak to me—
I must be shunned by all.
                              And I myself
Pronounced this malediction upon myself!

Think of it: I have touched you with these hands,          *295*
These hands that killed your husband. What defilement!

Am I all evil, then? It must be so,
Since I must flee from Thebes, yet never again
See my own countrymen, my own country,
For fear of joining my mother in marriage          *300*
And killing Polybos, my father.
                              Ah,
If I was created so, born to this fate.
Who could deny the savagery of God?

O holy majesty of heavenly powers!
May I never see that day! Never!                                    305
Rather let me vanish from the race of men
Than know the abomination destined me!
CHORAGOS:   We too, my lord, have felt dismay at this.
    But there is hope: you have yet to hear the shepherd.
OEDIPUS:   Indeed, I fear no other hope is left me.              310
IOCASTÊ:   What do you hope from him when he comes?
OEDIPUS:                                                  This much:
    If his account of the murder tallies with yours,
    Then I am cleared.
IOCASTÊ:                    What was it that I said
    Of such importance?
OEDIPUS:                    Why, "marauders," you said,
    Killed the King, according to this man's story.           315
    If he maintains that still, if there were several,
    Clearly the guilt is not mine: I was alone.
    But if he says one man, singlehanded, did it,
    Then the evidence all points to me.
IOCASTÊ:   You may be sure that he said there were
        several;                                              320
    And can he call back that story now? He cannot.
    The whole city heard it as plainly as I.
    But suppose he alters some detail of it:
    He cannot ever show that Laïos' death
    Fulfilled the oracle: for Apollo said                     325
    My child was doomed to kill him; and my child—
    Poor baby!—it was my child that died first.

    No. From now on, where oracles are concerned,
    I would not waste a second thought on any.
OEDIPUS:   You may be right.
                              But come: let someone go         330
    For the shepherd at once. This matter must be settled.
IOCASTÊ:   I will send for him.
    I would not wish to cross you in anything.
    And surely not in this.—Let us go in.

                                *Exeunt into the palace.*

# ODE II

CHORUS:   Let me be reverent in the ways of right,          *Strophe 1*
    Lowly the paths I journey on;
    Let all my words and actions keep
    The laws of the pure universe
    From highest Heaven handed down.                              5
    For Heaven is their bright nurse,
    Those generations of the realms of light;
    Ah, never of mortal kind were they begot,
    Nor are they slaves of memory, lost in sleep:
    Their Father is greater than Time, and ages not.            10

    The tyrant is a child of Pride                          *Antistrophe 1*
    Who drinks from his great sickening cup
    Recklessness and vanity,
    Until from his high crest headlong
    He plummets to the dust of hope.                            15
    That strong man is not strong.
    But let no fair ambition be denied;
    May God protect the wrestler for the State
    In government, in comely policy,
    Who will fear God, and on His ordinance wait.               20

    Haughtiness and the high hand of disdain                  *Strophe 2*
    Tempt and outrage God's holy law;
    And any mortal who dares hold
    No immortal Power in awe
    Will be caught up in a net of pain:                         25
    The price for which his levity is sold.
    Let each man take due earnings, then,
    And keep his hands from holy things,
    And from blasphemy stand apart—
    Else the crackling blast of heaven                          30
    Blows on his head, and on his desperate heart;
    Though fools will honor impious men,
    In their cities no tragic poet sings.

Shall we lose faith in Delphi's obscurities,          *Antistrophe 2*
We who have heard the world's core                                    35
Discredited, and the sacred wood
Of Zeus at Elis praised no more?
The deeds and the strange prophecies
Must make a pattern yet to be understood.
Zeus, if indeed you are lord of all,                                  40
Throned in light over night and day,
Mirror this in your endless mind:
Our masters call the oracle
Words on the wind, and the Delphic vision blind!
Their hearts no longer know Apollo,                                   45
And reverence for the gods has died away.

## SCENE III

*Enter Iocastê*

IOCASTÊ:   Princes of Thebes, it has occurred to me
To visit the altars of the gods, bearing
These branches as a suppliant, and this incense.
Our King is not himself: his noble soul
Is overwrought with fantasies of dread,                               5
Else he would consider
The new prophecies in the light of the old.
He will listen to any voice that speaks disaster,
And my advice goes for nothing.

*She approaches the altar, right.*

To you, then, Apollo,
Lycean lord, since you are nearest, I turn in prayer.               10
Receive these offerings, and grant us deliverance
From defilement. Our hearts are heavy with fear
When we see our leader distracted, as helpless sailors
Are terrified by the confusion of their helmsman.

*Enter Messenger.*

MESSENGER:   Friends, no doubt you can direct me:                    15
　　Where shall I find the house of Oedipus,
　　Or, better still, where is the King himself?
CHORAGOS:   It is this very place, stranger; he is inside.
　　This is his wife and mother of his children.
MESSENGER:   I wish her happiness in a happy house,                 20
　　Blest in all the fulfillment of her marriage.
IOCASTÊ:   I wish as much for you: your courtesy
　　Deserves a like good fortune. But now, tell me:
　　Why have you come? What have you to say to us?
MESSENGER:   Good news, my lady, for your house and your
　　　　husband.                                                    25
IOCASTÊ:   What news? Who sent you here?
MESSENGER:                                    I am from Corinth.
　　The news I bring ought to mean joy for you,
　　Though it may be you will find some grief in it.
IOCASTÊ:   What is it? How can it touch us in both ways?
MESSENGER:   The people of Corinth, they say,                       30
　　Intend to call Oedipus to be their king.
IOCASTÊ:   But old Polybos—is he not reigning still?
MESSENGER:   No. Death holds him in his sepulchre.
IOCASTÊ:   What are you saying? Polybos is dead?
MESSENGER:   If I am not telling the truth, may I die myself.       35
IOCASTÊ *(to a Maidservant)*:   Go in, go quickly; tell this to your
　　master.

　　O riddlers of God's will, where are you now!
　　This was the man whom Oedipus, long ago,
　　Feared so, fled so, in dread of destroying him—
　　But it was another fate by which he died.                      40

*Enter Oedipus, center.*

OEDIPUS:   Dearest Iocastê, why have you sent for me?
IOCASTÊ:   Listen to what this man says, and then tell me
　　What has become of the solemn prophecies.
OEDIPUS:   Who is this man? What is his news for me?
IOCASTÊ:   He has come from Corinth to announce your father's
　　death!                                                         45
OEDIPUS:   Is it true, stranger? Tell me in your own words.

MESSENGER:   I cannot say it more clearly: the King is dead.
OEDIPUS:   Was it by treason? Or by an attack of illness?
MESSENGER:   A little thing brings old men to their rest.
OEDIPUS:   It was sickness, then?
MESSENGER:                              Yes, and his many years.          50
OEDIPUS:   Ah!
    Why should a man respect the Pythian hearth,° or
    Give heed to the birds that jangle above his head?
    They prophesied that I should kill Polybos,
    Kill my own father; but he is dead and buried,          55
    And I am here—I never touched him, never,
    Unless he died in grief for my departure,
    And thus, in a sense, through me. No. Polybos
    Has packed the oracles off with him underground.
    They are empty words.
IOCASTÊ:                              Had I not told you so?          60
OEDIPUS:   You had; it was my faint heart that betrayed me.
IOCASTÊ:   From now on never think of those things again.
OEDIPUS:   And yet—must I not fear my mother's bed?
IOCASTÊ:   Why should anyone in this world be afraid,
    Since Fate rules us and nothing can be foreseen?          65
    A man should live only for the present day.
    Have no more fear of sleeping with your mother:
    How many men, in dreams, have lain with their mothers!
    No reasonable man is troubled by such things.
OEDIPUS:   That is true; only—          70
    If only my mother were not still alive!
    But she is alive. I cannot help my dread.
IOCASTÊ:   Yet this news of your father's death is wonderful.
OEDIPUS:   Wonderful. But I fear the living woman.
MESSENGER:   Tell me, who is this woman that you fear?          75
OEDIPUS:   It is Meropê, man; the wife of King Polybos.
MESSENGER:   Meropê? Why should you be afraid of her?
OEDIPUS:   An oracle of the gods, a dreadful saying.

---

Scene III   [52] **Pythian heart** Delphi (also called Pytho because a great snake had lived there), where Apollo spoke through a priestess

MESSENGER:  Can you tell me about it or are you sworn to
  silence?
OEDIPUS:  I can tell you, and I will.                                    80
  Apollo said through his prophet that I was the man
  Who should marry his own mother, shed his father's blood
  With his own hands. And so, for all these years
  I have kept clear of Corinth, and no harm has come—
  Though it would have been sweet to see my parents
    again.                                                               85
MESSENGER:  And is this the fear that drove you out of Corinth?
OEDIPUS:  Would you have me kill my father?
MESSENGER:                                    As for that
  You must be reassured by the news I gave you.
OEDIPUS:  If you could reassure me, I would reward you.
MESSENGER:  I had that in mind, I will confess: I thought       90
  I could count on you when you returned to Corinth.
OEDIPUS:  No: I will never go near my parents again.
MESSENGER:  Ah, son, you still do not know what you are
    doing—
OEDIPUS:  What do you mean? In the name of God tell me!
MESSENGER:  —If these are your reasons for not going home.     95
OEDIPUS:  I tell you, I fear the oracle may come true.
MESSENGER:  And guilt may come upon you through your
    parents?
OEDIPUS:  That is the dread that is always in my heart.
MESSENGER:  Can you not see that all your fears are groundless?
OEDIPUS:  How can you say that? They are my parents,
    surely?                                                             100
MESSENGER:  Polybos was not your father.
OEDIPUS:                                    Not my father?
MESSENGER:  No more your father than the man speaking to
    you.
OEDIPUS:  But you are nothing to me!
MESSENGER:                            Neither was he.
OEDIPUS:  Then why did he call me son?
MESSENGER:                              I will tell you:
  Long ago he had you from my hands, as a gift.                105
OEDIPUS:  Then how could he love me so, if I was not his?
MESSENGER:  He had no children, and his heart turned to you.

OEDIPUS:   What of you? Did you buy me? Did you find me by
    chance?
MESSENGER:   I came upon you in the crooked pass of Kithairon.
OEDIPUS:   And what were you doing there?
MESSENGER:                                  Tending my flocks.   *110*
OEDIPUS:   A wandering shepherd?
MESSENGER:                                  But your savior, son, that day.
OEDIPUS:   From what did you save me?
MESSENGER:                                  Your ankles should tell you that.
OEDIPUS:   Ah, stranger, why do you speak of that childhood
    pain?
MESSENGER:   I cut the bonds that tied your ankles together.
OEDIPUS:   I have had the mark as long as I can remember.   *115*
MESSENGER:   That was why you were given the name you
    bear.°
OEDIPUS:   God! Was it my father or my mother who did it?
    Tell me!
MESSENGER:   I do not know. The man who gave you to me
    Can tell you better than I.                                  *120*
OEDIPUS:   It was not you that found me, but another?
MESSENGER:   It was another shepherd gave you to me.
OEDIPUS:   Who was he? Can you tell me who he was?
MESSENGER:   I think he was said to be one of Laïos' people.
OEDIPUS:   You mean the Laïos who was king here
    years ago?                                                   *125*
MESSENGER:   Yes; King Laïos; and the man was one of his
    herdsmen.
OEDIPUS:   Is he still alive? Can I see him?
MESSENGER:                                  These men here
    Know best about such things.

OEDIPUS:                                  Does anyone here
    Know this shepherd that he is talking about?
    Have you seen him in the fields, or in the town?             *130*
    If you have, tell me. It is time things were made plain.

---

¹¹⁶ **name you bear** "Oedipus" means "swollen-foot."

CHORAGOS:  I think the man he means is that same shepherd
    You have already asked to see. Iocastê perhaps
    Could tell you something.
OEDIPUS:                   Do you know anything
    About him, Lady? Is he the man we have summoned?    *135*
    Is that the man this shepherd means?
IOCASTÊ:                 Why think of him?
    Forget this herdsman. Forget it all.
    This talk is a waste of time.
OEDIPUS:              How can you say that,
    When the clues to my true birth are in my hands?
IOCASTÊ:  For God's love, let us have no more questioning!    *140*
    Is your life nothing to you?
    My own is pain enough for me to bear.
OEDIPUS:  You need not worry. Suppose my mother a slave,
    And born of slaves: no baseness can touch you.
IOCASTÊ:  Listen to me, I beg you: do not do this thing!    *145*
OEDIPUS:  I will not listen; the truth must be made known.
IOCASTÊ:  Everything that I say is for your own good!
OEDIPUS:                  My own good
    Snaps my patience, then: I want none of it.
IOCASTÊ:  You are fatally wrong! May you never learn who you
    are!
OEDIPUS:  Go, one of you, and bring the shepherd here.    *150*
    Let us leave this woman to brag of her royal name.
IOCASTÊ:  Ah, miserable!
    That is the only word I have for you now.
    That is the only word I can ever have.

                                  *Exit into the palace.*

CHORAGOS:  Why has she left us, Oedipus? Why has
    she gone    *155*
    In such a passion of sorrow? I fear this silence:
    Something dreadful may come of it.
OEDIPUS:                 Let it come!
    However base my birth, I must know about it.
    The Queen, like a woman, is perhaps ashamed
    To think of my low origin. But I    *160*

Am a child of luck; I cannot be dishonored.
Luck is my mother; the passing months, my brothers,
Have seen me rich and poor. If this is so,
How could I wish that I were someone else?
How could I not be glad to know my birth?                    *165*

## ODE III

CHORUS:   If ever the coming time were known               *Strophe*
    To my heart's pondering,
    Kithairon, now by Heaven I see the torches
    At the festival of the next full moon,
    And see the dance, and hear the choir sing         *5*
    A grace to your gentle shade:
    Mountain where Oedipus was found.
    O mountain guard of a noble race!
    May the god who heals us lend his aid,
    And let that glory come to pass                     *10*
    For our king's cradling-ground.

    Of the nymphs that flower beyond the years,        *Antistrophe*
    Who bore you, royal child,
    To Pan of the hills or the timberline Apollo,
    Cold in delight where the upland clears,           *15*
    Or Hermês for whom Kyllenê's° heights are piled?
    Or flushed as evening cloud,
    Great Dionysos, roamer of mountains,
    He—was it he who found you there,
    And caught you up in his own proud                  *20*
    Arms from the sweet god-ravisher
    Who laughed by the Muses' fountains?

---

Ode III.   [16] **Hermês . . . Kyllenê's** Hermês, messenger of the gods, was said to have been born on Mt. Kyllenê.

# SCENE IV

OEDIPUS:   Sirs: though I do not know the man,
    I think I see him coming, this shepherd we want:
    He is old, like our friend here, and the men
    Bringing him seem to be servants of my house.
    But you can tell, if you have ever seen him.                    5

*Enter Shepherd escorted by servants.*

CHORAGOS:   I know him, he was Laïos' man. You can trust him.
OEDIPUS:   Tell me first, you from Corinth: is this the shepherd
    We were discussing?
MESSENGER:                This is the very man.
OEDIPUS *(to Shepherd)*:   Come here. No, look at me. You must
        answer
    Everything I ask. —You belonged to Laïos?                       10
SHEPHERD:   Yes: born his slave, brought up in his house.
OEDIPUS:   Tell me: what kind of work did you do for him?
SHEPHERD:   I was a shepherd of his, most of my life.
OEDIPUS:   Where mainly did you go for pasturage?
SHEPHERD:   Sometimes Kithairon, sometimes the hills
        near-by.                                                    15
OEDIPUS:   Do you remember ever seeing this man out there?
SHEPHERD:   What would he be doing there? This man?
OEDIPUS:   This man standing here. Have you ever seen him
        before?
SHEPHERD:   No. At least, not to my recollection.
MESSENGER:   And that is not strange, my lord. But
        I'll refresh                                                20
    His memory: he must remember when we two
    Spent three whole seasons together, March to September,
    On Kithairon or thereabouts. He had two flocks;
    I had one. Each autumn I'd drive mine home
    And he would go back with his to Laïos' sheepfold.—             25
    Is this not true, just as I have described it?
SHEPHERD:   True, yes; but it was all so long ago.
MESSENGER:   Well, then: do you remember, back in those days
    That you gave me a baby boy to bring up as my own?

SHEPHERD:   What if I did? What are you trying to say?   30
MESSENGER:   King Oedipus was once that little child.
SHEPHERD:   Damn you, hold your tongue!
OEDIPUS:                                                   No more of that!
It is your tongue needs watching, not this man's.
SHEPHERD:   My King, my Master, what is it I have done wrong?
OEDIPUS:   You have not answered his question about
        the boy.   35
SHEPHERD:   He does not know . . . He is only making
        trouble . . .
OEDIPUS:   Come, speak plainly, or it will go hard with you.
SHEPHERD:   In God's name, do not torture an old man!
OEDIPUS:   Come here, one of you; bind his arms behind him.
SHEPHERD:   Unhappy king! What more do you wish to learn?   40
OEDIPUS:   Did you give this man the child he speaks of?
SHEPHERD:                                                   I did.
And I would to God I had died that very day.
OEDIPUS:   You will die now unless you speak the truth.
SHEPHERD:   Yet if I speak the truth, I am worse than dead.
OEDIPUS:   Very well; since you insist upon delaying—   45
SHEPHERD:   No! I have told you already that I gave him the boy.
OEDIPUS:   Where did you get him? From your house? From
        somewhere else?
SHEPHERD:   Not from mine, no. A man gave him to me.
OEDIPUS:   Is that man here? Do you know whose slave he was?
SHEPHERD:   For God's love, my King, do not ask me
        any more!   50
OEDIPUS:   You are a dead man if I have to ask you again.
SHEPHERD:   Then . . . Then the child was from the palace of
        Laïos.
OEDIPUS:   A slave child? or a child of his own line?
SHEPHERD:   Ah, I am on the brink of dreadful speech!
OEDIPUS:   And I of dreadful hearing. Yet I must hear.   55
SHEPHERD:   If you must be told, then . . .
                                    They said it was Laïos' child,
But it is your wife who can tell you about that.
OEDIPUS:   My wife!—Did she give it to you?
SHEPHERD:                                                   My lord, she did.
OEDIPUS:   Do you know why?

SHEPHERD:                          I was told to get rid of it.
OEDIPUS:   An unspeakable mother!
SHEPHERD:                          There had beenprophecies . . .    60
OEDIPUS:   Tell me.
SHEPHERD:      It was said that the boy would kill his own father.
OEDIPUS:   Then why did you give him over to this old man?
SHEPHERD:   I pitied the baby, my King,
   And I thought that this man would take him far away
   To his own country.
                          He saved him—but for what a fate!    65
   For if you are what this man says you are,
   No man living is more wretched than Oedipus.
OEDIPUS:   Ah God!
   It was true!
             All the prophecies!
                    —Now,
   O Light, may I look on you for the last time!           70
   I, Oedipus,
   Oedipus, damned in his birth, in his marriage damned,
   Damned in the blood he shed with his own hand!

*He rushes into the palace.*

---

## ODE IV

---

CHORUS:   Alas for the seed of men.                    *Strophe 1*

   What measure shall I give these generations
   That breathe on the void and are void
   And exist and do not exist?

   Who bears more weight of joy                            5
   Than mass of sunlight shifting in images,
   Or who shall make his thought stay on
   That down time drifts away?

Your splendor is all fallen.

O naked brow of wrath and tears,    *10*
O change of Oedipus!
I who saw your days call no man blest—
Your great days like ghósts góne.

That mind was a strong bow.    *Antistrophe 1*
Deep, how deep you drew it then, hard archer,    *15*
At a dim fearful range,
And brought dear glory down!

You overcame the stranger—
The virgin with her hooking lion claws—
And though death sang, stood like a tower    *20*
To make pale Thebes take heart.

Fortress against our sorrow!

Divine king, giver of laws,
Majestic Oedipus!
No prince in Thebes had ever such renown,    *25*
No prince won such grace of power.

And now of all men ever known    *Strophe 2*
Most pitiful is this man's story:
His fortunes are most changed, his state
Fallen to a low slave's    *30*
Ground under bitter fate.

O Oedipus, most royal one!
The great door that expelled you to the light
Gave it night—ah, gave night to your glory:
As to the father, to the fathering son.    *35*

All understood too late.

How could that queen whom Laïos won,
The garden that he harrowed at his height,
Be silent when that act was done?

But all eyes fail before time's eye,                    *Antistrophe 2*  40
All actions come to justice there.
Though never willed, though far down the deep past,
Your bed, your dread sirings,
Are brought to book at last.
Child by Laïos doomed to die,                                        45
Then doomed to lose that fortunate little death,
Would God you never took breath in this air
That with my wailing lips I take to cry:

For I weep the world's outcast.

I was blind, and now I can tell why:                                 50
Asleep, for you had given ease of breath
To Thebes, while the false years went by.

---

# EXODOS

*Enter, from the palace, Second Messenger.*

SECOND MESSENGER:    Elders of Thebes, most honored in this
    land,
What horrors are yours to see and hear, what weight
Of sorrow to be endured, if, true to your birth,
You venerate the line of Labdakos!
I think neither Istros nor Phasis, those great rivers,               5
Could purify this place of the corruption
It shelters now, or soon must bring to light—
Evil not done unconsciously, but willed.

The greatest griefs are those we cause ourselves.
CHORAGOS:    Surely, friend, we have grief enough already;           10
    What new sorrow do you mean?
SECOND MESSENGER:                    The Queen is dead.
CHORAGOS:    Iocastê? Dead? But at whose hand?
SECOND MESSENGER:                                    Her own.
    The full horror of what happened you cannot know,

For you did not see it; but I, who did, will tell you
As clearly as I can how she met her death.                    15

When she had left us,
In passionate silence, passing through the court,
She ran to her apartment in the house,
Her hair clutched by the fingers of both hands.
She closed the doors behind her; then, by that bed          20
Where long ago the fatal son was conceived—
That son who should bring about his father's death—
We heard her call upon Laïos, dead so many years,
And heard her wail for the double fruit of her marriage,
A husband by her husband, children by her child.            25

Exactly how she died I do not know:
For Oedipus burst in moaning and would not let us
Keep vigil to the end: it was by him
As he stormed about the room that our eyes were caught.
From one to another of us he went, begging a sword,          30
Cursing the wife who was not his wife, the mother
Whose womb had carried his own children and himself.
I do not know: it was none of us aided him,
But surely one of the gods was in control!
For with a dreadful cry                                       35
He hurled his weight, as though wrenched out of himself,
At the twin doors: the bolts gave, and he rushed in.
And there we saw her hanging, her body swaying
From the cruel cord she had noosed about her neck.
A great sob broke from him heartbreaking to hear,            40
As he loosed the rope and lowered her to the ground.

I would blot out from my mind what happened next!
For the King ripped from her gown the golden brooches
That were her ornament, and raised them, and plunged
    them down
Straight into his own eyeballs, crying, "No more,            45
No more shall you look on the misery about me,
The horrors of my own doing! Too long you have known
The faces of those whom I should never have seen,
Too long been blind to those for whom I was searching!

From this hour, go in darkness!" And as he spoke,                    *50*
He struck at his eyes—not once, but many times;
And the blood spattered his beard,
Bursting from his ruined sockets like red hail.

So from the unhappiness of two this evil has sprung,
A curse on the man and woman alike. The old                          *55*
Happiness of the house of Labdakos
Was happiness enough: where is it today?
It is all wailing and ruin, disgrace, death—all
The misery of mankind that has a name—
And it is wholly and for ever theirs.                                *60*
CHORAGOS:   Is he in agony still? Is there no rest for him?
SECOND MESSENGER:   He is calling for someone to lead him to
        the gates
So that all the children of Kadmos may look upon
His father's murderer, his mother's—no,
I cannot say it!
                        And then he will leave Thebes,              *65*
Self-exiled, in order that the curse
Which he himself pronounced may depart from the house.
He is weak, and there is none to lead him,
So terrible is his suffering.
                        But you will see:
Look, the doors are opening; in a moment                            *70*
You will see a thing that would crush a heart of stone.

*The central door is opened; Oedipus, blinded, is led in.*

CHORAGOS:   Dreadful indeed for men to see.
    Never have my own eyes
    Looked on a sight so full of fear.

Oedipus!                                                            *75*
What madness came upon you, what daemon°
Leaped on your life with heavier
Punishment than a mortal man can bear?

---

Exodos.   ⁷⁶ **daemon** a spirit, not necessarily evil

No: I cannot even
Look at you, poor ruined one.                                    80
And I would speak, question, ponder,
If I were able. No.
You make me shudder.
OEDIPUS:   God. God.
Is there a sorrow greater?                                        85
Where shall I find harbor in this world?
My voice is hurled far on a dark wind.
What has God done to me?
CHORAGOS:   Too terrible to think of, or to see.

OEDIPUS:   O cloud of night,                          *Strophe 1*  90
Never to be turned away: night coming on,
I cannot tell how: night like a shroud!
My fair winds brought me here.
                              Oh God. Again
The pain of the spikes where I had sight,
The flooding pain                                                95
Of memory, never to be gouged out.
CHORAGOS:   This is not strange.
You suffer it all twice over, remorse in pain,
Pain in remorse.

OEDIPUS:   Ah dear friend                       *Antistrophe 1*  100
Are you faithful even yet, you alone?
Are you still standing near me, will you stay here,
Patient, to care for the blind?
                              The blind man!
Yet even blind I know who it is attends me,
By the voice's tone—                                            105
Though my new darkness hide the comforter.
CHORAGOS:   Oh fearful act!
What god was it drove you to rake black
Night across your eyes?

OEDIPUS:   Apollo. Apollo. Dear                    *Strophe 2*  110
Children, the god was Apollo.
He brought my sick, sick fate upon me.
But the blinding hand was my own!

How could I bear to see
When all my sight was horror everywhere?                     115
CHORAGOS:   Everywhere; that is true.
OEDIPUS:   And now what is left?
    Images? Love? A greeting even,
    Sweet to the senses? Is there anything?
    Ah, no, friends: lead me away.                           120
    Lead me away from Thebes.
                              Lead the great wreck
    And hell of Oedipus, whom the gods hate.
CHORAGOS:   Your fate is clear, you are not blind to that.
    Would God you had never found it out!

OEDIPUS:   Death take the man who unbound      *Antistrophe 2*  125
    My feet on that hillside
    And delivered me from death to life! What life?
    If only I had died,
    This weight of monstrous doom
    Could not have dragged me and my darlings down.          130
CHORAGOS:   I would have wished the same.
OEDIPUS:   Oh never to have come here
    With my father's blood upon me! Never
    To have been the man they call his mother's husband!
    Oh accurst! Oh child of evil,                            135
    To have entered that wretched bed—
                              the selfsame one!
    More primal than sin itself, this fell to me.
CHORAGOS:   I do not know how I can answer you.
    You were better dead than alive and blind.
OEDIPUS:   Do not counsel me any more. This punishment        140
    that I have laid upon myself is just.
    If I had eyes,
    I do not know how I could bear the sight
    Of my father, when I came to the house of Death,
    Or my mother: for I have sinned against them both        145
    So vilely that I could not make my peace
    By strangling my own life.
                              Or do you think my children,
    Born as they were born, would be sweet to my eyes?
    Ah never, never! Nor this town with its high walls,

Nor the holy images of the gods.
                              For I,                    150
Thrice miserable—Oedipus, noblest of all the line
Of Kadmos, have condemned myself to enjoy
These things no more, by my own malediction
Expelling that man whom the gods declared
To be a defilement in the house of Laïos.                155
After exposing the rankness of my own guilt,
How could I look men frankly in the eyes?
No, I swear it.
If I could have stifled my hearing at its source,
I would have done it and made all this body         160
A tight cell of misery, blank to light and sound:
So I should have been safe in a dark agony
Beyond all recollection.
                              Ah Kithairon!
Why did you shelter me? When I was cast upon you,
Why did I not die? Then I should never               165
Have shown the world my execrable birth.

Ah Polybos! Corinth, city that I believed
The ancient seat of my ancestors: how fair
I seemed, your child! And all the while this evil
Was cancerous within me!
                              For I am sick            170
In my daily life, sick in my origin.

O three roads, dark ravine, woodland and way
Where three roads met: you, drinking my father's blood,
My own blood, spilled by my own hand: can you remember
The unspeakable things I did there, and the things    175
I went on from there to do?
                              O marriage, marriage!
The act that engendered me, and again the act
Performed by the son in the same bed—
                              Ah, the net
Of incest, mingling fathers, brothers, sons,
With brides, wives, mothers: the last evil            180
That can be known by men: no tongue can say

How evil!
         No. For the love of God, conceal me
Somewhere far from Thebes; or kill me; or hurl me
Into the sea, away from men's eyes for ever.
Come, lead me. You need not fear to touch me.                    185
Of all men, I alone can bear this guilt.

*Enter Creon.*

CHORAGOS:   We are not the ones to decide; but Creon here
   May fitly judge of what you ask. He only
   Is left to protect the city in your place.
OEDIPUS:   Alas, how can I speak to him? What right have I      190
   To beg his courtesy whom I have deeply wronged?
CREON:   I have not come to mock you, Oedipus,
   Or to reproach you, either.
      *(To Attendants.)*           —You, standing there:
   If you have lost all respect for man's dignity,
   At least respect the flame of Lord Helios:                    195
   Do not allow this pollution to show itself
   Openly here, an affront to the earth
   And Heaven's rain and the light of day. No, take him
   Into the house as quickly as you can.
   For it is proper                                              200
   That only the close kindred see his grief.
OEDIPUS:   I pray you in God's name, since your courtesy
   Ignores my dark expectation, visiting
   With mercy this man of all men most execrable:
   Give me what I ask—for your good, not for mine.               205
CREON:   And what is it that you would have me do?
OEDIPUS:   Drive me out of this country as quickly as may be
   To a place where no human voice can ever greet me.
CREON:   I should have done that before now—only,
   God's will had not been wholly revealed to me.                210
OEDIPUS:   But his command is plain: the parricide
   Must be destroyed. I am that evil man.
CREON:   That is the sense of it, yes; but as things are,
   We had best discover clearly what is to be done.
OEDIPUS:   You would learn more about a man like me?            215
CREON:   You are ready now to listen to the god.

OEDIPUS:   I will listen. But it is to you
That I must turn for help. I beg you, hear me.

The woman in there—
Give her whatever funeral you think proper:                     220
She is your sister.
                              —But let me go, Creon!
Let me purge my father's Thebes of the pollution
Of my living here, and go out to the wild hills,
To Kithairon, that has won such fame with me,
The tomb my mother and father appointed for me,               225
And let me die there, as they willed I should.
And yet I know
Death will not ever come to me through sickness
Or in any natural way: I have been preserved
For some unthinkable fate. But let that be.                    230
As for my sons, you need not care for them.
They are men, they will find some way to live.
But my poor daughters, who have shared my table,
Who never before have been parted from their father—
Take care of them, Creon; do this for me.                     235
And will you let me touch them with my hands
A last time, and let us weep together?
Be kind, my lord,
Great prince, be kind!
                              Could I but touch them,
They would be mine again, as when I had my eyes.              240

*Enter Antigonê and Ismenê, attended.*

Ah, God!
Is it my dearest children I hear weeping?
Has Creon pitied me and sent my daughters?
CREON:   Yes, Oedipus: I knew that they were dear to you
In the old days, and know you must love them still.           245
OEDIPUS:   May God bless you for this—and be a friendlier
Guardian to you than he has been to me!

Children, where are you?
Come quickly to my hands: they are your brother's—

Hands that have brought your father's once clear eyes    250
To this way of seeing—
                        Ah dearest ones,
I had neither sight nor knowledge then, your father
By the woman who was the source of his own life!
And I weep for you—having no strength to see you—,
I weep for you when I think of the bitterness    255
That men will visit upon you all your lives.
What homes, what festivals can you attend
Without being forced to depart again in tears?
And when you come to marriageable age,
Where is the man, my daughters, who would dare    260
Risk the bane that lies on all my children?
Is there any evil wanting? Your father killed
His father; sowed the womb of her who bore him;
Engendered you at the fount of his own existence!
That is what they will say of you.
                        Then, whom    265
Can you ever marry? There are no bridegrooms for you,
And your lives must wither away in sterile dreaming.
O Creon, son of Menoikeus!
You are the only father my daughters have,
Since we, their parents, are both of us gone for ever.    270
They are your own blood: you will not let them
Fall into beggary and loneliness;
You will keep them from the miseries that are mine!
Take pity on them; see, they are only children,
Friendless except for you. Promise me this,    275
Great Prince, and give me your hand in token of it.

*Creon clasps his right hand.*

Children:
I could say much, if you could understand me,
But as it is, I have only this prayer for you:
Live where you can, be as happy as you can—    280
Happier, please God, than God has made your father!
CREON:   Enough. You have wept enough. Now go within.
OEDIPUS:   I must; but it is hard.
CREON:                        Time eases all things.

OEDIPUS:   But you must promise—
CREON:                                      Say what you desire.
OEDIPUS:   Send me from Thebes!
CREON:                                      God grant that I may!        285
OEDIPUS:   But since God hates me . . .
CREON:                                      No, he will grant your wish.
OEDIPUS:   You promise?
CREON:                        I cannot speak beyond my knowledge.
OEDIPUS:   Then lead me in.
CREON:                             Come now, and leave your children.
OEDIPUS:   No! Do not take them from me!
CREON:                                           Think no longer
That you are in command here, but rather think        290
How, when you were, you served your own destruction.

*(Exeunt into the house all but the Chorus; the Choragos chants
directly to the audience.)*

CHORAGOS:   Men of Thebes: look upon Oedipus.

This is the king who solved the famous riddle
And towered up, most powerful of men.
No mortal eyes but looked on him with envy,        295
Yet in the end ruin swept over him.

Let every man in mankind's frailty
Consider his last day; and let none
Presume on his good fortune until he find
Life, at his death, a memory without pain.        300

## WILLIAM SHAKESPEARE [1564–1616]

# The Tragedy of Hamlet, Prince of Denmark

### Dramatis Personae

CLAUDIUS, *King of Denmark*
HAMLET, *son to the late, and nephew to the present, King*
POLONIUS, *Lord Chamberlain*
HORATIO, *friend to Hamlet*
LAERTES, *son to Polonius*
VOLTEMAND
CORNELIUS
ROSENCRANTZ
GUILDENSTERN } *courtiers*
OSRIC
A GENTLEMAN
A PRIEST
MARCELLUS } *officers*
BARNARDO }
FRANCISCO, *a soldier*
REYNALDO, *servant to Polonius*
PLAYERS
TWO CLOWNS, *gravediggers*
FORTINBRAS, *Prince of Norway*
A NORWEGIAN CAPTAIN

ENGLISH AMBASSADORS
GERTRUDE, *Queen of Denmark, mother to Hamlet*
OPHELIA, *daughter to Polonius*
GHOST OF HAMLET'S FATHER
LORDS, LADIES, OFFICERS, SOLDIERS, SAILORS, MESSENGERS, ATTENDANTS

**SCENE.** *Elsinore**

---

This version is edited by Edward Hubler.
* It has been found useful to divide the play into acts and scenes. These divisions, however, are not found in the early printed versions of the play; they are purely editorial additions.

# ACT I

**S C E N E  I.**  *A guard platform of the castle.*

*Enter Barnardo and Francisco, two sentinels.*

BARNARDO:  Who's there?
FRANCISCO:  Nay, answer me. Stand and unfold*° yourself.
BARNARDO:  Long live the King!°
FRANCISCO:  Barnardo?
BARNARDO:  He.                                                                                  5
FRANCISCO:  You come most carefully upon your hour.
BARNARDO:  'Tis now struck twelve. Get thee to bed, Francisco.
FRANCISCO:  For this relief much thanks. 'Tis bitter cold,
    And I am sick at heart.
BARNARDO:  Have you had quiet guard?
FRANCISCO:                                                    Not a mouse stirring.   10
BARNARDO:  Well, good night.
    If you do meet Horatio and Marcellus,
    The rivals° of my watch, bid them make haste.

*Enter Horatio and Marcellus.*

FRANCISCO:  I think I hear them. Stand, ho! Who is there?
HORATIO:  Friends to this ground.
MARCELLUS:                                          And liegemen to the Dane.°  15
FRANCISCO:  Give you° good night.
MARCELLUS:                                          O, farewell, honest soldier.
    Who hath relieved you?
FRANCISCO:                              Barnardo hath my place.
    Give you good night.

*Exit Francisco.*

---

* The notes are Edward Hubler's for the New American Library edition of *Hamlet.*
I.i.   ² *unfold* disclose   ³ *Long live the King* (perhaps a password, perhaps a
greeting)   ¹³ *rivals* partners   ¹⁵ *liegemen to the Dane* loyal subjects to the King of
Denmark   ¹⁶ *Give you* God give you

MARCELLUS:                    Holla, Barnardo!
BARNARDO:                                   Say—
    What, is Horatio there?
HORATIO:                    A piece of him.
BARNARDO:  Welcome, Horatio. Welcome, good Marcellus.    20
MARCELLUS:  What, has this thing appeared again tonight?
BARNARDO:  I have seen nothing.
MARCELLUS:  Horatio says 'tis but our fantasy,
    And will not let belief take hold of him
    Touching this dreaded sight twice seen of us;    25
    Therefore I have entreated him along
    With us to watch the minutes of this night,
    That, if again this apparition come,
    He may approve° our eyes and speak to it.
HORATIO:  Tush, tush, 'twill not appear.
BARNARDO:                                   Sit down awhile,    30
    And let us once again assail your ears,
    That are so fortified against our story,
    What we have two nights seen.
HORATIO:                                   Well, sit we down,
    And let us hear Barnardo speak of this.
BARNARDO:  Last night of all,    35
    When yond same star that's westward from the pole°
    Had made his course t' illume that part of heaven
    Where now it burns, Marcellus and myself,
    The bell then beating one ———

*Enter Ghost.*

MARCELLUS:  Peace, break thee off. Look where it comes
    again.    40
BARNARDO:  In the same figure like the king that's dead.
MARCELLUS:  Thou art a scholar; speak to it, Horatio.
BARNARDO:  Looks 'a not like the king? Mark it, Horatio.
HORATIO:  Most like: it harrows me with fear and wonder.
BARNARDO:  It would be spoke to.
MARCELLUS:                                   Speak to it, Horatio.    45

--------

[29] *approve* confirm   [36] *pole* polestar

HORATIO:   What art thou that usurp'st this time of night,
    Together with that fair and warlike form
    In which the majesty of buried Denmark°
    Did sometimes march? By heaven I charge thee, speak.
MARCELLUS:   It is offended.
BARNARDO:                          See, it stalks away.                          50
HORATIO:   Stay! Speak, speak. I charge thee, speak.

*Exit Ghost.*


MARCELLUS:   'Tis gone and will not answer.
BARNARDO:   How now, Horatio? You tremble and look pale.
    Is not this something more than fantasy?
    What think you on't?                          55
HORATIO:   Before my God, I might not this believe
    Without the sensible and true avouch°
    Of mine own eyes.
MARCELLUS:               Is it not like the King?
HORATIO:   As thou art to thyself.
    Such was the very armor he had on                          60
    When he the ambitious Norway° combated:
    So frowned he once, when, in an angry parle,°
    He smote the sledded Polacks° on the ice.
    'Tis strange.
MARCELLUS:   Thus twice before, and jump° at this dread
    hour,                          65
    With martial stalk hath he gone by our watch.
HORATIO:   In what particular thought to work I know not;
    But, in the gross and scope° of my opinion,
    This bodes some strange eruption to our state.
MARCELLUS:   Good now, sit down, and tell me he that
    knows,                          70
    Why this same strict and most observant watch
    So nightly toils the subject° of the land,

---

[48] *buried Denmark* the buried King of Denmark   [57] *sensible and true avouch* sensory and true proof   [61] *Norway* King of Norway   [62] *parle* parley   [63] *sledded Polacks* Poles in sledges   [65] *jump* just   [68] *gross and scope* general drift   [72] *toils the subject* makes the subjects toil

And why such daily cast of brazen cannon
And foreign mart° for implements of war,
Why such impress° of shipwrights, whose sore task          75
Does not divide the Sunday from the week,
What might be toward° that this sweaty haste
Doth make the night joint-laborer with the day?
Who is't that can inform me?
HORATIO:                              That can I.
At least the whisper goes so: our last king,               80
Whose image even but now appeared to us,
Was, as you know, by Fortinbras of Norway,
Thereto pricked on by a most emulate pride,
Dared to the combat; in which our valiant Hamlet
(For so this side of our known world esteemed him)         85
Did slay this Fortinbras, who, by a sealed compact
Well ratified by law and heraldry,°
Did forfeit, with his life, all those his lands
Which he stood seized° of, to the conqueror;
Against the which a moiety competent°                      90
Was gagèd° by our King, which had returned
To the inheritance of Fortinbras,
Had he been vanquisher, as, by the same comart°
And carriage of the article designed,°
His fell to Hamlet. Now, sir, young Fortinbras,            95
Of unimprovèd° mettle hot and full,
Hath in the skirts° of Norway here and there
Sharked up° a list of lawless resolutes,°
For food and diet, to some enterprise
That hath a stomach in't;° which is no other,             100
As it doth well appear unto our state,
But to recover of us by strong hand
And terms compulsatory, those foresaid lands
So by his father lost; and this, I take it,

---

[74] *mart* trading   [75] *impress* forced service   [77] *toward* in preparation   [87] *law and heraldry* heraldic law (governing the combat)   [89] *seized* possessed   [90] *moiety competent* equal portion   [91] *gagèd* engaged, pledged   [93] *comart* agreement   [94] *carriage of the article designed* import of the agreement drawn up   [96] *unimprovèd* untried   [97] *skirts* borders   [98] *Sharked up* collected indiscriminately (as a shark gulps its prey)   [98] *resolutes* desperadoes   [100] *hath a stomach in't* i.e., requires courage

Is the main motive of our preparations,                    105
The source of this our watch, and the chief head°
Of this posthaste and romage° in the land.
BARNARDO:   I think it be no other but e'en so;
Well may it sort° that this portentous figure
Comes armèd through our watch so like the King    110
That was and is the question of these wars.
HORATIO:   A mote it is to trouble the mind's eye:
In the most high and palmy state of Rome,
A little ere the mightiest Julius fell,
The graves stood tenantless, and the sheeted dead    115
Did squeak and gibber in the Roman streets;°
As stars with trains of fire and dews of blood,
Disasters° in the sun; and the moist star,°
Upon whose influence Neptune's empire stands,
Was sick almost to doomsday with eclipse.            120
And even the like precurse° of feared events,
As harbingers° preceding still° the fates
And prologue to the omen° coming on,
Have heaven and earth together demonstrated
Unto our climatures° and countrymen.                 125

*Enter Ghost.*

But soft, behold, lo where it comes again!
I'll cross it,° though it blast me.—Stay, illusion.

*It spreads his° arms.*

If though hast any sound or use of voice,
Speak to me.
If there be any good thing to be done               130

---

¹⁰⁶ *head* fountainhead, origin   ¹⁰⁷ *romage* bustle   ¹⁰⁹ *sort* befit   ¹¹⁶ *Did squeak . . .*
*Roman streets* (the break in the sense which follows this line suggests that a line
has dropped out)   ¹¹⁸ *Disasters* threatening signs   ¹¹⁸ *moist star* moon   ¹²¹ *pre-*
*curse* precursor, foreshadowing   ¹²² *harbingers* forerunners   ¹²² *still* always
¹²³ *omen* calamity   ¹²⁵ *climatures* regions   ¹²⁷ *cross it* (1) cross its path, confront
it, (2) make the sign of the cross in front of it   ¹²⁷ ˢ·ᵈ· *his* i.e., its, the ghost's
(though possibly what is meant is that Horatio spreads his own arms, making a
cross of himself)

That may to thee do ease and grace to me,
Speak to me.
If thou art privy to thy country's fate,
Which happily° foreknowing may avoid,
O, speak!                                                                                    135
Or if thou hast uphoarded in thy life
Extorted° treasure in the womb of earth,
For which, they say, you spirits oft walk in death,

*The cock crows.*

Speak of it. Stay and speak. Stop it, Marcellus.
MARCELLUS:  Shall I strike at it with my partisan°?                    140
HORATIO:  Do, if it will not stand.
BARNARDO:                                   'Tis here.
HORATIO:                                                            'Tis here.
MARCELLUS:  'Tis gone.

                                                                    *Exit Ghost.*

We do it wrong, being so majestical,
To offer it the show of violence,
For it is as the air, invulnerable,                                           145
And our vain blows malicious mockery.
BARNARDO:  It was about to speak when the cock crew.
HORATIO:  And then it started, like a guilty thing
Upon a fearful summons. I have heard,
The cock, that is the trumpet to the morn,                          150
Doth with his lofty and shrill-sounding throat
Awake the god of day, and at his warning,
Whether in sea or fire, in earth or air,
Th' extravagant and erring° spirit hies
To his confine; and of the truth herein                                155
This present object made probation.°
MARCELLUS:  It faded on the crowing of the cock.
Some say that ever 'gainst° that season comes

---

[134] *happily* haply, perhaps   [137] *Extorted* ill-won   [140] *partisan* pike (a long-handled weapon)   [154] *extravagant and erring* out of bounds and wandering   [156] *probation* proof   [158] *'gainst* just before

Wherein our Savior's birth is celebrated,
This bird of dawning singeth all night long,                    160
And then, they say, no spirit dare stir abroad,
The nights are wholesome, then no planets strike,°
No fairy takes,° nor witch hath power to charm:
So hallowed and so gracious is that time.
HORATIO:   So have I heard and do in part believe it.          165
But look, the morn in russet mantle clad
Walks o'er the dew of yon high eastward hill.
Break we our watch up, and by my advice
Let us impart what we have seen tonight
Unto young Hamlet, for upon my life                            170
This spirit, dumb to us, will speak to him.
Do you consent we shall acquaint him with it,
As needful in our loves, fitting our duty?
MARCELLUS:   Let's do 't. I pray, and I this morning know
Where we shall find him most convenient.                       175

Exeunt.

**S C E N E  II.**   *The castle.*

*Flourish.° Enter Claudius, King of Denmark, Gertrude the Queen,*
*Councilors, Polonius and his son Laertes, Hamlet, cum aliis° [in-*
*cluding Voltemand and Cornelius].*

KING:   Though yet of Hamlet our dear brother's death
The memory be green, and that it us befitted
To bear our hearts in grief, and our whole kingdom
To be contracted in one brow of woe,
Yet so far hath discretion fought with nature                  5
That we with wisest sorrow think on him
Together with remembrance of ourselves.
Therefore our sometime sister,° now our Queen,
Th' imperial jointress° to this warlike state,

---

[162] *strike* exert an evil influence   [163] *takes* bewitches.   I.ii.   [s.d.] *Flourish* fanfare
of trumpets   [s.d.] *cum aliis* with others (Latin)   [8] *our sometime sister* my (the
royal "we") former sister-in-law   [9] *jointress* joint tenant, partner

Have we, as 'twere, with a defeated joy,           *10*
With an auspicious° and a dropping eye,
With mirth in funeral, and with dirge in marriage,
In equal scale weighing delight and dole,
Taken to wife. Nor have we herein barred
Your better wisdoms, which have freely gone      *15*
With this affair along. For all, our thanks.
Now follows that you know young Fortinbras,
Holding a weak supposal of our worth,
Or thinking by our late dear brother's death
Our state to be disjoint and out of frame,°        *20*
Colleaguèd with this dream of his advantage,°
He hath not failed to pester us with message,
Importing the surrender of those lands
Lost by his father, with all bands of law,
To our most valiant brother. So much for him.     *25*
Now for ourself and for this time of meeting.
Thus much the business is: we have here writ
To Norway, uncle of young Fortinbras—
Who, impotent and bedrid, scarcely hears
Of this his nephew's purpose—to suppress      *30*
His further gait° herein, in that the levies,
The lists, and full proportions° are all made
Out of his subject;° and we here dispatch
You, good Cornelius, and you, Voltemand,
For bearers of this greeting to old Norway,      *35*
Giving to you no further personal power
To business with the King, more than the scope
Of these delated articles° allow.
Farewell, and let your haste commend your duty.
CORNELIUS, VOLTEMAND:   In that, and all things, will we show
    our duty.                     *40*
KING:   We doubt it nothing. Heartily farewell.

                         *Exit Voltemand and Cornelius.*

---

[11] *auspicious* joyful   [20] *frame* order   [21] *advantage* superiority   [31] *gait* proceeding   [32] *proportions* supplies for war   [33] *Out of his subject* i.e., out of old Norway's subjects and realm   [38] *delated articles* detailed documents

And now, Laertes, what's the news with you?
You told us of some suit. What is't, Laertes?
You cannot speak of reason to the Dane
And lose your voice.° What wouldst thou beg, Laertes,          45
That shall not be my offer, not thy asking?
The head is not more native° to the heart,
The hand more instrumental to the mouth,
Than is the throne of Denmark to thy father.
What wouldst thou have, Laertes?

LAERTES:                                    My dread lord,          50
Your leave and favor to return to France,
From whence though willingly I came to Denmark
To show my duty in your coronation,
Yet now I must confess, that duty done,
My thoughts and wishes bend again toward France          55
And bow them to your gracious leave and pardon.

KING:   Have you your father's leave? What says Polonius?

POLONIUS:   He hath, my lord, wrung from me my slow leave
By laborsome petition, and at last
Upon his will I sealed my hard consent.°          60
I do beseech you give him leave to go.

KING:   Take thy fair hour, Laertes. Time be thine,
And thy best graces spend it at thy will.
But now, my cousin° Hamlet, and my son——

HAMLET [aside]:   A little more than kin, and less than kind!°          65

KING:   How is it that the clouds still hang on you?

HAMLET:   Not so, my lord. I am too much in the sun.°

QUEEN:   Good Hamlet, cast thy nighted color off,
And let thine eye look like a friend on Denmark.
Do not forever with thy vailèd° lids          70
Seek for thy noble father in the dust.
Thou know'st 'tis common; all that lives must die,
Passing through nature to eternity.

HAMLET:   Ay, madam, it is common.°

---

[45] *lose your voice* waste your breath   [47] *native* related   [60] *Upon his . . . hard consent* to his desire I gave my reluctant consent   [64] *cousin* kinsman   [65] *kind* pun on the meanings "kindly" and "natural"; though doubly related—*more than kin*—Hamlet asserts that he neither resembles Claudius in nature or feels kindly toward him   [67] *sun* sunshine of royal favor (with a pun on "son")   [70] *vailèd* lowered   [74] *common* (1) universal, (2) vulgar

QUEEN:                                     If it be,
   Why seems it so particular with thee?                    75
HAMLET:   Seems, madam? Nay, it is. I know not "seems."
   'Tis not alone my inky cloak, good mother,
   Nor customary suits of solemn black,
   Nor windy suspiration° of forced breath,
   No, nor the fruitful river in the eye,                        80
   Nor the dejected havior of the visage,
   Together with all forms, moods, shapes of grief,
   That can denote me truly. These indeed seem,
   For they are actions that a man might play,
   But I have that within which passes show;                     85
   These but the trappings and the suits of woe.
KING:   'Tis sweet and commendable in your nature, Hamlet,
   To give these mourning duties to your father,
   But you must know your father lost a father,
   That father lost, lost his, and the survivor bound            90
   In filial obligation for some term
   To do obsequious° sorrow, But to persever
   In obstinate condolement° is a course
   Of impious stubbornness. 'Tis unmanly grief.
   It shows a will most incorrect to heaven,                     95
   A heart unfortified, a mind impatient,
   An understanding simple and unschooled.
   For what we know must be and is as common
   As any the most vulgar° thing to sense,
   Why should we in our peevish opposition                      100
   Take it to heart? Fie, 'tis a fault to heaven,
   A fault against the dead, a fault to nature,
   To reason most absurd, whose common theme
   Is death of fathers, and who still hath cried,
   From the first corse° till he that died today,               105
   "This must be so." We pray you throw to earth
   This unprevailing° woe, and think of us
   As of a father, for let the world take note

---

[79] *windy suspiration* heavy sighing   [92] *obsequious* suitable to obsequies
(funerals)   [93] *condolement* mourning   [99] *vulgar* common   [105] *corse* corpse
[107] *unprevailing* unavailing

You are the most immediate to our throne,
And with no less nobility of love                                110
Than that which dearest father bears his son
Do I impart toward you. For your intent
In going back to school in Wittenberg,
It is most retrograde° to our desire,
And we beseech you, bend you° to remain              115
Here in the cheer and comfort of our eye,
Our chiefest courtier, cousin, and our son.
QUEEN:   Let not thy mother lose her prayers, Hamlet.
   I pray thee stay with us, go not to Wittenberg.
HAMLET:   I shall in all my best obey you, madam.        120
KING:   Why, 'tis a loving and a fair reply.
   Be as ourself in Denmark. Madam, come.
   This gentle and unforced accord of Hamlet
   Sits smiling to my heart, in grace whereof
   No jocund health that Denmark drinks today,       125
   But the great cannon to the clouds shall tell,
   And the King's rouse° the heaven shall bruit° again,
   Respeaking earthly thunder. Come away.

*Flourish. Exeunt all but Hamlet.*

HAMLET:   O that this too too sullied° flesh would melt,
   Thaw, and resolve itself into a dew,                    130
   Or that the Everlasting had not fixed
   His canon° 'gainst self-slaughter. O God, God,
   How weary, stale, flat, and unprofitable
   Seem to me all the uses of this world!
   Fie on't, ah, fie, 'tis an unweeded garden             135
   That grows to seed. Things rank and gross in nature
   Possess it merely.° That it should come to this:
   But two months dead, nay, not so much, not two,
   So excellent a king, that was to this

---

¹¹⁴ *retrograde* contrary   ¹¹⁵ *bend you* incline   ¹²⁷ *rouse* deep drink   ¹²⁷ *bruit* announce noisily   ¹²⁹ *sullied* (Q2 has *sallied*, here modernized to *sullied*, which makes sense and is therefore given; but the Folio reading, *solid*, which fits better with *melt*, is quite possibly correct)   ¹³² *canon* law   ¹³⁷ *merely* entirely

Hyperion° to a satyr, so loving to my mother                      140
That he might not beteem° the winds of heaven
Visit her face too roughly. Heaven and earth,
Must I remember? Why, she would hang on him
As if increase of appetite had grown
By what it fed on; and yet within a month—                        145
Let me not think on't; frailty, thy name is woman—
A little month, or ere those shoes were old
With which she followed my poor father's body
Like Niobe,° all tears, why she, even she—
O God, a beast that wants discourse of reason°                    150
Would have mourned longer—married with my uncle,
My father's brother, but no more like my father
Than I to Hercules. Within a month,
Ere yet the salt of most unrighteous tears
Had left the flushing° in her gallèd eyes,                        155
She married. O, most wicked speed, to post°
With such dexterity to incestuous° sheets!
It is not, nor it cannot come to good.
But break my heart, for I must hold my tongue.

*Enter Horatio, Marcellus, and Barnardo.*

HORATIO:   Hail to your lordship!
HAMLET:                              I am glad to see you well.    160
    Horatio—or I do forget myself.
HORATIO:   The same, my lord, and your poor servant ever.
HAMLET:   Sir, my good friend, I'll change° that name with you.
    And what make you from Wittenberg, Horatio?
    Marcellus?                                                    165
MARCELLUS:   My good lord!
HAMLET:   I am very glad to see you. [*To Barnardo.*] Good even,
    sir.
    But what, in faith, make you from Wittenberg?

---

¹⁴⁰ *Hyperion* the sun god, a model of beauty   ¹⁴¹ *beteem* allow   ¹⁴⁹ *Niobe* a
mother who wept profusely at the death of her children   ¹⁵⁰ *wants discourse of
reason* lacks reasoning power   ¹⁵⁵ *left the flushing* stopped reddening   ¹⁵⁶ *post*
hasten   ¹⁵⁷ *incestuous* canon law considered marriage with a deceased brother's
widow to be incestuous   ¹⁶³ *change* exchange

HORATIO:   A truant disposition, good my lord.

HAMLET:   I would not hear your enemy say so,                                170
Nor shall you do my ear that violence
To make it truster° of your own report
Against yourself. I know you are no truant.
But what is your affair in Elsinore?
We'll teach you to drink deep ere you depart.                             175

HORATIO:   My lord, I came to see your father's funeral.

HAMLET:   I prithee do not mock me, fellow student.
I think it was to see my mother's wedding.

HORATIO:   Indeed, my lord, it followed hard upon.

HAMLET:   Thrift, thrift, Horatio. The funeral baked meats               180
Did coldly furnish forth the marriage tables.
Would I had met my dearest° foe in heaven
Or ever I had seen that day, Horatio!
My father, methinks I see my father.

HORATIO:   Where, my lord?

HAMLET:                              In my mind's eye, Horatio.                185

HORATIO:   I saw him once. 'A° was a goodly king.

HAMLET:   'A was a man, take him for all in all,
I shall not look upon his like again.

HORATIO:   My lord, I think I saw him yesternight.

HAMLET:   Saw? Who?                                                             190

HORATIO:   My lord, the King your father.

HAMLET:                                        The King my father?

HORATIO:   Season your admiration° for a while
With an attent ear till I may deliver
Upon the witness of these gentlemen
This marvel to you.

HAMLET:                        For God's love let me hear!                    195

HORATIO:   Two nights together had these gentlemen,
Marcellus and Barnardo, on their watch
In the dead waste and middle of the night
Been thus encountered. A figure like your father,
Armèd at point exactly, cap-a-pe,°                                          200
Appears before them, and with solemn march
Goes slow and stately by them. Thrice he walked

---

172 *truster* believer   182 *dearest* most intensely felt   186 *'A* he   192 *Season your admiration* control your wonder   200 *cap-a-pe* head to foot

By their oppressed and fear-surprisèd eyes,
Within his truncheon's length,° whilst they, distilled°
Almost to jelly with the act° of fear,                                    205
Stand dumb and speak not to him. This to me
In dreadful° secrecy impart they did,
And I with them the third night kept the watch,
Where, as they had delivered, both in time,
Form of the thing, each word made true and good,         210
The apparition comes. I knew your father.
These hands are not much more like.
HAMLET:                                              But where was this?
MARCELLUS:   My lord, upon the platform where we watched.
HAMLET:   Did you not speak to it?
HORATIO:                                    My lord, I did;
But answer made it none. Yet once methought              215
It lifted up it° head and did address
Itself to motion like as it would speak:
But even then the morning cock crew loud,
And at the sound it shrunk in haste away
And vanished from our sight.
HAMLET:                                          'Tis very strange.          220
HORATIO:   As I do live, my honored lord, 'tis true,
And we did think it writ down in our duty
To let you know of it.
HAMLET:   Indeed, indeed, sirs, but this troubles me.
Hold you the watch tonight?
ALL:                                          We do, my lord.               225
HAMLET:   Armed, say you?
ALL:   Armed, my lord.
HAMLET:   From top to toe?
ALL:                                          My lord, from head to foot.
HAMLET:   Then saw you not his face.
HORATIO:   O, yes, my lord. He wore his beaver° up.          230
HAMLET:   What, looked he frowningly?
HORATIO:   A countenance more in sorrow than in anger.
HAMLET:   Pale or red?

---

²⁰⁴ *truncheon's length* space of a short staff   ²⁰⁴ *distilled* reduced   ²⁰⁵ *act*
action   ²⁰⁷ *dreadful* terrified   ²¹⁶ *it* its   ²³⁰ *beaver* visor, face guard

HORATIO:   Nay, very pale.
HAMLET:                     And fixed his eyes upon you?
HORATIO:   Most constantly.
HAMLET:                     I would I had been there.          235
HORATIO:   It would have much amazed you.
HAMLET:   Very like, very like. Stayed it long?
HORATIO:   While one with moderate haste might tell° a
    hundred.
BOTH:   Longer, longer.
HORATIO:   Not when I saw't.
HAMLET:                     His beard was grizzled,° no?       240
HORATIO:   It was as I have seen it in his life,
    A sable silvered.°
HAMLET:                I will watch tonight.
    Perchance 'twill walk again.
HORATIO:                     I warr'nt it will.
HAMLET:   If it assume my noble father's person,
    I'll speak to it though hell itself should gape            245
    And bid me hold my peace. I pray you all,
    If you have hitherto concealed this sight,
    Let it be tenable° in your silence still,
    And whatsomever else shall hap tonight,
    Give it an understanding but no tongue;                    250
    I will requite your loves. So fare you well.
    Upon the platform 'twixt eleven and twelve
    I'll visit you.
ALL:                Our duty to your honor.
HAMLET:   Your loves, as mine to you. Farewell.

*Exeunt [all but Hamlet].*

My father's spirit—in arms? All is not well.             255
I doubt° some foul play. Would the night were come!
Till then sit still, my soul. Foul deeds will rise,
Though all the earth o'erwhelm them, to men's eyes.

*Exit.*

---

²³⁸ *tell* count   ²⁴⁰ *grizzled* gray   ²⁴² *sable silvered* black mingled with white
²⁴⁸ *tenable* held   ²⁵⁶ *doubt* suspect

**S C E N E  III.**   *A room.*

*Enter Laertes and Ophelia, his sister.*

LAERTES:   My necessaries are embarked. Farewell.
   And, sister, as the winds give benefit
   And convoy° is assistant, do not sleep,
   But let me hear from you.
OPHELIA:             Do you doubt that?
LAERTES:   For Hamlet, and the trifling of his favor,       5
   Hold it a fashion and a toy° in blood,
   A violet in the youth of primy° nature,
   Forward,° not permanent, sweet, not lasting,
   The perfume and suppliance° of a minute,
   No more.
OPHELIA:   No more but so?
LAERTES:             Think it no more.       10
   For nature crescent° does not grow alone
   In thews° and bulk, but as this temple° waxes,
   The inward service of the mind and soul
   Grows wide withal. Perhaps he loves you now,
   And now no soil nor cautel° doth besmirch       15
   The virtue of his will; but you must fear,
   His greatness weighed,° his will is not his own.
   For he himself is subject to his birth.
   He may not, as unvalued° persons do,
   Carve for himself; for on his choice depends      20
   The safety and health of this whole state;
   And therefore must his choice be circumscribed
   Unto the voice and yielding of that body
   Whereof he is the head. Then if he says he loves you,
   It fits your wisdom so far to believe it      25
   As he in his particular act and place
   May give his saying deed, which is no further
   Than the main voice of Denmark goes withal.

---

I.iii.   ³ *convoy* conveyance   ⁶ *toy* idle fancy   ⁷ *primy* springlike   ⁸ *Forward*
premature   ⁹ *suppliance* diversion   ¹¹ *crescent* growing   ¹² *thews* muscles and
sinews   ¹² *temple* i.e., the body   ¹⁵ *cautel* deceit   ¹⁷ *greatness weighed* high rank
considered   ¹⁹ *unvalued* of low rank

Then weigh what loss your honor may sustain
If with too credent° ear you list his songs,                                    30
Or lose your heart, or your chaste treasure open
To his unmastered importunity.
Fear it, Ophelia, fear it, my dear sister,
And keep you in the rear of your affection,
Out of the shot and danger of desire.                                          35
The chariest maid is prodigal enough
If she unmask her beauty to the moon.
Virtue itself scapes not calumnious strokes.
The canker° galls the infants of the spring
Too oft before their buttons° be disclosed,                                    40
And in the morn and liquid dew of youth
Contagious blastments are most imminent.
Be wary then; best safety lies in fear;
Youth to itself rebels, though none else near.
OPHELIA:   I shall the effect of this good lesson keep                          45
As watchman to my heart, but, good my brother,
Do not, as some ungracious° pastors do,
Show me the steep and thorny way to heaven,
Whiles, like a puffed and reckless libertine,
Himself the primrose path of dalliance treads                                  50
And recks not his own rede.°

*Enter Polonius.*

LAERTES:                              O, fear me not.
I stay too long. But here my father comes.
A double blessing is a double grace;
Occasion smiles upon a second leave.
POLONIUS:   Yet here, Laertes? Aboard, aboard, for shame!                       55
The wind sits in the shoulder of your sail,
And you are stayed for. There—my blessing with thee,
And these few precepts in thy memory
Look thou character.° Give thy thoughts no tongue,

---

[30] *credent* credulous   [39] *canker* cankerworm   [40] *buttons* buds   [47] *ungracious* lacking grace   [51] *recks not his own rede* does not heed his own advice   [59] *character*
inscribe

Nor any unproportioned° thought his act.                                60
Be thou familiar, but by no means vulgar.
Those friends thou hast, and their adoption tried,
Grapple them unto thy soul with hoops of steel,
But do not dull thy palm with entertainment
Of each new-hatched, unfledged courage.° Beware        65
Of entrance to a quarrel; but being in,
Bear't that th' opposèd may beware of thee.
Give every man thine ear, but few thy voice;
Take each man's censure,° but reserve thy judgment.
Costly thy habits as thy purse can buy,                              70
But not expressed in fancy; rich, not gaudy,
For the apparel oft proclaims the man,
And they in France of the best rank and station
Are of a most select and generous, chief in that.°
Neither a borrower nor a lender be,                                  75
For loan oft loses both itself and friend,
And borrowing dulleth edge of husbandry.°
This above all, to thine own self be true,
And it must follow, as the night the day,
Thou canst not then be false to any man.                            80
Farewell. My blessing season this° in thee!
LAERTES:  Most humbly do I take my leave, my lord.
POLONIUS:  The time invites you. Go, your servants tend.°
LAERTES:  Farewell, Ophelia, and remember well
     What I have said to you.
OPHELIA:                          'Tis in my memory locked,          85
     And you yourself shall keep the key of it.
LAERTES:  Farewell.

                                                    *Exit Laertes.*


POLONIUS:  What is't, Ophelia, he hath said to you?
OPHELIA:  So please you, something touching the Lord Hamlet.

---

⁶⁰ *unproportioned* unbalanced   ⁶⁵ *courage* gallant youth   ⁶⁹ *censure* opinion
⁷⁴ *Are of . . . in that* show their fine taste and their gentlemanly instincts more in
that than in any other point of manners (Kittredge)   ⁷⁷ *husbandry* thrift   ⁸¹ *season this* make fruitful this (advice)   ⁸³ *tend* attend

POLONIUS:   Marry,° well bethought.                                    90
  'Tis told me he hath very oft of late
  Given private time to you, and you yourself
  Have of your audience been most free and bounteous.
  If it be so—as so 'tis put on me,
  And that in way of caution—I must tell you            95
  You do not understand yourself so clearly
  As it behooves my daughter and your honor.
  What is between you? Give me up the truth.
OPHELIA:   He hath, my lord, of late made many tenders°
  Of his affection to me.                                       100
POLONIUS:   Affection pooh! You speak like a green girl,
  Unsifted° in such perilous circumstance.
  Do you believe his tenders, as you call them?
OPHELIA:   I do not know, my lord, what I should think.
POLONIUS:   Marry, I will teach you. Think yourself a baby     105
  That you have ta'en these tenders for true pay
  Which are not sterling. Tender yourself more dearly,
  _Or (not to crack the wind of the poor phrase)
  Tend'ring it thus you'll tender me a fool.°
OPHELIA:   My lord, he hath importuned me with love          110
  In honorable fashion.
POLONIUS:   Ay, fashion you may call it. Go to, go to.
OPHELIA:   And hath given countenance to his speech, my lord,
  With almost all the holy vows of heaven.
POLONIUS:   Ay, springes to catch woodcocks.° I do know,     115
  When the blood burns, how prodigal the soul
  Lends the tongue vows. These blazes, daughter,
  Giving more light than heat, extinct in both,
  Even in their promise, as it is a-making,
  You must not take for fire. From this time             120
  Be something scanter of your maiden presence.
  Set your entreatments° at a higher rate

---

⁹⁰ *Marry* (a light oath, from "By the Virgin Mary")   ⁹⁹ *tenders* offers (in line 103 it has the same meaning, but in line 106 Polonius speaks of *tenders* in the sense of counters or chips; in line 109 *Tend'ring* means "holding," and *tender* means "give," "present")   ¹⁰² *Unsifted* untried   ¹⁰⁹ *tender me a fool* (1) present me with a fool, (2) present me with a baby   ¹¹⁵ *springes to catch woodcocks* snares to catch stupid birds   ¹²² *entreatments* interviews

Than a command to parley. For Lord Hamlet,
Believe so much in him that he is young,
And with a larger tether may he walk                          125
Than may be given you. In few, Ophelia,
Do not believe his vows, for they are brokers,°
Not of that dye° which their investments° show,
But mere implorators° of unholy suits,
Breathing like sanctified and pious bonds,°                   130
The better to beguile. This is for all:
I would not, in plain terms, from this time forth
Have you so slander° any moment leisure
As to give words or talk with the Lord Hamlet.
Look to't, I charge you. Come your ways.                      135
OPHELIA:   I shall obey, my lord.

                                                    *Exeunt.*

**S C E N E   IV.**   *A guard platform.*

*Enter Hamlet, Horatio, and Marcellus.*

HAMLET:   The air bites shrewdly;° it is very cold.
HORATIO:   It is a nipping and an eager° air.
HAMLET:   What hour now?
HORATIO:                         I think it lacks of twelve.
MARCELLUS:   No, it is struck.
HORATIO:   Indeed? I heard it not. It then draws near the
   season                                                     5
Wherein the spirit held his wont to walk.

*A flourish of trumpets, and two pieces go off.*

What does this mean, my lord?
HAMLET:   The King doth wake° tonight and takes his rouse,°
   Keeps wassail, and the swagg'ring upspring° reels,
   And as he drains his draughts of Rhenish° down            10

---

[127] *brokers* procurers   [128] *dye* i.e., kind   [128] *investments* garments   [129] *implorators* solicitors   [130] *bonds* pledges   [133] *slander* disgrace   I.iv.   [1] *shrewdly* bitterly   [2] *eager* sharp   [8] *wake* hold a revel by night   [8] *takes his rouse* carouses   [9] *upspring* (a dance)   [10] *Rhenish* Rhine wine

The kettledrum and trumpet thus bray out
The triumph of his pledge.°
HORATIO:                              Is it a custom?
HAMLET:    Ay, marry, is't,
But to my mind, though I am native here
And to the manner born, it is a custom                                    15
More honored in the breach than the observance.
This heavy-headed revel east and west
Makes us traduced and taxed of° other nations.
They clepe° us drunkards and with swinish phrase
Soil our addition,° and indeed it takes                                   20
From our achievements, though performed at height,
The pith and marrow of our attribute.°
So oft it chances in particular men
That for some vicious mole° of nature in them,
As in their birth, wherein they are not guilty,                          25
(Since nature cannot choose his origin)
By the o'ergrowth of some complexion,°
Oft breaking down the pales° and forts of reason,
Or by some habit that too much o'erleavens°
The form of plausive° manners, that (these men,                          30
Carrying, I say, the stamp of one defect,
Being nature's livery, or fortune's star° )
Their virtues else, be they as pure as grace,
As infinite as man may undergo,
Shall in the general censure° take corruption                            35
From that particular fault. The dram of evil
Doth all the noble substance of a doubt,
To his own scandal.°

*Enter Ghost.*

---

¹² *The triumph of his pledge* the achievement (of drinking a wine cup in one draught) of his toast   ¹⁸ *taxed of* blamed by   ¹⁹ *clepe* call   ²⁰ *addition* reputation (literally, "title of honor")   ²² *attribute* reputation   ²⁴ *mole* blemish   ²⁷ *complexion* natural disposition   ²⁸ *pales* enclosures   ¹²⁹ *o'erleavens* mixes with, corrupts   ³⁰ *plausive* pleasing   ³² *nature's livery, or fortune's star* nature's equipment (i.e., "innate"), or a person's destiny determined by the stars   ³⁵ *general censure* popular judgment   ³⁶⁻³⁸ *The dram . . . own scandal* (though the drift is clear, there is no agreement as to the exact meaning of these lines)

HORATIO:                    Look, my lord, it comes.
HAMLET:   Angels and ministers of grace defend us!
    Be thou a spirit of health° or goblin damned,                    40
    Bring with thee airs from heaven or blasts from hell,
    Be thy intents wicked or charitable,
    Thou com'st in such a questionable° shape
    That I will speak to thee. I'll call thee Hamlet,
    King, father, royal Dane. O, answer me!                          45
    Let me not burst in ignorance, but tell
    Why thy canonized° bones, hearsèd in death,
    Have burst their cerements,° why the sepulcher
    Wherein we saw thee quietly interred
    Hath oped his ponderous and marble jaws                          50
    To cast thee up again. What may this mean
    That thou, dead corse, again in complete steel,
    Revisits thus the glimpses of the moon,
    Making night hideous, and we fools of nature
    So horridly to shake our disposition°                            55
    With thoughts beyond the reaches of our souls?
    Say, why is this? Wherefore? What should we do?

*Ghost beckons Hamlet.*

HORATIO:   It beckons you to go away with it,
    As if it some impartment° did desire
    To you alone.
MARCELLUS:        Look with what courteous action                    60
    It waves you to a more removèd ground.
    But do not go with it.
HORATIO:                    No, by no means.
HAMLET:   It will not speak. Then I will follow it.
HORATIO:   Do not, my lord.
HAMLET:                      Why, what should be the fear?
    I do not set my life at a pin's fee,                             65
    And for my soul, what can it do to that,

---

[40] *spirit of health* good spirit   [43] *questionable* (1) capable of discourse,
(2) dubious   [47] *canonized* buried according to the canon or ordinance of the
church   [48] *cerements* waxed linen shroud   [55] *shake our disposition* disturb us
[59] *impartment* communication

Being a thing immortal as itself?
It waves me forth again. I'll follow it.
HORATIO:   What if it tempt you toward the flood, my lord,
Or to the dreadful summit of the cliff                                      70
That beetles° o'er his base into the sea,
And there assume some other horrible form,
Which might deprive your sovereignty of reason°
And draw you into madness? Think of it.
The very place puts toys° of desperation,                                  75
Without more motive, into every brain
That looks so many fathoms to the sea
And hears it roar beneath.
HAMLET:                                     It waves me still.
Go on; I'll follow thee.
MARCELLUS:   You shall not go, my lord.
HAMLET:                                                           Hold off your hands.   80
HORATIO:   Be ruled. You shall not go.
HAMLET:                                                   My fate cries out
And makes each petty artere° in this body
As hardy as the Nemean lion's nerve.°
Still am I called! Unhand me, gentlemen.
By heaven, I'll make a ghost of him that lets° me!             85
I say, away! Go on, I'll follow thee.

*Exit Ghost, and Hamlet.*

HORATIO:   He waxes desperate with imagination.
MARCELLUS:   Let's follow. 'Tis not fit thus to obey him.
HORATIO:   Have after! To what issue will this come?
MARCELLUS:   Something is rotten in the state of Denmark.   90
HORATIO:   Heaven will direct it.
MARCELLUS:                                     Nay, let's follow him.

*Exeunt.*

---

[71] *beetles* juts out   [73] *deprive your sovereignty of reason* destroy the sovereignty
of your reason   [75] *toys* whims, fancies   [82] *artere* artery   [83] *Nemean lion's nerve*
sinews of the mythical lion slain by Hercules   [85] *lets* hinders

**S C E N E   V.**   *The battlements.*

*Enter Ghost and Hamlet.*

HAMLET:   Whither wilt thou lead me? Speak; I'll go no further.
GHOST:   Mark me.
HAMLET:                 I will.
GHOST:                         My hour is almost come,
   When I to sulf'rous and tormenting flames
   Must render up myself.
HAMLET:                         Alas, poor ghost.
GHOST:   Pity me not, but lend thy serious hearing                     5
   To what I shall unfold.
HAMLET:                         Speak. I am bound to hear.
GHOST:   So art thou to revenge, when thou shalt hear.
HAMLET:   What?
GHOST:   I am thy father's spirit,
   Doomed for a certain term to walk the night,                     10
   And for the day confined to fast in fires,
   Till the foul crimes° done in my days of nature
   Are burnt and purged away. But that I am forbid
   To tell the secrets of my prison house,
   I could a tale unfold whose lightest word                      15
   Would harrow up thy soul, freeze thy young blood,
   Make thy two eyes like stars start from their spheres,°
   Thy knotted and combinèd locks to part,
   And each particular hair to stand an end
   Like quills upon the fearful porpentine.°                      20
   But this eternal blazon° must not be
   To ears of flesh and blood. List, list, O, list!
   If thou didst ever thy dear father love—
HAMLET:   O God!
GHOST:   Revenge his foul and most unnatural murder.                  25
HAMLET:   Murder?
GHOST:   Murder most foul, as in the best it is,
   But this most foul, strange, and unnatural.

---

I.v.   [12] *crimes* sins   [17] *spheres* in Ptolemaic astronomy, each planet was fixed in a hollow transparent shell concentric with the earth   [20] *fearful porpentine* timid porcupine   [21] *eternal blazon* revelation of eternity

HAMLET:  Haste me to know't, that I, with wings as swift
    As meditation° or the thoughts of love,              30
    May sweep to my revenge.
GHOST:                  I find thee apt,
    And duller shouldst thou be than the fat weed
    That roots itself in ease on Lethe wharf,°
    Wouldst thou not stir in this. Now, Hamlet, hear.
    'Tis given out that, sleeping in my orchard,        35
    A serpent stung me. So the whole ear of Denmark
    Is by a forgèd process° of my death
    Rankly abused. But know, thou noble youth,
    The serpent that did sting thy father's life
    Now wears his crown.
HAMLET:              O my prophetic soul!        40
    My uncle?
GHOST:  Ay, that incestuous, that adulterate° beast,
    With witchcraft of his wits, with traitorous gifts—
    O wicked wit and gifts, that have the power
    So to seduce!—won to his shameful lust        45
    The will of my most seeming-virtuous queen.
    O Hamlet, what a falling-off was there,
    From me, whose love was of that dignity
    That it went hand in hand even with the vow
    I made to her in marriage, and to decline        50
    Upon a wretch whose natural gifts were poor
    To those of mine.
    But virtue, as it never will be moved,
    Though lewdness° court it in a shape of heaven,
    So lust, though to a radiant angel linked,        55
    Will sate itself in a celestial bed
    And prey on garbage.
    But soft, methinks I scent the morning air;
    Brief let me be. Sleeping within my orchard,
    My custom always of the afternoon,        60
    Upon my secure° hour thy uncle stole

---

[30] *meditation* thought   [33] *Lethe wharf* bank of the river of forgetfulness in Hades   [37] *forgèd process* false account   [42] *adulterate* adulterous   [54] *lewdness* lust   [61] *secure* unsuspecting

With juice of cursed hebona° in a vial,
And in the porches of my ears did pour
The leperous distillment, whose effect
Holds such an enmity with blood of man          65
That swift as quicksilver it courses through
The natural gates and alleys of the body,
And with a sudden vigor it doth posset°
And curd, like eager° droppings into milk,
The thin and wholesome blood. So did it mine,          70
And a most instant tetter° barked about
Most lazarlike° with vile and loathsome crust
All my smooth body.
Thus was I, sleeping, by a brother's hand
Of life, of crown, of queen at once dispatched,          75
Cut off even in the blossoms of my sin,
Unhouseled, disappointed, unaneled,°
No reck'ning made, but sent to my account
With all my imperfections on my head.
O, horrible! O, horrible! Most horrible!          80
If thou has nature in thee, bear it not.
Let not the royal bed of Denmark be
A couch for luxury° and damnèd incest.
But howsomever thou pursues this act,
Taint not thy mind, nor let thy soul contrive          85
Against thy mother aught. Leave her to heaven
And to those thorns that in her bosom lodge
To prick and sting her. Fare thee well at once.
The glowworm shows the matin° to be near
And 'gins to pale his uneffectual fire.          90
Adieu, adieu, adieu. Remember me.

*Exit.*

HAMLET:   O all you host of heaven! O earth! What else?
And shall I couple hell? O fie! Hold, hold, my heart,

---

⁶² *hebona* a poisonous plant   ⁶⁸ *posset* curdle   ⁶⁹ *eager* acid   ⁷¹ *tetter* scab   ⁷² *lazarlike* leperlike   ⁷⁷ *Unhouseled, disappointed, unaneled* without the sacrament of communion, unabsolved, without extreme unction   ⁸³ *luxury* lust   ⁸⁹ *matin* morning

And you, my sinews, grow not instant old,
But bear me stiffly up. Remember thee?                          95
Ay, thou poor ghost, whiles memory holds a seat
In this distracted globe.° Remember thee?
Yea, from the table° of my memory
I'll wipe away all trivial fond° records,
All saws° of books, all forms, all pressures° past          100
That youth and observation copied there,
And thy commandment all alone shall live
Within the book and volume of my brain,
Unmixed with baser matter. Yes, by heaven!
O most pernicious woman!                                             105
O villain, villain, smiling, damnèd villain!
My tables—meet it is I set it down
That one may smile, and smile, and be a villain.
At least I am sure it may be so in Denmark. [*Writes.*]
So, uncle, there you are. Now to my word:                     110
It is "Adieu, adieu, remember me."
I have sworn't.
HORATIO AND MARCELLUS (*within*):   My lord, my lord!

*Enter Horatio and Marcellus.*

MARCELLUS:                            Lord Hamlet!
HORATIO:                                            Heavens secure him!
HAMLET:   So be it!
MARCELLUS:   Illo, ho, ho,° my lord!                          115
HAMLET:   Hillo, ho, ho, boy! Come, bird, come.
MARCELLUS:   How is't, my noble lord?
HORATIO:                                     What news, my lord?
HAMLET:   O, wonderful!
HORATIO:   Good my lord, tell it.
HAMLET:                            No, you will reveal it.
HORATIO:   Not I, my lord, by heaven.
MARCELLUS:                             Nor I, my lord.          120

---

[97] *globe* i.e., his head   [98] *table* tablet, notebook   [99] *fond* foolish   [100] *saws*
maxims   [100] *pressures* impressions   [115] *Illo, ho, ho* (falconer's call to his hawk)

HAMLET:   How say you then? Would heart of man once think
   it?
   But you'll be secret?
BOTH:                Ay, by heaven, my lord.
HAMLET:   There's never a villain dwelling in all Denmark
   But he's an arrant knave.
HORATIO:   There needs no ghost, my lord, come from
   the grave                                 125
   To tell us this.
HAMLET:        Why, right, you are in the right;
   And so, without more circumstance° at all,
   I hold it fit that we shake hands and part:
   You, as your business and desire shall point you,
   For every man hath business and desire         130
   Such as it is, and for my own poor part,
   Look you, I'll go pray.
HORATIO:   These are but wild and whirling words, my lord.
HAMLET:   I am sorry they offend you, heartily;
   Yes, faith, heartily.
HORATIO:         There's no offense, my lord.     135
HAMLET:   Yes, by Saint Patrick, but there is, Horatio,
   And much offense too. Touching this vision here,
   It is an honest ghost,° that let me tell you.
   For your desire to know what is between us,
   O'ermaster't as you may. And now, good friends,    140
   As you are friends, scholars, and soldiers,
   Give me one poor request.
HORATIO:   What is't, my lord? We will.
HAMLET:   Never make known what you have seen tonight.
BOTH:   My lord, we will not.
HAMLET:         Nay, but swear't.
HORATIO:               In faith,    145
   My lord, not I.
MARCELLUS:     Nor I, my lord—in faith.
HAMLET:   Upon my sword.
MARCELLUS:       We have sworn, my lord, already.
HAMLET:   Indeed, upon my sword, indeed.

---

[127] *circumstance* details   [138] *honest ghost* i.e., not a demon in his father's shape

*Ghost cries under the stage.*

GHOST:   Swear.
HAMLET:   Ha, ha, boy, say'st thou so? Art thou there,
    truepenny?°                                                                    150
    Come on. You hear this fellow in the cellarage.
    Consent to swear.
HORATIO:                   Propose the oath, my lord.
HAMLET:   Never to speak of this that you have seen.
    Swear by my sword.
GHOST [*beneath*]:   Swear.                                                  155
HAMLET:   *Hic et ubique?*° Then we'll shift our ground;
    Come hither, gentlemen,
    And lay your hands again upon my sword.
    Swear by my sword
    Never to speak of this that you have heard.                   160
GHOST [*beneath*]:   Swear by his sword.
HAMLET:   Well said, old mole! Canst work i' th' earth so fast?
    A worthy pioner!° Once more remove, good friends.
HORATIO:   O day and night, but this is wondrous strange!
HAMLET:   And therefore as a stranger give it welcome.              165
    There are more things in heaven and earth, Horatio,
    Than are dreamt of in your philosophy.
    But come:
    Here as before, never, so help you mercy,
    How strange or odd some'er I bear myself                     170
    (As I perchance hereafter shall think meet
    To put an antic disposition° on),
    That you, at such times seeing me, never shall
    With arms encumb'red° thus, or this headshake,
    Or by pronouncing of some doubtful phrase,                   175
    As "Well, well, we know," or "We could, an if we would,"
    Or "If we list to speak," or "There be, an if they might,"
    Or such ambiguous giving out, to note
    That you know aught of me—this do swear,
    So grace and mercy at your most need help you.              180

---

[150] *truepenny* honest fellow    [156] *Hic et ubique* here and everywhere (Latin)
[163] *pioner* digger of mines    [172] *antic disposition* fantastic behavior    [174] *encumb'red*
folded

GHOST [*beneath*]:   Swear.

[*They swear.*]

HAMLET:   Rest, rest, perturbèd spirit. So, gentlemen,
With all my love I do commend me° to you,
And what so poor a man as Hamlet is
May do t' express his love and friending to you,                    185
God willing, shall not lack. Let us go in together,
And still your fingers on your lips, I pray.
The time is out of joint. O cursèd spite,
That ever I was born to set it right!
Nay, come, let's go together.                                       190

*Exeunt.*

---

# ACT II

S C E N E  I.   *A room.*

*Enter old Polonius, with his man Reynaldo.*

POLONIUS:   Give him this money and these notes, Reynaldo.
REYNALDO:   I will, my lord.
POLONIUS:   You shall do marvell's° wisely, good Reynaldo,
Before you visit him, to make inquire
Of his behavior.
REYNALDO:            My lord, I did intend it.                       5
POLONIUS:   Marry, well said, very well said. Look you sir,
Inquire me first what Danskers° are in Paris,
And how, and who, what means, and where they keep,°
What company, at what expense; and finding
By this encompassment° and drift of question                        10
That they do know my son, come you more nearer
Than your particular demands° will touch it.

---

¹⁸³ *commend me* entrust myself   II.i.   ³ *marvell's* marvelous(ly)   ⁷ *Danskers*
Danes   ⁸ *keep* dwell   ¹⁰ *encompassment* circling   ¹² *demands* questions

Take you as 'twere some distant knowledge of him,
As thus, "I know his father and his friends,
And in part him." Do you mark this, Reynaldo?      15
REYNALDO:   Ay, very well, my lord.
POLONIUS:   "And in part him, but," you may say, "not well,
But if 't be he I mean, he's very wild,
Addicted so and so." And there put on him
What forgeries° you please; marry, none so rank      20
As may dishonor him—take heed of that—
But, sir, such wanton, wild, and usual slips
As are companions noted and most known
To youth and liberty.
REYNALDO:                        As gaming, my lord.
POLONIUS:   Ay, or drinking, fencing, swearing, quarreling,      25
Drabbing.° You may go so far.
REYNALDO:   My lord, that would dishonor him.
POLONIUS:   Faith, no, as you may season it in the charge.
You must not put another scandal on him,
That he is open to incontinency.°      30
That's not my meaning. But breathe his faults so quaintly°
That they may seem the taints of liberty,
The flash and outbreak of a fiery mind,
A savageness in unreclaimèd blood,
Of general assault.°
REYNALDO:                        But, my good lord—      35
POLONIUS:   Wherefore should you do this?
REYNALDO:                                    Ay, my lord,
I would know that.
POLONIUS:                        Marry, sir, here's my drift,
And I believe it is a fetch of warrant.°
You laying these slight sullies on my son
As 'twere a thing a little soiled i' th' working,      40
Mark you,
Your party in converse, him you would sound,
Having ever seen in the prenominate crimes°

---

²⁰ *forgeries* inventions   ²⁶ *Drabbing* wenching   ³⁰ *incontinency* habitual
licentiousness   ³¹ *quaintly* ingeniously, delicately   ³⁵ *Of general assault* common
to all men   ³⁸ *fetch of warrant* justifiable device   ⁴³ *Having . . . crimes* if he has
ever seen in the aforementioned crimes

The youth you breathe of guilty, be assured
He closes with you in this consequence.°                                    45
"Good sir," or so, or "friend," or "gentleman"—
According to the phrase or the addition°
Of man and country—
REYNALDO:                          Very good, my lord.
POLONIUS:  And then, sir, does 'a° this—'a does—
What was I about to say? By the mass, I was about        50
to say something! Where did I leave?
REYNALDO:  At "closes in the consequence," at "friend or so,"
and "gentlemen."
POLONIUS:  At "closes in the consequence"—Ay, marry!
He closes thus: "I know the gentleman;                          55
I saw him yesterday, or t'other day,
Or then, or then, with such or such, and, as you say,
There was 'a gaming, there o'ertook in's rouse,
There falling out at tennis"; or perchance,
"I saw him enter such a house of sale,"                          60
Videlicet,° a brothel, or so forth.
See you now—
Your bait of falsehood take this carp of truth,
And thus do we of wisdom and of reach,°
With windlasses° and with assays of bias,°                      65
By indirections find directions out.
So, by my former lecture and advice,
Shall you my son. You have me, have you not?
REYNALDO:  My lord, I have.
POLONIUS:                          God bye ye, fare ye well.
REYNALDO:  Good my lord.                                        70
POLONIUS:  Observe his inclination in yourself.°
REYNALDO:  I shall, my lord.
POLONIUS:  And let him ply his music.
REYNALDO:                          Well, my lord.
POLONIUS:  Farewell.

*Exit Reynaldo.*

**45 He closes . . . this consequence** he falls in with you in this conclusion   **47 addition** title   **49 a** he   **61 Videlicet** namely   **64 reach** far-reaching awareness(?)   **65 windlasses** circuitous courses   **65 assays of bias** indirect attempts (metaphor from bowling; *bias* = curved course)   **71 in yourself** for yourself

*Enter Ophelia.*

                    How now, Ophelia, what's the matter?
OPHELIA:   O my lord, my lord, I have been so affrighted!          75
POLONIUS:   With what, i' th' name of God?
OPHELIA:   My lord, as I was sewing in my closet,°
   Lord Hamlet, with his doublet all unbraced,°
   No hat upon his head, his stockings fouled,
   Ungartered, and down-gyvèd° to his ankle,                       80
   Pale as his shirt, his knees knocking each other,
   And with a look so piteous in purport,°
   As if he had been loosèd out of hell
   To speak of horrors—he comes before me.
POLONIUS:   Mad for thy love?
OPHELIA:                     My lord, I do not know,                85
   But truly I do fear it.
POLONIUS:             -        What said he?
OPHELIA:   He took me by the wrist and held me hard;
   Then goes he to the length of all his arm,
   And with his other hand thus o'er his brow
   He falls to such perusal of my face                             90
   As 'a would draw it. Long stayed he so.
   At last, a little shaking of mine arm,
   And thrice his head thus waving up and down,
   He raised a sigh so piteous and profound
   As it did seem to shatter all his bulk                          95
   And end his being. That done, he lets me go,
   And, with his head over his shoulder turned,
   He seemed to find his way without his eyes,
   For out o' doors he went without their helps,
   And to the last bended their light on me.                       100
POLONIUS:   Come, go with me. I will go seek the King.
   This is the very ecstasy° of love,
   Whose violent property fordoes° itself
   And leads the will to desperate undertakings
   As oft as any passions under heaven                             105

---

⁷⁷ *closet* private room   ⁷⁸ *doublet all unbraced* jacket entirely unlaced   ⁸⁰ *down-gyvèd* hanging down like fetters   ⁸² *purport* expression   ¹⁰² *ecstasy* madness ¹⁰³ *property fordoes* quality destroys

That does afflict our natures. I am sorry.
What, have you given him any hard words of late?
OPHELIA:   No, my good lord; but as you did command,
I did repel his letters and denied
His access to me.
POLONIUS:                 That hath made him mad.                    110
I am sorry that with better heed and judgment
I had not quoted° him. I feared he did but trifle
And meant to wrack thee; but beshrew my jealousy.°
By heaven, it is as proper° to our age
To cast beyond ourselves° in our opinions              115
As it is common for the younger sort
To lack discretion. Come, go we to the King.
This must be known, which, being kept close, might move
More grief to hide than hate to utter love.°
Come.                                                                  120

                                                            *Exeunt.*

**S C E N E  II.**   *The castle.*

*Flourish. Enter King and Queen, Rosencrantz, and Guildenstern
[with others].*

KING:   Welcome, dear Rosencrantz and Guildenstern.
Moreover that° we much did long to see you,
The need we have to use you did provoke
Our hasty sending. Something have you heard
Of Hamlet's transformation: so call it,                      5
Sith° nor th' exterior nor the inward man
Resembles that it was. What it should be,
More than his father's death, that thus hath put him
So much from th' understanding of himself,
I cannot dream of. I entreat you both                        10

---

[112] *quoted* noted   [113] *beshrew my jealousy* curse on my suspicions   [114] *proper*
natural   [115] *To cast beyond ourselves* to be overcalculating   [117–119] *Come, go . . .*
*utter love* (the general meaning is that while telling the King of Hamlet's love
may anger the King, more grief would come from keeping it secret)
II.ii   [2] *Moreover that* beside the fact that   [6] *Sith* since

That, being of so° young days brought up with him,
And sith so neighbored to his youth and havior,°
That you vouchsafe your rest° here in our court
Some little time, so by your companies
To draw him on to pleasures, and to gather                           15
So much as from occasion you may glean,
Whether aught to us unknown afflicts him thus,
That opened° lies within our remedy.

QUEEN:   Good gentlemen, he hath much talked of you,
And sure I am, two men there is not living                           20
To whom he more adheres. If it will please you
To show us so much gentry° and good will
As to expend your time with us awhile
For the supply and profit of our hope,
Your visitation shall receive such thanks                           25
As fits a king's remembrance.

ROSENCRANTZ:                         Both your Majesties
Might, by the sovereign power you have of us,
Put your dread pleasures more into command
Than to entreaty.

GUILDENSTERN:       But we both obey,
And here give up ourselves in the full bent°                        30
To lay our service freely at your feet,
To be commanded.

KING:   Thanks, Rosencrantz and gentle Guildenstern.

QUEEN:   Thanks, Guildenstern and gentle Rosencrantz.
And I beseech you instantly to visit                                 35
My too much changèd son. Go, some of you,
And bring these gentlemen where Hamlet is.

GUILDENSTERN:   Heavens make our presence and our practices
Pleasant and helpful to him!

QUEEN:                          Ay, amen!

*Exeunt Rosencrantz and Guildenstern*
*[with some Attendants].*

---

**11** *of so* from such   **12** *youth and havior* behavior in his youth   **13** *vouchsafe your rest* consent to remain   **18** *opened* revealed   **22** *gentry* courtesy   **30** *in the full bent* entirely (the figure is of a bow bent to its capacity)

*Enter Polonius.*

POLONIUS:   Th' ambassadors from Norway, my good lord,   40
   Are joyfully returned.
KING:   Thou still° hast been the father of good news.
POLONIUS:   Have I, my lord? Assure you, my good liege,
   I hold my duty, as I hold my soul,
   Both to my God and to my gracious king;   45
   And I do think, or else this brain of mine
   Hunts not the trail of policy so sure°
   As it hath used to do, that I have found
   The very cause of Hamlet's lunacy.
KING:   O, speak of that! That do I long to hear.   50
POLONIUS:   Give first admittance to th' ambassadors.
   My news shall be the fruit to that great feast.
KING:   Thyself do grace to them and bring them in.

[*Exit Polonius.*]

He tells me, my dear Gertrude, he hath found
The head and source of all your son's distemper.   55
QUEEN:   I doubt° it is no other but the main,°
   His father's death and our o'erhasty marriage.
KING:   Well, we shall sift him.

*Enter Polonius, Voltemand, and Cornelius.*

                        Welcome, my good friends.
   Say, Voltemand, what from our brother Norway?
VOLTEMAND:   Most fair return of greetings and desires.   60
   Upon our first,° he sent out to suppress
   His nephew's levies, which to him appeared
   To be a preparation 'gainst the Polack;
   But better looked into, he truly found
   It was against your Highness, whereat grieved,   65

---

⁴² *still* always   ⁴⁷ *Hunts not . . . so sure* does not follow clues of political doings with such sureness   ⁵⁶ *doubt* suspect   ⁵⁶ *main* principal point   ⁶¹ *first* first audience

That so his sickness, age, and impotence
Was falsely borne in hand,° sends out arrests
On Fortinbras; which he, in brief, obeys,
Receives rebuke from Norway, and in fine,°
Makes vow before his uncle never more                           70
To give th' assay° of arms against your Majesty.
Whereon old Norway, overcome with joy,
Gives him threescore thousand crowns in annual fee
And his commission to employ those soldiers,
So levied as before, against the Polack,                        75
With an entreaty, herein further shown, [*gives a paper*]
That it might please you to give quiet pass
Through your dominions for this enterprise,
On such regards of safety and allowance°
As therein are set down.
KING:                         It likes us well;                 80
And at our more considered time° we'll read,
Answer, and think upon this business.
Meantime, we thank you for your well-took labor.
Go to your rest; at night we'll feast together.
Most welcome home!

                              *Exeunt Ambassadors.*


POLONIUS:                 This business is well ended.          85
My liege and madam, to expostulate°
What majesty should be, what duty is,
Why day is day, night night, and time is time,
Were nothing but to waste night, day, and time.
Therefore, since brevity is the soul of wit,°                   90
And tediousness the limbs and outward flourishes,
I will be brief. Your noble son is mad.
Mad call I it, for, to define true madness,
What is't but to be nothing else but mad?
But let that go.

---

⁶⁷ *borne in hand* deceived   ⁶⁹ *in fine* finally   ⁷¹ *assay* trial   ⁷⁹ *regards of safety and allowance* i.e., conditions   ⁸¹ *considered time* time proper for considering   ⁸⁶ *expostulate* discuss   ⁹⁰ *wit* wisdom, understanding

QUEEN:             More matter, with less art.                                95
POLONIUS:   Madam, I swear I use no art at all.
  That he's mad, 'tis true: 'tis true 'tis pity,
  And pity 'tis 'tis true—a foolish figure.°
  But farewell it, for I will use no art.
  Mad let us grant him then; and now remains                         100
  That we find out the cause of this effect,
  Or rather say, the cause of this defect,
  For this effect defective comes by cause.
  Thus it remains, and the remainder thus.
  Perpend.°                                                           105
  I have a daughter: have, while she is mine,
  Who in her duty and obedience, mark,
  Hath given me this. Now gather, and surmise.

[*Reads*] *the letter.*

  "To the celestial, and my soul's idol, the most
  beautified Ophelia"—                                                110

That's an ill phrase, a vile phrase; "beautified" is a vile
phrase. But you shall hear. Thus:

  "In her excellent white bosom, these, &c."

QUEEN:   Came this from Hamlet to her?
POLONIUS:   Good madam, stay awhile. I will be faithful.                      115

  "Doubt thou the stars are fire,
    Doubt that the sun doth move;
  Doubt° truth to be a liar,
    But never doubt I love.

  O dear Ophelia, I am ill at these numbers.° I have            120
  not art to reckon my groans; but that I love thee
  best, O most best, believe it. Adieu.

        Thine evermore, most dear lady,
     whilst this machine° is to him, HAMLET."

---

⁹⁸ *figure* figure of rhetoric   ¹⁰⁵ *Perpend* consider carefully   ¹¹⁸ *Doubt* suspect
¹²⁰ *ill at these numbers* unskilled in verses   ¹²⁴ *machine* complex device (here, his
body)

This in obedience hath my daughter shown me,                    125
And more above° hath his solicitings,
As they fell out by time, by means, and place,
All given to mine ear.
KING:                      But how hath she
Received his love?
POLONIUS:              What do you think of me?
KING:   As of a man faithful and honorable.                     130
POLONIUS:   I would fain prove so. But what might you think,
When I had seen this hot love on the wing
(As I perceived it, I must tell you that,
Before my daughter told me), what might you,
Or my dear Majesty your Queen here, think,                       135
If I had played the desk or table book,°
Or given my heart a winking,° mute and dumb,
Or looked upon this love with idle sight?
What might you think? No, I went round to work
And my young mistress thus I did bespeak:                        140
"Lord Hamlet is a prince, out of thy star.°
This must not be." And then I prescripts gave her,
That she should lock herself from his resort,
Admit no messengers, receive no tokens.
Which done, she took the fruits of my advice,                   145
And he, repellèd, a short tale to make,
Fell into a sadness, then into a fast,
Thence to a watch,° thence into a weakness,
Thence to a lightness,° and, by this declension,
Into the madness wherein now he raves,                          150
And all we mourn for.
KING:                      Do you think 'tis this?
QUEEN:   It may be, very like.
POLONIUS:   Hath there been such a time, I would fain know
        that,
That I have positively said "'Tis so,"
When it proved otherwise?
KING:                      Not that I know.                     155

---

[126] *more above* in addition  [136] *played the desk or table book* i.e., been a passive recipient of secrets  [137] *winking* closing of the eyes  [141] *star* sphere  [148] *watch* wakefulness  [149] *lightness* mental derangement

POLONIUS [*pointing to his head and shoulder*]:   Take this from this,
    if this be otherwise.
    If circumstances lead me, I will find
    Where truth is hid, though it were hid indeed
    Within the center.°
KING:               How may we try it further?
POLONIUS:   You know sometimes he walks four hours
    together                                160
    Here in the lobby.
QUEEN:           So he does indeed.
POLONIUS:   At such a time I'll loose my daughter to him.
    Be you and I behind an arras° then.
    Mark the encounter. If he love her not,
    And be not from his reason fall'n thereon,         165
    Let me be no assistant for a state
    But keep a farm and carters.
KING:                   We will try it.

*Enter Hamlet reading on a book.*

QUEEN:   But look where sadly the poor wretch comes reading.
POLONIUS:   Away, I do beseech you both, away.

                                *Exit King and Queen.*

    I'll board him presently.° O, give me leave.        170
    How does my good Lord Hamlet?
HAMLET:   Well, God-a-mercy.
POLONIUS:   Do you know me, my lord?
HAMLET:   Excellent well. You are a fishmonger.°
POLONIUS:   Not I, my lord.                          175
HAMLET:   Then I would you were so honest a man.
POLONIUS:   Honest, my lord?
HAMLET:   Ay, sir. To be honest, as this world goes, is to be one
    man picked out of ten thousand.
POLONIUS:   That's very true, my lord.           180

---

159 *center* center of the earth   163 *arras* tapestry hanging in front of a wall
170 *board him presently* accost him at once   174 *fishmonger* dealer in fish (slang for
a procurer)

HAMLET:   For if the sun breed maggots in a dead dog, being
a good kissing carrion°—Have you a daughter?

POLONIUS:   I have, my lord.

HAMLET:   Let her not walk i' th' sun. Conception° is a blessing, but as your daughter may conceive, friend, look to't.          185

POLONIUS [aside]:   How say you by that? Still harping on
my daughter. Yet he knew me not at first. 'A said I was
a fishmonger. 'A is far gone, far gone. And truly in my
youth I suffered much extremity for love, very near
this. I'll speak to him again.—What do you read, my          190
lord?

HAMLET:   Words, words, words.

POLONIUS:   What is the matter,° my lord?

HAMLET:   Between who?

POLONIUS:   I mean the matter that you read, my lord.          195

HAMLET:   Slanders, sir; for the satirical rogue says here that
old men have gray beards, that their faces are wrinkled,
their eyes purging thick amber and plumtree gum, and
that they have a plentiful lack of wit, together with most
weak hams. All which, sir, though I most powerfully and          200
potently believe, yet I hold it not honesty° to have it thus
set down; for you yourself, sir, should be old as I am if,
like a crab, you could go backward.

POLONIUS [aside]:   Though this be madness, yet there is
method in't. Will you walk out of the air, my lord?          205

HAMLET:   Into my grave.

POLONIUS:   Indeed, that's out of the air. [Aside.] How preg-
nant° sometimes his replies are! A happiness° that often
madness hits on, which reason and sanity could not so
prosperously be delivered of. I will leave him and sud-          210
denly contrive the means of meeting between him and
my daughter.—My lord, I will take my leave of you.

HAMLET:   You cannot take from me anything that I will more
willingly part withal—except my life, except my life, except my life.          215

---

°182 *a good kissing carrion* (perhaps the meaning is "a good piece of flesh to kiss,"
but many editors emend *good* to *god*, taking the word to refer to the sun)
°184 *Conception* (1) understanding, (2) becoming pregnant   °193 *matter* (Polonius
means "subject matter," but Hamlet pretends to take the word in the sense of
"quarrel")   °201 *honesty* decency   °207–208 *pregnant* meaningful   °208 *happiness* apt
turn of phrase

*Enter Guildenstern and Rosencrantz.*

POLONIUS:   Fare you well, my lord.

HAMLET:   These tedious old fools!

POLONIUS:   You go to seek the Lord Hamlet? There he is.

ROSENCRANTZ [*to Polonius*]:   God save you, sir! [*Exit Polonius.*]

GUILDENSTERN:   My honored lord!                                          220

ROSENCRANTZ:   My most dear lord!

HAMLET:   My excellent good friends! How dost thou, Guildenstern? Ah, Rosencrantz! Good lads, how do you
both?

ROSENCRANTZ:   As the indifferent° children of the earth.      225

GUILDENSTERN:   Happy in that we are not overhappy. On
Fortune's cap we are not the very button.

HAMLET:   Nor the soles of her shoe?

ROSENCRANTZ:   Neither, my lord.

HAMLET:   Then you live about her waist, or in the middle     230
of her favors?

GUILDENSTERN:   Faith, her privates° we.

HAMLET:   In the secret parts of Fortune? O, most true! She
is a strumpet. What news?

ROSENCRANTZ:   None, my lord, but that the world's grown    235
honest.

HAMLET:   Then is doomsday near. But your news is not true.
Let me question more in particular. What have you, my
good friends, deserved at the hands of Fortune that she
sends you to prison hither?                                              240

GUILDENSTERN:   Prison, my lord?

HAMLET:   Denmark's a prison.

ROSENCRANTZ:   Then is the world one.

HAMLET:   A goodly one, in which there are many confines,
wards,° and dungeons, Denmark being one o' th' worst.       245

ROSENCRANTZ:   We think not so, my lord.

HAMLET:   Why, then 'tis none to you, for there is nothing

---

²²⁵ *indifferent* ordinary   ²³² *privates* ordinary men (with a pun on "private
parts")   ²⁴⁵ *wards* cells

either good or bad but thinking makes it so. To me it is
a prison.

ROSENCRANTZ:   Why then your ambition makes it one. 'Tis   250
too narrow for your mind.

HAMLET:   O God, I could be bounded in a nutshell and
count myself a king of infinite space, were it not that I
have bad dreams.

GUILDENSTERN:   Which dreams indeed are ambition, for the   255
very substance of the ambitious is merely the shadow of
a dream.

HAMLET:   A dream itself is but a shadow.

ROSENCRANTZ:   Truly, and I hold ambition of so airy and
light a quality that it is but a shadow's shadow.   260

HAMLET:   Then are our beggars bodies, and our monarchs
and outstretched heroes the beggars' shadows.° Shall we
to th' court? For, by my fay,° I cannot reason.

BOTH:   We'll wait upon you.

HAMLET:   No such matter. I will not sort you with the rest   265
of my servants, for, to speak to you like an honest man,
I am most dreadfully attended. But in the beaten way of
friendship, what make you at Elsinore?

ROSENCRANTZ:   To visit you, my lord; no other occasion.

HAMLET:   Beggar that I am, I am even poor in thanks, but I   270
thank you; and sure, dear friends, my thanks are too
dear a halfpenny.° Were you not sent for? Is it your own
inclining? Is it a free visitation? Come, come, deal justly
with me. Come, come; nay, speak.

GUILDENSTERN:   What should we say, my lord?   275

HAMLET:   Why anything—but to th' purpose. You were sent
for, and there is a kind of confession in your looks, which
your modesties have not craft enough to color. I know
the good King and Queen have sent for you.

ROSENCRANTZ:   To what end, my lord?   280

HAMLET:   That you must teach me. But let me conjure you
by the rights of our fellowship, by the consonancy of our
youth, by the obligation of our ever preserved love, and

---

**261–262** *Then are . . . beggars' shadows* i.e., by your logic, beggars (lacking ambition) are substantial, and great men are elongated shadows   **263** *fay* faith
**271–272** *too dear a halfpenny* i.e., not worth a halfpenny

by what more dear a better proposer can charge you
withal, be even and direct with me, whether you were     285
sent for or no.

ROSENCRANTZ [*aside to Guildenstern*]:   What say you?

HAMLET [*aside*]:   Nay then, I have an eye of you.—If you
love me, hold not off.

GUILDENSTERN:   My lord, we were sent for.     290

HAMLET:   I will tell you why; so shall my anticipation prevent your discovery,° and your secrecy to the King and
Queen molt no feather. I have of late, but wherefore I
know not, lost all my mirth, forgone all custom of exer-
cises; and indeed, it goes so heavily with my disposition     295
that this goodly frame, the earth, seems to me a sterile
promontory; this most excellent canopy, the air, look you,
this brave o'erhanging firmament, this majestical roof
fretted° with golden fire: why, it appeareth nothing to
me but a foul and pestilent congregation of vapors. What     300
a piece of work is a man, how noble in reason, how
infinite in faculties, in form and moving how express°
and admirable, in action how like an angel, in apprehension how like a god: the beauty of the world, the paragon
of animals; and yet to me, what is this quintessence of     305
dust? Man delights not me; nor woman neither, though
by your smiling you seem to say so.

ROSENCRANTZ:   My lord, there was no such stuff in my
thoughts.

HAMLET:   Why did ye laugh then, when I said "Man delights     310
not me"?

ROSENCRANTZ:   To think, my lord, if you delight not in man,
what lenten° entertainment the players shall receive from
you. We coted° them on the way, and hither are they
coming to offer you service.     315

HAMLET:   He that plays the king shall be welcome; his Majesty shall have tribute of me; the adventurous knight
shall use his foil and target;° the lover shall not sigh

---

²⁹¹⁻²⁹² *prevent your discovery* forestall your disclosure   ²⁹⁹ *fretted* adorned   ³⁰² *express* exact   ³¹³ *lenten* meager   ³¹⁴ *coted* overtook   ³¹⁸ *target* shield

gratis; the humorous man° shall end his part in peace;
the clown shall make those laugh whose lungs are tickle      *320*
o' th' sere;° and the lady shall say her mind freely, or°
the blank verse shall halt° for't. What players are they?

ROSENCRANTZ:   Even those you were wont to take such delight in, the tragedians of the city.

HAMLET:   How chances it they travel? Their residence, both      *325*
in reputation and profit, was better both ways.

ROSENCRANTZ:   I think their inhibition° comes by the means
of the innovation.°

HAMLET:   Do they hold the same estimation they did when
I was in the city? Are they so followed?      *330*

ROSENCRANTZ:   No indeed, are they not.

HAMLET:   How comes it? Do they grow rusty?

ROSENCRANTZ:   Nay, their endeavor keeps in the wonted
pace, but there is, sir, an eyrie° of children, little eyases,
that cry out on the top of question° and are most tyran-      *335*
nically° clapped for't. These are now the fashion, and so
berattle the common stages° (so they call them) that many
wearing rapiers are afraid of goosequills° and dare scarce
come thither.

HAMLET:   What, are they children? Who maintains 'em?      *340*
How are they escoted?° Will they pursue the quality° no
longer than they can sing? Will they not say afterwards,
if they should grow themselves to common players (as it
is most like, if their means are no better), their writers
do them wrong to make them exclaim against their own      *345*
succession?°

ROSENCRANTZ:   Faith, there has been much to-do on both
sides, and the nation holds it no sin to tarre° them to
controversy. There was, for a while, no money bid for

---

[319] *humorous man* i.e., eccentric man (among stock characters in dramas were men dominated by a "humor" or odd trait)   [320–321] *tickle o' th' sere* on hair trigger (*sere* = part of the gunlock)   [321] *or* else   [322] *halt* limp   [327] *inhibition* hindrance   [328] *innovation* (probably an allusion to the companies of child actors that had become popular and were offering serious competition to the adult actors)   [334] *eyrie* nest   [334–335] *eyases, that ... of question* unfledged hawks that cry shrilly above others in matter of debate   [335–336] *tyrannically* violently   [337] *berattle the common stages* cry down the public theaters (with the adult acting companies)   [338] *goosequills* pens (of satirists who ridicule the public theaters and their audiences)   [341] *escoted* finanacially supported   [341] *quality* profession of acting   [346] *succession* future   [348] *tarre* incite

argument° unless the poet and the player went to cuffs    350
in the question.

HAMLET:   Is't possible?

GUILDENSTERN:   O, there has been much throwing about of
brains.

HAMLET:   Do the boys carry it away?    355

ROSENCRANTZ:   Ay, that they do, my lord—Hercules and his
load° too.

HAMLET:   It is not very strange, for my uncle is King of
Denmark, and those that would make mouths at him
while my father lived give twenty, forty, fifty, a hundred    360
ducats apiece for his picture in little. 'Sblood,° there is
something in this more than natural, if philosophy could
find it out.

*A flourish.*

GUILDENSTERN:   There are the players.

HAMLET:   Gentlemen, you are welcome to Elsinore. Your    365
hands, come then. Th' appurtenance of welcome is fashion and ceremony. Let me comply° with you in this garb,°
lest my extent° to the players (which I tell you must show
fairly outwards) should more appear like entertainment
than yours. You are welcome. But my uncle-father and    370
aunt-mother are deceived.

GUILDENSTERN:   In what, my dear lord?

HAMLET:   I am but mad north-northwest:° when the wind
is southerly I know a hawk from a handsaw.°

*Enter Polonius.*

POLONIUS:   Well be with you, gentlemen.    375

HAMLET:   Hark you, Guildenstern, and you too; at each ear

---

³⁵⁰ *argument* plot of a play    ³⁵⁶⁻³⁵⁷ *Hercules and his load* i.e., the whole world
(with a reference to the Globe Theatre, which had a sign that represented Hercules bearing the globe)    ³⁶¹ *'Sblood* by God's blood    ³⁶⁷ *comply* be courteous
³⁶⁷ *garb* outward show    ³⁶⁸ *extent* behavior    ³⁷³ *north-northwest* i.e., on one point
of the compass only    ³⁷⁴ *hawk from a handsaw* (*hawk* can refer not only to a bird
but to a kind of pickax; *handsaw*—a carpenter's tool—may involve a similar pun
on "hernshaw," a heron)

a hearer. That great baby you see there is not yet out of
his swaddling clouts.

ROSENCRANTZ:   Happily° he is the second time come to
them, for they say an old man is twice a child.                          380

HAMLET:   I will prophesy he comes to tell me of the players.
Mark it.—You say right, sir; a Monday morning, 'twas
then indeed.

POLONIUS:   My lord, I have news to tell you.

HAMLET:   My lord, I have news to tell you. When Roscius°           385
was an actor in Rome—

POLONIUS:   The actors are come hither, my lord.

HAMLET:   Buzz, buzz.°

POLONIUS:   Upon my honor—

HAMLET:   Then came each actor on his ass—                           390

POLONIUS:   The best actors in the world, either for tragedy,
comedy, history, pastoral, pastoral-comical, historical-
pastoral, tragical-historical, tragical-comical-historical-
pastoral; scene individable,° or poem unlimited.° Seneca°
cannot be too heavy, nor Plautus° too light. For the law           395
of writ and the liberty,° these are the only men.

HAMLET:   O Jeptha, judge of Israel,° what a treasure hadst
thou!

POLONIUS:   What a treasure had he, my lord?

HAMLET:   Why,                                                        400

"One fair daughter, and no more,
    The which he lovèd passing well."

POLONIUS [*aside*]:   Still on my daughter.

HAMLET:   Am I not i' th' right, old Jeptha?

POLONIUS:   If you call me Jeptha, my lord, I have a daughter        405
that I love passing well.

---

[379] *Happily* perhaps    [385] *Roscius* (a famous Roman comic actor)    [388] *Buzz, buzz*
(an interjection, perhaps indicating that the news is old)    [394] *scene individable*
plays observing the unities of time, place, and action    [394] *poem unlimited* plays
not restricted by the tenets of criticism    [394] *Seneca* (Roman tragic dramatist)
[395] *Plautus* (Roman comic dramatist)    [395–396] *For the law of writ and the liberty*
(perhaps "for sticking to the text and for improvising"; perhaps "for classical
plays and for modern loosely written plays")    [397] *Jeptha, judge of Israel* (the title
of a ballad on the Hebrew judge who sacrificed his daughter; see Judges 11)

HAMLET:   Nay, that follows not.
POLONIUS:   What follows then, my lord?
HAMLET:   Why,

> "As by lot, God wot,"                              410

and then, you know,

> "It came to pass, as most like it was."

The first row of the pious chanson° will show you more,
for look where my abridgment° comes.

*Enter the Players.*

You are welcome, masters, welcome, all. I am glad to see      415
thee well. Welcome, good friends. O, old friend, why,
thy face is valanced° since I saw thee last. Com'st thou
to beard me in Denmark? What, my young lady° and
mistress? By'r Lady, your ladyship is nearer to heaven
than when I saw you last by the altitude of a chopine.°      420
Pray God your voice, like a piece of uncurrent gold, be
not cracked within the ring.°—Masters, you are all welcome. We'll e'en to't like French falconers, fly at anything
we see. We'll have a speech straight. Come, give us a
taste of your quality. Come, a passionate speech.            425
PLAYER:   What speech, my good lord?
HAMLET:   I heard thee speak me a speech once, but it was
never acted, or if it was, not above once, for the play, I
remember, pleased not the million; 'twas caviary to the
general,° but it was (as I received it, and others, whose      430
judgments in such matters cried in the top of° mine) an
excellent play, well digested in the scenes, set down with
as much modesty as cunning.° I remember one said there

---

[413] *row of the pious chanson* stanza of the scriptural song   [414] *abridgment* (1) i.e.,
entertainers, who abridge the time, (2) interrupters   [417] *valanced* fringed (with a
beard)   [418] *young lady* i.e., boy for female roles   [420] *chopine* thick-soled
shoe   [420–421] *like a piece . . . the ring* (a coin was unfit for legal tender if a crack
extended from the edge through the ring enclosing the monarch's head. Hamlet,
punning on *ring,* refers to the change of voice that the boy actor will undergo)
[429–430] *caviary to the general* i.e., too choice for the multitude   [431] *in the top of*
overtopping   [433] *modesty as a cunning* restraint as art

were no sallets° in the lines to make the matter savory;
nor no matter in the phrase that might indict the author      *435*
of affectation, but called it an honest method, as wholesome as sweet, and by very much more handsome than
fine.° One speech in't I chiefly loved. 'Twas Aeneas' tale
to Dido, and thereabout of it especially when he speaks
of Priam's slaughter. If it live in your memory, begin at      *440*
this line—let me see, let me see:

"The rugged Pyrrhus, like th' Hyrcanian beast°—"

'Tis not so; it begins with Pyrrhus:

"The rugged Pyrrhus, he whose sable° arms,
Black as his purpose, did the night resemble      *445*
When he lay couchèd in th' ominous horse,°
Hath now this dread and black complexion smeared
With heraldry more dismal.° Head to foot
Now is he total gules, horridly tricked°
With blood of fathers, mothers, daughters, sons,      *450*
Baked and impasted° with the parching streets,
That lend a tyrannous and a damnèd light
To their lord's murder. Roasted in wrath and fire,
And thus o'ersizèd° with coagulate gore,
With eyes like carbuncles, the hellish Pyrrhus      *455*
Old grandsire Priam seeks."

So, proceed you.
POLONIUS:   Fore God, my lord, well spoken, with good ac-
cent and good discretion.
PLAYER:                                      "Anon he finds him,      *460*
Striking too short at Greeks. His antique sword,
Rebellious to his arm, lies where it falls,
Repugnant to command.° Unequal matched,
Pyrrhus at Priam drives, in rage strikes wide,
But with the whiff and wind of his fell sword      *465*

---

[434] *sallets* salads, spicy jests   [437-438] *more handsome than fine* well-proportioned
rather than ornamented   [442] *Hyrcanian beast* i.e., tiger (Hyrcania was in
Asia)   [444] *sable* black   [446] *ominous horse* i.e., wooden horse at the siege of
Troy   [448] *dismal* ill-omened   [449] *total gules, horridly tricked* all red, horridly
adorned   [451] *impasted* encrusted   [454] *o'ersizèd* smeared over   [463] *Repugnant to
command* disobedient

Th' unnervèd father falls. Then senseless Ilium,°
Seeming to feel this blow, with flaming top
Stoops to his base,° and with a hideous crash
Takes prisoner Pyrrhus' ear. For lo, his sword,
Which was declining on the milky head                              470
Of reverend Priam, seemed i' th' air to stick.
So as a painted tyrant° Pyrrhus stood,
And like a neutral to his will and matter°
Did nothing.
But as we often see, against° some storm,                         475
A silence in the heavens, the rack° stand still,
The bold winds speechless, and the orb below
As hush as death, anon the dreadful thunder
Doth rend the region, so after Pyrrhus' pause,
A rousèd vengeance sets him new awork,                            480
And never did the Cyclops' hammers fall
On Mars's armor, forged for proof eterne,°
With less remorse than Pyrrhus' bleeding sword
Now falls on Priam.
Out, out, thou strumpet Fortune! All you gods,                    485
In general synod° take away her power,
Break all the spokes and fellies° from her wheel,
And bowl the round nave° down the hill of heaven,
As low as to the fiends."                                         490

POLONIUS:  This is too long.
HAMLET:  It shall to the barber's, with your beard.—Prithee
    say on. He's for a jig or a tale of bawdry, or he sleeps.
    Say on; come to Hecuba.                                       495

PLAYER:  "But who (ah woe!) had seen the mobled° queen—"

HAMLET:  "The mobled queen"?
POLONIUS:  That's good. "Mobled queen" is good.

PLAYER:  "Run barefoot up and down, threat'ning the flames

---

466 *senseless Ilium* insensate Troy    468 *Stoops to his base* collapses (*his* = its)
472 *painted tyrant* tyrant in a picture    473 *matter* task    475 *against* just before
476 *rack* clouds    482 *proof eterne* eternal endurance    486 *synod* council    487 *fellies*
rims    488 *nave* hub    494 *mobled* muffled

With bisson rheum;° a clout° upon that head
Where late the diadem stood, and for a robe,
About her lank and all o'erteemèd° loins,                    500
A blanket in the alarm of fear caught up—
Who this had seen, with tongue in venom steeped
'Gainst Fortune's state would treason have pronounced.
But if the gods themselves did see her then,
When she saw Pyrrhus make malicious sport              505
In mincing with his sword her husband's limbs,
The instant burst of clamor that she made
(Unless things mortal move them not at all)
Would have made milch° the burning eyes of heaven
And passion in the gods."                                            510

POLONIUS:   Look, whe'r° he has not turned his color, and
has tears in's eyes. Prithee no more.

HAMLET:   'Tis well. I'll have thee speak out the rest of this
soon. Good my lord, will you see the players well bestowed?° Do you hear? Let them be well used, for they     515
are the abstract and brief chronicles of the time. After
your death you were better have a bad epitaph than their
ill report while you live.

POLONIUS:   My lord, I will use them according to their de-
sert.                                                                                520

HAMLET:   God's bodkin,° man, much better! Use every man
after his desert, and who shall scape whipping? Use them
after your own honor and dignity. The less they deserve,
the more merit is in your bounty. Take them in.

POLONIUS:   Come, sirs.                                                525

HAMLET:   Follow him, friends. We'll hear a play tomorrow.
[*Aside to Player.*] Dost thou hear me, old friend? Can you
play *The Murder of Gonzago?*

PLAYER:   Ay, my lord.

HAMLET:   We'll ha't tomorrow night. You could for a need     530
study a speech of some dozen or sixteen lines which I
would set down and insert in't, could you not?

PLAYER:   Ay, my lord.

---

⁴⁹⁸ *bisson rheum* blinding tears   ⁴⁹⁸ *clout* rag   ⁵⁰⁰ *o'erteemèd* exhausted with
childbearing   ⁵⁰⁹ *milch* moist (literally, "milk-giving")   ⁵¹¹ *whe'r* whether
⁵¹⁴⁻⁵¹⁵ *bestowed* housed   ⁵²¹ *God's bodkin* by God's little body

HAMLET:   Very well. Follow that lord, and look you mock
    him not. My good friends, I'll leave you till night. You    535
    are welcome to Elsinore.

*Exeunt Polonius and Players.*

ROSENCRANTZ:   Good my lord.

*Exeunt [Rosencrantz and Guildenstern].*

HAMLET:   Ay, so, God bye to you.—Now I am alone.
    O, what a rogue and peasant slave am I!
    Is it not monstrous that this player here,    540
    But in a fiction, in a dream of passion,°
    Could force his soul so to his own conceit°
    That from her working all his visage wanned,
    Tears in his eyes, distraction in his aspect,
    A broken voice, and his whole function° suiting    545
    With forms° to his conceit? And all for nothing!
    For Hecuba!
    What's Hecuba to him, or he to Hecuba,
    That he should weep for her? What would he do
    Had he the motive and the cue for passion    550
    That I have? He would drown the stage with tears
    And cleave the general ear with horrid speech,
    Make mad the guilty and appall the free,°
    Confound the ignorant, and amaze indeed
    The very faculties of eyes and ears.    555
    Yet I,
    A dull and muddy-mettled° rascal, peak
    Like John-a-dreams,° unpregnant of° my cause,
    And can say nothing. No, not for a king,
    Upon whose property and most dear life    560
    A damned defeat was made. Am I a coward?
    Who calls me villain? Breaks my pate across?
    Plucks off my beard and blows it in my face?
    Tweaks me by the nose? Gives me the lie i' th' throat

---

[541] *dream of passion* imaginary emotion    [542] *conceit* imagination    [545] *function*
action    [546] *forms* bodily expressions    [553] *appall the free* terrify (make pale?) the
guiltless    [557] *muddy-mettled* weak-spirited    [557–558] *peak/Like John-a-dreams* mope
like a dreamer    [558] *unpregnant of* unquickened by

As deep as to the lungs? Who does me this?                              565
Ha, 'swounds,° I should take it, for it cannot be
But I am pigeon-livered° and lack gall
To make oppression bitter, or ere this
I should ha' fatted all the region kites°
With this slave's offal. Bloody, bawdy villain!                         570
Remorseless, treacherous, lecherous, kindless° villain!
O, vengeance!
Why, what an ass am I! This is most brave,°
That I, the son of a dear father murdered,
Prompted to my revenge by heaven and hell,                             575
Must, like a whore, unpack my heart with words
And fall a-cursing like a very drab,°
A stallion!° Fie upon't, foh! About,° my brains.
Hum—
I have heard that guilty creatures sitting at a play                    580
Have by the very cunning of the scene
Been struck so to the soul that presently°
They have proclaimed their malefactions.
For murder, though it have no tongue, will speak
With most miraculous organ. I'll have these players                     585
Play something like the murder of my father
Before mine uncle. I'll observe his looks,
I'll tent° him to the quick. If 'a do blench,°
I know my course. The spirit that I have seen
May be a devil, and the devil hath power                               590
T' assume a pleasing shape, yea, and perhaps
Out of my weakness and my melancholy,
As he is very potent with such spirits,
Abuses me to damn me. I'll have grounds
More relative° than this. The play's the thing                         595
Wherein I'll catch the conscience of the King.

                                                              *Exit.*

---

566 *'swounds* by God's wounds    567 *pigeon-livered* gentle as a dove    569 *region
kites* kites (scavenger birds) of the sky    571 *kindless* unnatural    573 *brave* fine
577 *drab* prostitute    578 *stallion* male prostitute (perhaps one should adopt the
Folio reading, *scullion* = kitchen wench)    578 *About* to work    582 *presently*
immediately    588 *tent* probe    588 *blench* flinch    595 *relative* (probably "pertinent,"
but possibly "able to be related plausibly")

# ACT III

**S C E N E  I.**  *The castle.*

*Enter King, Queen, Polonius, Ophelia, Rosencrantz, Guildenstern, Lords.*

KING:   And can you by no drift of conference°
  Get from him why he puts on this confusion,
  Grating so harshly all his days of quiet
  With turbulent and dangerous lunacy?
ROSENCRANTZ:   He does confess he feels himself distracted,      5
  But from what cause 'a will by no means speak.
GUILDENSTERN:   Nor do we find him forward to be sounded,°
  But with a crafty madness keeps aloof
  When we would bring him on to some confession
  Of his true state.
QUEEN:                    Did he receive you well?                    10
ROSENCRANTZ:   Most like a gentleman.
GUILDENSTERN:   But with much forcing of his disposition.°
ROSENCRANTZ:   Niggard of question,° but of our demands
  Most free in his reply.
QUEEN:                    Did you assay° him
  To any pastime?                                                      15
ROSENCRANTZ:   Madam, it so fell out that certain players
  We o'erraught° on the way; of these we told him,
  And there did seem in him a kind of joy
  To hear of it. They are here about the court,
  And, as I think, they have already order                            20
  This night to play before him.
POLONIUS:                              'Tis most true,
  And he beseeched me to entreat your Majesties
  To hear and see the matter.
KING:   With all my heart, and it doth much content me
  To hear him so inclined.                                            25

---

III.i   ¹ *drift of conference* management of conversation   ⁷ *forward to be sounded* willing to be questioned   ¹² *forcing of his disposition* effort   ¹³ *Niggard of question* uninclined to talk   ¹⁴ *assay* tempt   ¹⁷ *o'erraught* overtook

Good gentlemen, give him a further edge
And drive his purpose into these delights.
ROSENCRANTZ:   We shall, my lord.

*Exeunt Rosencrantz and Guildenstern.*

KING:                                    Sweet Gertrude, leave us too,
  For we have closely° sent for Hamlet hither,
  That he, as 'twere by accident, may here                              30
  Affront° Ophelia.
  Her father and myself (lawful espials°)
  Will so bestow ourselves that, seeing unseen,
  We may of their encounter frankly judge
  And gather by him, as he is behaved,                                    35
  If 't be th' affliction of his love or no
  That thus he suffers for.
QUEEN:                                  I shall obey you.
  And for your part, Ophelia, I do wish
  That your good beauties be the happy cause
  Of Hamlet's wildness. So shall I hope your virtues                     40
  Will bring him to his wonted way again,
  To both your honors.
OPHELIA:                            Madam, I wish it may.

*[Exit Queen.]*

POLONIUS:   Ophelia, walk you here.—Gracious, so please you,
  We will bestow ourselves. [*To Ophelia.*] Read on this book,
  That show of such an exercise may color°                               45
  Your loneliness. We are oft to blame in this,
  'Tis too much proved, that with devotion's visage
  And pious action we do sugar o'er
  The devil himself.
KING [*aside*]:            O, 'tis too true.
  How smart a lash that speech doth give my conscience!                  50
  The harlot's cheek, beautied with plast'ring art,

---

²⁹ *closely* secretly   ³¹ *Affront* meet face to face   ³² *espials* spies   ⁴⁵ *exercise may
color* act of devotion may give a plausible hue to (the book is one of devotion)

Is not more ugly to the thing that helps it
Than is my deed to my most painted word.
O heavy burden!
POLONIUS:   I hear him coming. Let's withdraw, my lord.          55

[*Exeunt King and Polonius.*]

*Enter Hamlet.*

HAMLET:   To be, or not to be: that is the question:
Whether 'tis nobler in the mind to suffer
The slings and arrows of outrageous fortune,
Or to take arms against a sea of troubles,
And by opposing end them. To die, to sleep—          60
No more—and by a sleep to say we end
The heartache, and the thousand natural shocks
That flesh is heir to! 'Tis a consummation
Devoutly to be wished. To die, to sleep—
To sleep—perchance to dream: ay, there's the rub,°          65
For in that sleep of death what dreams may come
When we have shuffled off this mortal coil,°
Must give us pause. There's the respect°
That makes calamity of so long life:°
For who would bear the whips and scorns of time,          70
Th' oppressor's wrong, the proud man's contumely,
The pangs of despised love, the law's delay,
The insolence of office, and the spurns
That patient merit of th' unworthy takes,
When he himself might his quietus° make          75
With a bare bodkin?° Who would fardels° bear,
To grunt and sweat under a weary life,
But that the dread of something after death
The undiscovered country, from whose bourn°
No traveler returns, puzzles the will,          80

---

[65] *rub* impediment (obstruction to a bowler's ball)    [67] *coil* (1) turmoil, (2) a ring of rope (here the flesh encircling the soul)    [68] *respect* consideration    [69] *makes calamity of so long life* (1) makes calamity so long-lived, (2) makes living so long a calamity    [75] *quietus* full discharge (a legal term)    [76] *bodkin* dagger    [76] *fardels* burdens    [79] *bourn* region

And makes us rather bear those ills we have,
Than fly to others that we know not of?
Thus conscience° does make cowards of us all,
And thus the native hue of resolution
Is sicklied o'er with the pale cast° of thought,                    85
And enterprises of great pitch° and moment,
With this regard° their currents turn awry,
And lose the name of action.—Soft you now,
The fair Ophelia!—Nymph, in thy orisons°
Be all my sins remembered.

OPHELIA:                          Good my lord,                       90
How does your honor for this many a day?

HAMLET:   I humbly thank you; well, well, well.

OPHELIA:   My lord, I have remembrances of yours
That I have longèd long to redeliver.
I pray you now, receive them.

HAMLET:                          No, not I,                            95
I never gave you aught.

OPHELIA:   My honored lord, you know right well you did,
And with them words of so sweet breath composed
As made these things more rich. Their perfume lost,
Take these again, for to the noble mind                              100
Rich gifts wax poor when givers prove unkind.
There, my lord.

HAMLET:   Ha, ha! Are you honest?°

OPHELIA:   My lord?

HAMLET:   Are you fair?                                              105

OPHELIA:   What means your lordship?

HAMLET:   That if you be honest and fair, your honesty
should admit no discourse to your beauty.°

OPHELIA:   Could beauty, my lord, have better commerce
than with honesty?                                                  110

HAMLET:   Ay, truly; for the power of beauty will sooner
transform honesty from what it is to a bawd° than the

---

[83] *conscience* self-consciousness, introspection   [85] *cast* color   [86] *pitch* height (a
term from falconry)   [87] *regard* consideration   [89] *orisons* prayers   [103] *Are you honest* (1) are you modest, (2) are you chaste, (3) have you integrity   [107–108] *your
honesty . . . to your beauty* your modesty should permit no approach to your
beauty   [112] *bawd* procurer

force of honesty can translate beauty into his likeness.
This was sometime a paradox, but now the time gives it
proof. I did love you once.    115
OPHELIA:   Indeed, my lord, you made me believe so.
HAMLET:   You should not have believed me, for virtue cannot so inoculate° our old stock but we shall relish of it.°
I loved you not.
OPHELIA:   I was the more deceived.    120
HAMLET:   Get thee to a nunnery. Why wouldst thou be a
breeder of sinners? I am myself indifferent honest,° but
yet I could accuse me of such things that it were better
my mother had not borne me: I am very proud, revenge-
ful, ambitious, with more offenses at my beck° than I    125
have thoughts to put them in, imagination to give them
shape, or time to act them in. What should such fellows
as I do crawling between earth and heaven? We are arrant
knaves all; believe none of us. Go thy ways to a nunnery.
Where's your father?    130
OPHELIA:   At home, my lord.
HAMLET:   Let the doors be shut upon him, that he may play
the fool nowhere but in's own house. Farewell.
OPHELIA:   O help him, you sweet heavens!
HAMLET:   If thou dost marry, I'll give thee this plague for thy    135
dowry: be thou as chaste as ice, as pure as snow, thou
shalt not escape calumny. Get thee to a nunnery. Go,
farewell. Or if thou wilt needs marry, marry a fool, for
wise men know well enough what monsters° you make
of them. To a nunnery, go, and quickly too. Farewell.    140
OPHELIA:   Heavenly powers, restore him!
HAMLET:   I have heard of your paintings, well enough. God
hath given you one face, and you make yourselves another. You jig and amble, and you lisp; you nickname
God's creatures and make your wantonness your igno-    145
rance.° Go to, I'll no more on't; it hath made me mad. I

---

¹¹⁸ *inoculate* graft    ¹¹⁸ *relish of it* smack of it (our old sinful nature)    ¹²² *indifferent honest* moderately virtuous    ¹²⁵ *beck* call    ¹³⁹ *monsters* horned beasts,
cuckolds    ¹⁴⁵⁻¹⁴⁶ *make your wantonness your ignorance* excuse your wanton
speech by pretending ignorance

say we will have no moe° marriage. Those that are married already—all but one—shall live. The rest shall keep
as they are. To a nunnery, go.

*Exit.*

OPHELIA:   O what a noble mind is here o'erthrown!          150
The courtier's, soldier's, scholar's, eye, tongue, sword,
Th' expectancy and rose° of the fair state,
The glass of fashion, and the mold of form,°
Th' observed of all observers, quite, quite down!
And I, of ladies most deject and wretched,                 155
That sucked the honey of his musicked vows,
Now see that noble and most sovereign reason
Like sweet bells jangled, out of time and harsh,
That unmatched form and feature of blown° youth
Blasted with ecstasy.° O, woe is me                        160
T' have seen what I have seen, see what I see!

*Enter King and Polonius.*

KING:   Love? His affections° do not that way tend,
Nor what he spake, though it lacked form a little,
Was not like madness. There's something in his soul
O'er which his melancholy sits on brood,                   165
And I do doubt° the hatch and the disclose
Will be some danger; which for to prevent,
I have in quick determination
Thus set it down: he shall with speed to England
For the demand of our neglected tribute.                   170
Haply the seas, and countries different,
With variable objects, shall expel
This something-settled° matter in his heart,
Whereon his brains still beating puts him thus
From fashion of himself. What think you on't?             175

---

<sup>147</sup> *moe* more   <sup>152</sup> *expectancy and rose* i.e., fair hope   <sup>153</sup> *The glass . . . of form* the mirror of fashion, and the pattern of excellent behavior   <sup>159</sup> *blown* blooming   <sup>160</sup> *ecstasy* madness   <sup>162</sup> *affections* inclinations   <sup>166</sup> *doubt* fear   <sup>173</sup> *something-settled* somewhat settled

POLONIUS:   It shall do well. But yet do I believe
 The origin and commencement of his grief
 Sprung from neglected love. How now, Ophelia?
 You need not tell us what Lord Hamlet said;
 We heard it all. My lord, do as you please,     *180*
 But if you hold it fit, after the play,
 Let his queen mother all alone entreat him
 To show his grief. Let her be round° with him,
 And I'll be placed, so please you, in the ear
 Of all their conference. If she find him not,°    *185*
 To England send him, or confine him where
 Your wisdom best shall think.
KING:          It shall be so.
 Madness in great ones must not unwatched go.

                   *Exeunt.*

**S C E N E  II.** *The castle.*

*Enter Hamlet and three of the Players.*

HAMLET:   Speak the speech, I pray you, as I pronounced it
to you, trippingly on the tongue. But if you mouth it, as
many of our players do, I had as lief the town crier spoke
my lines. Nor do not saw the air too much with your
hand, thus, but use all gently, for in the very torrent,  *5*
tempest, and (as I may say) whirlwind of your passion,
you must acquire and beget a temperance that may give
it smoothness. O, it offends me to the soul to hear a
robustious periwig-pated° fellow tear a passion to tatters,
to very rags, to split the ears of the groundlings,° who  *10*
for the most part are capable of° nothing but inexplicable
dumb shows° and noise. I would have such a fellow

---

[183] *round* blunt [185] *find him not* does not find him out III.ii. [9] *robustious peri-*
*wig-pated* boisterous wig-headed [10] *groundlings* those who stood in the pit of
the theater (the poorest and presumably most ignorant of the audience) [11] *are*
*capable of* are able to understand [12] *dumb shows* (it had been the fashion for
actors to preface plays or parts of plays with silent mime)

whipped for o'erdoing Termagant. It out-herods Herod.°
Pray you avoid it.

PLAYER:   I warrant your honor.                                    15

HAMLET:   Be not too tame neither, but let your own discretion be your tutor. Suit the action to the word, the word
to the action, with this special observance, that you o'er-
step not the modesty of nature. For anything so o'erdone
is from° the purpose of playing, whose end, both at the    20
first and now, was and is, to hold, as'twere, the mirror
up to nature; to show virtue her own feature, scorn her
own image, and the very age and body of the time his
form and pressure.° Now, this overdone, or come tardy
off, though it makes the unskillful laugh, cannot but      25
make the judicious grieve, the censure of the which one
must in your allowance o'erweigh a whole theater of
others. O, there be players that I have seen play, and
heard others praise, and that highly (not to speak it
profanely), that neither having th' accent of Christians,  30
nor the gait of Christian, pagan, nor man, have so strut-
ted and bellowed that I have thought some of Nature's
journeymen° had made men, and not made them well,
they imitated humanity so abominably.

PLAYER:   I hope we have reformed that indifferently° with  35
us, sir.

HAMLET:   O, reform it altogether! And let those that play
your clowns speak no more than is set down for them,
for there be of them that will themselves laugh, to set on
some quantity of barren spectators to laugh too, though    40
in the meantime some necessary question of the play be
then to be considered. That's villainous and shows a most
pitiful ambition in the fool that uses it. Go make you
ready.

*Exit Players.*

*Enter Polonius, Guildenstern, and Rosencrantz.*

---

[13] *Termagant . . . Herod* (boisterous characters in the old mystery plays)   [20] *from*
contrary to   [24] *pressure* image, impress   [33] *journeymen* workers not yet masters
of their craft   [35] *indifferently* tolerably

How now, my lord? Will the King hear this piece of      45
   work?
POLONIUS:   And the Queen too, and that presently.
HAMLET:   Bid the players make haste.

                                       *Exit Polonius.*

Will you two help to hasten them?
ROSENCRANTZ:   Ay, my lord.      50

                                       *Exeunt they two.*

HAMLET:   What, ho, Horatio!

*Enter Horatio.*

HORATIO:   Here, sweet lord, at your service.
HAMLET:   Horatio, thou art e'en as just a man
   As e'er my conversation coped withal.°
HORATIO:   O, my dear lord—
HAMLET:                  Nay, do not think I flatter.      55
   For what advancement° may I hope from thee,
   That no revenue hast but thy good spirits
   To feed and clothe thee? Why should the poor be flattered?
   No, let the candied° tongue lick absurd pomp,
   And crook the pregnant° hinges of the knee      60
   Where thrift° may follow fawning. Dost thou hear?
   Since my dear soul was mistress of her choice
   And could of men distinguish her election,
   S' hath sealed thee° for herself, for thou hast been
   As one, in suff'ring all, that suffers nothing,      65
   A man that Fortune's buffets and rewards
   Hast ta'en with equal thanks; and blest are those
   Whose blood° and judgment are so well commeddled°
   That they are not a pipe for Fortune's finger
   To sound what stop she please. Give me that man      70

---

<sup>54</sup> *coped withal* met with   <sup>56</sup> *advancement* promotion   <sup>59</sup> *candied* sugared,
flattering   <sup>60</sup> *pregnant* (1) pliant, (2) full of promise of good fortune   <sup>61</sup> *thrift*
profit   <sup>64</sup> *S' hath sealed thee* she (the soul) has set a mark on you   <sup>68</sup> *blood*
passion   <sup>68</sup> *commeddled* blended

That is not passion's slave, and I will wear him
In my heart's core, ay, in my heart of heart,
As I do thee. Something too much of this—
There is a play tonight before the King.
One scene of it comes near the circumstance           75
Which I have told thee, of my father's death.
I prithee, when thou seest that act afoot,
Even with the very comment° of thy soul
Observe my uncle. If his occulted° guilt
Do not itself unkennel in one speech,                 80
It is a damnèd ghost that we have seen,
And my imaginations are as foul
As Vulcan's stithy.° Give him heedful note,
For I mine eyes will rivet to his face,
And after we will both our judgments join             85
In censure of his seeming.°
HORATIO:                          Well, my lord.
If 'a steal aught the whilst this play is playing,
And scape detecting, I will pay the theft.

*Enter Trumpets and Kettledrums, King, Queen, Polonius, Ophelia,*
*Rosencrantz, Guildenstern, and other Lords attendant with his*
*Guard carrying torches. Danish March. Sound a Flourish.*

HAMLET:   They are coming to the play: I must be idle;°
Get you a place.                                      90
KING:   How fares our cousin Hamlet?
HAMLET:   Excellent, i' faith, of the chameleon's dish;° I eat the
air, promise-crammed; you cannot feed capons so.
KING:   I have nothing with this answer. Hamlet; these words
are not mine.                                         95
HAMLET:   No, nor mine now. [*To Polonius.*] My lord, you played
once i' th' university, you say?
POLONIUS:   That did I, my lord, and was accounted a good
actor.

---

<sup>78</sup> *very comment* deepest wisdom   <sup>79</sup> *occulted* hidden   <sup>83</sup> *stithy* forge, smithy
<sup>86</sup> *censure of his seeming* judgment on his looks   <sup>89</sup> *be idle* play the fool   <sup>92</sup> *the*
*chameleon's dish* air (on which chameleons were thought to live)

HAMLET:   What did you enact?
POLONIUS:   I did enact Julius Caesar. I was killed i' th' Capitol;   *100*
   Brutus killed me.
HAMLET:   It was a brute part of him to kill so capital a calf
   there. Be the players ready?
ROSENCRANTZ:   Ay, my lord. They stay upon your patience.
QUEEN:   Come hither, my dear Hamlet, sit by me.   *105*
HAMLET:   No, good mother. Here's metal more attractive.°
POLONIUS [*to the king*]:   O ho! Do you mark that?
HAMLET:   Lady, shall I lie in your lap?

[*He lies at Ophelia's feet.*]

OPHELIA:   No, my lord.
HAMLET:   I mean, my head upon your lap?   *110*
OPHELIA:   Ay, my lord.
HAMLET:   Do you think I meant country matters?°
OPHELIA:   I think nothing, my lord.
HAMLET:   That's a fair thought to lie between maids' legs.
OPHELIA:   What is, my lord?   *115*
HAMLET:   Nothing.
OPHELIA:   You are merry, my lord.
HAMLET:   Who, I?
OPHELIA:   Ay, my lord.
HAMLET:   O God, your only jig-maker!° What should a man   *120*
   do but be merry? For look you how cheerfully my mother
   looks, and my father died within's two hours.
OPHELIA:   Nay, 'tis twice two months, my lord.
HAMLET:   So long? Nay then, let the devil wear black, for
   I'll have a suit of sables.° O heavens! Die two months   *125*
   ago, and not forgotten yet? Then there's hope a great
   man's memory may outlive his life half a year. But, by'r
   Lady, 'a must build churches then, or else shall 'a suffer
   not thinking on, with the hobbyhorse,° whose epitaph is
   "For O, for O, the hobbyhorse is forgot!"   *130*

---

[106] *attractive* magnetic   [112] *country matters* rustic doings (with a pun on the vulgar word for the pudendum)   [120] *jig-maker* composer of songs and dances (often a Fool, who performed them)   [125] *sables* (pun on "black" and "luxurious furs")   [129] *hobbyhorse* mock horse worn by a performer in the morris dance

*The trumpets sound. Dumb show follows:*

*Enter a King and a Queen very lovingly, the Queen embracing
him, and he her. She kneels; and makes show of protestation unto
him. He takes her up, and declines his head upon her neck. He lies
him down upon a bank of flowers. She, seeing him asleep, leaves
him. Anon comes in another man: takes off his crown, kisses it,
pours poison in the sleeper's ears, and leaves him. The Queen returns, finds the King dead, makes passionate action. The poisoner,
with some three or four, come in again, seem to condole with her.
The dead body is carried away. The poisoner woos the Queen with
gifts; she seems harsh awhile, but in the end accepts love.*

*Exeunt.*

OPHELIA:  What means this, my lord?
HAMLET:  Marry, this is miching mallecho;° it means mischief.
OPHELIA:  Belike this show imports the argument° of the play.

*Enter Prologue.*

HAMLET:  We shall know by this fellow. The players cannot
keep counsel; they'll tell all.                                    135
OPHELIA:  Will 'a tell us what this show meant?
HAMLET:  Ay, or any show that you will show him. Be not
you ashamed to show, he'll not shame to tell you what
it means.
OPHELIA:  You are naught,° you are naught; I'll mark the play.   140
PROLOGUE:  For us, and for our tragedy,
Here stooping to your clemency.
We beg your hearing patiently.

[*Exit.*]

HAMLET:  Is this a prologue, or the posy of a ring?°
OPHELIA:  'Tis brief, my lord.                                      145
HAMLET:  As woman's love.

---

[132] *miching mallecho* sneaking mischief  [133] *argument* plot  [140] *naught* wicked,
improper  [144] *posy of a ring* motto inscribed in a ring

*Enter [two Players as] King and Queen.*

PLAYER KING:   Full thirty times hath Phoebus' cart° gone round
Neptune's salt wash° and Tellus'° orbèd ground,
And thirty dozen moons with borrowed sheen
About the world have times twelve thirties been,                    150
Since love our hearts, and Hymen did our hands,
Unite commutual in most sacred bands.
PLAYER QUEEN:   So many journeys may the sun and moon
Make us again count o'er ere love be done!
But woe is me, you are so sick of late,                             155
So far from cheer and from your former state,
That I distrust° you. Yet, though I distrust,
Discomfort you, my lord, it nothing must.
For women fear too much, even as they love,
And women's fear and love hold quantity,                           160
In neither aught, or in extremity.°
Now what my love is, proof° hath made you know,
And as my love is sized, my fear is so.
Where love is great, the littlest doubts are fear;
Where little fears grow great, great love grows there.             165
PLAYER KING:   Faith, I must leave thee, love, and shortly too;
My operant° powers their functions leave to do:
And thou shalt live in this fair world behind,
Honored, beloved, and haply one as kind
For husband shalt thou—
PLAYER QUEEN:                    O, confound the rest!               170
Such love must needs be treason in my breast.
In second husband let me be accurst!
None wed the second but who killed the first.
HAMLET [*aside*]:   That's wormwood.°
PLAYER QUEEN:   The instances° that second marriage move°          175

---

[147] *Phoebus' cart* the sun's chariot   [148] *Neptune's salt wash* the sea   [148] *Tellus* Roman goddess of the earth   [157] *distrust* am anxious about   [160–161] *And women's . . . in extremity* (perhaps the idea is that women's anxiety is great or little in proportion to their love. The previous line, unrhymed, may be a false start that Shakespeare neglected to delete)   [162] *proof* experience   [167] *operant* active   [174] *wormwood* a bitter herb   [175] *instances* motives   [175] *move* induce

Are base respects of thrift,° but none of love.
A second time I kill my husband dead
When second husband kisses me in bed.

PLAYER KING:   I do believe you think what now you speak,
But what we do determine oft we break.                              *180*
Purpose is but the slave to memory,
Of violent birth, but poor validity,°
Which now like fruit unripe sticks on the tree,
But fall unshaken when they mellow be.
Most necessary 'tis that we forget                                  *185*
To pay ourselves what to ourselves is debt.
What to ourselves in passion we propose,
The passion ending, doth the purpose lose.
The violence of either grief or joy
Their own enactures° with themselves destroy:                      *190*
Where joy most revels, grief doth most lament;
Grief joys, joy grieves, on slender accident.
This world is not for aye, nor 'tis not strange
That even our loves should with our fortunes change,
For 'tis a question left us yet to prove,                          *195*
Whether love lead fortune, or else fortune love.
The great man down, you mark his favorite flies;
The poor advanced makes friends of enemies;
And hitherto doth love on fortune tend,
For who not needs shall never lack a friend;                       *200*
And who in want a hollow friend doth try,
Directly seasons him° his enemy.
But, orderly to end where I begun,
Our wills and fates do so contrary run
That our devices still are overthrown;                             *205*
Our thoughts are ours, their ends none of our own.
So think thou wilt no second husband wed,
But die thy thoughts when thy first lord is dead.

PLAYER QUEEN:   Nor earth to give me food, nor heaven light,
Sport and repose lock from me day and night,                       *210*
To desperation turn my trust and hope,
An anchor's° cheer in prison be my scope,

---

[176] *respects of thrift* considerations of profit   [182] *validity* strength   [190] *enactures* acts   [202] *seasons him* ripens him into   [212] *anchor's* anchorite's, hermit's

Each opposite that blanks° the face of joy
Meet what I would have well, and it destroy:
Both here and hence pursue me lasting strife,                    215
If, once a widow, ever I be wife!
HAMLET:   If she should break it now!
PLAYER KING:   'Tis deeply sworn. Sweet, leave me here awhile;
My spirits grow dull, and fain I would beguile
The tedious day with sleep.
PLAYER QUEEN:                           Sleep rock thy brain,       220

[*He*] *sleeps.*

And never come mischance between us twain!

*Exit.*

HAMLET:   Madam, how like you this play?
QUEEN:   The lady doth protest too much, methinks.
HAMLET:   O, but she'll keep her word.
KING:   Have you heard the argument?° Is there no offense in't?   225
HAMLET:   No, no, they do but jest, poison in jest; no offense
i' th' world.
KING:   What do you call this play?
HAMLET:   *The Mousetrap.* Marry, how? Tropically.° This play
is the image of a murder done in Vienna: Gonzago is the        230
Duke's name; his wife, Baptista. You shall see anon. 'Tis
a knavish piece of work, but what of that? Your Majesty,
and we that have free° souls, it touches us not. Let the
galled jade winch;° our withers are unwrung.

*Enter Lucianus.*

This is one Lucianus, nephew to the King.                       235
OPHELIA:   You are as good as a chorus, my lord.
HAMLET:   I could interpret° between you and your love, if I
could see the puppets dallying.

---

[213] *opposite that blanks* adverse thing that blanches   [225] *argument* plot   [229] *Tropically* figuratively (with a pun on "trap")   [233] *free* innocent   [234] *galled jade winch* chafed horse wince   [237] *interpret* (like a showman explaining the action of puppets)

OPHELIA: You are keen,° my lord, you are keen.
HAMLET: It would cost you a groaning to take off mine edge. 240
OPHELIA: Still better, and worse.
HAMLET: So you mistake° your husbands.—Begin, murderer. Leave thy damnable faces and begin. Come, the croaking raven doth bellow for revenge.
LUCIANUS: Thoughts black, hands apt, drugs fit, and time agreeing,                    245
Confederate season,° else no creature seeing,
Thou mixture rank, of midnight weeds collected,
With Hecate's ban° thrice blasted, thrice infected,
Thy natural magic and dire property°
On wholesome life usurps immediately.                    250

*Pours the poison in his ears.*

HAMLET: 'A poisons him i' th' garden for his estate. His name's Gonzago. The story is extant, and written in very choice Italian. You shall see anon how the murderer gets the love of Gonzago's wife.
OPHELIA: The King rises.                    255
HAMLET: What, frighted with false fire?°
QUEEN: How fares my lord?
POLONIUS: Give o'er the play.
KING: Give me some light. Away!
POLONIUS: Lights, lights, lights!                    260

*Exeunt all but Hamlet and Horatio.*

HAMLET:        Why, let the strucken deer go weep,
                    The hart ungallèd play:
                For some must watch, while some must sleep;
                    Thus runs the world away.
        Would not this, sir, and a forest of feathers°—if the rest    265
        of my fortunes turn Turk° with me—with two Provincial

---

²³⁹ *keen* (1) sharp, (2) sexually aroused    ²⁴² *mistake* err in taking    ²⁴⁶ *Confederate season* the opportunity allied with me    ²⁴⁸ *Hecate's ban* the curse of the goddess of sorcery    ²⁴⁹ *property* nature    ²⁵⁶ *false fire* blank discharge of firearms    ²⁶⁵ *feathers* (plumes were sometimes part of a costume)    ²⁶⁶ *turn Turk* i.e., go bad, treat me badly

roses° on my razed° shoes, get me a fellowship in a cry°
of players?
HORATIO:   Half a share.
HAMLET:   A whole one, I.                                        270

    For thou dost know, O Damon dear,
        This realm dismantled was
    Of Jove himself; and now reigns here
        A very, very—pajock.°
HORATIO:   You might have rhymed.°                              275
HAMLET:   O good Horatio, I'll take the ghost's word for a
thousand pound. Didst perceive?
HORATIO:   Very well, my lord.
HAMLET:   Upon the talk of poisoning?
HORATIO:   I did very well note him.                            280
HAMLET:   Ah ha! Come, some music! Come, the recorders!°

    For if the King like not the comedy,
    Why then, belike he likes it not, perdy.°

Come, some music!

*Enter Rosencrantz and Guildenstern.*

GUILDENSTERN:   Good my lord, vouchsafe me a word with
    you.                                                  285
HAMLET:   Sir, a whole history.
GUILDENSTERN:   The King, sir—
HAMLET:   Ay, sir, what of him?
GUILDENSTERN:   Is in his retirement marvelous distemp'red.
HAMLET:   With drink, sir?                                       290
GUILDENSTERN:   No, my lord, with choler.°
HAMLET:   Your wisdom should show itself more richer to
signify this to the doctor, for me to put him to his pur-
gation would perhaps plunge him into more choler.

---

<sup>266–267</sup> ***Provincial roses*** rosettes like the roses of Provence(?)   <sup>267</sup> ***razed*** orna-
mented with slashes   <sup>267</sup> ***cry*** pack, company   <sup>274</sup> ***pajock*** peacock   <sup>275</sup> ***You might***
***have rhymed*** i.e., rhymed "was" with "ass"   <sup>281</sup> ***recorders*** flutelike instruments
   <sup>283</sup> ***perdy*** by God (French: *par dieu*)   <sup>291</sup> ***choler*** anger (but Hamlet pretends to
take the word in its sense of "biliousness")

GUILDENSTERN: Good my lord, put your discourse into 295
some frame,° and start not so wildly from my affair.

HAMLET: I am tame, sir; pronounce.

GUILDENSTERN: The Queen, your mother, in most great affliction of spirit hath sent me to you.

HAMLET: You are welcome. 300

GUILDENSTERN: Nay, good my lord, this courtesy is not of
the right breed. If it shall please you to make me a wholesome answer, I will do your mother's commandment: if
not, your pardon and my return shall be the end of my
business. 305

HAMLET: Sir, I cannot.

ROSENCRANTZ: What, my lord?

HAMLET: Make you a wholesome° answer; my wit's dis-
eased. But, sir, such answer as I can make, you shall
command, or rather, as you say, my mother. Therefore 310
no more, but to the matter. My mother, you say—

ROSENCRANTZ: Then thus she says: your behavior hath
struck her into amazement and admiration.°

HAMLET: O wonderful son, that can so stonish a mother!
But is there no sequel at the heels of this mother's ad- 315
miration? Impart.

ROSENCRANTZ: She desires to speak with you in her closet
ere you go to bed.

HAMLET: We shall obey, were she ten times our mother.
Have you any further trade with us? 320

ROSENCRANTZ: My lord, you once did love me.

HAMLET: And do still, by these pickers and stealers.°

ROSENCRANTZ: Good my lord, what is your cause of distemper? You do surely bar the door upon your own liberty,
if you deny your griefs to your friend. 325

HAMLET: Sir, I lack advancement.°

ROSENCRANTZ: How can that be, when you have the voice
of the King himself for your succession in Denmark?

*Enter the Players with recorders.*

---

²⁹⁶ *frame* order, control   ³⁰⁸ *wholesome* sane   ³¹³ *admiration* wonder   ³²² *pickers
and stealers* i.e., hands (with reference to the prayer; "Keep my hands from
picking and stealing")   ³²⁶ *advancement* promotion

HAMLET: Ay, sir, but "while the grass grows"—the proverb°
is something musty. O, the recorders. Let me see one.   *330*
To withdraw° with you—why do you go about to recover
the wind° of me as if you would drive me into a toil?°
GUILDENSTERN: O my lord, if my duty be too bold, my love
is too unmannerly.°
HAMLET: I do not well understand that. Will you play upon   *335*
this pipe?
GUILDENSTERN: My lord, I cannot.
HAMLET: I pray you.
GUILDENSTERN: Believe me, I cannot.
HAMLET: I do beseech you.   *340*
GUILDENSTERN: I know no touch of it, my lord.
HAMLET: It is as easy as lying. Govern these ventages° with
your fingers and thumb, give it breath with your mouth,
and it will discourse most eloquent music. Look you,
these are the stops.   *345*
GUILDENSTERN: But these cannot I command to any utt'r-
ance of harmony; I have not the skill.
HAMLET: Why, look you now, how unworthy a thing you
make of me! You would play upon me; you would seem
to know my stops; you would pluck out the heart of my   *350*
mystery; you would sound me from my lowest note to
the top of my compass;° and there is much music, excellent voice, in this little organ,° yet cannot you make it
speak. 'Sblood, do you think I am easier to be played on
than a pipe? Call me what instrument you will, though   *355*
you can fret° me, you cannot play upon me.

*Enter Polonius.*

God bless you, sir!

---

²²⁹ *proverb* ("While the grass groweth, the horse starveth")   ³³¹ *withdraw* speak
in private   ³³¹⁻³³² *recover the wind* get on the windward side (as in hunting)
³³² *toil* snare   ³³³⁻³³⁴ *if my duty . . . too unmannerly* i.e., if these questions seem
rude, it is because my love for you leads me beyond good manners   ³⁴² *ventages*
vents, stops on a recorder   ³⁵² *compass* range of voice   ³⁵³ *organ* i.e., the
recorder   ³⁵⁶ *fret* vex (with a pun alluding to the frets, or ridges, that guide the
fingering on some instruments)

POLONIUS:   My lord, the Queen would speak with you, and presently.

HAMLET:   Do you see yonder cloud that's almost in shape    360
of a camel?

POLONIUS:   By th' mass and 'tis, like a camel indeed.

HAMLET:   Methinks it is like a weasel.

POLONIUS:   It is backed like a weasel.

HAMLET:   Or like a whale.    365

POLONIUS:   Very like a whale.

HAMLET:   Then I will come to my mother by and by. [*Aside.*]
They fool me to the top of my bent.°—I will come by and
by.°

POLONIUS:   I will say so.    370

*Exit.*

HAMLET:   "By and by" is easily said. Leave me, friends.

[*Exeunt all but Hamlet.*]

'Tis now the very witching time of night,
When churchyards yawn, and hell itself breathes out
Contagion to this world. Now could I drink hot blood
And do such bitter business as the day    375
Would quake to look on. Soft, now to my mother.
O heart, lose not the nature; let not ever
The soul of Nero° enter this firm bosom.
Let me be cruel, not unnatural;
I will speak daggers to her, but use none.    380
My tongue and soul in this be hypocrites:
How in my words somever she be shent,°
To give them seals° never, my soul, consent!

*Exit.*

---

[368]  *They fool . . . my bent* they compel me to play the fool to the limit of my capacity   [368–369] *by and by* very soon   [378] *Nero* (Roman emperor who had his mother murdered)   [382] *shent* rebuked   [383] *give them seals* confirm them with deeds

**S C E N E  III.**  *The castle.*

*Enter King, Rosencrantz, and Guildenstern.*

KING:  I like him not, nor stands it safe with us
To let his madness range. Therefore prepare you.
I your commission will forthwith dispatch,
And he to England shall along with you.
The terms° of our estate may not endure                    5
Hazard so near's° as doth hourly grow
Out of his brows.
GUILDENSTERN:          We will ourselves provide.
Most holy and religious fear it is
To keep those many many bodies safe
That live and feed upon your Majesty.                      10
ROSENCRANTZ:   The single and peculiar° life is bound
With all the strength and armor of the mind
To keep itself from noyance,° but much more
That spirit upon whose weal depends and rests
The lives of many. The cess of majesty°                    15
Dies not alone, but like a gulf° doth draw
What's near it with it; or it is a massy wheel
Fixed on the summit of the highest mount,
To whose huge spokes ten thousand lesser things
Are mortised and adjoined, which when it falls,           20
Each small annexment, petty consequence,
Attends° the boist'rous ruin. Never alone
Did the King sigh, but with a general groan.
KING:  Arm° you, I pray you, to this speedy voyage,
For we will fetters put about this fear,                    25
Which now goes too free-footed.
ROSENCRANTZ:                           We will haste us.

*Exeunt Gentlemen.*

---

III.iii.   ⁵ *terms* conditions   ⁶ *near's* near us   ¹¹ *peculiar* individual, private
¹³ *noyance* injury   ¹⁵ *cess of majesty* cessation (death) of a king   ¹⁶ *gulf*
whirlpool   ²² *Attends* waits on, participates in   ²⁴ *Arm* prepare

*Enter Polonius.*

POLONIUS:   My lord, he's going to his mother's closet.°
Behind the arras I'll convey myself
To hear the process.° I'll warrant she'll tax him home,°
And, as you said, and wisely was it said,                    30
'Tis meet that some more audience than a mother,
Since nature makes them partial, should o'erhear
The speech of vantage.° Fare you well, my liege.
I'll call upon you ere you go to bed
And tell you what I know.
KING:                                  Thanks, dear my lord.        35

                                  *Exit* [*Polonius*].

O, my offense is rank, it smells to heaven;
It hath the primal eldest curse° upon't,
A brother's murder. Pray can I not,
Though inclination be as sharp as will.
My stronger guilt defeats my strong intent,                  40
And like a man to double business bound
I stand in pause where I shall first begin,
And both neglect. What if this cursèd hand
Were thicker than itself with brother's blood,
Is there not rain enough in the sweet heavens               45
To wash it white as snow? Whereto serves mercy
But to confront° the visage of offense?
And what's in prayer but this twofold force,
To be forestallèd ere we come to fall,
Or pardoned being down? Then I'll look up.                   50
My fault is past. But, O, what form of prayer
Can serve my turn? "Forgive me my foul murder"?
That cannot be, since I am still possessed
Of those effects° for which I did the murder,
My crown, mine own ambition, and my queen.                  55

---

[27] *closet* private room   [29] *process* proceedings   [29] *tax him home* censure him
sharply   [33] *of vantage* from an advantageous place   [37] *primal eldest curse* (curse
of Cain, who killed Abel)   [47] *confront* oppose   [54] *effects* things gained

May one be pardoned and retain th' offense?
In the corrupted currents of this world
Offense's gilded hand may shove by justice,
And oft 'tis seen the wicked prize itself
Buys out the law. But 'tis not so above.                          60
There is no shuffling;° there the action lies
In his true nature, and we ourselves compelled,
Even to the teeth and forehead of our faults,
To give in evidence. What then? What rests?°
Try what repentance can. What can it not?                         65
Yet what can it when one cannot repent?
O wretched state! O bosom black as death!
O limèd° soul, that struggling to be free
Art more engaged!° Help, angels! Make assay.°
Bow, stubborn knees, and, heart with strings of steel,            70
Be soft as sinews of the newborn babe.
All may be well. [*He kneels.*]

*Enter Hamlet.*

HAMLET:   Now might I do it pat, now 'a is a-praying,
And now I'll do't. And so 'a goes to heaven,
And so am I revenged. That would be scanned.°                     75
A villain kills my father, and for that
I, his sole son, do this same villain send
To heaven.
Why, this is hire and salary, not revenge.
'A took my father grossly, full of bread,°                        80
With all his crimes broad blown,° as flush° as May;
And how his audit° stands, who knows save heaven?
But in our circumstance and course of thought,
'Tis heavy with him; and am I then revenged,
To take him in the purging of his soul,                           85
When he is fit and seasoned for his passage?
No.

---

⁶¹ *shuffling* trickery   ⁶⁴ *rests* remains   ⁶⁸ *limèd* caught (as with birdlime, a sticky substance spread on boughs to snare birds)   ⁶⁹ *engaged* ensnared   ⁶⁹ *assay* an attempt   ⁷⁵ *would be scanned* ought to be looked into   ⁸⁰ *bread* i.e., worldly gratification   ⁸¹ *crimes broad blown* sins in full bloom   ⁸¹ *flush* vigorous   ⁸² *audit* account

Up, sword, and know thou a more horrid hent.°
When he is drunk asleep, or in his rage,
Or in th' incestuous pleasure of his bed,                    90
At game a-swearing, or about some act
That has no relish° of salvation in't—
Then trip him, that his heels may kick at heaven,
And that his soul may be as damned and black
As hell, whereto it goes. My mother stays.                   95
This physic° but prolongs thy sickly days.

                                              *Exit.*

KING [*rises*]:   My words fly up, my thoughts remain below.
    Words without thoughts never to heaven go.

                                              *Exit.*

**S C E N E   IV.**   *The Queen's closet.*

*Enter [Queen] Gertrude and Polonius.*

POLONIUS:   'A will come straight. Look you lay home° to him.
    Tell him his pranks have been too broad° to bear with,
    And that your Grace hath screened and stood between
    Much heat and him. I'll silence me even here.
    Pray you be round with him.                              5
HAMLET (*within*):   Mother, Mother, Mother!
QUEEN:   I'll warrant you; fear me not. Withdraw; I hear him
    coming.

                        [*Polonius hides behind the arras.*]

*Enter Hamlet.*

HAMLET:   Now, mother, what's the matter?
QUEEN:   Hamlet, thou hast thy father much offended.         10

---

[88] *hent* grasp (here, occasion for seizing)   [92] *relish* flavor   [96] *physic* (Claudius'
purgation by prayer, as Hamlet thinks in line 85)   III.iv.   [1] *lay home* thrust (rebuke) him sharply   [2] *broad* unrestrained

HAMLET:   Mother, you have my father much offended.
QUEEN:   Come, come, you answer with an idle° tongue.
HAMLET:   Go, go, you question with a wicked tongue.
QUEEN:   Why, how now, Hamlet?
HAMLET:                                     What's the matter now?
QUEEN:   Have you forgot me?
HAMLET:                                     No, by the rood,° not so!          15
    You are the Queen, your husband's brother's wife,
    And, would it were not so, you are my mother.
QUEEN:   Nay, then I'll set those to you that can speak.
HAMLET:   Come, come, and sit you down. You shall not budge.
    You go not till I set you up a glass°                          20
    Where you may see the inmost part of you!
QUEEN:   What wilt thou do? Thou wilt not murder me?
    Help, ho!
POLONIUS [*behind*]:   What, ho! Help!
HAMLET [*draws*]:   How now? A rat? Dead for a ducat, dead!   25

[*Makes a pass through the arras and*] *kills Polonius.*

POLONIUS [*behind*]:   O, I am slain!
QUEEN:                                     O me, what hast thou done?
HAMLET:   Nay, I know not. Is it the King?
QUEEN:   O, what a rash and bloody deed is this!
HAMLET:   A bloody deed—almost as bad, good Mother,
    As kill a king, and marry with his brother.                    30
QUEEN:   As kill a king?
HAMLET:                                     Ay, lady, it was my word.

[*Lifts up the arras and sees Polonius.*]

Thou wretched, rash, intruding fool, farewell!
I took thee for thy better. Take thy fortune.
Thou find'st to be too busy is some danger.—
Leave wringing of your hands. Peace, sit you down       35
And let me wring your heart, for so I shall
If it be made of penetrable stuff,

---

¹² *idle* foolish   ¹⁵ *rood* cross   ²⁰ *glass* mirror

If damnèd custom have not brazed° it so
That it be proof° and bulwark against sense.°
QUEEN:   What have I done that thou dar'st wag thy tongue          40
In noise so rude against me?
HAMLET:                                        Such an act
That blurs the grace and blush of modesty,
Calls virtue hypocrite, takes off the rose
From the fair forehead of an innocent love,
And sets a blister° there, makes marriage vows          45
As false as dicers' oaths. O, such a deed
As from the body of contraction° plucks
The very soul, and sweet religion makes
A rhapsody° of words! Heaven's face does glow
O'er this solidity and compound mass          50
With heated visage, as against the doom
Is thoughtsick at the act.°
QUEEN:                                        Ay me, what act,
That roars so loud and thunders in the index?°
HAMLET:   Look here upon this picture, and on this,
The counterfeit presentment° of two brothers.          55
See what a grace was seated on this brow:
Hyperion's curls, the front° of Jove himself,
An eye like Mars, to threaten and command,
A station° like the herald Mercury
New lighted on a heaven-kissing hill—          60
A combination and a form indeed
Where every god did seem to set his seal
To give the world assurance of a man.
This was your husband. Look you now what follows.
Here is your husband, like a mildewed ear          65
Blasting his wholesome brother. Have you eyes?
Could you on this fair mountain leave to feed,
And batten° on this moor? Ha! Have you eyes?

----

<sup>38</sup> *brazed* hardened like brass   <sup>39</sup> *proof* armor   <sup>39</sup> *sense* feeling   <sup>45</sup> *sets a blister*
brands (as a harlot)   <sup>47</sup> *contraction* marriage contract   <sup>49</sup> *rhapsody* senseless
string   <sup>49–52</sup> *Heaven's face . . . the act* i.e., the face of heaven blushes over this
earth (compounded of four elements), the face hot, as if Judgment Day were
near, and it is thoughtsick at the act   <sup>53</sup> *index* prologue   <sup>55</sup> *counterfeit present-
ment* represented image   <sup>57</sup> *front* forehead   <sup>59</sup> *station* bearing   <sup>68</sup> *batten* feed
gluttonously

You cannot call it love, for at your age
The heyday° in the blood is tame, it's humble,                    70
And waits upon the judgment, and what judgment
Would step from this to this? Sense° sure you have,
Else could you not have motion, but sure that sense
Is apoplexed,° for madness would not err,
Nor sense to ecstasy° was ne'er so thralled              75
But it reserved some quantity of choice
To serve in such a difference. What devil wast
That thus hath cozened you at hoodman-blind?°
Eyes without feeling, feeling without sight,
Ears without hands or eyes, smelling sans° all,          80
Or but a sickly part of one true sense
Could not so mope.°
O shame, where is thy blush? Rebellious hell,
If thou canst mutine in a matron's bones,
To flaming youth let virtue be as wax                    85
And melt in her own fire. Proclaim no shame
When the compulsive ardor° gives the charge,
Since frost itself as actively doth burn,
And reason panders will.°

QUEEN:                           O Hamlet, speak no more.
Thou turn'st mine eyes into my very soul,                 90
And there I see such black and grainèd° spots
As will not leave their tinct.°

HAMLET:                         Nay, but to live
In the rank sweat of an enseamèd° bed,
Stewed in corruption, honeying and making love
Over the nasty sty—

QUEEN:                  O, speak to me no more.            95
These words like daggers enter in my ears.
No more, sweet Hamlet.

HAMLET:                   A murderer and a villain,
A slave that is not twentieth part the tithe°

---

⁷⁰ *heyday* excitement   ⁷² *Sense* feeling   ⁷⁴ *apoplexed* paralyzed   ⁷⁵ *ecstasy* madness   ⁷⁸ *cozened you at hoodman-blind* cheated you at blindman's buff   ⁸⁰ *sans* without   ⁸² *mope* be stupid   ⁸⁷ *compulsive ardor* compelling passion   ⁸⁹ *reason panders will* reason acts as a procurer for desire   ⁹¹ *grainèd* dyed in grain (fast dyed)   ⁹² *tinct* color   ⁹³ *enseamèd* (perhaps "soaked in grease," i.e., sweaty; perhaps "much wrinkled")   ⁹⁸ *tithe* tenth part

Of your precedent lord, a vice° of kings,
A cutpurse of the empire and the rule,                          100
That from a shelf the precious diadem stole
And put it in his pocket—
QUEEN:                              No more.

*Enter Ghost.*

HAMLET:   A king of shreds and patches—
    Save me and hover o'er me with your wings,
    You heavenly guards! What would your gracious figure?   105
QUEEN:   Alas, he's mad.
HAMLET:   Do you not come your tardy son to chide,
    That, lapsed in time and passion, lets go by
    Th' important acting of your dread command?
    O, say!                                                 110
GHOST:   Do not forget. This visitation
    Is but to whet thy almost blunted purpose.
    But look, amazement on thy mother sits.
    O, step between her and her fighting soul!
    Conceit° in weakest bodies strongest works.             115
    Speak to her, Hamlet.
HAMLET:                          How is it with you, lady?
QUEEN:   Alas, how is't with you,
    That you do bend your eye on vacancy,
    And with th' incorporal° air do hold discourse?
    Forth at your eyes your spirits wildly peep,            120
    And as the sleeping soldiers in th' alarm
    Your bedded hair° like life in excrements°
    Start up and stand an end.° O gentle son,
    Upon the heat and flame of thy distemper
    Sprinkle cool patience. Whereon do you look?            125
HAMLET:   On him, on him! Look you, how pale he glares!
    His form and cause conjoined, preaching to stones,
    Would make them capable.°—Do not look upon me,

---

⁹⁹ *vice* (like the Vice, a fool and mischiefmaker in the old morality plays)
¹¹⁵ *Conceit* imagination   ¹¹⁹ *incorporal* bodiless   ¹²² *bedded hair* hairs laid flat
¹²² *excrements* outgrowths (here, the hair)   ¹²³ *an end* on end   ¹²⁸ *capable* receptive

Lest with this piteous action you convert
My stern effects.° Then what I have to do                        *130*
Will want true color; tears perchance for blood.
QUEEN:   To whom do you speak this?
HAMLET:                                        Do you see nothing there?
QUEEN:   Nothing at all; yet all that is I see.
HAMLET:   Nor did you nothing hear?
QUEEN:                                        No, nothing but ourselves.
HAMLET:   Why, look you there! Look how it steals away!        *135*
My father, in his habit° as he lived!
Look where he goes even now at the portal!

                                        *Exit Ghost.*


QUEEN:   This is the very coinage of your brain.
This bodiless creation ecstasy
Is very cunning in.
HAMLET:                   Ecstasy?                                 *140*
My pulse as yours doth temperately keep time
And makes as healthful music. It is not madness
That I have uttered. Bring me to the test,
And I the matter will reword, which madness
Would gambol° from. Mother, for love of grace,              *145*
Lay not that flattering unction° to your soul,
That not your trespass but my madness speaks.
It will but skin and film the ulcerous place
Whiles rank corruption, mining° all within,
Infects unseen. Confess yourself to heaven,                 *150*
Repent what's past, avoid what is to come,
And do not spread the compost° on the weeds
To make them ranker. Forgive me this my virtue.
For in the fatness of these pursy° times
Virtue itself of vice must pardon beg,                       *155*
Yea, curb° and woo for leave to do him good.

---

[129–130] *convert/My stern effects* divert my stern deeds    [136] *habit* garment (Q1,
though a "bad" quarto, is probably correct in saying that at line 102 the ghost
enters "in his nightgown," i.e., dressing gown)    [145] *gambol* start away    [146] *unction* ointment    [149] *mining* undermining    [152] *compost* fertilizing substance
[154] *pursy* bloated    [156] *curb* bow low

QUEEN:   O Hamlet, thou hast cleft my heart in twain.
HAMLET:   O, throw away the worser part of it,
   And live the purer with the other half.
   Good night—but go not to my uncle's bed.            160
   Assume a virtue, if you have it not.
   That monster custom, who all sense doth eat,
   Of habits devil, is angel yet in this,
   That to the use° of actions fair and good
   He likewise gives a frock or livery°            165
   That aptly is put on. Refrain tonight,
   And that shall lend a kind of easiness
   To the next abstinence; the next more easy;
   For use almost can change the stamp of nature,
   And either° the devil, or throw him out            170
   With wondrous potency. Once more, good night,
   And when you are desirous to be blest,
   I'll blessing beg of you.—For this same lord,
   I do repent; but heaven hath pleased it so,
   To punish me with this, and this with me,           175
   That I must be their° scourge and minister.
   I will bestow° him and will answer well
   The death I gave him. So again, good night.
   I must be cruel only to be kind.
   Thus bad begins, and worse remains behind.         180
   One word more, good lady.
QUEEN:                    What shall I do?
HAMLET:   Not this, by no means, that I bid you do:
   Let the bloat King tempt you again to bed,
   Pinch wanton on your cheek, call you his mouse,
   And let him, for a pair of reechy° kisses,         185
   Or paddling in your neck with his damned fingers,
   Make you to ravel° all this matter out,
   That I essentially am not in madness,

---

[164] *use* practice   [165] *livery* characteristic garment (punning on "habits" in line 163)   [170] *either* (probably a word is missing after *either*; among suggestions are "master," "curb," and "house"; but possibly *either* is a verb meaning "make easier")   [176] *their* i.e., the heavens'   [177] *bestow* stow, lodge   [185] *reechy* foul (literally "smoky")   [187] *ravel* unravel, reveal

But mad in craft. 'Twere good you let him know,
For who that's but a queen, fair, sober, wise,                          190
Would from a paddock,° from a bat, a gib,°
Such dear concernings hide? Who would do so?
No, in despite of sense and secrecy,
Unpeg the basket on the house's top,
Let the birds fly, and like the famous ape,                            195
To try conclusions,° in the basket creep
And break your own neck down.
QUEEN:   Be thou assured, if words be made of breath,
And breath of life, I have no life to breathe
What thou hast said to me.                                             200
HAMLET:   I must to England; you know that?
QUEEN:                                            Alack,
I had forgot. 'Tis so concluded on.
HAMLET:   There's letters sealed, and my two school-fellows,
Whom I will trust as I will adders fanged,
They bear the mandate;° they must sweep my way                         205
And marshal me to knavery. Let it work;
For 'tis the sport to have the enginer
Hoist with his own petar,° and 't shall go hard
But I will delve one yard below their mines
And blow them at the moon. O, 'tis most sweet                          210
When in one line two crafts° directly meet.
This man shall set me packing:
I'll lug the guts into the neighbor room.
Mother, good night. Indeed, this counselor
Is now most still, most secret, and most grave,                        215
Who was in life a foolish prating knave.
Come, sir, to draw toward an end with you.
Good night, Mother.

> [*Exit the Queen. Then*] *exit Hamlet,*
> *tugging in Polonius.*

---

[191] *paddock* toad   [193] *gib* tomcat   [196] *To try conclusions* to make experiments
[205] *mandate* command   [208] *petar* bomb   [211] *crafts* (1) boats, (2) acts of guile, crafty
schemes

# ACT IV

**S C E N E  I.** *The castle.*

*Enter King and Queen, with Rosencrantz and Guildenstern.*

KING:   There's matter in these sighs. These profound heaves
　　You must translate; 'tis fit we understand them.
　　Where is your son?
QUEEN:   Bestow this place on us a little while.

　　　　　　　　　[*Exeunt Rosencrantz and Guildenstern.*]

　　Ah, mine own lord, what have I seen tonight!　　　　　　5
KING:   What, Gertrude? How does Hamlet?
QUEEN:   Mad as the sea and wind when both contend
　　Which is the mightier. In his lawless fit,
　　Behind the arras hearing something stir,
　　Whips out his rapier, cries, "A rat, a rat!"　　　　　10
　　And in this brainish apprehension° kills
　　The unseen good old man.
KING:　　　　　　　　　　　O heavy deed!
　　It had been so with us, had we been there.
　　His liberty is full of threats to all,
　　To you yourself, to us, to every one.　　　　　　　15
　　Alas, how shall this bloody deed be answered?
　　It will be laid to us, whose providence°
　　Should have kept short, restrained, and out of haunt°
　　This mad young man. But so much was our love
　　We would not understand what was most fit,　　　　　20
　　But, like the owner of a foul disease,
　　To keep it from divulging, let it feed
　　Even on the pith of life. Where is he gone?
QUEEN:   To draw apart the body he hath killed;
　　O'er whom his very madness, like some ore　　　　　25

─────────

IV.i.  <sup>11</sup> ***brainish apprehension*** mad imagination　<sup>17</sup> *providence* foresight　<sup>18</sup> *out
of haunt* away from association with others

Among a mineral° of metals base,
Shows itself pure. 'A weeps for what is done.
KING:   O Gertrude, come away!
The sun no sooner shall the mountains touch
But we will ship him hence, and this vile deed                          30
We must with all our majesty and skill
Both countenance and excuse. Ho, Guildenstern!

*Enter Rosencrantz and Guildenstern.*

Friends both, go join you with some further aid:
Hamlet in madness hath Polonius slain,
And from his mother's closet hath he dragged him.                        35
Go seek him out; speak fair, and bring the body
Into the chapel. I pray you haste in this.

[*Exeunt Rosencrantz and Guildenstern.*]

Come, Gertrude, we'll call up our wisest friends
And let them know both what we mean to do
And what's untimely done . . .°                                          40
Whose whisper o'er the world's diameter,
As level as the cannon to his blank°
Transports his poisoned shot, may miss our name
And hit the woundless° air. O, come away!
My soul is full of discord and dismay.                                   45

*Exeunt.*

**S C E N E  II.**   *The castle.*

*Enter Hamlet.*

HAMLET:   Safely stowed.
GENTLEMEN (*within*):   Hamlet! Lord Hamlet!
HAMLET:   But soft, what noise? Who calls on Hamlet?
O, here they come.

---

²⁵⁻²⁶ *ore/Among a mineral* vein of gold in a mine    ⁴⁰ *done* . . . (evidently something has dropped out of the text. Cappell's conjecture, "So, haply slander," is
usually printed)    ⁴² *blank* white center of a target    ⁴⁴ *woundless* invulnerable

*Enter Rosencrantz and Guildenstern.*

ROSENCRANTZ:   What have you done, my lord, with the dead
   body?                                             5

HAMLET:   Compounded it with dust, whereto 'tis kin.

ROSENCRANTZ:   Tell us where 'tis, that we may take it thence
   And bear it to the chapel.

HAMLET:   Do not believe it.

ROSENCRANTZ:   Believe what?             10

HAMLET:   That I can keep your counsel and not mine own.
   Besides, to be demanded of° a sponge, what replication°
   should be made by the son of a king?

ROSENCRANTZ:   Take you me for a sponge, my lord?

HAMLET:   Ay, sir, that soaks up the King's countenance,° his   15
   rewards, his authorities. But such officers do the King
   best service in the end. He keeps them, like an ape, in
   the corner of his jaw, first mouthed, to be last swallowed.
   When he needs what you have gleaned, it is but squeezing you and, sponge, you shall be dry again.   20

ROSENCRANTZ:   I understand you not, my lord.

HAMLET:   I am glad of it: a knavish speech sleeps in a foolish
   ear.

ROSENCRANTZ:   My lord, you must tell us where the body is
   and go with us to the King.   25

HAMLET:   The body is with the King, but the King is not
   with the body.° The King is a thing—

GUILDENSTERN:   A thing, my lord?

HAMLET:   Of nothing. Bring me to him. Hide fox, and all
   after.°   30

*Exeunt.*

**S C E N E   III.**   *The castle.*

*Enter King, and two or three.*

KING:   I have sent to seek him and to find the body:
   How dangerous is it that this man goes loose!

---

IV.ii.   [12] *demanded of* questioned by   [12] *replication* reply   [15] *countenance*
favor   [26–27] *The body . . . body* i.e., the body of authority is with Claudius, but
spiritually he is not the true king   [29–30] *Hide fox, and all after* (a cry in a game
such as hide-and-seek; Hamlet runs from the stage)

Yet must not we put the strong law on him:
He's loved of the distracted° multitude,
Who like not in their judgment, but their eyes,                    5
And where 'tis so, th' offender's scourge is weighed,
But never the offense. To bear° all smooth and even,
This sudden sending him away must seem
Deliberate pause.° Diseases desperate grown
By desperate appliance are relieved,                               10
Or not at all.

*Enter Rosencrantz, [Guildenstern,] and all the rest.*

How now? What hath befall'n?
ROSENCRANTZ:   Where the dead body is bestowed, my lord,
We cannot get from him.
KING:                          But where is he?
RESENCRANTZ:   Without, my lord; guarded, to know your
    pleasure.
KING:   Bring him before us.
ROSENCRANTZ:                       Ho! Bring in the lord.          15

*They enter.*

KING:   Now, Hamlet, where's Polonius?
HAMLET:   At supper.
KING:   At supper? Where?
HAMLET:   Not where he eats, but where 'a is eaten. A certain
    convocation of politic° worms are e'en at him. Your worm    20
    is your only emperor for diet. We fat all creatures else to
    fat us, and we fat ourselves for maggots. Your fat king
    and your lean beggar is but variable service°—two dishes,
    but to one table. That's the end.
KING:   Alas, alas!                                                25
HAMLET:   A man may fish with the worm that hath eat of a
    king, and eat of the fish that hath fed of that worm.
KING:   What dost thou mean by this?

---

IV.iii.   ⁴ *distracted* bewildered senseless   ⁷ *bear* carry out   ⁹ *pause* planning
²⁰ *politic* statesmanlike, shrewd   ²³ *variable service* different courses

HAMLET:   Nothing but to show you how a king may go a
   progress° through the guts of a beggar.                          30
KING:   Where is Polonius?
HAMLET:   In heaven. Send thither to see. If your messenger
   find him not there, seek him i' th' other place yourself.
   But if indeed you find him not within this month, you
   shall nose him as you go up the stairs into the lobby.          35
KING [*to Attendants*]:   Go seek him there.
HAMLET:   'A will stay till you come.

*[Exeunt Attendants.]*

KING:   Hamlet, this deed, for thine especial safety,
   Which we do tender° as we dearly grieve
   For that which thou hast done, must send thee hence           40
   With fiery quickness. Therefore prepare thyself.
   The bark is ready and the wind at help,
   Th' associates tend,° and everything is bent
   For England.
HAMLET:          For England?
KING:                          Ay, Hamlet.
HAMLET:                                  Good.
KING:   So is it, if thou knew'st our purposes.                    45
HAMLET:   I see a cherub° that sees them. But come, for England!
   Farewell, dear Mother.
KING:   Thy loving father, Hamlet.
HAMLET:   My mother—father and mother is man and wife,
   man and wife is one flesh, and so, my mother. Come,           50
   for England!

*Exit.*

KING:   Follow him at foot;° tempt him with speed abroad.
   Delay it not; I'll have him hence tonight.
   Away! For everything is sealed and done
   That else leans° on th' affair. Pray you make haste.          55

*[Exeunt all but the King.]*

---

[30] *progress* royal journey   [39] *tender* hold dear   [43] *tend* wait   [46] *cherub* angel of
knowledge   [52] *at foot* closely   [55] *leans* depends

And, England, if my love thou hold'st at aught—
As my great power thereof may give thee sense,
Since yet thy cicatrice° looks raw and red
After the Danish sword, and thy free awe°
Pays homage to us—thou mayst not coldly set          60
Our sovereign process,° which imports at full
By letters congruing to that effect
The present° death of Hamlet. Do it, England,
For like the hectic° in my blood he rages,
And thou must cure me. Till I know 'tis done,        65
How'er my haps,° my joys were ne'er begun.

*Exit.*

S C E N E  **IV.**   *A plain in Denmark.*

*Enter Fortinbras with his Army over the stage.*

FORTINBRAS:   Go, Captain, from me greet the Danish king.
Tell him that by his license Fortinbras
Craves the conveyance of° a promised march
Over his kingdom. You know the rendezvous.
If that his Majesty would aught with us,              5
We shall express our duty in his eye;°
And let him know so.
CAPTAIN:                     I will do't, my lord.
FORTINBRAS:   Go softly° on.

[*Exeunt all but the Captain.*]

*Enter Hamlet, Rosencrantz, &c.*

HAMLET:   Good sir, whose powers° are these?
CAPTAIN:   They are of Norway, sir.                   10
HAMLET:   How purposed, sir, I pray you?

---

58 *cicatrice* scar   59 *free awe* uncompelled submission   60–61 *coldly set/Our sovereign process* regard slightly our royal command   63 *present* instant   64 *hectic* fever   66 *haps* chances, fortunes   IV.iv.   3 *conveyance of* escort for   6 *in his eye* before his eyes (i.e., in his presence)   8 *softly* slowly   9 *powers* forces

CAPTAIN: Against some part of Poland.

HAMLET: Who commands them, sir?

CAPTAIN: The nephew to old Norway, Fortinbras.

HAMLET: Goes it against the main° of Poland, sir,         15
Or for some frontier?

CAPTAIN: Truly to speak, and with no addition,°
We go to gain a little patch of ground
That hath in it no profit but the name.
To pay five ducats, five, I would not farm it,         20
Nor will it yield to Norway or the Pole
A ranker° rate, should it be sold in fee.°

HAMLET: Why, then the Polack never will defend it.

CAPTAIN: Yes, it is already garrisoned.

HAMLET: Two thousand souls and twenty thousand ducats   25
Will not debate° the question of this straw.
This is th' imposthume° of much wealth and peace,
That inward breaks, and shows no cause without
Why the man dies. I humbly thank you sir.

CAPTAIN: God bye you, sir.

[*Exit.*]

ROSENCRANTZ:                    Will't please you go, my lord?   30

HAMLET: I'll be with you straight. Go a little before.

[*Exeunt all but Hamlet.*]

How all occasions do inform against me
And spur my dull revenge! What is a man,
If his chief good and market° of his time
Be but to sleep and feed? A beast, no more.         35
Sure he that made us with such large discourse,°
Looking before and after, gave us not
That capability and godlike reason
To fust° in us unused. Now, whether it be
Bestial oblivion,° or some craven scruple         40

---

¹⁵ *main* main part   ¹⁷ *with no addition* plainly   ²² *ranker* higher   ²² *in fee*
outright   ²⁶ *debate* settle   ²⁷ *imposthume* abscess, ulcer   ³⁴ *market* profit   ³⁶ *discourse* understanding   ³⁹ *fust* grow moldy   ⁴⁰ *oblivion* forgetfulness

Of thinking too precisely on th' event°—
A thought which, quartered, hath but one part wisdom
And ever three parts coward—I do not know
Why yet I live to say, "This thing's to do,"
Sith I have cause, and will, and strength, and means    45
To do't. Examples gross° as earth exhort me.
Witness this army of such mass and charge,°
Led by a delicate and tender prince,
Whose spirit, with divine ambition puffed,
Makes mouths at the invisible event,°    50
Exposing what is mortal and unsure
To all that fortune, death, and danger dare,
Even for an eggshell. Rightly to be great
Is not° to stir without great argument,°
But greatly° to find quarrel in a straw    55
When honor's at the stake. How stand I then,
That have a father killed, a mother stained,
Excitements° of my reason and my blood,
And let all sleep, while to my shame I see
The imminent death of twenty thousand men    60
That for a fantasy and trick of fame°
Go to their graves like beds, fight for a plot
Whereon the numbers cannot try the cause,
Which is not tomb enough and continent°
To hide the slain? O, from this time forth,    65
My thoughts be bloody, or be nothing worth!

                                                   *Exit.*

**S C E N E   V.**    *The castle.*

*Enter Horatio, [Queen] Gertrude, and a Gentleman.*

QUEEN:   I will not speak with her.
GENTLEMAN:   She is importunate, indeed distract.
    Her mood will needs be pitied.

---

[41] *event* outcome    [46] *gross* large, obvious    [47] *charge* expense    [50] *Makes mouths at
the invisible event* makes scornful faces at (is contemptuous of) the unseen
outcome    [54] *not* (the sense seems to require "not not")    [54] *argument* reason
[55] *greatly* i.e., nobly    [58] *Excitements* incentives    [61] *fantasy and trick of fame* illusion and trifle of reputation    [64] *continent* receptacle, container

QUEEN:                          What would she have?
GENTLEMAN:   She speaks much of her father, says she hears
   There's tricks i' th' world, and hems, and beats her heart,   5
   Spurns enviously at straws,° speaks things in doubt°
   That carry but half sense. Her speech is nothing,
   Yet the unshapèd use of it doth move
   The hearers to collection;° they yawn° at it,
   And botch the words up fit to their own thoughts,            10
   Which, as her winks and nods and gestures yield them,
   Indeed would make one think there might be thought,
   Though nothing sure, yet much unhappily.
HORATIO:   'Twere good she were spoken with, for she may
   strew
   Dangerous conjectures in ill-breeding minds.                 15
QUEEN:   Let her come in.

                             *[Exit Gentleman.]*

   *[Aside.]* To my sick soul (as sin's true nature is)
   Each toy seems prologue to some great amiss;°
   So full of artless jealousy° is guilt
   It spills° itself in fearing to be spilt.                    20

   *Enter Ophelia [distracted].*

OPHELIA:   Where is the beauteous majesty of Denmark?
QUEEN:   How now, Ophelia?
OPHELIA:   *(She sings.)*

   How should I your truelove know
      From another one?
   By his cockle hat° and staff                                 25
      And his sandal shoon.°

---

IV.v.   ⁶ *Spurns enviously at straws* objects spitefully to insignificant matters   ⁶ *in doubt* uncertainly   ⁸⁻⁹ *Yet the ... to collection* i.e., yet the formless manner of it moves her listeners to gather up some sort of meaning   ⁹ *yawn* gape (?)   ¹⁸ *amiss* misfortune   ¹⁹ *artless jealousy* crude suspicion   ²⁰ *spills* destroys   ²⁵ *cockle hat* (a cockleshell on the hat was the sign of a pilgrim who had journeyed to shrines overseas. The association of lovers and pilgrims was a common one.)   ²⁶ *shoon* shoes

QUEEN:   Alas, sweet lady, what imports this song?
OPHELIA:   Say you? Nay, pray you mark.

> He is dead and gone, lady,                              *(Song.)*
>     He is dead and gone;                                     30
> At his head a grass-green turf,
>     At his heels a stone.

> O, ho!

QUEEN:   Nay but Ophelia—
OPHELIA:   Pray you mark. [*Sings.*]                         35

> White his shroud as the mountain snow—

*Enter King.*

QUEEN:   Alas, look here, my lord.
OPHELIA:

>     Larded° all with sweet flowers                     *(Song.)*
>     Which bewept to the grave did not go
>         With truelove showers.                                40

KING:   How do you, pretty lady?
OPHELIA:   Well, God dild° you! They say the owl was a
   baker's daughter.° Lord, we know what we are, but know
   not what we may be. God be at your table!
KING:   Conceit° upon her father.                            45
OPHELIA:   Pray let's have no words of this, but when they
   ask you what it means, say you this:

>     Tomorrow is Saint Valentine's day.°                *(Song.)*
>         All in the morning betime,
>     And I a maid at your window,                           50
>         To be your Valentine.

>     Then up he rose and donned his clothes
>         And dupped° the chamber door,

---

[38] *Larded* decorated    [42] *dild* yield, i.e., reward    [42] *baker's daughter* (an allusion to
a tale of a baker's daughter who begrudged bread to Christ and was turned into
an owl)    [45] *Conceit* brooding    [48] *Saint Valentine's day* Feb. 14 (the notion was
that a bachelor would become the truelove of the first girl he saw on this
day)    [53] *dupped* opened (did up)

Let in the maid, that out a maid
    Never departed more.               55

KING:  Pretty Ophelia.
OPHELIA:  Indeed, la, without an oath, I'll make an end on't:

[*Sings.*]

By Gis° and by Saint Charity,
    Alack, and fie for shame!
Young men will do't if they come to't,        60
    By Cock,° they are to blame.
Quoth she, "Before you tumbled me
    You promised me to wed."

He answers:

"So would I 'a' done, by yonder sun,        65
    An thou hadst not come to my bed."

KING:  How long hath she been thus?
OPHELIA:  I hope all will be well. We must be patient, but I
cannot choose but weep to think they would lay him i'
th' cold ground. My brother shall know of it; and so I    70
thank you for your good counsel. Come, my coach! Good
night, ladies, good night. Sweet ladies, good night, good
night.

                            *Exit.*

KING:  Follow her close; give her good watch, I pray you.

                    [*Exit Horatio.*]

O, this is the poison of deep grief; it springs        75
All from her father's death—and now behold!
O Gertrude, Gertrude.
When sorrows come, they come not single spies,
But in battalions; first, her father slain;
Next, your son gone, and he most violent author      80
Of his own just remove; the people muddied,°

---

<sup>58</sup> *Gis* (contraction of "Jesus")   <sup>61</sup> *Cock* (1) God, (2) phallus   <sup>81</sup> *muddied* muddled

Thick and unwholesome in their thoughts and whispers
For good Polonius' death, and we have done but greenly°
In huggermugger° to inter him; poor Ophelia
Divided from herself and her fair judgment,                                 85
Without the which we are pictures of mere beasts;
Last, and as much containing as all these,
Her brother is in secret come from France,
Feeds on his wonder,° keeps himself in clouds,
And wants not buzzers° to infect his ear                                   90
With pestilent speeches of his father's death,
Wherein necessity, of matter beggared,°
Will nothing stick° our person to arraign
In ear and ear. O my dear Gertrude, this,
Like to a murd'ring piece,° in many places                                 95
Gives me superfluous death.

                                        *A noise within.*

*Enter a Messenger.*


QUEEN:                            Alack, what noise is this?
KING:   Attend, where are my Switzers?° Let them guard the
        door.
    What is the matter?
MESSENGER:              Save yourself, my lord.
    The ocean, overpeering of his list,°                                   100
    Eats not the flats with more impiteous haste
    Than young Laertes, in a riotous head,°
    O'erbears your officers. The rabble call him lord,
    And, as the world were now but to begin,
    Antiquity forgot, custom not known,                                    105
    The ratifiers and props of every word,
    They cry, "Choose we! Laertes shall be king!"

---

[83] *greenly* foolishly    [84] *huggermugger* secret haste    [89] *wonder* suspicion    [90] *wants not buzzers* does not lack talebearers    [92] *of matter beggared* unprovided with facts    [93] *Will nothing stick* will not hesitate    [95] *murd'ring piece* (a cannon that shot a kind of shrapnel)    [97] *Switzers* Swiss guards    [99] *list* shore    [101] *in a riotous head* with a rebellious force

Caps, hands, and tongues applaud it to the clouds,
"Laertes shall be king! Laertes king!"

*A noise within.*

QUEEN:   How cheerfully on the false trail they cry!
O, this is counter,° you false Danish dogs!                    110

*Enter Laertes with others.*

KING:   The doors are broke.
LAERTES:   Where is this king?—Sirs, stand you all without.
ALL:   No, let's come in.
LAERTES:                    I pray you give me leave.
ALL:   We will, we will.
LAERTES:   I thank you. Keep the door.

[*Exeunt his Followers.*]

O thou vile King,                    115
Give me my father.
QUEEN:                    Calmly, good Laertes.
LAERTES:   That drop of blood that's calm proclaims me bastard,
Cries cuckold° to my father, brands the harlot
Even here between the chaste unsmirchèd brow
Of my true mother.
KING:                    What is the cause, Laertes,                    120
That thy rebellion looks so giantlike?
Let him go, Gertrude. Do not fear° our person.
There's such divinity doth hedge a king
That treason can but peep to° what it would,
Acts little of his will. Tell me, Laertes,                    125
Why thou art thus incensed. Let him go, Gertrude.
Speak, man.
LAERTES:   Where is my father?
KING:                    Dead.

---

¹¹⁰ *counter* (a hound runs counter when he follows the scent backward from the prey)   ¹¹⁸ *cuckold* man whose wife is unfaithful   ¹²² *fear* fear for   ¹²⁴ *peep to* i.e., look at from a distance

QUEEN:                                   But not by him.
KING:   Let him demand his fill.
LAERTES:   How came he dead? I'll not be juggled with.          130
   To hell allegiance, vows to the blackest devil,
   Conscience and grace to the profoundest pit!
   I dare damnation. To this point I stand,
   That both the worlds I give to negligence,°
   Let come what comes, only I'll be revenged          135
   Most throughly for my father.
KING:                                   Who shall stay you?
LAERTES:   My will, not all the world's.
   And for my means. I'll husband them° so well
   They shall go far with little.
KING:                                   Good Laertes,
   If you desire to know the certainty          140
   Of your dear father, is't writ in your revenge
   That swoopstake° you will draw both friend and foe,
   Winner and loser?
LAERTES:   None but his enemies.
KING:                                   Will you know them then?
LAERTES:   To his good friends thus wide I'll ope my arms          145
   And like the kind life-rend'ring pelican°
   Repast° them with my blood.
KING:                                   Why, now you speak
   Like a good child and a true gentleman.
   That I am guiltless of your father's death,
   And am most sensibly° in grief for it,          150
   It shall as level to your judgment 'pear
   As day does to your eye.

*A noise within: "Let her come in."*

LAERTES:   How now? What noise is that?

*Enter Ophelia.*

---

[134] *That both . . . to negligence* i.e., I care not what may happen (to me) in this world or the next   [138] *husband them* use them economically   [142] *swoopstake* in a clean sweep   [146] *pelican* (thought to feed its young with its own blood)   [147] *Repast* feed   [150] *sensibly* acutely

O heat, dry up my brains; tears seven times salt
Burn out the sense and virtue° of mine eye!                    155
By heaven, thy madness shall be paid with weight
Till our scale turn the beam.° O rose of May,
Dear maid, kind sister, sweet Ophelia!
O heavens, is't possible a young maid's wits
Should be as mortal as an old man's life?                      160
Nature is fine° in love, and where 'tis fine,
It sends some precious instance° of itself
After the thing it loves.

OPHELIA:

    They bore him barefaced on the bier          *(Song.)*
        Hey non nony, nony, hey nony                165
    And in his grave rained many a tear—

Fare you well, my dove!

LAERTES:   Hadst thou thy wits, and didst persuade revenge,
It could not move thus.

OPHELIA:   You must sing "A-down a-down, and you call    170
him a-down-a." O, how the wheel° becomes it! It is the
false steward, that stole his master's daughter.

LAERTES:   This nothing's more than matter.°

OPHELIA:   There's rosemary, that's for remembrance. Pray
you, love, remember. And there is pansies, that's for   175
thoughts.

LAERTES:   A document° in madness, thoughts and remembrance fitted.

OPHELIA:   There's fennel° for you, and columbines. There's
rue for you, and here's some for me. We may call it herb   180
of grace o' Sundays. O, you must wear your rue with a
difference. There's a daisy. I would give you some violets, but they withered all when my father died. They
say 'a made a good end.

                                                  *[Sings.]*

---

[155] *virtue* power   [157] *turn the beam* weigh down the bar (of the balance)   [161] *fine* refined, delicate   [162] *instance* sample   [171] *wheel* (of uncertain meaning, but probably a turn or dance of Ophelia's, rather than Fortune's wheel)   [173] *This nothing's more than matter* this nonsense has more meaning than matters of consequence   [177] *document* lesson   [179] *fennel* (the distribution of flowers in the

For bonny sweet Robin is all my joy. 185

LAERTES: Thought and affliction, passion, hell itself,
She turns to favor° and to prettiness.

OPHELIA:

And will 'a not come again? (*Song.*)
And will 'a not come again?
No, no, he is dead, 190
Go to thy deathbed,
He never will come again.

His beard was as white as snow,
All flaxen was his poll.°
He is gone, he is gone, 195
And we cast away moan.
God 'a' mercy on his soul!

And of all Christian souls, I pray God. God bye you.

[*Exit.*]

LAERTES: Do you see this, O God?

KING: Laertes, I must commune with your grief, 200
Or you deny me right. Go but apart,
Make choice of whom your wisest friends you will,
And they shall hear and judge 'twixt you and me.
If by direct or by collateral° hand
They find us touched,° we will our kingdom give, 205
Our crown, our life, and all that we call ours,
To you in satisfaction; but if not,
Be you content to lend your patience to us,
And we shall jointly labor with your soul
To give it due content.

LAERTES:                     Let this be so. 210
His means of death, his obscure funeral—

---

ensuing lines has symbolic meaning, but the meaning is disputed. Perhaps *fennel*, flattery; *columbines*, cuckoldry; *rue*, sorrow for Ophelia and repentance for the Queen; *daisy*, dissembling; *violets*, faithfulness. For other interpretations, see J. W. Lever in *Review of English Studies*, New Series 3 [1952], pp. 123–29) [187] *favor* charm, beauty [194] *All flaxen was his poll* white as flax was his head [204] *collateral* indirect [205] *touched* implicated

No trophy, sword, nor hatchment° o'er his bones,
No noble rite nor formal ostentation°—
Cry to be heard, as 'twere from heaven to earth,
That I must call't in question.

KING:                                    So you shall;                    *215*
And where th' offense is, let the great ax fall.
I pray you go with me.

*Exeunt.*

### S C E N E  VI.   *The castle.*

*Enter Horatio and others.*

HORATIO:   What are they that would speak with me?

GENTLEMAN:   Seafaring men, sir. They say they have letters for
you.

HORATIO:   Let them come in.

[*Exit Attendant.*]

I do not know from what part of the world                    *5*
I should be greeted, if not from Lord Hamlet.

*Enter Sailors.*

SAILOR:   God bless you, sir.

HORATIO:   Let Him bless thee too.

SAILOR:   'A shall, sir, an't please Him. There's a letter for
you, sir—it came from th' ambassador that was bound          *10*
for England—if your name be Horatio, as I am let to
know it is.

HORATIO [*reads the letter*]:

"Horatio, when thou shalt have overlooked° this, give
these fellows some means to the King. They have letters
for him. Ere we were two days old at sea, a pirate of        *15*
very warlike appointment° gave us chase. Finding our-

---

²¹² *hatchment* tablet bearing the coat of arms of the dead   ²¹³ *ostentation*
ceremony   IV.vi.   ¹³ *overlooked* surveyed   ¹⁶ *appointment* equipment

selves too slow of sail, we put on a compelled valor, and
in the grapple I boarded them. On the instant they got
clear of our ship; so I alone became their prisoner. They
have dealt with me like thieves of mercy, but they knew       20
what they did: I am to do a good turn for them. Let the
King have the letters I have sent, and repair thou to me
with as much speed as thou wouldest fly death. I have
words to speak in thine ear will make thee dumb; yet are
they much too light for the bore° of the matter. These       25
good fellows will bring thee where I am. Rosencrantz
and Guildenstern hold their course for England. Of them
I have much to tell thee. Farewell.
He that thou knowest thine, HAMLET."

Come, I will give you way for these your letters,            30
And do't the speedier that you may direct me
To him from whom you brought them.

*Exeunt.*

## S C E N E  VII.   *The castle.*

*Enter King and Laertes.*

KING:   Now must your conscience my acquittance seal,
    And you must put me in your heart for friend,
    Sith you have heard, and with a knowing ear,
    That he which hath your noble father slain
    Pursued my life.
LAERTES:            It well appears. But tell me          5
    Why you proceeded not against these feats
    So criminal and so capital° in nature,
    As by your safety, greatness, wisdom, all things else,
    You mainly° were stirred up.
KING:               O, for two special reasons,
    Which may to you perhaps seem much unsinewed,°      10

---

²⁵ *bore* caliber (here, "importance")   IV.vii.   ⁷ *capital* deserving death   ⁹ *mainly*
powerfully   ¹⁰ *unsinewed* weak

But yet to me they're strong. The Queen his mother
Lives almost by his looks, and for myself—
My virtue or my plague, be it either which—
She is so conjunctive° to my life and soul,
That, as the star moves not but in his sphere,                    15
I could not but by her. The other motive
Why to a public count° I might not go
Is the great love the general gender° bear him,
Who, dipping all his faults in their affection,
Would, like the spring that turneth wood to stone,°                20
Convert his gyves° to graces; so that my arrows,
Too slightly timbered° for so loud a wind,
Would have reverted to my bow again,
And not where I had aimed them.

LAERTES:   And so have I a noble father lost,                       25
A sister driven into desp'rate terms,°
Whose worth, if praises may go back again,°
Stood challenger on mount of all the age
For her perfections. But my revenge will come.

KING:   Break not your sleeps for that. You must not think         30
That we are made of stuff so flat and dull
That we can let our beard be shook with danger,
And think it pastime. You shortly shall hear more.
I loved your father, and we love ourself,
And that, I hope, will teach you to imagine—                       35

*Enter a Messenger with letters.*

How now? What news?

MESSENGER:                      Letters, my lord, from Hamlet:
These to your Majesty; this to the Queen.

KING:   From Hamlet? Who brought them?

MESSENGER:   Sailors, my lord, they say; I saw them not.
They were given me by Claudio; he received them                    40
Of him that brought them.

---

[14] *conjunctive* closely united   [17] *count* reckoning   [18] *general gender* common
people   [20] *spring that turneth wood to stone* (a spring in Shakespeare's county
was so charged with lime that it would petrify wood placed in it)   [21] *gyves*
fetters   [22] *timbered* shafted   [26] *terms* conditions   [27] *go back again* revert to what
is past

KING:                              Laertes, you shall hear them.—
Leave us. [*Reads.*]

*Exit Messenger.*

"High and mighty, you shall know I am set naked° on
your kingdom. Tomorrow shall I beg leave to see your
kingly eyes; when I shall (first asking your pardon there-        *45*
unto) recount the occasion of my sudden and more
strange return.
                                                HAMLET."

What should this mean? Are all the rest come back?
Or is it some abuse,° and no such thing?                          *50*
KING:                              'Tis Hamlet's character.° "Naked"!
And in a postscript here, he says "alone."
Can you devise° me?
LAERTES:   I am lost in it, my lord. But let him come.
It warms the very sickness in my heart                           *55*
That I shall live and tell him to his teeth,
"Thus did'st thou."
KING:                        If it be so, Laertes
(As how should it be so? How otherwise?),
Will you be ruled by me?
LAERTES:                        Ay, my lord,
So you will not o'errule me to a peace.                          *60*
KING:   To thine own peace. If he be now returned,
As checking at° his voyage, and that he means
No more to undertake it, I will work him
To an exploit now ripe in my device,
Under the which he shall not choose but fall;                    *65*
And for his death no wind of blame shall breathe,
But even his mother shall uncharge the practice°
And call it accident.
LAERTES:                        My lord, I will be ruled;
The rather if you could devise it so
That I might be the organ.

---

[43] *naked* destitute   [50] *abuse* deception   [51] *character* handwriting   [53] *devise*
advise   [62] *checking at* turning away from (a term in falconry)   [67] *uncharge the*
*practice* not charge the device with treachery

KING:                              It falls right.                              70
   You have been talked of since your travel much,
   And that in Hamlet's hearing, for a quality
   Wherein they say you shine. Your sum of parts
   Did not together pluck such envy from him
   As did that one, and that, in my regard,                              75
   Of the unworthiest siege.°
LAERTES:                              What part is that, my lord?
KING:   A very riband in the cap of youth,
   Yet needful too, for youth no less becomes
   The light and careless livery that it wears
   Than settled age his sables and his weeds,°                              80
   Importing health and graveness. Two months since
   Here was a gentleman of Normandy.
   I have seen myself, and served against, the French,
   And they can° well on horseback, but this gallant
   Had witchcraft in't. He grew unto his seat,                              85
   And to such wondrous doing brought his horse
   As had he been incorpsed and deminatured
   With the brave beast. So far he topped my thought
   That I, in forgery° of shapes and tricks,
   Come short of what he did.
LAERTES:                              A Norman was't?                              90
KING:   A Norman.
LAERTES:   Upon my life, Lamord.
KING:                              The very same.
LAERTES:   I know him well. He is the brooch° indeed
   And gem of all the nation.
KING:   He made confession° of you,                              95
   And gave you such a masterly report,
   For art and exercise in your defense,
   And for your rapier most especial,
   That he cried out 'twould be a sight indeed
   If one could match you. The scrimers° of their nation                              100
   He swore had neither motion, guard, nor eye,
   If you opposed them. Sir, this report of his

---

[76] *seige* rank   [80] *sables and his weeds* i.e., sober attire   [84] *can* do   [89] *forgery* invention   [93] *brooch* ornament   [95] *confession* report   [100] *scrimers* fencers

Did Hamlet so envenom with his envy
That he could nothing do but wish and beg
Your sudden coming o'er to play with you.                              105
Now, out of this—
LAERTES:                          What out of this, my lord?
KING:   Laertes, was your father dear to you?
Or are you like the painting of a sorrow,
A face without a heart?
LAERTES:                          Why ask you this?
KING:   Not that I think you did not love your father,               110
But that I know love is begun by time,
And that I see, in passages of proof.°
Time qualifies° the spark and fire of it.
There lives within the very flame of love
A kind of wick or snuff° that will abate it,                          115
And nothing is at a like goodness still,°
For goodness, growing to a plurisy,°
Dies in his own too-much. That we would do
We should do when we would, for this "would" changes,
And hath abatements and delays as many                               120
As there are tongues, are hands, are accidents,
And then this "should" is like a spendthrift sigh,°
That hurts by easing. But to the quick° of th' ulcer—
Hamlet comes back; what would you undertake
To show yourself in deed your father's son                           125
More than in words?
LAERTES:                          To cut his throat i' th' church!
KING:   No place indeed should murder sanctuarize;°
Revenge should have no bounds. But, good Laertes,
Will you do this? Keep close within your chamber.
Hamlet returned shall know you are come home.                        130
We'll put on those° shall praise your excellence
And set a double varnish on the fame
The Frenchman gave you, bring you in fine° together

---

¹¹² *passages of proof* proved cases    ¹¹³ *qualifies* diminishes    ¹¹⁵ *snuff* residue of
burnt wick (which dims the light)    ¹¹⁶ *still* always    ¹¹⁷ *plurisy* fullness,
excess    ¹²² *spendthrift sigh* (sighing provides ease, but because it was thought to
thin the blood and so shorten life it was spendthrift)    ¹²³ *quick* sensitive
flesh    ¹²⁷ *sanctuarize* protect    ¹³¹ *We'll put on those* we'll incite persons who
¹³³ *in fine* finally

And wager on your heads. He, being remiss,
Most generous, and free from all contriving,                    135
Will not peruse the foils, so that with ease,
Or with a little shuffling, you may choose
A sword unbated,° and, in a pass of practice,°
Requite him for your father.

LAERTES:                        I will do't.
And for that purpose I'll anoint my sword.                      140
I bought an unction of a mountebank,°
So mortal that, but dip a knife in it,
Where it draws blood, no cataplasm° so rare,
Collected from all simples° that have virtue°
Under the moon, can save the thing from death                  145
That is but scratched withal. I'll touch my point
With this contagion, that, if I gall him slightly,
It may be death.

KING:                        Let's further think of this,
Weigh what convenience both of time and means
May fit us to our shape.° If this should fail,                  150
And that our drift look through° our bad performance,
'Twere better not assayed. Therefore this project
Should have a back or second, that might hold
If this did blast in proof.° Soft, let me see.
We'll make a solemn wager on your cunnings—                     155
I ha't!
When in your motion you are hot and dry—
As make your bouts more violent to that end—
And that he calls for drink, I'll have prepared him
A chalice for the nonce,° whereon but sipping,                  160
If he by chance escape your venomed stuck,°
Our purpose may hold there.—But stay, what noise?

*Enter Queen.*

---

[138] *unbated* not blunted   [138] *pass of practice* treacherous thrust   [141] *mountebank*
quack   [143] *cataplasm* poultice   [144] *simples* medicinal herbs   [144] *virtue* power (to
heal)   [150] *shape* role   [151] *drift look through* purpose show through   [154] *blast in
proof* burst (fail) in performance   [160] *nonce* occasion   [161] *stuck* thrust

QUEEN:   One woe doth tread upon another's heel.
   So fast they follow. Your sister's drowned, Laertes.
LAERTES:   Drowned! O, where?                                                165
QUEEN:   There is a willow grows askant° the brook,
   That shows his hoar° leaves in the glassy stream:
   Therewith° fantastic garlands did she make
   Of crowflowers, nettles, daisies, and long purples,
   That liberal° shepherds give a grosser name,                         170
   But our cold maids do dead men's fingers call them.
   There on the pendent boughs her crownet° weeds
   Clamb'ring to hang, an envious sliver° broke,
   When down her weedy trophies and herself
   Fell in the weeping brook. Her clothes spread wide,                   175
   And mermaidlike awhile they bore her up,
   Which time she chanted snatches of old lauds,°
   As one incapable° of her own distress,
   Or like a creature native and indued°
   Unto that element. But long it could not be                          180
   Till that her garments, heavy with their drink,
   Pulled the poor wretch from her melodious lay
   To muddy death.
LAERTES:                            Alas, then she is drowned?
QUEEN:   Drowned, drowned.
LAERTES:   Too much of water hast thou, poor Ophelia,                        185
   And therefore I forbid my tears; but yet
   It is our trick;° nature her custom holds,
   Let shame say what it will: when these are gone,
   The woman° will be out. Adieu, my lord.
   I have a speech o' fire, that fain would blaze,                       190
   But that this folly drowns it.

*Exit.*

KING:                            Let's follow, Gertrude.
   How much I had to do to calm his rage!

---

¹⁶⁶ *askant* aslant   ¹⁶⁷ *hoar* silver-gray   ¹⁶⁸ *Therewith* i.e., with willow twigs
¹⁷⁰ *liberal* free-spoken, coarse-mouthed   ¹⁷² *crownet* coronet   ¹⁷³ *envious sliver*
malicious branch   ¹⁷⁷ *lauds* hymns   ¹⁷⁸ *incapable* unaware   ¹⁷⁹ *indued* in harmony with   ¹⁸⁷ *trick* trait, way   ¹⁸⁹ *woman* i.e., womanly part of me

Now fear I this will give it start again;
Therefore let's follow.

*Exeunt.*

---

# ACT V

**S C E N E  I.**  *A churchyard.*

*Enter two Clowns.°*

CLOWN:  Is she to be buried in Christian burial when she
willfully seeks her own salvation?
OTHER:  I tell thee she is. Therefore make her grave straight.°
The crowner° hath sate on her, and finds it Christian
burial.                                                                                                      5
CLOWN:  How can that be, unless she drowned herself in
her own defense?
OTHER:  Why, 'tis found so.
CLOWN:  It must be *se offendendo;*° it cannot be else. For here
lies the point: if I drown myself wittingly, it argues an      10
act, and an act hath three branches—it is to act, to do,
to perform. Argal,° she drowned herself wittingly.
OTHER:  Nay, but hear you, Goodman Delver.
CLOWN:  Give me leave. Here lies the water—good. Here
stands the man—good. If the man go to this water and   15
drown himself, it is, will he nill he,° he goes; mark you
that. But if the water come to him and drown him, he
drowns not himself. Argal, he that is not guilty of his
own death, shortens not his own life.
OTHER:  But is this law?                                                                              20
CLOWN:  Ay marry, is't—crowner's quest° law.
OTHER:  Will you ha' the truth on't? If this had not been a

---

V.i.   ˢ·ᵈ· *Clowns* rustics   ³ *straight* straightway   ⁴ *crowner* coroner   ⁹ *se offen-*
*dendo* (blunder for *se defendendo,* a legal term meaning "in self-defense")   ¹² *Argal*
(blunder for Latin *ergo,* "therefore")   ¹⁶ *will he nill he* will he or will he not
(whether he will or will not)   ²¹ *quest* inquest

gentlewoman, she should have been buried out o' Christian burial.

CLOWN: Why, there thou say'st. And the more pity that 25
great folk should have count'nance° in this world to
drown or hang themselves more than their even-Christen.° Come, my spade. There is no ancient gentlemen
but gard'ners, ditchers, and gravemakers. They hold up°
Adam's profession. 30

OTHER: Was he a gentleman?

CLOWN: 'A was the first that ever bore arms.°

OTHER: Why, he had none.

CLOWN: What, art a heathen? How dost thou understand
the Scripture? The Scripture says Adam digged. Could 35
he dig without arms? I'll put another question to thee. If
thou answerest me not to the purpose, confess thyself—

OTHER: Go to.

CLOWN: What is he that builds stronger than either the
mason, the shipwright, or the carpenter? 40

OTHER: The gallowsmaker, for that frame outlives a thousand tenants.

CLOWN: I like thy wit well, in good faith. The gallows does
well. But how does it well? It does well to those that do
ill. Now thou dost ill to say the gallows is built stronger 45
than the church. Argal, the gallows may do well to thee.
To't again, come.

OTHER: Who builds stronger than a mason, a shipwright,
or a carpenter?

CLOWN: Ay, tell me that, and unyoke.° 50

OTHER: Marry, now I can tell.

CLOWN: To't.

OTHER: Mass,° I cannot tell.

*Enter Hamlet and Horatio afar off.*

---

²⁶ *count'nance* privilege   ²⁷⁻²⁸ *even-Christen* fellow Christian   ²⁹ *hold up* keep up
³² *bore arms* had a coat of arms (the sign of a gentleman)   ⁵⁰ *unyoke* i.e., stop
work for the day   ⁵³ *Mass* by the mass

CLOWN:   Cudgel thy brains no more about it, for your dull
   ass will not mend his pace with beating. And when you   55
   are asked this question next, say "a gravemaker." The
   houses he makes lasts till doomsday. Go, get thee in,
   and fetch me a stoup° of liquor.

[*Exit Other Clown.*]

In youth when I did love, did love                    [*Song.*]
   Methought it was very sweet                             60
To contract—O—the time for—a—my behove,°
   O, methought there—a—was nothing—a—meet.
HAMLET:   Has this fellow no feeling of his business? 'A sings
   in gravemaking.
HORATIO:   Custom hath made it in him a property of easiness.°   65
HAMLET:   'Tis e'en so. The hand of little employment hath
   the daintier sense.°
CLOWN:

But age with his stealing steps                        (*Song.*)
   Hath clawed me in his clutch,
And hath shipped me into the land,                      70
   As if I had never been such.

[*Throws up a skull.*]

HAMLET:   That skull had a tongue in it, and could sing once.
   How the knave jowls° it to the ground, as if 'twere Cain's
   jawbone, that did the first murder! This might be the
   pate of a politician, which this ass now o'erreaches,° one   75
   that would circumvent God, might it not?
HORATIO:   It might, my lord.
HAMLET:   Or of a courtier, which could say "Good morrow,
   sweet lord! How dost thou, sweet lord?" This might be

---

⁵⁸ *stoup* tankard   ⁶¹ *behove* advantage   ⁶⁵ *in him a property of easiness* easy for
him   ⁶⁶⁻⁶⁷ *hath the daintier sense* is more sensitive (because it is not calloused)
   ⁷³ *jowls* hurls   ⁷⁵ *o'erreaches* (1) reaches over, (2) has the advantage over

my Lord Such-a-one, that praised my Lord Such-a-one's    80
horse when 'a went to beg it, might it not?
HORATIO:   Ay, my lord.
HAMLET:   Why e'en so, and now my Lady Worm's, chapless,° and knocked about the mazzard° with a sexton's
spade. Here's fine revolution, an we had the trick to see't.    85
Did these bones cost no more the breeding but to play
at loggets° with them? Mine ache to think on't.
CLOWN:

> A pickax and a spade, a spade,                    *(Song.)*
>     For and a shrouding sheet;
> O, a pit of clay for to be made                    90
>     For such a guest is meet.

[*Throws up another skull.*]

HAMLET:   There's another. Why may not that be the skull
of a lawyer? Where be his quiddities° now, his quillities,°
his cases, his tenures,° and his tricks? Why does he suffer
this mad knave now to knock him about the sconce° with    95
a dirty shovel, and will not tell him of his action of
battery? Hum! This fellow might be in's time a great
buyer of land, with his statutes, his recognizances, his
fines,° his double vouchers, his recoveries. Is this the
fine° of his fines, and the recovery of his recoveries, to    100
have his fine pate full of fine dirt? Will his vouchers
vouch him no more of his purchases, and double ones
too, than the length and breadth of a pair of indentures?°
The very conveyances° of his lands will scarcely lie in
this box, and must th' inheritor himself have no more,    105
ha?
HORATIO:   Not a jot more, my lord.

---

**83–84** *chapless* lacking the lower jaw   **84** *mazzard* head   **87** *loggets* (a game in
which small pieces of wood were thrown at an object)   **93** *quiddities* subtle arguments (from Latin *quidditas,* "whatness")   **93** *quillities* fine distinctions   **94** *tenures*
legal means of holding land   **95** *sconce* head   **98–99** *his statutes, his recognizances,*
*his fines* his documents giving a creditor control of a debtor's land, his bonds of
surety, his documents changing an entailed estate into fee simple (unrestricted
ownership)   **100** *fine* end   **103** *indentures* contracts   **104** *conveyances* legal documents for the transference of land

HAMLET:   Is not parchment made of sheepskins?
HORATIO:   Ay, my lord, and of calveskins too.
HAMLET:   They are sheep and calves which seek out assur- 110
ance° in that. I will speak to this fellow. Whose grave's
this, sirrah?
CLOWN:   Mine, sir. [*Sings.*]

> O, pit of clay for to be made
> For such a guest is meet.                                    115

HAMLET:   I think it be thine indeed, for thou liest in't.
CLOWN:   You lie out on't, sir, and therefore 'tis not yours.
For my part, I do not lie in't, yet it is mine.
HAMLET:   Thou dost lie in't, to be in't and say it is thine.
'Tis for the dead, not for the quick;° therefore thou liest. 120
CLOWN:   'Tis a quick lie, sir; 'twill away again from me to you.
HAMLET:   What man dost thou dig it for?
CLOWN:   For no man, sir.
HAMLET:   What woman then?
CLOWN:   For none neither.                                       125
HAMLET:   Who is to be buried in't?
CLOWN:   One that was a woman, sir; but, rest her soul, she's
dead.
HAMLET:   How absolute° the knave is! We must speak by
the card,° or equivocation° will undo us. By the Lord, 130
Horatio, this three years I have took note of it, the age
is grown so picked° that the toe of the peasant comes so
near the heel of the courtier he galls his kibe.° How long
hast thou been a gravemaker?
CLOWN:   Of all the days i' th' year, I came to't that day that 135
our last king Hamlet overcame Fortinbras.
HAMLET:   How long is that since?
CLOWN:   Cannot you tell that? Every fool can tell that. It
was that very day that young Hamlet was born—he that
is mad, and sent into England.                                  140

---

110–111 *assurance* safety   120 *quick* living   129 *absolute* positive, decided   129–130 *by
the card* by the compass card, i.e., exactly   130 *equivocation* ambiguity   132 *picked*
refined   133 *kibe* sore on the back of the heel

HAMLET:   Ay, marry, why was he sent into England?

CLOWN:   Why, because 'a was mad. 'A shall recover his wits
there; or, if 'a do not, 'tis no great matter there.

HAMLET:   Why?

CLOWN:   'Twill not be seen in him there. There the men are   145
as mad as he.

HAMLET:   How came he mad?

CLOWN:   Very strangely, they say.

HAMLET:   How strangely?

CLOWN:   Faith, e'en with losing his wits.   150

HAMLET:   Upon what ground?

CLOWN:   Why, here in Denmark. I have been sexton here,
man and boy, thirty years.

HAMLET:   How long will a man lie i' th' earth ere he rot?

CLOWN:   Faith, if 'a be not rotten before 'a die (as we have   155
many pocky corses° nowadays that will scarce hold the
laying in), 'a will last you some eight year or nine year.
A tanner will last you nine year.

HAMLET:   Why he, more than another?

CLOWN:   Why, sir, his hide is so tanned with his trade that   160
'a will keep out water a great while, and your water is a
sore decayer of your whoreson dead body. Here's a skull
now hath lien you i' th' earth three and twenty years.

HAMLET:   Whose was it?

CLOWN:   A whoreson mad fellow's it was. Whose do you   165
think it was?

HAMLET:   Nay, I know not.

CLOWN:   A pestilence on him for a mad rogue! 'A poured a
flagon of Rhenish on my head once. This same skull, sir,
was, sir, Yorick's skull, the King's jester.   170

HAMLET:   This?

CLOWN:   E'en that.

HAMLET:   Let me see [*Takes the skull.*] Alas, poor Yorick!
I knew him, Horatio, a fellow of infinite jest, of most
excellent fancy. He hath borne me on his back a thou-   175
sand times. And now how abhorred in my imagination
it is? My gorge rises at it. Here hung those lips that I

---

[156] *pocky corses* bodies of persons who had been infected with the pox (syphilis)

have kissed I know not how oft. Where be your gibes
now? Your gambols, your songs, your flashes of merriment that were wont to set the table on a roar? Not      *180*
one now to mock your own grinning? Quite chapfall'n?°
Now get you to my lady's chamber, and tell her, let
her paint an inch thick, to this favor° she must come.
Make her laugh at that. Prithee, Horatio, tell me one
thing.                                                      *185*
HORATIO:   What's that, my lord?
HAMLET:   Dost thou think Alexander looked o' this fashion
   i' th' earth?
HORATIO:   E'en so.
HAMLET:   And smelt so? Pah! [*Puts down the skull.*]        *190*
HORATIO:   E'en so, my lord.
HAMLET:   To what base uses we may return, Horatio! Why
   may not imagination trace the noble dust of Alexander
   till a' find it stopping a bunghole?
HORATIO:   'Twere to consider too curiously,° to consider so.   *195*
HAMLET:   No, faith, not a jot, but to follow him thither with
   modesty enough,° and likelihood to lead it; as thus: Al-
   exander died, Alexander was buried, Alexander retur-
   neth to dust; the dust is earth; of earth we make loam;
   and why of that loam whereto he was converted might   *200*
   they not stop a beer barrel?
   Imperious Caesar, dead and turned to clay,
   Might stop a hole to keep the wind away
   O, that that earth which kept the world in awe
   Should patch a wall t' expel the winter's flaw!°        *205*
   But soft, but soft awhile! Here comes the King.

*Enter King, Queen, Laertes, and a coffin, with Lords attendant*
[*and a Doctor of Divinity*].

The Queen, the courtiers. Who is this they follow?
And with such maimèd° rites? This doth betoken

---

[182] *chapfall'n* (1) down in the mouth, (2) jawless   [183] *favor* facial appearance
[195] *curiously* minutely   [196–197] *with modesty enough* without exaggeration
[205] *flaw* gust   [208] *maimèd* incomplete

The corse they follow did with desp'rate hand
Fordo it° own life. 'Twas of some estate.°                                210
Couch° we awhile, and mark.

[*Retires with Horatio.*]

LAERTES:   What ceremony else?
HAMLET:                                      That is Laertes,
    A very noble youth. Mark.
LAERTES:   What ceremony else?
DOCTOR:   Her obsequies have been as far enlarged                        215
    As we have warranty. Her death was doubtful,°
    And, but that great command o'ersways the order,
    She should in ground unsanctified been lodged
    Till the last trumpet. For charitable prayers,
    Shards,° flints, and pebbles should be thrown on her.            220
    Yet here she is allowed her virgin crants,°
    Her maiden strewments,° and the bringing home
    Of bell and burial.
LAERTES:   Must there no more be done?
DOCTOR:                                      No more be done.
    We should profane the service of the dead                        225
    To sing a requiem and such rest to her
    As to peace-parted souls.
LAERTES:                                      Lay her i' th' earth,
    And from her fair and unpolluted flesh
    May violets spring! I tell thee, churlish priest,
    A minist'ring angel shall my sister be                           230
    When thou liest howling!
HAMLET:                                      What, the fair Ophelia?
QUEEN:   Sweets to the sweet! Farewell. [*Scatters flowers.*]
    I hoped thou shouldst have been my Hamlet's wife.
    I thought thy bride bed to have decked, sweet maid,
    And not have strewed thy grave.
LAERTES:                                      O, treble woe                  235
    Fall ten times treble on that cursèd head

---

[210] *Fordo it* destroy its   [210] *estate* high rank   [211] *Couch* hide   [216] *doubtful* suspicious   [220] *Shards* broken pieces of pottery   [221] *crants* garlands   [222] *strewments* i.e., of flowers

Whose wicked deed thy most ingenious sense°
Deprived thee of! Hold off the earth awhile,
Till I have caught her once more in mine arms.

*Leaps in the grave.*

Now pile your dust upon the quick and dead                     240
Till of this flat a mountain you have made
T'o'ertop old Pelion° or the skyish head
Of blue Olympus.
HAMLET [*coming forward*]:    What is he whose grief
    Bears such an emphasis, whose phrase of sorrow         245
    Conjures the wand'ring stars,° and makes them stand
    Like wonder-wounded hearers? This is I,
    Hamlet the Dane.
LAERTES:                    The devil take thy soul!

*[Grapples with him.]°*

HAMLET:    Thou pray'st not well.
    I prithee take thy fingers from my throat,                   250
    For, though I am not splenitive° and rash,
    Yet have I in me something dangerous,
    Which let thy wisdom fear. Hold off thy hand.
KING:    Pluck them asunder.
QUEEN:                    Hamlet, Hamlet!
ALL:    Gentlemen!
HORATIO:              Good my lord, be quiet.                    255

*Attendants part them.*

---

[237] *most ingenious sense* finely endowed mind    [242] *Pelion* (according to classical
legend, giants in their fight with the gods sought to reach heaven by piling
Mount Pelion and Mount Ossa on Mount Olympus)    [246] *wand'ring stars*
planets    [248 s.d.] *Grapples with him* (Q1, a bad quarto, presumably reporting a
version that toured, has a previous direction saying "Hamlet leaps in after
Laertes." Possibly he does so, somewhat hysterically. But such a direction—absent from the two good texts, Q2 and F—makes Hamlet the aggressor, somewhat
contradicting his next speech. Perhaps Laertes leaps out of the grave to attack
Hamlet)    [251] *splenitive* fiery (the spleen was thought to be the seat of anger)

HAMLET:   Why, I will fight with him upon this theme
        Until my eyelids will no longer wag.
QUEEN:   O my son, what theme?
HAMLET:   I loved Ophelia. Forty thousand brothers
        Could not with all their quantity of love                    260
        Make up my sum. What wilt thou do for her?
KING:   O, he is mad, Laertes.
QUEEN:   For love of God forbear him.
HAMLET:   'Swounds, show me what thou't do.
        Woo't weep? Woo't fight? Woo't fast? Woo't tear thyself?   265
        Woo't drink up eisel?° Eat a crocodile?
        I'll do't. Dost thou come here to whine?
        To outface me with leaping in her grave?
        Be buried quick with her, and so will I.
        And if thou prate of mountains, let them throw             270
        Millions of acres on us, till our ground,
        Singeing his pate against the burning zone,°
        Make Ossa like a wart! Nay, an thou'lt mouth,
        I'll rant as well as thou.
QUEEN:                         This is mere madness;
        And thus a while the fit will work on him.                   275
        Anon, as patient as the female dove
        When that her golden couplets are disclosed,°
        His silence will sit drooping.
HAMLET:                         Hear you, sir.
        What is the reason that you use me thus?
        I loved you ever. But it is no matter.                       280
        Let Hercules himself do what he may,
        The cat will mew, and dog will have his day.
KING:   I pray thee, good Horatio, wait upon him.

                                    *Exit Hamlet and Horatio.*

        [*To Laertes.*] Strengthen your patience in our last night's
             speech.
        We'll put the matter to the present push.°                   285

---

[266] *eisel* vinegar   [272] *burning zone* sun's orbit   [277] *golden couplets are disclosed*
(the dove lays two eggs, and the newly hatched [*disclosed*] young are covered
with golden down)   [285] *present push* immediate test

Good Gertrude, set some watch over your son.
This grave shall have a living° monument.
An hour of quiet shortly shall we see;
Till then in patience our proceeding be.

*Exeunt.*

**S C E N E  II.**   *The castle.*

*Enter Hamlet and Horatio.*

HAMLET:   So much for this, sir; now shall you see the other.
   You do remember all the circumstance?
HORATIO:   Remember it, my lord!
HAMLET:   Sir, in my heart there was a kind of fighting
   That would not let me sleep. Methought I lay 5
   Worse than the mutines in the bilboes.° Rashly
   (And praised be rashness for it) let us know,
   Our indiscretion sometimes serves us well
   When our deep plots do pall,° and that should learn us
   There's a divinity that shapes our ends, 10
   Rough-hew them how we will.
HORATIO:               That is most certain.
HAMLET:   Up from my cabin,
   My sea gown scarfed about me, in the dark
   Groped I to find out them, had my desire,
   Fingered° their packet, and in fine° withdrew 15
   To mine own room again, making so bold,
   My fears forgetting manners, to unseal
   Their grand commission; where I found, Horatio—
   Ah, royal knavery!—an exact command.
   Larded° with many several sorts of reasons, 20
   Importing Denmark's health, and England's too,
   With, ho, such bugs and goblins in my life,°
   That on the supervise,° no leisure bated,°

---

[287] *living* lasting (with perhaps also a reference to the plot against Hamlet's life) V.ll.   [6] *mutines in the bilboes* mutineers in fetters   [9] *pall* fail   [15] *Fingered* stole   [15] *in fine* finally   [20] *Larded* enriched   [22] *such bugs and goblins in my life* such bugbears and imagined terrors if I were allowed to live   [23] *supervise* reading   [23] *leisure bated* delay allowed

No, not to stay the grinding of the ax,
My head should be struck off.
HORATIO:                                              Is't possible?                    25
HAMLET:   Here's the commission; read it at more leisure.
    But wilt thou hear now how I did proceed?
HORATIO:   I beseech you.
HAMLET:   Being thus benetted round with villains,
    Or° I could make a prologue to my brains,                          30
    They had begun the play. I sat me down,
    Devised a new commission, wrote it fair.
    I once did hold it, as our statists° do,
    A baseness to write fair,° and labored much
    How to forget that learning, but, sir, now                          35
    It did me yeoman's service. Wilt thou know
    Th' effect° of what I wrote?
HORATIO:                                   Ay, good my lord.
HAMLET:   An earnest conjuration from the King,
    As England was his faithful tributary,
    As love between them like the palm might flourish,          40
    As peace should still her wheaten garland wear
    And stand a comma° 'tween their amities,
    And many suchlike as's of great charge,°
    That on the view and knowing of these contents,
    Without debatement further, more or less,                          45
    He should those bearers put to sudden death,
    Not shriving° time allowed.
HORATIO:                                   How was this sealed?
HAMLET:   Why, even in that was heaven ordinant.°
    I had my father's signet in my purse,
    Which was the model° of that Danish seal,                        50
    Folded the writ up in the form of th' other,
    Subscribed it, gave't th' impression, placed it safely,
    The changeling never known. Now, the next day
    Was our sea fight, and what to this was sequent
    Thou knowest already.                                                         55

---

<sup>30</sup> *Or* ere   <sup>33</sup> *statists* statesmen   <sup>34</sup> *fair* clearly   <sup>37</sup> *effect* purport   <sup>42</sup> *comma*
link   <sup>43</sup> *great charge* (1) serious exhortation, (2) heavy burden (punning on *as's*
and "asses")   <sup>47</sup> *shriving* absolution   <sup>48</sup> *ordinant* ruling   <sup>50</sup> *model* counterpart

HORATIO:   So Guildenstern and Rosencrantz go to't.
HAMLET:   Why, man, they did make love to this employment.
   They are not near my conscience; their defeat
   Does by their own insinuation° grow.
   'Tis dangerous when the baser nature comes        60
   Between the pass° and fell° incensèd points
   Of mighty opposites.
HORATIO:                Why, what a king is this!
HAMLET:   Does it not, think thee, stand me now upon°—
   He that hath killed my king, and whored my mother,
   Popped in between th' election° and my hopes,        65
   Thrown out his angle° for my proper life,°
   And with such coz'nage°—is't not perfect conscience
   To quit° him with this arm? And is't not to be damned
   To let this canker of our nature come
   In further evil?        70
HORATIO:   It must be shortly known to him from England
   What is the issue of the business there.
HAMLET:   It will be short; the interim's mine,
   And a man's life's no more than to say "one."
   But I am very sorry, good Horatio,        75
   That to Laertes I forgot myself,
   For by the image of my cause I see
   The portraiture of his. I'll court his favors.
   But sure the bravery° of his grief did put me
   Into a tow'ring passion.
HORATIO:            Peace, who comes here?        80

*Enter young Osric, a courtier.*

OSRIC:   Your lordship is right welcome back to Denmark.
HAMLET:   I humbly thank you, sir. [*Aside to Horatio.*] Dost
   know this waterfly?
HORATIO [*aside to Hamlet*]:   No, my good lord.
HAMLET [*aside to Horatio*]:   Thy state is the more gracious,   85

---

⁵⁹ *insinuation* meddling   ⁶¹ *pass* thrust   ⁶¹ *fell* cruel   ⁶³ *stand me now upon* become incumbent upon me   ⁶⁵ *election* (the Danish monarchy was elective)
⁶⁶ *angle* fishing line   ⁶⁶ *my proper life* my own life   ⁶⁷ *coz'nage* trickery   ⁶⁸ *quit*
pay back   ⁷⁹ *bravery* bravado

for 'tis a vice to know him. He hath much land, and
fertile. Let a beast be lord of beasts, and his crib shall
stand at the king's mess.° 'Tis a chough,° but, as I say,
spacious° in the possession of dirt.

OSRIC:   Sweet lord, if your lordship were at leisure, I should     90
impart a thing to you from his Majesty.

HAMLET:   I will receive it, sir, with all diligence of spirit. Put
your bonnet to his right use. 'Tis for the head.

OSRIC:   I thank your lordship, it is very hot.

HAMLET:   No, believe me, 'tis very cold; the wind is northerly.     95

OSRIC:   It is indifferent cold, my lord, indeed.

HAMLET:   But yet methinks it is very sultry and hot for my
complexion.°

OSRIC:   Exceedingly, my lord; it is very sultry, as 'twere—I
cannot tell how. But, my lord, his Majesty bade me sig-     100
nify to you that 'a has laid a great wager on your head.
Sir, this is the matter—

HAMLET:   I beseech you remember.

[*Hamlet moves him to put on his hat.*]

OSRIC:   Nay, good my lord; for my ease, in good faith. Sir,
here is newly come to court Laertes—believe me, an     105
absolute gentleman, full of most excellent differences,°
of very soft society and great showing. Indeed, to speak
feelingly° of him, he is the card° or calendar of gentry;
for you shall find in him the continent° of what part a
gentleman would see.     110

HAMLET:   Sir, his definement° suffers no perdition° in you,
though, I know, to divide him inventorially would dozy°
th' arithmetic of memory, and yet but yaw neither in
respect of his quick sail.° But, in the verity of extolment,

---

[88] *mess* table   [88] *chough* jackdaw (here chatterer)   [89] *spacious* well off   [98] *complexion* temperament   [106] *differences* distinguishing characteristics   [108] *feelingly*
justly   [108] *card* chart   [109] *continent* summary   [111] *definement* description   [111] *per-
dition* loss   [112] *dozy* dizzzy   [113-114] *and yet . . . quick sail* i.e., and yet only stag-
ger despite all (*yaw neither*) in trying to overtake his virtues

I take him to be a soul of great article,° and his infusion°    *115*
of such dearth and rareness as, to make true diction° of
him, his semblable° is his mirror, and who else would
trace him, his umbrage,° nothing more.

OSRIC:   Your lordship speaks most infallibly of him.

HAMLET:   The concernancy,° sir? Why do we wrap the gen-    *120*
tleman in our more rawer breath?

OSRIC:   Sir?

HORATIO:   Is't not possible to understand in another tongue?
You will to't,° sir, really.

HAMLET:   What imports the nomination of this gentleman?    *125*

OSRIC:   Of Laertes?

HORATIO [*aside to Hamlet*]:   His purse is empty already. All's
golden words are spent.

HAMLET:   Of him, sir.

OSRIC:   I know you are not ignorant—    *130*

HAMLET:   I would you did, sir; yet, in faith, if you did, it
would not much approve° me. Well, sir?

OSRIC:   You are not ignorant of what excellence Laertes is—

HAMLET:   I dare not confess that, lest I should compare with
him in excellence; but to know a man well were to know    *135*
himself.

OSRIC:   I mean, sir, for his weapon; but in the imputation°
laid on him by them, in his meed° he's unfellowed.

HAMLET:   What's his weapon?

OSRIC:   Rapier and dagger.    *140*

HAMLET:   That's two of his weapons—but well.

OSRIC:   The King, sir, hath wagered with him six Barbary
horses, against the which he has impawned,° as I take
it, six French rapiers and poniards, with their assigns,°
as girdle, hangers,° and so. Three of the carriages,° in    *145*
faith, are very dear to fancy, very responsive° to the hilts,

---

[115] *article* (literally, "item," but here perhaps "traits" or "importance")   [116] *infu-sion* essential quality   [117] *diction* description   [117] *semblable* likeness   [118] *umbrage* shadow   [120] *concernancy* meaning   [124] *will to't* will get there   [132] *approve* commend   [137] *imputation* reputation   [138] *meed* merit   [143] *impawned* wagered   [144] *assigns* accompaniments   [145] *hangers* straps hanging the sword to the belt   [145] *carriages* an affected word for hangers   [146] *responsive* corresponding

most delicate carriages, and of very liberal conceit.°

HAMLET:   What call you the carriages?

HORATIO [*aside to Hamlet*]:   I knew you must be edified by
the margent° ere you had done.                                         *150*

OSRIC:   The carriages, sir, are the hangers.

HAMLET:   The phrase would be more germane to the matter
if we could carry a cannon by our sides. I would it might
be hangers till then. But on! Six Barbary horses against
six French swords, their assigns, and three liberal-con-     *155*
ceited carriages—that's the French bet against the Danish. Why is this all impawned, as you call it?

OSRIC:   The King, sir, hath laid, sir, that in a dozen passes
between yourself and him he shall not exceed you three
hits; he hath laid on twelve for nine, and it would come     *160*
to immediate trial if your lordship would vouchsafe the
answer.

HAMLET:   How if I answer no?

OSRIC:   I mean, my lord, the opposition of your person in trial.

HAMLET:   Sir, I will walk here in the hall. If it please his     *165*
Majesty, it is the breathing time of day with me.° Let the
foils be brought, the gentleman willing, and the King
hold his purpose, I will win for him an I can; if not, I
will gain nothing but my shame and the odd hits.

OSRIC:   Shall I deliver you e'en so?                                   *170*

HAMLET:   To this effect, sir, after what flourish your nature
will.

OSRIC:   I commend my duty to your lordship.

HAMLET:   Yours, yours.

[*Exit Osric.*]

He does well to commend it himself; there are no tongues *175*
else for's turn.

HORATIO:   This lapwing° runs away with the shell on his
head.

---

[147] *liberal conceit* elaborate design   [150] *margent* i.e., marginal (explanatory
comment)   [166] *breathing time of day with me* time when I take exercise   [177] *lapwing* (the new-hatched lapwing was thought to run around with half its shell on
its head)

HAMLET:  'A did comply, sir, with his dug° before 'a sucked
  it. Thus has he, and many more of the same breed that        *180*
  I know the drossy age dotes on, only got the tune of the
  time and, out of an habit of encounter,° a kind of yeasty°
  collection, which carries them through and through the
  most fanned and winnowed opinions; and do but blow
  them to their trial, the bubbles are out.°                   *185*

*Enter a Lord.*

LORD:  My lord, his Majesty commended him to you by
  young Osric, who brings back to him that you attend
  him in the hall. He sends to know if your pleasure hold
  to play with Laertes, or that you will take longer time.
HAMLET:  I am constant to my purposes; they follow the       *190*
  King's pleasure. If his fitness speaks, mine is ready; now
  or whensoever, provided I be so able as now.
LORD:  The King and Queen and all are coming down.
HAMLET:  In happy time.
LORD:  The Queen desires you to use some gentle entertain-   *195*
  ment° to Laertes before you fall to play.
HAMLET:  She well instructs me.

                                              [*Exit Lord.*]

HORATIO:  You will lose this wager, my lord.
HAMLET:  I do not think so. Since he went into France I have
  been in continual practice. I shall win at the odds. But     *200*
  thou wouldst not think how ill all's here about my heart.
  But it is no matter.
HORATIO:  Nay, good my lord—
HAMLET:  It is but foolery, but it is such a kind of gain-
  giving° as would perhaps trouble a woman.                    *205*

---

[179] *'A did comply, sir, with his dug* he was ceremoniously polite to his mother's
breast   [182] *out of an habit of encounter* out of his own superficial way of meeting
and conversing with people   [182] *yeasty* frothy   [185] *the bubbles are out* i.e., they
are blown away (the reference is to the "yeasty collection")   [195-196] *to use some
gentle entertainment* to be courteous   [204-205] *gain-giving* misgiving

HORATIO:  If your mind dislike anything, obey it. I will forestall their repair hither and say you are not fit.
HAMLET:  Not a whit, we defy augury. There is special providence in the fall of a sparrow.° If it be now, 'tis not to
come; if it be not to come, it will be now; if it be not now,    210
yet it will come. The readiness is all. Since no man of
aught he leaves knows, what is't to leave betimes?° Let
be.

*A table prepared. [Enter] Trumpets, Drums, and Officers with
cushions; King, Queen, [Osric,] and all the State, [with] foils, daggers, [and stoups of wine borne in]; and Laertes.*

KING:  Come, Hamlet, come, and take this hand from me.

*[The King puts Laertes' hand into Hamlet's.]*

HAMLET:  Give me your pardon, sir. I have done you wrong,    215
But pardon't, as you are a gentleman.
This presence° knows, and you must needs have heard,
How I am punished with a sore distraction.
What I have done
That might your nature, honor, and exception°    220
Roughly awake, I here proclaim was madness.
Was't Hamlet wronged Laertes? Never Hamlet.
If Hamlet from himself be ta'en away,
And when he's not himself does wrong Laertes,
Then Hamlet does it not, Hamlet denies it.    225
Who does it then? His madness. If't be so,
Hamlet is of the faction° that is wronged;
His madness is poor Hamlet's enemy.
Sir, in this audience,
Let my disclaiming from a purposed evil    230
Free me so far in your most generous thoughts
That I have shot my arrow o'er the house
And hurt my brother.

---

[209] *the fall of a sparrow* (cf. Matthew 10:29 "Are not two sparrows sold for a
farthing? and one of them shall not fall on the ground without your Father")
[212] *betimes* early   [217] *presence* royal assembly   [220] *exception* disapproval   [227] *faction* party, side

LAERTES:                         I am satisfied in nature,
Whose motive in this case should stir me most
To my revenge. But in my terms of honor                    235
I stand aloof, and will no reconcilement
Till by some elder masters of known honor
I have a voice and precedent° of peace
To keep my name ungored. But till that time
I do receive your offered love like love,                   240
And will not wrong it.
HAMLET:                         I embrace it freely,
And will this brother's wager frankly play.
Give us the foils. Come on.
LAERTES:                         Come, one for me.
HAMLET:   I'll be your foil,° Laertes. In mine ignorance
Your skill shall, like a star i' th' darkest night,         245
Stick fiery off° indeed.
LAERTES:                    You mock me, sir.
HAMLET:   No, by this hand.
KING:   Give them the foils, young Osric, Cousin Hamlet,
You know the wager?
HAMLET:                         Very well, my lord.
Your grace has laid the odds o' th' weaker side.            250
KING:   I do not fear it, I have seen you both;
But since he is bettered,° we have therefore odds.
LAERTES:   This is too heavy; let me see another.
HAMLET:   This likes me well. These foils have all a length?

*Prepare to play.*

OSRIC:   Ay, my good lord.                                    255
KING:   Set me the stoups of wine upon that table.
If Hamlet give the first or second hit,
Or quit° in answer of the third exchange,
Let all the battlements their ordnance fire.
The King shall drink to Hamlet's better breath,             260

---

²³⁸ *voice and precedent* authoritative opinion justified by precedent   ²⁴⁴ *foil* (1)
blunt sword, (2) background (of metallic leaf) for a jewel   ²⁴⁶ *Stick fiery off* stand
out brilliantly   ²⁵² *bettered* has improved (in France)   ²⁵⁸ *quit* repay, hit back

And in the cup an union° shall he throw
Richer than that which four successive kings
In Denmark's crown have worn. Give me the cups,
And let the kettle° to the trumpet speak,
The trumpet to the cannoneer without,                                265
The cannons to the heavens, the heaven to earth,
"Now the King drinks to Hamlet." Come, begin.

*Trumpets the while.*

And you, the judges, bear a wary eye.
HAMLET:   Come on, sir.
LAERTES:                    Come, my lord!

*They play.*

HAMLET:                              One!
LAERTES:                                    No.
HAMLET:                                          Judgment?
OSRIC:   A hit, a very palpable hit.

*Drum, trumpets, and shot. Flourish; a piece goes off.*

LAERTES:                          Well, again.                         270
KING:   Stay, give me drink. Hamlet, this pearl is thine.
    Here's to thy health. Give him the cup.
HAMLET:   I'll play this bout first; set it by awhile.
    Come.

[*They play.*]

                  Another hit. What say you?
LAERTES:   A touch, a touch; I do confess't.                          275
KING:   Our son shall win.
QUEEN:                        He's fat,° and scant of breath.
    Here, Hamlet, take my napkin, rub thy brows.
    The Queen carouses to thy fortune, Hamlet.

---

²⁶¹ *union* pearl   ²⁶⁴ *kettle* kettledrum   ²⁷⁶ *fat* (1) sweaty, (2) out of training

HAMLET:   Good madam!
KING:                         Gertrude, do not drink.
QUEEN:   I will, my lord; I pray you pardon me. [*Drinks.*]        280
KING [*aside*]:   It is the poisoned cup; it is too late.
HAMLET:   I dare not drink yet, madam—by and by.
QUEEN:   Come, let me wipe thy face.
LAERTES:   My lord, I'll hit him now.
KING:                                   I do not think't.
LAERTES [*aside*]:   And yet it is almost against my conscience.   285
HAMLET:   Come for the third, Laertes. You do but dally.
    I pray you pass with your best violence;
    I am sure you make a wanton° of me.

    [*They*] *play.*

LAERTES:   Say you so? Come on.
OSRIC:   Nothing neither way.                                           290
LAERTES:   Have at you now!

    *In scuffling they change rapiers,* [*and both are wounded.*]

KING:                                   Part them. They are incensed.
HAMLET:   Nay, come—again!

    [*The Queen falls.*]

OSRIC:                             Look to the Queen there, ho!
HORATIO:   They bleed on both sides. How is it, my lord?
OSRIC:   How is't, Laertes?
LAERTES:   Why, as a woodcock to mine own springe,° Osric.   295
    I am justly killed with mine own treachery.
HAMLET:   How does the Queen?
KING:                             She sounds° to see them bleed.
QUEEN:   No, no, the drink, the drink! O my dear Hamlet!
    The drink, the drink! I am poisoned.

                                                    [*Dies.*]

HAMLET:   O villainy! Ho! Let the door be locked.                    300
Treachery! Seek it out.

[*Laertes falls.*]

LAERTES:   It is here, Hamlet. Hamlet, thou art slain;
No med'cine in the world can do thee good.
In thee there is not half an hour's life.
The treacherous instrument is in thy hand,              305
Unbated and envenomed. The foul practice°
Hath turned itself on me. Lo, here I lie,
Never to rise again. Thy mother's poisoned.
I can no more. The King, the King's to blame.
HAMLET:   The point envenomed too?                             310
Then, venom, to thy work.

*Hurts the King.*

ALL:   Treason! Treason!
KING:   O, yet defend me, friends. I am but hurt.
HAMLET:   Here, thou incestuous, murd'rous, damnèd Dane,
Drink off this potion. Is thy union here?               315
Follow my mother.

*King dies.*

LAERTES:                 He is justly served.
It is a poison tempered° by himself.
Exchange forgiveness with me, noble Hamlet.
Mine and my father's death come not upon thee,
Nor thine on me!                                       320

*Dies.*

HAMLET:   Heaven make thee free of it! I follow thee.
I am dead, Horatio. Wretched Queen, adieu!
You that look pale and tremble at this chance,
That are but mutes° or audience to this act,

---

306 *practice* deception   317 *tempered* mixed   324 *mutes* performers who have no
words to speak

Had I but time (as this fell sergeant,° Death,                    325
Is strict in his arrest) O, I could tell you—
But let it be. Horatio, I am dead;
Thou livest; report me and my cause aright
To the unsatisfied.°
HORATIO:                    Never believe it.
I am more an antique Roman° than a Dane.                          330
Here's yet some liquor left.
HAMLET:                              As th' art a man,
Give me the cup. Let go. By heaven, I'll ha't!
O God, Horatio, what a wounded name,
Things standing thus unknown, shall live behind me!
If thou didst ever hold me in thy heart,                          335
Absent thee from felicity° awhile,
And in this harsh world draw thy breath in pain,
To tell my story.

*A march afar off. [Exit Osric.]*

What warlike noise is this?

*Enter Osric.*

OSRIC:   Young Fortinbras, with conquest come from Poland,
To th' ambassadors of England gives                              340
This warlike volley.
HAMLET:                              O, I die, Horatio!
The potent poison quite o'ercrows° my spirit.
I cannot live to hear the news from England,
But I do prophesy th' election lights
On Fortinbras. He has my dying voice.                             345
So tell him, with th' occurrents,° more and less,
Which have solicited°—the rest is silence.

*Dies.*

---

³²⁵ *fell sergeant* dread sheriff's officer   ³²⁹ *unsatisfied* uninformed   ³³⁰ *antique Roman* (with reference to the old Roman fashion of suicide)   ³³⁶ *felicity* i.e., the felicity of death   ³⁴² *o'ercrows* overpowers (as a triumphant cock crows over its weak opponent)   ³⁴⁶ *occurrents* occurrences   ³⁴⁷ *solicited* incited

HORATIO:   Now cracks a noble heart. Good night, sweet Prince,
And flights of angels sing thee to thy rest.

[*March within.*]

Why does the drum come hither?                                    350

*Enter Fortinbras, with the Ambassadors with Drum, Colors, and
Attendants.*

FORTINBRAS:   Where is this sight?
HORATIO:                                      What is it you would see?
If aught of woe or wonder, cease your search.
FORTINBRAS:   This quarry° cries on havoc.° O proud Death,
What feast is toward° in thine eternal cell
That thou so many princes at a shot                                355
So bloodily hast struck?
AMBASSADOR:                            The sight is dismal;
And our affairs from England come too late.
The ears are senseless that should give us hearing
To tell him his commandment is fulfilled,
That Rosencrantz and Guildenstern are dead.                       360
Where should we have our thanks?
HORATIO:                                         Not from his° mouth
Had it th' ability of life to thank you.
He never gave commandment for their death.
But since, so jump° upon this bloody question,
You from the Polack wars, and you from England,                   365
Are here arrived, give order that these bodies
High on a stage° be placèd to the view,
And let me speak to th' yet unknowing world
How these things came about. So shall you hear
Of carnal, bloody, and unnatural acts,                            370
Of accidental judgments, casual° slaughters,
Of deaths put on by cunning and forced cause,
And, in this upshot, purposes mistook

---

³⁵³ *quarry* heap of slain bodies    ³⁵³ *cries on havoc* proclaims general
slaughter    ³⁵⁴ *toward* in preparation    ³⁶¹ *his* (Claudius')    ³⁶⁴ *jump* precisely
³⁶⁷ *stage* platform    ³⁷¹ *casual* not humanly planned, chance

Fall'n on th' inventors' heads. All this can I
Truly deliver.
FORTINBRAS:       Let us haste to hear it,                                375
And call the noblest to the audience.
For me, with sorrow I embrace my fortune.
I have some rights of memory° in this kingdom,
Which now to claim my vantage doth invite me.
HORATIO:   Of that I shall have also cause to speak,                380
And from his mouth whose voice will draw on° more.
But let this same be presently performed,
Even while men's minds are wild, lest more mischance
On° plots and errors happen.
FORTINBRAS:                           Let four captains
Bear Hamlet like a soldier to the stage,                                385
For he was likely, had he been put on,°
To have proved most royal; and for his passage°
The soldiers' music and the rite of war
Speak loudly for him.
Take up the bodies. Such a sight as this                                390
Becomes the field,° but here shows much amiss.
Go, bid the soldiers shoot.

*Exeunt marching;*
*after the which a peal of ordnance are shot off.*

*Finis*

---

[378] *rights of memory* remembered claims   [381] *voice will draw on* vote will
influence   [384] *On* on top of   [386] *put on* advanced (to the throne)   [387] *passage*
death   [391] *field* battlefield

# HENRIK IBSEN [1828–1906]

# A Doll's House

### List of Characters

TORVALD HELMER, *a lawyer*
NORA, *his wife*
DR. RANK
MRS. LINDE
KROGSTAD
*The Helmers' three small children*
ANNE-MARIE, *the children's nurse*
*A housemaid*
*A porter*

S C E N E:   *The Helmers' living room.*

---

## ACT I

---

*A pleasant, tastefully but not expensively furnished, living room.
A door on the rear wall, right, leads to the front hall, another door,
left, to Helmer's study. Between the two doors a piano. A third
door in the middle of the left wall; further front a window. Near the
window a round table with easy chairs and a small couch. Towards
the rear of the right wall a fourth door; further front a tile stove
with a rocking chair and a couple of arm chairs in front of it.
Between the stove and the side door a small table. Copperplate etch-
ings on the walls. A whatnot with porcelain figurines and other
small objects. A small bookcase with deluxe editions. A rug on the
floor; fire in the stove. Winter day.*

*The doorbell rings, then the sound of the front door opening. Nora,*

---

Translated by Otto Reinert.

*dressed for outdoors, enters, humming cheerfully. She carries several packages, which she puts down on the table, right. She leaves the door to the front hall open; there a Porter is seen holding a Christmas tree and a basket. He gives them to the Maid, who has let them in.*

NORA:   Be sure to hide the Christmas tree, Helene. The children mustn't see it before tonight when we've trimmed it. (*Opens her purse; to the Porter.*) How much?

PORTER:   Fifty øre.

NORA:   Here's a crown. No, keep the change. (*The Porter thanks her, leaves. Nora closes the door. She keeps laughing quietly to herself as she takes off her coat, etc. She takes a bag of macaroons from her pocket and eats a couple. She walks cautiously over to the door to the study and listens.*) Yes, he's home. (*Resumes her humming, walks over to the table, right.*)

HELMER (*in his study*):   Is that my little lark twittering out there?

NORA (*opening some of the packages*):   That's right.

HELMER:   My squirrel bustling about?

NORA:   Yes.

HELMER:   When did squirrel come home?

NORA:   Just now. (*Puts the bag of macaroons back in her pocket, wipes her mouth.*) Come out here, Torvald. I want to show you what I've bought.

HELMER:   I'm busy! (*After a little while he opens the door and looks in, pen in hand.*) Bought, eh? All that? So little wastrel has been throwing money around again?

NORA:   Oh but Torvald, this Christmas we can be a little extravagant, can't we? It's the first Christmas we don't have to scrimp.

HELMER:   I don't know about that. We certainly don't have money to waste.

NORA:   Yes, Torvald, we do. A little, anyway. Just a tiny little bit? Now that you're going to get that big salary and make lots and lots of money.

HELMER:   Starting at New Year's, yes. But payday isn't till the end of the quarter.

NORA:   That doesn't matter. We can always borrow.

HELMER:   Nora! (*Goes over to her and playfully pulls her ear.*) There you go being irresponsible again. Suppose I borrowed a thousand crowns today and you spent it all for Christmas and on New Year's Eve a tile hit me in the head and laid me out cold.

NORA (*putting her hand over his mouth*):   I won't have you say such horrid things.

HELMER:   But suppose it happened. Then what?

NORA:   If it did, I wouldn't care whether we owed money or not.

HELMER:   But what about the people I had borrowed from?

NORA:   Who cares about them! They are strangers.

HELMER:   Nora, Nora, you are a woman. No, really! You know how I feel about that. No debts! A home in debt isn't a free home, and if it isn't free it isn't beautiful. We've managed nicely so far, you and I, and that's the way we'll go on. It won't be for much longer.

NORA (*walks over toward the stove*):   All right, Torvald. Whatever you say.

HELMER (*follows her*):   Come, come, my little songbird mustn't droop her wings. What's this? Can't have a pouty squirrel in the house, you know. (*Takes out his wallet.*) Nora, what do you think I have here?

NORA (*turns around quickly*):   Money!

HELMER:   Here. (*Gives her some bills.*) Don't you think I know Christmas is expensive?

NORA (*counting*):   Ten—twenty—thirty—forty. Thank you, thank you, Torvald. This helps a lot.

HELMER:   I certainly hope so.

NORA:   It does, it does. But I want to show you what I got. It was cheap, too. Look. New clothes for Ivar. And a sword. And a horse and trumpet for Bob. And a doll and a little bed for Emmy. It isn't any good, but it wouldn't last, anyway. And here's some dress material and scarves for the maids. I feel bad about old Anne-Marie, though. She really should be getting much more.

HELMER:   And what's in here?

NORA (*cries*):   Not till tonight!

HELMER:   I see. But now what does my little prodigal have in mind for herself?

NORA:   Oh, nothing. I really don't care.

HELMER:   Of course you do. Tell me what you'd like. Within reason.

NORA:   Oh, I don't know. Really, I don't. The only thing—

HELMER:   Well?

NORA (*fiddling with his buttons, without looking at him*):   If you really want to give me something, you might—you could—

HELMER:   All right, let's have it.

NORA (*quickly*):   Some money, Torvald. Just as much as you think you can spare. Then I'll buy myself something one of these days.

HELMER:   No, really Nora—

NORA:   Oh yes, please, Torvald. Please? I'll wrap the money in pretty gold paper and hang it on the tree. Won't that be nice?

HELMER:   What's the name for little birds that are always spending money?

NORA:   Wastrels, I know. But please let's do it my way, Torvald. Then I'll have time to decide what I need most. Now that's sensible, isn't it?

HELMER (*smiling*):   Oh, very sensible. That is, if you really bought yourself something you could use. But it all disappears in the household expenses or you buy things you don't need. And then you come back to me for more.

NORA:   Oh, but Torvald—

HELMER:   That's the truth, dear little Nora, and you know it. (*Puts his arm around her.*) My wastrel is a little sweetheart, but she does go through an awful lot of money awfully fast. You've no idea how expensive it is for a man to keep a wastrel.

NORA:   That's not fair, Torvald. I really save all I can.

HELMER (*laughs*):   Oh, I believe that. All you can. Meaning, exactly nothing!

NORA (*hums, smiles mysteriously*):   You don't know all the things we songbirds and squirrels need money for, Torvald.

HELMER:   You know, you're funny. Just like your father. You're always looking for ways to get money, but as soon as you do it runs through your fingers and you can never say what you spent it for. Well, I guess I'll just have to take you the way you are. It's in your blood. Yes, that sort of thing is hereditary, Nora.

NORA:   In that case, I wish I had inherited many of Daddy's qualities.

HELMER:   And I don't want you any different from just what you are—my own sweet little songbird. Hey!—I think I just noticed something. Aren't you looking—what's the word?—a little—sly—?

NORA:  I am?

HELMER:  You definitely are. Look at me.

NORA *(looks at him)*:  Well?

HELMER *(wagging a finger)*:  Little sweet-tooth hasn't by any chance been on a rampage today, has she?

NORA:  Of course not. Whatever makes you think that?

HELMER:  A little detour by the pastryshop maybe?

NORA:  No, I assure you, Torvald—

HELMER:  Nibbled a little jam?

NORA:  Certainly not!

HELMER:  Munched a macaroon or two?

NORA:  No, really, Torvald, I honestly—

HELMER:  All right. Of course I was only joking.

NORA *(walks toward the table, right)*:  You know I wouldn't do anything to displease you.

HELMER:  I know. And I have your promise. *(Over to her.)* All right, keep your little Christmas secrets to yourself, Nora darling. They'll all come out tonight, I suppose, when we light the tree.

NORA:  Did you remember to invite Rank?

HELMER:  No, but there's no need to. He knows he'll have dinner with us. Anyway, I'll see him later this morning. I'll ask him then. I did order some good wine. Oh Nora, you've no idea how much I'm looking forward to tonight!

NORA:  Me too. And the children, Torvald! They'll have such a good time!

HELMER:  You know, it *is* nice to have a good, safe job and a comfortable income. Feels good just thinking about it. Don't you agree?

NORA:  Oh, it's wonderful!

HELMER:  Remember last Christmas? For three whole weeks you shut yourself up every evening till long after midnight, making ornaments for the Christmas tree and I don't know what else. Some big surprise for all of us, anyway. I'll be damned if I've ever been so bored in my whole life!

NORA:  I wasn't bored at all.

HELMER *(smiling)*:  But you've got to admit you didn't have much to show for it in the end.

NORA:  Oh, don't tease me again about that! Could I help it that the cat got in and tore up everything?

HELMER:  Of course you couldn't, my poor little Nora. You just wanted to please the rest of us, and that's the important thing. But I am glad the hard times are behind us. Aren't you?

NORA:   Oh yes. I think it's just wonderful.

HELMER:   This year I won't be bored and lonely. And you won't have to strain your dear eyes and your delicate little hands—

NORA *(claps her hands)*:   No I won't, will I, Torvald? Oh, how wonderful, how lovely, to hear you say that! *(Puts her arm under his.)* Let me tell you how I think we should arrange things, Torvald. Soon as Christmas is over—*(The doorbell rings.)* Someone's at the door. *(Straightens things up a bit.)* A caller, I suppose. Bother!

HELMER:   Remember, I'm not home for visitors.

THE MAID *(in the door to the front hall)*:   Ma'am, there's a lady here—

NORA:   All right. Ask her to come in.

THE MAID *(to Helmer)*:   And the Doctor just arrived.

HELMER:   Is he in the study?

THE MAID:   Yes, sir.

*Helmer exits into his study. The Maid shows Mrs. Linde in and closes the door behind her as she leaves. Mrs. Linde is in travel dress.*

MRS. LINDE *(timid and a little hesitant)*:   Good morning, Nora.

NORA *(uncertainly)*:   Good morning.

MRS. LINDE:   I don't believe you know who I am.

NORA:   No—I'm not sure—Though I know I should—Of course! Kristine! It's you!

MRS. LINDE:   Yes, it's me.

NORA:   And I didn't even recognize you! I had no idea! *(In a lower voice.)* You've changed, Kristine.

MRS. LINDE:   I'm sure I have. It's been nine or ten long years.

NORA:   Has it really been that long? Yes, you're right. I've been so happy these last eight years. And now you're here. Such a long trip in the middle of winter. How brave!

MRS. LINDE:   I got in on the steamer this morning.

NORA:   To have some fun over the holidays, of course. That's lovely. For we *are* going to have fun. But take off your coat! You aren't cold, are you? *(Helps her.)* There, now! Let's sit down here by the fire and just relax and talk. No, you sit there. I want the rocking chair. (*Takes her hands.*) And now you've got your old face back. It was just for a minute, right at first—Though you are a little more pale, Kristine. And maybe a little thinner.

MRS. LINDE:  And much, much older, Nora.

NORA:  Maybe a little older. Just a teeny-weeny bit, not much. (*Interrupts herself, serious.*) Oh, but how thoughtless of me, chatting away like this! Sweet, good Kristine, can you forgive me?

MRS. LINDE:  Forgive you what, Nora?

NORA (*in a low voice*):  You poor dear, you lost your husband, didn't you?

MRS. LINDE:  Three years ago, yes.

NORA:  I know. I saw it in the paper. Oh please believe me, Kristine. I really meant to write you, but I never got around to it. Something was always coming up.

MRS. LINDE:  Of course, Nora. I understand.

NORA:  No, that wasn't very nice of me. You poor thing, all you must have been through. And he didn't leave you much, either, did he?

MRS. LINDE:  No.

NORA:  And no children?

MRS. LINDE:  No.

NORA:  Nothing at all, in other words?

MRS. LINDE:  Not so much as a sense of loss—a grief to live on—

NORA (*incredulous*):  But Kristine, how can that *be*?

MRS. LINDE (*with a sad smile, strokes Nora's hair*):  That's the way it sometimes is, Nora.

NORA:  All alone. How awful for you. I have three darling children. You can't see them right now, though; they're out with their nurse. But now you must tell me everything—

MRS. LINDE:  No, no; I'd rather listen to you.

NORA:  No, you begin. Today I won't be selfish. Today I'll think only of you. Except there's one thing I've just got to tell you first. Something marvelous that's happened to us just these last few days. You haven't heard, have you?

MRS. LINDE:  No; tell me.

NORA:  Just think. My husband's been made manager of the Mutual Bank.

MRS. LINDE:  Your husband—! Oh, I'm so glad!

NORA:   Yes, isn't that great? You see, private law practice is so uncertain, especially when you won't have anything to do with cases that aren't—you know—quite nice. And of course Torvald won't do that, and I quite agree with him. Oh, you've no idea how delighted we are! He takes over at New Year's, and he'll be getting a big salary and all sorts of extras. From now on we'll be able to live in quite a different way—exactly as we like. Oh, Kristine! I feel so carefree and happy! It's lovely to have lots and lots of money and not have to worry about a thing! Don't you agree?

MRS. LINDE:   It would be nice to have enough, at any rate.

NORA:   No, I don't mean just enough. I mean lots and lots!

MRS. LINDE *(smiles)*:   Nora, Nora, when are you going to be sensible? In school you spent a great deal of money.

NORA *(quietly laughing)*:   Yes, and Torvald says I still do. *(Raises her finger at Mrs. Linde.)* But "Nora, Nora" isn't so crazy as you all think. Believe me, we've had nothing to be extravagant with. We've both had to work.

MRS. LINDE:   You too?

NORA:   Yes. Oh, it's been little things mostly—sewing, crocheting, embroidery—that sort of thing. *(Casually.)* And other things too. You know, of course, that Torvald left government service when we got married? There was no chance of promotion in his department, and of course he had to make more money than he had been making. So for the first few years he worked altogether too hard. He had to take jobs on the side and work night and day. It turned out to be too much for him. He became seriously ill. The doctors told him he needed to go south.

MRS. LINDE:   That's right; you spent a year in Italy, didn't you?

NORA:   Yes, we did. But you won't believe how hard it was to get away. Ivar had just been born. But of course we had to go. Oh, it was a wonderful trip. And it saved Torvald's life. But it took a lot of money, Kristine.

MRS. LINDE:   I'm sure it did.

NORA:   Twelve hundred specie dollars. Four thousand eight hundred crowns. That's a lot of money.

MRS. LINDE:   Yes. So it's lucky you have it when something like that happens.

NORA:   Well, actually we got the money from Daddy.

MRS. LINDE: I see. That was about the time your father died, I believe.

NORA: Yes, just about then. And I couldn't even go and take care of him. I was expecting little Ivar any day. And I had poor Torvald to look after, desperately sick and all. My dear, good Daddy! I never saw him again, Kristine. That's the saddest thing that's happened to me since I got married.

MRS. LINDE: I know you were very fond of him. But then you went to Italy?

NORA: Yes, for now we had the money, and the doctors urged us to go. So we left about a month later.

MRS. LINDE: And when you came back your husband was well again?

NORA: Healthy as a horse!

MRS. LINDE: But—the doctor?

NORA: What do you mean?

MRS. LINDE: I thought the maid said it was the doctor, that gentleman who came the same time I did.

NORA: Oh, that's Dr. Rank. He doesn't come as a doctor. He's our closest friend. He looks in at least once every day. No, Torvald hasn't been sick once since then. And the children are strong and healthy, too, and so am I. (*Jumps up and claps her hands.*) Oh God, Kristine! Isn't it wonderful to be alive and happy! Isn't it just lovely!—But now I'm being mean again, talking only about myself and my things. (*Sits down on a footstool close to Mrs. Linde and puts her arms on her lap.*) Please, don't be angry with me! Tell me, is it really true that you didn't care for your husband? Then why did you marry him?

MRS. LINDE: Mother was still alive then, but she was bedridden and helpless. And I had my two younger brothers to look after. I didn't think I had the right to turn him down.

NORA: No, I suppose not. So he had money then?

MRS. LINDE: He was quite well off, I think. But it was an uncertain business, Nora. When he died, the whole thing collapsed and there was nothing left.

NORA: And then—?

MRS. LINDE: Well, I had to manage as best I could. With a little store and a little school and anything else I could think of. The last three years have been one long work day for me, Nora, without any rest. But now it's over. My poor mother doesn't need me any more. She passed away. And the boys are on their own too. They've both got jobs and support themselves.

NORA:   What a relief for you—

MRS. LINDE:   No, not relief. Just a great emptiness. Nobody to live for any more. (*Gets up, restlessly.*) That's why I couldn't stand it any longer in that little hole. Here in town it has to be easier to find something to keep me busy and occupy my thoughts. With a little luck I should be able to find a permanent job, something in an office—

NORA:   Oh but Kristine, that's exhausting work, and you look worn out already. It would be much better for you to go to a resort.

MRS. LINDE (*walks over to the window*):   I don't have a Daddy who can give me the money, Nora.

NORA (*getting up*):   Oh, don't be angry with me.

MRS. LINDE (*over to her*):   Dear Nora, don't *you* be angry with *me*. That's the worst thing about my kind of situation: you become so bitter. You've nobody to work for, and yet you have to look out for yourself, somehow. You've got to keep on living, and so you become selfish. Do you know—when you told me about your husband's new position I was delighted not so much for your sake as for my own.

NORA:   Why was that? Oh, I see. You think maybe Torvald can give you a job?

MRS. LINDE:   That's what I had in mind.

NORA:   And he will too, Kristine. Just leave it to me. I'll be ever so subtle about it. I'll think of something nice to tell him, something he'll like. Oh I so much want to help you.

MRS. LINDE:   That's very good of you, Nora—making an effort like that for me. Especially since you've known so little trouble and hardship in your own life.

NORA:   I—?—have known so little—?

MRS. LINDE (*smiling*):   Oh well, a little sewing or whatever it was. You're still a child, Nora.

NORA (*with a toss of her head, walks away*):   You shouldn't sound so superior.

MRS. LINDE:   I shouldn't?

NORA:   You're just like all the others. None of you think I'm good for anything really serious.

MRS. LINDE:   Well, now—

NORA:   That I've never been through anything difficult.

MRS. LINDE:   But Nora! You just told me all your troubles!

NORA:   That's nothing. (*Lowers her voice.*) I haven't told you about *it*.

MRS. LINDE:   It? What's that? What do you mean?

NORA:   You patronize me, Kristine, and that's not fair. You're proud that you worked so long and so hard for your mother.

MRS. LINDE:   I don't think I patronize anyone. But it *is* true that I'm both proud and happy that I could make mother's last years comparatively easy.

NORA:   And you're proud of all you did for your brothers.

MRS. LINDE:   I think I have the right to be.

NORA:   And so do I. But now I want to tell you something, Kristine. I have something to be proud and happy about too.

MRS. LINDE:   I don't doubt that for a moment. But what exactly do you mean?

NORA:   Not so loud! Torvald mustn't hear—not for anything in the world. Nobody must know about this, Kristine. Nobody but you.

MRS. LINDE:   But what is it?

NORA:   Come here. (*Pulls her down on the couch beside her.*) You see, I *do* have something to be proud and happy about. I've saved Torvald's life.

MRS. LINDE:   Saved—? How do you mean—"saved"?

NORA:   I told you about our trip to Italy. Torvald would have died if he hadn't gone.

MRS. LINDE:   I understand that. And so your father gave you the money you needed.

NORA (*smiles*):   Yes, that's what Torvald and all the others think. But—

MRS. LINDE:   But what?

NORA:   Daddy didn't give us a penny. *I* raised that money.

MRS. LINDE:   *You* did? That whole big amount?

NORA:   Twelve hundred specie dollars. Four thousand eight hundred crowns. *Now* what do you say?

MRS. LINDE:   But Nora, how could you? Did you win in the state lottery?

NORA (*contemptuously*):   State lottery! (*Snorts.*) What is so great about that?

MRS. LINDE:   Where did it come from then?

NORA *(humming and smiling, enjoying her secret)*: Hmmm. Tra-la-la-la-la!

MRS. LINDE:   You certainly couldn't have borrowed it.

NORA:   Oh? And why not?

MRS. LINDE:   A wife can't borrow money without her husband's consent.

NORA *(with a toss of her head)*:   Oh, I don't know—take a wife with a little bit of a head for business—a wife who knows how to manage things—

MRS. LINDE:   But Nora, I don't understand at all—

NORA:   You don't have to. I didn't say I borrowed the money, did I? I could have gotten it some other way. *(Leans back.)* An admirer may have given it to me. When you're as tolerably goodlooking as I am—

MRS. LINDE:   Oh, you're crazy.

NORA:   I think you're dying from curiosity, Kristine.

MRS. LINDE:   I'm beginning to think you've done something very foolish, Nora.

NORA *(sits up)*:   Is it foolish to save your husband's life?

MRS. LINDE:   I say it's foolish to act behind his back.

NORA:   But don't you see: he couldn't be told! You're missing the whole point, Kristine. We couldn't even let him know how seriously ill he was. The doctors came to *me* and told me his life was in danger, that nothing could save him but a stay in the south. Don't you think I tried to work on him? I told him how lovely it would be if I could go abroad like other young wives. I cried and begged. I said he'd better remember what condition I was in, that he had to be nice to me and do what I wanted. I even hinted he could borrow the money. But that almost made him angry with me. He told me I was being irresponsible and that it was his duty as my husband not to give in to my moods and whims—I think that's what he called it. All right, I said to myself, you've got to be saved somehow, and so I found a way—

MRS. LINDE:   And your husband never learned from your father that the money didn't come from him?

NORA:   Never. Daddy died that same week. I thought of telling him all about it and ask him not to say anything. But since he was so sick—It turned out I didn't have to—

MRS. LINDE:   And you've never told your husband?

NORA:   Of course not! Good heavens, how could I? He, with his strict principles! Besides, you know how men are. Torvald would find it embarrassing and humiliating to learn that he owed me anything. It would upset our whole relationship. Our happy, beautiful home would no longer be what it is.

MRS. LINDE:   Aren't you ever going to tell him?

NORA (*reflectively, half smiling*):   Yes—one day, maybe. Many, many years from now, when I'm no longer young and pretty. Don't laugh! I mean when Torvald no longer feels about me the way he does now, when he no longer thinks it's fun when I dance for him and put on costumes and recite for him. Then it will be good to have something in reserve—(*Interrupts herself* ) Oh, I'm just being silly! That day will never come.—Well, now, Kristine, what do you think of my great secret? Don't you think I'm good for something too?—By the way, you wouldn't believe all the worry I've had because of it. It's been very hard to meet my obligations on schedule. You see, in business there's something called quarterly interest and something called installments on the principal, and those are terribly hard to come up with. I've had to save a little here and a little there, whenever I could. I couldn't use much of the housekeeping money, for Torvald has to eat well. And I couldn't use what I got for clothes for the children. They have to look nice, and I didn't think it would be right to spend less than I got—the sweet little things!

MRS. LINDE:   Poor Nora! So you had to take it from your own allowance?

NORA:   Yes, of course. After all, it was my affair. Every time Torvald gave me money for a new dress and things like that, I never used more than half of it. I always bought the cheapest, simplest things for myself. Thank God, everything looks good on me, so Torvald never noticed. But it was hard many times, Kristine, for it's fun to have pretty clothes. Don't you think?

MRS. LINDE:   Certainly.

NORA:   Anyway, I had other ways of making money too. Last winter I was lucky enough to get some copying work. So I locked the door and sat up writing every night till quite late. God! I often got so tired—! But it was great fun, too, working and making money. It was almost like being a man.

MRS. LINDE: But how much have you been able to pay off this way?

NORA: I couldn't tell you exactly. You see, it's very difficult to keep track of business like that. All I know is I have been paying off as much as I've been able to scrape together. Many times I didn't know what to do. (*Smiles.*) Then I used to imagine a rich old gentleman had fallen in love with me—

MRS. LINDE: What! What old gentleman?

NORA: Phooey! And now he was dead and they were reading his will, and there it said in big letters, "All my money is to be paid in cash immediately to the charming Mrs. Nora Helmer."

MRS. LINDE: But dearest Nora—who was this old gentleman?

NORA: For heaven's sake, Kristine, don't you see! There was no old gentleman. He was just somebody I made up when I couldn't think of any way to raise the money. But never mind him. The old bore can be anyone he likes to for all I care. I have no use for him or his last will, for now I don't have a single worry in the world. (*Jumps up.*) Dear God, what a lovely thought that is! To be able to play and have fun with the children, to have everything nice and pretty in the house, just the way Torvald likes it! Not a care! And soon spring will be here, and the air will be blue and high. Maybe we can travel again. Maybe I'll see the ocean again! Oh, yes, yes!—it's wonderful to be alive and happy!

*The doorbell rings.*

MRS. LINDE (*getting up*): There's the doorbell. Maybe I better be going.

NORA: No, please stay. I'm sure it's just someone for Torvald—

THE MAID (*in the hall door*): Excuse me, ma'am. There's a gentleman here who'd like to see Mr. Helmer.

NORA: You mean the bank manager.

THE MAID: Sorry, ma'am; the bank manager. But I didn't know— since the Doctor is with him—

NORA: Who is the gentleman?

KROGSTAD (*appearing in the door*): It's just me, Mrs. Helmer.

*Mrs. Linde starts, looks, turns away toward the window.*

NORA (*takes a step toward him, tense, in a low voice*):  You? What do you want? What do you want with my husband?

KROGSTAD:  Bank business—in a way. I have a small job in the Mutual, and I understand your husband is going to be our new manager—

NORA:  So it's just—

KROGSTAD:  Just routine business, ma'am. Nothing else.

NORA:  All right. In that case, why don't you go through the door to the office.

*Dismisses him casually as she closes the door. Walks over to the stove and tends the fire.*

MRS. LINDE:  Nora—who was that man?

NORA:  His name's Krogstad. He's a lawyer.

MRS. LINDE:  So it *was* him.

NORA:  Do you know him?

MRS. LINDE:  I used to—many years ago. For a while he clerked in our part of the country.

NORA:  Right. He did.

MRS. LINDE:  He has changed a great deal.

NORA:  I believe he had a very unhappy marriage.

MRS. LINDE:  And now he's a widower, isn't he?

NORA:  With many children. There now; it's burning nicely again. (*Closes the stove and moves the rocking chair a little to the side.*)

MRS. LINDE:  They say he's into all sorts of business.

NORA:  Really? Maybe so. I wouldn't know. But let's not think about business. It's such a bore.

DR. RANK (*appears in the door to Helmer's study*):  No, I don't want to be in the way. I'd rather talk to your wife a bit. (*Closes the door and notices Mrs. Linde.*) Oh, I beg your pardon. I believe I'm in the way here too.

NORA:  No, not at all. (*Introduces them.*) Dr. Rank. Mrs. Linde.

RANK:  Aha. A name often heard in this house. I believe I passed you on the stairs coming up.

MRS. LINDE:  Yes. I'm afraid I climb stairs very slowly. They aren't good for me.

RANK:  I see. A slight case of inner decay, perhaps?

MRS. LINDE:  Overwork, rather.

RANK:   Oh, is that all? And now you've come to town to relax at all the parties?

MRS. LINDE:   I have come to look for a job.

RANK:   A proven cure for overwork, I take it?

MRS. LINDE:   One has to live, Doctor.

RANK:   Yes, that seems to be the common opinion.

NORA:   Come on, Dr. Rank—you want to live just as much as the rest of us.

RANK:   Of course I do. Miserable as I am, I prefer to go on being tortured as long as possible. All my patients feel the same way. And that's true of the moral invalids too. Helmer is talking with a specimen right this minute.

MRS. LINDE *(in a low voice)*:   Ah!

NORA:   What do you mean?

RANK:   Oh, this lawyer, Krogstad. You don't know him. The roots of his character are decayed. But even he began by saying something about having *to live*—as if it were a matter of the highest importance.

NORA:   Oh? What did he want with Torvald?

RANK:   I don't really know. All I heard was something about the bank.

NORA:   I didn't know that Krog—that this Krogstad had anything to do with the Mutual Bank.

RANK:   Yes, he seems to have some kind of job there. (*To Mrs. Linde.*) I don't know if you are familiar in your part of the country with the kind of person who is always running around trying to sniff out cases of moral decrepitude and as soon as he finds one puts the individual under observation in some excellent position or other. All the healthy ones are left out in the cold.

MRS. LINDE:   I should think it's the sick who need looking after the most.

RANK *(shrugs his shoulders)*:   There we are. That's the attitude that turns society into a hospital.

*Nora, absorbed in her own thoughts, suddenly starts giggling and clapping her hands.*

RANK:   What's so funny about that? Do you even know what society is?

NORA: What do I care about your stupid society! I laughed at something entirely different—something terribly amusing. Tell me, Dr. Rank—all the employees in the Mutual Bank, from now on they'll all be dependent on Torvald, right?

RANK: Is that what you find so enormously amusing?

NORA (*smiles and hums*): That's my business, that's my business! (*Walks around.*) Yes, I do think it's fun that we—that Torvald is going to have so much influence on so many people's lives. (*Brings out the bag of macaroons.*) Have a macaroon, Dr. Rank.

RANK: Well, well—macaroons. I thought they were banned around here.

NORA: Yes, but these were some that Kristine gave me.

MRS. LINDE: What! I?

NORA: That's all right. Don't look so scared. You couldn't know that Torvald won't let me have them. He's afraid they'll ruin my teeth. But who cares! Just once in a while—! Right, Dr. Rank? Have one! (*Puts a macaroon into his mouth.*) You too, Kristine. And one for me. A very small one. Or at most two. (*Walks around again.*) Yes, I really feel very, very happy. Now there's just one thing I'm dying to do.

RANK: Oh? And what's that?

NORA: Something I'm dying to say so Torvald could hear.

RANK: And why can't you?

NORA: I don't dare to, for it's not nice.

MRS. LINDE: Not nice?

RANK: In that case, I guess you'd better not. But surely to the two of us—? What is it you'd like to say for Helmer to hear?

NORA: I want to say, "Goddammit!"

RANK: Are you out of your mind!

MRS. LINDE: For heaven's sake, Nora!

RANK: Say it. Here he comes.

NORA (*hiding the macaroons*): Shhh!

*Helmer enters from his study, carrying his hat and overcoat.*

NORA (*going to him*): Well, dear, did you get rid of him?

HELMER: Yes, he just left.

NORA: Torvald, I want you to meet Kristine. She's just come to town.

HELMER:   Kristine—? I'm sorry; I don't think—

NORA:   Mrs. Linde, Torvald dear. Mrs. Kristine Linde.

HELMER:   Ah, yes. A childhood friend of my wife's, I suppose.

MRS. LINDE:   Yes, we've known each other for a long time.

NORA:   Just think; she has come all this way to see you.

HELMER:   I'm not sure I understand—

MRS. LINDE:   Well, not really—

NORA:   You see, Kristine is an absolutely fantastic secretary, and she would so much like to work for a competent executive and learn more than she knows already—

HELMER:   Very sensible, I'm sure, Mrs. Linde.

NORA:   So when she heard about your appointment—they got a wire about it—she came here as fast as she could. How about it, Torvald? Couldn't you do something for Kristine? For my sake. Please?

HELMER:   Quite possibly. I take it you're a widow, Mrs. Linde?

MRS. LINDE:   Yes.

HELMER:   And you've had office experience?

MRS. LINDE:   Some—yes.

HELMER:   In that case I think it's quite likely that I'll be able to find you a position.

NORA *(claps her hands)*:   I knew it! I knew it!

HELMER:   You've arrived at a most opportune time, Mrs. Linde.

MRS. LINDE:   Oh, how can I ever thank you—

HELMER:   Not at all, not at all. (*Puts his coat on.*) But today you'll have to excuse me—

RANK:   Wait a minute; I'll come with you. (*Gets his fur coat from the front hall, warms it by the stove.*)

NORA:   Don't be long, Torvald.

HELMER:   An hour or so; no more.

NORA:   Are you leaving, too, Kristine?

MRS. LINDE *(putting on her things)*:   Yes, I'd better go and find a place to stay.

HELMER:   Good. Then we'll be going the same way.

NORA *(helping her)*:   I'm sorry this place is so small, but I don't think we very well could—

MRS. LINDE:   Of course! Don't be silly, Nora. Goodbye, and thank you for everything.

NORA:   Goodbye. We'll see you soon. You'll be back this evening, of course. And you too, Dr. Rank; right? If you feel well enough? Of course you will. Just wrap yourself up.

*General small talk as all exit into the hall. Children's voices are heard on the stairs.*

NORA:   There they are! There they are! (*She runs and opens the door. The nurse Anne-Marie enters with the children.*)
NORA:   Come in! Come in! (*Bends over and kisses them.*) Oh, you sweet, sweet darlings! Look at them, Kristine! Aren't they beautiful?
RANK:   No standing around in the draft!
HELMER:   Come along, Mrs. Linde. This place isn't fit for anyone but mothers right now.

*Dr. Rank, Helmer, and Mrs. Linde go down the stairs. The Nurse enters the living room with the children. Nora follows, closing the door behind her.*

NORA:   My, how nice you all look! Such red cheeks! Like apples and roses. (*The children all talk at the same time.*) You've had so much fun? I bet you have. Oh, isn't that nice! You pulled both Emmy and Bob on your sleigh? Both at the same time? That's very good, Ivar. Oh, let me hold her for a minute, Anne-Marie. My sweet little doll baby! (*Takes the smallest of the children from the Nurse and dances with her.*) Yes, yes, of course; Mama'll dance with you too, Bob. What? You threw snowballs? Oh, I wish I'd been there! No, no; I want to take their clothes off, Anne-Marie. Please let me; I think it's so much fun. You go on in. You look frozen. There's hot coffee on the stove.

*The Nurse exits into the room to the left. Nora takes the children's wraps off and throws them all around. They all keep telling her things at the same time.*

NORA:   Oh, really? A big dog ran after you? But it didn't bite you. Of course not. Dogs don't bite sweet little doll babies. Don't peck at the packages, Ivar! What's in them? Wouldn't you like to know! No, no; that's something terrible! Play? You want to play? What do you want to play? Okay, let's play hide-and-seek. Bob hides first. You want *me* to? All right. I'll go first.

*Laughing and shouting, Nora and the children play in the living room and in the adjacent room, right. Finally, Nora hides herself under the table; the children rush in, look for her, can't find her. They hear her low giggle, run to the table, lift the rug that covers it, see her. General hilarity. She crawls out, pretends to scare them. New delight. In the meantime there has been a knock on the door between the living room and the front hall, but nobody has noticed. Now the door is opened halfway; Krogstad appears. He waits a little. The playing goes on.*

KROGSTAD:  Pardon me, Mrs. Helmer—
NORA *(with a muted cry turns around, jumps up)*:  Ah! What do you want?
KROGSTAD:  I'm sorry. The front door was open. Somebody must have forgotten to close it—
NORA *(standing up)*:  My husband isn't here, Mr. Krogstad.
KROGSTAD:  I know.
NORA:  So what do you want?
KROGSTAD:  I'd like a word with you.
NORA:  With—? *(To the children in a low voice.)* Go in to Anne-Marie. What? No, the strange man won't do anything bad to Mama. When he's gone we'll play some more.

*She takes the children into the room to the left and closes the door.*

NORA *(tense, troubled)*:  You want to speak to me?
KROGSTAD:  Yes I do.
NORA:  Today—? It isn't the first of the month yet.
KROGSTAD:  No, it's Christmas Eve. It's up to you what kind of holiday you'll have.
NORA:  What do you want? I can't possibly—
KROGSTAD:  Let's not talk about that just yet. There's something else. You do have a few minutes, don't you?
NORA:  Yes. Yes, of course. That is—
KROGSTAD:  Good. I was sitting in Olsen's restaurant when I saw your husband go by.
NORA:  Yes—?

KROGSTAD:  —with a lady.

NORA:  What of it?

KROGSTAD:  May I be so free as to ask: wasn't that lady Mrs. Linde?

NORA:  Yes.

KROGSTAD:  Just arrived in town?

NORA:  Yes, today.

KROGSTAD:  She's a good friend of yours, I understand?

NORA:  Yes, she is. But I fail to see—

KROGSTAD:  I used to know her myself.

NORA:  I know that.

KROGSTAD:  So you know about that. I thought as much. In that case, let me ask you a simple question. Is Mrs. Linde going to be employed in the bank?

NORA:  What makes you think you have the right to cross-examine me like this, Mr. Krogstad—you, one of my husband's employees? But since you ask, I'll tell you. Yes, Mrs. Linde is going to be working in the bank. And it was I who recommended her, Mr. Krogstad. Now you know.

KROGSTAD:  So I was right.

NORA *(walks up and down)*:  After all, one does have a little influence, you know. Just because you're a woman, it doesn't mean that—Really, Mr. Krogstad, people in a subordinate position should be careful not to offend someone who—oh well—

KROGSTAD:  —has influence?

NORA:  Exactly.

KROGSTAD *(changing his tone)*:  Mrs. Helmer, I must ask you to be good enough to use your influence on my behalf.

NORA:  What do you mean?

KROGSTAD:  I want you to make sure that I am going to keep my subordinate position in the bank.

NORA:  I don't understand. Who is going to take your position away from you?

KROGSTAD:  There's no point in playing ignorant with me, Mrs. Helmer. I can very well appreciate that your friend would find it unpleasant to run into me. So now I know who I can thank for my dismissal.

NORA:  But I assure you—

KROGSTAD:  Never mind. Just want to say you still have time. I advise you to use your influence to prevent it.

NORA: But Mr. Krogstad, I don't have any influence—none at all.

KROGSTAD: No? I thought you just said—

NORA: Of course I didn't mean it that way. I! Whatever makes you think that I have any influence of that kind on my husband?

KROGSTAD: I went to law school with your husband. I have no reason to think that the bank manager is less susceptible than other husbands.

NORA: If you're going to insult my husband, I'll ask you to leave.

KROGSTAD: You're brave, Mrs. Helmer.

NORA: I'm not afraid of you any more. After New Year's I'll be out of this thing with you.

KROGSTAD (*more controlled*): Listen, Mrs. Helmer. If necessary, I'll fight as for my life to keep my little job in the bank.

NORA: So it seems.

KROGSTAD: It isn't just the money; that's really the smallest part of it. There is something else—Well, I guess I might as well tell you. It's like this. I'm sure you know, like everybody else, that some years ago I committed—an impropriety.

NORA: I believe I've heard it mentioned.

KROGSTAD: The case never came to court, but from that moment all doors were closed to me. So I took up the kind of business you know about. I had to do something, and I think I can say about myself that I have not been among the worst. But now I want to get out of all that. My sons are growing up. For their sake I must get back as much of my good name as I can. This job in the bank was like the first rung on the ladder. And now your husband wants to kick me down and leave me back in the mud again.

NORA: But I swear to you, Mr. Krogstad; it's not at all in my power to help you.

KROGSTAD: That's because you don't want to. But I have the means to force you.

NORA: You don't mean you're going to tell my husband I owe you money?

KROGSTAD: And if I did?

NORA: That would be a mean thing to do. (*Almost crying.*) That secret, which is my joy and my pride—for him to learn about

it in such a coarse and ugly manner—to learn it from you—!
It would be terribly unpleasant for me.

KROGSTAD:   Just unpleasant?

NORA *(heatedly)*:   But go ahead! Do it! It will be worse for you
than for me. When my husband realizes what a bad person
you are, you'll be sure to lose your job.

KROGSTAD:   I asked you if it was just domestic unpleasantness
you were afraid of?

NORA:   When my husband finds out, of course he'll pay off the
loan, and then we won't have anything more to do with you.

KROGSTAD *(stepping closer)*:   Listen, Mrs. Helmer—either you have
a very bad memory, or you don't know much about business.
I think I had better straighten you out on a few things.

NORA:   What do you mean?

KROGSTAD:   When your husband was ill, you came to me to borrow twelve hundred dollars.

NORA:   I knew nobody else.

KROGSTAD:   I promised to get you the money—

NORA:   And you did.

KROGSTAD:   I promised to get you the money on certain conditions. At the time you were so anxious about your husband's
health and so set on getting him away that I doubt very much
that you paid much attention to the details of our transaction.
That's why I remind you of them now. Anyway, I promised
to get you the money if you would sign an I.O.U., which I
drafted.

NORA:   And which I signed.

KROGSTAD:   Good. But below your signature I added a few lines,
making your father security for the loan. Your father was
supposed to put his signature to those lines.

NORA:   Supposed to—? He did.

KROGSTAD:   I had left the date blank. That is, your father was to
date his own signature. You recall that, don't you, Mrs. Helmer?

NORA:   I guess so—

KROGSTAD:   I gave the note to you. You were to mail it to your
father. Am I correct?

NORA:   Yes.

KROGSTAD:   And of course you did so right away, for no more than five or six days later you brought the paper back to me, signed by your father. Then I paid you the money.

NORA:   Well? And haven't I been keeping up with the payments?

KROGSTAD:   Fairly well, yes. But to get back to what we were talking about—those were difficult days for you, weren't they, Mrs. Helmer?

NORA:   Yes, they were.

KROGSTAD:   Your father was quite ill, I believe.

NORA:   He was dying.

KROGSTAD:   And died shortly afterwards?

NORA:   That's right.

KROGSTAD:   Tell me, Mrs. Helmer; do you happen to remember the date of your father's death? I mean the exact day of the month?

NORA:   Daddy died on September 29.

KROGSTAD:   Quite correct. I have ascertained that fact. That's why there is something peculiar about this (*takes out a piece of paper*), which I can't account for.

NORA:   Peculiar? How? I don't understand—

KROGSTAD:   It seems very peculiar, Mrs. Helmer, that your father signed this promissory note three days after his death.

NORA:   How so? I don't see what—

KROGSTAD:   Your father died on September 29. Now look. He has dated his signature October 2. Isn't that odd?

*Nora remains silent.*

KROGSTAD:   Can you explain it?

*Nora is still silent.*

KROGSTAD:   I also find it striking that the date and the month and the year are not in your father's handwriting but in a hand I think I recognize. Well, that might be explained. Your father may have forgotten to date his signature and somebody else may have done it here, guessing at the date before he had learned of your father's death. That's all right. It's only the signature itself that matters. And that is genuine, isn't it, Mrs. Helmer? Your father did put his name to this note?

NORA (*after a brief silence tosses her head back and looks defiantly at him*): No, he didn't. *I* wrote Daddy's name.

KROGSTAD: Mrs. Helmer—do you realize what a dangerous admission you just made?

NORA: Why? You'll get your money soon.

KROGSTAD: Let me ask you something. Why didn't you mail this note to your father?

NORA: Because it was impossible. Daddy was sick—you know that. If I had asked him to sign it, I would have had to tell him what the money was for. But I couldn't tell him, as sick as he was, that my husband's life was in danger. That was impossible. Surely you can see that.

KROGSTAD: Then it would have been better for you if you had given up your trip abroad.

NORA: No, that was impossible! That trip was to save my husband's life. I couldn't give it up.

KROGSTAD: But didn't you realize that what you did amounted to fraud against me?

NORA: I couldn't let that make any difference. I didn't care about you at all. I hated the way you made all those difficulties for me, even though you knew the danger my husband was in. I thought you were cold and unfeeling.

KROGSTAD: Mrs. Helmer, obviously you have no clear idea of what you have done. Let me tell you that what I did that time was no more and no worse. And it ruined my name and reputation.

NORA: You! Are you trying to tell me that you did something brave once in order to save your wife's life?

KROGSTAD: The law doesn't ask about motives.

NORA: Then it's a bad law.

KROGSTAD: Bad or not—if I produce this note in court you'll be judged according to the law.

NORA: I refuse to believe you. A daughter shouldn't have the right to spare her dying old father worry and anxiety? A wife shouldn't have the right to save her husband's life? I don't know the laws very well, but I'm sure that somewhere they make allowance for cases like that. And you, a lawyer, don't know that? I think you must be a bad lawyer, Mr. Krogstad.

KROGSTAD: That may be. But business—the kind of business you and I have with one another—don't you think I know something about that? Very well. Do what you like. But let me tell you this: if I'm going to be kicked out again, you'll keep me company. (*He bows and exits through the front hall.*)

NORA (*pauses thoughtfully; then, with a defiant toss of her head*):   Oh, nonsense! Trying to scare me like that! I'm not all that silly. (*Starts picking up the children's clothes; soon stops.*) But—? No! That's impossible! I did it for love!

THE CHILDREN (*in the door to the left*):   Mama, the strange man just left. We saw him.

NORA:   Yes, yes; I know. But don't tell anybody about the strange man. Do you hear? Not even Daddy.

THE CHILDREN:   We won't. But now you'll play with us again, won't you, Mama?

NORA:   No, not right now.

THE CHILDREN:   But Mama—you promised.

NORA:   I know, but I can't just now. Go to your own room. I've so much to do. Be nice now, my little darlings. Do as I say. (*She nudges them gently into the other room and closes the door. She sits down on the couch, picks up a piece of embroidery, makes a few stitches, then stops.*) No! (*Throws the embroidery down, goes to the hall door and calls out.*) Helene! Bring the Christmas tree in here, please! (*Goes to the table, left, opens the drawer, halts.*) No—that's impossible!

THE MAID (*with the Christmas tree*):   Where do you want it, ma'am?

NORA:   There. The middle of the floor.

THE MAID:   You want anything else?

NORA:   No, thanks. I have everything I need. (*The Maid goes out. Nora starts trimming the tree.*) I want candles—and flowers— That awful man! Oh, nonsense! There's nothing wrong. This will be a lovely tree. I'll do everything you want me to, Torvald. I'll sing for you—dance for you—

*Helmer, a bundle of papers under his arm, enters from outside.*

NORA:   Ah—you're back already?

HELMER:   Yes. Has anybody been here?

NORA:   Here? No.

HELMER:   That's funny. I saw Krogstad leaving just now.

NORA:   Oh? Oh yes, that's right. Krogstad was here for just a moment.

HELMER:   I can tell from your face that he came to ask you to put in a word for him.

NORA:   Yes.

HELMER:   And it was supposed to be your own idea, wasn't it? You were not to tell me he'd been here. He asked you that too, didn't he?

NORA:   Yes, Torvald, but—

HELMER:   Nora, Nora, how could you! Talk to a man like that and make him promises! And lying to me about it afterwards—!

NORA:   Lying—?

HELMER:   Didn't you say nobody had been here? (*Shakes his finger at her.*) My little songbird must never do that again. Songbirds are supposed to have clean beaks to chirp with—no false notes. (*Puts his arm around her waist.*) Isn't that so? Of course it is. (*Lets her go.*) And that's enough about that. (*Sits down in front of the fireplace.*) Ah, it's nice and warm in here. (*Begins to leaf through his papers.*)

NORA (*busy with the tree; after a brief pause*):   Torvald.

HELMER:   Yes.

NORA:   I'm looking forward so much to the Stenborgs' costume party day after tomorrow.

HELMER:   And I can't wait to find out what you're going to surprise me with.

NORA:   Oh, that silly idea!

HELMER:   Oh?

NORA:   I can't think of anything. It all seems so foolish and pointless.

HELMER:   Ah, my little Nora admits that?

NORA (*behind his chair, her arms on the back of the chair*):   Are you very busy, Torvald?

HELMER:   Well—

NORA:   What are all those papers?

HELMER:   Bank business.

NORA:   Already?

HELMER:   I've asked the board to give me the authority to make certain changes in organization and personnel. That's what I'll be doing over the holidays. I want it all settled before New Year's.

NORA:   So that's why this poor Krogstad—

HELMER:   Hm.

NORA *(leisurely playing with the hair on his neck)*:   If you weren't so busy, Torvald, I'd ask you for a great big favor.

HELMER:   Let's hear it, anyway.

NORA:   I don't know anyone with better taste than you, and I want so much to look nice at the party. Couldn't you sort of take charge of me, Torvald, and decide what I'll wear—Help me with my costume?

HELMER:   Aha! Little Lady Obstinate is looking for someone to rescue her?

NORA:   Yes, Torvald. I won't get anywhere without your help.

HELMER:   All right. I'll think about it. We'll come up with something.

NORA:   Oh, you *are* nice! *(Goes back to the Christmas tree. A pause.)* Those red flowers look so pretty—Tell me, was it really all that bad what this Krogstad fellow did?

HELMER:   He forged signatures. Do you have any idea what that means?

NORA:   Couldn't it have been because he felt he had to?

HELMER:   Yes, or like so many others he may simply have been thoughtless. I'm not so heartless as to condemn a man absolutely because of a single imprudent act.

NORA:   Of course not, Torvald!

HELMER:   People like him can redeem themselves morally by openly confessing their crime and taking their punishment.

NORA:   Punishment?

HELMER:   But that was not the way Krogstad chose. He got out of it with tricks and evasions. That's what has corrupted him.

NORA:   So you think that if—?

HELMER:   Can't you imagine how a guilty person like that has to lie and fake and dissemble wherever he goes—putting on a mask before everybody he's close to, even his own wife and children. It's this thing with the children that's the worst part of it, Nora.

NORA:   Why is that?

HELMER:   Because when a man lives inside such a circle of stinking lies he brings infection into his own home and contaminates his whole family. With every breath of air his children inhale the germs of something ugly.

NORA *(moving closer behind him)*:   Are you sure of that?

HELMER:   Of course I am. I have seen enough examples of that in my work. Nearly all young criminals have had mothers who lied.

NORA:   Why mothers—particularly?

HELMER:   Most often mothers. But of course fathers tend to have the same influence. Every lawyer knows that. And yet, for years this Krogstad has been poisoning his own children in an atmosphere of lies and deceit. That's why I call him a lost soul morally. (*Reaches out for her hands.*) And that's why my sweet little Nora must promise me never to take his side again. Let's shake on that.—What? What's this? Give me your hand. There! Now that's settled. I assure you, I would find it impossible to work in the same room with that man. I feel literally sick when I'm around people like that.

NORA (*withdraws her hand and goes to the other side of the Christmas tree*):   It's so hot in here. And I have so much to do.

HELMER (*gets up and collects his papers*):   Yes, and I really should try to get some of this reading done before dinner. I must think about your costume too. And maybe just possibly I'll have something to wrap in gilt paper and hang on the Christmas tree. (*Puts his hands on her head.*) Oh my adorable little songbird! (*Enters his study and closes the door.*)

NORA (*after a pause, in a low voice*):   It's all a lot of nonsense. It's not that way at all. It's impossible. It has to be impossible.

THE NURSE (*in the door, left*):   The little ones are asking ever so nicely if they can't come in and be with their mamma.

NORA:   No, no, no! Don't let them in here! You stay with them, Anne-Marie.

THE NURSE:   If you say so, ma'am. (*Closes the door.*)

NORA (*pale with terror*):   Corrupt my little children—! Poison my home—? (*Brief pause; she lifts her head.*) That's not true. Never. Never in a million years.

# ACT II

*The same room. The Christmas tree is in the corner by the piano, stripped shabby-looking, with burnt-down candles. Nora's outside clothes are on the couch. Nora is alone. She walks around restlessly. She stops by the couch and picks up her coat.*

NORA (*drops the coat again*):   There's somebody now! (*Goes to the door, listens.*) No. Nobody. Of course not—not on Christmas. And not tomorrow either[1]—But perhaps—(*Opens the door and looks.*) No, nothing in the mailbox. All empty. (*Comes forward.*) How silly I am! Of course he isn't serious. Nothing like that could happen. After all, I have three small children.

*The Nurse enters from the room, left, carrying a big carton.*

THE NURSE:   Well, at last I found it—the box with your costume.
NORA:   Thanks. Just put it on the table.
NURSE (*does so*):   But it's all a big mess, I'm afraid.
NORA:   Oh, I wish I could tear the whole thing to little pieces!
NURSE:   Heavens! It's not as bad as all that. It can be fixed all right. All it takes is a little patience.
NORA:   I'll go over and get Mrs. Linde to help me.
NURSE:   Going out again? In this awful weather? You'll catch a cold.
NORA:   That might not be such a bad thing. How are the children?
NURSE:   The poor little dears are playing with their presents, but—
NORA:   Do they keep asking for me?
NURSE:   Well, you know, they're used to being with their mamma.
NORA:   I know. But Anne-Marie, from now on I can't be with them as much as before.
NURSE:   Oh well. Little children get used to everything.
NORA:   You think so? Do you think they'll forget their mamma if I were gone altogether?
NURSE:   Goodness me—gone altogether?
NORA:   Listen, Anne-Marie—something I've wondered about. How could you bring yourself to leave your child with strangers?
NURSE:   But I had to, if I were to nurse you.
NORA:   Yes, but how could you *want* to?
NURSE:   When I could get such a nice place? When something like that happens to a poor young girl, she'd better be grateful

---

[1] In Norway both December 25 and 26 are legal holidays. [Translator's note.]

for whatever she gets. For *he* didn't do a thing for me—the louse!

NORA:   But your daughter has forgotten all about you, hasn't she?

NURSE:   Oh no! Not at all! She wrote to me both when she was confirmed and when she got married.

NORA *(putting her arms around her neck)*:   You dear old thing—you were a good mother to me when I was little.

NURSE:   Poor little Nora had no one else, you know.

NORA:   And if my little ones didn't, I know you'd—oh, I'm being silly! *(Opens the carton.)* Go in to them, please. I really should— Tomorrow you'll see how pretty I'll be.

NURSE:   I know. There won't be anybody at that party half as pretty as you, ma'am. *(Goes out, left.)*

NORA *(begins to take clothes out of the carton; in a moment she throws it all down)*:   If only I dared to go out. If only I knew nobody would come. That nothing would happen while I was gone.— How silly! Nobody'll come. Just don't think about it. Brush the muff. Beautiful gloves. Beautiful gloves. Forget it. Forget it. One, two, three, four, five, six—*(Cries out.)* There they are! *(Moves toward the door, stops irresolutely.)*

*Mrs. Linde enters from the hall. She has already taken off her coat.*

NORA:   Oh, it's you, Kristine. There's no one else out there, is there? I'm so glad you're here.

MRS. LINDE:   They told me you'd asked for me.

NORA:   I just happened to walk by. I need your help with something—badly. Let's sit here on the couch. Look. Torvald and I are going to a costume party tomorrow night—at Consul Stenborg's upstairs—and Torvald wants me to go as a Neapolitan fisher girl and dance the tarantella. I learned it when we were on Capri.

MRS. LINDE:   Well, well! So you'll be putting on a whole show?

NORA:   Yes. Torvald thinks I should. Look, here's the costume. Torvald had it made for me while we were there. But it's all so torn and everything. I just don't know—

MRS. LINDE:   Oh, that can be fixed. It's not that much. The trimmings have come loose in a few places. Do you have needle and thread? Ah, here we are. All set.

NORA:   I really appreciate it, Kristine.

MRS. LINDE *(sewing)*:   So you'll be in disguise tomorrow night, eh? You know—I may come by for just a moment, just to look at you.—Oh dear. I haven't even thanked you for the nice evening last night.

NORA *(gets up, moves around)*:   Oh, I don't know. I don't think last night was as nice as it usually is.—You should have come to town a little earlier, Kristine.—Yes, Torvald knows how to make it nice and pretty around here.

MRS. LINDE:   You too, I should think. After all, you're your father's daughter. By the way, is Dr. Rank always as depressed as he was last night?

NORA:   No, last night was unusual. He's a very sick man, you know—very sick. Poor Rank, his spine is rotting away. Tuberculosis, I think. You see, his father was a nasty old man with mistresses and all that sort of thing. Rank has been sickly ever since he was a little boy.

MRS. LINDE *(dropping her sewing to her lap)*:   But dearest Nora, where have you learned about things like that?

NORA *(still walking about)*:   Oh, you know—with three children you sometimes get to talk with—other wives. Some of them know quite a bit about medicine. So you pick up a few things.

MRS. LINDE *(resumes her sewing; after a brief pause)*:   Does Dr. Rank come here every day?

NORA:   Every single day. He's Torvald's oldest and best friend, after all. And my friend too, for that matter. He's part of the family, almost.

MRS. LINDE:   But tell me, is he quite sincere? I mean, isn't he the kind of man who likes to say nice things to people?

NORA:   No, not at all. Rather the opposite, in fact. What makes you say that?

MRS. LINDE:   When you introduced us yesterday, he told me he'd often heard my name mentioned in this house. But later on it was quite obvious that your husband really had no idea who I was. So how could Dr. Rank—?

NORA:   You're right, Kristine, but I can explain that. You see, Torvald loves me so very much that he wants me all to himself. That's what he says. When we were first married he got almost jealous when I as much as mentioned anybody from back home that I was fond of. So of course I soon stopped doing that. But with Dr. Rank I often talk about home. You see, he likes to listen to me.

MRS. LINDE:   Look here, Nora. In many ways you're still a child. After all, I'm quite a bit older than you and have had more experience. I want to give you a piece of advice. I think you should get out of this thing with Dr. Rank.

NORA:   Get out of what thing?

MRS. LINDE:   Several things in fact, if you want my opinion. Yesterday you said something about a rich admirer who was going to give you money—

NORA:   One who doesn't exist, unfortunately. What of it?

MRS. LINDE:   Does Dr. Rank have money?

NORA:   Yes, he does.

MRS. LINDE:   And no dependents?

NORA:   No. But—?

MRS. LINDE:   And he comes here every day?

NORA:   Yes, I told you that already.

MRS. LINDE:   But how can that sensitive man be so tactless?

NORA:   I haven't the slightest idea what you're talking about.

MRS. LINDE:   Don't play games with me, Nora. Don't you think I know who you borrowed the twelve hundred dollars from?

NORA:   Are you out of your mind! The very idea—! A friend of both of us who sees us every day—! What a dreadfully— uncomfortable position that would be!

MRS. LINDE:   So it really isn't Dr. Rank?

NORA:   Most certainly not! I would never have dreamed of asking him—not for a moment. Anyway, he didn't have any money then. He inherited it afterwards.

MRS. LINDE:   Well, I still think it may have been lucky for you, Nora dear.

NORA:   The idea! It would never have occurred to me to ask Dr. Rank—Though I'm sure that if I *did* ask him—

MRS. LINDE:   But of course you wouldn't.

NORA:   Of course not. I can't imagine that that would ever be necessary. But I am quite sure that if I told Dr. Rank—

MRS. LINDE:   Behind your husband's back?

NORA:   I must get out of—this other thing. That's also behind his back. I must get out of it.

MRS. LINDE:   That's what I told you yesterday. But—

NORA (*walking up and down*):   A man manages these things so much better than a woman—

MRS. LINDE:   One's husband, yes.

NORA:   Silly, silly! (*Stops.*) When you've paid off all you owe, you get your I.O.U. back; right?

MRS. LINDE:   Yes, of course.

NORA:   And you can tear it into a hundred thousand little pieces and burn it—that dirty, filthy, paper!

MRS. LINDE (*looks hard at her, puts down her sewing, rises slowly*):   Nora—you're hiding something from me.

NORA:   Can you tell?

MRS. LINDE:   Something's happened to you, Nora, since yesterday morning. What is it?

NORA (*going to her*):   Kristine! (*Listens.*) Shhh. Torvald just came back. Listen. Why don't you go in to the children for a while. Torvald can't stand having sewing around. Get Anne-Marie to help you.

MRS. LINDE (*gathers some of the sewing things together*):   All right, but I'm not leaving here till you and I have talked.

*She goes out left, just as Helmer enters from the front hall.*

NORA (*towards him*):   I have been waiting and waiting for you, Torvald.

HELMER:   Was that the dressmaker?

NORA:   No, it was Kristine. She's helping me with my costume. Oh Torvald, just wait till you see how nice I'll look!

HELMER:   I told you. Pretty good idea I had, wasn't it?

NORA:   Lovely! And wasn't it nice of me to go along with it?

HELMER (*his hand under her chin*):   Nice? To do what your husband tells you? All right, you little rascal; I know you didn't mean it that way. But don't let me interrupt you. I suppose you want to try it on.

NORA:   And you'll be working?

HELMER:   Yes. (*Shows her a pile of papers.*) Look. I've been down to the bank. (*Is about to enter his study.*)

NORA:   Torvald.

HELMER (*halts*):   Yes?

NORA:   What if your little squirrel asked you ever so nicely—

HELMER:   For what?

NORA:  Would you do it?

HELMER:  Depends on what it is.

NORA:  Squirrel would run around and do all sorts of fun tricks if you'd be nice and agreeable.

HELMER:  All right. What is it?

NORA:  Lark would chirp and twitter in all the rooms, up and down—

HELMER:  So what? Lark does that anyway.

NORA:  I'll be your elfmaid and dance for you in the moonlight, Torvald.

HELMER:  Nora, don't tell me it's the same thing you mentioned this morning?

NORA *(closer to him)*:  Yes, Torvald. I beg you!

HELMER:  You really have the nerve to bring that up again?

NORA:  Yes. You've got to do as I say. You *must* let Krogstad keep his job.

HELMER:  My dear Nora. It's his job I intend to give to Mrs. Linde.

NORA:  I know. And that's ever so nice of you. But can't you just fire somebody else?

HELMER:  This is incredible! You just don't give up, do you? Because you make some foolish promise, *I* am supposed to—!

NORA:  That's not the reason, Torvald. It's for your own sake. That man writes for the worst newspapers. You've said so yourself. There's no telling what he may do to you. I'm scared to death of him.

HELMER:  Ah, I understand. You're afraid because of what happened before.

NORA:  What do you mean?

HELMER:  You're thinking of your father, of course.

NORA:  Yes. Yes, you're right. Remember the awful things they wrote about Daddy in the newspapers. I really think they might have forced him to resign if the ministry hadn't sent you to look into the charges and if you hadn't been so helpful and understanding.

HELMER:  My dear little Nora, there is a world of difference between your father and me. Your father's official conduct was not above reproach. Mine is, and I intend for it to remain that way as long as I hold my position.

NORA:  Oh, but you don't know what vicious people like that may think of. Oh, Torvald! Now all of us could be so happy together here in our own home, peaceful and carefree. Such a good life, Torvald, for you and me and the children! That's why I implore you—

HELMER:   And it's exactly because you plead for him that you make it impossible for me to keep him. It's already common knowledge in the bank that I intend to let Krogstad go. If it gets out that the new manager has changed his mind because of his wife—

NORA:   Yes? What then?

HELMER:   No, of course, that wouldn't matter at all as long as little Mrs. Pighead here got her way! Do you want me to make myself look ridiculous before my whole staff—make people think I can be swayed by just anybody—by outsiders? Believe me, I would soon enough find out what the consequences would be! Besides, there's another thing that makes it absolutely impossible for Krogstad to stay on in the bank now that I'm in charge.

NORA:   What's that?

HELMER:   I suppose in a pinch I could overlook his moral short-comings—

NORA:   Yes, you could; couldn't you, Torvald?

HELMER:   And I understand he's quite a good worker, too. But we've known each other for a long time. It's one of those imprudent relationships you get into when you're young that embarrass you for the rest of your life. I guess I might as well be frank with you: he and I are on a first name basis. And that tactless fellow never hides the fact even when other people are around. Rather, he seems to think it entitles him to be familiar with me. Every chance he gets he comes out with his damn "Torvald, Torvald." I'm telling you, I find it most awkward. He would make my position in the bank intolerable.

NORA:   You don't really mean any of this, Torvald.

HELMER:   Oh? I don't? And why not?

NORA:   No, for it's all so petty.

HELMER:   What! Petty? You think I'm being petty!

NORA:   No, I *don't* think you are petty, Torvald dear. That's exactly why I—

HELMER:   Never mind. You think my reasons are petty, so it follows that I must be petty too. Petty! Indeed! By God, I'll put an end to this right now! (*Opens the door to the front hall and calls out.*) Helene!

NORA:    What are you doing?

HELMER (*searching among his papers*):    Making a decision. (*The Maid enters.*) Here. Take this letter. Go out with it right away. Find somebody to deliver it. But quick. The address is on the envelope. Wait. Here's money.

THE MAID:    Very good, sir. (*She takes the letter and goes out.*)

HELMER (*collecting his papers*):    There now, little Mrs. Obstinate!

NORA (*breathless*):    Torvald—what was that letter?

HELMER:    Krogstad's dismissal.

NORA:    Call it back, Torvald! There's still time! Oh Torvald, please—call it back! For my sake, for your own sake, for the sake of the children! Listen to me, Torvald! Do it! You don't know what you're doing to all of us!

HELMER:    Too late.

NORA:    Yes. Too late.

HELMER:    Dear Nora, I forgive you this fear you're in, although it really is an insult to me. Yes, it is! It's an insult to think that I am scared of a shabby scrivener's revenge. But I forgive you, for it's such a beautiful proof how much you love me. (*Takes her in his arms.*) And that's the way it should be, my sweet darling. Whatever happens, you'll see that when things get really rough I have both strength and courage. You'll find out that I am man enough to shoulder the whole burden.

NORA (*terrified*):    What do you mean by that?

HELMER:    All of it, I tell you—

NORA (*composed*):    You'll never have to do that.

HELMER:    Good. Then we'll share the burden, Nora—like husband and wife, the way it ought to be. (*Caresses her.*) Now are you satisfied? There, there, there. Not that look in your eyes—like a frightened dove. It's all your own foolish imagination.— Why don't you practice the tarantella—and your tambourine, too. I'll be in the inner office and close both doors, so I won't hear you. You can make as much noise as you like. (*Turning in the doorway.*) And when Rank comes, tell him where to find me. (*He nods to her, enters his study carrying his papers, and closes the door.*)

NORA (*transfixed by terror, whispers*):    He would do it. He'll do it.

He'll do it in spite of the whole world.—No, this mustn't
happen. Anything rather than that! There must be a way—!
(*The doorbell rings.*) Dr. Rank! Anything rather than that! Anything—anything at all!

*She passes her hand over her face, pulls herself together, and opens
the door to the hall. Dr. Rank is out there, hanging up his coat.
Darkness begins to fall during the following scene.*

NORA: Hello there, Dr. Rank. I recognized your ringing. Don't
go in to Torvald yet. I think he's busy.

RANK: And you?

NORA (*as he enters and she closes the door behind him*): You know I
always have time for you.

RANK: Thanks. I'll make use of that as long as I can.

NORA: What do you mean by that—As long as you can?

RANK: Does that frighten you?

NORA: Well, it's a funny expression. As if something was going
to happen.

RANK: Something is going to happen that I've long been expecting. But I admit I hadn't thought it would come quite so soon.

NORA (*seizes his arm*): What is it you've found out? Dr. Rank—
tell me!

RANK (*sits down by the stove*): I'm going downhill fast. There's
nothing to do about that.

NORA (*with audible relief*): So it's *you*—

RANK: Who else? No point in lying to myself. I'm in worse shape
than any of my other patients, Mrs. Helmer. These last few
days I've been conducting an audit on my inner condition.
Bankrupt. Chances are that within a month I'll be rotting up
in the cemetery.

NORA: Shame on you! Talking that horrid way!

RANK: The thing itself is horrid—damn horrid. The worst of it,
though, is all that other horror that comes first. There is only
one more test I need to make. After that I'll have a pretty good
idea when I'll start coming apart. There is something I want
to say to you. Helmer's refined nature can't stand anything
hideous. I don't want him in my sick room.

NORA: Oh, but Dr. Rank—

RANK: I don't want him there. Under no circumstance. I'll close my door to him. As soon as I have full certainty that the worst is about to begin I'll give you my card with a black cross on it. Then you'll know the last horror of destruction has started.

NORA: Today you're really quite impossible. And I had hoped you'd be in a particularly good mood.

RANK: With death on my hands? Paying for someone else's sins? Is there justice in that? And yet there isn't a single family that isn't ruled by that same law of ruthless retribution, in one way or another.

NORA (*puts her hands over her ears*): Poppycock! Be fun! Be fun!

RANK: Well, yes. You may just as well laugh at the whole thing. My poor, innocent spine is suffering for my father's frolics as a young lieutenant.

NORA (*over by the table, left*): Right. He was addicted to asparagus and goose liver paté, wasn't he?

RANK: And truffles.

NORA: Of course. Truffles. And oysters too, I think.

RANK: And oysters. Obviously.

NORA: And all the port and champagne that go with it. It's really too bad that goodies like that ruin your backbone.

RANK: Particularly an unfortunate backbone that never enjoyed any of it.

NORA: Ah yes, that's the saddest part of it all.

RANK (*looks searchingly at her*): Hm—

NORA (*after a brief pause*): Why did you smile just then?

RANK: No, it was you that laughed.

NORA: No, it was you that smiled, Dr. Rank!

RANK (*gets up*): You're more of a mischief-maker than I thought.

NORA: I feel in the mood for mischief today.

RANK: So it seems.

NORA (*with both her hands on his shoulders*): Dear, dear Dr. Rank, don't you go and die and leave Torvald and me.

RANK: Oh, you won't miss me for very long. Those who go away are soon forgotten.

NORA (*with an anxious look*): Do you believe that?

RANK: You'll make new friends, and then—

NORA: Who'll make new friends?

RANK: Both you and Helmer, once I'm gone. You yourself seem to have made a good start already. What was this Mrs. Linde doing here last night?

NORA: Aha—Don't tell me you're jealous of poor Kristine?

RANK: Yes, I am. She'll be my successor in this house. As soon as I have made my excuses, that woman is likely to—

NORA: Shh—not so loud. She's in there.

RANK: Today too? There you are!

NORA: She's mending my costume. My God, you really *are* unreasonable. (*Sits down on the couch.*) Now be nice, Dr. Rank. Tomorrow you'll see how beautifully I'll dance, and then you are to pretend I'm dancing just for you—and for Torvald too, of course. (*Takes several items out of the carton.*) Sit down, Dr. Rank; I want to show you something.

RANK (*sitting down*): What?

NORA: Look.

RANK: Silk stockings.

NORA: Flesh-colored. Aren't they lovely? Now it's getting dark in here; but tomorrow—No, no. You only get to see the foot. Oh well, you might as well see all of it.

RANK: Hmm.

NORA: Why do you look so critical? Don't you think they'll fit?

RANK: That's something I can't possibly have a reasoned opinion about.

NORA (*looks at him for a moment*): Shame on you. (*Slaps his ear lightly with the stocking.*) That's what you get. (*Puts the things back in the carton.*)

RANK: And what other treasures are you going to show me?

NORA: Nothing at all, because you're naughty. (*She hums a little and rummages in the carton.*)

RANK (*after a brief silence*): When I sit here like this, talking confidently with you, I can't imagine—I can't possibly imagine what would have become of me if I hadn't had you and Helmer.

NORA (*smiles*): Well, yes—I do believe you like being with us.

RANK (*in a lower voice, lost in thought*): And then to have to go away from it all—

NORA: Nonsense. You are not going anywhere.

RANK (*as before*): —and not to leave behind as much as a poor little token of gratitude, hardly a brief memory of someone missed, nothing but a vacant place that anyone can fill.

NORA: And what if I were to ask you—? No—

RANK: Ask me what?

NORA: For a great proof of your friendship—

RANK: Yes, yes—?

NORA: No, I mean—for an enormous favor—

RANK: Would you really for once make me as happy as all that?

NORA: But you don't even know what it is.

RANK: Well, then; tell me.

NORA: Oh, but I can't, Dr. Rank. It's altogether too much to ask—It's advice and help and a favor—

RANK: So much the better. I can't even begin to guess what it is you have in mind. So for heaven's sake tell me! Don't you trust me?

NORA: Yes. I trust you more than anyone else I know. You are my best and most faithful friend. I know that. So I will tell you. All right, Dr. Rank. There is something you can help me prevent. You know how much Torvald loves me—beyond all words. Never for a moment would he hesitate to give his life for me.

RANK (*leaning over to her*): Nora—do you really think he's the only one—?

NORA (*with a slight start*): Who—?

RANK: —would gladly give his life for you.

NORA (*heavily*): I see.

RANK: I have sworn an oath to myself to tell you before I go. I'll never find a better occasion.—All right, Nora; now you know. And now you also know that you can confide in me more than in anyone else.

NORA (*gets up; in a calm, steady voice*): Let me get by.

RANK (*makes room for her but remains seated*): Nora—

NORA (*in the door to the front hall*): Helene, bring the lamp in here, please. (*Walks over to the stove.*) Oh, dear Dr. Rank. That really wasn't very nice of you.

RANK (*gets up*): That I have loved you as much as anybody—was that not nice?

NORA: No, not that. But that you told me. There was no need for that.

RANK: What do you mean? Have you known—?


*The Maid enters with the lamp, puts it on the table, and goes out.*


RANK: Nora—Mrs. Helmer—I'm asking you: did you know?

NORA: Oh, how can I tell what I knew and didn't know! I really can't say—But that you could be so awkward, Dr. Rank! Just when everything was so comfortable.

RANK: Well, anyway, now you know that I'm at your service with my life and soul. And now you must speak.

NORA (*looks at him*): After what just happened?

RANK: I beg of you—let me know what it is.

NORA: There is nothing I can tell you now.

RANK: Yes, yes. You mustn't punish me this way. Please let me do for you whatever anyone *can* do.

NORA: Now there is nothing you can do. Besides, I don't think I really need any help, anyway. It's probably just my imagination. Of course that's all it is. I'm sure of it! (*Sits down in the rocking chair, looks at him, smiles.*) Well, well, well, Dr. Rank! What a fine gentleman you turned out to be! Aren't you ashamed of yourself, now that we have light?

RANK: No, not really. But perhaps I ought to leave—and not come back?

NORA: Don't be silly; of course not! You'll come here exactly as you have been doing. You know perfectly well that Torvald can't do without you.

RANK: Yes, but what about you?

NORA: Oh, I always think it's perfectly delightful when you come.

RANK: That's the very thing that misled me. You are a riddle to me. It has often seemed to me that you'd just as soon be with me as with Helmer.

NORA: Well, you see, there are people you love, and then there are other people you'd almost rather be with.

RANK: Yes, there is something in that.

NORA: When I lived at home with Daddy, of course I loved him most. But I always thought it was so much fun to sneak off down to the maids' room, for they never gave me good advice and they always talked about such fun things.

RANK: Aha! So it's *their* place I have taken.

NORA (*jumps up and goes over to him*): Oh dear, kind Dr. Rank, you know very well I didn't mean it that way. Can't you see that with Torvald it is the way it used to be with Daddy?

*The Maid enters from the front hall.*

THE MAID: Ma'am! (*Whispers to her and gives her a caller's card.*)
NORA (*glances at the card*): Ah! (*Puts it in her pocket.*)

RANK: Anything wrong?

NORA: No, no; not at all. It's nothing—just my new costume—

RANK: But your costume is lying right there!

NORA: Oh yes, that one. But this is another one. I ordered it. Torvald mustn't know—

RANK: Aha. So that's the great secret.

NORA: That's it. Why don't you go in to him, please. He's in the inner office. And keep him there for a while—

RANK: Don't worry. He won't get away. (*Enters Helmer's study.*)

NORA (*to The Maid*): You say he's waiting in the kitchen?

THE MAID: Yes. He came up the back stairs.

NORA: But didn't you tell him there was somebody with me?

THE MAID: Yes, but he wouldn't listen.

NORA: He won't leave?

THE MAID: No, not till he's had a word with you, ma'am.

NORA: All right. But try not to make any noise. And, Helene— don't tell anyone he's here. It's supposed to be a surprise for my husband.

THE MAID: I understand, ma'am— (*She leaves.*)

NORA: The terrible is happening. It's happening, after all. No, no, no. It can't happen. It won't happen. (*She bolts the study door.*)

*The Maid opens the front hall door for Krogstad and closes the door behind him. He wears a fur coat for traveling, boots, and a fur hat.*

NORA (*toward him*): Keep your voice down. My husband's home.

KROGSTAD: That's all right.

NORA: What do you want?

KROGSTAD: To find out something.

NORA: Be quick, then. What is it?

KROGSTAD: I expect you know I've been fired.

NORA: I couldn't prevent it, Mr. Krogstad. I fought for you as long and as hard as I could, but it didn't do any good.

KROGSTAD: Your husband doesn't love you any more than that? He knows what I can do to you, and yet he runs the risk—

NORA: Surely you didn't think I'd tell him?

KROGSTAD: No, I really didn't. It wouldn't be like Torvald Helmer to show that kind of guts—

NORA: Mr. Krogstad, I insist that you show respect for my husband.

KROGSTAD: By all means. All due respect. But since you're so anxious to keep this a secret, may I assume that you are a little better informed than yesterday about exactly what you have done?

NORA:   Better than *you* could ever teach me.

KROGSTAD:   Of course. Such a bad lawyer as I am—

NORA:   What do you want of me?

KROGSTAD:   I just wanted to find out how you are, Mrs. Helmer. I've been thinking about you all day. You see, even a bill collector, a pen pusher, a—anyway, someone like me—even he has a little of what they call a heart.

NORA:   Then show it. Think of my little children.

KROGSTAD:   Have you and your husband thought of mine? Never mind. All I want to tell you is that you don't need to take this business too seriously. I have no intention of bringing charges right away.

NORA:   Oh no, you wouldn't; would you? I knew you wouldn't.

KROGSTAD:   The whole thing can be settled quite amiably. Nobody else needs to know anything. It will be between the three of us.

NORA:   My husband must never find out about this.

KROGSTAD:   How are you going to prevent that? Maybe you can pay me the balance on the loan?

NORA:   No, not right now.

KROGSTAD:   Or do you have a way of raising the money one of these next few days?

NORA:   None I intend to make use of.

KROGSTAD:   It wouldn't do you any good, anyway. Even if you had the cash in your hand right this minute, I wouldn't give you your note back. It wouldn't make any difference *how* much money you offered me.

NORA:   Then you'll have to tell me what you plan to use the note *for*.

KROGSTAD:   Just keep it; that's all. Have it on hand, so to speak. I won't say a word to anybody else. So if you've been thinking about doing something desperate—

NORA:   I have.

KROGSTAD:   —like leaving house and home—

NORA:   I have!

KROGSTAD:   —or even something worse—

NORA:   How did you know?

KROGSTAD:  —then: don't.

NORA:  How did you know I was thinking of *that*?

KROGSTAD:  Most of us do, right at first. I did, too, but when it came down to it I didn't have the courage—

NORA *(tonelessly)*:  Nor do I.

KROGSTAD *(relieved)*:  See what I mean? I thought so. You don't either.

NORA:  I don't. I don't.

KROGSTAD:  Besides, it would be very silly of you. Once that first domestic blow-up is behind you—. Here in my pocket is a letter for your husband.

NORA:  Telling him everything?

KROGSTAD:  As delicately as possible.

NORA *(quickly)*:  He mustn't get that letter. Tear it up. I'll get you the money somehow.

KROGSTAD:  Excuse me, Mrs. Helmer. I thought I just told you—

NORA:  I'm not talking about the money I owe you. Just let me know how much money you want from my husband, and I'll get it for you.

KROGSTAD:  I want no money from your husband.

NORA:  Then, what *do* you want?

KROGSTAD:  I'll tell you, Mrs. Helmer. I want to rehabilitate myself; I want to get up in the world; and your husband is going to help me. For a year and a half I haven't done anything disreputable. All that time I have been struggling with the most miserable circumstances. I was content to work my way up step by step. Now I've been kicked out, and I'm no longer satisfied just getting my old job back. I want more than that; I want to get to the top. I'm being quite serious. I want the bank to take me back but in a higher position. I want your husband to create a new job for me—

NORA:  He'll never do that!

KROGSTAD:  He will. I know him. He won't dare not to. And once I'm back inside and he and I are working together, you'll see! Within a year I'll be the manager's right hand. It will be Nils Krogstad and not Torvald Helmer who'll be running the Mutual Bank!

NORA:  You'll never see that happen!

KROGSTAD:  Are you thinking of—?

NORA:  Now I *do* have the courage.

KROGSTAD:   You can't scare me. A fine, spoiled lady like you—

NORA:   You'll see, you'll see!

KROGSTAD:   Under the ice, perhaps? Down into that cold, black water? Then spring comes, and you float up again—hideous, can't be identified, hair all gone—

NORA:   You don't frighten me.

KROGSTAD:   Nor you me. One doesn't do that sort of thing, Mrs. Helmer. Besides, what good would it do? He'd still be in my power.

NORA:   Afterwards? When I'm no longer—?

KROGSTAD:   Aren't you forgetting that your reputation would be in my hands?

*Nora stares at him, speechless.*

KROGSTAD:   All right; now I've told you what to expect. So don't do anything foolish. When Helmer gets my letter I expect to hear from him. And don't you forget that it's your husband himself who forces me to use such means again. That I'll never forgive him. Goodbye, Mrs. Helmer. (*Goes out through the hall.*)

NORA (*at the door, opens it a little, listens*):   He's going. And no letter. Of course not! That would be impossible! (*Opens the door more.*) What's he doing? He's still there. Doesn't go down. Having second thoughts—? Will he—?

*The sound of a letter dropping into the mailbox. Then Krogstad's steps are heard going down the stairs, gradually dying away.*

NORA (*with a muted cry runs forward to the table by the couch; brief pause*):   In the mailbox. (*Tiptoes back to the door to the front hall.*) There it is. Torvald, Torvald—now we're lost!

MRS. LINDE (*enters from the left, carrying Nora's Capri costume*):   There now. I think it's all fixed. Why don't we try it on you—

NORA (*in a low, hoarse voice*):   Kristine, come here.

MRS. LINDE:   What's wrong with you? You look quite beside yourself.

NORA:   Come over here. Do you see that letter? There, look— through the glass in the mailbox.

MRS. LINDE:   Yes, yes; I see it.

NORA:   That letter is from Krogstad.

MRS. LINDE:   Nora—it was Krogstad who lent you the money!

NORA:   Yes, and now Torvald will find out about it.

MRS. LINDE:   Oh believe me, Nora. That's the best thing for both of you.

NORA:   There's more to it than you know. I forged a signature—

MRS. LINDE:   Oh my God—!

NORA:   I just want to tell you this, Kristine, that you must be my witness.

MRS. LINDE:   Witness? How? Witness to what?

NORA:   If I lose my mind—and that could very well happen—

MRS. LINDE:   Nora!

NORA:   —or if something were to happen to me—something that made it impossible for me to be here—

MRS. LINDE:   Nora, Nora! You're not yourself!

NORA:   —and if someone were to take all the blame, assume the whole responsibility—Do you understand—?

MRS. LINDE:   Yes, yes; but how can you think—!

NORA:   —then you are to witness that that's not so, Kristine. I am not beside myself. I am perfectly rational, and what I'm telling you is that nobody else has known about this. I've done it all by myself, the whole thing. Just remember that.

MRS. LINDE:   I will. But I don't understand any of it.

NORA:   Oh, how could you! For it's the wonderful that's about to happen.

MRS. LINDE:   The wonderful?

NORA:   Yes, the wonderful. But it's so terrible, Kristine. It mustn't happen for anything in the whole world!

MRS. LINDE:   I'm going over to talk to Krogstad right now.

NORA:   No, don't. Don't go to him. He'll do something bad to you.

MRS. LINDE:   There was a time when he would have done anything for me.

NORA:   He!

MRS. LINDE:   Where does he live?

NORA:   Oh, I don't know—Yes, wait a minute— (*Reaches into her pocket.*) here's his card—But the letter, the letter—

HELMER (*in his study, knocks on the door*):   Nora!

NORA (*cries out in fear*):   Oh, what is it? What do you want?

HELMER:   That's all right. Nothing to be scared about. We're not coming in. For one thing, you've bolted the door, you know. Are you modeling your costume?

NORA:   Yes, yes; I am. I'm going to be so pretty, Torvald.

MRS. LINDE (*having looked at the card*):   He lives just around the corner.

NORA:   Yes, but it's no use. Nothing can save us now. The letter is in the mailbox.

MRS. LINDE:   And your husband has the key?

NORA:   Yes. He always keeps it with him.

MRS. LINDE:   Krogstad must ask for his letter back, unread. He's got to think up some pretext or other—

NORA:   But this is just the time of day when Torvald—

MRS. LINDE:   Delay him. Go in to him. I'll be back as soon as I can. (*She hurries out through the hall door.*)

NORA (*walks over to Helmer's door, opens it, and peeks in*):   Torvald!

HELMER (*still offstage*):   Well, well! So now one's allowed in one's own living room again. Come on, Rank. Now we'll see— (*In the doorway.*) But what's this?

NORA:   What, Torvald dear?

HELMER:   Rank prepared me for a splendid metamorphosis.

RANK (*in the doorway*):   That's how I understood it. Evidently I was mistaken.

NORA:   Nobody gets to admire me in my costume before tomorrow.

HELMER:   But, dearest Nora—you look all done in. Have you been practicing too hard?

NORA:   No, I haven't practiced at all.

HELMER:   But you'll have to, you know.

NORA:   I know it, Torvald. I simply must. But I can't do a thing unless you help me. I have forgotten everything.

HELMER:   Oh it will all come back. We'll work on it.

NORA:   Oh yes, please, Torvald. You just have to help me. Promise? I am so nervous. That big party—. You mustn't do anything else tonight. Not a bit of business. Don't even touch a pen. Will you promise, Torvald?

HELMER:   I promise. Tonight I'll be entirely at your service—you helpless little thing.—Just a moment, though. First I want to— (*Goes to the door to the front hall.*)

NORA:   What are you doing out there?

HELMER:   Just looking to see if there's any mail.

NORA:   No, no! Don't, Torvald!

HELMER:   Why not?
NORA:   Torvald, I beg you. There is no mail.
HELMER:   Let me just look, anyway. (*Is about to go out.*)

*Nora by the piano, plays the first bars of the tarantella dance.*

HELMER (*halts at the door*):   Aha!
NORA:   I won't be able to dance tomorrow if I don't get to practice
   with you.
HELMER (*goes to her*):   Are you really all that scared, Nora dear?
NORA:   Yes, so terribly scared. Let's try it right now. There's still
   time before we eat. Oh please, sit down and play for me,
   Torvald. Teach me, coach me, the way you always do.
HELMER:   Of course I will, my darling, if that's what you want.
   (*Sits down at the piano.*)

*Nora takes the tambourine out of the carton, as well as a long,
many-colored shawl. She quickly drapes the shawl around herself,
then leaps into the middle of the floor.*

NORA:   Play for me! I want to dance!

*Helmer plays and Nora dances. Dr. Rank stands by the piano be-
hind Helmer and watches.*

HELMER (*playing*):   Slow down, slow down!
NORA:   Can't!
HELMER:   Not so violent, Nora!
NORA:   It has to be this way.
HELMER (*stops playing*):   No, no. This won't do at all.
NORA (*laughing, swinging her tambourine*):   What did I tell you?
RANK:   Why don't you let me play?
HELMER (*getting up*):   Good idea. Then I can direct her better.

*Rank sits down at the piano and starts playing. Nora dances more
and more wildly. Helmer stands over by the stove, repeatedly cor-
recting her. She doesn't seem to hear. Her hair comes loose and falls
down over her shoulders. She doesn't notice but keeps on dancing.
Mrs. Linde enters.*

MRS. LINDE (*stops by the door, dumbfounded*):   Ah—!

NORA (*dancing*):   We're having such fun, Kristine!

HELMER:   My dearest Nora, you're dancing as if it were a matter of life and death!

NORA:   It is! It is!

HELMER:   Rank, stop. This is sheer madness. Stop it, I say!

*Rank stops playing; Nora suddenly stops dancing.*

HELMER (*goes over to her*):   If I hadn't seen it I wouldn't have believed it. You've forgotten every single thing I ever taught you.

NORA (*tosses away the tambourine*):   See? I told you.

HELMER:   Well! You certainly need coaching.

NORA:   Didn't I tell you I did? Now you've seen for yourself. I'll need your help till the very minute we're leaving for the party. Will you promise, Torvald?

HELMER:   You can count on it.

NORA:   You're not to think of anything except me—not tonight and not tomorrow. You're not to read any letters—not to look in the mailbox—

HELMER:   Ah, I see. You're still afraid of that man.

NORA:   Yes—yes, that too.

HELMER:   Nora, I can tell from looking at you. There's a letter from him out there.

NORA:   I don't know. I think so. But you're not to read it now. I don't want anything ugly to come between us before it's all over.

RANK (*to Helmer in a low voice*):   Better not argue with her.

HELMER (*throws his arm around her*):   The child shall have her way. But tomorrow night, when you've done your dance—

NORA:   Then you'll be free.

THE MAID (*in the door, right*):   Dinner can be served any time, ma'am.

NORA:   We want champagne. Helene.

THE MAID:   Very good, ma'am. (*Goes out.*)

HELMER:   Aha! Having a party, eh?

NORA:   Champagne from now till sunrise! (*Calls out.*) And some macaroons, Helene. Lots!—just this once.

HELMER (*taking her hands*):   There, there—I don't like this wild—

frenzy—Be my own sweet little lark again, the way you always are.

NORA:  Oh, I will. But you go on in. You too, Dr. Rank. Kristine, please help me put up my hair.

RANK *(in a low voice to Helmer as they go out)*:  You don't think she is—you know—expecting—?

HELMER:  Oh no. Nothing like that. It's just this childish fear I was telling you about. *(They go out, right.)*

NORA:  Well?

MRS. LINDE:  Left town.

NORA:  I saw it in your face.

MRS. LINDE:  He'll be back tomorrow night. I left him a note.

NORA:  You shouldn't have. I don't want you to try to stop anything. You see, it's a kind of ecstasy, too, this waiting for the wonderful.

MRS. LINDE:  But what is it you're waiting *for*?

NORA:  You wouldn't understand. Why don't you go in to the others. I'll be there in a minute.

*Mrs. Linde enters the dining room, right.*

NORA *(stands still for a little while, as if collecting herself; she looks at her watch)*:  Five o'clock. Seven hours till midnight. Twenty-four more hours till next midnight. Then the tarantella is over. Twenty-four plus seven—thirty-one more hours to live.

HELMER *(in the door, right)*:  What's happening to my little lark?

NORA *(to him, with open arms)*:  Here's your lark!

---

# ACT III

---

*The same room. The table by the couch and the chairs around it have been moved to the middle of the floor. A lighted lamp is on the table. The door to the front hall is open. Dance music is heard from upstairs.*

*Mrs. Linde is seated by the table, idly leafing through the pages of a book. She tries to read but seems unable to concentrate. Once or twice she turns her head in the direction of the door, anxiously listening.*

MRS. LINDE *(looks at her watch)*:   Not yet. It's almost too late. If only he hasn't—(*Listens again.*) Ah! There he is. (*She goes to the hall and opens the front door carefully. Quiet footsteps on the stairs. She whispers.*) Come in. There's nobody here.

KROGSTAD *(in the door)*:   I found your note when I got home. What's this all about?

MRS. LINDE:   I've got to talk to you.

KROGSTAD:   Oh? And it has to be here?

MRS. LINDE:   It couldn't be at my place. My room doesn't have a separate entrance. Come in. We're all alone. The maid is asleep and the Helmers are at a party upstairs.

KROGSTAD *(entering)*:   Really? The Helmers are dancing tonight, are they?

MRS. LINDE:   And why not?

KROGSTAD:   You're right. Why not, indeed.

MRS. LINDE:   All right, Krogstad. Let's talk, you and I.

KROGSTAD:   I didn't know we had anything to talk about.

MRS. LINDE:   We have much to talk about.

KROGSTAD:   I didn't think so.

MRS. LINDE:   No, because you've never really understood me.

KROGSTAD:   What was there to understand? What happened was perfectly commonplace. A heartless woman jilts a man when she gets a more attractive offer.

MRS. LINDE:   Do you think I'm all that heartless? And do you think it was easy for me to break with you?

KROGSTAD:   No?

MRS. LINDE:   You really thought it was?

KROGSTAD:   If it wasn't, why did you write the way you did that time?

MRS. LINDE:   What else could I do? If I had to make a break, I also had the duty to destroy whatever feelings you had for me.

KROGSTAD *(clenching his hands)*:   So that's the way it was. And you did—*that*—just for money!

MRS. LINDE:   Don't forget I had a helpless mother and two small brothers. We couldn't wait for you, Krogstad. You know yourself how uncertain your prospects were then.

KROGSTAD:   All right. But you still didn't have the right to throw me over for somebody else.

MRS. LINDE:   I don't know. I have asked myself that question many times. Did I have that right?

KROGSTAD *(in a lower voice)*:   When I lost you I lost my footing. Look at me now. A shipwrecked man on a raft.

MRS. LINDE:   Rescue may be near.

KROGSTAD:   It *was* near. Then you came between.

MRS. LINDE:   I didn't know that, Krogstad. Only today did I find out it's your job I'm taking over in the bank.

KROGSTAD:   I believe you when you say so. But now that you *do* know, aren't you going to step aside?

MRS. LINDE:   No, for it wouldn't do you any good.

KROGSTAD:   Whether it would or not—*I* would do it.

MRS. LINDE:   I have learned common sense. Life and hard necessity have taught me that.

KROGSTAD:   And life has taught me not to believe in pretty speeches.

MRS. LINDE:   Then life has taught you a very sensible thing. But you do believe in actions, don't you?

KROGSTAD:   How do you mean?

MRS. LINDE:   You referred to yourself just now as a shipwrecked man.

KROGSTAD:   It seems to me I had every reason to do so.

MRS. LINDE:   And I am a shipwrecked woman. No one to grieve for, no one to care for.

KROGSTAD:   You made your choice.

MRS. LINDE:   I had no other choice that time.

KROGSTAD:   Let's say you didn't. What then?

MRS. LINDE:   Krogstad, how would it be if we two shipwrecked people got together?

KROGSTAD:   What's this!

MRS. LINDE:   Two on one wreck are better off than each on his own.

KROGSTAD:   Kristine!

MRS. LINDE:   Why do you think I came to town?

KROGSTAD:   Surely not because of me?

MRS. LINDE:   If I'm going to live at all I must work. All my life, for as long as I can remember, I have worked. That's been my one and only pleasure. But now that I'm all alone in the world

I feel nothing but this terrible emptiness and desolation. There is no joy in working just for yourself. Krogstad—give me someone and something to work for.

KROGSTAD:    I don't believe this. Only hysterical females go in for that kind of high-minded self-sacrifice.

MRS. LINDE:    Did you ever know me to be hysterical?

KROGSTAD:    You really could do this? Listen—do you know about my past? All of it?

MRS. LINDE:    Yes, I do.

KROGSTAD:    Do you also know what people think of me around here?

MRS. LINDE:    A little while ago you sounded as if you thought that together with me you might have become a different person.

KROGSTAD:    I'm sure of it.

MRS. LINDE:    Couldn't that still be?

KROGSTAD:    Kristine—do you know what you are doing? Yes, I see you do. And you think you have the courage?

MRS. LINDE:    I need someone to be a mother to, and your children need a mother. You and I need one another. Nils, I believe in you—in the real you. Together with you I dare to do anything.

KROGSTAD (*seizes her hands*):    Thanks, thanks, Kristine—now I know I'll raise myself in the eyes of others.—Ah, but I forget—!

MRS. LINDE (*listening*):    Shh!—There's the tarantella. You must go; hurry!

KROGSTAD:    Why? What is it?

MRS. LINDE:    Do you hear what they're playing up there? When that dance is over they'll be down.

KROGSTAD:    All right. I'm leaving. The whole thing is pointless, anyway. Of course you don't know what I'm doing to the Helmers.

MRS. LINDE:    Yes, Krogstad; I do know.

KROGSTAD:    Still, you're brave enough—?

MRS. LINDE:    I very well understand to what extremes despair can drive a man like you.

KROGSTAD:    If only it could be undone!

MRS. LINDE:    It could, for your letter is still out there in the mailbox.

KROGSTAD:    Are you sure?

MRS. LINDE:    Quite sure. But—

KROGSTAD (*looks searchingly at her*):  Maybe I'm beginning to understand. You want to save your friend at any cost. Be honest with me. That's it, isn't it?

MRS. LINDE:  Krogstad, you may sell yourself once for somebody else's sake, but you don't do it twice.

KROGSTAD:  I'll demand my letter back.

MRS. LINDE:  No, no.

KROGSTAD:  Yes, of course. I'll wait here till Helmer comes down. Then I'll ask him for my letter. I'll tell him it's just about my dismissal—that he shouldn't read it.

MRS. LINDE:  No, Krogstad. You are not to ask for that letter back.

KROGSTAD:  But tell me—wasn't that the real reason you wanted to meet me here?

MRS. LINDE:  At first it was, because I was so frightened. But that was yesterday. Since then I have seen the most incredible things going on in this house. Helmer must learn the whole truth. This miserable secret must come out in the open; those two must come to a full understanding. They simply can't continue with all this concealment and evasion.

KROGSTAD:  All right; if you want to take that chance. But there is one thing I *can* do, and I'll do that right now.

MRS. LINDE (*listening*):  But hurry! Go! The dance is over. We aren't safe another minute.

KROGSTAD:  I'll be waiting for you downstairs.

MRS. LINDE:  Yes, do. You must see me home.

KROGSTAD:  I've never been so happy in my whole life. (*He leaves through the front door. The door between the living room and the front hall remains open.*)

MRS. LINDE (*straightens up the room a little and gets her things ready*):  What a change! Oh yes!—what a change! People to work for—to live for—a home to bring happiness to. I can't wait to get to work—! If only they'd come soon—(*Listens.*) Ah, there they are. Get my coat on—(*Puts on her coat and hat.*)

*Helmer's and Nora's voices are heard outside. A key is turned in the lock, and Helmer almost forces Nora into the hall. She is dressed in her Italian costume, with a big black shawl over her shoulders. He is in evening dress under an open black domino.*

NORA (*in the door, still resisting*):  No, no, no! I don't want to! I want to go back upstairs. I don't want to leave so early.

HELMER:   But dearest Nora—

NORA:   Oh please, Torvald—please! I'm asking you as nicely as I can—just another hour!

HELMER:   Not another minute, sweet. You know we agreed. There now. Get inside. You'll catch a cold out here. (*She still resists, but he guides her gently into the room.*)

MRS. LINDE:   Good evening.

NORA:   Kristine!

HELMER:   Ah, Mrs. Linde. Still here?

MRS. LINDE:   I know. I really should apologize, but I so much wanted to see Nora in her costume.

NORA:   You've been waiting up for me?

MRS. LINDE:   Yes, unfortunately I didn't get here in time. You were already upstairs, but I just didn't feel like leaving till I had seen you.

HELMER (*removing Nora's shawl*):   Yes, do take a good look at her, Mrs. Linde. I think I may say she's worth looking at. Isn't she lovely?

MRS. LINDE:   She certainly is—

HELMER:   Isn't she a miracle of loveliness, though? That was the general opinion at the party, too. But dreadfully obstinate—that she is, the sweet little thing. What can we do about that? Will you believe it—I practically had to use force to get her away.

NORA:   Oh Torvald, you're going to be sorry you didn't give me even half an hour more.

HELMER:   See what I mean, Mrs. Linde? She dances the tarantella—she is a tremendous success—quite deservedly so, though perhaps her performance was a little too natural—I mean, more than could be reconciled with the rules of art. But all right! The point is: she's a success, a tremendous success. So should I let her stay after that? Spoil the effect? Of course not. So I take my lovely little Capri girl—I might say, my capricious little Capri girl—under my arm—a quick turn around the room—a graceful bow in all directions, and—as they say in the novels—the beautiful apparition is gone. A finale should always be done for effect, Mrs. Linde, but there doesn't seem to be any way of getting that into Nora's head. Poooh—! It's hot in here. (*Throws his cloak down on a chair and opens the door to his room.*) Why, it's dark in here! Of course. Excuse me—(*Goes inside and lights a couple of candles.*)

NORA *(in a hurried, breathless whisper)*:    Well?

MRS. LINDE *(in a low voice)*:    I have talked to him.

NORA:    And—?

MRS. LINDE:    Nora—you've got to tell your husband everything.

NORA *(no expression in her voice)*:    I knew it.

MRS. LINDE:    You have nothing to fear from Krogstad. But you must speak.

NORA:    I'll say nothing.

MRS. LINDE:    Then the letter will.

NORA:    Thank you, Kristine. Now I know what I have to do. Shh!

HELMER *(returning)*:    Well, Mrs. Linde, have you looked your fill?

MRS. LINDE:    Yes. And now I'll say goodnight.

HELMER:    So soon? Is that your knitting?

MRS. LINDE *(takes it)*:    Yes, thank you. I almost forgot.

HELMER:    So you knit, do you?

MRS. LINDE:    Oh yes.

HELMER:    You know—you ought to take up embroidery instead.

MRS. LINDE:    Oh? Why?

HELMER:    Because it's so much more beautiful. Look. You hold the embroidery so—in your left hand. Then with your right you move the needle—like this—in an easy, elongated arc— you see?

MRS. LINDE:    Maybe you're right—

HELMER:    Knitting, on the other hand, can never be anything but ugly. Look here: arms pressed close to the sides—the needles going up and down—there's something Chinese about it somehow—. That really was an excellent champagne they served us tonight.

MRS. LINDE:    Well, goodnight, Nora. And don't be obstinate any more.

HELMER:    Well said, Mrs. Linde!

MRS. LINDE:    Goodnight, sir.

HELMER *(sees her to the front door)*:    Goodnight, goodnight. I hope you'll get home all right? I'd be very glad to—but of course you don't have far to walk, do you? Goodnight, goodnight. *(She leaves. He closes the door behind her and returns to the living room.)* There! At last we got rid of her. She really is an incredible bore, that woman.

NORA:    Aren't you very tired, Torvald?

HELMER:    No, not in the least.

NORA:    Not sleepy either?

HELMER:  Not at all. Quite the opposite. I feel enormously—animated. How about you? Yes, you do look tired and sleepy.

NORA:  Yes, I am very tired. Soon I'll be asleep.

HELMER:  What did I tell you? I was right, wasn't I? Good thing I didn't let you stay any longer.

NORA:  Everything you do is right.

HELMER *(kissing her forehead)*:  Now my little lark is talking like a human being. But did you notice what splendid spirits Rank was in tonight?

NORA:  Was he? I didn't notice. I didn't get to talk with him.

HELMER:  Nor did I—hardly. But I haven't seen him in such a good mood for a long time. *(Looks at her, comes closer to her.)* Ah! It does feel good to be back in our own home again, to be quite alone with you—my young, lovely, ravishing woman!

NORA:  Don't look at me like that, Torvald!

HELMER:  Am I not to look at my most precious possession? All that loveliness that is mine, nobody's but mine, all of it mine.

NORA *(walks to the other side of the table)*:  I won't have you talk to me like that tonight.

HELMER *(follows her)*:  The tarantella is still in your blood. I can tell. That only makes you all the more alluring. Listen! The guests are beginning to leave. *(Softly.)* Nora—soon the whole house will be quiet.

NORA:  Yes, I hope so.

HELMER:  Yes, don't you, my darling? Do you know—when I'm at a party with you, like tonight—do you know why I hardly ever talk to you, why I keep away from you, only look at you once in a while—a few stolen glances—do you know why I do that? It's because I pretend that you are my secret love, my young, secret bride-to-be, and nobody has the slightest suspicion that there is anything between us.

NORA:  Yes, I know. All your thoughts are with me.

HELMER:  Then when we're leaving and I lay your shawl around your delicate young shoulders—around that wonderful curve of your neck—then I imagine you're my young bride, that we're coming away from the wedding, that I am taking you to my home for the first time—that I am alone with you for the first time—quite alone with you, you young, trembling beauty! I have desired you all evening—there hasn't been a longing in me that hasn't been for you. When you were dancing the tarantella, chasing, inviting—my blood was on fire; I couldn't stand it any longer—that's why I brought you down so early—

NORA:  Leave me now, Torvald. Please! I don't want all this.

HELMER:  What do you mean? You're only playing your little teasing bird game with me; aren't you, Nora? Don't want to? I'm your husband, aren't I?

*There is a knock on the front door.*

NORA *(with a start)*:  Did you hear that—?

HELMER *(on his way to the hall)*:  Who is it?

RANK *(outside)*:  It's me. May I come in for a moment?

HELMER *(in a low voice, annoyed)*:  Oh, what does he want now? *(Aloud.)* Just a minute. *(Opens the door.)* Well! How good of you not to pass by our door.

RANK:  I thought I heard your voice, so I felt like saying hello. *(Looks around.)* Ah yes—this dear, familiar room. What a cozy, comfortable place you have here, you two.

HELMER:  Looked to me as if you were quite comfortable upstairs too.

RANK:  I certainly was. Why not? Why not enjoy all you can in this world? As much as you can for as long as you can, anyway. Excellent wine.

HELMER:  The champagne, particularly.

RANK:  You noticed that too? Incredible how much I managed to put away.

NORA:  Torvald drank a lot of champagne tonight, too.

RANK:  Did he?

NORA:  Yes, he did, and then he's always so much fun afterwards.

RANK:  Well, why not have some fun in the evening after a well spent day?

HELMER:  Well spent? I'm afraid I can't claim that.

RANK *(slapping him lightly on the shoulder)*:  But you see, I can!

NORA:  Dr. Rank, I believe you must have been conducting a scientific test today.

RANK:  Exactly.

HELMER:  What do you know—little Nora talking about scientific tests!

NORA:  May I congratulate you on the result?

RANK:  You may indeed.

NORA:   It was a good one?

RANK:   The best possible for both doctor and patient—certainty.

NORA *(a quick query)*:   Certainty?

RANK:   Absolute certainty. So why shouldn't I have myself an enjoyable evening afterwards?

NORA:   I quite agree with you, Dr. Rank. You should.

HELMER:   And so do I. If only you don't pay for it tomorrow.

RANK:   Oh well—you get nothing for nothing in this world.

NORA:   Dr. Rank—you are fond of costume parties, aren't you?

RANK:   Yes, particularly when there is a reasonable number of amusing disguises.

NORA:   Listen—what are the two of us going to be the next time?

HELMER:   You frivolous little thing! Already thinking about the next party!

RANK:   You and I? That's easy. You'll be Fortune's Child.

HELMER:   Yes, but what is a fitting costume for that?

RANK:   Let your wife appear just the way she always is.

HELMER:   Beautiful. Very good indeed. But how about yourself? Don't you know what you'll go as?

RANK:   Yes, my friend. I know precisely what I'll be.

HELMER:   Yes?

RANK:   At the next masquerade I'll be invisible.

HELMER:   That's a funny idea.

RANK:   There's a certain big, black hat—you've heard about the hat that makes you invisible, haven't you? You put that on, and nobody can see you.

HELMER *(suppressing a smile)*:   I guess that's right.

RANK:   But I'm forgetting what I came for. Helmer, give me a cigar—one of your dark Havanas.

HELMER:   With the greatest pleasure. *(Offers him his case.)*

RANK *(takes one and cuts off the tip)*:   Thanks.

NORA *(striking a match)*:   Let me give you a light.

RANK:   Thanks. *(She holds the match; he lights his cigar.)* And now goodbye!

HELMER:   Goodbye, goodbye, my friend.

NORA:   Sleep well, Dr. Rank.

RANK:   I thank you.

NORA:   Wish me the same.

RANK:   You? Well, if you really want me to—. Sleep well. And thanks for the light. *(He nods to both of them and goes out.)*

HELMER (*in a low voice*):   He had had quite a bit to drink.
NORA (*absently*):   Maybe so.

*Helmer takes out his keys and goes out into the hall.*

NORA:   Torvald—what are you doing out there?
HELMER:   Got to empty the mailbox. It is quite full. There
wouldn't be room for the newspapers in the morning—
NORA:   Are you going to work tonight?
HELMER:   You know very well I won't.—Say! What's this? Some-
body's been at the lock.
NORA:   The lock—?
HELMER:   Yes. Why, I wonder. I hate to think that any of the
maids—. Here's a broken hairpin. It's one of yours, Nora.
NORA (*quickly*):   Then it must be one of the children.
HELMER:   You better make damn sure they stop that. Hm, hm.—
There! I got it open, finally. (*Gathers up the mail, calls out to the
kitchen.*) Helene?—Oh Helene—turn out the light here in the
hall, will you? (*He comes back into the living room and closes the
door.*) Look how it's been piling up. (*Shows her the bundle of
letters. Starts leafing through it.*) What's this?
NORA (*by the window*):   The letter! Oh no, no, Torvald!
HELMER:   Two calling cards—from Rank.
NORA:   From Dr. Rank?
HELMER (*looking at them*):   "Doctor medicinae Rank." They were
on top. He must have put them there when he left just now.
NORA:   Anything written on them?
HELMER:   A black cross above the name. Look. What a macabre
idea. Like announcing his own death.
NORA:   That's what it is.
HELMER:   Hm? You know about this? Has he said anything to
you?
NORA:   That card means he has said goodbye to us. He'll lock
himself up to die.
HELMER:   My poor friend. I knew of course he wouldn't be with
me very long. But so soon—. And hiding himself away like a
wounded animal—
NORA:   When it has to be, it's better it happens without words.
Don't you think so, Torvald?
HELMER (*walking up and down*):   He'd grown so close to us. I find

it hard to think of him as gone. With his suffering and loneliness he was like a clouded background for our happy sunshine. Well, it may be better this way. For him, at any rate.
(*Stops.*) And perhaps for us, too, Nora. For now we have
nobody but each other. (*Embraces her.*) Oh you—my beloved
wife! I feel I just can't hold you close enough. Do you know,
Nora—many times I have wished some great danger threatened you, so I could risk my life and blood and everything—
everything, for your sake.

NORA (*frees herself and says in a strong and firm voice*):   I think you
should go and read your letters now, Torvald.

HELMER:   No, no—not tonight. I want to be with you, my darling.

NORA:   With the thought of your dying friend—?

HELMER:   You are right. This has shaken both of us. Something
not beautiful has come between us. Thoughts of death and
dissolution. We must try to get over it—out of it. Till then—
we'll each go to our own room.

NORA (*her arms around his neck*):   Torvald—goodnight! Goodnight!

HELMER (*kisses her forehead*):   Goodnight, my little songbird. Sleep
well, Nora. Now I'll read my letters. (*He goes into his room,
carrying the mail. Closes the door.*)

NORA (*her eyes desperate, her hands groping, finds Helmer's domino and
throws it around her; she whispers, quickly, brokenly,
hoarsely*):   Never see him again. Never. Never. Never. (*Puts
her shawl over her head.*) And never see the children again,
either. Never; never.—The black, icy water—fathomless—
this—! If only it was all over.—Now he has it. Now he's
reading it. No, no; not yet. Torvald—goodbye—you—the children—

*She is about to hurry through the hall, when Helmer flings open
the door to his room and stands there with an open letter in his
hand.*

HELMER:   Nora!

NORA (*cries out*):   Ah—!

HELMER:   What is it? You know what's in this letter?

NORA:   Yes, I do! Let me go! Let me out!

HELMER (*holds her back*):   Where do you think you're going?

NORA *(trying to tear herself loose from him)*:   I won't let you save me, Torvald!

HELMER *(tumbles back)*:   True! Is it true what he writes? Oh my God! No, no—this can't possibly be true.

NORA:   It is true. I have loved you more than anything else in the whole world.

HELMER:   Oh, don't give me any silly excuses.

NORA *(taking a step towards him)*:   Torvald—

HELMER:   You wretch! What have you done!

NORA:   Let me go. You are not to sacrifice yourself for me. You are not to take the blame.

HELMER:   No more playacting. *(Locks the door to the front hall.)* You'll stay here and answer me. Do you understand what you have done? Answer me! Do you understand?

NORA *(gazes steadily at him with an increasingly frozen expression)*:   Yes. Now I'm beginning to understand.

HELMER *(walking up and down)*:   What a dreadful awakening. All these years—all these eight years—she, my pride and my joy— a hypocrite, a liar—oh worse! worse!—a criminal! Oh, the bottomless ugliness in all this! Damn! Damn! Damn!

*Nora, silent, keeps gazing at him.*

HELMER *(stops in front of her)*:   I ought to have guessed that something like this would happen. I should have expected it. All your father's loose principles—Silence! You have inherited every one of your father's loose principles. No religion, no morals, no sense of duty—. Now I am being punished for my leniency with him. I did it for your sake, and this is how you pay me back.

NORA:   Yes. This is how.

HELMER:   You have ruined all my happiness. My whole future— that's what you have destroyed. Oh, it's terrible to think about. I am at the mercy of an unscrupulous man. He can do with me whatever he likes, demand anything of me, command me and dispose of me just as he pleases—I dare not say a word! To go down so miserably, to be destroyed—all because of an irresponsible woman!

NORA:   When I am gone from the world, you'll be free.

HELMER:   No noble gestures, please. Your father was always full of such phrases too. What good would it do me if you were gone from the world, as you put it? Not the slightest good at all. He could still make the whole thing public, and if he did I wouldn't be surprised if people thought I'd put you up to it. They might even think it was my idea—that it was I who urged you to do it! And for all this I have you to thank—you, whom I've borne on my hands through all the years of our marriage. *Now* do you understand what you've done to me?

NORA *(with cold calm)*:   Yes.

HELMER:   I just can't get it into my head that this is happening; it's all so incredible. But we have to come to terms with it somehow. Take your shawl off. Take it off, I say! I have to satisfy him one way or another. The whole affair must be kept quiet at whatever cost.—And as far as you and I are concerned, nothing must seem to have changed. I'm talking about appearances, of course. You'll go on living here; that goes without saying. But I won't let you bring up the children; I dare not trust you with them.—Oh! Having to say this to one I have loved so much, and whom I still—! But all that is past. It's not a question of happiness any more but of hanging on to what can be salvaged—pieces, appearances—*(The doorbell rings.)*

HELMER *(jumps)*:   What's that? So late. Is the worst—? Has he—! Hide, Nora! Say you're sick.

*Nora doesn't move. Helmer opens the door to the hall.*

THE MAID *(half dressed, out in the hall)*:   A letter for your wife, sir.

HELMER:   Give it to me. *(Takes the letter and closes the door.)* Yes, it's from him. But I won't let you have it. I'll read it myself.

NORA:   Yes—you read it.

HELMER *(by the lamp)*:   I hardly dare. Perhaps we're lost, both you and I. No; I've got to know. *(Tears the letter open, glances through it, looks at an enclosure; a cry of joy.)* Nora!

*Nora looks at him with a question in her eyes.*

HELMER:   Nora!—No, I must read it again.—Yes, yes; it is so! I'm saved! Nora, I'm saved!

NORA:   And I?

HELMER:  You too, of course; we're both saved, both you and I. Look! He's returning your note. He writes that he's sorry, he regrets, a happy turn in his life—oh, it doesn't matter what he writes. We're saved, Nora! Nobody can do anything to you now. Oh Nora, Nora—. No, I want to get rid of this disgusting thing first. Let me see—(*Looks at the signature.*) No, I don't want to see it. I don't want it to be more than a bad dream, the whole thing. (*Tears up the note and both letters, throws the pieces in the stove, and watches them burn.*) There! Now it's gone.—He wrote that ever since Christmas Eve—. Good God, Nora, these must have been three terrible days for you.

NORA:  I have fought a hard fight these last three days.

HELMER:  And been in agony and seen no other way out than—. No, we won't think of all that ugliness. We'll just rejoice and tell ourselves it's over, it's all over! Oh, listen to me, Nora. You don't seem to understand. It's over. What *is* it? Why do you look like that—that frozen expression on your face? Oh my poor little Nora, don't you think I know what it is? You can't make yourself believe that I have forgiven you. But I have, Nora; I swear to you, I have forgiven you for everything. Of course I know that what you did was for love of me.

NORA:  That is true.

HELMER:  You have loved me the way a wife ought to love her husband. You just didn't have the wisdom to judge the means. But do you think I love you any less because you don't know how to act on your own? Of course not. Just lean on me. I'll advise you; I'll guide you. I wouldn't be a man if I didn't find you twice as attractive because of your womanly helplessness. You mustn't pay any attention to the hard words I said to you right at first. It was just that first shock when I thought everything was collapsing all around me. I have forgiven you, Nora. I swear to you—I really have forgiven you.

NORA:  I thank you for your forgiveness. (*She goes out through the door, right.*)

HELMER:  No, stay—(*Looks into the room she entered.*) What are you doing in there?

NORA (*within*):  Getting out of my costume.

HELMER (*by the open door*):  Good, good. Try to calm down and compose yourself, my poor little frightened songbird. Rest safely; I have broad wings to cover you with. (*Walks around near the door.*) What a nice and cozy home we have, Nora. Here's shelter for you. Here I'll keep you safe like a hunted dove I have rescued from the hawk's talons. Believe me: I'll know how to quiet your beating heart. It will happen by and by, Nora; you'll see. Why, tomorrow you'll look at all this in quite a different light. And soon everything will be just the way it was before. I won't need to keep reassuring you that I have forgiven you; you'll feel it yourself. Did you really think I could have abandoned you, or even reproached you? Oh, you don't know a real man's heart, Nora. There is something unspeakably sweet and satisfactory for a man to know deep in himself that he has forgiven his wife—forgiven her in all the fullness of his honest heart. You see, that way she becomes his very own all over again—in a double sense, you might say. He has, so to speak, given her a second birth; it is as if she had become his wife and his child, both. From now on that's what you'll be to me, you lost and helpless creature. Don't worry about a thing, Nora. Only be frank with me, and I'll be your will and your conscience.—What's this? You're not in bed? You've changed your dress—!

NORA *(in an everyday dress)*:   Yes, Torvald. I have changed my dress.

HELMER:   But why—now—this late?

NORA:   I'm not going to sleep tonight.

HELMER:   But my dear Nora—

NORA *(looks at her watch)*:   It isn't all that late. Sit down here with me, Torvald. You and I have much to talk about. (*Sits down at the table.*)

HELMER:   Nora—what is this all about? That rigid face—

NORA:   Sit down. This will take a while. I have much to say to you.

HELMER *(sits down, facing her across the table)*:   You worry me, Nora. I don't understand you.

NORA:   No, that's just it. You don't understand me. And I have never understood you—not till tonight. No, don't interrupt me. Just listen to what I have to say.—This is a settling of accounts, Torvald.

HELMER:   What do you mean by that?

NORA *(after a brief silence)*:   Doesn't one thing strike you, now that we are sitting together like this?

HELMER:   What would that be?

NORA:   We have been married for eight years. Doesn't it occur to you that this is the first time that you and I, husband and wife, are having a serious talk?

HELMER:   Well—serious—. What do you mean by that?

NORA:   For eight whole years—longer, in fact—ever since we first met, we have never talked seriously to each other about a single serious thing.

HELMER:   You mean I should forever have been telling you about worries you couldn't have helped me with anyway?

NORA:   I am not talking about worries. I'm saying we have never tried seriously to get to the bottom of anything together.

HELMER:   But dearest Nora, I hardly think that would have been something *you*—

NORA:   That's the whole point. You have never understood me. Great wrong has been done to me, Torvald. First by Daddy and then by you.

HELMER:   What! By us two? We who have loved you more deeply than anyone else?

NORA *(shakes her head)*:   You never loved me—neither Daddy nor you. You only thought it was fun to be in love with me.

HELMER:   But, Nora—what an expression to use!

NORA:   That's the way it has been, Torvald. When I was home with Daddy, he told me all his opinions, and so they became my opinions too. If I disagreed with him I kept it to myself, for he wouldn't have liked that. He called me his little doll baby, and he played with me the way I played with my dolls. Then I came to your house—

HELMER:   What a way to talk about our marriage!

NORA *(imperturbably)*:   I mean that I passed from Daddy's hands into yours. You arranged everything according to your taste, and so I came to share it—or I pretended to; I'm not sure which. I think it was a little of both, now one and now the other. When I look back on it now, it seems to me I've been living here like a pauper—just a hand-to-mouth kind of existence. I have earned my keep by doing tricks for you, Torvald. But that's the way you wanted it. You have great sins against me to answer for, Daddy and you. It's your fault that nothing has become of me.

HELMER:   Nora, you're being both unreasonable and ungrateful. Haven't you been happy here?

NORA:   No, never. I thought I was, but I wasn't.

HELMER:   Not—not happy!

NORA:   No; just having fun. And you have always been very good to me. But our home has never been more than a playroom. I have been your doll wife here, just the way I used to be Daddy's doll child. And the children have been my dolls. I thought it was fun when you played with me, just as they thought it was fun when I played with them. That's been our marriage, Torvald.

HELMER:   There is something in what you are saying—exaggerated and hysterical though it is. But from now on things will be different. Playtime is over; it's time for growing up.

NORA:   Whose growing up—mine or the children's?

HELMER:   Both yours and the children's, Nora darling.

NORA:   Oh Torvald, you're not the man to bring me up to be the right kind of wife for you.

HELMER:   How can you say that?

NORA:   And I—? What qualifications do I have for bringing up the children?

HELMER:   Nora!

NORA:   You said so yourself a minute ago—that you didn't dare to trust me with them.

HELMER:   In the first flush of anger, yes. Surely, you're not going to count that.

NORA:   But you were quite right. I am *not* qualified. Something else has to come first. Somehow I have to grow up myself. And you are not the man to help me do that. That's a job I have to do by myself. And that's why I'm leaving you.

HELMER (*jumps up*):   What did you say!

NORA:   I have to be by myself if I am to find out about myself and about all the other things too. So I can't stay here with you any longer.

HELMER:   Nora, Nora!

NORA:   I'm leaving now. I'm sure Kristine will put me up for tonight.

HELMER:   You're out of your mind! I won't let you! I forbid you!

NORA:   You can't forbid me anything any more; it won't do any good. I'm taking my own things with me. I won't accept anything from you, either now or later.

HELMER:   But this is madness!

NORA:   Tomorrow I'm going home—I mean back to my old hometown. It will be easier for me to find some kind of job there.

HELMER:   Oh, you blind, inexperienced creature—!

NORA:   I must see to it that I get experience, Torvald.

HELMER:   Leaving your home, your husband, your children! Not a thought of what people will say!

NORA:   I can't worry about that. All I know is that I have to leave.

HELMER:   Oh, this is shocking! Betraying your most sacred duties like this!

NORA:   And what do you consider my most sacred duties?

HELMER:   Do I need to tell you that? They are your duties to your husband and your children.

NORA:   I have other duties equally sacred.

HELMER:   You do not. What duties would they be?

NORA:   My duties to myself.

HELMER:   You are a wife and a mother before you are anything else.

NORA:   I don't believe that any more. I believe I am first of all a human being, just as much as you—or at any rate that I must try to become one. Oh, I know very well that most people agree with you, Torvald, and that it says something like that in all the books. But what people say and what the books say is no longer enough for me. I have to think about these things myself and see if I can't find the answers.

HELMER:   You mean to tell me you don't know what your proper place in your own home is? Don't you have a reliable guide in such matters? Don't you have religion?

NORA:   Oh but Torvald—I don't really know what religion is.

HELMER:   What are you saying!

NORA:   All I know is what the Reverend Hansen told me when he prepared me for confirmation. He said that religion was *this* and it was *that.* When I get by myself, away from here, I'll have to look into that, too. I have to decide if what the Reverend Hansen said was right, or anyway if it is right for me.

HELMER:   Oh, this is unheard of in a young woman! If religion can't guide you, let me appeal to your conscience. For surely you have moral feelings? Or—answer me—maybe you don't?

NORA:   Well, you see, Torvald, I don't really know what to say. I just don't know. I am confused about these things. All I know is that my ideas are quite different from yours. I have just found out that the laws are different from what I thought they were, but in no way can I get it into my head that those laws are right. A woman shouldn't have the right to spare her dying old father or save her husband's life! I just can't believe that.

HELMER:   You speak like a child. You don't understand the society you live in.

NORA:   No, I don't. But I want to find out about it. I have to make up my mind who is right, society or I.

HELMER:   You are sick, Nora; you have a fever. I really don't think you are in your right mind.

NORA:   I have never felt so clearheaded and sure of myself as I do tonight.

HELMER:   And clearheaded and sure of yourself you're leaving your husband and children?

NORA:   Yes.

HELMER:   Then there is only one possible explanation.

NORA:   What?

HELMER:   You don't love me any more.

NORA:   No, that's just it.

HELMER:   Nora! Can you say that?

NORA:   I am sorry, Torvald, for you have always been so good to me. But I can't help it. I don't love you any more.

HELMER (*with forced composure*):   And this too is a clear and sure conviction?

NORA:   Completely clear and sure. That's why I don't want to stay here any more.

HELMER:   And are you ready to explain to me how I came to forfeit your love?

NORA:   Certainly I am. It was tonight, when the wonderful didn't happen. That was when I realized you were not the man I thought you were.

HELMER:   You have to explain. I don't understand.

NORA:   I have waited patiently for eight years, for I wasn't such a fool that I thought the wonderful is something that happens any old day. Then this—thing—came crashing in on me, and then there wasn't a doubt in my mind that now—now comes the wonderful. When Krogstad's letter was in that mailbox, never for a moment did it even occur to me that you would submit to his conditions. I was so absolutely certain that you would say to him: make the whole thing public—tell everybody. And when that had happened—

HELMER:  Yes, then what? When I had surrendered my own wife to shame and disgrace—!

NORA:  When that had happened, I was absolutely certain that you would stand up and take the blame and say, "I'm the guilty one."

HELMER:  Nora!

NORA:  You mean I never would have accepted such a sacrifice from you? Of course not. But what would my protests have counted against yours? *That* was the wonderful I was waiting for in hope and terror. And to prevent that I was going to kill myself.

HELMER:  I'd gladly work nights and days for you, Nora—endure sorrow and want for your sake. But nobody sacrifices his *honor* for his love.

NORA:  A hundred thousand women have done so.

HELMER:  Oh, you think and talk like a silly child.

NORA:  All right. But you don't think and talk like the man I can live with. When you had gotten over your fight—not because of what threatened *me* but because of the risk to *you*—and the whole danger was past, then you acted as if nothing at all had happened. Once again I was your little songbird, your doll, just as before, only now you had to handle her even more carefully, because she was so frail and weak. (*Rises.*) Torvald— that moment I realized that I had been living here for eight years with a stranger and had borne him three children—Oh, I can't stand thinking about it! I feel like tearing myself to pieces!

HELMER (*heavily*):  I see it, I see it. An abyss has opened up between us.—Oh but Nora—surely it can be filled?

NORA:  The way I am now I am no wife for you.

HELMER:  I have it in me to change.

NORA:  Perhaps—if your doll is taken from you.

HELMER:  To part—to part from you! No, no, Nora! I can't grasp that thought!

NORA (*goes out, right*):  All the more reason why it has to be. (*She returns with her outdoor clothes and a small bag, which she sets down on the chair by the table.*)

HELMER:  Nora, Nora! Not now! Wait till tomorrow.

NORA (*putting on her coat*):  I can't spend the night in a stranger's rooms.

HELMER: But couldn't we live here together like brother and sister—?

NORA *(tying on her hat)*: You know very well that wouldn't last long—. (*Wraps her shawl around her.*) Goodbye, Torvald. I don't want to see the children. I know I leave them in better hands than mine. The way I am now I can't be anything to them.

HELMER: But some day, Nora—some day?

NORA: How can I tell? I have no idea what's going to become of me.

HELMER: But you're still my wife, both as you are now and as you will be.

NORA: Listen, Torvald—when a wife leaves her husband's house, the way I am doing now, I have heard he has no more legal responsibilities for her. At any rate, I now release you from all responsibility. You are not to feel yourself obliged to me for anything, and I have no obligations to you. There has to be full freedom on both sides. Here is your ring back. Now give me mine.

HELMER: Even this?

NORA: Even this.

HELMER: Here it is.

NORA: There. So now it's over. I'm putting the keys here. The maids know everything about the house—better than I. To-morrow, after I'm gone, Kristine will come over and pack my things from home. I want them sent after me.

HELMER: Over! It's all over! Nora, will you never think of me?

NORA: I'm sure I'll often think of you and the children and this house.

HELMER: May I write to you, Nora?

NORA: No—never. I won't have that.

HELMER: But send you things—? You must let me.

NORA: Nothing, nothing.

HELMER: —help you, when you need help—

NORA: I told you, no; I won't have it. I'll accept nothing from strangers.

HELMER: Nora—can I never again be more to you than a stranger?

NORA *(picks up her bag)*: Oh Torvald—then the most wonderful of all would have to happen—

HELMER: Tell me what that would be—!

NORA:   For that to happen, both you and I would have to change
so that—Oh Torvald; I no longer believe in the wonderful.
HELMER:   But I *will* believe. Tell me! Change, so that—?
NORA:   So that our living together would become a true marriage.
Goodbye. (*She goes out through the hall.*)
HELMER (*sinks down on a chair near the door and covers his face
with his hands*):   Nora! Nora! (*Looks around him and gets up.*)
All empty. She's gone. (*With sudden hope.*) The most wonder-
ful—?!

*From downstairs comes the sound of a heavy door slamming shut.*

# ANTON CHEKHOV [1860–1904]

# A Marriage Proposal

## Characters

STEPAN STEPANOVITCH TSCHUBUKOV, *a country farmer*
NATALIA STEPANOVNA, *his daughter (aged 25)*
IVAN VASSILIYITCH LOMOV, *Tschubukov's neighbor*

*Scene:* Reception room in Tschubukov's country home, Russia.

*Time:* The present.

*Scene:* The reception room in Tschubukov's home. Tschubukov discovered as the curtain rises.

*(Enter Lomov, wearing a dress-suit.)*

TSCHUB *(going toward him and greeting him):* Who is this I see? My dear fellow! Ivan Vassiliyitch! I'm so glad to see you! *(Shakes hands.)* But this is a surprise! How are you?

LOMOV: Thank you! And how are you?

TSCHUB: Oh, so-so, my friend. Please sit down. It isn't right to forget one's neighbor. But tell me, why all this ceremony? Dress clothes, white gloves and all? Are you on your way to some engagement, my good fellow?

LOMOV: No, I have no engagement except with you, Stepan Stepanovitch.

TSCHUB: But why in evening clothes, my friend? This isn't New Years!

LOMOV: You see, it's simply this, that—*(Composing himself.)* I have come to you, Stepan Stepanovitch, to trouble you with a request. It is not the first time I have had the honor of turning to you for assistance, and you have always, that is—I beg your

---

An English version by Hilmar Baukhage and Barrett H. Clark.

pardon, I am a bit excited! I'll take a drink of water first, dear Stepan Stepanovitch. *(He drinks.)*

TSCHUB *(aside):*   He's come to borrow money! I won't give him any! *(To Lomov.)* What is it, then, dear Lomov?

LOMOV:   You see—dear—Stepanovitch, pardon me, Stepan—Stepan—dearvitch—I mean—I am terribly nervous, as you will be so good as to see—! What I mean to say—you are the only one who can help me, though I don't deserve it, and—and I have no right whatever to make this request of you.

TSCHUB:   Oh, don't beat about the bush, my dear fellow. Tell me!

LOMOV:   Immediately—in a moment. Here it is, then: I have come to ask for the hand of your daughter, Natalia Stepanovna.

TSCHUB *(joyfully):*   Angel! Ivan Vassiliyitch! Say that once again! I didn't quite hear it!

LOMOV:   I have the honor to beg—

TSCHUB *(interrupting):*   My dear, dear man! I am so happy that everything is so—everything! *(Embraces and kisses him.)* I have wanted this to happen for so long. It has been my dearest wish! *(He represses a tear.)* And I have always loved you, my dear fellow, as my own son! May God give you His blessings and His grace and—I always wanted it to happen. But why am I standing here like a blockhead? I am completely dumbfounded with pleasure, completely dumbfounded. My whole being—I'll call Natalia—

LOMOV:   Dear Stepan Stepanovitch, what do you think? May I hope for Natalia Stepanovna's acceptance?

TSCHUB:   Really! A fine boy like you—and you think she won't accept on the minute? Lovesick as a cat and all that—! *(He goes out, right.)*

LOMOV:   I'm cold. My whole body is trembling as though I was going to take my examination! But the chief thing is to settle matters! If a person meditates too much, or hesitates, or talks about it, waits for an ideal or for true love, he never gets it. Brrr! It's cold! Natalia is an excellent housekeeper, not at all bad-looking, well educated—what more could I ask? I'm so excited my ears are roaring! *(He drinks water.)* And not to marry, that won't do! In the first place, I'm thirty-five—a critical age, you might say. In the second place, I must live a well-regulated life. I have a weak heart, continual palpitation, and I am very sensitive and always getting excited. My lips begin to tremble and the pulse in my right temple throbs terribly. But the worst of all is sleep! I hardly lie down and begin to doze before something in my left side begins to pull and tug, and something begins to hammer in my left shoulder—and in my head, too! I jump up like a madman, walk about a little, lie down again, but the moment I fall asleep I have a terrible cramp in the side. And so it is all night long!

*(Enter Natalia Stepanovna.)*

NATALIA:   Ah! It's you. Papa said to go in: there was a dealer in there who'd come to buy something. Good afternoon, Ivan Vassiliyitch.

LOMOV:   Good day, my dear Natalia Stepanovna.

NATALIA:   You must pardon me for wearing my apron and this old dress: we are working to-day. Why haven't you come to see us oftener? You've not been here for so long! Sit down. *(They sit down.)* Won't you have something to eat?

LOMOV:   Thank you, I have just had lunch.

NATALIA:   Smoke, do, there are the matches. To-day it is beautiful and only yesterday it rained so hard that the workmen couldn't do a stroke of work. How many bricks have you cut? Think of it! I was so anxious that I had the whole field mowed, and now I'm sorry I did it, because I'm afraid the hay will rot. It would have been better if I had waited. But what on earth is this? You are in evening clothes! The latest cut! Are you on your way to a ball? And you seem to be looking better, too—really. Why are you dressed up so gorgeously?

LOMOV *(excited)*:   You see, my dear Natalia Stepanovna—it's simply this: I have decided to ask you to listen to me—of course it will be a surprise, and indeed you'll be angry, but I—*(Aside.)* How fearfully cold it is!

NATALIA:   What is it? *(A pause.)* Well?

LOMOV:   I'll try to be brief. My dear Natalia Stepanovna, as you know, for many years, since my childhood, I have had the honor to know your family. My poor aunt and her husband, from whom, as you know, I inherited the estate, always had the greatest respect for your father and your poor mother. The Lomovs and the Tschubukovs have been for decades on the friendliest, indeed the closest, terms with each other, and furthermore my property, as you know, adjoins your own. If you will be so good as to remember, my meadows touch your birch woods.

NATALIA:   Pardon the interruption. You said "my meadows"— but are they yours?

LOMOV:   Yes, they belong to me.

NATALIA:   What nonsense! The meadows belong to us—not to you!

LOMOV:   No, to me! Now, my dear Natalia Stepanovna!

NATALIA:   Well, that is certainly news to me. How do they belong to you?

LOMOV:   How? I am speaking of the meadows lying between your birch woods and my brick-earth.

NATALIA:   Yes, exactly. They belong to us.

LOMOV:   No, you are mistaken, my dear Natalia Stepanovna, they belong to me.

NATALIA:   Try to remember exactly, Ivan Vassiliyitch. Is it so long ago that you inherited them?

LOMOV:   Long ago! As far back as I can remember they have always belonged to us.

NATALIA:   But that isn't true! You'll pardon my saying so.

LOMOV:   It is all a matter of record, my dear Natalia Stepanovna. It is true that at one time the title to the meadows was disputed, but now everyone knows they belong to me. There is no room for discussion. Be so good as to listen: my aunt's grandmother put these meadows, free from all costs, into the hands of your father's grandfather's peasants for a certain time while they were making bricks for my grandmother. These people used the meadows free of cost for about forty years, living there as they would on their own property. Later, however, when—

NATALIA:   There's not a word of truth in that! My grandfather, and my great-grandfather, too, knew that their estate reached back to the swamp, so that the meadows belong to us. What further discussion can there be? I can't understand it. It is really most annoying.

LOMOV:   I'll show you the papers, Natalia Stepanovna.

NATALIA:   No, either you are joking, or trying to lead me into a discussion. That's not at all nice! We have owned this property for nearly three hundred years, and now all at once we hear that it doesn't belong to us. Ivan Vassiliyitch, you will pardon me, but I really can't believe my ears. So far as I am concerned, the meadows are worth very little. In all they don't contain more than five acres and they are worth only a few hundred roubles, say three hundred, but the injustice of the thing is what affects me. Say what you will, I can't bear injustice.

LOMOV:   Only listen until I have finished, please! The peasants of your respected father's grandfather, as I have already had the honor to tell you, baked bricks for my grandmother. My aunt's grandmother wished to do them a favor—

NATALIA:   Grandfather! Grandmother! Aunt! I know nothing about them. All I know is that the meadows belong to us, and that ends the matter.

LOMOV:   No, they belong to me!

NATALIA:   And if you keep on explaining it for two days, and put on five suits of evening clothes, the meadows are still ours, ours, ours! I don't want to take your property, but I refuse to give up what belongs to us!

LOMOV:   Natalia Stepanovna, I don't need the meadows, I am only concerned with the principle. If you are agreeable, I beg of you, accept them as a gift from me!

NATALIA:   But I can give them to you, because they belong to me! That is very peculiar, Ivan Vassiliyitch! Until now we have considered you as a good neighbor and a good friend; only last year we lent you our threshing machine so that we couldn't thresh until November, and now you treat us like thieves! You offer to give me my own land. Excuse me, but neighbors don't treat each other that way. In my opinion, it's a very low trick—to speak frankly—

LOMOV:   According to you I'm a usurper, then, am I? My dear lady, I have never appropriated other people's property, and I shall permit no one to accuse me of such a thing! (*He goes quickly to the bottle and drinks water.*) The meadows are mine!

NATALIA:   That's not the truth! They are mine!

LOMOV:   Mine!

NATALIA:   Eh? I'll prove it to you! This afternoon I'll send my reapers into the meadows.

LOMOV:   W—h—a—t?

NATALIA:   My reapers will be there to-day!

LOMOV:   And I'll chase them off!

NATALIA:  If you dare!

LOMOV:  The meadows are mine, you understand? Mine!

NATALIA:  Really, you needn't scream so! If you want to scream and snort and rage you may do it at home, but here please keep yourself within the limits of common decency.

LOMOV:  My dear lady, if it weren't that I were suffering from palpitation of the heart and hammering of the arteries in my temples, I would deal with you very differently! *(In a loud voice.)* The meadows belong to me!

NATALIA:  Us!

LOMOV:  Me! *(Enter Tschubukov, right.)*

TSCHUB:  What's going on here? What is he yelling about?

NATALIA:  Papa, please tell this gentleman to whom the meadows belong, to us or to him?

TSCHUB *(to Lomov):*  My dear fellow, the meadows are ours.

LOMOV:  But, merciful heavens, Stepan Stepanovitch, how do you make that out? You at least might be reasonable. My aunt's grandmother gave the use of the meadows free of cost to your grandfather's peasants; the peasants lived on the land for forty years and used it as their own, but later when—

TSCHUB:  Permit me, my dear friend. You forget that your grandmother's peasants never paid, because there had been a lawsuit over the meadows, and everyone knows that the meadows belong to us. You haven't looked at the map.

LOMOV:  I'll prove to you that they belong to me!

TSCHUB:  Don't try to prove it, my dear fellow.

LOMOV:  I will!

TSCHUB:  My good fellow, what are you shrieking about? You can't prove anything by yelling, you know. I don't ask for anything that belongs to you, nor do I intend to give up anything of my own. Why should I? If it has gone so far, my dear man, that you really intend to claim the meadows, I'd rather give them to the peasants than you, and I certainly shall!

LOMOV:  I can't believe it! By what right can you give away property that doesn't belong to you?

TSCHUB:  Really, you must allow me to decide what I am to do with my own land! I'm not accustomed, young man, to have people address me in that tone of voice. I, young man, am twice your age, and I beg you to address me respectfully.

LOMOV:   No! No! You think I'm a fool! You're making fun of me! You call my property yours and then expect me to stand quietly by and talk to you like a human being. That isn't the way a good neighbor behaves, Stepan Stepanovitch! You are no neighbor, you're no better than a landgrabber. That's what you are!

TSCHUB:   Wh—at? What did he say?

NATALIA:   Papa, send the reapers into the meadows this minute!

TSCHUB *(to Lomov):*   What was that you said, sir?

NATALIA:   The meadows belong to us and I won't give them up! I won't give them up! I won't give them up!

LOMOV:   We'll see about that! I'll prove in court that they belong to me.

TSCHUB:   In court! You may sue in court, sir, if you like! Oh, I know you, you are only waiting to find an excuse to go to law! You're an intriguer, that's what you are! Your whole family were always looking for quarrels. The whole lot!

LOMOV:   Kindly refrain from insulting my family. The entire race of Lomov has always been honorable! And never has one been brought to trial for embezzlement, as your dear uncle was!

TSCHUB:   And the whole Lomov family were insane!

NATALIA:   Every one of them!

TSCHUB:   Your grandmother was a dipsomaniac, and the younger aunt, Nastasia Michailovna, ran off with an architect.

LOMOV:   And your mother limped. *(He puts his hand over his heart.)* Oh, my side pains! My temples are bursting! Lord in Heaven! Water!

TSCHUB:   And your dear father was a gambler—and a glutton!

NATALIA:   And your aunt was a gossip like few others!

LOMOV:   And you are an intriguer. Oh, my heart! And it's an open secret that you cheated at the elections—my eyes are blurred! Where is my hat?

NATALIA:   Oh, how low! Liar! Disgusting thing!

LOMOV:   Where's the hat—? My heart! Where shall I go? Where is the door—? Oh—it seems—as though I were dying! I can't— my legs won't hold me—*(Goes to the door.)*

TSCHUB *(following him):*   May you never darken my door again!

NATALIA:   Bring your suit to court! We'll see! *(Lomov staggers out, center.)*

TSCHUB *(angrily):*   The devil!

NATALIA:  Such a good-for-nothing! And then they talk about being good neighbors!

TSCHUB:  Loafer! Scarecrow! Monster!

NATALIA:  A swindler like that takes over a piece of property that doesn't belong to him and then dares to argue about it!

TSCHUB:  And to think that this fool dares to make a proposal of marriage!

NATALIA:  What? A proposal of marriage?

TSCHUB:  Why, yes! He came here to make you a proposal of marriage!

NATALIA:  Why didn't you tell me that before?

TSCHUB:  That's why he had on his evening clothes! The poor fool!

NATALIA:  Proposal for me? Oh! *(Falls into an armchair and groans.)* Bring him back! Bring him back!

TSCHUB:  Bring whom back?

NATALIA:  Faster, faster, I'm sinking! Bring him back! *(She becomes hysterical.)*

TSCHUB:  What is it? What's wrong with you? *(His hands to his head.)* I'm cursed with bad luck! I'll shoot myself! I'll hang myself!

NATALIA:  I'm dying! Bring him back!

TSCHUB:  Bah! In a minute! Don't bawl! *(He rushes out, center.)*

NATALIA *(groaning):*  What have they done to me? Bring him back! Bring him back!

TSCHUB *(comes running in):*  He's coming at once! The devil take him! Ugh! Talk to him yourself, I can't.

NATALIA *(groaning):*  Bring him back!

TSCHUB:  He's coming, I tell you! "Oh, Lord! What a task it is to be the father of a grown daughter!" I'll cut my throat! I really will cut my throat! We've argued with the fellow, insulted him, and now we've thrown him out—and you did it all, you!

NATALIA:  No, you! You haven't any manners, you are brutal! If it weren't for you, he wouldn't have gone!

TSCHUB:  Oh, yes, I'm to blame! If I shoot or hang myself, re- member *you'll* be to blame. You forced me to it! You! *(Lomov appears in the doorway.)* There, talk to him yourself! *(He goes out.)*

LOMOV:  Terrible palpitation!—My leg is lamed! My side hurts me—

NATALIA:   Pardon us, we were angry, Ivan Vassiliyitch. I remember now—the meadows really belong to you.

LOMOV:   My heart is beating terribly! My meadows—my eyelids tremble—*(They sit down.)* We were wrong. It was only the principle of the thing—the property isn't worth much to me, but the principle is worth a great deal.

NATALIA:   Exactly, the principle! Let us talk about something else.

LOMOV:   Because I have proofs that my aunt's grandmother had, with the peasants of your good father—

NATALIA:   Enough, enough. *(Aside.)* I don't know how to begin. *(To Lomov.)* Are you going hunting soon?

LOMOV:   Yes, heath-cock shooting, respected Natalia Stepanovna. I expect to begin after the harvest. Oh, did you hear? My dog, Ugadi, you know him—limps!

NATALIA:   What a shame! How did that happen?

LOMOV:   I don't know. Perhaps it's a dislocation, or maybe he was bitten by some other dog. *(He sighs.)* The best dog I ever had—to say nothing of his price! I paid Mironov a hundred and twenty-five roubles for him.

NATALIA:   That was too much to pay, Ivan Vassiliyitch.

LOMOV:   In my opinion it was very cheap. A wonderful dog!

NATALIA:   Papa paid eighty-five roubles for his Otkatai, and Otkatai is much better than your Ugadi.

LOMOV:   Really? Otkatai is better than Ugadi? What an idea! *(He laughs).* Otkatai better than Ugadi!

NATALIA:   Of course he is better. It is true Otkatai is still young; he isn't full-grown yet, but in the pack or on the leash with two or three, there is no better than he, even—

LOMOV:   I really beg your pardon, Natalia Stepanovna, but you quite overlooked the fact that he has a short lower jaw, and a dog with a short lower jaw can't snap.

NATALIA:   Short lower jaw? That's the first time I ever heard that!

LOMOV:   I assure you, his lower jaw is shorter than the upper.

NATALIA:   Have you measured it?

LOMOV:   I have measured it. He is good at running, though.

NATALIA:   In the first place, our Otkatai is pure-bred, a full-blooded son of Sapragavas and Stameskis, and as for your mongrel, nobody could ever figure out his pedigree; he's old and ugly, and as skinny as an old hag.

LOMOV:   Old, certainly! I wouldn't take five of your Otkatais for him! Ugadi is a dog and Otkatai is—it is laughable to argue about it! Dogs like your Otkatai can be found by the dozens at any dog dealer's, a whole pound-full!

NATALIA: Ivan Vassiliyitch, you are very contrary to-day. First our meadows belong to you and then Ugadi is better than Otkatai. I don't like it when a person doesn't say what he really thinks. You know perfectly well that Otkatai is a hundred times better than your silly Ugadi. What makes you keep on saying he isn't?

LOMOV: I can see, Natalia Stepanovna, that you consider me either a blindman or a fool. But at least you may as well admit that Otkatai has a short lower jaw!

LOMOV: It isn't so!

LOMOV: Yes, a short lower jaw!

NATALIA (*loudly*): It's not so!

LOMOV: What makes you scream, my dear lady?

NATALIA: What makes you talk such nonsense? It's disgusting! It is high time that Ugadi was shot, and yet you compare him with Otkatai!

LOMOV: Pardon me, but I can't carry on this argument any longer. I have palpitation of the heart!

NATALIA: I have always noticed that the hunters who do the most talking know the least about hunting.

LOMOV: My dear lady, I beg of you to be still. My heart is bursting! (*He shouts.*) Be still!

NATALIA: I won't be still until you admit that Otkatai is better! (*Enter Tschubukov.*)

TSCHUB: Well, has it begun again?

NATALIA: Papa, say frankly, on your honor, which dog is better: Otkatai or Ugadi?

LOMOV: Stepan Stepanovitch, I beg of you, just answer this: has your dog a short lower jaw or not? Yes or no?

TSCHUB: And what if he has? Is it of such importance? There is no better dog in the whole country.

LOMOV: My Ugadi is better. Tell the truth, now!

TSCHUB: Don't get so excited, my dear fellow! Permit me. Your Ugadi certainly has his good points. He is from a good breed, has a good stride, strong haunches, and so forth. But the dog, if you really want to know it, has two faults; he is old and he has a short lower jaw.

LOMOV:   Pardon me, I have palpitation of the heart!—Let us keep to facts—just remember in Maruskin's meadows, my Ugadi kept ear to ear with the Count Rasvachai and your dog.

TSCHUB:   He was behind, because the Count struck him with his whip.

LOMOV:   Quite right. All the other dogs were on the fox's scent, but Otkatai found it necessary to bite a sheep.

TSCHUB:   That isn't so!—I am sensitive about that and beg you to stop this argument. He struck him because everybody looks on a strange dog of good blood with envy. Even you, sir, aren't free from the sin. No sooner do you find a dog better than Ugadi than you begin to—this, that—his, mine—and so forth! I remember distinctly.

LOMOV:   I remember something, too!

TSCHUB *(mimicking him):*   I remember something, too! What do you remember?

LOMOV:   Palpitation! My leg is lame—I can't—

NATALIA:   Palpitation! What kind of hunter are you? You ought to stay in the kitchen by the stove and wrestle with the potato peelings, and not go fox-hunting! Palpitation!

TSCHUB:   And what kind of hunter are you? A man with your diseases ought to stay at home and not jolt around in the saddle. If you were a hunter—! But you only ride round in order to find out about other people's dogs, and make trouble for everyone. I am sensitive! Let's drop the subject. Besides, you're no hunter.

LOMOV:   You only ride around to flatter the Count!—My heart! You intriguer! Swindler!

TSCHUB:   And what of it? *(Shouting.)* Be still!

LOMOV:   Intriguer!

TSCHUB:   Baby! Puppy! Walking drug-store!

LOMOV:   Old rat! Jesuit! Oh, I know you!

TSCHUB:   Be still! Or I'll shoot you—with my worst gun, like a partridge! Fool! Loafer!

LOMOV:   Everyone knows that—oh, my heart!—that your poor late wife beat you. My leg—my temples—Heavens—I'm dying—I—

TSCHUB:   And your housekeeper wears the trousers in your house!

LOMOV: Here—here—there—there—my heart has burst! My shoulder is torn apart. Where is my shoulder? I'm dying! *(He falls into a chair.)* The doctor! *(Faints.)*

TSCHUB: Baby! Half-baked clam! Fool!

NATALIA: Nice sort of hunter you are! You can't even sit on a horse. *(To Tschub.)* Papa, what's the matter with him? *(She screams.)* Ivan Vassiliyitch! He is dead!

LOMOV: I'm ill! I can't breathe! Air!

NATALIA: He is dead! *(She shakes Lomov in the chair.)* Ivan Vassiliyitch! What have we done! He is dead! *(She sinks into a chair.)* The doctor—doctor! *(She goes into hysterics.)*

TSCHUB: Ahh! What is it? What's the matter with you?

NATALIA *(groaning):* He's dead!—Dead!

TSCHUB: Who is dead? Who? *(Looking at Lomov.)* Yes, he is dead! Good God! Water! The doctor! *(Holding the glass to Lomov's lips.)* Drink! No, he won't drink! He's dead! What a terrible situation! Why didn't I shoot myself? Why have I never cut my throat? What am I waiting for now? Only give me a knife! Give me a pistol! *(Lomov moves.)* He's coming to! Drink some water—there!

LOMOV: Sparks! Mists! Where am I?

TSCHUB: Get married! Quick, and then go to the devil. She's willing! *(He joins the hands of Lomov and Natalia.)* She's agreed! Only leave me in peace!

LOMOV: Wh—What? *(Getting up.)* Whom?

TSCHUB: She's willing! Well? Kiss each other and—the devil take you both!

NATALIA *(groans):* He lives! Yes, yes, I'm willing!

TSCHUB: Kiss each other!

LOMOV: Eh? Whom? *(Natalia and Lomov kiss.)* Very nice—! Pardon me, but what is this for? Oh, yes, I understand! My heart—sparks—I am happy, Natalia Stepanovna. *(He kisses her hand.)* My leg is lame!

NATALIA: I'm happy, too!

TSCHUB: Ahh! A load off my shoulders! Ahh!

NATALIA: And now at least you'll admit that Ugadi is worse than Otkatai!

LOMOV: Better!

NATALIA: Worse!

TSCHUB: Now the domestic joys have begun.—Champagne!
LOMOV: Better!
NATALIA: Worse, worse, worse!
TSCHUB *(trying to drown them out):* Champagne, champagne!

*Curtain*

# JOHN MILLINGTON SYNGE [1871–1909]

# Riders to the Sea

## List of Characters

MAURYA, *an old woman*
BARTLEY, *her son*
CATHLEEN, *her daughter*
NORA, *a younger daughter*
Men and women

**S C E N E:** *An Island off the West of Ireland.*

*Cottage kitchen, with nets, oil-skins, spinning-wheel, some new boards standing by the wall, etc. Cathleen, a girl of about twenty, finishes kneading cake, and puts it down in the pot-oven by the fire; then wipes her hands, and begins to spin at the wheel. Nora, a young girl, puts her head in at the door.*

NORA *(in a low voice):* Where is she?
CATHLEEN: She's lying down, God help her, and may be sleeping, if she's able.

*Nora comes in softly, and takes a bundle from under her shawl.*

CATHLEEN *(spinning the wheel rapidly):* What is it you have?
NORA: The young priest is after bringing them. It's a shirt and a plain stocking were got off a drowned man in Donegal.

*Cathleen stops her wheel with a sudden movement, and leans out to listen.*

NORA: We're to find out if it's Michael's they are, some time herself will be down looking by the sea.
CATHLEEN: How would they be Michael's, Nora? How would he go the length of that way to the far north?

NORA: The young priest says he's known the like of it. "If it's Michael's they are," says he, "you can tell herself he's got a clean burial by the grace of God, and if they're not his, let no one say a word about them, for she'll be getting her death," says he, "with crying and lamenting."

*The door which Nora half-closed is blown open by a gust of wind.*

CATHLEEN *(looking out anxiously):* Did you ask him would he stop Bartley going this day with the horses to the Galway fair?

NORA: "I won't stop him," says he, "but let you not be afraid. Herself does be saying prayers half through the night, and the Almighty God won't leave her destitute," says he, "with no son living."

CATHLEEN: Is the sea bad by the white rocks, Nora?

NORA: Middling bad, God help us. There's a great roaring in the west, and it's worse it'll be getting when the tide's turned to the wind.

*She goes over to the table with the bundle.*

Shall I open it now?

CATHLEEN: Maybe she'd wake up on us, and come in before we'd done. *(Coming to the table.)* It's a long time we'll be, and the two of us crying.

NORA *(goes to the inner door and listens):* She's moving about on the bed. She'll be coming in a minute.

CATHLEEN: Give me the ladder, and I'll put them up in the turf-loft, the way she won't know of them at all, and maybe when the tide turns she'll be going down to see would he be floating from the east.

*They put the ladder against the gable of the chimney; Cathleen goes up a few steps and hides the bundle in the turf-loft. Maurya comes from the inner room.*

MAURYA *(looking up at Cathleen and speaking querulously):* Isn't it turf enough you have for this day and evening?

CATHLEEN:  There's a cake baking at the fire for a short space *(throwing down the turf)* and Bartley will want it when the tide turns if he goes to Connemara.

*Nora picks up the turf and puts it round the pot-oven.*

MAURYA *(sitting down on a stool at the fire):*  He won't go this day with the wind rising from the south and west. He won't go this day, for the young priest will stop him surely.

NORA:  He'll not stop him, mother, and I heard Eamon Simon and Stephen Pheety and Colum Shawn saying he would go.

MAURYA:  Where is he itself?

NORA:  He went down to see would there be another boat sailing in the week, and I'm thinking it won't be long till he's here now, for the tide's turning at the green head, and the hooker's[1] tacking from the east.

CATHLEEN:  I hear some one passing the big stones.

NORA *(looking out):*  He's coming now, and he in a hurry.

BARTLEY *(comes in and looks round the room. Speaking sadly and quietly):*  Where is the bit of new rope, Cathleen, was bought in Connemara?

CATHLEEN *(coming down):*  Give it to him, Nora; it's on a nail by the white boards. I hung it up this morning, for the pig with the black feet was eating it.

NORA *(giving him a rope):*  Is that it, Bartley?

MAURYA:  You'd do right to leave that rope, Bartley, hanging by the boards. *(Bartley takes the rope.)* It will be wanting in this place, I'm telling you, if Michael is washed up to-morrow morning, or the next morning, or any morning in the week, for it's a deep grave we'll make him by the grace of God.

BARTLEY *(beginning to work with the rope):*  I've no halter the way I can ride down on the mare, and I must go now quickly. This is the one boat going for two weeks or beyond it, and the fair will be a good fair for horses I heard them saying below.

MAURYA:  It's a hard thing they'll be saying below if the body is washed up and there's no man in it to make the coffin, and I

---

[1] Sailboat's.

after giving a big price for the finest white boards you'd find in Connemara.

*She looks round at the boards.*

BARTLEY:   How would it be washed up, and we after looking each day for nine days, and a strong wind blowing a while back from the west and south?

MAURYA:   If it wasn't found itself, the wind is raising the sea, and there was a star up against the moon, and it rising in the night. If it was a hundred horses, or a thousand horses you had itself, what is the price of a thousand horses against a son where there is one son only?

BARTLEY *(working at the halter, to Cathleen):*   Let you go down each day, and see the sheep aren't jumping in on the rye, and if the jobber comes you can sell the pig with the black feet if there is a good price going.

MAURYA:   How would the like of her get a good price for a pig?

BARTLEY *(to Cathleen):*   If the west wind holds with the last bit of the moon let you and Nora get up weed enough for another cock for the kelp.[2] It's hard set we'll be from this day with no one in it but one man to work.

MAURYA:   It's hard set we'll be surely the day you're drownd'd with the rest. What way will I live and the girls with me, and I an old woman looking for the grave?

*Bartley lays down the halter, takes off his old coat, and puts on a newer one of the same flannel.*

BARTLEY *(to Nora):*   Is she coming to the pier?

NORA *(looking out):*   She's passing the green head and letting fall her sails.

BARTLEY *(getting his purse and tobacco):*   I'll have half an hour to go down, and you'll see me coming again in two days, or in three days, or maybe in four days if the wind is bad.

MAURYA *(turning round to the fire, and putting her shawl over her*

---

[2] Seaweed (used for fertilizer).

*head):*   Isn't it a hard and cruel man won't hear a word from an old woman, and she holding him from the sea?

CATHLEEN:   It's the life of a young man to be going on the sea, and who would listen to an old woman with one thing and she saying it over?

BARTLEY *(taking the halter):*   I must go now quickly. I'll ride down on the red mare, and the gray pony'll run behind me. . . . The blessing of God on you.

*He goes out.*

MAURYA *(crying out as he is in the door):*   He's gone now, God spare us, and we'll not see him again. He's gone now, and when the black night is falling I'll have no son left me in the world.

CATHLEEN:   Why wouldn't you give him your blessing and he looking round in the door? Isn't it sorrow enough is on every one in this house without your sending him out with an unlucky word behind him, and a hard word in his ear?

*Maurya takes up the tongs and begins raking the fire aimlessly without looking round.*

NORA *(turning towards her):*   You're taking away the turf from the cake.

CATHLEEN *(crying out):*   The Son of God forgive us, Nora, we're after forgetting his bit of bread.

*She comes over to the fire.*

NORA:   And it's destroyed he'll be going till dark night, and he after eating nothing since the sun went up.

CATHLEEN *(turning the cake out of the oven):*   It's destroyed he'll be, surely. There's no sense left on any person in a house where an old woman will be talking for ever.

*Maurya sways herself on her stool.*

CATHLEEN *(cutting off some of the bread and rolling it in a cloth; to Maurya):*   Let you go down now to the spring well and give him this and he passing. You'll see him then and the dark word will be broken, and you can say "God speed you," the way he'll be easy in his mind.

MAURYA (*taking the bread*):   Will I be in it as soon as himself?

CATHLEEN:   If you go now quickly.

MAURYA (*standing up unsteadily*):   It's hard set I am to walk.

CATHLEEN (*looking at her anxiously*):   Give her the stick, Nora, or maybe she'll slip on the big stones.

NORA:   What stick?

CATHLEEN:   The stick Michael brought from Connemara.

MAURYA (*taking a stick Nora gives her*):   In the big world the old people do be leaving things after them for their sons and children, but in this place it is the young men do be leaving things behind for them that do be old.

*She goes out slowly. Nora goes over to the ladder.*

CATHLEEN:   Wait, Nora, maybe she'd turn back quickly. She's that sorry, God help her, you wouldn't know the thing she'd do.

NORA:   Is she gone around by the bush?

CATHLEEN (*looking out*):   She's gone now. Throw it down quickly, for the Lord knows when she'll be out of it again.

NORA (*getting the bundle from the loft*):   The young priest said he'd be passing to-morrow, and we might go down and speak to him below if it's Michael's they are surely.

CATHLEEN (*taking the bundle*):   Did he say what way they were found?

NORA (*coming down*):   "There were two men," says he, "and they rowing round with poteen[3] before the cocks crowed, and the oar of one of them caught the body, and they passing the black cliffs of the north."

CATHLEEN (*trying to open the bundle*):   Give me a knife, Nora, the strings perished with the salt water, and there's a black knot on it you wouldn't loosen in a week.

NORA (*giving her a knife*):   I've heard tell it was a long way to Donegal.

CATHLEEN (*cutting the string*):   It is surely. There was a man in here a while ago—the man sold us that knife—and he said if

---

[3] Illegal whiskey.

you set off walking from the rock beyond, it would be seven days you'd be in Donegal.

NORA:   And what time would a man take, and he floating?

*Cathleen opens the bundle and takes out a bit of a stocking. They look at them eagerly.*

CATHLEEN *(in a low voice):*   The Lord spare us, Nora! isn't it a queer hard thing to say if it's his they are surely?

NORA:   I'll get his shirt off the hook the way we can put the one flannel on the other. *(She looks through some clothes hanging in the corner.)* It's not with them, Cathleen, and where will it be?

CATHLEEN:   I'm thinking Bartley put it on him in the morning, for his own shirt was heavy with the salt in it. *(Pointing to the corner.)* There's a bit of a sleeve was of the same stuff. Give me that and it will do.

*Nora brings it to her and they compare the flannel.*

CATHLEEN:   It's the same stuff, Nora; but if it is itself aren't there great rolls of it in the shops of Galway, and isn't it many another man may have a shirt of it as well as Michael himself?

NORA *(who has taken up the stocking and counted the stitches, crying out):*   It's Michael, Cathleen, it's Michael; God spare his soul, and what will herself say when she hears this story, and Bartley on the sea?

CATHLEEN *(taking the stocking):*   It's a plain stocking.

NORA:   It's the second one of the third pair I knitted, and I put up three score stitches, and I dropped four of them.

CATHLEEN *(counts the stitches):*   It's that number is in it. *(Crying out.)* Ah, Nora, isn't it a bitter thing to think of him floating that way to the far north, and no one to keen[4] him but the black hags that do be flying on the sea?

NORA *(swinging herself round, and throwing out her arms on the clothes):*   And isn't it a pitiful thing when there is nothing left of a man who was a great rower and fisher, but a bit of an old shirt and a plain stocking!

---

[4] Lament.

CATHLEEN (*after an instant*):   Tell me is herself coming, Nora? I hear a little sound on the path.

NORA (*looking out*):   She is, Cathleen. She's coming up to the door.

CATHLEEN:   Put these things away before she'll come in. Maybe it's easier she'll be after giving her blessing to Bartley, and we won't let on we've heard anything the time he's on the sea.

NORA (*helping Cathleen to close the bundle*):   We'll put them here in the corner.

*They put them into a hole in the chimney corner. Cathleen goes back to the spinning-wheel.*

NORA:   Will she see it was crying I was?

CATHLEEN:   Keep your back to the door the way the light'll not be on you.

*Nora sits down at the chimney corner, with her back to the door. Maurya comes in very slowly, without looking at the girls, and goes over to her stool at the other side of the fire. The cloth with the bread is still in her hand. The girls look at each other, and Nora points to the bundle of bread.*

CATHLEEN (*after spinning for a moment*):   You didn't give him his bit of bread?

*Maurya begins to keen softly, without turning round.*

CATHLEEN:   Did you see him riding down?

*Maurya goes on keening.*

CATHLEEN (*a little impatiently*):   God forgive you; isn't it a better thing to raise your voice and tell what you seen, than to be making lamentation for a thing that's done? Did you see Bartley, I'm saying to you.

MAURYA (*with a weak voice*):   My heart's broken from this day.

CATHLEEN (*as before*):   Did you see Bartley?

MAURYA:   I seen the fearfulest thing.

CATHLEEN (*leaves her wheel and looks out*):   God forgive you; he's riding the mare now over the green head, and the gray pony behind him.

MAURYA (*starts, so that her shawl falls back from her head and shows her white tossed hair. With a frightened voice*):  The gray pony behind him.

CATHLEEN (*coming to the fire*):  What is it ails you, at all?

MAURYA (*speaking very slowly*):  I've seen the fearfulest thing any person has seen, since the day Bride Dara seen the dead man with the child in his arms.

CATHLEEN AND NORA:  Uah.

*They crouch down in front of the old woman at the fire.*

NORA:  Tell us what it is you seen.

MAURYA:  I went down to the spring well, and I stood there saying a prayer to myself. Then Bartley came along, and he riding on the red mare with the gray pony behind him. (*She puts up her hands, as if to hide something from her eyes.*) The Son of God spare us, Nora!

CATHLEEN:  What is it you seen?

MAURYA:  I seen Michael himself.

CATHLEEN (*speaking softly*):  You did not, mother; it wasn't Michael you seen, for his body is after being found in the far north, and he's got a clean burial by the grace of God.

MAURYA (*a little defiantly*):  I'm after seeing him this day, and he riding and galloping. Bartley came first on the red mare; and I tried to say "God speed you," but something choked the words in my throat. He went by quickly; and "the blessing of God on you," says he, and I could say nothing. I looked up then, and I crying, at the gray pony, and there was Michael upon it—with fine clothes on him, and new shoes on his feet.

CATHLEEN (*begins to keen*):  It's destroyed we are from this day. It's destroyed, surely.

NORA:  Didn't the young priest say the Almighty God wouldn't leave her destitute with no son living?

MAURYA (*in a low voice, but clearly*):  It's little the like of him knows of the sea. . . . Bartley will be lost now, and let you call in Eamon and make me a good coffin out of the white boards, for I won't live after them. I've had a husband, and a husband's father, and six sons in this house—six fine men, though it was a hard birth I had with every one of them and they coming to the world—and some of them were found and some of them were not found, but they're gone now the lot of them. . . . There were Stephen, and Shawn, were lost in the great wind, and found after in the Bay of Gregory of the Golden Mouth, and carried up the two of them on the one plank, and in by that door.

*She pauses for a moment, the girls start as if they heard something through the door that is half open behind them.*

NORA *(in a whisper):*   Did you hear that, Cathleen? Did you hear a noise in the north-east?

CATHLEEN *(in a whisper):*   There's some one after crying out by the seashore.

MAURYA *(continues without hearing anything):*   There was Sheamus and his father, and his own father again, were lost in a dark night, and not a stick or sign was seen of them when the sun went up. There was Patch after was drowned out of a curagh[5] that turned over. I was sitting here with Bartley, and he a baby, lying on my two knees, and I seen two women, and three women, and four women coming in, and they crossing themselves, and not saying a word. I looked out then, and there were men coming after them, and they holding a thing in the half of a red sail, and water dripping out of it—it was a dry day, Nora—and leaving a track to the door.

*She pauses again with her hand stretched out towards the door. It opens softly and old women begin to come in, crossing themselves on the threshold, and kneeling down in front of the stage with red petticoats over their heads.*

MAURYA *(half in a dream, to Cathleen):*   Is it Patch, or Michael, or what is it at all?

CATHLEEN:   Michael is after being found in the far north, and when he is found there how could he be here in this place?

MAURYA:   There does be a power of young men floating round in the sea, and what way would they know if it was Michael

---

[5] Unstable vessel of tarred canvas on a wood frame; canoe.

they had, or another man like him, for when a man is nine days in the sea, and the wind blowing, it's hard set his own mother would be to say what man was it.

CATHLEEN:   It's Michael, God spare him, for they're after sending us a bit of his clothes from the far north.

*She reaches out and hands Maurya the clothes that belonged to Michael. Maurya stands up slowly and takes them in her hand. Nora looks out.*

NORA:   They're carrying a thing among them and there's water dripping out of it and leaving a track by the big stones.

CATHLEEN *(in a whisper to the women who have come in):*   Is it Bartley it is?

ONE OF THE WOMEN:   It is surely, God rest his soul.

*Two younger women come in and pull out the table. Then men carry in the body of Bartley, laid on a plank, with a bit of sail over it, and lay it on the table.*

CATHLEEN *(to the women, as they are doing so):*   What way was he drowned?

ONE OF THE WOMEN:   The gray pony knocked him into the sea, and he was washed out where there is a great surf on the white rocks.

*Maurya has gone over and knelt down at the head of the table. The women are keening softly and swaying themselves with a slow movement. Cathleen and Nora kneel at the other end of the table. The men kneel near the door.*

MAURYA *(raising her head and speaking as if she did not see the people around her):*   They're all gone now, and there isn't anything more the sea can do to me. . . . I'll have no call now to be up crying and praying when the wind breaks from the south, and you can hear the surf is in the east, and the surf is in the west, making a great stir with the two noises, and they hitting one on the other. I'll have no call now to be going down and getting Holy Water in the dark nights after Samhain,[6] and I won't care what way the sea is when the other women will be keening. *(To Nora.)* Give me the Holy Water, Nora, there's a small cup still on the dresser.

*Nora gives it to her.*

MAURYA *(drops Michael's clothes across Bartley's feet, and sprinkles the Holy Water over him):* It isn't that I haven't prayed for you, Bartley, to the Almighty God. It isn't that I haven't said prayers in the dark night till you wouldn't know what I'ld be saying; but it's a great rest I'll have now, and it's time surely. It's a great rest I'll have now, and great sleeping in the long nights after Samhain, if it's only a bit of wet flour we do have to eat, and maybe a fish that would be stinking.

*She kneels down again, crossing herself, and saying prayers under her breath.*

CATHLEEN *(to an old man):* Maybe yourself and Eamon would make a coffin when the sun rises. We have fine white boards herself bought, God help her, thinking Michael would be found, and I have a new cake you can eat while you'll be working.

THE OLD MAN *(looking at the boards):* Are there nails with them?

CATHLEEN: There are not, Colum; we didn't think of the nails.

ANOTHER MAN: It's a great wonder she wouldn't think of the nails, and all the coffins she's seen made already.

CATHLEEN: It's getting old she is, and broken.

*Maurya stands up again very slowly and spreads out the pieces of Michael's clothes beside the body, sprinkling them with the last of the Holy Water.*

NORA *(in a whisper to Cathleen):* She's quiet now and easy; but the day Michael was drowned you could hear her crying out from this to the spring well. It's fonder she was of Michael, and would any one have thought that?

---

[6] All Saints' Day, November 1.

CATHLEEN (*slowly and clearly*):   An old woman will be soon tired with anything she will do, and isn't it nine days herself is after crying and keening, and making great sorrow in the house?

MAURYA (*puts the empty cup mouth downwards on the table, and lays her hands together on Bartley's feet*):   They're all together this time, and the end is come. May the Almighty God have mercy on Bartley's soul, and on Michael's soul, and on the souls of Sheamus and Patch, and Stephen and Shawn (*bending her head*); and may He have mercy on my soul, Nora, and on the soul of every one is left living in the world.

*She pauses, and the keen rises a little more loudly from the women, then sinks away.*

MAURYA (*continuing*):   Michael has a clean burial in the far north, by the grace of the Almighty God. Bartley will have a fine coffin out of the white boards, and a deep grave surely. What more can we want than that? No man at all can be living for ever, and we must be satisfied.

*She kneels down again and the curtain falls slowly.*

# SUSAN GLASPELL [1882–1948]

# Trifles

## SCENE

*The kitchen in the now abandoned farmhouse of John Wright, a gloomy kitchen, and left without having been put in order—unwashed pans under the sink, a loaf of bread outside the bread-box, a dish-towel on the table—other signs of incompleted work. At the rear the outer door opens and the Sheriff comes in followed by the County Attorney and Hale. The Sheriff and Hale are men in middle life, the county Attorney is a young man; all are much bundled up and go at once to the stove. They are followed by the two women— the Sheriff's wife first; she is a slight wiry woman, with a thin nervous face. Mrs. Hale is larger and would ordinarily be called more comfortable looking, but she is disturbed now and looks fearfully about as she enters. The women have come in slowly, and stand close together near the door.*

COUNTY ATTORNEY (*rubbing his hands*):   This feels good. Come up to the fire, ladies.

MRS. PETERS (*after taking a step forward*):   I'm not—cold.

SHERIFF (*unbuttoning his overcoat and stepping away from the stove as if to mark the beginning of official business*):   Now, Mr. Hale, before we move things about, you explain to Mr. Henderson just what you saw when you came here yesterday morning.

COUNTY ATTORNEY:   By the way, has anything been moved? Are things just as you left them yesterday?

SHERIFF (*looking about*):   It's just the same. When it dropped below zero last night I thought I'd better send Frank out this morning to make a fire for us—no use getting pneumonia with a big case on, but I told him not to touch anything except the stove— and you know Frank.

COUNTY ATTORNEY:   Somebody should have been left here yesterday.

SHERIFF:   Oh—yesterday. When I had to send Frank to Morris Center for that man who went crazy—I want you to know I had my hands full yesterday. I knew you could get back from Omaha by to-day and as long as I went over everything here myself—

COUNTY ATTORNEY: Well, Mr. Hale, tell just what happened when you came here yesterday morning.

HALE: Harry and I had started to town with a load of potatoes. We came along the road from my place and as I got here I said, "I'm going to see if I can't get John Wright to go in with me on a party telephone." I spoke to Wright about it once before and he put me off, saying folks talked too much anyway, and all he asked was peace and quiet—I guess you know about how much he talked himself; but I thought maybe if I went to the house and talked about it before his wife, though I said to Harry that I didn't know as what his wife wanted made much difference to John—

COUNTY ATTORNEY: Let's talk about that later, Mr. Hale. I do want to talk about that, but tell now just what happened when you got to the house.

HALE: I didn't hear or see anything; I knocked at the door, and still it was all quiet inside. I knew they must be up, it was past eight o'clock. So I knocked again, and I thought I heard somebody say "Come in." I wasn't sure, I'm not sure yet, but I opened the door—this door (*indicating the door by which the two women are still standing*) and there in that rocker—(*pointing to it*) sat Mrs. Wright.

(*They all look at the rocker.*)

COUNTY ATTORNEY: What—was she doing?

HALE: She was rockin' back and forth. She had her apron in her hand and was kind of—pleating it.

COUNTY ATTORNEY: And how did she—look?

HALE: Well, she looked queer.

COUNTY ATTORNEY: How do you mean—queer?

HALE: Well, as if she didn't know what she was going to do next. And kind of done up.

COUNTY ATTORNEY: How did she seem to feel about your coming?

HALE: Why, I don't think she minded—one way or other. She didn't pay much attention. I said, "How do, Mrs. Wright, it's cold, ain't it?" And she said "Is it?"—and went on kind of pleating at her apron. Well, I was surprised; she didn't ask me to come up to the stove, or to set down, but just sat there, not even looking at me, so I said, "I want to see John." And then she—laughed. I guess you would call it a laugh. I thought of Harry and the team outside, so I said a little sharp: "Can't I see John?" "No," she says, kind o' dull like. "Ain't he home?" says I. "Yes," says she, "he's home." "Then why can't I see him?" I asked her out of patience. "'Cause he's dead," says she. *"Dead?"* says I. She just nodded her head, not getting a bit excited, but rockin' back and forth. "Why—where is he?" says I, not knowing what to say. She just pointed upstairs— like that (*himself pointing to the room above*). I got up, with the idea of going up there. I walked from there to here—then I says, "Why, what did he die of?" "He died of a rope round his neck," says she, and just went on pleatin' at her apron. Well, I went out and called Harry. I thought I might—need help. We went upstairs and there he was lyin'—

COUNTY ATTORNEY:    I think I'd rather have you go into that up- stairs, where you can point it all out. Just go on now with the rest of the story.

HALE:    Well, my first thought was to get that rope off. It looked . . . (*Stops, his face twitches.*) . . . but Harry, he went up to him, and he said, "No, he's dead all right, and we'd better not touch anything." So we went back down stairs. She was still sitting that same way. "Has anybody been notified?" I asked. "No," says she, unconcerned. "Who did this, Mrs. Wright?" said Harry. He said it business-like—and she stopped pleatin' of her apron. "I don't know," she says. "You don't *know?*" says Harry. "No," says she. "Weren't you sleepin' in the bed with him?" says Harry. "Yes," says she, "but I was on the inside." "Somebody slipped a rope round his neck and stran- gled him and you didn't wake up?" says Harry. "I didn't wake up," she said after him. We must 'a looked as if we didn't see how that could be, for after a minute she said, "I sleep sound." Harry was going to ask her more questions, but I said maybe we ought to let her tell her story first to the coroner, or the sheriff, so Harry went fast as he could to Rivers' place, where there's a telephone.

COUNTY ATTORNEY: And what did Mrs. Wright do when she knew that you had gone for the coroner?

HALE: She moved from that chair to this over here . . . (*Pointing to a small chair in the corner.*) . . . and just sat there with her hands held together and looking down. I got a feeling that I ought to make some conversation, so I said I had come in to see if John wanted to put in a telephone, and at that she started to laugh, and then she stopped and looked at me—scared. (*The County Attorney, who has had his notebook out, makes a note.*) I dunno, maybe it wasn't scared. I wouldn't like to say it was. Soon Harry got back, and then Dr. Lloyd came, and you, Mr. Peters, and so I guess that's all I know that you don't.

COUNTY ATTORNEY (*looking around*): I guess we'll go upstairs first—and then out to the barn and around there. (*To the Sheriff.*) You're convinced that there was nothing important here—nothing that would point to any motive?

SHERIFF: Nothing here but kitchen things.

(*The County Attorney, after again looking around the kitchen, opens the door of a cupboard closet. He gets up on a chair and looks on a shelf. Pulls his hand away, sticky.*)

COUNTY ATTORNEY: Here's a nice mess.

(*The women draw nearer.*)

MRS. PETERS (*to the other woman*): Oh, her fruit; it did freeze. (*To the Lawyer.*) She worried about that when it turned so cold. She said the fire'd go out and her jars would break.

SHERIFF: Well, can you beat the women! Held for murder and worryin' about her preserves.

COUNTY ATTORNEY: I guess before we're through she may have something more serious than preserves to worry about.

HALE: Well, women are used to worrying over trifles.

(*The two women move a little closer together.*)

COUNTY ATTORNEY (*with the gallantry of a young politician*):   And yet, for all their worries, what would we do without the ladies? (*The women do not unbend. He goes to the sink, takes a dipperful of water from the pail and, pouring it into a basin, washes his hands. Starts to wipe them on the roller-towel, turns it for a cleaner place.*) Dirty towels! (*Kicks his foot against the pans under the sink.*) Not much of a housekeeper, would you say, ladies?

MRS. HALE (*stiffly*):   There's a great deal of work to be done on a farm.

COUNTY ATTORNEY:   To be sure. And yet . . . (*With a little bow to her.*) . . . I know there are some Dickson county farmhouses which do not have such roller towels.

(*He gives it a pull to expose its full length again.*)

MRS. HALE:   Those towels get dirty awful quick. Men's hands aren't always as clean as they might be.

COUNTY ATTORNEY:   Ah, loyal to your sex, I see. But you and Mrs. Wright were neighbors. I suppose you were friends, too.

MRS. HALE (*shaking her head*):   I've not seen much of her of late years. I've not been in this house—it's more than a year.

COUNTY ATTORNEY:   And why was that? You didn't like her?

MRS. HALE:   I like her all well enough. Farmers' wives have their hands full, Mr. Henderson. And then—

COUNTY ATTORNEY:   Yes—?

MRS. HALE (*looking about*):   It never seemed a very cheerful place.

COUNTY ATTORNEY:   No—it's not cheerful. I shouldn't say she had the homemaking instinct.

MRS. HALE:   Well, I don't know as Wright had, either.

COUNTY ATTORNEY:   You mean that they didn't get on very well?

MRS. HALE:   No, I don't mean anything. But I don't think a place'd be any cheerful for John Wright's being in it.

COUNTY ATTORNEY:   I'd like to talk more of that a little later. I want to get the lay of things upstairs now.

(*He goes to the left, where three steps lead to a stair door.*)

SHERIFF:   I suppose anything Mrs. Peters does'll be all right. She was to take in some clothes for her, you know, and a few little things. We left in such a hurry yesterday.

COUNTY ATTORNEY: Yes, but I would like to see what you take, Mrs. Peters, and keep an eye out for anything that might be of use to us.

MRS. PETERS: Yes, Mr. Henderson.

*(The women listen to the men's steps on the stairs, then look about the kitchen.)*

MRS. HALE: I'd hate to have men coming into my kitchen, snooping around and criticizing.

*(She arranges the pans under sink which the Lawyer had shoved out of place.)*

MRS. PETERS: Of course it's no more than their duty.

MRS. HALE: Duty's all right, but I guess that deputy sheriff that came out to make the fire might have got a little of this on. *(Gives the roller towel a pull.)* Wish I'd thought of that sooner. Seems mean to talk about her for not having things slicked up when she had to come away in such a hurry.

MRS. PETERS *(who has gone to a small table in the left rear corner of the room, and lifted one end of a towel that covers a pan):* She had bread set. *(Stands still.)*

MRS. HALE *(eyes fixed on a loaf of bread beside the bread-box, which is on a low shelf at the other side of the room. Moves slowly toward it.):* She was going to put this in there. *(Picks up loaf, then abruptly drops it. In a manner of returning to familiar things.)* It's a shame about her fruit. I wonder if it's all gone. *(Gets up on the chair and looks.)* I think there's some here that's all right, Mrs. Peters. Yes—here; *(Holding it toward the window.)* this is cherries, too. *(Looking again.)* I declare I believe that's the only one. *(Gets down, bottle in her hand. Goes to the sink and wipes it off on the outside.)* She'll feel awful bad after all her hard work in the hot weather. I remember the afternoon I put up my cherries last summer.

*(She puts the bottle on the big kitchen table, center of the room, front table. With a sigh, is about to sit down in the rocking-chair. Before she is seated realizes what chair it is: with a slow look at it, steps back. The chair which she has touched rocks back and forth.)*

MRS. PETERS:   Well, I must get those things from the front room closet. (*She goes to the door at the right, but after looking into the other room, steps back.*) You coming with me, Mrs. Hale? You could help me carry them.

(*They go in the other room: reappear, Mrs. Peters carrying a dress and skirt, Mrs. Hale following with a pair of shoes.*)

MRS. PETERS:   My, it's cold in there.

(*She puts the clothes on the big table, and hurries to the stove.*)

MRS. HALE (*examining the skirt*):   Wright was close. I think maybe that's why she kept so much to herself. She didn't even belong to the Ladies' Aid. I suppose she felt she couldn't do her part, and then you don't enjoy things when you feel shabby. She used to wear pretty clothes and be lively, when she was Minnie Foster, one of the town girls singing in the choir. But that— oh, that was thirty years ago. This all you was to take in?

MRS. PETERS:   She said she wanted an apron. Funny thing to want, for there isn't much to get you dirty in jail, goodness knows. But I suppose just to make her feel more natural. She said they was in the top drawer in this cupboard. Yes, here. And then her little shawl that always hung behind the door. (*Opens stair door and looks.*) Yes, here it is.

(*Quickly shuts door leading upstairs.*)

MRS. HALE (*abruptly moving toward her*):   Mrs. Peters?

MRS. PETERS:   Yes, Mrs. Hale?

MRS. HALE:   Do you think she did it?

MRS. PETERS (*in a frightened voice*):   Oh, I don't know.

MRS. HALE:   Well, I don't think she did. Asking for an apron and her little shawl. Worrying about her fruit.

MRS. PETERS (*starts to speak, glances up, where footsteps are heard in the room above. In a low voice*):   Mr. Peters says it looks bad for her. Mr. Henderson is awful sarcastic in a speech and he'll make fun of her sayin' she didn't wake up.

MRS. HALE:   Well, I guess John Wright didn't wake when they was slipping that rope under his neck.

MRS. PETERS:   No, it's strange. It must have been done awful crafty and still. They say it was such a—funny way to kill a man, rigging it all up like that.

MRS. HALE:   That's just what Mr. Hale said. There was a gun in the house. He says that's what he can't understand.

MRS. PETERS:   Mr. Henderson said coming out that what was needed for the case was a motive; something to show anger, or—sudden feeling.

MRS. HALE (*who is standing by the table*):   Well, I don't see any signs of anger around here. (*She puts her hand on the dish towel which lies on the table, stands looking down at table, one half of which is clean, the other half messy.*) It's wiped here. (*Makes a move as if to finish work, then turns and looks at loaf of bread outside the bread-box. Drops towel. In that voice of coming back to familiar things.*) Wonder how they are finding things upstairs? I hope she had it a little more red-up up there. You know, it seems kind of *sneaking.* Locking her up in town and then coming out here and trying to get her own house to turn against her!

MRS. PETERS:   But, Mrs. Hale, the law is the law.

MRS. HALE:   I s'pose 'tis. (*Unbuttoning her coat.*) Better loosen up your things, Mrs. Peters. You won't feel them when you go out.

(*Mrs. Peters takes off her fur tippet, goes to hang it on hook at back of room, stands looking at the under part of the small corner table.*)

MRS. PETERS:   She was piecing a quilt. (*She brings the large sewing basket and they look at the bright pieces.*)

MRS. HALE:   It's log cabin pattern. Pretty, isn't it? I wonder if she was goin' to quilt it or just knot it?

(*Footsteps have been heard coming down the stairs. The Sheriff enters, followed by Hale and the County Attorney.*)

SHERIFF:   They wonder if she was going to quilt it or just knot it.

(*The men laugh, the women look abashed.*)

COUNTY ATTORNEY *(rubbing his hands over the stove):*   Frank's fire didn't do much up there, did it? Well, let's go out to the barn and get that cleared up.

*(The men go outside.)*

MRS. HALE *(resentfully):*   I don't know as there's anything so strange, our takin' up our time with little things while we're waiting for them to get the evidence. *(She sits down at the big table smoothing out a block with decision.)* I don't see as it's anything to laugh about.

MRS. PETERS *(apologetically):*   Of course they've got awful important things on their minds.

*(Pulls up a chair and joins Mrs. Hale at the table.)*

MRS. HALE *(examining another block):*   Mrs. Peters, look at this one. Here, this is the one she was working on, and look at the sewing! All the rest of it has been so nice and even. And look at this! It's all over the place! Why, it looks as if she didn't know what she was about!

*(After she has said this they look at each other, then start to glance back at the door. After an instant Mrs. Hale has pulled at a knot and ripped the sewing.)*

MRS. PETERS:   Oh, what are you doing, Mrs. Hale?

MRS. HALE *(mildly):*   Just pulling out a stich or two that's not sewed very good. *(Threading a needle.)* Bad sewing always made me fidgety.

MRS. PETERS *(nervously):*   I don't think we ought to touch things.

MRS. HALE:   I'll just finish up this end. *(Suddenly stopping and leaning forward.)* Mrs. Peters?

MRS. PETERS:   Yes, Mrs. Hale?

MRS. HALE:   What do you suppose she was so nervous about?

MRS. PETERS:   Oh—I don't know. I don't know as she was nervous. I sometimes sew awful queer when I'm just tired. *(Mrs. Hale starts to say something, looks at Mrs. Peters, then goes on sewing.)* Well, I must get these things wrapped up. They may be through sooner than we think. *(Putting apron and other things *together.*) I wonder where I can find a piece of paper, and string.

Mrs. Hale:   In that cupboard, maybe.

Mrs. Peters (*looking in cupboard*):   Why, here's a bird-cage. (*Holds it up.*) Did she have a bird, Mrs. Hale?

Mrs. Hale:   Why, I don't know whether she did or not—I've not been here for so long. There was a man around last year selling canaries cheap, but I don't know as she took one; maybe she did. She used to sing real pretty herself.

Mrs. Peters (*glancing around*):   Seems funny to think of a bird here. But she must have had one, or why should she have a cage? I wonder what happened to it?

Mrs. Hale:   I s'pose maybe the cat got it.

Mrs. Peters:   No, she didn't have a cat. She's got that feeling some people have about cats—being afraid of them. My cat got in her room and she was real upset and asked me to take it out.

Mrs. Hale:   My sister Bessie was like that. Queer, ain't it?

Mrs. Peters (*examining the cage*):   Why, look at this door. It's broke. One hinge is pulled apart.

Mrs. Hale (*looking too*):   Looks as if some one must have been rough with it.

Mrs. Peters:   Why, yes.

(*She brings the cage forward and puts it on the table.*)

Mrs. Hale:   I wish if they're going to find any evidence they'd be about it. I don't like this place.

Mrs. Peters:   But I'm awful glad you came with me, Mrs. Hale. It would be lonesome for me sitting here alone.

Mrs. Hale:   It would, wouldn't it? (*Dropping her sewing.*) But I tell you what I do wish, Mrs. Peters. I wish I had come over some times when *she* was here. I—(*Looking around the room.*)—wish I had.

Mrs. Peters:   But of course you were awful busy, Mrs. Hale—your house and your children.

Mrs. Hale:   I could've come. I stayed away because it weren't cheerful—and that's why I ought to have come. I—I've never liked this place. Maybe because it's down in a hollow and you don't see the road. I dunno what it is, but it's a lonesome

place and always was. I wish I had come over to see Minnie
Foster sometimes. I can see now—

*(Shakes her head.)*

MRS. PETERS:   Well, you mustn't reproach yourself, Mrs. Hale.
  Somehow we just don't see how it is with other folks until—
  something comes up.

MRS. HALE:   Not having children makes less work—but it makes
  a quiet house, and Wright out to work all day, and no company
  when he did come in. Did you know John Wright, Mrs. Peters?

MRS. PETERS:   Not to know him; I've seen him in town. They say
  he was a good man.

MRS. HALE:   Yes—good; he didn't drink, and kept his word as
  well as most, I guess, and paid his debts. But he was a hard
  man, Mrs. Peters. Just to pass the time of day with him.
  *(Shivers.)* Like a raw wind that gets to the bone. *(Pauses, her
  eye falling on the cage.)* I should think she would 'a wanted a
  bird. But what do you suppose went with it?

MRS. PETERS:   I don't know, unless it got sick and died.

*(She reaches over and swings the broken door, swings it again, both
women watch it.)*

MRS. HALE:   You weren't raised round here, were you? *(Mrs.
  Peters shakes her head.)* You didn't know—her?

MRS. PETERS:   Not till they brought her yesterday.

MRS. HALE:   She—come to think of it, she was kind of like a bird
  herself—real sweet and pretty, but kind of timid and—fluttery.
  How—she—did—change. *(Silence; then as if struck by a happy
  thought and relieved to get back to every day things.)* Tell you what,
  Mrs. Peters, why don't you take the quilt in with you? It might
  take up her mind.

MRS. PETERS:   Why, I think that's a real nice idea, Mrs. Hale.
  There couldn't possibly be any objection to it, could there?
  Now, just what would I take? I wonder if her patches are in
  here—and her things.

*(They look in the sewing basket.)*

MRS. HALE:   Here's some red. I expect this has got sewing things in it. (*Brings out a fancy box.*) What a pretty box. Looks like something somebody would give you. Maybe her scissors are in here. (*Opens box. Suddenly puts her hand to her nose.*) Why— (*Mrs. Peters bends nearer, then turns her face away.*) There's something wrapped up in this piece of silk.

MRS. PETERS:   Why, this isn't her scissors.

MRS. HALE (*lifting the silk*):   Oh, Mrs. Peters—it's—

(*Mrs. Peters bends closer.*)

MRS. PETERS:   It's the bird.

MRS. HALE (*jumping up*):   But, Mrs. Peters—look at it. Its neck! Look at its neck! It's all—other side *to*.

MRS. PETERS:   Somebody—wrung—its neck.

(*Their eyes meet. A look of growing comprehension, of horror. Steps are heard outside. Mrs. Hale slips box under quilt pieces, and sinks into her chair. Enter Sheriff and County Attorney. Mrs. Peters rises.*)

COUNTY ATTORNEY (*as one turning from serious things to little pleasantries*):   Well, ladies, have you decided whether she was going to quilt it or knot it?

MRS. PETERS:   We think she was going to—knot it.

COUNTY ATTORNEY:   Well, that's interesting, I'm sure. (*Seeing the bird-cage.*) Has the bird flown?

MRS. HALE (*putting more quilt pieces over the box*):   We think the— cat got it.

COUNTY ATTORNEY (*preoccupied*):   Is there a cat?

(*Mrs. Hale glances in a quick covert way at Mrs. Peters.*)

MRS. PETERS:   Well, not now. They're superstitious, you know. They leave.

COUNTY ATTORNEY (*to Sheriff Peters, continuing an interrupted conversation*):   No sign at all of any one having come from the outside. Their own rope. Now let's go up again and go over it piece by piece. (*They start upstairs.*) It would have to have been some one who knew just the—

*(Mrs. Peters sits down. The two women sit there not looking at one another, but as if peering into something and at the same time holding back. When they talk now it is in the manner of feeling their way over strange ground, as if afraid of what they are saying, but as if they cannot help saying it.)*

MRS. HALE: She liked the bird. She was going to bury it in that pretty box.

MRS. PETERS *(in a whisper):* When I was a girl—my kitten—there was a boy took a hatchet, and before my eyes—and before I could get there—*(Covers her face an instant.)* If they hadn't held me back I would have—*(Catches herself, looks upstairs where steps are heard, falters weakly.)*—hurt him.

MRS. HALE *(with a slow look around her):* I wonder how it would seem never to have had any children around. *(Pause.)* No, Wright wouldn't like the bird—a thing that sang. She used to sing. He killed that, too.

MRS. PETERS *(moving uneasily):* We don't know who killed the bird.

MRS. HALE: I knew John Wright.

MRS. PETERS: It was an awful thing was done in this house that night, Mrs. Hale. Killing a man while he slept, slipping a rope around his neck that choked the life out of him.

MRS. HALE: His neck. Choked the life out of him.

*(Her hand goes out and rests on the bird-cage.)*

MRS. PETERS *(with rising voice):* We don't know who killed him. We don't *know.*

MRS. HALE *(her own feeling not interrupted):* If there'd been years and years of nothing, then a bird to sing to you, it would be awful—still, after the bird was still.

MRS. PETERS *(something within her speaking):* I know what stillness is. When we homesteaded in Dakota, and my first baby died—after he was two years old, and me with no other then—

MRS. HALE *(moving):* How soon do you suppose they'll be through, looking for the evidence?

MRS. PETERS: I know what stillness is. *(Pulling herself back.)* The law has got to punish crime, Mrs. Hale.

MRS. HALE *(not as if answering that):* I wish you'd seen Minnie

Foster when she wore a white dress with blue ribbons and stood up there in the choir and sang. (*A look around the room.*) Oh, I *wish* I'd come over here once in a while. That was a crime! That was a crime! Who's going to punish that?

MRS. PETERS (*looking upstairs*):   We mustn't—take on.

MRS. HALE:   I might have known she needed help! I know how things can be—for women. I tell you, it's queer, Mrs. Peters. We live close together and we live far apart. We all go through the same things—it's all just a different kind of the same thing. (*Brushes her eyes, noticing the bottle of fruit, reaches out for it.*) If I was you I wouldn't tell her her fruit was gone. Tell her it *ain't.* Tell her it's all right. Take this in to prove it to her. She— she may never know whether it was broke or not.

MRS. PETERS (*takes the bottle, looks about for something to wrap it in; takes petticoat from the clothes brought from the other room, very nervously begins winding this around the bottle. In a false voice*):   My, it's a good thing the men couldn't hear us. Wouldn't they just laugh. Getting all stirred up over a little thing like a—dead canary. As if that could have anything to do with—with—wouldn't they *laugh!*

(*The men are heard coming down stairs.*)

MRS. HALE (*under her breath*):   Maybe they would—maybe they wouldn't.

COUNTY ATTORNEY:   No, Peters, it's all perfectly clear except a reason for doing it. But you know juries when it comes to women. If there was some definite thing. Something to show—something to make a story about—a thing that would connect up with this strange way of doing it.

(*The women's eyes meet for an instant. Enter Hale from outer door.*)

HALE:   Well, I've got the team around. Pretty cold out there.

COUNTY ATTORNEY:   I'm going to stay here a while by myself. (*To the Sheriff.*) You can send Frank out for me, can't you? I want to go over everything. I'm not satisfied that we can't do better.

SHERIFF:   Do you want to see what Mrs. Peters is going to take in?

*(The Lawyer goes to the table, picks up the apron, laughs.)*

COUNTY ATTORNEY:   Oh, I guess they're not very dangerous things the ladies have picked out. *(Moves a few things about, disturbing the quilt pieces which cover the box. Steps back.)* No, Mrs. Peters doesn't need supervising. For that matter, a sheriff's wife is married to the law. Ever think of it that way, Mrs. Peters?

MRS. PETERS:   Not—just that way.

SHERIFF *(chuckling)*:   Married to the law. *(Moves toward the other room.)* I just want you to come in here a minute, George. We ought to take a look at these windows.

COUNTY ATTORNEY *(scoffingly)*:   Oh, windows!

SHERIFF:   We'll be right out, Mr. Hale.

*(Hale goes outside. The Sheriff follows the County Attorney into the other room. Then Mrs. Hale rises, hands tight together, looking intensely at Mrs. Peters, whose eyes make a slow turn, finally meeting Mrs. Hale's. A moment Mrs. Hale holds her, then her own eyes point the way to where the box is concealed. Suddenly Mrs. Peters throws back quilt pieces and tries to put the box in the bag she is wearing. It is too big. She opens box, starts to take bird out, cannot touch it, goes to pieces, stands there helpless. Sound of a knob turning in the other room. Mrs. Hale snatches the box and puts it in the pocket of her big coat. Enter County Attorney and Sheriff.)*

COUNTY ATTORNEY *(facetiously)*:   Well, Henry, at least we found out that she was not going to quilt it. She was going to—what is it you call it, ladies?

MRS. HALE *(her hand against her pocket)*:   We call it—knot it, Mr. Henderson.

*(Curtain)*

# TENNESSEE WILLIAMS [1911–1983]

## The Glass Menagerie

*Nobody, not even the rain, has such small hands.*
*—E. E. Cummings*

### List of Characters

AMANDA WINGFIELD, *the mother. A little woman of great but confused vitality clinging frantically to another time and place. Her characterization must be carefully created, not copied from type. She is not paranoiac, but her life is paranoia. There is much to admire in Amanda, and as much to love and pity as there is to laugh at. Certainly she has endurance and a kind of heroism, and though her foolishness makes her unwittingly cruel at times, there is tenderness in her slight person.*

LAURA WINGFIELD, *her daughter. Amanda, having failed to establish contact with reality, continues to live vitally in her illusions, but Laura's situation is even graver. A childhood illness has left her crippled, one leg slightly shorter than the other, and held in a brace. This defect need not be more than suggested on the stage. Stemming from this, Laura's separation increases till she is like a piece of her own glass collection, too exquisitely fragile to move from the shelf.*

TOM WINGFIELD, *her son. And the narrator of the play. A poet with a job in a warehouse. His nature is not remorseless, but to escape from a trap he has to act without pity.*

JIM O'CONNOR, *the gentleman caller. A nice, ordinary, young man.*


**Scene:** *An alley in St. Louis.*

**Part I:** *Preparation for a Gentleman Caller.*
**Part II:** *The Gentleman Calls.*

**Time:** *Now and the Past.*

*781*

# SCENE I

*The Wingfield apartment is in the rear of the building, one of those vast hive-like conglomerations of cellular living-units that flower as warty growths in overcrowded urban centers of lower middle-class population and are symptomatic of the impulse of this largest and fundamentally enslaved section of American society to avoid fluidity and differentiation and to exist and function as one interfused mass of automatism.*

*The apartment faces an alley and is entered by a fire-escape, a structure whose name is a touch of accidental poetic truth, for all of these huge buildings are always burning with the slow and implacable fires of human desperation. The fire-escape is included in the set—that is, the landing of it and steps descending from it.*

*The scene is memory and is therefore nonrealistic. Memory takes a lot of poetic license. It omits some details; others are exaggerated, according to the emotional value of the articles it touches, for memory is seated predominantly in the heart. The interior is therefore rather dim and poetic.*

*At the rise of the curtain, the audience is faced with the dark, grim rear wall of the Wingfield tenement. This building, which runs parallel to the footlights, is flanked on both sides by dark, narrow alleys which run into murky canyons of tangled clotheslines, garbage cans and the sinister latticework of neighboring fire-escapes. It is up and down these side alleys that exterior entrances and exits are made, during the play. At the end of Tom's opening commentary, the dark tenement wall slowly reveals (by means of a transparency) the interior of the ground floor Wingfield apartment.*

*Downstage is the living room, which also serves as a sleeping room for Laura, the sofa unfolding to make her bed. Upstage, center, and divided by a wide arch or second proscenium with transparent faded portieres (or second curtain), is the dining room. In an old-fashioned what-not in the living room are seen scores of transparent glass animals. A blown-up photograph of the father hangs on the wall of the living room, facing the audience, to the left of the archway. It is the face of a very handsome young man in a doughboy's First World War cap. He is gallantly smiling, ineluctably smiling, as if to say, "I will be smiling forever."*

*The audience hears and sees the opening scene in the dining room*

*through both the transparent fourth wall of the building and the
transparent gauze portieres of the dining-room arch. It is during
this revealing scene that the fourth wall slowly ascends, out of
sight. This transparent exterior wall is not brought down again
until the very end of the play, during Tom's final speech.*

*The narrator is an undisguised convention of the play. He takes
whatever license with dramatic convention as is convenient to his
purposes.*

*Tom enters dressed as a merchant sailor from alley, stage left, and
strolls across the front of the stage to the fire-escape. There he stops
and lights a cigarette. He addresses the audience.*

Toм:    Yes, I have tricks in my pocket, I have things up my sleeve.
But I am the opposite of a stage magician. He gives you illusion
that has the appearance of truth. I give you truth in the pleasant disguise of illusion. To begin with, I turn back time. I
reverse it to that quaint period, the thirties, when the huge
middle class of America was matriculating in a school for the
blind. Their eyes had failed them, or they had failed their
eyes, and so they were having their fingers pressed forcibly
down on the fiery Braille alphabet of a dissolving economy. In
Spain there was revolution. Here there was only shouting and
confusion. In Spain there was Guernica.[1] Here there were
disturbances of labor, sometimes pretty violent, in otherwise
peaceful cities such as Chicago, Cleveland, Saint Louis. . . .
This is the social background of the play.

**(Music.)**

The play is memory. Being a memory play, it is dimly lighted,
it is sentimental, it is not realistic. In memory everything seems
to happen to music. That explains the fiddle in the wings. I
am the narrator of the play, and also a character in it. The
other characters are my mother, Amanda, my sister, Laura,
and a gentleman caller who appears in the final scenes. He is
the most realistic character in the play, being an emissary from
a world of reality that we were somehow set apart from. But
since I have a poet's weakness for symbols, I am using this

---

[1] A Spanish town destroyed by German bombers during the Spanish Civil War.

character also as a symbol; he is the long delayed but always expected something that we live for. There is a fifth character in the play who doesn't appear except in this larger-than-life photograph over the mantel. This is our father who left us a long time ago. He was a telephone man who fell in love with long distances; he gave up his job with the telephone company and skipped the light fantastic out of town. . . . The last we heard of him was a picture post-card from Mazatlan, on the Pacific coast of Mexico, containing a message of two words— "Hello—Goodbye!" and no address. I think the rest of the play will explain itself. . . .

*Amanda's voice becomes audible through the portieres.*

**(Legend On Screen: "Où Sont Les Neiges."[2])**

*He divides the portieres and enters the upstage area.*

*Amanda and Laura are seated at a drop-leaf table. Eating is indicated by gestures without food or utensils. Amanda faces the audience. Tom and Laura are seated in profile.*

*The interior has lit up softly and through the scrim we see Amanda and Laura seated at the table in the upstage area.*

AMANDA (*calling*):   Tom?
TOM:   Yes, Mother.
AMANDA:   We can't say grace until you come to the table!
TOM:   Coming, Mother. (*He bows slightly and withdraws, reappearing a few moments later in his place at the table.*)
AMANDA (*to her son*):   Honey, don't *push* with your *fingers*. If you have to push with something, the thing to push with is a crust of bread. And chew—chew! Animals have sections in their stomachs which enable them to digest food without mastication, but human beings are supposed to chew their food before they swallow it down. Eat food leisurely, son, and really enjoy it. A well-cooked meal has lots of delicate flavors that have to

---

[2] "Mais où sont les neiges d'antans?" ("But where are the snows of yesteryear?") is the refrain of *Ballade des Dames du Tants Jadis* by Frech poet François Villon (1431–c.1463). The refrain was translated by the 19th-century Italian/English poet Dante Gabriel Rossetti as *The Ballad of Dead Ladies.*

be held in the mouth for appreciation. So chew your food and give your salivary glands a chance to function!

*Tom deliberately lays his imaginary fork down and pushes his chair back from the table.*

TOM:   I haven't enjoyed one bite of this dinner because of your constant directions on how to eat it. It's you that makes me rush through meals with your hawk-like attention to every bite I take. Sickening—spoils my appetite—all this discussion of animals' secretion—salivary glands—mastication!

AMANDA *(lightly):*   Temperament like a Metropolitan star! (*He rises and crosses downstage.*) You're not excused from the table.

TOM:   I am getting a cigarette.

AMANDA:   You smoke too much.

*Laura rises.*

LAURA:   I'll bring in the blanc mange.

*He remains standing with his cigarette by the portieres during the following.*

AMANDA *(rising):*   No, sister, no, sister—you be the lady this time and I'll be the darky.

LAURA:   I'm already up.

AMANDA:   Resume your seat, little sister—I want you to stay fresh and pretty—for gentlemen callers!

LAURA:   I'm not expecting any gentlemen callers.

AMANDA *(crossing out to kitchenette. Airily):*   Sometimes they come when they are least expected! Why, I remember one Sunday afternoon in Blue Mountain—(*Enters kitchenette.*)

TOM:   I know what's coming!

LAURA:   Yes. But let her tell it.

TOM:   Again?

LAURA:   She loves to tell it.

*Amanda returns with bowl of dessert.*

AMANDA:  One Sunday afternoon in Blue Mountain—your
mother received—*seventeen!*—gentlemen callers! Why, sometimes there weren't chairs enough to accommodate them all.
We had to send the nigger over to bring in folding chairs from
the parish house.

TOM *(remaining at portieres):*  How did you entertain those gentlemen callers?

AMANDA:  I understood the art of conversation!

TOM:  I bet you could talk.

AMANDA:  Girls in those days *knew* how to talk, I can tell you.

TOM:  Yes?

*(Image: Amanda As A Girl On A Porch Greeting Callers.)*

AMANDA:  They knew how to entertain their gentlemen callers.
It wasn't enough for a girl to be possessed of a pretty face and
a graceful figure—although I wasn't slighted in either respect.
She also needed to have a nimble wit and a tongue to meet
all occasions.

TOM:  What did you talk about?

AMANDA:  Things of importance going on in the world! Never
anything coarse or common or vulgar. (*She addresses Tom as
though he were seated in the vacant chair at the table though he
remains by portieres. He plays this scene as though he held the book.*)
My callers were gentlemen—all! Among my callers were some
of the most prominent young planters of the Mississippi
Delta—planters and sons of planters!

*Tom motions for music and a spot of light on Amanda.*

*Her eyes lift, her face glows, her voice becomes rich and elegiac.*

*(Screen Legend: "Où Sont Les Neiges.")*

There was young Champ Laughlin who later became vice-
president of the Delta Planters Bank. Hadley Stevenson who
was drowned in Moon Lake and left his widow one hundred
and fifty thousand in Government bonds. There were the
Cutrere brothers, Wesley and Bates. Bates was one of my

bright particular beaux! He got in a quarrel with that wild Wainright boy. They shot it out on the floor of Moon Lake Casino. Bates was shot through the stomach. Died in the ambulance on his way to Memphis. His widow was also well-provided for, came into eight or ten thousand acres, that's all. She married him on the rebound—never loved her—carried my picture on him the night he died! And there was that boy that every girl in the Delta had set her cap for! That beautiful, brilliant young Fitzhugh boy from Green County!

TOM:  What did he leave his widow?

AMANDA:  He never married! Gracious, you talk as though all of my old admirers had turned up their toes to the daisies!

TOM:  Isn't this the first you mentioned that still survives?

AMANDA:  That Fitzhugh boy went North and made a fortune—came to be known as the Wolf of Wall Street! He had the Midas touch, whatever he touched turned to gold! And I could have been Mrs. Duncan J. Fitzhugh, mind you! But—I picked your *father!*

LAURA *(rising):*  Mother, let me clear the table.

AMANDA:  No dear, you go in front and study your typewriter chart. Or practice your shorthand a little. Stay fresh and pretty!—It's almost time for our gentlemen callers to start arriving. *(She flounces girlishly toward the kitchenette.)* How many do you suppose we're going to entertain this afternoon?

*Tom throws down the paper and jumps up with a groan.*

LAURA *(alone in the dining room):*  I don't believe we're going to receive any, Mother.

AMANDA *(reappearing, airily):*  What? No one—not one? You must be joking! *(Laura nervously echoes her laugh. She slips in a fugitive manner through the half-open portieres and draws them gently behind her. A shaft of very clear light is thrown on her face against the faded tapestry of the curtains.)* **(Music: "The Glass Menagerie" Under Faintly.)** *(Lightly.)* Not one gentleman caller? It can't be true! There must be a flood, there must have been a tornado!

LAURA:  It isn't a flood, it's not a tornado, Mother. I'm just not popular like you were in Blue Mountain. . . . *(Tom utters another groan. Laura glances at him with a faint, apologetic smile. Her voice catching a little.*) Mother's afraid I'm going to be an old maid.

**(*This Scene Dims Out With "Glass Menagerie" Music.*)**

---

## SCENE II

"Laura, Haven't You Ever Liked Some Boy?"

*On the dark stage the screen is lighted with the image of blue roses. Gradually Laura's figure becomes apparent and the screen goes out. The music subsides.*

*Laura is seated in the delicate ivory chair at the small clawfoot table.*

*She wears a dress of soft violet material for a kimono—her hair tied back from her forehead with a ribbon.*

*She is washing and polishing her collection of glass.*

*Amanda appears on the fire-escape steps. At the sound of her ascent, Laura catches her breath, thrusts the bowl of ornaments away and seats herself stiffly before the diagram of the typewriter keyboard as though it held her spellbound. Something has happened to Amanda. It is written in her face as she climbs to the landing: a look that is grim and hopeless and a little absurd.*

*She has on one of those cheap or imitation velvety-looking cloth coats with imitation fur collar. Her hat is five or six years old, one of those dreadful cloche hats that were worn in the late twenties, and she is clasping an enormous black patent-leather pocketbook with nickel clasp and initials. This is her full-dress outfit, the one she usually wears to the D.A.R.*[3]

*Before entering she looks through the door.*

*She purses her lips, opens her eyes wide, rolls them upward and shakes her head.*

*Then she slowly lets herself in the door. Seeing her mother's expression Laura touches her lips with a nervous gesture.*

---

[3] Daughters of the American Revolution.

LAURA:   Hello, Mother, I was—(*She makes a nervous gesture toward the chart on the wall. Amanda leans against the shut door and stares at Laura with a martyred look.*)

AMANDA:   Deception? Deception? (*She slowly removes her hat and gloves, continuing the swift suffering stare. She lets the hat and gloves fall on the floor—a bit of acting.*)

LAURA (*shakily*):   How was the D.A.R. meeting? (*Amanda slowly opens her purse and removes a dainty white handkerchief which she shakes out delicately and delicately touches to her lips and nostrils.*) Didn't you go to the D.A.R. meeting, Mother?

AMANDA (*faintly, almost inaudibly*):   —No.—No. (*Then more forcibly.*) I did not have the strength—to go to the D.A.R. In fact, I did not have the courage! I wanted to find a hole in the ground and hide myself in it forever! (*She crosses slowly to the wall and removes the diagram of the typewriter keyboard. She holds it in front of her for a second, staring at it sweetly and sorrowfully— then bites her lips and tears it in two pieces.*)

LAURA (*faintly*):   Why did you do that, Mother? (*Amanda repeats the same procedure with the chart of the Gregg Alphabet.[4]*) Why are you—

AMANDA:   Why? Why? How old are you, Laura?

LAURA:   Mother, you know my age.

AMANDA:   I thought that you were an adult; it seems that I was mistaken. (*She crosses slowly to the sofa and sinks down and stares at Laura.*)

LAURA:   Please don't stare at me, Mother.

*Amanda closes her eyes and lowers her head. Count ten.*

AMANDA:   What are we going to do, what is going to become of us, what is the future?

*Count ten.*

LAURA:   Has something happened, Mother? (*Amanda draws a long breath and takes out the handkerchief again. Dabbing process.*) Mother, has—something happened?

---

[4] Shorthand symbols.

AMANDA:   I'll be all right in a minute. I'm just bewildered—*(count five)*—by life. . . .

LAURA:   Mother, I wish that you would tell me what's happened.

AMANDA:   As you know, I was supposed to be inducted into my office at the D.A.R. this afternoon. *(Image: A Swarm Of Typewriters.)* But I stopped off at Rubicam's Business College to speak to your teachers about you having a cold and ask them what progress they thought you were making down there.

LAURA:   Oh. . . .

AMANDA:   I went to the typing instructor and introduced myself as your mother. She didn't know who you were. Wingfield, she said. We don't have any such student enrolled at the school! I assured her she did, that you had been going to classes since early in January. "I wonder," she said, "if you could be talking about that terribly shy little girl who dropped out of school after only a few days' attendance?" "No," I said, "Laura, my daughter, has been going to school every day for the past six weeks!" "Excuse me," she said. She took the attendance book out and there was your name, unmistakably printed, and all the dates you were absent until they decided that you had dropped out of school. I still said, "No, there must have been some mistake! There must have been some mix-up in the records!" And she said, "No—I remember her perfectly now. Her hand shook so that she couldn't hit the right keys! The first time we gave a speed-test, she broke down completely—was sick at the stomach and almost had to be carried into the wash-room! After that morning she never showed up any more. We phoned the house but never got any answer"—while I was working at Famous and Barr, I suppose, demonstrating those—Oh! I felt so weak I could barely keep on my feet. I had to sit down while they got me a glass of water! Fifty dollars' tuition, all of our plans—my hopes and ambitions for you—just gone up the spout, just gone up the spout like that. *(Laura draws a long breath and gets awkwardly to her feet. She crosses to the victrola and winds it up.)* What are you doing?

LAURA:   Oh! *(She releases the handle and returns to her seat.)*

AMANDA:   Laura, where have you been going when you've gone out pretending that you were going to business college?

LAURA:   I've just been going out walking.

AMANDA:   That's not true.

LAURA:   It is. I just went walking.

AMANDA:   Walking? Walking? In winter? Deliberately courting pneumonia in that light coat? Where did you walk to, Laura?

LAURA:   It was the lesser of two evils, Mother. *(Image: Winter Scene In Park.)* I couldn't go back up. I—threw up—on the floor!

AMANDA:   From half past seven till after five every day you mean to tell me you walked around in the park, because you wanted to make me think that you were still going to Rubicam's Business College?

LAURA:   It wasn't as bad as it sounds. I went inside places to get warmed up.

AMANDA:   Inside where?

LAURA:   I went in the art museum and the bird-houses at the Zoo. I visited the penguins every day! Sometimes I did without lunch and went to the movies. Lately I've been spending most of my afternoons in the Jewel-box, that big glass house where they raise the tropical flowers.

AMANDA:   You did all this to deceive me, just for the deception? *(Laura looks down.)* Why?

LAURA:   Mother, when you're disappointed, you get that awful suffering look on your face, like the picture of Jesus' mother in the museum!

AMANDA:   Hush!

LAURA:   I couldn't face it.

*Pause. A whisper of strings.*

*(Legend: "The Crust Of Humility.")*

AMANDA *(hopelessly fingering the huge pocketbook):*   So what are we going to do the rest of our lives? Stay home and watch the parades go by? Amuse ourselves with the glass menagerie, darling? Eternally play those worn-out phonograph records your father left as a painful reminder of him? We won't have a business career—we've given that up because it gave us nervous indigestion! *(Laughs wearily.)* What is there left but dependency all our lives? I know so well what becomes of unmarried women who aren't prepared to occupy a position.

I've seen such pitiful cases in the South—barely tolerated spinsters living upon the grudging patronage of sister's husband or brother's wife!—stuck away in some little mousetrap of a room—encouraged by one in-law to visit another—little birdlike women without any nest—eating the crust of humility all their life! Is that the future that we've mapped out for ourselves? I swear it's the only alternative I can think of! It isn't a very pleasant alternative, is it? Of course—some girls *do marry*. (*Laura twists her hands nervously.*) Haven't you ever liked some boy?

LAURA:    Yes. I liked one once. (*Rises.*) I came across his picture a while ago.

AMANDA (*with some interest*):    He gave you his picture?

LAURA:    No, it's in the year-book.

AMANDA (*disappointed*):    Oh—a high-school boy.

*(Screen Image: Jim As A High-School Hero Bearing A Silver Cup.)*

LAURA:    Yes. His name was Jim. (*Laura lifts the heavy annual from the clawfoot table.*) Here he is in *The Pirates of Penzance.*

AMANDA (*absently*):    The what?

LAURA:    The operetta the senior class put on. He had a wonderful voice and we sat across the aisle from each other Mondays, Wednesdays and Fridays in the Aud. Here he is with the silver cup for debating! See him grin?

AMANDA (*absently*):    He must have had a jolly disposition.

LAURA:    He used to call me—Blue Roses.

*(Image: Blue Roses.)*

AMANDA:    Why did he call you such a name as that?

LAURA:    When I had that attack of pleurosis—he asked me what was the matter when I came back. I said pleurosis—he thought that I said Blue Roses! So that's what he always called me after that. Whenever he saw me, he'd holler, "Hello, Blue Roses!" I didn't care for the girl that he went out with. Emily Meisenbach. Emily was the best-dressed girl at Soldan. She never struck me, though, as being sincere. . . . It says in the Personal

Section—they're engaged. That's—six years ago! They must be married by now.

AMANDA:  Girls that aren't cut out for business careers usually wind up married to some nice man. (*Gets up with a spark of revival.*) Sister, that's what you'll do!

*Laura utters a startled, doubtful laugh. She reaches quickly for a piece of glass.*

LAURA:  But, Mother—

AMANDA:  Yes? (*Crossing to photograph.*)

LAURA (*in a tone of frightened apology*):  I'm—crippled!

*(Image: Screen.)*

AMANDA:  Nonsense! Laura, I've told you never, never to use that word. Why, you're not crippled, you just have a little defect—hardly noticeable, even! When people have some slight disadvantage like that, they cultivate other things to make up for it—develop charm—and vivacity—and—*charm!* That's all you have to do! (*She turns again to the photograph.*) One thing your father had *plenty of*—was *charm!*

*Tom motions to the fiddle in the wings.*

*(The Scene Fades Out With Music.)*

## SCENE III

*(Legend On The Screen: "After The Fiasco—")*

*Tom Speaks from the fire-escape landing.*

TOM:  After the fiasco at Rubicam's Business College, the idea of getting a gentleman caller for Laura began to play a more important part in Mother's calculations. It became an obsession. Like some archetype of the universal unconscious, the image of the gentleman caller haunted our small apartment. . . . *(Image: Young Man At Door With Flowers.)* An evening at home rarely passed without some allusion to this image, this specter, this hope. . . . Even when he wasn't mentioned, his presence hung in Mother's preoccupied look and in my sister's frightened, apologetic manner—hung like a sentence passed upon the Wingfields! Mother was a woman of action as well as words. She began to take logical steps in the planned direction. Late that winter and in the early spring—realizing that extra money would be needed to properly feather the nest and plume the bird—she conducted a vigorous campaign on the telephone, roping in subscribers to one of those magazines for matrons called *The Home-maker's Companion*, the type of journal that features the serialized sublimations of ladies of letters who think in terms of delicate cup-like breasts, slim, tapering waists, rich, creamy thighs, eyes like wood-smoke in autumn, fingers that soothe and caress like strains of music, bodies as powerful as Etruscan sculpture.

*(Screen Image: Glamor Magazine Cover.)*

*Amanda enters with phone on long extension cord. She is spotted in the dim stage.*

AMANDA:   Ida Scott? This is Amanda Wingfield! We *missed* you at the D.A.R. last Monday! I said to myself: She's probably suffering with that sinus condition! How is that sinus condition? Horrors! Heaven have mercy!—You're a Christian martyr, yes, that's what you are, a Christian martyr! Well, I just now happened to notice that your subscription to the *Companion's* about to expire! Yes, it expires with the next issue, honey!—just when that wonderful new serial by Bessie Mae Hopper is getting off to such an exciting start. Oh, honey, it's something that you can't miss! You remember how *Gone With the Wind* took everybody by storm? You simply couldn't go out if you hadn't read it. All everybody *talked* was Scarlett O'Hara. Well, this is a book that critics already compare to *Gone With the Wind*. It's the *Gone With the Wind* of the post-World War generation!—What?—Burning?—Oh, honey, don't

let them burn, go take a look in the oven and I'll hold the
wire! Heavens—I think she's hung up!

*(Dim Out.)*

*(Legend On Screen: "You Think I'm In Love With Continental
Shoemakers?")*

*Before the stage is lighted, the violent voices of Tom and Amanda
are heard. They are quarreling behind the portieres. In front of
them stands Laura with clenched hands and panicky expression.*

*A clear pool of light on her figure throughout this scene.*

TOM:   What in Christ's name am I—
AMANDA *(shrilly):*   Don't you use that—
TOM:   Supposed to do!
AMANDA:   Expression! Not in my—
TOM:   Ohhh!
AMANDA:   Presence! Have you gone out of your senses?
TOM:   I have, that's true, *driven* out!
AMANDA:   What is the matter with you, you—big—big—IDIOT!
TOM:   Look—I've got *no thing*, no single thing—
AMANDA:   Lower your voice!
TOM:   In my life here that I can call my OWN! Everything is—
AMANDA:   Stop that shouting!
TOM:   Yesterday you confiscated my books! You had the nerve
      to—
AMANDA:   I took that horrible novel back to the library—yes! That
      hideous book by that insane Mr. Lawrence.[5] *(Tom laughs
      wildly.)* I cannot control the output of diseased minds or people
      who cater to them—*(Tom laughs still more wildly.)* BUT I WON'T
      ALLOW SUCH FILTH BROUGHT INTO MY HOUSE! No, no, no, no,
      no!
TOM:   House, house! Who pays rent on it, who makes a slave of
      himself to—
AMANDA *(fairly screeching):*   Don't you DARE to—
TOM:   No, no, I musn't say things! *I've* got to just—
AMANDA:   Let me tell you—

---

[5] British poet and novelist D. H. Lawrence [1885–1930].

Tom:   I don't want to hear any more! (*He tears the portieres open. The upstage area is lit with a turgid smokey red glow.*)

*Amanda's hair is in metal curlers and she wears a very old bath-robe, much too large for her slight figure, a relic of the faithless Mr. Wingfield.*

*An upright typewriter and a wild disarray of manuscripts are on the drop-leaf table. The quarrel was probably precipitated by Aman-da's interruption of his creative labor. A chair lying overthrown on the floor.*

*Their gesticulating shadows are cast on the ceiling by the fiery glow.*

Amanda:   You *will* hear more, you—

Tom:   No, I won't hear more, I'm going out!

Amanda:   You come right back in—

Tom:   Out, out out! Because I'm—

Amanda:   Come back here, Tom Wingfield! I'm not through talking to you!

Tom:   Oh, go—

Laura (*desperately*):   Tom!

Amanda:   You're going to listen, and no more insolence from you! I'm at the end of my patience! (*He comes back toward her.*)

Tom:   What do you think I'm at? Aren't I supposed to have any patience to reach the end of, Mother? I know, I know. It seems unimportant to you, what I'm *doing*—what I *want* to do—having a little *difference* between them! You don't think that—

Amanda:   I think you've been doing things that you're ashamed of. That's why you act like this. I don't believe that you go every night to the movies. Nobody goes to the movies night after night. Nobody in their right minds goes to the movies as often as you pretend to. People don't go to the movies at nearly midnight, and movies don't let out at two A.M. Come in stumbling. Muttering to yourself like a maniac! You get three hours' sleep and then go to work. Oh, I can picture the way you're doing down there. Moping, doping, because you're in no condition.

Tom (*wildly*):   No, I'm in no condition!

Amanda:   What right have you got to jeopardize your job? Jeopardize the security of us all? How do you think we'd manage if you were—

Tom:  Listen! You think I'm crazy *about* the *warehouse?* (*He bends fiercely toward her slight figure.*) You think I'm in love with the Continental Shoemakers? You think I want to spend fifty-five years down there in that—*celotex interior!* with—*fluorescent— tubes!* Look! I'd rather somebody picked up a crowbar and battered out my brains—than go back mornings! I *go!* Every time you come in yelling that God damn *"Rise and Shine!" "Rise and Shine!"* I say to myself "How *lucky dead* people are!" But I get up. I *go!* For sixty-five dollars a month I give up all that I dream of doing and being *ever!* And you say self—*self's* all I ever think of. Why, listen, if self is what I thought of, Mother, I'd be where he is—GONE! (*Pointing to father's picture.*) As far as the system of transportation reaches! (*He starts past her. She grabs his arm.*) Don't grab at me, Mother!

Amanda:  Where are you going?

Tom:  I'm going to the *movies!*

Amanda:  I don't believe that lie!

Tom (*crouching toward her, overtowering her tiny figure. She backs away, gasping*):  I'm going to opium dens! Yes, opium dens, dens of vice and criminals' hang-outs, Mother. I've joined the Hogan gang, I'm a hired assassin, I carry a tommy-gun in a violin case! I run a string of cat-houses in the Valley! They call me Killer, Killer Wingfield, I'm leading a double-life, a simple, honest warehouse worker by day, by night a dynamic *czar* of the *underworld, Mother.* I go to gambling casinos, I spin away fortunes on the roulette table! I wear a patch over one eye and a false mustache, sometimes I put on green whiskers. On those occasions they call me—*El Diablo!* Oh, I could tell you things to make you sleepless! My enemies plan to dynamite this place. They're going to blow us all sky-high some night! I'll be glad, very happy, and so will you! You'll go up, up on a broomstick, over Blue Mountain with seventeen gentlemen callers! You ugly—babbling old—*witch.* . . . (*He goes through a series of violent, clumsy movements, seizing his overcoat, lunging to the door, pulling it fiercely open. The women watch him, aghast. His arm catches in the sleeve of the coat as he struggles to pull it on. For a moment he is pinioned by the bulky garment. With an outraged groan he tears the coat off again, splitting the shoulders of it, and hurls it across the room. It strikes against the shelf of Laura's glass collection, there is a tinkle of shattering glass. Laura cries out as if wounded.)*

**(Music Legend: "The Glass Menagerie.")**

LAURA *(shrilly):*   My glass!—menagerie. . . . *(She covers her face and turns away.)*

*But Amanda is still stunned and stupefied by the "ugly witch" so that she barely notices this occurrence. Now she recovers her speech.*

AMANDA *(in an awful voice):*   I won't speak to you—until you apologize! *(She crosses through portieres and draws them together behind her. Tom is left with Laura. Laura clings weakly to the mantel with her face averted. Tom stares at her stupidly for a moment. Then he crosses to shelf. Drops awkwardly to his knees to collect the fallen glass, glancing at Laura as if he would speak but couldn't.)*
*"The Glass Menagerie" steals in as*

**(The Scene Dims Out.)**

---

## SCENE IV

*The interior is dark. Faint light in the alley.*

*A deep-voiced bell in a church is tolling the hour of five as the scene commences.*

*Tom appears at the top of the alley. After each solemn boom of the bell in the tower, he shakes a little noise-maker or rattle as if to express the tiny spasm of man in contrast to the sustained power and dignity of the Almighty. This and the unsteadiness of his advance make it evident that he has been drinking.*

*As he climbs the few steps to the fire-escape landing light steals up inside. Laura appears in night-dress, observing Tom's empty bed in the front room.*

*Tom fishes in his pockets for the door-key, removing a motley as-*

*sortment of articles in the search, including a perfect shower of movie-ticket stubs and an empty bottle. At last he finds the key, but just as he is about to insert it, it slips from his fingers. He strikes a match and crouches below the door.*

TOM (*bitterly*):    One crack—and it falls through!

*Laura opens the door.*

LAURA:    Tom! Tom, what are you doing?

TOM:    Looking for a door-key.

LAURA:    Where have you been all this time?

TOM:    I have been to the movies.

LAURA:    All this time at the movies?

TOM:    There was a very long program. There was a Garbo picture and a Mickey Mouse and a travelogue and a newsreel and a preview of coming attractions. And there was an organ solo and a collection for the milk-fund—simultaneously—which ended up in a terrible fight between a fat lady and an usher!

LAURA (*innocently*):    Did you have to stay through everything?

TOM:    Of course! And, oh, I forgot! There was a big stage show! The headliner on this stage show was Malvolio the Magician. He performed wonderful tricks, many of them, such as pouring water back and forth between pitchers. First it turned to wine and then it turned to beer and then it turned to whiskey. I know it was whiskey it finally turned into because he needed somebody to come up out of the audience to help him, and I came up—both shows! It was Kentucky Straight Bourbon. A very generous fellow, he gave souvenirs. (*He pulls from his back pocket a shimmering rainbow-colored scarf.*) He gave me this. This is his magic scarf. You can have it, Laura. You wave it over a canary cage and you get a bowl of gold-fish. You wave it over the gold-fish bowl and they fly away canaries. . . . But the wonderfullest trick of all was the coffin trick. We nailed him into a coffin and he got out of the coffin without removing one nail. (*He has come inside.*) There is a trick that would come in handy for me—get me out of this 2 by 4 situation! (*Flops onto bed and starts removing shoes.*)

LAURA:    Tom—Shhh!

TOM:    What you shushing me for?

LAURA:  You'll wake up Mother.

TOM:  Goody, goody! Pay'er back for all those "Rise an' Shines." (*Lies down, groaning.*) You know it don't take much intelligence to get yourself into a nailed-up coffin, Laura. But who in hell ever got himself out of one without removing one nail?

*As if in answer, the father's grinning photograph lights up.*

**(Scene Dims Out.)**

*Immediately following: The church bell is heard striking six. At the sixth stroke the alarm clock goes off in Amanda's room, and after a few moments we hear her calling: "Rise and Shine! Rise and Shine! Laura, go tell your brother to rise and shine!"*

TOM (*sitting up slowly*):  I'll rise—but I won't shine.

*The light increases.*

AMANDA:  Laura, tell your brother his coffee is ready.

*Laura slips into front room.*

LAURA:  Tom! it's nearly seven. Don't make Mother nervous. (*He stares at her stupidly. Beseechingly.*) Tom, speak to Mother this morning. Make up with her, apologize, speak to her!

TOM:  She won't to me. It's her that started not speaking.

LAURA:  If you just say you're sorry she'll start speaking.

TOM:  Her not speaking—is that such a tragedy?

LAURA:  Please—please!

AMANDA (*calling from kitchenette*):  Laura, are you going to do what I asked you to do, or do I have to get dressed and go out myself?

LAURA:  Going, going—soon as I get on my coat! (*She pulls on a shapeless felt hat with nervous, jerky movement, pleadingly glancing at Tom. Rushes awkwardly for coat. The coat is one of Amanda's inaccurately made-over, the sleeves too short for Laura.*) Butter and what else?

AMANDA (*entering upstage*):  Just butter. Tell them to charge it.

LAURA:  Mother, they make such faces when I do that.

AMANDA:  Sticks and stones may break my bones, but the expression on Mr. Garfinkel's face won't harm us! Tell your brother his coffee is getting cold.

LAURA *(at door):*  Do what I asked you, will you, will you, Tom?

*He looks sullenly away.*

AMANDA:  Laura, go now or just don't go at all!

LAURA *(rushing out):*  Going—going! (*A second later she cries out. Tom springs up and crosses to the door. Amanda rushes anxiously in. Tom opens the door.*)

TOM:  Laura?

LAURA:  I'm all right. I slipped, but I'm all right.

AMANDA *(peering anxiously after her):*  If anyone breaks a leg on those fire-escape steps, the landlord ought to be sued for every cent he possesses! (*She shuts door. Remembers she isn't speaking and returns to other room.*)

*As Tom enters listlessly for his coffee, she turns her back to him and stands rigidly facing the window on the gloomy gray vault of the areaway. Its light on her face with its aged but childish features is cruelly sharp, satirical as a Daumier[6] print.*

**(Music Under: "Ave Maria.")**

*Tom glances sheepishly but sullenly at her averted figure and slumps at the table. The coffee is scalding hot; he sips it and gasps and spits it back in the cup. At his gasp, Amanda catches her breath and half turns. Then catches herself and turns back to window.*

*Tom blows on his coffee, glancing sidewise at his mother. She clears her throat. Tom clears his. He starts to rise. Sinks back down again, scratches his head, clears his throat again. Amanda coughs. Tom raises his cup in both hands to blow on it, his eyes staring over the rim of it at his mother for several moments. Then he*

---

[6] Honoré Daumier [1808–1879], a French satirist, caricaturist, and painter.

*slowly sets the cup down and awkwardly and hesitantly rises from the chair.*

TOM (*hoarsely*):   Mother. I—I apologize. Mother. (*Amanda draws a quick, shuddering breath. Her face works grotesquely. She breaks into childlike tears.*) I'm sorry for what I said, for everything that I said, I didn't mean it.

AMANDA (*sobbingly*):   My devotion has made me a witch and so I make myself hateful to my children!

TOM:   No, you *don't*.

AMANDA:   I worry so much, don't sleep, it makes me nervous!

TOM (*gently*):   I understand that.

AMANDA:   I've had to put up a solitary battle all these years. But you're my right-hand bower! Don't fall down, don't fail!

TOM (*gently*):   I try, Mother.

AMANDA (*with great enthusiasm*):   Try and you will SUCCEED! (*The notion makes her breathless.*) Why, you—you're just *full* of natural endowments! Both of my children—they're *unusual* children! Don't you think I know it? I'm so—*proud!* Happy and—feel I've—so much to be thankful for but—Promise me one thing, son!

TOM:   What, Mother?

AMANDA:   Promise, son, you'll—never be a drunkard!

TOM (*turns to her grinning*):   I will never be a drunkard, Mother.

AMANDA:   That's what frightened me so, that you'd be drinking! Eat a bowl of Purina!

TOM:   Just coffee, Mother.

AMANDA:   Shredded wheat biscuit?

TOM:   No. No, Mother, just coffee.

AMANDA:   You can't put in a day's work on an empty stomach. You've got ten minutes—don't gulp! Drinking too-hot liquids makes cancer of the stomach. . . . Put cream in.

TOM:   No, thank you.

AMANDA:   To cool it.

TOM:   No! No, thank you, I want it black.

AMANDA:   I know, but it's not good for you. We have to do all that we can to build ourselves up. In these trying times we live in, all that we have to cling to is—each other. . . . That's why it's so important to—Tom, I—I sent out your sister so I could discuss something with you. If you hadn't spoken I would have spoken to you. (*Sits down.*)

TOM (*gently*):   What is it, Mother, that you want to discuss?

AMANDA:   Laura!

*Tom puts his cup down slowly.*

**(*Legend On Screen: "Laura."*)**

**(*Music: "The Glass Menagerie."*)**

TOM:   —Oh.—Laura . . .

AMANDA (*touching his sleeve*):   You know how Laura is. So quiet but—still water runs deep! She notices things and I think she—broods about them. (*Tom looks up.*) A few days ago I came in and she was crying.

TOM:   What about?

AMANDA:   You.

TOM:   Me?

AMANDA:   She has an idea that you're not happy here.

TOM:   What gave her that idea?

AMANDA:   What gives her any idea? However, you do act strangely. I—I'm not criticizing, understand *that!* I know your ambitions do not lie in the warehouse, that like everybody in the whole wide world—you've had to—make sacrifices, but—Tom—Tom—life's not easy, it calls for—Spartan endurance! There's so many things in my heart that I cannot describe to you! I've never told you but I—*loved* your father. . . .

TOM (*gently*):   I know that, Mother.

AMANDA:   And you—when I see you taking after his ways! Staying out late—and—well, you *had* been drinking the night you were in that—terrifying condition! Laura says that you hate the apartment and that you go out nights to get away from it! Is that true, Tom?

TOM:   No. You say there's so much in your heart that you can't describe to me. That's true of me, too. There's so much in my heart that I can't describe to *you!* So let's respect each other's—

AMANDA:   But, why—*why*, Tom—are you always so *restless?* Where do you go to, nights?

TOM: I—go to the movies.

AMANDA: Why do you go to the movies so much, Tom?

TOM: I go to the movies because—I like adventure. Adventure is something I don't have much of at work, so I go to the movies.

AMANDA: But, Tom, you go to the movies *entirely too much!*

TOM: I like a lot of adventure.

*Amanda looks baffled, then hurt. As the familiar inquisition resumes he becomes hard and impatient again. Amanda slips back into her querulous attitude toward him.*

**(Image On Screen: Sailing Vessel With Jolly Roger.)**

AMANDA: Most young men find adventure in their careers.

TOM: Then most young men are not employed in a warehouse.

AMANDA: The world is full of young men employed in warehouses and offices and factories.

TOM: Do all of them find adventure in their careers?

AMANDA: They do or they do without it! Not everybody has a craze for adventure.

TOM: Man is by instinct a lover, a hunter, a fighter, and none of those instincts are given much play at the warehouse!

AMANDA: Man is by instinct! Don't quote instinct to me! Instinct is something that people have got away from! It belongs to animals! Christian adults don't want it!

TOM: What do Christian adults want, then, Mother?

AMANDA: Superior things! Things of the mind and the spirit! Only animals have to satisfy instincts! Surely your aims are somewhat higher than theirs! Than monkeys—pigs—

TOM: I reckon they're not.

AMANDA: You're joking. However, that isn't what I wanted to discuss.

TOM *(rising):* I haven't much time.

AMANDA *(pushing his shoulders):* Sit down.

TOM: You want me to punch in red at the warehouse, Mother?

AMANDA: You have five minutes. I want to talk about Laura.

**(Legend: "Plans And Provisions.")**

Tom:    All right! What about Laura?

Amanda:    We have to be making plans and provisions for her. She's older than you, two years, and nothing has happened. She just drifts along doing nothing. It frightens me terribly how she just drifts along.

Tom:    I guess she's the type that people call home girls.

Amanda:    There's no such type, and if there is, it's a pity! That is unless the home is hers, with a husband!

Tom:    What?

Amanda:    Oh, I can see the handwriting on the wall as plain as I see the nose in front of my face! It's terrifying! More and more you remind me of your father! He was out all hours without explanation—Then *left! Goodbye!* And me with the bag to hold. I saw that letter you got from the Merchant Marine. I know what you're dreaming of. I'm not standing here blindfolded. Very well, then. Then *do* it! But not till there's somebody to take your place.

Tom:    What do you mean?

Amanda:    I mean that as soon as Laura has got somebody to take care of her, married, a home of her own, independent—why, then you'll be free to go wherever you please, on land, on sea, whichever way the wind blows! But until that time you've got to look out for your sister. I don't say me because I'm old and don't matter! I say for your sister because she's young and dependent. I put her in business college—a dismal failure! Frightened her so it made her sick to her stomach. I took her over to the Young People's League at the church. Another fiasco. She spoke to nobody, nobody spoke to her. Now all she does is fool with those pieces of glass and play those worn-out records. What kind of a life is that for a girl to lead!

Tom:    What can I do about it?

Amanda:    Overcome selfishness! Self, self, self is all that you ever think of! (*Tom springs up and crosses to get his coat. It is ugly and bulky. He pulls on a cap with earmuffs.*) Where is your muffler? Put your wool muffler on! (*He snatches it angrily from the closet and tosses it around his neck and pulls both ends tight.*) Tom! I haven't said what I had in mind to ask you.

Tom:    I'm too late to—

Amanda (*catching his arms—very importunately. Then shyly*):    Down at the warehouse, aren't there some—nice young men?

ToM:  No!
AMANDA:  There *must* be—*some*.
ToM:  Mother—

*Gesture.*

AMANDA:  Find out one that's clean-living—doesn't drink and—
ask him out for sister!
ToM:  What?
AMANDA:  For *sister!* To *meet!* Get *acquainted!*
ToM *(stamping to door):*  Oh, my *go-osh!*
AMANDA:  Will you? *(He opens door. Imploringly.)* Will you? *(He
starts down.)* Will you? *Will* you, dear?
ToM *(calling back):*  YES!

*Amanda closes the door hesitantly and with a troubled but faintly
hopeful expression.*

**(Screen Image: Glamor Magazine Cover.)**

*Spot Amanda at phone.*

AMANDA:  Ella Cartwright? This is Amanda Wingfield! How are
you, honey? How is that kidney condition? *(Count five.)* Horrors! *(Count five.)* You're a Christian martyr, yes, honey, that's
what you are, a Christian martyr! Well, I just happened to
notice in my little red book that your subscription to the *Companion* has just run out! I knew that you wouldn't want to miss
out on the wonderful serial starting in this new issue. It's by
Bessie Mae Hopper, the first thing she's written since *Honey-
moon for Three.* Wasn't that a strange and interesting story?
Well, this one is even lovelier, I believe. It has a sophisticated
society background. It's all about the horsey set on Long Island!

**(Fade Out.)**

# SCENE V

*(Legend On Screen: "Annunciation.")* Fade with music.

*It is early dusk of a spring evening. Supper has just been finished in the Wingfield apartment. Amanda and Laura in light colored dresses are removing dishes from the table, in the upstage area, which is shadowy, their movements formalized almost as a dance or ritual, their moving forms as pale and silent as moths.*

*Tom, in white shirt and trousers, rises from the table and crosses toward the fire-escape.*

AMANDA *(as he passes her):*   Son, will you do me a favor?
TOM:   What?
AMANDA:   Comb your hair! You look so pretty when your hair is combed! *(Tom slouches on sofa with evening paper. Enormous caption "Franco Triumphs."[7])* There is only one respect in which I would like you to emulate your father.
TOM:   What respect is that?
AMANDA:   The care he always took of his appearance. He never allowed himself to look untidy. *(He throws down the paper and crosses to fire-escape.)* Where are you going?
TOM:   I'm going out to smoke.
AMANDA:   You smoke too much. A pack a day at fifteen cents a pack. How much would that amount to in a month? Thirty times fifteen is how much, Tom? Figure it out and you will be astounded at what you could save. Enough to give you a night-school course in accounting at Washington U! Just think what a wonderful thing that would be for you, son!

*Tom is unmoved by the thought.*

TOM:   I'd rather smoke. *(He steps out on landing, letting the screen door slam.)*

---

[7] Francisco Franco [1892–1975] led Republican forces to victory over the Loyalists in 1939, thus ending the Spanish Civil War.

AMANDA *(sharply):*  I know! That's the tragedy of it. . . . (*Alone, she turns to look at her husband's picture.*)

**(Dance Music: "All The World Is Waiting For The Sunrise!")**

TOM *(to the audience):*  Across the alley from us was the Paradise Dance Hall. On evenings in spring the windows and doors were open and the music came outdoors. Sometimes the lights were turned out except for a large glass sphere that hung from the ceiling. It would turn slowly about and filter the dusk with delicate rainbow colors. Then the orchestra played a waltz or a tango, something that had a slow and sensuous rhythm. Couples would come outside, to the relative privacy of the alley. You could see them kissing behind ashpits and telephone poles. This was the compensation for lives that passed like mine, without any change or adventure. Adventure and change were imminent in this year. They were waiting around the corner for all these kids. Suspended in the mist over Berchtesgaden,[8] caught in the folds of Chamberlain's[9] umbrella—In Spain there was Guernica! But here there was only hot swing music and liquor, dance halls, bars, and movies, and sex that hung in the gloom like a chandelier and flooded the world with brief, deceptive rainbows. . . . All the world was waiting for bombardments!

*Amanda turns from the picture and comes outside.*

AMANDA *(sighing):*  A fire-escape landing's a poor excuse for a porch. (*She spreads a newspaper on a step and sits down, gracefully and demurely as if she were settling into a swing on a Mississippi veranda.*) What are you looking at?
TOM:  The moon.
AMANDA:  Is there a moon this evening?
TOM:  It's rising over Garfinkel's Delicatessen.
AMANDA:  So it is! A little silver slipper of a moon. Have you made a wish on it yet?

---

[8] Adolf Hilter's armored villa in the German Alps.
[9] British Prime Minister Neville Chamberlain [1869–1940], who advocated a policy of appeasement in dealing with Hitler's aggression.

Tom:  Um-hum.

Amanda:  What did you wish for?

Tom:  That's a secret.

Amanda:  A secret, huh? Well, I won't tell mine either. I will be just as mysterious as you.

Tom:  I bet I can guess what yours is.

Amanda:  Is my head so transparent?

Tom:  You're not a sphinx.

Amanda:  No, I don't have secrets. I'll tell you what I wished for on the moon. Success and happiness for my precious children! I wish for that whenever there's a moon, and when there isn't a moon, I wish for it, too.

Tom:  I thought perhaps you wished for a gentleman caller.

Amanda:  Why do you say that?

Tom:  Don't you remember asking me to fetch one?

Amanda:  I remember suggesting that it would be nice for your sister if you brought home some nice young man from the warehouse. I think I've made that suggestion more than once.

Tom:  Yes, you have made it repeatedly.

Amanda:  Well?

Tom:  We are going to have one.

Amanda:  *What?*

Tom:  A gentleman caller!

*(The Annunciation Is Celebrated With Music.)*

*Amanda rises.*

*(Image On Screen: Caller With Bouquet.)*

Amanda:  You mean you have asked some nice young man to come over?

Tom:  Yep. I've asked him to dinner.

Amanda:  You really did?

Tom:  I did!

Amanda:  You did, and did he—*accept?*

Tom:  He did!

Amanda:  Well, well—well, well! That's—lovely!

Tom:  I thought that you would be pleased.

Amanda:  It's definite, then?

TOM:   Very definite.

AMANDA:   Soon?

TOM:   Very soon.

AMANDA:   For heaven's sake, stop putting on and tell me some things, will you?

TOM:   What things do you want me to tell you?

AMANDA:   Naturally I would like to know when he's *coming!*

TOM:   He's coming tomorrow.

AMANDA:   *Tomorrow?*

TOM:   Yep. Tomorrow.

AMANDA:   But, Tom!

TOM:   Yes, Mother?

AMANDA:   Tomorrow gives me no time!

TOM:   Time for what?

AMANDA:   Preparations! Why didn't you phone me at once, as soon as you asked him, the minute that he accepted? Then, don't you see, I could have been getting ready!

TOM:   You don't have to make any fuss.

AMANDA:   Oh, Tom, Tom, Tom, of course I have to make a fuss! I want things nice, not sloppy! Not thrown together. I'll certainly have to do some fast thinking, won't I?

TOM:   I don't see why you have to think at all.

AMANDA:   You just don't know. We can't have a gentleman caller in a pig-sty! All my wedding silver has to be polished, the monogrammed table linen ought to be laundered! The windows have to be washed and fresh curtains put up. And how about clothes? We have to *wear* something, don't we?

TOM:   Mother, this boy is no one to make a fuss over!

AMANDA:   Do you realize he's the first young man we've introduced to your sister? It's terrible, dreadful, disgraceful that poor little sister has never received a single gentleman caller! Tom, come inside! (*She opens the screen door.*)

TOM:   What for?

AMANDA:   I want to ask you some things.

TOM:   If you're going to make such a fuss, I'll call it off, I'll tell him not to come.

AMANDA:   You certainly won't do anything of the kind. Nothing offends people worse than broken engagements. It simply means I'll have to work like a Turk! We won't be brilliant, but we'll pass inspection. Come on inside. (*Tom follows, groaning.*) Sit down.

TOM:   Any particular place you would like me to sit?

AMANDA:   Thank heavens I've got that new sofa! I'm also making payments on a floor lamp I'll have sent out! And put the chintz covers on, they'll brighten things up! Of course I'd hoped to have these walls re-papered. . . . What is the young man's name?

TOM:   His name is O'Connor.

AMANDA:   That, of course, means fish—tomorrow is Friday! I'll have that salmon loaf—with Durkee's dressing! What does he do? He works at the warehouse?

TOM:   Of course! How else would I—

AMANDA:   Tom, he—doesn't drink?

TOM:   Why do you ask me that?

AMANDA:   Your father *did!*

TOM:   Don't get started on that!

AMANDA:   He *does* drink, then?

TOM:   Not that I know of!

AMANDA:   Make sure, be certain! The last thing I want for my daughter's a boy who drinks!

TOM:   Aren't you being a little premature? Mr. O'Connor has not yet appeared on the scene!

AMANDA:   But will tomorrow. To meet your sister, and what do I know about his character? Nothing! Old maids are better off than wives of drunkards!

TOM:   Oh, my God!

AMANDA:   Be still!

TOM (*leaning forward to whisper*):   Lots of fellows meet girls whom they don't marry!

AMANDA:   Oh, talk sensibly, Tom—and don't be sarcastic! (*She has gotten a hairbrush.*)

TOM:   What are you doing?

AMANDA:   I'm brushing that cow-lick down! What is this young man's position at the warehouse?

TOM (*submitting grimly to the brush and the interrogation*):   This young man's position is that of a shipping clerk, Mother.

AMANDA:   Sounds to me like a fairly responsible job, the sort of a job *you* would be in if you just had more *get-up.* What is his salary? Have you got any idea?

TOM:   I would judge it to be approximatley eighty-five dollars a month.

AMANDA:   Well—not princely, but—

TOM:   Twenty more than I make.

AMANDA:   Yes, how well I know! But for a family man, eighty-five dollars a month is not much more than you can just get by on. . . .

TOM:   Yes, but Mr. O'Connor is not a family man.

AMANDA:   He might be, mightn't he? Some time in the future?

TOM:   I see. Plans and provisions.

AMANDA:   You are the only young man that I know of who ignores the fact that the future becomes the present, the present the past, and the past turns into everlasting regret if you don't plan for it!

TOM:   I will think that over and see what I can make of it.

AMANDA:   Don't be supercilious with your mother! Tell me some more about this—what do you call him?

TOM:   James D. O'Connor. The D. is for Delaney.

AMANDA:   Irish on *both* sides! *Gracious!* And doesn't drink?

TOM:   Shall I call him up and ask him right this minute?

AMANDA:   The only way to find out about those things is to make discreet inquiries at the proper moment. When I was a girl in Blue Mountain and it was suspected that a young man drank, the girl whose attentions he had been receiving, if any girl *was*, would sometimes speak to the minister of his church, or rather her father would if her father was living, and sort of feel him out on the young man's character. That is the way such things are discreetly handled to keep a young woman from making a tragic mistake!

TOM:   Then how did you happen to make a tragic mistake?

AMANDA:   That innocent look of your father's had everyone fooled! He *smiled*—the world was *enchanted!* No girl can do worse than put herself at the mercy of a handsome appearance! I hope that Mr. O'Connor is not too good-looking.

TOM:   No, he's not too good-looking. He's covered with freckles and hasn't too much of a nose.

AMANDA:   He's not right-down homely, though?

TOM:   Not right-down homely. Just medium homely, I'd say.

AMANDA:   Character's what to look for in a man.

TOM:   That's what I've always said, Mother.

AMANDA:   You've never said anything of the kind and I suspect you would never give it a thought.

TOM:   Don't be suspicious of me.

AMANDA:   At least I hope he's the type that's up and coming.

TOM:   I think he really goes in for self-improvement.

AMANDA:   What reason have you to think so?

TOM:   He goes to night school.

AMANDA *(beaming)*:   Splendid! What does he do, I mean study?

TOM:   Radio engineering and public speaking!

AMANDA:   Then he has visions of being advanced in the world! Any young man who studies public speaking is aiming to have an executive job some day! And radio engineering? A thing for the future! Both of these facts are very illuminating. Those are the sort of things that a mother should know concerning any young man who comes to call on her daughter. Seriously or—not.

TOM:   One little warning. He doesn't know about Laura. I didn't let on that we had dark ulterior motives. I just said, why don't you come have dinner with us? He said okay and that was the whole conversation.

AMANDA:   I bet it was! You're eloquent as an oyster. However, he'll know about Laura when he gets here. When he sees how lovely and sweet and pretty she is, he'll thank his lucky stars he was asked to dinner.

TOM:   Mother, you mustn't expect too much of Laura.

AMANDA:   What do you mean?

TOM:   Laura seems all those things to you and me because she's ours and we love her. We don't even notice she's crippled any more.

AMANDA:   Don't say crippled! You know that I never allow that word to be used!

TOM:   But face facts, Mother. She is and—that's not all—

AMANDA:   What do you mean "not all"?

TOM:   Laura is very different from other girls.

AMANDA:   I think the difference is all to her advantage.

TOM:   Not quite all—in the eyes of others—strangers—she's terribly shy and lives in a world of her own and those things make her seem a little peculiar to people outside the house.

AMANDA:   Don't say peculiar.

TOM:   Face the facts. She is.

*(The Dance-Hall Music Changes To A Tango That Has A Minor And Somewhat Ominous Tone.)*

AMANDA:   In what way is she peculiar—may I ask?

TOM (*gently*):   She lives in a world of her own—a world of—little glass ornaments, Mother. . . . (*Gets up. Amanda remains holding brush, looking at him, troubled.*) She plays old phonograph records and—that's about all—(*He glances at himself in the mirror and crosses to door.*)

AMANDA (*sharply*):   Where are you going?

TOM:   I'm going to the movies. (*Out screen door.*)

AMANDA:   Not to the movies, every night to the movies! (*Follows quickly to screen door.*) I don't believe you always go to the movies! (*He is gone. Amanda looks worriedly after him for a moment. Then vitality and optimism return and she turns from the door. Crossing to portieres.*) Laura! Laura! (*Laura answers from kitchenette.*)

LAURA:   Yes, Mother.

AMANDA:   Let those dishes go and come in front! (*Laura appears with dish towel. Gaily.*) Laura, come here and make a wish on the moon!

LAURA (*entering*):   Moon—moon?

AMANDA:   A little silver slipper of a moon. Look over your left shoulder, Laura, and make a wish! (*Laura looks faintly puzzled as if called out of sleep. Amanda seizes her shoulders and turns her at an angle by the door.*) Now! Now, darling, wish!

LAURA:   What shall I wish for, Mother?

AMANDA (*her voice trembling and her eyes suddenly filling with tears*):   Happiness! Good Fortune!

*The violin rises and the stage dims out.*

---

## SCENE VI

*(Image: High School Hero.)*

TOM:   And so the following evening I brought Jim home to dinner. I had known Jim slightly in high school. In high school Jim was a hero. He had tremendous Irish good nature and vitality with the scrubbed and polished look of white chinaware. He seemed to move in a continual spotlight. He was a star in basketball, captain of the debating club, president of the senior class and the glee club and he sang the male lead in the annual light operas. He was always running or bounding, never just walking. He seemed always at the point of defeating the law of gravity. He was shooting with such velocity through his adolescence that you would logically expect him to arrive at nothing short of the White House by the time he was thirty. But Jim apparently ran into more interference after his graduation from Soldan. His speed had definitely slowed. Six years after he left high school he was holding a job that wasn't much better than mine.

*(Image: Clerk.)*

He was the only one at the warehouse with whom I was on friendly terms. I was valuable to him as someone who could remember his former glory, who had seen him win basketball games and the silver cup in debating. He knew of my secret practice of retiring to a cabinet of the washroom to work on poems when business was slack in the warehouse. He called me Shakespeare. And while the other boys in the warehouse regarded me with suspicious hostility, Jim took a humorous attitude toward me. Gradually his attitude affected the others, their hostility wore off and they also began to smile at me as people smile at an oddly fashioned dog who trots across their path at some distance.

    I knew that Jim and Laura had known each other at Soldan, and I had heard Laura speak admiringly of his voice. I didn't know if Jim remembered her or not. In high school Laura had been as unobtrusive as Jim had been astonishing. If he did remember Laura, it was not as my sister, for when I asked him to dinner, he grinned and said, "You know, Shakespeare, I never thought of you as having folks!"

    He was about to discover that I did. . . .

*(Light Up Stage.)*

*(Legend On Screen: "The Accent Of A Coming Foot.")*

*Friday evening. It is about five o'clock of a late spring evening which comes "scattering poems in the sky."*

*A delicate lemony light is in the Wingfield apartment.*

*Amanda has worked like a Turk in preparation for the gentleman caller. The results are astonishing. The new floor lamp with its rose-silk shade is in place, a colored paper lantern conceals the broken light fixture in the ceiling, new billowing white curtains are at the windows, chintz covers are on chairs and sofa, a pair of new sofa pillows make their initial appearance.*

*Open boxes and tissue paper are scattered on the floor.*

*Laura stands in the middle with lifted arms while Amanda crouches before her, adjusting the hem of the new dress, devout and ritualistic. The dress is colored and designed by memory. The arrangement of Laura's hair is changed; it is softer and more becoming. A fragile, unearthly prettiness has come out in Laura: she is like a piece of translucent glass touched by light, given a momentary radiance, not actual, not lasting.*

AMANDA (*impatiently*):   Why are you trembling?

LAURA:   Mother, you've made me so nervous!

AMANDA:   How have I made you nervous?

LAURA:   By all this fuss! You make it seem so important!

AMANDA:   I don't understand you, Laura. You couldn't be satisfied with just sitting home, and yet whenever I try to arrange something for you, you seem to resist it. (*She gets up.*) Now take a look at yourself. No, wait! Wait just a moment—I have an idea!

LAURA:   What is it now?

*Amanda produces two powder puffs which she wraps in handkerchiefs and stuffs in Laura's bosom.*

LAURA:   Mother, what are you doing?

AMANDA:   They call them "Gay Deceivers"!

LAURA:   I won't wear them!

AMANDA:   You will!

LAURA:   Why should I?

AMANDA:   Because, to be painfully honest, your chest is flat.

LAURA:   You make it seem like we were setting a trap.

AMANDA:   All pretty girls are a trap, a pretty trap, and men expect them to be. *(Legend:"A Pretty Trap.")* Now look at yourself, young lady. This is the prettiest you will ever be! I've got to fix myself now! You're going to be surprised by your mother's appearance! (*She crosses through portieres, humming gaily.*)

*Laura moves slowly to the long mirror and stares solemnly at herself. A wind blows the white curtains inward in a slow, graceful motion and with a faint, sorrowful sighing.*

AMANDA *(off stage):* It isn't dark enough yet. (*She turns slowly before the mirror with a troubled look.*)

**(Legend On Screen: "This Is My Sister: Celebrate Her With Strings!" Music.)**

AMANDA *(laughing, off ):* I'm going to show you something. I'm going to make a spectacular appearance!
LAURA:  What is it, Mother?
AMANDA:  Possess your soul in patience—you will see! Something I've resurrected from that old trunk! Styles haven't changed so terribly much after all. . . . (*She parts the portieres.*) Now just look at your mother! (*She wears a girlish frock of yellowed voile with a blue silk sash. She carries a bunch of jonquils—the legend of her youth is nearly revived. Feverishly.*) This is the dress in which I led the cotillion. Won the cakewalk twice at Sunset Hill, wore one spring to the Governor's ball in Jackson! See how I sashayed around the ballroom, Laura? (*She raises her skirt and does a mincing step around the room*). I wore it on Sundays for my gentlemen callers! I had it on the day I met your father— I had malaria fever all that spring. The change of climate from East Tennessee to the Delta—weakened resistance—I had a little temperature all the time—not enough to be serious—just enough to make me restless and giddy! Invitations poured in—parties all over the Delta!—"Stay in bed," said Mother, "you have fever!"—but I just wouldn't.—I took quinine but kept on going, going!—Evenings, dances!—Afternoons, long, long rides! Picnics—lovely!—So lovely, that country in May.— All lacy with dogwood, literally flooded with jonquils!—That was the spring I had the craze for jonquils. Jonquils became an absolute obsession. Mother said, "Honey, there's no more

room for jonquils." And still I kept bringing in more jonquils. Whenever, wherever I saw them, I'd say, "Stop! Stop! I see jonquils!" I made the young men help me gather the jonquils! It was a joke, Amanda and her jonquils! Finally there were no more vases to hold them, every available space was filled with jonquils. No vases to hold them? All right, I'll hold them myself! And then I—(*She stops in front of the picture.*) (*Music.*) met your father! Malaria fever and jonquils and then— this—boy. . . . (*She switches on the rose-colored lamp.*) I hope they get here before it starts to rain. (*She crosses upstage and places the jonquils in bowl on table.*) I gave your brother a little extra change so he and Mr. O'Connor could take the service car home.

LAURA (*with altered look*):    What did you say his name was?
AMANDA:    O'Connor.
LAURA:    What is his first name?
AMANDA:    I don't remember. Oh, yes, I do. It was—Jim!

*Laura sways slightly and catches hold of a chair.*

**(Legend On Screen: "Not Jim!")**

LAURA (*faintly*):    Not—Jim!
AMANDA:    Yes, that was it, it was Jim! I've never known a Jim that wasn't nice!

**(Music: Ominous.)**

LAURA:    Are you sure his name is Jim O'Connor?
AMANDA:    Yes. Why?
LAURA:    Is he the one that Tom used to know in high school?
AMANDA:    He didn't say so. I think he just got to know him at the warehouse.
LAURA:    There was a Jim O'Connor we both knew in high school—(*Then, with effort.*) If that is the one that Tom is bring-ing to dinner—you'll have to excuse me, I won't come to the table.
AMANDA:    What sort of nonsense is this?
LAURA:    You asked me once if I'd ever liked a boy. Don't you remember I showed you this boy's picture?
AMANDA:    You mean the boy you showed me in the year book?

LAURA:  Yes, that boy.

AMANDA:  Laura, Laura, were you in love with that boy?

LAURA:  I don't know, Mother. All I know is I couldn't sit at the table if it was him!

AMANDA:  It won't be him! It isn't the least bit likely. But whether it is or not, you will come to the table. You will not be excused.

LAURA:  I'll have to be, Mother.

AMANDA:  I don't intend to humor your silliness, Laura. I've had too much from you and your brother, both! So just sit down and compose yourself till they come. Tom has forgotten his key so you'll have to let them in, when they arrive.

LAURA *(panicky):*  Oh, Mother—*you* answer the door!

AMANDA *(lightly):*  I'll be in the kitchen—busy!

LAURA:  Oh, Mother, please answer the door, don't make me do it!

AMANDA *(crossing into kitchenette):*  I've got to fix the dressing for the salmon. Fuss, fuss—silliness!—over a gentleman caller!

*Door swings shut. Laura is left alone.*

**(Legend: "Terror!")**

*She utters a low moan and turns off the lamp—sits stiffly on the edge of the sofa, knotting her fingers together.*

**(Legend On Screen: "The Opening Of A Door!")**

*Tom and Jim appear on the fire-escape steps and climb to landing. Hearing their approach, Laura rises with a panicky gesture. She retreats to the portieres.*

*The doorbell. Laura catches her breath and touches her throat. Low drums.*

AMANDA *(calling):*  Laura, sweetheart! The door!

*Laura stares at it without moving.*

JIM:  I think we just beat the rain.

TOM:  Uh-huh. *(He rings again, nervously. Jim whistles and fishes for a cigarette.)*

AMANDA *(very, very gaily):*   Laura, that is your brother and Mr. O'Connor! Will you let them in, darling?

*Laura crosses toward the kitchenette door.*

LAURA *(breathlessly):*   Mother—you go to the door!

*Amanda steps out of kitchenette and stares furiously at Laura. She points imperiously at the door.*

LAURA:   Please, please!
AMANDA *(in a fierce whisper):*   What is the matter with you, you silly thing?
LAURA *(desperately):*   Please, you answer it, *please!*
AMANDA:   I told you I wasn't going to humor you, Laura. Why have you chosen this moment to lose your mind?
LAURA:   Please, please, please, you go!
AMANDA:   You'll have to go to the door because I can't!
LAURA *(despairingly):*   I can't either!
AMANDA:   Why?
LAURA:   I'm *sick!*
AMANDA:   I'm sick, too—of your nonsense! Why can't you and your brother be normal people? Fantastic whims and behavior! *(Tom gives a long ring.)* Preposterous goings on! Can you give me one reason—*(Calls out lyrically.)* COMING! JUST ONE SEC-OND!—why should you be afraid to open a door? Now you answer it, Laura!
LAURA:   Oh, oh, oh . . . *(She returns through the portieres. Darts to the victrola and winds it frantically and turns it on.)*
AMANDA:   Laura Wingfield, you march right to that door!
LAURA:   Yes—yes, Mother!

*A faraway, scratchy rendition of "Dardanella" softens the air and gives her strength to move through it. She slips to the door and draws it cautiously open.*
*Tom enters with the caller, Jim O'Connor.*

TOM:   Laura, this is Jim. Jim, this is my sister, Laura.
JIM *(stepping inside):*   I didn't know that Shakespeare had a sister!

LAURA *(retreating stiff and trembling from the door):*   How—how do you do?

JIM *(heartily extending his hand):*   Okay!

*Laura touches it hesitantly with hers.*

JIM:   Your hand's *cold,* Laura!

LAURA:   Yes, well—I've been playing the victrola. . . .

JIM:   Must have been playing classical music on it! You ought to play a little hot swing music to warm you up!

LAURA:   Excuse me—I haven't finished playing the victrola. . . .

*She turns awkwardly and hurries into the front room. She pauses a second by the victrola. Then catches her breath and darts through the portieres like a frightened deer.*

JIM *(grinning):*   What was the matter?

TOM:   Oh—with Laura? Laura is—terribly shy.

JIM:   Shy, huh? It's unusual to meet a shy girl nowadays. I don't believe you ever mentioned you had a sister.

TOM:   Well, now you know. I have one. Here is the *Post Dispatch.* You want a piece of it?

JIM:   Uh-huh.

TOM:   What piece? The comics?

JIM:   Sports! *(Glances at it.)* Ole Dizzy Dean is on his bad behavior.

TOM *(disinterest):*   Yeah? *(Lights cigarette and crosses back to fire-escape door.)*

JIM:   Where are *you* going?

TOM:   I'm going out on the terrace.

JIM *(goes after him):*   You know, Shakespeare—I'm going to sell you a bill of goods!

TOM:   What goods?

JIM:   A course I'm taking.

TOM:   Huh?

JIM:   In public speaking! You and me, we're not the warehouse type.

TOM:   Thanks—that's good news. But what has public speaking got to do with it?

JIM:   It fits you for—executive positions!

Tom:   Awww.

Jim:   I tell you it's done a helluva lot for me.

*(Image: Executive At Desk.)*

Tom:   In what respect?

Jim:   In every! Ask yourself what is the difference between you an' me and men in the office down front? Brains?—No!—Ability?—No! Then what? Just one little thing—

Tom:   What is that one little thing?

Jim:   Primarily it amounts to—social poise! Being able to square up to people and hold your own on any social level!

Amanda *(off stage):*   Tom?

Tom:   Yes, Mother?

Amanda:   Is that you and Mr. O'Connor?

Tom:   Yes, Mother.

Amanda:   Well, you just make yourselves comfortable in there.

Tom:   Yes, Mother.

Amanda:   Ask Mr. O'Connor if he would like to wash his hands.

Jim:   Aw—no—no—thank you—I took care of that at the warehouse. Tom—

Tom:   Yes?

Jim:   Mr. Mendoza was speaking to me about you.

Tom:   Favorably?

Jim:   What do you think?

Tom:   Well—

Jim:   You're going to be out of a job if you don't wake up.

Tom:   I am waking up—

Jim:   You show no signs.

Tom:   The signs are interior.

*(Image On Screen: The Sailing Vessel With Jolly Roger Again.)*

Tom:   I'm planning to change. (*He leans over the rail speaking with quiet exhilaration. The incandescent marquees and signs of the first-run movie houses light his face from across the alley. He looks like a voyager.*) I'm right at the point of committing myself to a future that doesn't include the warehouse and Mr. Mendoza or even a night-school course in public speaking.

JIM:  What are you gassing about?

TOM:  I'm tired of the movies.

JIM:  Movies!

TOM:  Yes, movies! Look at them—(*A wave toward the marvels of Grand Avenue.*) All of those glamorous people—having adventures—hogging it all, gobbling the whole thing up! You know what happens? People go to the *movies* instead of *moving!* Hollywood characters are supposed to have all the adventures for everybody in America, while everybody in America sits in a dark room and watches them have them! Yes, until there's a war. That's when adventure becomes available to the masses! *Everyone's* dish, not only Gable's! Then the people in the dark room come out of the dark room to have some adventures themselves—Goody, goody—It's our turn now, to go to the South Sea Island—to make a safari—to be exotic, far-off—But I'm not patient. I don't want to wait till then. I'm tired of the *movies* and I am *about* to *move!*

JIM *(incredulously):*  Move?

TOM:  Yes.

JIM:  When?

TOM:  Soon!

JIM:  Where? Where?

*(Theme Three: Music Seems To Answer The Question, While Tom Thinks It Over. He Searches Among His Pockets.)*

TOM:  I'm starting to boil inside. I know I seem dreamy, but inside—well, I'm boiling! Whenever I pick up a shoe, I shudder a little thinking how short life is and what I am doing!— Whatever that means. I know it doesn't mean shoes—except as something to wear on a traveler's feet! (*Finds paper.*) Look—

JIM:  What?

TOM:  I'm a member.

JIM *(reading):*  The Union of Merchant Seamen.

TOM:  I paid my dues this month, instead of the light bill.

JIM:  You will regret it when they turn the lights off.

TOM:  I won't be here.

JIM:  How about your mother?

TOM:  I'm like my father. The bastard son of a bastard! See how he grins? And he's been absent going on sixteen years!

JIM:   You're just talking, you drip. How does your mother feel
about it?

TOM:   Shhh—Here comes Mother! Mother is not acquainted with
my plans!

AMANDA *(enters portieres):*   Where are you all?

TOM:   On the terrace, Mother.

*They start inside. She advances to them. Tom is distinctly shocked
at her appearance. Even Jim blinks a little. He is making his first
contact with girlish Southern vivacity and in spite of the night-
school course in public speaking is somewhat thrown off the beam
by the unexpected outlay of social charm.*

*Certain responses are attempted by Jim but are swept aside by
Amanda's gay laughter and chatter. Tom is embarrassed but after
the first shock Jim reacts very warmly. Grins and chuckles, is altogether won over.*

**(Image: Amanda As A Girl.)**

AMANDA *(coyly smiling, shaking her girlish ringlets):*   Well, well,
well, so this is Mr. O'Connor. Introductions entirely unnec-
essary. I've heard so much about you from my boy. I finally
said to him, Tom—good gracious!—why don't you bring this
paragon to supper? I'd like to meet this nice young man at the
warehouse!—Instead of just hearing him sing your praises so
much! I don't know why my son is so standoffish—that's not
Southern behavior! Let's sit down and—I think we could stand
a little more air in here! Tom, leave the door open. I felt a nice
fresh breeze a moment ago. Where has it gone? Mmm, so
warm already! And not quite summer, even. We're going to
burn up when summer really gets started. However, we're
having—we're having a very light supper. I think light things
are better fo' this time of year. The same as light clothes are.
Light clothes an' light food are what warm weather calls fo'.
You know our blood gets so thick during th' winter—it takes
a while fo' us to *adjust* ou'selves!—when the season changes
. . . It's come so quick this year. I wasn't prepared. All of a
sudden—heavens! Already summer!—I ran to the trunk an'

pulled out this light dress—Terribly old! Historical almost! But
feels so good—so good an' co-ol, y'know. . . .

TOM:  Mother—

AMANDA:  Yes, honey?

TOM:  How about—supper?

AMANDA:  Honey, you go ask Sister if supper is ready! You know
that Sister is in full charge of supper! Tell her you hungry boys
are waiting for it. (*To Jim.*) Have you met Laura?

JIM:  She—

AMANDA:  Let you in? Oh, good, you've met already! It's rare for
a girl as sweet an' pretty as Laura to be domestic! But Laura
is, thank heavens, not only pretty but also very domestic. I'm
not at all. I never was a bit. I never could make a thing but
angel-food cake. Well, in the South we had so many servants.
Gone, gone, gone. All vestiges of gracious living! Gone completely! I wasn't prepared for what the future brought me. All
of my gentlemen callers were sons of planters and so of course
I assumed that I would be married to one and raise my family
on a large piece of land with plenty of servants. But man
proposes—and woman accepts the proposal!—To vary that
old, old saying a little bit—I married no planter! I married a
man who worked for the telephone company!—that gallantly
smiling gentleman over there! (*Points to the picture.*) A telephone man who—fell in love with long distance!—Now he
travels and I don't even know where!—But what am I going
on for about my—tribulations! Tell me yours—I hope you don't
have any! Tom?

TOM (*returning*):  Yes, Mother?

AMANDA:  Is supper nearly ready?

TOM:  It looks to me like supper is on the table.

AMANDA:  Let me look—(*She rises prettily and looks through portieres.*) Oh, lovely—But where is Sister?

TOM:  Laura is not feeling well and she says that she thinks she'd
better not come to the table.

AMANDA:  What?—Nonsense!—Laura? Oh, Laura!

LAURA (*off stage, faintly*):  Yes, Mother.

AMANDA:  You really must come to the table. We won't be seated
until you come to the table! Come in, Mr. O'Connor. You sit
over there and I'll—Laura? Laura Wingfield! You're keeping

us waiting, honey! We can't say grace until you come to the
table!

*The back door is pushed weakly open and Laura comes in. She is
obviously quite faint, her lips trembling, her eyes wide and staring.
She moves unsteadily toward the table.*

**(Legend: "Terror!")**

*Outside a summer storm is coming abruptly. The white curtains
billow inward at the windows and there is a sorrowful murmur and
deep blue dusk.*
*Laura suddenly stumbles—She catches at a chair with a faint moan.*

TOM:   Laura!

AMANDA:   Laura! (*There is a clap of thunder.*) **(Legend: "Ah!")** (*Despairingly.*) Why, Laura, you *are* sick, darling! Tom, help your
sister into the living room, dear! Sit in the living room, Laura—
rest on the sofa. Well! (*To the gentleman caller.*) Standing over
the hot stove made her ill!—I told her that it was just too warm
this evening, but—(*Tom comes back in. Laura is on the sofa.*) Is
Laura all right now?

TOM:   Yes.

AMANDA:   What *is* that? Rain? A nice cool rain has come up! (*She
gives the gentleman caller a frightened look.*) I think we may—
have grace—now . . . (*Tom looks at her stupidly.*) Tom, honey—
you say grace!

TOM:   Oh . . . "For these and all thy mercies—" (*They bow their
heads, Amanda stealing a nervous glance at Jim. In the living room
Laura, stretched on the sofa, clenches her hand to her lips, to hold
back a shuddering sob.*) God's Holy Name be praised—

**(The Scene Dims Out.)**

---

## S C E N E   VII

### A Souvenir

*Half an hour later. Dinner is just being finished in the upstage area
which is concealed by the drawn portieres.*

*As the curtain rises Laura is still huddled upon the sofa, her feet drawn under her, her head resting on a pale blue pillow, her eyes wide and mysteriously watchful. The new floor lamp with its shade of rose-colored silk gives a soft, becoming light to her face, bringing out the fragile, unearthly prettiness which usually escapes attention. There is a steady murmur of rain, but it is slackening and stops soon after the scene beings; the air outside becomes pale and luminous as the moon breaks out.*

*A moment after the curtain rises, the lights in both rooms flicker and go out.*

JIM:   Hey, there, Mr. Light Bulb!

*Amanda laughs nervously.*

**(Legend: "Suspension Of A Public Service.")**

AMANDA:   Where was Moses when the lights went out? Ha-ha. Do you know the answer to that one, Mr. O'Connor?

JIM:   No, Ma'am, what's the answer?

AMANDA:   In the dark! (*Jim laughs appreciatively.*) Everybody sit still. I'll light the candles. Isn't it lucky we have them on the table? Where's a match? Which of you gentlemen can provide a match?

JIM:   Here.

AMANDA:   Thank you, sir.

JIM:   Not at all, Ma'am!

AMANDA:   I guess the fuse has burnt out. Mr. O'Connor, can you tell a burnt-out fuse? I know I can't and Tom is a total loss when it comes to mechanics. (*Sound: Getting Up: Voices Recede A Little To Kitchenette.*) Oh, be careful you don't bump into something. We don't want our gentleman caller to break his neck. Now wouldn't that be a fine howdy-do?

JIM:   Ha-ha! Where is the fuse-box?

AMANDA:   Right here next to the stove. Can you see anything?

JIM:   Just a minute.

AMANDA:   Isn't electricity a mysterious thing? Wasn't it Benjamin Franklin who tied a key to a kite? We live in such a mysterious universe, don't we? Some people say that science clears up all

the mysteries for us. In my opinion it only creates more! Have
you found it yet?

JIM:   No, Ma'am. All these fuses look okay to me.

AMANDA:   Tom!

TOM:   Yes, Mother?

AMANDA:   That light bill I gave you several days agō. The one I
told you we got the notices about?

TOM:   Oh.—Yeah.

*(Legend: "Ha!")*

AMANDA:   You didn't neglect to pay it by any chance?

TOM:   Why, I—

AMANDA:   Didn't! I might have known it!

JIM:   Shakespeare probably wrote a poem on that light bill, Mrs.
Wingfield.

AMANDA:   I might have known better than to trust him with it!
There's such a high price for negligence in this world!

JIM:   Maybe the poem will win a ten-dollar prize.

AMANDA:   We'll just have to spend the remainder of the evening
in the nineteenth century, before Mr. Edison made the Mazda
lamp!

JIM:   Candlelight is my favorite kind of light.

AMANDA:   That shows you're romantic! But that's no excuse for
Tom. Well, we got through dinner. Very considerate of them
to let us get through dinner before they plunged us into everlasting darkness, wasn't it, Mr. O'Connor?

JIM:   Ha-ha!

AMANDA:   Tom, as a penalty for your carelessness you can help
me with the dishes.

JIM:   Let me give you a hand.

AMANDA:   Indeed you will not!

JIM:   I ought to be good for something.

AMANDA:   Good for something? *(Her tone is rhapsodic.) You?* Why,
Mr. O'Connor, nobody, *nobody's* given me this much entertainment in years—as you have!

JIM:   Aw, now, Mrs. Wingfield!

AMANDA:   I'm not exaggerating, not one bit! But Sister is all by
her lonesome. You go keep her company in the parlor! I'll give
you this lovely old candelabrum that used to be on the altar

at the church of the Heavenly Rest. It was melted a little out
of shape when the church burnt down. Lightning struck it
one spring. Gypsy Jones was holding a revival at the time
and he intimated that the church was destroyed because the
Episcopalians gave card parties.

JIM:   Ha-ha.

AMANDA:   And how about coaxing Sister to drink a little wine? I
think it would be good for her! Can you carry both at once?

JIM:   Sure. I'm Superman!

AMANDA:   Now, Thomas, get into this apron!

*The door of kitchenette swings closed on Amanda's gay laughter;
the flickering light approaches the portieres.*

*Laura sits up nervously as he enters. Her speech at first is low and
breathless from the almost intolerable strain of being alone with a
stranger.*

**(Legend: "I Don't Suppose You Remember Me At All!")**

*In her first speeches in this scene, before Jim's warmth overcomes
her paralyzing shyness, Laura's voice is thin and breathless as
though she has run up a steep flight of stairs.*

*Jim's attitude is gently humorous. In playing this scene it should be
stressed that while the incident is apparently unimportant, it is to
Laura the climax of her secret life.*

JIM:   Hello, there, Laura.

LAURA *(faintly):*   Hello. *(She clears her throat.)*

JIM:   How are you feeling now? Better?

LAURA:   Yes. Yes, thank you.

JIM:   This is for you. A little dandelion wine. *(He extends it toward
her with extravagant gallantry.)*

LAURA:   Thank you.

JIM:   Drink it—but don't get drunk! *(He laughs heartily. Laura takes
the glass uncertainly; laughs shyly.)* Where shall I set the candles?

LAURA:   Oh—oh, anywhere . . .

JIM:   How about here on the floor? Any objections?

LAURA:   No.

JIM:   I'll spread a newspaper under to catch the drippings. I like to sit on the floor. Mind if I do?

LAURA:   Oh, no.

JIM:   Give me a pillow?

LAURA:   What?

JIM:   A pillow!

LAURA:   Oh . . . (*Hands him one quickly.*)

JIM:   How about you? Don't you like to sit on the floor?

LAURA:   Oh—yes.

JIM:   Why don't you, then?

LAURA:   I—will.

JIM:   Take a pillow! (*Laura does. Sits on the other side of the candelabrum. Jim crosses his legs and smiles engagingly at her.*) I can't hardly see you sitting way over there.

LAURA:   I can—see you.

JIM:   I know, but that's not fair, I'm in the limelight. (*Laura moves her pillow closer.*) Good! Now I can see you! Comfortable?

LAURA:   Yes.

JIM:   So am I. Comfortable as a cow. Will you have some gum?

LAURA:   No, thank you.

JIM:   I think that I will indulge, with your permission. (*Musingly unwraps it and holds it up.*) Think of the fortune made by the guy that invented the first piece of chewing gum. Amazing, huh? The Wrigley Building is one of the sights of Chicago.— I saw it summer before last when I went up to the Century of Progress. Did you take in the Century of Progress?

LAURA:   No, I didn't.

JIM:   Well, it was quite a wonderful exposition. What impressed me most was the Hall of Science. Gives you an idea of what the future will be in America, even more wonderful than the present time is! (*Pause. Smiling at her.*) Your brother tells me you're shy. Is that right, Laura?

LAURA:   I—don't know.

JIM:   I judge you to be an old-fashioned type of girl. Well, I think that's a pretty good type to be. Hope you don't think I'm being too personal—do you?

LAURA (*hastily, out of embarrassment*):   I believe I *will* take a piece of gum, if you—don't mind. (*Clearing her throat.*) Mr. O'Connor, have you—kept up with your singing?

JIM:   Singing? Me?

LAURA:   Yes. I remember what a beautiful voice you had.

JIM:   When did you hear me sing?

*(Voice Offstage In The Pause.)*

VOICE *(offstage):*
>    O blow, ye winds, heigh-ho,
>    A-roving I will go!
>    I'm off to my love
>    With a boxing glove—
>    Ten thousand miles away!

JIM:   You say you've heard me sing?

LAURA:   Oh, yes! Yes, very often . . . I—don't suppose you re-member me—at all?

JIM *(smiling doubtfully):*   You know I have an idea I've seen you before. I had that idea soon as you opened the door. It seemed almost like I was about to remember your name. But the name that I started to call you—wasn't a name! And so I stopped myself before I said it.

LAURA:   Wasn't it—Blue Roses?

JIM *(springs up, grinning):*   Blue Roses! My gosh, yes—Blue Roses! That's what I had on my tongue when you opened the door! Isn't it funny what tricks your memory plays? I didn't connect you with the high school somehow or other. But that's where it was; it was high school. I didn't even know you were Shake-speare's sister! Gosh, I'm sorry.

LAURA:   I didn't expect you to. You—barely knew me!

JIM:   But we did have a speaking acquaintance, huh?

LAURA:   Yes, we—spoke to each other.

JIM:   When did you recognize me?

LAURA:   Oh, right away!

JIM:   Soon as I came in the door?

LAURA:   When I heard your name I thought it was probably you. I knew that Tom used to know you a little in high school. So when you came in the door—Well, then I was—sure.

JIM:   Why didn't you *say* something, then?

LAURA *(breathlessly):*   I didn't know what to say, I was—too sur-prised!

JIM:   For goodness' sakes! You know, this sure is funny!

LAURA:   Yes! Yes, isn't it, though . . .

JIM:   Didn't we have a class in something together?

LAURA:   Yes, we did.

JIM:   What class was that?

LAURA:   It was—singing—Chorus!

JIM:   Aw!

LAURA:   I sat across the aisle from you in the Aud.

JIM:   Aw.

LAURA:   Mondays, Wednesdays and Fridays.

JIM:   Now I remember—you always came in late.

LAURA:   Yes, it was so hard for me, getting upstairs. I had that brace on my leg—it clumped so loud!

JIM:   I never heard any clumping.

LAURA *(wincing at the recollection):*   To me it sounded like—thunder!

JIM:   Well, well, well. I never even noticed.

LAURA:   And everybody was seated before I came in. I had to walk in front of all those people. My seat was in the back row. I had to go clumping all the way up the aisle with everyone watching!

JIM:   You shouldn't have been self-conscious.

LAURA:   I know, but I was. It was always such a relief when the singing started.

JIM:   Aw, yes, I've placed you now! I used to call you Blue Roses. How was it that I got started calling you that?

LAURA:   I was out of school a little while with pleurosis. When I came back you asked me what was the matter. I said I had pleurosis—you thought I said Blue Roses. That's what you always called me after that!

JIM:   I hope you didn't mind.

LAURA:   Oh, no—I liked it. You see, I wasn't acquainted with many—people. . . .

JIM:   As I remember you sort of stuck by yourself.

LAURA:   I—I—never had much luck at—making friends.

JIM:   I don't see why you wouldn't.

LAURA:   Well, I—started out badly.

JIM:   You mean being—

LAURA:   Yes, it sort of—stood between me—

JIM:   You shouldn't have let it!

LAURA:   I know, but it did, and—

JIM:   You were shy with people!

LAURA:   I tried not to be but never could—

JIM:   Overcome it?

LAURA:   No, I—I never could!

JIM:   I guess being shy is something you have to work out of kind of gradually.

LAURA *(sorrowfully)*:   Yes—I guess it—

JIM:   Takes time!

LAURA:   Yes—

JIM:   People are not so dreadful when you know them. That's what you have to remember! And everybody has problems, not just you, but practically everybody has got some problems. You think of yourself as having the only problems, as being the only one who is disappointed. But just look around you and you will see lots of people as disappointed as you are. For instance, I hoped when I was going to high school that I would be further along at this time, six years later, than I am now—You remember that wonderful write-up I had in *The Torch?*

LAURA:   Yes! (*She rises and crosses to table.*)

JIM:   It said I was bound to succeed in anything I went into! (*Laura returns with the annual.*) Holy Jeez! *The Torch!* (*He accepts it reverently. They smile across it with mutual wonder. Laura crouches beside him and they begin to turn through it. Laura's shyness is dissolving in his warmth.*)

LAURA:   Here you are in *Pirates of Penzance!*

JIM *(wistfully)*:   I sang the baritone lead in that operetta.

LAURA *(rapidly)*:   So—*beautifully!*

JIM *(protesting)*:   Aw—

LAURA:   Yes, yes—beautifully—beautifully!

JIM:   You heard me?

LAURA:   All three times!

JIM:   No!

LAURA:   Yes!

JIM:   All three performances?

LAURA *(looking down)*:   Yes.

JIM:   Why?

LAURA:   I—wanted to ask you to—autograph my program.

JIM:   Why didn't you ask me to?

LAURA:   You were always surrounded by your own friends so much that I never had a chance to.

JIM:   You should have just—

LAURA:   Well, I—thought you might think I was—

JIM:   Thought I might think you was—what?

LAURA:   Oh—

JIM *(with reflective relish):*   I was beleaguered by females in those days.

LAURA:   You were terribly popular!

JIM:   Yeah—

LAURA:   You had such a—friendly way—

JIM:   I was spoiled in high school.

LAURA:   Everybody—liked you!

JIM:   Including you?

LAURA:   I—yes, I—I did, too—*(She gently closes the book in her lap.)*

JIM:   Well, well, well!—Give me that program, Laura. *(She hands it to him. He signs it with a flourish.)* There you are—better late than never!

LAURA:   Oh, I—what a—surprise!

JIM:   My signature isn't worth very much right now. But some day—maybe—it will increase in value! Being disappointed is one thing and being discouraged is something else. I am disappointed but I'm not discouraged. I'm twenty-three years old. How old are you?

LAURA:   I'll be twenty-four in June.

JIM:   That's not old age!

LAURA:   No, but—

JIM:   You finished high school?

LAURA *(with difficulty):*   I didn't go back.

JIM:   You mean you dropped out?

LAURA:   I made bad grades in my final examinations. *(She rises and replaces the book and the program. Her voice strained.)* How is—Emily Meisenbach getting along?

JIM:   Oh, that kraut-head!

LAURA:   Why do you call her that?

JIM:   That's what she was.

LAURA:   You're not still—going with her?

JIM:   I never see her.

LAURA:   It said in the Personal Section that you were—engaged!

JIM:   I know, but I wasn't impressed by that—propaganda!

LAURA:  It wasn't—the truth?
JIM:  Only in Emily's optimistic opinion!
LAURA:  Oh—

*(Legend: "What Have You Done Since High School?")*

*Jim lights a cigarette and leans indolently back on his elbows smiling at Laura with a warmth and charm which light her inwardly with altar candles. She remains by the table and turns in her hands a piece of glass to cover her tumult.*

JIM *(after several reflective puffs on a cigarette):*  What have you done since high school? *(She seems not to hear him.)* Huh? *(Laura looks up.)* I said what have you done since high school, Laura?
LAURA:  Nothing much.
JIM:  You must have been doing something these six long years.
LAURA:  Yes.
JIM:  Well, then, such as what?
LAURA:  I took a business course at business college—
JIM:  How did that work out?
LAURA:  Well, not very—well—I had to drop out, it gave me— indigestion—

*Jim laughs gently.*

JIM:  What are you doing now?
LAURA:  I don't do anything—much. Oh, please don't think I sit around doing nothing! My glass collection takes up a good deal of my time. Glass is something you have to take good care of.
JIM:  What did you say—about glass?
LAURA:  Collection I said—I have one—*(She clears her throat and turns away again, acutely shy.)*
JIM *(abruptly):*  You know what I judge to be the trouble with you? Inferiority complex! Know what that is? That's what they call it when someone low-rates himself! I understand it because I had it, too. Although my case was not so aggravated as yours seems to be. I had it until I took up public speaking, developed my voice, and learned that I had an aptitude for science. Before that time I never thought of myself as being outstanding in

any way whatsoever! Now I've never made a regular study of it, but I have a friend who says I can analyze people better than doctors that make a profession of it. I don't claim that to be necessarily true, but I can sure guess a person's psychology, Laura! (*Takes out his gum.*) Excuse me, Laura. I always take it out when the flavor is gone. I'll use this scrap of paper to wrap it in. I know how it is to get it stuck on a shoe. Yep— that's what I judge to be your principal trouble. A lack of confidence in yourself as a person. You don't have the proper amount of faith in yourself. I'm basing that fact on a number of your remarks and also on certain observations I've made. For instance that clumping you thought was so awful in high school. You say that you even dreaded to walk into class. You see what you did? You dropped out of school, you gave up an education because of a clump, which as far as I know was practically nonexistent! A little physical defect is what you have. Hardly noticeable even! Magnified thousands of times by imagination! You know what my strong advice to you is? Think of yourself as *superior* in some way!

LAURA:   In what way would I think?

JIM:   Why, man alive, Laura! Just look about you a little. What do you see? A world full of common people! All of 'em born and all of 'em going to die! Which of them has one-tenth of your good points! Or mine! Or anyone else's, as far as that goes—Gosh! Everybody excels in some one thing. Some in many! (*Unconsciously glances at himself in the mirror.*) All you've got to do is discover in what! Take me, for instance. (*He adjusts his tie at the mirror.*) My interest happens to lie in electrodynamics. I'm taking a course in radio engineering at night school, Laura, on top of a fairly responsible job at the warehouse. I'm taking that course and studying public speaking.

LAURA:   Ohhhh.

JIM:   Because I believe in the future of television! (*Turning back to her.*) I wish to be ready to go up right along with it. Therefore I'm planning to get in on the ground floor. In fact, I've already made the right connections and all that remains is for the industry itself to get under way! Full steam—(*His eyes are starry.*) Knowledge—Zzzzzp! Money—Zzzzzzp!—Power! That's the cycle democracy is built on! (*His attitude is convincingly dynamic. Laura stares at him, even her shyness eclipsed in her ab-*

*solute wonder. He suddenly grins.*) I guess you think I think a lot of myself!

LAURA:   No—o-o-o, I—

JIM:   Now how about you? Isn't there something you take more interest in than anything else?

LAURA:   Well, I do—as I said—have my—glass collection—

*A peal of girlish laughter from the kitchen.*

JIM:   I'm not right sure I know what you're talking about. What kind of glass is it?

LAURA:   Little articles of it, they're ornaments mostly! Most of them are little animals made out of glass, the tiniest little animals in the world. Mother calls them a glass menagerie! Here's an example of one, if you'd like to see it! This one is one of the oldest. It's nearly thirteen. (*He stretches out his hand.*) **(Music: "The Glass Menagerie.")**   Oh, be careful—if you breathe, it breaks!

JIM:   I'd better not take it. I'm pretty clumsy with things.

LAURA:   Go on, I trust you with him! (*Places it in his palm.*) There now—you're holding him gently! Hold him over the light, he loves the light! You see how the light shines through him?

JIM:   It sure does shine!

LAURA:   I shouldn't be partial, but he is my favorite one.

JIM:   What kind of a thing is this one supposed to be?

LAURA:   Haven't you noticed the single horn on his forehead?

JIM:   A unicorn, huh?

LAURA:   Mmm-hmmm!

JIM:   Unicorns, aren't they extinct in the modern world?

LAURA:   I know!

JIM:   Poor little fellow, he must feel sort of lonesome.

LAURA (*smiling*):   Well, if he does he doesn't complain about it. He stays on a shelf with some horses that don't have horns and all of them seem to get along nicely together.

JIM:   How do you know?

LAURA (*lightly*):   I haven't heard any arguments among them!

JIM (*grinning*):   No arguments, huh? Well, that's a pretty good sign! Where shall I set him?

LAURA:   Put him on the table. They all like a change of scenery once in a while!

JIM (*stretching*):   Well, well, well, well—Look how big my shadow is when I stretch!

LAURA:   Oh, oh, yes—it stretches across the ceiling!

JIM (*crossing to door*):   I think it's stopped raining. (*Opens fire-escape door.*) Where does the music come from?

LAURA:   From the Paradise Dance Hall across the alley.

JIM:   How about cutting the rug a little, Miss Wingfield?

LAURA:   Oh, I—

JIM:   Or is your program filled up? Let me have a look at it. (*Grasps imaginary card.*) Why, every dance is taken! I'll just have to scratch some out. *(Waltz Music: "La Golondrina.")* Ahhh, a waltz! (*He executes some sweeping turns by himself then holds his arms toward Laura.*)

LAURA (*breathlessly*):   I—can't dance!

JIM:   There you go, that inferiority stuff!

LAURA:   I've never danced in my life!

JIM:   Come on, try!

LAURA:   Oh, but I'd step on you!

JIM:   I'm not made out of glass.

LAURA:   How—how—how do we start?

JIM:   Just leave it to me. You hold your arms out a little.

LAURA:   Like this?

JIM:   A little bit higher. Right. Now don't tighten up, that's the main thing about it—relax.

LAURA (*laughing breathlessly*):   It's hard not to.

JIM:   Okay.

LAURA:   I'm afraid you can't budge me.

JIM:   What do you bet I can't? (*He swings her into motion.*)

LAURA:   Goodness, yes, you can!

JIM:   Let yourself go, now, Laura, just let yourself go.

LAURA:   I'm—

JIM:   Come on!

LAURA:   Trying!

JIM:   Not so stiff—Easy does it!

LAURA:   I know but I'm—

JIM:   Loosen th' backbone! There now, that's a lot better.

LAURA:   Am I?

JIM:   Lots, lots better! (*He moves her about the room in a clumsy waltz.*)

LAURA:   Oh, my!

JIM:  Ha-ha!

LAURA:  Goodness, yes you can!

JIM:  Ha-ha-ha! (*They suddenly bump into the table. Jim stops.*) What did we hit on?

LAURA:  Table.

JIM:  Did something fall off it? I think—

LAURA:  Yes.

JIM:  I hope it wasn't the little glass horse with the horn!

LAURA:  Yes.

JIM:  Aw, aw, aw. Is it broken?

LAURA:  Now it is just like all the other horses.

JIM:  It's lost its—

LAURA:  Horn! It doesn't matter. Maybe it's a blessing in disguise.

JIM:  You'll never forgive me. I bet that that was your favorite piece of glass.

LAURA:  I don't have favorites much. It's no tragedy, Freckles. Glass breaks so easily. No matter how careful you are. The traffic jars the shelves and things fall off them.

JIM:  Still I'm awfully sorry that I was the cause.

LAURA (*smiling*):  I'll just imagine he had an operation. The horn was removed to make him feel less—freakish! (*They both laugh.*) Now he will feel more at home with the other horses, the ones that don't have horns. . .

JIM:  Ha-ha, that's very funny! (*Suddenly serious.*) I'm glad to see that you have a sense of humor. You know—you're—well—very different! Surprisingly different from anyone else I know! (*His voice becomes soft and hesitant with a genuine feeling.*) Do you mind me telling you that? (*Laura is abashed beyond speech.*) You make me feel sort of—I don't know how to put it! I'm usually pretty good at expressing things, but—This is something that I don't know how to say! (*Laura touches her throat and clears it— turns the broken unicorn in her hands.*) (*Even softer.*) Has anyone ever told you that you were pretty? **(Pause: Music.)** (*Laura looks up slowly, with wonder, and shakes her head.*) Well, you are! In a very different way from anyone else. And all the nicer because of the difference, too. (*His voice becomes low and husky. Laura turns away, nearly faint with the novelty of her emotions.*) I wish that you were my sister. I'd teach you to have some confidence in yourself. The different people are not like other people, but being different is nothing to be ashamed of. Because other people are not such wonderful people. They're one hundred times one thousand. You're one times one! They walk all over the earth. You just stay here. They're common as—weeds, but—you—well, you're—*Blue Roses!*

*(Image On Screen: Blue Roses.)*

*(Music Changes.)*

LAURA:   But blue is wrong for—roses . . .
JIM:   It's right for you—You're—pretty!
LAURA:   In what respect am I pretty?
JIM:   In all respects—believe me! Your eyes—your hair—are pretty! Your hands are pretty! (*He catches hold of her hand.*) You think I'm making this up because I'm invited to dinner and have to be nice. Oh, I could do that! I could put on an act for you, Laura, and say lots of things without being very sincere. But this time I am. I'm talking to you sincerely. I happened to notice you had this inferiority complex that keeps you from feeling comfortable with people. Somebody needs to build your confidence up and make you proud instead of shy and turning away and—blushing—Somebody ought to—ought to—*kiss* you, Laura! (*His hand slips slowly up her arm to her shoulder.*) **(Music Swells Tumultuously.)** (*He suddenly turns her about and kisses her on the lips. When he releases her Laura sinks on the sofa with a bright, dazed look. Jim backs away and fishes in his pocket for a cigarette.*) **(Legend On Screen: "Souvenir.")** Stumble-john! (*He lights the cigarette, avoiding her look. There is a peal of girlish laughter from Amanda in the kitchen. Laura slowly raises and opens her hand. It still contains the little broken glass animal. She looks at it with a tender, bewildered expression.*) Stumble-john! I shouldn't have done that—That was way off the beam. You don't smoke, do you? (*She looks up, smiling, not hearing the question. He sits beside her a little gingerly. She looks at him speechlessly—waiting. He coughs decorously and moves a little farther aside as he considers the situation and senses her feelings, dimly, with perturbation. Gently.*) Would you—care for a—mint? (*She doesn't seem to hear him but her look grows brighter even.*) Peppermint—Life Saver? My pocket's a regular drug store— wherever I go . . . (*He pops a mint in his mouth. Then gulps and*

*decides to make a clean breast of it. He speaks slowly and gingerly.*)
Laura, you know, if I had a sister like you, I'd do the same
thing as Tom. I'd bring out fellows—introduce her to them.
The right type of boys of a type to—appreciate her. Only—
well—he made a mistake about me. Maybe I've got no call to
be saying this. That may not have been the idea in having me
over. But what if it was? There's nothing wrong about that.
The only trouble is that in my case—I'm not in a situation to—
do the right thing. I can't take down your number and say I'll
phone. I can't call up next week and—ask for a date. I thought
I had better explain the situation in case you misunderstood
it and—hurt your feelings. . . . (*Pause. Slowly, very slowly,
Laura's look changes, her eyes returning slowly from his to the
ornament in her palm.*)

*Amanda utters another gay laugh in the kitchen.*

LAURA (*faintly*):   You—won't—call again?
JIM:   No, Laura, I can't. (*He rises from the sofa.*) As I was just
explaining. I've—got strings on me, Laura, I've—been going
steady! I go out all the time with a girl named Betty. She's a
home-girl like you, and Catholic, and Irish, and in a great
many ways we—get along fine. I met her last summer on a
moonlight boat trip up the river to Alton, on the *Majestic*.
Well—right away from the start it was—love! (**Legend:
Love!**) (*Laura sways slightly forward and grips the arm of the sofa.
He fails to notice, now enrapt in his own comfortable being.*) Being
in love has made a new man of me! (*Leaning stiffly forward,
clutching the arm of the sofa, Laura struggles visibly with her storm.
But Jim is oblivious, she is a long way off.*) The power of love is
really pretty tremendous! Love is something that—changes the
whole world, Laura! (*The storm abates a little and Laura leans
back. He notices her again.*) It happened that Betty's aunt took
sick, she got a wire and had to go to Centralia. So Tom—when
he asked me to dinner—I naturally just accepted the invitation,
not knowing that you—that he—that I—(*He stops awkwardly.*)
Huh—I'm a stumble-john! (*He flops back on the sofa. The. holy
candles in the altar of Laura's face have been snuffed out! There is a
look of almost infinite desolation. Jim glances at her uneasily.*) I wish
that you would—say something. (*She bites her lip which was*

*trembling and then bravely smiles. She opens her hand again on the broken glass ornament. Then she gently takes his hand and raises it level with her own. She carefully places the unicorn in the palm of his hand, then pushes his fingers closed upon it.*) What are you— doing that for? You want me to have him?—Laura? (*She nods.*) What for?

LAURA:   A—souvenir . . .

*She rises unsteadily and crouches beside the victrola to wind it up.*

**(Legend On Screen: "Things Have A Way Of Turning Out So Badly.")**

**(Or Image: "Gentleman Caller Waving Good-Bye!—Gaily.")**

*At this moment Amanda rushes brightly back in the front room. She bears a pitcher of fruit punch in an old-fashioned cut-glass pitcher and a plate of macaroons. The plate has a gold border and poppies painted on it.*

AMANDA:   Well, well, well! Isn't the air delightful after the shower? I've made you children a little liquid refreshment. (*Turns gaily to the gentleman caller.*) Jim, do you know that song about lemonade?

"Lemonade, lemonade
Made in the shade and stirred with a spade—
Good enough for any old maid!"

JIM (*uneasily*):   Ha-ha! No—I never heard it.
AMANDA:   Why, Laura! You look so serious!
JIM:   We were having a serious conversation.
AMANDA:   Good! Now you're better acquainted!
JIM (*uncertainly*):   Ha-ha! Yes.
AMANDA:   You modern young people are much more serious- minded than my generation. I was so gay as a girl!
JIM:   You haven't changed, Mrs. Wingfield.
AMANDA:   Tonight I'm rejuvenated! The gaiety of the occasion, Mr. O'Connor! (*She tosses her head with a peal of laughter. Spills lemonade.*) Oooo! I'm baptizing myself!
JIM:   Here—let me—

AMANDA (*setting the pitcher down*):   There now. I discovered we had some maraschino cherries. I dumped them in, juice and all!

JIM:   You shouldn't have gone to that trouble, Mrs. Wingfield.

AMANDA:   Trouble, trouble? Why it was loads of fun! Didn't you hear me cutting up in the kitchen? I bet your ears were burning! I told Tom how outdone with him I was for keeping you to himself so long a time! He should have brought you over much, much sooner! Well, now that you've found your way, I want you to be a very frequent caller! Not just occasional but all the time. Oh, we're going to have a lot of gay times together! I see them coming! Mmm, just breathe that air! So fresh, and the moon's so pretty! I'll skip back out—I know where my place is when young folks are having a—serious conversation!

JIM:   Oh, don't go out, Mrs. Wingfield. The fact of the matter is I've got to be going.

AMANDA:   Going, now? You're joking! Why, it's only the shank of the evening, Mr. O'Connor!

JIM:   Well, you know how it is.

AMANDA:   You mean you're a young workingman and have to keep workingmen's hours. We'll let you off early tonight. But only on the condition that next time you stay later. What's the best night for you? Isn't Saturday night the best night for you workingmen?

JIM:   I have a couple of time-clocks to punch, Mrs. Wingfield. One at morning, another one at night!

AMANDA:   My, but you *are* ambitious! You work at night, too?

JIM:   No, Ma'am, not work but—Betty! (*He crosses deliberately to pick up his hat. The band at the Paradise Dance Hall goes into a tender waltz.*)

AMANDA:   Betty? Betty? Who's—Betty! (*There is an ominous cracking sound in the sky.*)

JIM:   Oh, just a girl. The girl I go steady with! (*He smiles charmingly. The sky falls.*)

**(Legend: "The Sky Falls.")**

AMANDA (*a long-drawn exhalation*):   Ohhhh . . . Is it a serious romance, Mr. O'Connor?

JIM:   We're going to be married the second Sunday in June.

AMANDA:   Ohhhh—how nice! Tom didn't mention that you were engaged to be married.

JIM:   The cat's not out of the bag at the warehouse yet. You know how they are. They call you Romeo and stuff like that. (*He stops at the oval mirror to put on his hat. He carefully shapes the brim and the crown to give a discreetly dashing effect.*) It's been a wonderful evening, Mrs. Wingfield. I guess this is what they mean by Southern hospitality.

AMANDA:   It really wasn't anything at all.

JIM:   I hope it don't seem like I'm rushing off. But I promised Betty I'd pick her up at the Wabash depot, an' by the time I get my jalopy down there her train'll be in. Some women are pretty upset if you keep 'em waiting.

AMANDA:   Yes, I know—The tyranny of women! (*Extends her hand.*) Goodbye, Mr. O'Connor. I wish you luck—and happiness—and success! All three of them, and so does Laura!— Don't you, Laura?

LAURA:   Yes!

JIM (*taking her hand*):   Goodbye, Laura. I'm certainly going to treasure that souvenir. And don't you forget the good advice I gave you. (*Raises his voice to a cheery shout.*) So long, Shakespeare! Thanks again, ladies—Good night!

*He grins and ducks jauntily out.*

*Still bravely grimacing, Amanda closes the door on the gentleman caller. Then she turns back to the room with a puzzled expression. She and Laura don't dare to face each other. Laura crouches beside the victrola to wind it.*

AMANDA (*faintly*):   Things have a way of turning out so badly. I don't believe that I would play the victrola. Well, well—well— Our gentleman caller was engaged to be married! Tom!

TOM (*from back*):   Yes, Mother?

AMANDA:   Come in here a minute. I want to tell you something awfully funny.

TOM (*enters with macaroon and a glass of the lemonade*):   Has the gentleman caller gotten away already?

AMANDA:   The gentleman caller has made an early departure. What a wonderful joke you played on us!

TOM:   How do you mean?

AMANDA:   You didn't mention that he was engaged to be married.

TOM:   Jim? Engaged?

AMANDA:   That's what he just informed us.

TOM:   I'll be jiggered! I didn't know about that.

AMANDA:   That seems very peculiar.

TOM:   What's peculiar about it?

AMANDA:   Didn't you call him your best friend down at the warehouse?

TOM:   He is, but how did I know?

AMANDA:   It seems extremely peculiar that you wouldn't know your best friend was going to be married!

TOM:   The warehouse is where I work, not where I know things about people!

AMANDA:   You don't know things anywhere! You live in a dream; you manufacture illusions! (*He crosses to door.*) Where are you going?

TOM:   I'm going to the movies.

AMANDA:   That's right, now that you've had us make such fools of ourselves. The effort, the preparations, all the expense! The new floor lamp, the rug, the clothes for Laura! All for what? To entertain some other girl's fiancé! Go to the movies, go! Don't think about us, a mother deserted, an unmarried sister who's crippled and has no job! Don't let anything interfere with your selfish pleasure! Just go, go, go—to the movies!

TOM:   All right, I will! The more you shout about my selfishness to me the quicker I'll go, and I won't go to the movies!

AMANDA:   Go, then! Then go to the moon—you selfish dreamer!

*Tom smashes his glass on the floor. He plunges out on the fire-escape, slamming the door. Laura screams—cut by door.*

*Dance-hall music up. Tom goes to the rail and grips it desperately, lifting his face in the chill white moonlight penetrating the narrow abyss of the alley.*

**(Legend On Screen: "And So Good-Bye . . .")**

*Tom's closing speech is timed with the interior pantomime. The interior scene is played as though viewed through sound-proof glass. Amanda appears to be making a comforting speech to Laura who is huddled upon the sofa. Now that we cannot hear the mother's speech, her silliness is gone and she has dignity and tragic beauty. Laura's dark hair hides her face until at the end of the speech she lifts it to smile at her mother. Amanda's gestures are slow and graceful, almost dancelike, as she comforts the daughter. At the end of her speech she glances a moment at the father's picture—then withdraws through the portieres. At close of Tom's speech, Laura blows out the candles, ending the play.*

TOM:   I didn't go to the moon, I went much further—for time is the longest distance between two places—Not long after that I was fired for writing a poem on the lid of a shoe-box. I left Saint Louis. I descended the steps of this fire-escape for a last time and followed, from then on, in my father's footsteps, attempting to find in motion what was lost in space—I traveled around a great deal. The cities swept about me like dead leaves, leaves that were brightly colored but torn away from the branches. I would have stopped, but I was pursued by something. It always came upon me unawares, taking me altogether by surprise. Perhaps it was a familiar bit of music. Perhaps it was only a piece of transparent glass—Perhaps I am walking along a street at night, in some strange city, before I have found companions. I pass the lighted window of a shop where perfume is sold. The window is filled with pieces of colored glass, tiny transparent bottles in delicate colors, like bits of a shattered rainbow. Then all at once my sister touches my shoulder. I turn around and look into her eyes . . . Oh, Laura, Laura, I tried to leave you behind me, but I am more faithful than I intended to be! I reach for a cigarette, I cross the street, I run into the movies or a bar, I buy a drink, I speak to the nearest stranger—anything that can blow your candles out! *(Laura bends over the candles.)*—for nowadays the world is lit by lightning! Blow out your candles, Laura—and so goodbye . . .

*She blows the candles out.*

**(The Scene Dissolves.)**

## PRODUCTION NOTES

Being a "memory play," *The Glass Menagerie* can be presented with
unusual freedom of convention. Because of its considerably delicate or tenuous material, atmospheric touches and subtleties of
direction play a particularly important part. Expressionism and all
other unconventional techniques in drama have only one valid
aim, and that is a closer approach to truth. When a play employs
unconventional techniques, it is not, or certainly shouldn't be,
trying to escape its responsibility of dealing with reality, or interpreting experience, but is actually or should be attempting to find
a closer approach, a more penetrating and vivid expression of
things as they are. The straight realistic play with its genuine
frigidaire and authentic ice cubes, its characters that speak exactly
as its audience speaks, corresponds to the academic landscape and
has the same virtue of a photographic likeness. Everyone should
know nowadays the unimportance of the photographic in art: that
truth, life, or reality is an organic thing which the poetic imagination can represent or suggest, in essence, only through transformation, through changing into other forms than those which
were merely present in appearance.

These remarks are not meant as comments only on this particular play. They have to do with a conception of a new, plastic
theater which must take the place of the exhausted theater of
realistic conventions if the theater is to resume vitality as a part of
our culture.

## The Screen Device

There is *only one important difference between the original and acting
version of the play* and that is the *omission* in the latter of the device
which I tentatively included in my *original* script. This device was
the use of a screen on which were projected magic-lantern slides
bearing images or titles. I do not regret the omission of this device
from the . . . Broadway production. The extraordinary power of
Miss Taylor's performance made it suitable to have the utmost
simplicity in the physical production. But I think it may be interesting to some readers to see how this device was conceived. So
I am putting it into the published manuscript. These images and
legends, projected from behind, were cast on a section of wall

between the front-room and dining-room areas, which should be indistinguishable from the rest when not in use.

The purpose of this will probably be apparent. It is to give accent to certain values in each scene. Each scene contains a particular point (or several) which is structurally the most important. In an episodic play, such as this, the basic structure or narrative line may be obscured from the audience; the effect may seem fragmentary rather than architectural. This may not be the fault of the play so much as a lack of attention in the audience. The legend or image upon the screen will strengthen the effect of what is merely allusion in the writing and allow the primary point to be made more simply and lightly than if the entire responsibility were on the spoken lines. Aside from this structural value, I think the screen will have a definite emotional appeal, less definable but just as important. An imaginative producer or director may invent many other uses for this device than those indicated in the present script. In fact the possibilities of the device seem much larger to me than the instance of this play can possibly utilize.

## The Music

Another extra-literary accent in this play is provided by the use of music. A single recurring tune, "The Glass Menagerie," is used to give emotional emphasis to suitable passages. This tune is like circus music, not when you are on the grounds or in the immediate vicinity of the parade, but when you are at some distance and very likely thinking of something else. It seems under those circumstances to continue almost interminably and it weaves in and out of your preoccupied consciousness; then it is the lightest, most delicate music in the world and perhaps the saddest. It expresses the surface vivacity of life with the underlying strain of immutable and inexpressible sorrow. When you look at a piece of delicately spun glass you think of two things: how beautiful it is and how easily it can be broken. Both of those ideas should be woven into the recurring tune, which dips in and out of the play as if it were carried on a wind that changes. It serves as a thread of connection and allusion between the narrator with his separate point in time and space and the subject of his story. Between each episode it returns as reference to the emotion, nostalgia, which is the first condition of the play. It is primarily Laura's music and therefore comes out most clearly when the play focuses upon her and the lovely fragility of glass which is her image.

## The Lighting

The lighting in the play is not realistic. In keeping with the atmosphere of memory, the stage is dim. Shafts of light are focused on selected areas or actors, sometimes in contradistinction to what is the apparent center. For instance, in the quarrel scene between Tom and Amanda, in which Laura has no active part, the clearest pool of light is on her figure. This is also true of the supper scene. The light upon Laura should be distinct from the others, having a peculiar pristine clarity such as light used in early religious portraits of female saints or madonnas. A certain correspondence to light in religious paintings, such as El Greco's,[10] where the figures are radiant in atmosphere that is relatively dusky, could be effectively used throughout the play. (It will also permit a more effective use of the screen.) A free, imaginative use of light can be of enormous value in giving a mobile, plastic quality to plays of a more or less static nature.

---

[10] A Greek painter [1541–1614] who worked mostly in Spain and was known for his use of unearthly lighting in his works.

# EUGÈNE IONESCO [b. 1912]

# The Lesson

## The Characters

THE PROFESSOR, *aged 50 to 60*
THE YOUNG PUPIL, *aged 18*
THE MAID, *aged 45 to 50*


S C E N E:  *The office of the old professor, which also serves as a dining room. To the left, a door opens onto the apartment stairs; upstage, to the right, another door opens onto a corridor of the apartment. Upstage, a little left of center, a window, not very large, with plain curtains; on the outside sill of the window are ordinary potted plants. The low buildings with red roofs of a small town can be seen in the distance. The sky is grayish-blue. On the right stands a provincial buffet. The table doubles as a desk, it stands at stage center. There are three chairs around the table, and two more stand on each side of the window. Light-colored wallpaper, some shelves with books.*

[*When the curtain rises the stage is empty, and it remains so for a few moments. Then we hear the doorbell ring.*]

VOICE OF THE MAID [*from the corridor*]:   Yes. I'm coming.

[*The Maid comes in, after having run down the stairs. She is stout, aged 45 to 50, red-faced, and wears a peasant woman's cap. She rushes in, slamming the door to the right behind her, and dries her hands on her apron as she runs towards the door on the left. Meanwhile we hear the doorbell ring again.*]

MAID:   Just a moment, I'm coming.

[*She opens the door. A young Pupil, aged 18, enters. She is wearing a gray student's smock, a small white collar, and carries a student's satchel under her arm.*]

---

Translated by Donald M. Allen.

MAID:   Good morning, miss.
PUPIL:   Good morning, madam. Is the Professor at home?
MAID:   Have you come for the lesson?
PUPIL:   Yes, I have.
MAID:   He's expecting you. Sit down for a moment. I'll tell him you're here.
PUPIL:   Thank you.

[*She seats herself near the table, facing the audience; the hall door is to her left; her back is to the door, through which the Maid hurriedly exits, calling:*]
MAID:   Professor, come down please, your pupil is here.
VOICE OF THE PROFESSOR [*rather reedy*]:   Thank you. I'm coming . . . in just a moment . . .

[*The Maid exits; the Pupil draws in her legs, holds her satchel on her lap, and waits demurely. She casts a glance or two around the room, at the furniture, at the ceiling too. Then she takes a notebook out of her satchel, leafs through it, and stops to look at a page for a moment as though reviewing a lesson, as though taking a last look at her homework. She seems to be a well-brought-up girl, polite, but lively, gay, dynamic; a fresh smile is on her lips. During the course of the play she progressively loses the lively rhythm of her movement and her carriage, she becomes withdrawn. From gay and smiling she becomes progressively sad and morose; from very lively at the beginning, she becomes more and more fatigued and somnolent. Towards the end of the play her face must clearly express a nervous depression; her way of speaking shows the effects of this, her tongue becomes thick, words come to her memory with difficulty and emerge from her mouth with as much difficulty; she comes to have a manner vaguely paralyzed, the beginning of aphasia. Firm and determined at the beginning, so much so as to appear to be almost aggressive, she becomes more and more passive, until she is almost a mute and inert object, seemingly inanimate in the Professor's hands, to such an extent that when he makes his final gesture, she no longer reacts. Insensible, her reflexes deadened, only her eyes in an expressionless face will show inexpressible astonishment and fear. The transition from one manner to the other must of course be made imperceptibly.*

*The Professor enters. He is a little old man with a little white beard. He wears pince-nez, a black skullcap, a long black schoolmaster's coat, trousers and shoes of black, detachable white collar, a black tie. Excessively polite, very timid, his voice deadened by his timidity, very proper, very much the teacher. He rubs his hands together constantly; occasionally a lewd gleam comes into his eyes and is quickly repressed.*

*During the course of the play his timidity will disappear progressively, imperceptibly; and the lewd gleams in his eyes will become a steady devouring flame in the end. From a manner that is inoffensive at the start, the Professor becomes more and more sure of himself, more and more nervous, aggressive, dominating, until he is able to do as he pleases with the Pupil, who has become, in his hands, a pitiful creature. Of course, the voice of the Professor must change too, from thin and reedy, to stronger and stronger, until at the end it is extremely powerful, ringing, sonorous, while the Pupil's voice changes from the very clear and ringing tones that she has at the beginning of the play until it is almost inaudible. In these first scenes the Professor might stammer very slightly.]*

PROFESSOR:   Good morning, young lady. You . . . I expect that you . . . that you are the new pupil?

PUPIL [*turns quickly with a lively and self-assured manner; she gets up, goes toward the Professor, and gives him her hand*]:   Yes, Professor. Good morning, Professor. As you see, I'm on time. I didn't want to be late.

PROFESSOR:   That's fine, miss. Thank you, you didn't really need to hurry. I am very sorry to have kept you waiting . . . I was just finishing up . . . well . . . I'm sorry . . . You will excuse me, won't you? . . .

PUPIL:   Oh, certainly, Professor. It doesn't matter at all, Professor.

PROFESSOR:   Please excuse me . . . Did you have any trouble finding the house?

PUPIL:   No . . . Not at all. I just asked the way. Everybody knows you around here.

PROFESSOR:   For thirty years I've lived in this town. You've not been here for long? How do you find it?

PUPIL:   It's all right. The town is attractive and even agreeable, there's a nice park, a boarding school, a bishop, nice shops and streets . . .

PROFESSOR:   That's very true, young lady. And yet, I'd just as soon live somewhere else. In Paris, or at least Bordeaux.

PUPIL:   Do you like Bordeaux?

PROFESSOR:   I don't know. I've never seen it.

PUPIL:   But you know Paris?

PROFESSOR:   No, I don't know it either, young lady, but if you'll permit me, can you tell me, Paris is the capital city of . . . miss?

PUPIL [*searching her memory for a moment, then, happily guessing*]:   Paris is the capital city of . . . France?

PROFESSOR:   Yes, young lady, bravo, that's very good, that's perfect. My congratulations. You have your French geography at your finger tips. You know your chief cities.

PUPIL:   Oh! I don't know them all yet, Professor, it's not quite that easy, I have trouble learning them.

PROFESSOR:   Oh! it will come . . . you mustn't give up . . . young lady . . . I beg your pardon . . . have patience . . . little by little . . . You will see, it will come in time . . . What a nice day it is today . . . or rather, not so nice . . . Oh! but then yes it is nice. In short, it's not too bad a day, that's the main thing . . . ahem . . . ahem . . . it's not raining and it's not snowing either.

PUPIL:   That would be most unusual, for it's summer now.

PROFESSOR:   Excuse me, miss I was just going to say so . . . but as you will learn, one must be ready for anything.

PUPIL:   I guess so, Professor.

PROFESSOR:   We can't be sure of anything, young lady, in this world.

PUPIL:   The snow falls in the winter. Winter is one of the four seasons. The other three are . . . uh . . . spr . . .

PROFESSOR:   Yes?

PUPIL:   . . . ing, and then summer . . . and . . . uh . . .

PROFESSOR:   It begins like "automobile," miss.

PUPIL:   Ah, yes, autumn . . .

PROFESSOR:   That's right miss. That's a good answer, that's perfect. I am convinced that you will be a good pupil. You will make real progress. You are intelligent, you seem to me to be well informed, and you've a good memory.

PUPIL:   I know my seasons, don't I, Professor?

PROFESSOR:   Yes, indeed, miss . . . or almost. But it will come in time. In any case, you're coming along. Soon you'll know all the seasons, even with your eyes closed. Just as I do.

PUPIL: It's hard.

PROFESSOR: Oh, no. All it takes is a little effort, a little good will, miss. You will see. It will come, you may be sure of that.

PUPIL: Oh, I do hope so, Professor. I have a great thirst for knowledge. My parents also want me to get an education. They want me to specialize. They consider a little general culture, even if it is solid, is no longer enough, in these times.

PROFESSOR: Your parents, miss, are perfectly right. You must go on with your studies. Forgive me for saying so, but it is very necessary. Our contemporary life has become most complex.

PUPIL: And so very complicated too . . . My parents are fairly rich, I'm lucky. They can help me in my work, help me in my very advanced studies.

PROFESSOR: And you wish to qualify for . . . ?

PUPIL: Just as soon as possible, for the first doctor's orals. They're in three weeks' time.

PROFESSOR: You already have your high school diploma, if you'll pardon the question?

PUPIL: Yes, Professor, I have my science diploma and my arts diploma, too.

PROFESSOR: Ah, you're very far advanced, even perhaps too advanced for your age. And which doctorate do you wish to qualify for? In the physical sciences or in moral philosophy?

PUPIL: My parents are very much hoping—if you think it will be possible in such a short time—they very much hope that I can qualify for the total doctorate.

PROFESSOR: The total doctorate? . . . You have great courage, young lady, I congratulate you sincerely. We will try, miss, to do our best. In any case, you already know quite a bit, and at so young an age too.

PUPIL: Oh, Professor.

PROFESSOR: Then, if you'll permit me, pardon me, please, I do think that we ought to get to work. We have scarcely any time to lose.

PUPIL: Oh, but certainly, Professor, I want to. I beg you to.

PROFESSOR: Then, may I ask you to sit down . . . there . . . Will you permit me, miss, that is if you have no objections, to sit down opposite you?

PUPIL: Oh, of course, Professor, please do.

PROFESSOR:  Thank you very much, miss. [*They sit down facing each other at the table, their profiles to the audience.*] There we are. Now have you brought your books and notebooks?

PUPIL [*taking notebooks and books out of her satchel*]:  Yes, Professor. Certainly, I have brought all that we'll need.

PROFESSOR:  Perfect, miss. This is perfect. Now, if this doesn't bore you . . . shall we begin?

PUPIL:  Yes, indeed, Professor, I am at your disposal.

PROFESSOR:  At my disposal? [*A gleam comes into his eyes and is quickly extinguished; he begins to make a gesture that he suppresses at once.*] Oh, miss, it is I who am at *your* disposal. I am only your humble servant.

PUPIL:  Oh, Professor . . .

PROFESSOR:  If you will . . . now . . . we . . . we . . . I . . . I will begin by making a brief examination of your knowledge, past and present, so that we may chart our future course . . . Good. How is your perception of plurality?

PUPIL:  It's rather vague . . . confused.

PROFESSOR:  Good. We shall see.

[*He rubs his hands together. The Maid enters, and this appears to irritate the Professor. She goes to the buffet and looks for something, lingering.*]

PROFESSOR:  Now, miss, would you like to do a little arithmetic, that is if you want to . . .

PUPIL:  Oh, yes, Professor. Certainly, I ask nothing better.

PROFESSOR:  It is rather a new science, a modern science, properly speaking, it is more a method than a science . . . And it is also a therapy. [*To the Maid:*] Have you finished, Marie?

MAID:  Yes, Professor, I've found the plate. I'm just going . . .

PROFESSOR:  Hurry up then. Please go along to the kitchen, if you will.

MAID:  Yes, Professor, I'm going. [*She starts to go out.*] Excuse me, Professor, but take care, I urge you to remain calm.

PROFESSOR:  You're being ridiculous, Marie. Now, don't worry.

MAID:  That's what you always say.

PROFESSOR:  I will not stand for your insinuations. I know perfectly well how to comport myself. I am old enough for that.

MAID:   Precisely, Professor. You will do better not to start the young lady on arithmetic. Arithmetic is tiring, exhausting.

PROFESSOR:   Not at my age. And anyhow, what business is it of yours? This is my concern. And I know what I'm doing. This is not your department.

MAID:   Very well, Professor. But you can't say that I didn't warn you.

PROFESSOR:   Marie, I can get along without your advice.

MAID:   As you wish, Professor. [*She exits.*]

PROFESSOR:   Miss, I hope you'll pardon this absurd interruption . . . Excuse this woman . . . She is always afraid that I'll tire myself. She fusses over my health.

PUPIL:   Oh, that's quite all right, Professor. It shows that she's very devoted. She loves you very much. Good servants are rare.

PROFESSOR:   She exaggerates. Her fears are stupid. But let's return to our arithmetical knitting.

PUPIL:   I'm following you, Professor.

PROFESSOR [*wittily*]:   Without leaving your seat!

PUPIL [*appreciating his joke*]:   Like you, Professor.

PROFESSOR:   Good. Let us arithmetize a little now.

PUPIL:   Yes, gladly, Professor.

PROFESSOR:   It wouldn't be too tiresome for you to tell me . . .

PUPIL:   Not at all, Professor, go on.

PROFESSOR:   How much are one and one?

PUPIL:   One and one make two.

PROFESSOR [*marveling at the Pupil's knowledge*]:   Oh, but that's very good. You appear to me to be well along in your studies. You should easily achieve the total doctorate, miss.

PUPIL:   I'm so glad. Especially to have someone like you tell me this.

PROFESSOR:   Let's push on: how much are two and one?

PUPIL:   Three.

PROFESSOR:   Three and one?

PUPIL:   Four.

PROFESSOR:   Four and one?

PUPIL:   Five.

PROFESSOR:   Five and one?

PUPIL:   Six.

PROFESSOR:   Six and one?

PUPIL:   Seven.

PROFESSOR:   Seven and one?

PUPIL:   Eight.

PROFESSOR:   Seven and one?

PUPIL:   Eight again.

PROFESSOR:   Very well answered. Seven and one?

PUPIL:   Eight once more.

PROFESSOR:   Perfect. Excellent. Seven and one?

PUPIL:   Eight again. And sometimes nine.

PROFESSOR:   Magnificent. You are magnificent. You are exquisite. I congratulate you warmly, miss. There's scarcely any point in going on. At addition you are a past master. Now, let's look at subtraction. Tell me, if you are not exhausted, how many are four minus three?

PUPIL:   Four minus three? . . . Four minus three?

PROFESSOR:   Yes. I mean to say: subtract three from four.

PUPIL:   That makes . . . seven?

PROFESSOR:   I am sorry but I'm obliged to contradict you. Four minus three does not make seven. You are confused: four plus three makes seven, four minus three does not make seven . . . This is not addition anymore, we must subtract now.

PUPIL [*trying to understand*]:   Yes . . . yes . . .

PROFESSOR:   Four minus three makes . . . How many? . . . How many?

PUPIL:   Four?

PROFESSOR:   No, miss, that's not it.

PUPIL:   Three, then.

PROFESSOR:   Not that either, miss . . . Pardon, I'm sorry . . . I ought to say, that's not it . . . excuse me.

PUPIL:   Four minus three . . . Four minus three . . . Four minus three? . . . But now doesn't that make ten?

PROFESSOR:   Oh, certainly not, miss. It's not a matter of guessing, you've got to think it out. Let's try to deduce it together. Would you like to count?

PUPIL:   Yes, Professor. One . . . two . . . uh . . .

PROFESSOR:   You know how to count? How far can you count up to?

PUPIL:   I can count to . . . to infinity.

PROFESSOR:   That's not possible, miss.

PUPIL:   Well then, let's say to sixteen.

PROFESSOR:   That is enough. One must know one's limits. Count then, if you will, please.

PUPIL:   One . . . two . . . and after two, comes three . . . then four . . .

PROFESSOR:   Stop there, miss. Which number is larger? Three or four?

PUPIL:   Uh . . . three or four? Which is the larger? The larger of three or four? In what sense larger?

PROFESSOR:   Some numbers are smaller and others are larger. In the larger numbers there are more units than in the small . . .

PUPIL:   Than in the small numbers?

PROFESSOR:   Unless the small ones have smaller units. If they are very small, then there might be more units in the small numbers than in the large . . . if it is a question of other units . . .

PUPIL:   In that case, the small numbers can be larger than the large numbers?

PROFESSOR:   Let's not go into that. That would take us much too far. You must realize simply that more than numbers are involved here . . . there are also magnitudes, totals, there are groups, there are heaps, heaps of such things as plums, trucks, geese, prune pits, etc. To facilitate our work, let's merely suppose that we have only equal numbers, then the bigger numbers will be those that have the most units.

PUPIL:   The one that has the most is the biggest? Ah, I understand, Professor, you are identifying quality with quantity.

PROFESSOR:   That is too theoretical, miss, too theoretical. You needn't concern yourself with that. Let us take an example and reason from a definite case. Let's leave the general conclusions for later. We have the number four and the number three, and each has always the same number of units. Which number will be larger, the smaller or the larger?

PUPIL:   Excuse me, Professor . . . What do you mean by the larger number? Is it the one that is not so small as the other?

PROFESSOR:   That's it, miss, perfect. You have understood me very well.

PUPIL:   Then, it is four.

PROFESSOR:   What is four—larger or smaller than three?

PUPIL:   Smaller . . . no, larger.

PROFESSOR:   Excellent answer. How many units are there between three and four? . . . Or between four and three, if you prefer?

PUPIL:   There aren't any units, Professor, between three and four. Four comes immediately after three; there is nothing at all between three and four!

PROFESSOR:   I haven't made myself very well understood. No doubt, it is my fault. I've not been sufficiently clear.

PUPIL:   No, Professor, it's my fault.

PROFESSOR:   Look here. Here are three matches. And here is another one, that makes four. Now watch carefully—we have four matches. I take one away, now how many are left?

[*We don't see the matches, nor any of the objects that are mentioned. The Professor gets up from the table, writes on the imaginary blackboard with an imaginary piece of chalk, etc.*]

PUPIL:   Five. If three and one make four, four and one make five.

PROFESSOR:   That's not it. That's not it at all. You always have a tendency to add. But one must be able to subtract too. It's not enough to integrate, you must also disintegrate. That's the way life is. That's philosophy. That's science. That's progress, civilization.

PUPIL:   Yes, Professor.

PROFESSOR:   Let's return to our matches. I have four of them. You see, there are really four. I take one away, and there remain only . . .

PUPIL:   I don't know, Professor.

PROFESSOR:   Come now, think. It's not easy, I admit. Nevertheless, you've had enough training to make the intellectual effort required to arrive at an understanding. So?

PUPIL:   I can't get it, Professor. I don't know, Professor.

PROFESSOR:   Let us take a simpler example. If you had two noses, and I pulled one of them off . . . how many would you have left?

PUPIL:   None.

PROFESSOR:   What do you mean, none?

PUPIL:   Yes, it's because you haven't pulled off any, that's why I have one now. If you had pulled it off, I wouldn't have it anymore.

PROFESSOR:   You've not understood my example. Suppose that you have only one ear.

PUPIL:   Yes, and then?

PROFESSOR:   If I gave you another one, how many would you have then?

PUPIL:   Two.

PROFESSOR:   Good. And if I gave you still another ear. How many would you have then?

PUPIL:   Three ears.

PROFESSOR:   Now, I take one away . . . and there remain . . . how many ears?

PUPIL:   Two.

PROFESSOR:   Good. I take away still another one, how many do you have left?

PUPIL:   Two.

PROFESSOR:   No. You have two, I take one away, I eat one up, then how many do you have left?

PUPIL:   Two.

PROFESSOR:   I eat one of them . . . one.

PUPIL:   Two.

PROFESSOR:   One.

PUPIL:   Two.

PROFESSOR:   One!

PUPIL:   Two!

PROFESSOR:   One!!!

PUPIL:   Two!!!

PROFESSOR:   One!!!

PUPIL:   Two!!!

PROFESSOR:   One!!!

PUPIL:   Two!!!

PROFESSOR:   No. No. That's not right. The example is not . . . it's not convincing. Listen to me.

PUPIL:   Yes, Professor.

PROFESSOR:   You've got . . . you've got . . . you've got . . .

PUPIL:   Ten fingers!

PROFESSOR:   If you wish. Perfect. Good. You have then ten fingers.

PUPIL:   Yes, Professor.

PROFESSOR:   How many would you have if you had only five of them?

PUPIL:   Ten, Professor.

PROFESSOR:   That's not right!

PUPIL:   But it is, Professor.

PROFESSOR:   I tell you it's not!

PUPIL:   You just told me that I had ten . . .

PROFESSOR:   I also said, immediately afterwards, that you had five!

PUPIL:   I don't have five, I've got ten!

PROFESSOR:   Let's try another approach . . . for purposes of subtraction let's limit ourselves to the numbers from one to five . . . Wait now, miss, you'll soon see. I'm going to make you understand.

[*The Professor begins to write on the imaginary blackboard. He moves it closer to the pupil, who turns around in order to see it.*]

PROFESSOR:   Look here, miss . . . [*He pretends to draw a stick on the blackboard and the number 1 below the stick; then two sticks and the number 2 below, then three sticks and the number 3 below, then four sticks with the number 4 below.*] You see . . .

PUPIL:   Yes, Professor.

PROFESSOR:   These are sticks, miss, sticks. This is one stick, these are two sticks, and three sticks, then four sticks, then five sticks. One stick, two sticks, three sticks, four and five sticks, these are numbers. When we count the sticks, each stick is a unit, miss . . . What have I just said?

PUPIL:   "A unit, miss! What have I just said?"

PROFESSOR:   Or a figure! Or a number! One, two, three, four, five, these are the elements of numeration, miss.

PUPIL [*hesistant*]:   Yes, Professor. The elements, figures, which are sticks, units and numbers . . .

PROFESSOR:   At the same time . . . that's to say, in short—the whole of arithmetic is there.

PUPIL:   Yes, Professor. Good, Professor. Thanks, Professor.

PROFESSOR:   Now, count, if you will please, using these elements . . . add and subtract . . .

PUPIL [*as though trying to impress them on her memory*]:   Sticks are really figures and numbers are units?

PROFESSOR:   Hmm . . . so to speak. And then?

PUPIL:   One could subtract two units from three units, but can one subtract two twos from three threes? And two figures from four numbers? And three numbers from one unit?

PROFESSOR:   No, miss.

PUPIL:   Why, Professor?

PROFESSOR:   Because, miss.

PUPIL:   Because why, Professor? Since one is the same as the other?

PROFESSOR:   That's the way it is, miss. It can't be explained. This is only comprehensible through internal mathematical reasoning. Either you have it or you don't.

PUPIL:   So much the worse for me.

PROFESSOR:   Listen to me, miss, if you don't achieve a profound understanding of these principles, these arithmetical archetypes, you will never be able to perform correctly the functions of a polytechnician. Still less will you be able to teach a course in a polytechnical school . . . or the primary grades. I realize that this is not easy, it is very, very abstract . . . obviously . . . but unless you can comprehend the primary elements, how do you expect to be able to calculate mentally—and this is the least of the things that even an ordinary engineer must be able to do—how much, for example, are three billion seven hundred fifty-five million nine hundred ninety-eight thousand two hundred fifty-one, multiplied by five billion one hundred sixty-two million three hundred and three thousand five hundred and eight?

PUPIL [*very quickly*]:   That makes nineteen quintillion three hundred ninety quadrillion two trillion eight hundred forty-four billion two hundred nineteen million one hundred sixty-four thousand five hundred and eight . . .

PROFESSOR [*astonished*]:   No. I don't think so. That must make nineteen quintillion three hundred ninety quadrillion two trillion eight hundred forty-four billion two hundred nineteen million one hundred sixty-four thousand five hundred and nine . . .

PUPIL:   . . . No . . . five hundred and eight . . .

PROFESSOR [*more and more astonished, calculating mentally*]:   Yes . . . you are right . . . the result is indeed . . . [*He mumbles unintelligibly:*] . . . quintillion, quadrillion, trillion, billion, million . . . [*Clearly:*] one hundred sixty-four thousand five hundred and eight . . . [*Stupefied:*] But how did you know that, if you don't know the principles of arithmetical reasoning?

PUPIL:   It's easy. Not being able to rely on my reasoning, I've memorized all the products of all possible multiplications.

PROFESSOR: That's pretty good . . . However, permit me to confess to you that that doesn't satisfy me, miss, and I do not congratulate you: in mathematics and in arithmetic especially, the thing that counts—for in arithmetic it is always necessary to count—the thing that counts is, above all, understanding . . . It is by mathematical reasoning, simultaneously inductive and deductive, that you ought to arrive at this result—as well as at any other result. Mathematics is the sworn enemy of memory, which is excellent otherwise, but disastrous, arithmetically speaking! . . . That's why I'm not happy with this . . . this won't do, not at all . . .

PUPIL [*desolated*]: No, Professor.

PROFESSOR: Let's leave it for the moment. Let's go on to another exercise . . .

PUPIL: Yes, Professor.

MAID [*entering*]: Hmm, hmm, Professor . . .

PROFESSOR [*who doesn't hear her*]: It is unfortunate, miss, that you aren't further along in specialized mathematics . . .

MAID [*taking him by the sleeve*]: Professor! Professor!

PROFESSOR: I fear that you will not be able to qualify for the total doctor's orals . . .

PUPIL: Yes, Professor, it's too bad!

PROFESSOR: Unless you . . . [*To the Maid:*] Let me be, Marie . . . Look here, why are you bothering me? Go back to the kitchen! To your pots and pans! Go away! Go away! [*To the Pupil:*] We will try to prepare you at least for the partial doctorate . . .

MAID: Professor! . . . Professor! . . . [*She pulls his sleeve.*]

PROFESSOR [*to the Maid*]: Now leave me alone! Let me be! What's the meaning of this? . . . [*To the Pupil:*] I must therefore teach you, if you really do insist on attempting the partial doctorate . . .

PUPIL: Yes, Professor.

PROFESSOR: . . . The elements of linguistics and of comparative philology . . .

MAID: No, Professor, no! . . . You mustn't do that! . . .

PROFESSOR: Marie, you're going too far!

MAID: Professor, especially not philology, philology leads to calamity . . .

PUPIL [*astonished*]: To calamity? [*Smiling, a little stupidly:*] That's hard to believe.

PROFESSOR [*to the Maid*]:   That's enough now! Get out of here!
MAID:   All right, Professor, all right. But you can't say that I didn't warn you! Philology leads to calamity!
PROFESSOR:   I'm an adult, Marie!
PUPIL:   Yes, Professor.
MAID:   As you wish.

[*She exits.*]

PROFESSOR:   Let's continue, miss.
PUPIL:   Yes, Professor.
PROFESSOR:   I want you to listen now with the greatest possible attention to a lecture I have prepared . . .
PUPIL:   Yes, Professor!
PROFESSOR:   . . . Thanks to which, in fifteen minutes' time, you will be able to acquire the fundamental principles of the linguistic and comparative philology of the neo-Spanish languages.
PUPIL:   Yes, Professor, oh good!

[*She claps her hands.*]

PROFESSOR [*with authority*]:   Quiet! What do you mean by that?
PUPIL:   I'm sorry, Professor.

[*Slowly, she replaces her hands on the table.*]

PROFESSOR:   Quiet! [*He gets up, walks up and down the room, his hands behind his back; from time to time he stops at stage center or near the Pupil, and underlines his words with a gesture of his hand; he orates, but without being too emotional. The Pupil follows him with her eyes, occasionally with some difficulty, for she has to turn her head far around; once or twice, not more, she turns around completely.*] And now, miss, Spanish is truly the mother tongue which gave birth to all the neo-Spanish languages, of which Spanish, Latin, Italian, our own French, Portuguese, Romanian, Sardinian or Sardanapalian, Spanish and neo-Spanish—and also, in certain of its aspects, Turkish, which is otherwise very close to Greek, which is only logical, since it is a fact that Turkey is a neighbor of Greece and Greece is even closer to Turkey than you are to me—this is only one more illustration of the very important linguistic law which states that geography and philology are twin sisters . . . You may take notes, miss.

PUPIL [*in a dull voice*]:   Yes, Professor!

PROFESSOR:   That which distinguishes the neo-Spanish languages from each other and their idioms from other linguistic groups, such as the group of languages called Austrian and neo-Austrian or Hapsburgian, as well as the Esperanto, Helvetian, Monacan, Swiss, Andorran, Basque, and jai alai groups, and also the groups of diplomatic and technical languages—that which distinguishes them, I repeat, is their striking resemblance which makes it so hard to distinguish them from each other—I'm speaking of the neo-Spanish languages which one is able to distinguish from each other, however, only thanks to their distinctive characteristics, absolutely indisputable proofs of their extraordinary resemblance, which renders indisputable their common origin, and which, at the same time, differentiates them profoundly—through the continuation of the distinctive traits which I've just cited.

PUPIL:   Oooh! Ye-e-e-s-s-s, Professor!

PROFESSOR:   But let's not linger over generalities . . .

PUPIL [*regretfully, but won over*]:   Oh, Professor . . .

PROFESSOR:   This appears to interest you. All the better, all the better.

PUPIL:   Oh, yes, Professor . . .

PROFESSOR:   Don't worry, miss. We will come back to it later . . . That is if we come back to it at all. Who can say?

PUPIL [*enchanted in spite of everything*]:   Oh, yes, Professor.

PROFESSOR:   Every tongue—you must know this, miss, and remember it *until the hour of your death* . . .

PUPIL:   Oh! yes, Professor, until the hour of my death . . . Yes, Professor . . .

PROFESSOR:   . . . And this, too, is a fundamental principle, every tongue is at bottom nothing but language, which necessarily implies that it is composed of sounds, or . . .

PUPIL:   Phonemes . . .

PROFESSOR:   Just what I was going to say. Don't parade your knowledge. You'd do better to listen.

PUPIL:   All right, Professor. Yes, Professor.

PROFESSOR:   The sounds, miss, must be seized on the wing as they fly so that they'll not fall on deaf ears. As a result, when you set out to articulate, it is recommended, insofar as possible, that you lift up your neck and chin very high, and rise up on the tips of your toes, you see, this way . . .

PUPIL: Yes, Professor.

PROFESSOR: Keep quiet. Remain seated, don't interrupt me . . . And project the sounds very loudly with all the force of your lungs in conjunction with that of your vocal cords. Like this, look: "Butterfly," "Eureka," "Trafalgar," "Papaya." This way, the sounds become filled with a warm air that is lighter than the surrounding air so that they can fly without danger of falling on deaf ears, which are veritable voids, tombs of sonorities. If you utter several sounds at an accelerated speed, they will automatically cling to each other, constituting thus syllables, words, even sentences, that is to say groupings of various importance, purely irrational assemblages of sounds, denuded of all sense, but for that very reason the more capable of maintaining themselves without danger at a high altitude in the air. By themselves, words charged with significance will fall, weighted down by their meaning, and in the end they always collapse, fall . . .

PUPIL: . . . On deaf ears.

PROFESSOR: That's it, but don't interrupt . . . and into the worst confusion . . . Or else burst like balloons. Therefore, miss . . . [*The Pupil suddenly appears to be unwell.*] What's the matter?

PUPIL: I've got a toothache, Professor.

PROFESSOR: That's not important. We're not going to stop for anything so trivial. Let us go on . . .

PUPIL [*appearing to be in more and more pain*]: Yes, Professor.

PROFESSOR: I draw your attention in passing to the consonants that change their nature in combinations. In this case *f* becomes *v*, *d* becomes *t*, *g* becomes *k*, and vice versa, as in these examples that I will cite for you: "That's all right," "hens and chickens," "Welsh rabbit," "lots of nothing," "not at all."[1]

PUPIL: I've got a toothache.

PROFESSOR: Let's continue.

PUPIL: Yes.

---

[1] All to be heavily elided. [Translator's note.]

PROFESSOR:   To resume: it takes years and years to learn to pronounce. Thanks to science, we can achieve this in a few minutes. In order to project words, sounds and all the rest, you must realize that it is necessary to pitilessly expel air from the lungs, and make it pass delicately, caressingly, over the vocal cords, which, like harps or leaves in the wind, will suddenly shake, agitate, vibrate, vibrate, vibrate or uvulate, or fricate or jostle against each other, or sibilate, sibilate, placing everything in movement, the uvula, the tongue, the palate, the teeth . . .

PUPIL:   I have a toothache.

PROFESSOR:   . . . And the lips . . . Finally the words come out through the nose, the mouth, the ears, the pores, drawing along with them all the organs that we have named, torn up by the roots, in a powerful, majestic flight, which is none other than what is called, improperly, the voice, whether modulated in singing or transformed into a terrible symphonic storm with a whole procession . . . of garlands of all kinds of flowers, of sonorous artifices: labials, dentals, occlusives, palatals, and others, some caressing, some bitter or violent.

PUPIL:   Yes, Professor, I've got a toothache.

PROFESSOR:   Let's go on, go on. As for the neo-Spanish languages, they are closely related, so closely to each other, that they can be considered as true second cousins. Moreover, they have the same mother: Spanishe, with a mute *e*. That is why it is so difficult to distinguish them from one another. That is why it is so useful to pronounce carefully, and to avoid errors in pronunciation. Pronunciation itself is worth a whole language. A bad pronunciation can get you into trouble. In this connection, permit me, parenthetically, to share a personal experience with you. [*Slight pause. The Professor goes over his memories for a moment; his features mellow, but he recovers at once.*] I was very young, little more than a child. It was during my military service. I had a friend in the regiment, a vicomte, who suffered from a rather serious defect in his pronunciation: he could not pronounce the letter *f*. Instead of *f*, he said *f*. Thus, instead of "Birds of a feather flock together," he said: "Birds of a feather flock together." He pronounced filly instead of filly, Firmin instead of Firmin, French bean instead of French bean, go frig yourself instead of go frig yourself, farrago instead of farrago, fee fi fo fum instead of fee fi fo fum, Philip instead of Philip, fictory instead of fictory, February instead of February, March-April instead of March-April, Gerard de Nerval and not as is correct—Gerard de Nerval, Mirabeau instead of Mirabeau, etc., instead of etc., and thus instead of etc., instead of etc., and thus and so forth. However, he managed to conceal his fault so effectively that, thanks to the hats he wore, no one ever noticed it.

PUPIL: Yes, I've got a toothache.

PROFESSOR [*abruptly changing his tone, his voice hardening*]: Let's go on. We'll first consider the points of similarity in order the better to apprehend, later on, that which distinguishes all these languages from each other. The differences can scarcely be recognized by people who are not aware of them. Thus, all the words of all the languages . . .

PUPIL: Uh, yes? . . . I've got a toothache.

PROFESSOR: Let's continue . . . are always the same, just as all the suffixes, all the prefixes, all the terminations, all the roots . . .

PUPIL: Are the roots of words square?

PROFESSOR: Square or cube. That depends.

PUPIL: I've got a toothache.

PROFESSOR: Let's go on. Thus, to give you an example which is little more than an illustration, take the word "front" . . .

PUPIL: How do you want me to take it?

PROFESSOR: However you wish, so long as you take it, but above all do not interrupt.

PUPIL: I've got a toothache.

PROFESSOR: Let's continue . . . I said: Let's continue. Take now the word "front." Have you taken it?

PUPIL: Yes, yes, I've got it. My teeth, my teeth . . .

PROFESSOR: The word "front" is the root of "frontispiece." It is also to be found in "affronted." "Ispiece" is the suffix, and "af" the prefix. They are so called because they do not change. They don't want to.

PUPIL: I've got a toothache.

PROFESSOR: Let's go on. [*Rapidly:*] These prefixes are of Spanish origin. I hope you noticed that, did you?

PUPIL: Oh, how my tooth aches.

PROFESSOR: Let's continue. You've surely also noticed that

they've not changed in French. And now, young lady, nothing has succeeded in changing them in Latin either, nor in Italian, nor in Portuguese, nor in Sardanapalian, nor in Sardanapali, nor in Romanian, nor in neo-Spanish, nor in Spanish, nor even in the Oriental: front, frontispiece, affronted, always the same word, invariably with the same root, the same suffix, the same prefix, in all the languages I have named. And it is always the same for all words.

PUPIL:   In all languages, these words mean the same thing? I've got a toothache.

PROFESSOR:   Absolutely. Moreover, it's more a notion than a word. In any case, you have always the same signification, the same composition, the same sound structure, not only for this word, but for all conceivable words, in all languages. For one single notion is expressed by one and the same word, and its synonyms, in all countries. Forget about your teeth.

PUPIL:   I've got a toothache. Yes, yes, yes.

PROFESSOR:   Good, let's go on. I tell you, let's go on . . . How would you say, for example, in French: the roses of my grandmother are as yellow as my grandfather who was Asiatic?

PUPIL:   My teeth ache, ache, ache.

PROFESSOR:   Let's go on, let's go on, go ahead and answer, anyway.

PUPIL:   In French?

PROFESSOR:   In French.

PUPIL:   Uhh . . . I should say in French: the roses of my grandmother are . . . ?

PROFESSOR:   As yellow as my grandfather who was Asiatic . . .

PUPIL:   Oh well, one would say, in French, I believe, the roses . . . of my . . . how do you say "grandmother" in French?

PROFESSOR:   In French? Grandmother.

PUPIL:   The roses of my grandmother are as yellow—in French, is it "yellow"?

PROFESSOR:   Yes, of course!

PUPIL:   Are as yellow as my grandfather when he got angry.

PROFESSOR:   No . . . who was A . . .

PUPIL:   . . . siatic . . . I've got a toothache.

PROFESSOR:   That's it.

PUPIL:   I've got a tooth . . .

PROFESSOR:   Ache . . . so what . . . let's continue! And now trans-

late the same sentence into Spanish, then into neo-Spanish
. . .

PUPIL:   In Spanish . . . this would be: the roses of my grandmother are as yellow as my grandfather who was Asiatic.

PROFESSOR:   No. That's wrong.

PUPIL:   And in neo-Spanish: the roses of my grandmother are as
yellow as my grandfather who was Asiatic.

PROFESSOR:   That's wrong. That's wrong. That's wrong. You have
inverted it, you've confused Spanish with neo-Spanish, and
neo-Spanish with Spanish . . . Oh . . . no . . . it's the other
way around . . .

PUPIL:   I've got a toothache. You're getting mixed up.

PROFESSOR:   You're the one who is mixing me up. Pay attention
and take notes. I will say the sentence to you in Spanish, then
in neo-Spanish, and finally, in Latin. You will repeat after me.
Pay attention, for the resemblances are great. In fact, they are
identical resemblances. Listen, follow carefully . . .

PUPIL:   I've got a tooth . . .

PROFESSOR:   . . . Ache.

PUPIL:   Let us go on . . . Ah! . . .

PROFESSOR:   . . . In Spanish: the roses of my grandmother are as
yellow as my grandfather who was Asiatic; in Latin: the roses
of my grandmother are as yellow as my grandfather who was
Asiatic. Do you detect the differences? Translate this into . . .
Romanian.

PUPIL:   The . . . how do you say "roses" in Romanian?

PROFESSOR:   But "roses," what else?

PUPIL:   It's not "roses"? Oh, how my tooth aches!

PROFESSOR:   Certainly not, certainly not, since "roses" is a translation in Oriental of the French word "roses," in Spanish
"roses," do you get it? In Sardanapali, "roses" . . .

PUPIL:   Excuse me, Professor, but . . . Oh, my toothache! . . . I
don't get the difference.

PROFESSOR:   But it's so simple! So simple! It's a matter of having
a certain experience, a technical experience and practice in
these diverse languages, which are so diverse in spite of the
fact that they present wholly identical characteristics. I'm
going to try to give you a key . . .

PUPIL:   Toothache . . .

PROFESSOR:   That which differentiates these languages, is neither the words, which are absolutely the same, nor the structure of the sentence which is everywhere the same, nor the intonation, which does not offer any differences, nor the rhythm of the language . . . that which differentiates them . . . are you listening?

PUPIL:   I've got a toothache.

PROFESSOR:   Are you listening to me, young lady? Aah! We're going to lose our temper.

PUPIL:   You're bothering me, Professor. I've got a toothache.

PROFESSOR:   Son of a cocker spaniel! Listen to me!

PUPIL:   Oh well . . . yes . . . yes . . . go on . . .

PROFESSOR:   That which distinguishes them from each other, on the one hand, and from their mother, Spanishe with its mute *e*, on the other hand . . . is . . .

PUPIL [*grimacing*]:   Is what?

PROFESSOR:   Is an intangible thing. Something intangible that one is able to perceive only after very long study, with a great deal of trouble and after the broadest experience . . .

PUPIL:   Ah?

PROFESSOR:   Yes, young lady. I cannot give you any rule. One must have a feeling for it, and well, that's it. But in order to have it, one must study, study, and then study some more.

PUPIL:   Toothache.

PROFESSOR:   All the same, there are some specific cases where words differ from one language to another . . . but we cannot base our knowledge on these cases, which are, so to speak, exceptional.

PUPIL:   Oh, yes? . . . Oh, Professor, I've got a toothache.

PROFESSOR:   Don't interrupt! Don't make me lose my temper! I can't answer for what I'll do. I was saying, then . . . Ah, yes, the exceptional cases, the so-called easily distinguished . . . or facilely distinguished . . . or conveniently . . . if you prefer . . . I repeat, if you prefer, for I see that you're not listening to me . . .

PUPIL:   I've got a toothache.

PROFESSOR:   I say then: in certain expressions in current usage, certain words differ totally from one language to another, so much so that the language employed is, in this case, considerably easier to identify. I'll give you an example: the neo-Spanish expression, famous in Madrid: "My country is the new Spain," becomes in Italian: "My country is . . .

PUPIL:   The new Spain.

PROFESSOR:   No! "My country is Italy." Tell me now, by simple deduction, how do you say "Italy" in French?

PUPIL:   I've got a toothache.

PROFESSOR:   But it's so easy: for the word "Italy," in French we have the word "France," which is an exact translation of it. My country is France. And "France" in Oriental: "Orient!" My country is the Orient. And "Orient" in Portuguese: "Portugal!" The Oriental expression: My country is the Orient is translated then in the same fashion into Portuguese: My country is Portugal! And so on . . .

PUPIL:   Oh, no more, no more. My teeth . . .

PROFESSOR:   Ache! ache! ache! . . . I'm going to pull them out, I will! One more example. The word "capital"—it takes on, according to the language one speaks, a different meaning. That is to say that when a Spaniard says: "I reside in the capital," the word "capital" does not mean at all the same thing that a Portuguese means when he says: "I reside in the capital." All the more so in the case of a Frenchman, a neo-Spaniard, a Romanian, a Latin, a Sardanapali . . . Whenever you hear it, young lady—young lady, I'm saying this for you! Pooh! Whenever you hear the expression: "I reside in the capital," you will immediately and easily know whether this is Spanish or Spanish, neo-Spanish, French, Oriental, Romanian, or Latin, for it is enough to know which metropolis is referred to by the person who pronounces the sentence . . . at the very moment he pronounces it . . . But these are almost the only precise examples that I can give you . . .

PUPIL:   Oh dear! My teeth . . .

PROFESSOR:   Silence! Or I'll bash in your skull!

PUPIL:   Just try to! Skulldugger!

[*The Professor seizes her wrist and twists it.*]

PUPIL:   Oww!

PROFESSOR:   Keep quiet now! Not a word!

PUPIL [*whimpering*]:   Toothache . . .

PROFESSOR: One thing that is the most . . . how shall I say it? . . . the most paradoxical . . . yes . . . that's the word . . . the most paradoxical thing, is that a lot of people who are completely illiterate speak these different languages . . . do you understand? What did I just say?

PUPIL: "Speak these different languages! What did I just say?"

PROFESSOR: You were lucky that time! . . . The common people speak a Spanish full of neo-Spanish words that they are entirely unaware of, all the while believing that they are speaking Latin . . . or they speak Latin, full of Oriental words, all the while believing that they're speaking Romanian . . . or Spanish, full of neo-Spanish, all the while believing that they're speaking Sardanapali, or Spanish . . . Do you understand?

PUPIL: Yes! yes! yes! yes! What more do you want . . . ?

PROFESSOR: No insolence, my pet, or you'll be sorry . . . [*In a rage:*] But the worst of all, young lady, is that certain people, for example, in a Latin that they suppose is Spanish, say: "Both my kidneys are of the same kidney," in addressing themselves to a Frenchman who does not know a word of Spanish, but the latter understands it as if it were his own language. For that matter he thinks it is his own language. And the Frenchman will reply, in French: "Me too, sir, mine are too," and this will be perfectly comprehensible to a Spaniard, who will feel certain that the reply is in pure Spanish and that Spanish is being spoken . . . when, in reality, it was neither Spanish nor French, but Latin in the neo-Spanish dialect . . . Sit still, young lady, don't fidget, stop tapping your feet . . .

PUPIL: I've got a toothache.

PROFESSOR: How do you account for the fact that, in speaking without knowing which language they speak, or even while each of them believes that he is speaking another, the common people understand each other at all?

PUPIL: I wonder.

PROFESSOR: It is simply one of the inexplicable curiosities of the vulgar empiricism of the common people—not to be confused with experience!—a paradox, a non-sense, one of the aberrations of human nature, it is purely and simply instinct—to put it in a nutshell . . . That's what is involved here.

PUPIL: Hah! hah!

PROFESSOR:   Instead of staring at the flies while I'm going to all this trouble . . . you would do much better to try to be more attentive . . . it is not I who is going to qualify for the partial doctor's orals . . . I passed mine a long time ago . . . and I've won my total doctorate, too . . . and my supertotal diploma . . . Don't you realize that what I'm saying is for your own good?

PUPIL:   Toothache!

PROFESSOR:   Ill-mannered . . . It can't go on like this, it won't do, it won't do, it won't do . . .

PUPIL:   I'm . . . listening . . . to you . . .

PROFESSOR:   Ahah! In order to learn to distinguish all the different languages, as I've told you, there is nothing better than practice . . . Let's take them up in order. I am going to try to teach you all the translations of the word "knife."

PUPIL:   Well, all right . . . if you want . . .

PROFESSOR [*calling the Maid*]:   Marie! Marie! She's not there . . . Marie! Marie! . . . Marie, where are you? [*He opens the door on the right.*] Marie! . . .

[*He exits. The Pupil remains alone several minutes, staring into space, wearing a stupefied expression.*]

PROFESSOR [*offstage, in a shrill voice*]:   Marie! What are you up to? Why don't you come! When I call you, you must come! [*He re-enters, followed by Marie.*] It is I who gives the orders, do you hear? [*He points at the Pupil:*] She doesn't understand anything, that girl. She doesn't understand!

MAID:   Don't get into such a state, sir, you know where it'll end! You're going to go too far, you're going to go too far.

PROFESSOR:   I'll be able to stop in time.

MAID:   That's what you always say. I only wish I could see it.

PUPIL:   I've got a toothache.

MAID:   You see, it's starting, that's the symptom!

PROFESSOR:   What symptom? Explain yourself? What do you mean?

PUPIL [*in a spiritless voice*]:   Yes, what do you mean? I've got a toothache.

MAID:   The final symptom! The chief symptom!

PROFESSOR:   Stupid! stupid! stupid! [*The Maid starts to exit.*] Don't go away like that! I called you to help me find the Spanish, neo-Spanish, Portuguese, French, Oriental, Romanian, Sardanapali, Latin and Spanish knives.

MAID [*severely*]:   Don't ask me. [*She exits.*]

PROFESSOR [*makes a gesture as though to protest, then refrains, a little helpless. Suddenly, he remembers*]:   Ah! [*He goes quickly to the drawer where he finds a big knife, invisible or real according to the preference of the director. He seizes it and brandishes it happily.*] Here is one, young lady, here is a knife. It's too bad that we only have this one, but we're going to try to make it serve for all the languages, anyway! It will be enough if you will pronounce the word "knife" in all the languages, while looking at the object, very closely, fixedly, and imagining that it is in the language that you are speaking.

PUPIL:   I've got a toothache.

PROFESSOR [*almost singing, chanting*]:   Now, say "kni," like "kni," "fe," like "fe" . . . And look, look, look at it, watch it . . .

PUPIL:   What is this one in? French, Italian or Spanish?

PROFESSOR:   That doesn't matter now . . . That's not your concern. Say: "kni."

PUPIL:   "Kni."

PROFESSOR:   . . . "fe" . . . Look.

[*He brandishes the knife under the Pupil's eyes.*]

PUPIL:   "fe" . . .

PROFESSOR:   Again . . . Look at it.

PUPIL:   Oh, no! My God! I've had enough. And besides, I've got a toothache, my feet hurt me, I've got a headache.

PROFESSOR [*abruptly*]:   Knife . . . look . . . knife . . . look . . . knife . . . look . . .

PUPIL:   You're giving me an earache, too. Oh, your voice! It's so piercing!

PROFESSOR:   Say: knife . . . kni . . . fe . . .

PUPIL:   No! My ears hurts, I hurt all over . . .

PROFESSOR:   I'm going to tear them off, your ears, that's what I'm going to do to you, and then they won't hurt you anymore, my pet.

PUPIL:   Oh . . . you're hurting me, oh, you're hurting me . . .

PROFESSOR:   Look, come on, quickly, repeat after me: "kni" . . .

PUPIL:   Oh, since you insist . . . knife . . . knife . . . [*In a lucid moment, ironically:*] Is that neo-Spanish . . . ?

PROFESSOR:   If you like, yes, it's neo-Spanish, but hurry up . . . we haven't got time . . . And then, what do you mean by that insidious question? What are you up to?

PUPIL [*becoming more and more exhausted, weeping, desperate, at the same time both exasperated and in a trance*]:   Ah!

PROFESSOR:   Repeat, watch. [*He imitates a cuckoo:*] Knife, knife . . . knife, knife . . . knife, knife . . . knife, knife . . .

PUPIL:   Oh, my head . . . aches . . . [*With her hand she caressingly touches the parts of her body as she names them:*] . . . My eyes . . .

PROFESSOR [*like a cuckoo*]:   Knife, knife . . . knife, knife . . .

[*They are both standing. The Professor still brandishes his invisible knife, nearly beside himself, as he circles around her in a sort of scalp dance, but it is important that this not be exaggerated and that his dance steps be only suggested. The Pupil stands facing the audience, then recoils in the direction of the window, sickly, languid, victimized.*]

PROFESSOR:   Repeat, repeat: knife . . . knife . . . knife . . .

PUPIL:   I've got a pain . . . my throat, neck . . . oh, my shoulders . . . my breast . . . knife . . .

PROFESSOR:   Knife . . . knife . . . knife . . .

PUPIL:   My hips . . . knife . . . my thighs . . . kni . . .

PROFESSOR:   Pronounce it carefully . . . knife . . . knife . . .

PUPIL:   Knife . . . my throat . . .

PROFESSOR:   Knife . . . knife . . .

PUPIL:   Knife . . . my shoulders . . . my arms, my breast, my hips . . . knife . . . knife . . .

PROFESSOR:   That's right . . . Now, you're pronouncing it well . . .

PUPIL:   Knife . . . my breast . . . my stomach . . .

PROFESSOR [*changing his voice*]:   Pay attention . . . don't break my window . . . the knife kills . . .

PUPIL [*in a weak voice*]:   Yes, yes, . . . the knife kills?

PROFESSOR [*striking the Pupil with a very spectacular blow of the knife*]:   Aaah! That'll teach you!

[*Pupil also cries "Aah!" then falls, flopping in an immodest position onto a chair which, as though by chance, is near the window.*]

*The murderer and his victim shout "Aaah!" at the same moment. After the first blow of the knife, the Pupil flops onto the chair, her legs spread wide and hanging over both sides of the chair. The Professor remains standing in front of her, his back to the audience. After the first blow, he strikes her dead with a second slash of the knife, from bottom to top. After that blow a noticeable convulsion shakes his whole body.]*

PROFESSOR [*winded, mumbling*]:  Bitch . . . Oh, that's good, that does me good . . . Ah! Ah! I'm exhausted . . . I can scarcely breathe . . . Aah! [*He breathes with difficulty; he falls—fortunately a chair is there; he mops his brow, mumbles some incomprehensible words; his breathing becomes normal. He gets up, looks at the knife in his hand, looks at the young girl, then as though he were waking up, in a panic:*] What have I done! What's going to happen to me now! What's going to happen! Oh! dear! Oh dear, I'm in trouble! Young lady, young lady, get up! [*He is agitated, still holding onto the invisible knife, which he doesn't know what to do with.*] Come now, young lady, the lesson is over . . . you may go . . . you can pay another time . . . Oh! she is dead . . . dea-ead . . . And by my knife . . . She is dea-ead . . . It's terrible. [*He calls the Maid:*] Marie! Marie! My good Marie, come here! Ah! ah! [*The door on the right opens a little and Marie appears.*] No . . . don't come in . . . I made a mistake . . . I don't need you, Marie . . . I don't need you anymore . . . do you understand? . . .

[*Maid enters wearing a stern expression, without saying a word. She sees the corpse.*]

PROFESSOR [*in a voice less and less assured*]:  I don't need you, Marie . . .

MAID [*sarcastic*]:  Then, you're satisfied with your pupil, she's profited by your lesson?

PROFESSOR [*holding the knife behind his back*]:  Yes, the lesson is finished . . . but . . . she . . . she's still there . . . she doesn't want to leave . . .

MAID [*very harshly*]:  Is that a fact? . . .

PROFESSOR [*trembling*]:  It wasn't I . . . it wasn't I . . . Marie . . . No . . . I assure you . . . it wasn't I, my little Marie . . .

MAID:   And who was it? Who was it then? Me?

PROFESSOR:   I don't know . . . maybe . . .

MAID:   Or the cat?

PROFESSOR:   That's possible . . . I don't know . . .

MAID:   And today makes it the fortieth time! . . . And every day it's the same thing! Every day! You should be ashamed, at your age . . . and you're going to make yourself sick! You won't have any pupils left. That will serve you right.

PROFESSOR [*irritated*]:   It wasn't my fault! She didn't want to learn! She was disobedient! She was a bad pupil! She didn't want to learn!

MAID:   Liar! . . .

PROFESSOR [*craftily approaching the Maid, holding the knife behind his back*]:   It's none of your business! [*He tries to strike her with a great blow of the knife; the Maid seizes his wrist in mid-gesture and twists it; the Professor lets the knife fall to the floor*]: . . . I'm sorry!

MAID [*gives him two loud, strong slaps; the Professor falls onto the floor, on his prat; he sobs*]:   Little murderer! bastard! You're disgusting! You wanted to do that to me? I'm not one of your pupils, not me! [*She pulls him up by the collar, picks up his skullcap and puts it on his head; he's afraid she'll slap him again and holds his arm up to protect his face, like a child.*] Put the knife back where it belongs, go on! [*The Professor goes and puts it back in the drawer of the buffet, then comes back to her.*] Now didn't I warn you, just a little while ago: arithmetic leads to philology, and philology leads to crime . . .

PROFESSOR:   You said "to calamity"!

MAID:   It's the same thing.

PROFESSOR:   I didn't understand you. I thought that "calamity" was a city and that you meant that philology leads to the city of Calamity . . .

MAID:   Liar! Old fox! An intellectual like you is not going to make a mistake in the meanings of words. Don't try to pull the wool over my eyes.

PROFESSOR [*sobbing*]:   I didn't kill her on purpose!

MAID:   Are you sorry at least?

PROFESSOR:   Oh, yes, Marie, I swear it to you!

MAID:   I can't help feeling sorry for you! Ah! you're a good boy in spite of everything! I'll try to fix this. But don't start it again . . . It could give you a heart attack . . .

PROFESSOR:  Yes, Marie! What are we going to do, now?

MAID:  We're going to bury her . . . along with the thirty-nine others . . . and that will make forty coffins . . . I'll call the undertakers and my lover, Father Auguste . . . I'll order the wreaths . . .

PROFESSOR:  Yes, Marie, thank you very much.

MAID:  Well, that's that. And perhaps it won't be necessary to call Auguste, since you yourself are something of a priest at times, if one can believe the gossip.

PROFESSOR:  In any case, don't spend too much on the wreaths. She didn't pay for her lesson.

MAID:  Don't worry . . . The least you can do is cover her up with a smock, she's not decent that way. And then we'll carry her out . . .

PROFESSOR:  Yes, Marie, yes. [*He covers up the body.*] There's a chance that we'll get pinched . . . with forty coffins . . . Don't you think . . . people will be surprised . . . Suppose they ask us what's inside them?

MAID:  Don't worry so much. We'll say that they're empty. And besides, people won't ask questions, they're used to it.

PROFESSOR:  Even so . . .

MAID [*she takes out an armband with an insignia, perhaps the Nazi swastika*]:  Wait, if you're afraid, wear this, then you won't have anything more to be afraid of. [*She puts the armband around his arm.*] . . . That's good politics.

PROFESSOR:  Thanks, my little Marie. With this, I won't need to worry . . . You're a good girl, Marie . . . very loyal . . .

MAID:  That's enough. Come on, sir. Are you all right?

PROFESSOR:  Yes, my little Marie. [*The Maid and the Professor take the body of the young girl, one by the shoulders, the other by the legs, and move towards the door on the right.*] Be careful. We don't want to hurt her.

[*They exit. The stage remains empty for several moments. We hear the doorbell ring at the left.*]

VOICE OF THE MAID:  Just a moment, I'm coming!

[*She appears as she was at the beginning of the play, and goes towards the door. The doorbell rings again.*]

MAID [*aside*]:   She's certainly in a hurry, this one! [*Aloud:*] Just a moment! [*She goes to the door on the left, and opens it.*] Good morning, miss! You are the new pupil? You have come for the lesson? The Professor is expecting you. I'll go tell him that you've come. He'll be right down. Come in, miss, come in!

# Ed Bullins [b. 1935]

# A Son, Come Home

A *Son, Come Home* was first produced at the American Place Theatre on March 26th, 1968. It was directed by Robert MacBeth, with scenery by John Jay Moore and lighting by Roger Morgan. The cast was as follows:

| | |
|---|---|
| Mother, *early 50's* | Estelle Evans |
| Son, *30 years old* | Wayne Grice |
| The Girl | Kelly-Marie Berry |
| The Boy | Gary Bolling |

Music for the production was composed by Gordon Watkins.

*The Boy and the Girl wear black tights and shirts. They move the action of the play and express the Mother's and the Son's moods and tensions. They become various embodiments recalled from memory and history: they enact a number of personalities and move from mood to mood.*

*The players are Black.*

*At rise: Scene: Bare stage but for two chairs positioned so as not to interfere with the actions of the Boy and the Girl.*

*The Mother enters, sits in chair and begins to use imaginary iron and board. She hums a spiritual as she works.*

MOTHER:   You came three times . . . Michael? It took you three times to find me at home?

*(The Girl enters, turns and peers through the cracked, imaginary door)*

SON'S VOICE *(Offstage):*   Is Mrs. Brown home?
GIRL *(An old woman):*   What?

MOTHER: It shouldn't have taken you three times. I told you that I would be here by two and you should wait, Michael.

*(The Son enters, passes the Girl and takes his seat upon the other chair.*

*The Boy enters, stops on other side of the imaginary door and looks through at the Girl)*

BOY: Is Mrs. Brown in?

GIRL: Miss Brown ain't come in yet. Come back later . . . She'll be in before dark.

MOTHER: It shouldn't have taken you three times . . . You should listen to me, Michael. Standin' all that time in the cold.

SON: It wasn't cold, Mother.

MOTHER: I told you that I would be here by two and you should wait, Michael.

BOY: Please tell Mrs. Brown that her son's in town to visit her.

GIRL: You little Miss Brown's son? Well, bless the Lord.

*(Calls over her shoulder)*

Hey, Mandy, do you hear that? Little Miss Brown upstairs got a son . . . a great big boy . . . He's come to visit her.

BOY: You'll tell her, won't you?

GIRL: Sure, I'll tell her.

*(Grins and shows gums)*

I'll tell her soon as she gets in.

MOTHER: Did you get cold, Michael?

SON: No, Mother. I walked around some . . . sightseeing.

BOY: I walked up Twenty-third Street toward South. I had phoned that I was coming.

MOTHER: Sightseeing? But this is your home, Michael . . . always has been.

BOY: Just before I left New York I phoned that I was taking the bus. Two hours by bus, that's all. That's all it takes. Two hours.

SON: This town seems so strange. Different than how I remember it.

MOTHER:   Yes, you have been away for a good while . . . How long has it been, Michael?

BOY:   Two hours down the Jersey Turnpike, the trip beginning at the New York Port Authority Terminal . . .

SON:   . . . and then straight down through New Jersey to Philadelphia . . .

GIRL:   . . . and home . . . Just imagine . . . little Miss Brown's got a son who's come home.

SON:   Yes, home . . . an anachronism.

MOTHER:   What did you say, Michael?

BOY:   He said . . .

GIRL *(Late teens)*:   What's an anachronism, Mike?

SON:   Anachronism: 1: an error in chronology; *esp:* a chronological misplacing of persons, events, objects, or customs in regard to each other 2: a person or a thing that is chronologically out of place—anachronistic/ *also* anachronic/ *or* anachronous—anachronistically/ *also* anachronously.

MOTHER:   I was so glad to hear you were going to school in California.

BOY:   College.

GIRL:   Yes, I understand.

MOTHER:   How long have you been gone, Michael?

SON:   Nine years.

BOY:   Nine years it's been. I wonder if she'll know me . . .

MOTHER:   You've put on so much weight, son. You know that's not healthy.

GIRL *(20 years old)*:   And that silly beard . . . how . . .

SON:   Oh . . . I'll take it off. I'm going on a diet tomorrow.

BOY:   I wonder if I'll know her.

SON:   You've put on some yourself, Mother.

MOTHER:   Yes, the years pass. Thank the Lord.

BOY:   I wonder if we've changed much.

GIRL:   Yes, thank the Lord.

SON:   The streets here seem so small.

MOTHER:   Yes, it seems like that when you spend a little time in Los Angeles.

GIRL:   I spent eighteen months there with your aunt when she was sick. She had nobody else to help her . . . she was so lonely. And you were in the service . . . away. You've always been away.

BOY:   In Los Angeles the boulevards, the avenues, the streets . . .

SON: . . . are wide. Yes, they have some wide ones out West. Here, they're so small and narrow. I wonder how cars get through on both sides.

MOTHER: Why, you know how . . . we lived on Derby Street for over ten years, didn't we?

SON: Yeah, that was almost an alley.

MOTHER: Did you see much of your aunt before you left Los Angeles?

SON: What?

GIRL *(Middle-aged woman) (To Boy)*: Have you found a job yet, Michael?

MOTHER: Your aunt. My sister.

BOY: Nawh, not yet . . . Today I just walked downtown . . . quite a ways . . . this place is plenty big, ain't it?

SON: I don't see too much of Aunt Sophie.

MOTHER: But you're so much alike.

GIRL: Well, your bags are packed and are sitting outside the door.

BOY: My bags?

MOTHER: You shouldn't be that way, Michael. You shouldn't get too far away from your family.

SON: Yes, Mother.

BOY: But I don't have any money. I had to walk downtown today. That's how much money I have. I've only been here a week.

GIRL: I packed your bags, Michael.

MOTHER: You never can tell when you'll need or want your family, Michael.

SON: That's right, Mother.

MOTHER: You and she are so much alike.

BOY: Well, goodbye, Aunt Sophie.

GIRL:


*(Silence)*


MOTHER: All that time in California and you hardly saw your aunt. My baby sister.

BOY: Tsk tsk tsk.

SON: I'm sorry, Mother.

MOTHER: In the letters I'd get from both of you there'd be no mention of the other. All these years. Did you see her again?

SON: Yes.

GIRL *(On telephone)*:   Michael? Michael who? . . . Ohhh . . . Bernice's boy.

MOTHER:   You didn't tell me about this, did you?

SON:   No, I didn't.

BOY:   Hello, Aunt Sophie. How are you?

GIRL:   I'm fine, Michael. How are you? You're looking well.

BOY:   I'm getting on okay.

MOTHER:   I prayed for you.

SON:   Thank you.

MOTHER:   Thank the Lord, Michael.

BOY:   Got me a job working for the city.

GIRL:   You did now.

BOY:   Yes, I've brought you something.

GIRL:   What's this, Michael . . . ohhh . . . it's money.

BOY:   It's for the week I stayed with you.

GIRL:   Fifty dollars. But, Michael, you didn't have to.

MOTHER:   Are you still writing that radical stuff, Michael?

SON:   Radical?

MOTHER:   Yes . . . that stuff you write and send me all the time in those little books.

SON:   My poetry, Mother?

MOTHER:   Yes, that's what I'm talking about.

SON:   No.

MOTHER:   Praise the Lord, son. Praise the Lord. Didn't seem like anything I had read in school.

BOY *(On telephone)*:   Aunt Sophie? . . . Aunt Sophie? . . . It's me, Michael . . .

GIRL:   Michael?

BOY:   Yes . . . Michael . . .

GIRL:   Oh . . . Michael . . . yes . . .

BOY:   I'm in jail, Aunt Sophie . . . I got picked up for drunk driving.

GIRL:   You did . . . how awful . . .

MOTHER:   When you going to get your hair cut, Michael?

BOY:   Aunt Sophie . . . will you please come down and sign my bail. I've got the money . . . I just got paid yesterday . . . They're holding more than enough for me . . . but the law says that someone has to sign for it.

MOTHER:   You look almost like a hoodlum, Michael.

BOY:   All you need to do is come down and sign . . . and I can get out.

MOTHER: What you tryin' to be . . . a savage or something? Are you keeping out of trouble, Michael?

GIRL: Ohhh . . . Michael . . . I'm sorry but I can't do nothin' like that . . .

BOY: But all you have to do is sign . . . I've got the money and everything.

GIRL: I'm sorry . . . I can't stick my neck out.

BOY: But, Aunt Sophie . . . if I don't get back to work I'll lose my job and everything . . . please . . .

GIRL: I'm sorry, Michael . . . I can't stick my neck out . . . I have to go now . . . Is there anyone I can call?

BOY: No.

GIRL: I could call your mother. She wouldn't mind if I reversed the charges on her, would she? I don't like to run my bills up.

BOY: No thanks.

MOTHER: You and your aunt are so much alike.

SON: Yes, Mother. Our birthdays are in the same month.

MOTHER: Yes, that year was so hot . . . so hot and I was carrying you . . .

*(As the Mother speaks the Boy comes over and takes her by the hand and leads her from the chair, and they stroll around the stage, arm in arm.*

*The Girl accompanies them and she and the Boy enact scenes from the Mother's mind)*

. . . carrying you, Michael . . . and you were such a big baby . . . kicked all the time. But I was happy. Happy that I was having a baby of my own. . . . I worked as long as I could and bought you everything you might need . . . diapers . . . and bottles . . . and your own spoon . . . and even toys . . . and even books . . . And it was so hot in Philadelphia that year . . . Your Aunt Sophie used to come over and we'd go for walks . . . sometimes up on the avenue . . . I was living in West Philly then . . . in that old terrible section they called "The Bottom." That's where I met your father.

GIRL: You're such a fool, Bernice. No nigger . . . man or boy's . . . ever going to do a thing to me like that.

MOTHER: Everything's going to be all right, Sophia.

GIRL:   But what is he going to do? How are you going to take care of a baby by yourself?

MOTHER:   Everything's going to be all right, Sophia. I'll manage.

GIRL:   You'll manage? How? Have you talked about marriage?

MOTHER:   Oh, please, Sophia!

GIRL:   What do you mean "please"? Have you?

MOTHER:   I just can't. He might think . . .

GIRL:   Think! That dirty nigger better think. He better think before he really messes up. And you better too. You got this baby comin' on. What are you going to do?

MOTHER:   I don't know . . . I don't know what I can do.

GIRL:   Is he still tellin' you those lies about . . .

MOTHER:   They're not lies.

GIRL:   Haaaa . . .

MOTHER:   They're not.

GIRL:   Some smooth-talkin' nigger comes up from Georgia and tells you he escaped from the chain gang and had to change his name so he can't get married 'cause they might find out . . . What kinda shit is that, Bernice?

MOTHER:   Please, Sophia. Try and understand. He loves me. I can't hurt him.

GIRL:   Loves you . . . and puts you through this?

MOTHER:   Please . . . I'll talk to him . . . Give me a chance.

GIRL:   It's just a good thing you got a family, Bernice. It's just a good thing. You know that, don't cha?

MOTHER:   Yes, . . . yes, I do . . . but please don't say anything to him.

SON:   I've only seen my father about a half dozen times that I remember, Mother. What was he like?

MOTHER:   Down in The Bottom . . . that's where I met your father. I was young and hinkty then. Had big pretty brown legs and a small waist. Everybody used to to call me Bernie . . . and me and my sister would go to Atlantic City on the weekends and work as waitresses in the evenings and sit all afternoon on the black part of the beach at Boardwalk and Atlantic . . . getting blacker . . . and having the times of our lives. Your father probably still lives down in The Bottom . . . perched over some bar down there . . . drunk to the world . . . I can see him now . . . He had good white teeth then . . . not how they turned later when he started in drinkin' that wine and wouldn't stop . . . he was so nice then.

BOY:   Awwww, listen, kid. I got my problems too.

GIRL:   But Andy . . . I'm six months gone . . . and you ain't done nothin'.

BOY:   Well, what can I do?

GIRL:   Don't talk like that . . . What can you do? . . . You know what you can do.

BOY:   You mean marry you? Now lissen, sweetheart . . .

GIRL:   But what about our baby?

BOY:   Your baby.

GIRL:   Don't talk like that! It took more than me to get him.

BOY:   Well . . . look . . . I'll talk to you later, kid. I got to go to work now.

GIRL:   That's what I got to talk to you about too, Andy. I need some money.

BOY:   Money! Is somethin' wrong with your head, woman? I ain't got no money.

GIRL:   But I can't work much longer, Andy. You got to give me some money. Andy . . . you just gotta.

BOY:   Woman . . . all I got to *ever* do is die and go to hell.

GIRL:   Well, you gonna do that, Andy. You sho are . . . you know that, don't you? . . . You know that.

MOTHER:   . . . Yes, you are, man. Praise the Lord. We all are . . . All of us . . . even though he ain't come for you yet to make you pay. Maybe he's waitin' for us to go together so I can be a witness to the retribution that's handed down. A witness to all that He'll bestow upon your sinner's head . . . A witness! . . . That's what I am, Andy! Do you hear me? . . . A witness!

SON:   Mother . . . what's wrong? What's the matter?

MOTHER:   Thank the Lord that I am not blinded and will see the fulfillment of divine . . .

SON:   Mother!

MOTHER:   Oh . . . is something wrong, Michael?

SON:   You're shouting and walking around . . .

MOTHER:   Oh . . . it's nothing, son. I'm just feeling the power of the Lord.

SON:   Oh . . . is there anything I can get you, Mother?

MOTHER:   No, nothing at all.

*(She sits again and irons)*

SON:   Where's your kitchen? . . . I'll get you some coffee . . . the way you like it. I bet I still remember how to fix it.

MOTHER:   Michael . . . I don't drink anything like that no more.

SON:   No?

MOTHER:   Not since I joined the service of the Lord.

SON:   Yeah? . . . Well, do you mind if I get myself a cup?

MOTHER:   Why, I don't have a kitchen. All my meals are prepared for me.

SON:   Oh . . . I thought I was having dinner with you.

MOTHER:   No. There's nothing like that here.

SON:   Well, could I take you out to a restaurant? . . . Remember how we used to go out all the time and eat? I've never lost my habit of liking to eat out. Remember . . . we used to come down to this part of town and go to restaurants. They used to call it home cooking then . . . now, at least where I been out West and up in Harlem . . . we call it soul food. I bet we could find a nice little restaurant not four blocks from here, Mother. Remember that old man's place we used to go to on Nineteenth and South? I bet he's dead now . . . but . . .

MOTHER:   I don't even eat out no more, Michael.

SON:   No?

MOTHER:   Sometimes I take a piece of holy bread to work . . . or some fruit . . . if it's been blessed by my Spiritual Mother.

SON:   I see.

MOTHER:   Besides . . . we have a prayer meeting tonight.

SON:   On Friday?

MOTHER:   Every night. You'll have to be going soon.

SON:   Oh.

MOTHER:   You're looking well.

SON:   Thank you.

MOTHER:   But you look tired.

SON:   Do I?

MOTHER:   Yes, those rings around your eyes might never leave. Your father had them.

SON:   Did he?

MOTHER:   Yes . . . and cowlicks . . . deep cowlicks on each side on his head.

SON:   Yes . . . I remember.

MOTHER:   Do you?

*(The Boy and the Girl take crouching positions behind and in front of them. They are in a streetcar. The Boy behind the Mother and Son, the Girl across the aisle, a passenger)*

MOTHER *(Young woman) (To the Boy)*:  Keep your damn hands off him, Andy!

BOY *(chuckles)*:  Awww, c'mon . . . Bernie. I ain't seen him since he was in the crib.

MOTHER:  And you wouldn't have seen neither of us . . . if I had anything to do with it . . . Ohhh . . . why did I get on this trolley?

BOY:  C'mon . . . Bernie . . . don't be so stuckup.

MOTHER:  Don't even talk to us . . . and stop reaching after him.

BOY:  Awww . . . c'mon . . . Bernie. Let me look at him.

MOTHER:  Leave us alone. Look . . . people are looking at us.

*(The Girl across the aisle has been peeking at the trio but looks toward front at the mention of herself)*

BOY:  Hey, big boy . . . do you know who I am?

MOTHER:  Stop it, Andy! Stop it, I say . . . Mikie . . . don't pay any attention to him . . . you hear?

BOY:  Hey, big boy . . . know who I am? . . . I'm your daddy. Hey, there . . .

MOTHER:  Shut up . . . shut up, Andy . . . you nothin' to us.

BOY:  Where you livin' at . . . Bernie? Let me come on by and see the little guy, huh?

MOTHER:  No! You're not comin' near us . . . ever . . . you hear?

BOY:  But I'm his father . . . look . . . Bernie . . . I've been an ass the way I've acted but . . .

MOTHER:  He ain't got no father.

BOY:  Oh, come off that nonsense, woman.

MOTHER:  Mikie ain't got no father . . . his father's dead . . . you hear?

BOY:  Dead?

MOTHER:  Yes, dead. My son's father's dead.

BOY:  What you talkin' about? . . . He's the spittin' image of me.

MOTHER:  Go away . . . leave us alone, Andrew.

BOY:  See there . . . he's got the same name as me. His first name is Michael after your father . . . and Andrew after me.

MOTHER:  No, stop that, you hear?

BOY:  Michael Andrew . . .

MOTHER:  You never gave him no name . . . his name is Brown
. . . Brown. The same as mine . . . and my sister's . . . and
my daddy . . . You never gave him nothin' . . . and you're
dead . . . go away and get buried.

BOY:  You know that trouble I'm in . . . I got a wife down there,
Bernie. I don't care about her . . . what could I do?

MOTHER *(Rises, pulling up the Son)*:  We're leavin' . . . don't you
try and follow us . . . you hear, Andy? C'mon . . . Mikie . . .
watch your step now.

BOY:  Well . . . bring him around my job . . . you know where I
work. That's all . . . bring him around on payday.

MOTHER *(Leaving)*:  We don't need anything from you . . . I'm
working . . . just leave us alone.

*(The Boy turns to the Girl)*

BOY *(Shrugs)*:  That's the way it goes . . . I guess. Ships passing
on the trolley car . . . Hey . . . don't I know you from up
around 40th and Market?

*(The Girl turns away)*

SON:  Yeah . . . I remember him. He always had liquor on his
breath.

MOTHER:  Yes . . . he did. I'm glad that stuff ain't got me no more
. . . Thank the Lord.

GIRL *(35 years old)*:  You want to pour me another drink, Michael?

BOY *(15 years old)*:  You drink too much, Mother.

GIRL:  Not as much as some other people I know.

BOY:  Well, me and the guys just get short snorts, Mother. But
you really hide some port.

GIRL:  Don't forget you talkin' to your mother. You gettin' more
like your father every day.

BOY:  Is that why you like me so much?

GIRL *(Grins drunkenly)*:  Oh, hush up now, boy . . . and pour me
a drink.

BOY:  There's enough here for me too.

GIRL:  That's okay . . . when Will comes in he'll bring something.

SON:  How is Will, Mother?

MOTHER:  I don't know . . . haven't seen Will in years.

SON:  Mother.

MOTHER:  Yes, Michael.

SON:  Why you and Will never got married? . . . You stayed together for over ten years.

MOTHER:  Oh, don't ask me questions like that, Michael.

SON:  But why not?

MOTHER:  It's just none of your business.

SON:  But you could be married now . . . not alone in this room . . .

MOTHER:  Will had a wife and child in Chester . . . you know that.

SON:  He could have gotten a divorce, Mother . . . Why . . .

MOTHER:  Because he just didn't . . . that's why.

SON:  You never hear from him?

MOTHER:  Last I heard . . . Will had cancer.

SON:  Oh, he did.

MOTHER:  Yes.

SON:  Why didn't you tell me? . . . You could have written.

MOTHER:  Why?

SON:  So I could have known.

MOTHER:  So you could have known? Why?

SON:  Because Will was like a father to me . . . the only one I've really known.

MOTHER:  A father? And you chased him away as soon as you got big enough.

SON:  Don't say that, Mother.

MOTHER:  You made me choose between you and Will.

SON:  Mother.

MOTHER:  The quarrels you had with him . . . the mean tricks you used to play . . . the lies you told to your friends about Will . . . He wasn't much . . . when I thought I had a sense of humor I us'ta call him just plain Will. But we was his family.

SON:  Mother, listen.

MOTHER:  And you drove him away . . . and he didn't lift a hand to stop you.

SON:  Listen, Mother.

MOTHER:  As soon as you were big enough you did all that you could to get me and Will separated.

Son: Listen.
Mother: All right, Michael . . . I'm listening.

*(Pause)*

Son: Nothing.

*(Pause. Lifts an imaginary object)*

Is this your tambourine?
Mother: Yes.
Son: Do you play it?
Mother: Yes.
Son: Well?
Mother: Everything I do in the service of the Lord I do as well as He allows.
Son: You play it at your meetings.
Mother: Yes, I do. We celebrate the life He has bestowed upon us.
Son: I guess that's where I get it from.
Mother: Did you say something, Michael?
Son: Yes. My musical ability.
Mother: Oh . . . you've begun taking your piano lessons again?
Son: No . . . I was never any good at that.
Mother: Yes, three different teachers and you never got past the tenth lesson.
Son: You have a good memory, Mother.
Mother: Sometimes, son. Sometimes.
Son: I play an electric guitar in a combo.
Mother: You do? That's nice.
Son: That's why I'm in New York. We got a good break and came East.
Mother: That's nice, Michael.
Son: I was thinking that Sunday I could rent a car and come down to get you and drive you up to see our show. You'll get back in plenty of time to rest for work Monday.
Mother: No, I'm sorry. I can't do that.
Son: But you would like it, Mother. We could have dinner up in Harlem, then go down and . . .

MOTHER:   I don't do anything like that any more, Michael.

SON:   You mean you wouldn't come to see me play even if I were appearing here in Philly?

MOTHER:   That's right, Michael. I wouldn't come. I'm past all that.

SON:   Oh, I see.

MOTHER:   Yes, thank the Lord.

SON:   But it's my life, Mother.

MOTHER:   Good . . . then you have something to live for.

SON:   Yes.

MOTHER:   Well, you're a man now, Michael . . . I can no longer live it for you. Do the best with what you have.

SON:   Yes . . . Yes, I will, Mother.

GIRL'S VOICE *(Offstage)*:   Sister Brown . . . Sister Brown . . . hello.

MOTHER *(Uneasy; peers at watch)*:   Oh . . . it's Mother Ellen . . . I didn't know it was so late.

GIRL *(Enters)*:   Sister Brown . . . how are you this evening?

MOTHER:   Oh, just fine, Mother.

GIRL:   Good. It's nearly time for dinner.

MOTHER:   Oh, yes, I know.

GIRL:   We don't want to keep the others waiting at meeting . . . do we?

MOTHER:   No, we don't.

GIRL *(Self-assured)*:   Hello, son.

SON:   Hello.

MOTHER:   Oh, Mother . . . Mother . . .

GIRL:   Yes, Sister Brown, what is it?

MOTHER:   Mother . . . Mother . . . this is . . . this is . . .

*(Pause)*

. . . this is . . .

SON:   Hello, I'm Michael. How are you?

MOTHER *(Relieved)*:   Yes, Mother . . . This is Michael . . . my son.

GIRL:   Why, hello, Michael. I've heard so much about you from your mother. She prays for you daily.

SON *(Embarrassed)*:   Oh . . . good.

GIRL *(Briskly)*:   Well . . . I have to be off to see about the others.

MOTHER:   Yes, Mother Ellen.

GIRL *(as she exists; chuckles)*:   Have to tell everyone that you won't be keeping us waiting, Bernice.

*(Silence)*

SON:   Well, I guess I better be going, Mother.
MOTHER:   Yes.
SON:   I'll write.
MOTHER:   Please do.
SON:   I will.
MOTHER:   You're looking well . . . Thank the Lord.
SON:   Thank you, so are you, Mother.

*(He moves toward her and hesitates)*

MOTHER:   You're so much like your aunt. Give her my best . . . won't you?
SON:   Yes, I will, Mother.
MOTHER:   Take care of yourself, son.
SON:   Yes, Mother. I will.

*(The Son exits. The Mother stands looking after him as the lights go slowly down to . . .)*

*Blackness*

# MARSHA NORMAN [b.1947]

## 'night, Mother

### List of Characters

JESSIE CATES, *in her late thirties or early forties, is pale and vaguely unsteady physically. It is only in the last year that Jessie has gained control of her mind and body, and tonight she is determined to hold on to that control. She wears pants and a long black sweater with deep pockets, which contain scraps of paper, and there may be a pencil behind her ear or a pen clipped to one of the pockets of the sweater.*

*As a rule, Jessie doesn't feel much like talking. Other people have rarely found her quirky sense of humor amusing. She has a peaceful energy on this night, a sense of purpose, but is clearly aware of the time passing moment by moment. Oddly enough, Jessie has never been as communicative or as enjoyable as she is on this evening, but we must know she has not always been this way. There is a familiarity between these two women that comes from having lived together for a long time. There is a shorthand to the talk and a sense of routine comfort in the way they relate to each other physically. Naturally, there are also routine aggravations.*

THELMA CATES, *"Mama," is Jessie's mother, in her late fifties or early sixties. She has begun to feel her age and so takes it easy when she can, or when it serves her purpose to let someone help her. But she speaks quickly and enjoys talking. She believes that* things *are what she says they are. Her sturdiness is more a mental quality than a physical one, finally. She is chatty and nosy, and this is* her *house.*

*The play takes place in a relatively new house built way out on a country road, with a living room and connecting kitchen, and a center hall that leads off to the bedrooms. A pull cord in the hall ceiling releases a ladder which leads to the attic. One of these bedrooms opens directly onto the hall, and its entry should be visible to everyone in the audience. It should be, in fact, the focal point of the entire set, and the lighting should make it disappear completely at*

*times and draw the entire set into it at others. It is a point of both
threat and promise. It is an ordinary door that opens onto absolute
nothingness. That door is the point of all the action, and the utmost
care should be given to its design and construction.*

*The living room is cluttered with magazines and needlework cata-
logues, ashtrays and candy dishes. Examples of Mama's needlework
are everywhere—pillows, afghans, and quilts, doilies and rugs, and
they are quite nice examples. The house is more comfortable than
messy, but there is quite a lot to keep in place here. It is more
personal than charming. It is not quaint. Under no circumstances
should the set and its dressing make a judgment about the intelligence or taste of Jessie and Mama. It should simply indicate that
they are very specific real people who happen to live in a particular
part of the country. Heavy accents, which would further distance
the audience from Jessie and Mama, are also wrong.*

*The time is the present, with the action beginning about 8:15.
Clocks onstage in the kitchen and on a table in the living room
should run throughout the performance and be visible to the audience.*

*There will be no intermission.*

*Mama stretches to reach the cupcakes in a cabinet in the kitchen.
She can't see them, but she can feel around for them, and she's
eager to have one, so she's working pretty hard at it. This may be
the most serious exercise Mama ever gets. She finds a cupcake, the
coconut-covered, raspberry-and-marshmallow-filled kind known as a
snowball, but sees that there's one missing from the package. She
calls to Jessie, who is apparently somewhere else in the house.*

MAMA (*unwrapping the cupcake*):   Jessie, it's the last snowball,
sugar. Put it on the list. O.K.? And we're out of Hershey bars,
and where's that peanut brittle? I think maybe Dawson's been
in it again. I ought to put a big mirror on the refrigerator door.
That'll keep him out of my treats, won't it? You hear me,
honey? (*Then more to herself.*) I hate it when the coconut falls
off. Why does the coconut fall off?

*Jessie enters from her bedroom, carrying a stack of newspapers.*

JESSIE:   We got any old towels?
MAMA:   There you are!
JESSIE (*holding a towel that was on the stack of newspapers*):   Towels

you don't want anymore. (*Picking up Mama's snowball wrapper*) How about this swimming towel Loretta gave us? Beach towel, that's the name of it. You want it? (*Mama shakes her head no.*)

MAMA:   What have you been doing in there?

JESSIE:   And a big piece of plastic like a rubber sheet or something. Garbage bags would do if there's enough.

MAMA:   Don't go making a big mess, Jessie. It's eight o'clock already.

JESSIE:   Maybe an old blanket or towels we got in a soap box sometime?

MAMA:   I said don't make a mess. Your hair is black enough, hon.

JESSIE (*continuing to search the kitchen cabinets, finding two or three more towels to add to her stack*):   It's not for my hair, Mama. What about some old pillows anywhere, or a foam cushion out of a yard chair would be real good.

MAMA:   You haven't forgot what night it is, have you? (*Holding up her fingernails.*) They're all chipped, see? I've been waiting all week, Jess. It's Saturday night, sugar.

JESSIE:   I know. I got it on the schedule.

MAMA (*crossing to the living room*):   You want me to wash 'em now or are you making your mess first? (*Looking at the snowball.*) We're out of these. Did I say that already?

JESSIE:   There's more coming tomorrow. I ordered you a whole case.

MAMA (*checking the TV Guide*):   A whole case will go stale, Jessie.

JESSIE:   They can go in the freezer till you're ready for them. Where's Daddy's gun?

MAMA:   In the attic.

JESSIE:   Where in the attic? I looked your whole nap and couldn't find it anywhere.

MAMA:   One of his shoeboxes, I think.

JESSIE:   Full of shoes. I looked already.

MAMA:   Well, you didn't look good enough, then. There's that box from the ones he wore to the hospital. When he died, they told me I could have them back, but I never did like those shoes.

JESSIE (*pulling them out of her pocket*):   I found the bullets. They were in an old milk can.

MAMA (*as Jessie starts for the hall*):   Dawson took the shotgun, didn't he? Hand me that basket, hon.

JESSIE (*getting the basket for her*):   Dawson better not've taken that pistol.

MAMA (*stopping her again*):   Now my glasses, please. (*Jessie returns to get the glasses.*) I told him to take those rubber boots, too, but he said they were for fishing. I told him to take up fishing.

*Jessie reaches for the cleaning spray, and cleans Mama's glasses for her.*

JESSIE:   He's just too lazy to climb up there, Mama. Or maybe he's just being smart. That floor's not very steady.

MAMA (*getting out a piece of knitting*):   It's not a floor at all, hon, it's a board now and then. Measure this for me. I need six inches.

JESSIE (*as she measures*):   Dawson could probably use some of those clothes up there. Somebody should have them. You ought to call the Salvation Army before the whole thing falls in on you. Six inches exactly.

MAMA:   It's plenty safe! As long as you don't go up there.

JESSIE (*turning to go again*):   I'm careful.

MAMA:   What do you want the gun for, Jess?

JESSIE (*not returning this time. Opening the ladder in the hall*):   Protection. (*She steadies the ladder as Mama talks.*)

MAMA:   You take the TV way too serious, hon. I've never seen a criminal in my life. This is way too far to come for what's out here to steal. Never seen a one.

JESSIE (*taking her first step up*):   Except for Ricky.

MAMA:   Ricky is mixed up. That's not a crime.

JESSIE:   Get your hands washed. I'll be right back. And get 'em real dry. You dry your hands till I get back or it's no go, all right?

MAMA:   I thought Dawson told you not to go up those stairs.

JESSIE (*going up*):   He did.

MAMA:   I don't like the idea of a gun, Jess.

JESSIE (*calling down from the attic*):   Which shoebox, do you remember?

MAMA:   Black.

JESSIE:   The box was black?

MAMA:   The shoes were black.

JESSIE:   That doesn't help much, Mother.

MAMA:  I'm not trying to help, sugar. (*No answer.*) We don't have anything anybody'd want, Jessie. I mean, I don't even want what we got, Jessie.

JESSIE:  Neither do I. Wash your hands. (*Mama gets up and crosses to stand under the ladder.*)

MAMA:  You come down from there before you have a fit. I can't come up and get you, you know.

JESSIE:  I know.

MAMA:  We'll just hand it over to them when they come, how's that? Whatever they want, the criminals.

JESSIE:  That's a good idea, Mama.

MAMA:  Ricky will grow out of this and be a real fine boy, Jess. But I have to tell you, I wouldn't want Ricky to know we had a gun in the house.

JESSIE:  Here it is. I found it.

MAMA:  It's just something Ricky's going through. Maybe he's in with some bad people. He just needs some time, sugar. He'll get back in school or get a job or one day you'll get a call and he'll say he's sorry for all the trouble he's caused and invite you out for supper someplace dress-up.

JESSIE (*coming back down the steps*):  Don't worry. It's not for him, it's for me.

MAMA:  I didn't think you would shoot your own boy, Jessie. I know you've felt like it, well, we've all felt like shooting somebody, but we don't do it. I just don't think we need . . .

JESSIE (*interrupting*):  Your hands aren't washed. Do you want a manicure or not?

MAMA:  Yes, I do, but . . .

JESSIE (*crossing to the chair*):  Then wash your hands and don't talk to me any more about Ricky. Those two rings he took were the last valuable things *I* had, so now he's started in on other people, door to door. I hope they put him away sometime. I'd turn him in myself if I knew where he was.

MAMA:  You don't mean that.

JESSIE:  Every word. Wash your hands and that's the last time I'm telling you.

*Jessie sits down with the gun and starts cleaning it, pushing the cylinder out, checking to see that the chambers and barrel are empty, then putting some oil on a small patch of cloth and pushing*

*it through the barrel with the push rod that was in the box. Mama
goes to the kitchen and washes her hands, as instructed, trying not
to show her concern about the gun.*

MAMA:   I shoulda got you to bring down that milk can. Agnes
Fletcher sold hers to somebody with a flea market for forty
dollars apiece.

JESSIE:   I'll go back and get it in a minute. There's a wagon wheel
up there, too. There's even a churn. I'll get it all if you want.

MAMA *(coming over, now, taking over now)*:   What are you doing?

JESSIE:   The barrel has to be clean, mama. Old powder, dust gets
in it . . .

MAMA:   What for?

JESSIE:   I told you.

MAMA *(reaching for the gun)*:   And I told you, we don't get criminals out here.

JESSIE *(quickly pulling it to her)*:   And I told you . . . *(Then trying to
be calm.)* The gun is for me.

MAMA:   Well, you can have it if you want. When I die, you'll get
it all, anyway.

JESSIE:   I'm going to kill myself, Mama

MAMA *(returning to the sofa)*:   Very funny. Very funny.

JESSIE:   I am.

MAMA:   You are not! Don't even say such a thing, Jessie.

JESSIE:   How would you know if I didn't say it? You want it to be
a surprise? You're lying there in your bed or maybe you're
just brushing your teeth and you hear this . . . noise down
the hall?

MAMA:   Kill yourself.

JESSIE:   Shoot myself. In a couple of hours.

MAMA:   It must be time for your medicine.

JESSIE:   Took it already.

MAMA:   What's the matter with you?

JESSIE:   Not a thing. Feel fine.

MAMA:   You feel fine. You're just going to kill yourself.

JESSIE:   Waited until I felt good enough, in fact.

MAMA:   Don't make jokes, Jessie. I'm too old for jokes.

JESSIE:   It's not a joke, Mama.

*Mama watches for a moment in silence.*

MAMA:   That gun's no good, you know. He broke it right before he died. He dropped it in the mud one day.

JESSIE:   Seems O.K. (*She spins the chamber, cocks the pistol, and pulls the trigger. The gun is not yet loaded, so all we hear is the click, but it will definitely work. It's also obvious that Jessie knows her way around a gun. Mama cannot speak.*) I had Cecil's all ready in there, just in case I couldn't find this one, but I'd rather use Daddy's.

MAMA:   Those bullets are at least fifteen years old.

JESSIE (*pulling out another box*):   These are from last week.

MAMA:   Where did you get those?

JESSIE:   Feed store Dawson told me about.

MAMA:   Dawson!

JESSIE:   I told him I was worried about prowlers. He said he thought it was a good idea. He told me what kind to ask for.

MAMA:   If he had any idea . . .

JESSIE:   He took it as a compliment. He thought I might be taking an interest in things. He got through telling me all about the bullets and then he said we ought to talk like this more often.

MAMA:   And where was I while this was going on?

JESSIE:   On the phone with Agnes. About the milk can, I guess. Anyway, I asked Dawson if he thought they'd send me some bullets and he said he'd just call for me, because he knew they'd send them if he told them to. And he was absolutely right. Here they are.

MAMA:   How could he do that?

JESSIE:   Just trying to help, Mama.

MAMA:   And then I told you where the gun was.

JESSIE (*smiling, enjoying this joke*):   See? Everybody's doing what they can.

MAMA:   You told me it was for protection!

JESSIE:   It *is*! I'm still doing your nails, though. Want to try that new Chinaberry color?

MAMA:   Well, I'm calling Dawson right now. We'll just see what he has to say about this little stunt.

JESSIE:   Dawson doesn't have any more to do with this.

MAMA:   He's your brother.

JESSIE:   And that's all.

MAMA (*stands up, moves toward the phone*):   Dawson will put a stop to this. Yes he will. He'll take the gun away.

JESSIE:   If you call him, I'll just have to do it before he gets here. Soon as you hang up the phone, I'll just walk in the bedroom and lock the door. Dawson will get here just in time to help you clean up. Go ahead, call him. Then call the police. Then call the funeral home. Then call Loretta and see if *she'll* do your nails.

MAMA:   You will not! This is crazy talk, Jessie!

*Mama goes directly to the telephone and starts to dial, but Jessie is fast, coming up behind her and taking the receiver out of her hand, putting it back down.*

JESSIE *(firm and quiet)*:   I said no. This is private. Dawson is not invited.

MAMA:   Just me.

JESSIE:   I don't want anybody else over here. Just you and me. If Dawson comes over, it'll make me feel stupid for not doing it ten years ago.

MAMA:   I think we better call the doctor. Or how about the ambulance. You like that one driver, I know. What's his name, Timmy? Get you somebody to talk to.

JESSIE *(going back to her chair)*:   I'm through talking, Mama. You're it. No more.

MAMA:   We're just going to sit around like every other night in the world and then you're going to kill yourself? *(Jessie doesn't answer.)* You'll miss. *(Again there is no response.)* You'll just wind up a vegetable. How would you like that? Shoot your ear off? You know what the doctor said about getting excited. You'll cock the pistol and have a fit.

JESSIE:   I think I can kill myself, Mama.

MAMA:   You're not going to kill yourself, Jessie. You're not even upset! *(Jessie smiles, or laughs quietly, and Mama tries a different approach.)* People don't really kill themselves, Jessie. No, mam, doesn't make sense, unless you're retarded or deranged, and you're as normal as they come, Jessie, for the most part. We're all *afraid* to die.

JESSIE:   I'm not, Mama. I'm cold all the time, anyway.

MAMA:   That's ridiculous.

JESSIE:   It's exactly what I want. It's dark and quiet.

MAMA:   So is the back yard, Jessie! Close your eyes. Stuff cotton in your ears. Take a nap! It's quiet in your room. I'll leave the TV off all night.

JESSIE:  So quiet I don't know it's quiet. So nobody can get me.

MAMA:  You don't know what dead is like. It might not be quiet at all. What if it's like an alarm clock and you can't wake up so you can't shut if off. Ever.

JESSIE:  Dead is everybody and everything I ever knew, gone. Dead is dead quiet.

MAMA:  It's a sin. You'll go to hell.

JESSIE:  Uh-huh.

MAMA:  You will!

JESSIE:  Jesus was a suicide, if you ask me.

MAMA:  You'll go to hell just for saying that. Jessie!

JESSIE *(with genuine surprise)*:  I didn't know I thought that.

MAMA:  Jessie!

*Jessie doesn't answer. She puts the now-loaded gun back in the box and crosses to the kitchen. But Mama is afraid she's headed for the bedroom.*

MAMA *(in a panic)*:  You can't use my towels! They're my towels. I've had them for a long time. I like my towels.

JESSIE:  I asked you if you wanted that swimming towel and you said you didn't.

MAMA:  And you can't use your father's gun, either. It's mine now, too. And you can't do it in my house.

JESSIE:  Oh, come on.

MAMA:  No. You can't do it. I won't let you. The house is in my name.

JESSIE:  I have to go in the bedroom and lock the door behind me so they won't arrest you for killing me. They'll probably test your hands for gunpowder, anyway, but you'll pass.

MAMA:  Not in my house!

JESSIE:  If I'd known you were going to act like this, I wouldn't have told you.

MAMA:  How am I supposed to act? Tell you to go ahead? O.K. by me, sugar? Might try it myself. What took you so long?

JESSIE:  There's just no point in fighting me over it, that's all. Want some coffee?

MAMA:   Your birthday's coming up, Jessie. Don't you want to know what we got you?

JESSIE:   You got me dusting powder, Loretta got me a new house-coat, pink probably, and Dawson got me new slippers, too small, but they go with the robe, he'll say. (*Mama cannot speak.*) Right? (*Apparently Jessie is right.*) Be back in a minute.

*Jessie takes the gun box, puts it on top of the stack of towels and garbage bags, and takes them into her bedroom. Mama, alone for a moment, goes to the phone, picks up the receiver, looks toward the bedroom, starts to dial, and then replaces the receiver in its cradle as Jessie walks back into the room. Jessie wonders, silently. They have lived together for so long there is very rarely any reason for one to ask what the other was about to do.*

MAMA:   I started to, but I didn't. I didn't call him.

JESSIE:   Good. Thank you.

MAMA (*starting over, a new approach*):   What's this all about, Jessie?

JESSIE:   About?

*Jessie now begins the next task she had "on the schedule," which is refilling all the candy jars, taking the empty papers out of the boxes of chocolates, etc. Mama generally snitches when Jessie does this. Not tonight, though. Nevertheless, Jessie offers.*

MAMA:   What did I do?

JESSIE:   Nothing. Want a caramel?

MAMA (*ignoring the candy*):   You're mad at me.

JESSIE:   Not a bit. I am worried about you, but I'm going to do what I can before I go. We're not just going to sit around tonight. I made a list of things.

MAMA:   What things?

JESSIE:   How the washer works. Things like that.

MAMA:   I know how the washer works. You put the clothes in. You put the soap in. You turn it on. You wait.

JESSIE:   You do something else. You don't just wait.

MAMA:   Whatever else you find to do, you're still mainly waiting. The waiting's the worst part of it. The waiting's what you pay somebody else to do, if you can.

JESSIE (*nodding*):   O.K. Where do we keep the soap?

MAMA:   I could find it.

JESSIE:   See?

MAMA:   If you're mad about doing the wash, we can get Loretta to do it.

JESSIE:   Oh now, that might be worth staying to see.

MAMA:   She'd never in her life, would she?

JESSIE:   Nope.

MAMA:   What's the matter with her?

JESSIE:   She thinks she's better than we are. She's not.

MAMA:   Maybe if she didn't wear that yellow all the time.

JESSIE:   The washer repair number is on a little card taped to the side of the machine.

MAMA:   Loretta doesn't ever have to come over again. Dawson can just leave her at home when he comes. And we don't ever have to see Dawson either if he bothers you. Does he bother you?

JESSIE:   Sure he does. Be sure you clean out the lint tray every time you use the dryer. But don't ever put your house shoes in, it'll melt the soles.

MAMA:   What does Dawson do, that bothers you?

JESSIE:   He just calls me Jess like he knows who he's talking to. He's always wondering what I do all day. I mean, I wonder that myself, but it's my day, so it's mine to wonder about, not his.

MAMA:   Family is just accident, Jessie. It's nothing personal, hon. They don't mean to get on your nerves. They don't even mean to be your family, they just are.

JESSIE:   They know too much.

MAMA:   About what?

JESSIE:   They know things about you, and they learned it before you had a chance to say whether you wanted them to know it or not. They were there when it happened and it don't belong to them, it belongs to you, only they got it. Like my mail-order bra got delivered to their house.

MAMA:   By accident!

JESSIE:   All the same . . . they opened it. They saw the little rosebuds on it. (*Offering her another candy.*) Chewy mint?

MAMA (*shaking her head no*):   What do they know about you? I'll tell them never to talk about it again. Is it Ricky or Cecil or

your fits or your hair is falling out or you drink too much
coffee or you never go out of the house or what?

JESSIE: I just don't like their talk. The account at the grocery is in
Dawson's name when you call. The number's on a whole list
of numbers on the back cover of the phone book.

MAMA: Well! Now we're getting somewhere. They're none of
them ever setting foot in this house again.

JESSIE: It's not them, Mother. I wouldn't kill myself just to get
away from them.

MAMA: You leave the room when they come over, anyway.

JESSIE: I stay as long as I can. Besides, it's you they come to see.

MAMA: That's because I stay in the room when they come.

JESSIE: It's not them.

MAMA: Then what is it?

JESSIE (*checking the list on her note pad*): The grocery won't deliver
on Saturday anymore. And if you want your order the same
day, you have to call before ten. And they won't deliver less
than fifteen dollars' worth. What I do is tell them what we
need and tell them to add on cigarettes until it gets to fifteen
dollars.

MAMA: It's Ricky. You're trying to get through to him.

JESSIE: If I thought I could do that, I would stay.

MAMA: Make him sorry he hurt you, then. That's it, isn't it?

JESSIE: He's hurt me. I've hurt him. We're about even.

MAMA: You'll be telling him killing is O.K. with you, you know.
Want him to start killing next? Nothing wrong with it. Mom
did it.

JESSIE: Only a matter of time, anyway, Mama. When the call
comes, you let Dawson handle it.

MAMA: Honey, nothing says those calls are always going to be
some new trouble he's into. You could get one that he's got a
job, that he's getting married, or how about he's joined the
army, wouldn't that be nice?

JESSIE: If you call the Sweet Tooth before you call the grocery,
that Susie will take your fudge next door to the grocery and
it'll all come out together. Be sure you talk to Susie, though.
She won't let them put it in the bottom of a sack like that one
time, remember?

MAMA: Ricky could come over, you know. What if he calls us?

JESSIE:  It's not Ricky, Mama.

MAMA:  Or anybody could call us, Jessie.

JESSIE:  Not on Saturday night, Mama.

MAMA:  Then what is it? Are you sick? If your gums are swelling again, we can get you to the dentist in the morning.

JESSIE:  No. Can you order your medicine or do you want Dawson to? I've got a note to him. I'll add that to it if you want.

MAMA:  Your eyes don't look right. I thought so yesterday.

JESSIE:  That was just the ragweed. I'm not sick.

MAMA:  Epilepsy is sick, Jessie

JESSIE:  It won't kill me. (*A pause.*) If it would, I wouldn't have to.

MAMA:  You don't *have* to.

JESSIE:  No, I don't. That's what I like about it.

MAMA:  Well, I won't let you!

JESSIE:  It's not up to you.

MAMA:  Jessie!

JESSIE:  I want to hang a big sign around my neck, like Daddy's on the barn. GONE FISHING.

MAMA:  You don't like it here.

JESSIE (*smiling*):  Exactly.

MAMA:  I meant here in my house.

JESSIE:  I know you did.

MAMA:  You never should have moved back in here with me. If you'd kept your little house or found another place when Cecil left you, you'd have made some new friends at least. Had a life to lead. Had your own things around you. Give Ricky a place to come see you. You never should've come here.

JESSIE:  Maybe.

MAMA:  But I didn't force you, did I?

JESSIE:  If it was a mistake, we made it together. You took me in. I appreciate that.

MAMA:  You didn't have any business being by yourself right then, but I can see how you might want a place of your own. A grown woman should . . .

JESSIE:  Mama . . . I'm just not having a very good time and I don't have any reason to think it'll get anything but worse. I'm tired. I'm hurt. I'm sad. I feel used.

MAMA:  Tired of what?

JESSIE:  It all.

MAMA:  What does that mean?

JESSIE:  I can't say it any better.

MAMA:  Well, you'll have to say it better because I'm not letting you alone till you do. What were those other things? Hurt . . . (*Before Jessie can answer.*) You had this all ready to say to me, didn't you? Did you write this down? How long have you been thinking about this?

JESSIE:  Off and on, ten years. On all the time, since Christmas.

MAMA:  What happened at Christmas?

JESSIE:  Nothing.

MAMA:  So why Christmas?

JESSIE:  That's it. On the nose.

*A pause. Mama knows exactly what Jessie means. She was there, too, after all.*

JESSIE (*putting the candy sacks away*):  See where all this is? Red hots up front, sour balls and horehound mixed together in this one sack. New packages of toffee and licorice right in back there.

MAMA:  Go back to your list. You're hurt by what?

JESSIE (*Mama knows perfectly well*):  Mama . . .

MAMA:  O.K. Sad about what? There's nothing real sad going on right now. If it was after your divorce or something, that would make sense.

JESSIE (*looking at her list, then opening the drawer*):  Now, this drawer has everything in it that there's no better place for. Extension cords, batteries for the radio, extra lighters, sandpaper, masking tape, Elmer's glue, thumbtacks, that kind of stuff. The mousetraps are under the sink, but you call Dawson if you've got one and let him do it.

MAMA:  Sad about what?

JESSIE:  The way things are.

MAMA:  Not good enough. What things?

JESSIE:  Oh, everything from you and me to Red China.

MAMA:  I think we can leave the Chinese out of this.

JESSIE (*crosses back into the living room*):  There's extra light bulbs in a box in the hall closet. And we've got a couple of packages of fuses in the fuse box. There's candles and matches in the top of the broom closet, but if the lights go out, just call Dawson and sit tight. But don't open the refrigerator door.

Things will stay cool in there as long as you keep the door shut.

MAMA:    I asked you a question.

JESSIE:    I read the paper. I don't like how things are. And they're not any better out there than they are in here.

MAMA:    If you're doing this because of the newspapers, I can sure fix that!

JESSIE:    There's just more of it on TV.

MAMA *(kicking the television set)*:    Take it out, then!

JESSIE:    You wouldn't do that.

MAMA:    Watch me.

JESSIE:    What would you do all day?

MAMA *(desperately)*:    Sing. *(Jessie laughs.)* I would, too. You want to watch? I'll sing till morning to keep you alive, Jessie, please!

JESSIE:    No. *(Then affectionately.)* It's a funny idea, though. What do you sing?

MAMA *(has no idea how to answer this)*:    We've got a good life here!

JESSIE *(going back into the kitchen)*:    I called this morning and canceled the papers, except for Sunday, for your puzzles; you'll still get that one.

MAMA:    Let's get another dog, Jessie! You liked a big dog, now, didn't you? That King dog, didn't you?

JESSIE *(washing her hands)*:    I did like that King dog, yes.

MAMA:    I'm so dumb. He's the one run under the tractor.

JESSIE:    That makes him dumb, not you.

MAMA:    For bringing it up.

JESSIE:    It's O.K. Handi-Wipes and sponges under the sink.

MAMA:    We could get a new dog and keep him in the house. Dogs are cheap!

JESSIE *(getting big pill jars out of the cabinet)*:    No.

MAMA:    Something for you to take care of.

JESSIE:    I've had you, Mama.

MAMA *(frantically starting to fill pill bottles)*:    You do too much for me. I can fill pill bottles all day, Jessie, and change the shelf paper and wash the floor when I get through. You just watch me. You don't have to do another thing in this house if you don't want to. You don't have to take care of me, Jessie.

JESSIE:    I know that. You've just been letting me do it so I'll have something to do, haven't you?

MAMA *(realizing this was a mistake)*:    I don't do it as well as you. I just meant if it tires you out or makes you feel used . . .

JESSIE:   Mama, I know you used to ride the bus. Riding the bus and it's hot and bumpy and crowded and too noisy and more than anything in the world you want to get off and the only reason in the world you don't get off is it's still fifty blocks from where you're going? Well, I can get off right now if I want to, because even if I ride fifty more years and get off then, it's the same place when I step down to it. Whenever I feel like it, I can get off. As soon as I've had enough, it's my stop. I've had enough.

MAMA:   You're feeling sorry for yourself!

JESSIE:   The plumber's helper is under the sink, too.

MAMA:   You're not having a good time! Whoever promised you a good time? Do you think I've had a good time?

JESSIE:   I think you're pretty happy, yeah. You have things you like to do.

MAMA:   Like what?

JESSIE:   Like crochet.

MAMA:   I'll teach you to crochet.

JESSIE:   I can't do any of that nice work, Mama.

MAMA:   Good time don't come looking for you, Jessie. You could work some puzzles or put in a garden or go to the store. Let's call a taxi and go to the A&P!

JESSIE:   I shopped you up for about two weeks already. You're not going to need toilet paper till Thanksgiving.

MAMA *(interrupting)*:   You're acting like some little brat, Jessie. You're mad and everybody's boring and you don't have any-thing to do and you don't like me and you don't like going out and you don't like staying in and you never talk on the phone and you don't watch TV and you're miserable and it's your own sweet fault.

JESSIE:   And it's time I did something about it.

MAMA:   Not something like killing yourself. Something like . . . buying us all new dishes! I'd like that. Or maybe the doctor would let you get a driver's license now, or I know what let's do right this minute, let's rearrange the furniture.

JESSIE:   I'll do that. If you want. I always thought if the TV was somewhere else, you wouldn't get such a glare on it during the day. I'll do whatever you want before I go.

MAMA *(badly frightened by those words)*:   You could get a job!

JESSIE:   I took that telephone sales job and I didn't even make enough money to pay the phone bill, and I tried to work at the gift shop at the hospital and they said I made people real uncomfortable smiling at them the way I did.

MAMA:  You could keep books. You kept your dad's books.

JESSIE:  But nobody ever checked them.

MAMA:  When he died, they checked them.

JESSIE:  And that's when they took the books away from me.

MAMA:  That's because without him there wasn't any business, Jessie!

JESSIE (*putting the pill bottles away*):  You know I couldn't work. I can't do anything. I've never been around people my whole life except when I went to the hospital. I could have a seizure any time. What good would a job do? The kind of job I could get would make me feel worse.

MAMA:  Jessie!

JESSIE:  It's true!

MAMA:  It's what you think is true!

JESSIE (*struck by the clarity of that*):  That's right. It's what I think is true.

MAMA (*hysterically*):  But I can't do anything about that!

JESSIE (*quietly*):  No. You can't. (*Mama slumps, if not physically, at least emotionally.*) And I can't do anything either, about my life, to change it, make it better, make me feel better about it. Like it better, make it work. But I can stop it. Shut it down, turn it off like the radio when there's nothing on I want to listen to. It's all I really have that belongs to me and I'm going to say what happens to it. And it's going to stop. And I'm going to stop it. So. Let's just have a good time.

MAMA:  Have a good time.

JESSIE:  We can't go on fussing all night. I mean, I could ask you things I always wanted to know and you could make me some hot chocolate. The old way.

MAMA (*in despair*):  It takes cocoa, Jessie.

JESSIE (*gets it out of the cabinet*):  I bought cocoa, Mama. And I'd like to have a caramel apple and do your nails.

MAMA:  You didn't eat a bite of supper.

JESSIE:  Does that mean I can't have a caramel apple?

MAMA:  Of course not. I mean . . . (*Smiling a little.*) Of course you can have a caramel apple.

JESSIE:  I thought I could.

MAMA:  I make the best caramel apples in the world.

JESSIE:   I know you do.

MAMA:   Or used to. And you don't get cocoa like mine anywhere anymore.

JESSIE:   It takes time, I know, but . . .

MAMA:   The salt is the trick.

JESSIE:   Trouble and everything.

MAMA (*backing away toward the stove*):   It's no trouble. What trouble? You put it in the pan and stir it up. All right. Fine. Caramel apples. Cocoa. O.K.

*Jessie walks to the counter to retrieve her cigarettes as Mama looks for the right pan. There are brief near-smiles, and maybe Mama clears her throat. We have a truce, for the moment. A genuine but nevertheless uneasy one. Jessie, who has been in constant motion since the beginning, now seems content to sit.*

*Mama starts looking for a pan to make the cocoa, getting out all the pans in the cabinets in the process. It looks like she's making a mess on purpose so Jessie will have to put them all away again. Mama is buying time, or trying to, and entertaining.*

JESSIE:   You talk to Agnes today?

MAMA:   She's calling me from a pay phone this week. God only knows why. She has a perfectly good Trimline at home.

JESSIE (*laughing*):   Well, how is she?

MAMA:   How is she every day, Jessie? Nuts.

JESSIE:   Is she really crazy or just silly?

MAMA:   No, she's really crazy. She was probably using the pay phone because she had another little fire problem at home.

JESSIE:   Mother . . .

MAMA:   I'm serious! Agnes Fletcher's burned down every house she ever lived in. Eight fires, and she's due for a new one any day now.

JESSIE (*laughing*):   No!

MAMA:   Wouldn't surprise me a bit.

JESSIE (*laughing*):   Why didn't you tell me this before? Why isn't she locked up somewhere?

MAMA:   'Cause nobody ever got hurt, I guess. Agnes woke everybody up to watch the fires as soon as she set 'em. One time she set out porch chairs and served lemonade.

JESSIE (*shaking her head*):   Real lemonade?

MAMA:   The houses they lived in, you knew they were going to fall down anyway, so why wait for it, is all I could ever make out about it. Agnes likes a feeling of accomplishment.

JESSIE:   Good for her.

MAMA *(finding the pan she wants)*:   Why are you asking about Agnes? One cup or two?

JESSIE:   One. She's your friend. No marshmallows.

MAMA *(getting the milk, etc.)*:   You have to have marshmallows. That's the old way, Jess. Two or three? Three is better.

JESSIE:   Three, then. Her whole house burns up? Her clothes and pillows and everything? I'm not sure I believe this.

MAMA:   When she was a girl, Jess, not now. Long time ago. But she's still got it in her, I'm sure of it.

JESSIE:   She wouldn't burn her house down now. Where would she go? She can't get Buster to build her a new one, he's dead. How could she burn it up?

MAMA:   Be exciting, though, if she did. You never know.

JESSIE:   You do too know, Mama. She wouldn't do it.

MAMA *(forced to admit, but reluctant)*:   I guess not.

JESSIE:   What else? Why does she wear all those whistles around her neck?

MAMA:   Why does she have a house full of birds?

JESSIE:   I didn't know she had a house full of birds!

MAMA:   Well, she does. And she says they just follow her home. Well, I know for a fact she's still paying on the last parrot she bought. You gotta keep your life filled up, she says. She says a lot of stupid things. *(Jessie laughs, Mama continues, convinced she's getting somewhere.)* It's all that okra she eats. You can't just willy-nilly eat okra two meals a day and expect to get away with it. Made her crazy.

JESSIE:   She really eats okra twice a day? Where does she get it in the winter?

MAMA:   Well, she eats it a lot. Maybe not two meals, but . . .

JESSIE:   More than the average person.

MAMA *(beginning to get irritated)*:   I don't know how much okra the average person eats.

JESSIE:   Do you know how much okra Agnes eats?

MAMA:   No.

JESSIE:   How many birds does she have?

MAMA:   Two.

JESSIE:   Then what are the whistles for?

MAMA:   They're not real whistles. Just little plastic ones on a necklace she won playing Bingo, and I only told you about it because I thought I might get a laugh out of you for once even if it wasn't the truth, Jessie. Things don't have to be true to talk about 'em, you know.

JESSIE:   Why won't she come over here?

*Mama is suddenly quiet, but the cocoa and milk are in the pan now, so she lights the stove and starts stirring.*

MAMA:   Well now, what a good idea. We should've had more cocoa. Cocoa is perfect.

JESSIE:   Except you don't like milk.

MAMA (*another attempt, but not as energetic*):   I hate milk. Coats your throat as bad as okra. Something just downright disgusting about it.

JESSIE:   It's because of me, isn't it?

MAMA:   No, Jess.

JESSIE:   Yes, Mama.

MAMA:   O.K. Yes, then, but she's crazy. She's as crazy as they come. She's a lunatic.

JESSIE:   What is it exactly? Did I say something, sometime? Or did she see me have a fit and's afraid I might have another one if she came over, or what?

MAMA:   I guess.

JESSIE:   You guess what? What's she ever said? She must've given you some reason.

MAMA:   Your hands are cold.

JESSIE:   What difference does that make?

MAMA:   "Like a corpse," she says, "and I'm gonna be one soon enough as it is."

JESSIE:   That's crazy.

MAMA:   That's Agnes. "Jessie's shook the hand of death and I can't take the chance it's catching, Thelma, so I ain't comin' over, and you can understand or not, but I ain't comin'. I'll come up the driveway, but that's as far as I go."

JESSIE (*laughing, relieved*):   I thought she didn't like me! She's scared of me! How about that! Scared of me.

MAMA:   I could make her come over here, Jessie. I could call her up right now and she could bring the birds and come visit. I didn't know you ever thought about her at all. I'll tell her she just has to come and she'll come, all right. She owes me one.

JESSIE: No. That's all right. I just wondered about it. When I'm in the hospital, does she come over here?

MAMA: Her kitchen is just a tiny thing. When she comes over here, she feels like . . . (*Toning it down a little.*) Well, we all like a change of scene, don't we?

JESSIE (*playing along*): Sure we do. Plus there's no birds diving around.

MAMA: I hate those birds. She says I don't understand them. What's there to understand about birds?

JESSIE: Why Agnes likes them, for one thing. Why they stay with her when they could be outside with the other birds. What their singing means. How they fly. What they think Agnes is.

MAMA: Why do you have to know so much about things, Jessie? There's just not that much *to* things that I could ever see.

JESSIE: That you could ever *tell*, you mean. You didn't have to lie to me about Agnes.

MAMA: I didn't lie. You never asked before!

JESSIE: You lied about setting fire to all those houses and about how many birds she has and how much okra she eats and why she won't come over here. If I have to keep dragging the truth out of you, this is going to take all night.

MAMA: That's fine with me. I'm not a bit sleepy.

JESSIE: Mama . . .

MAMA: All right. Ask me whatever you want. Here.

*They come to an awkward stop, as the cocoa is ready and Mama pours it into the cups Jessie has set on the table.*

JESSIE (*as Mama takes her first sip*): Did you love Daddy?

MAMA: No.

JESSIE (*pleased that Mama understands the rules better now*): I didn't think so. Were you really fifteen when you married him?

MAMA: The way he told it? I'm sitting in the mud, he comes along, drags me in the kitchen, "She's been there ever since"?

JESSIE: Yes.

MAMA: No. It was a big fat lie, the whole thing. He just thought it was funnier that way. God, this milk in here.

JESSIE: The cocoa helps.

MAMA (*pleased that they agree on this, at least*):    Not enough, though, does it? You can still taste it, can't you?

JESSIE:    Yeah, it's pretty bad. I thought it was my memory that was bad, but it's not. It's the milk, all right.

MAMA:    It's a real waste of chocolate. You don't have to finish it.

JESSIE (*putting her cup down*):    Thanks, though.

MAMA:    I should've known not to make it. I knew you wouldn't like it. You never did like it.

JESSIE:    You didn't ever love him, or he did something and you stopped loving him, or what?

MAMA:    He felt sorry for me. He wanted a plain country woman and that's what he married, and then he held it against me the rest of my life like I was supposed to change and surprise him somehow. Like I remember this one day he was standing on the porch and I told him to get a shirt on and he went in and got one and then he said, real peaceful, but to the point, "You're right, Thelma. If God had meant for people to go around without any clothes on, they'd have been born that way."

JESSIE (*sees Mama's hurt*):    He didn't mean anything by that, Mama.

MAMA:    He never said a word he didn't have to, Jessie. That was probably all he'd said to me all day, Jessie. So if he said it, there was something to it, but I never did figure that one out. What did that mean?

JESSIE:    I don't know. I liked him better than you did, but I didn't know him any better.

MAMA:    How could I love him, Jessie. I didn't have a thing he wanted. (*Jessie doesn't answer.*) He got his share, though. You loved him enough for both of us. You followed him around like some . . . Jessie, all the man ever did was farm and sit . . . and try to think of somebody to sell the farm to.

JESSIE:    Or make me a boyfriend out of pipe cleaners and sit back and smile like the stick man was about to dance and wasn't I going to get a kick out of that. Or sit up with a sick cow all night and leave me a chain of sleepy stick elephants on my bed in the morning.

MAMA:    Or just sit.

JESSIE:    I liked him sitting. Big old faded blue man in the chair. Quiet.

MAMA:    Agnes gets more talk out of her birds than I got from the two of you. He could've had that GONE FISHING sign around his neck in that chair. I saw him stare off at the water. I saw him look at the weather rolling in. I got where I could practically see that boat myself. But you, you knew what he was thinking about and you're going to tell me.

JESSIE:   I don't know, Mama! His life, I guess. His corn. His boots. Us. Things. You know.

MAMA:   No, I don't know, Jessie! You had those quiet little conversations after supper every night. What were you whispering about?

JESSIE:   We weren't whispering, you were just across the room.

MAMA:   What did you talk about?

JESSIE:   We talked about why black socks are warmer than blue socks. Is that something to go tell Mother? You were just jealous because I'd rather talk to him than wash the dishes with you.

MAMA:   I was jealous because you'd rather talk to him than anything! (*Jessie reaches across the table for the small clock and starts to wind it.*) If I had died instead of him, he wouldn't have taken you in like I did.

JESSIE:   I wouldn't have expected him to.

MAMA:   Then what would you have done?

JESSIE:   Come visit.

MAMA:   Oh, I see. He died and left you stuck with me and you're mad about it.

JESSIE (*getting up from the table*):   Not anymore. He didn't mean to. I didn't have to come here. We've been through this.

MAMA:   He felt sorry for you, too, Jessie, don't kid yourself about that. He said you were a runt and he said it from the day you were born and he said you didn't have a chance.

JESSIE (*getting the canister of sugar and starting to refill the sugar bowl*):   I know he loved me.

MAMA:   What if he did? It didn't change anything.

JESSIE:   It didn't have to. I miss him.

MAMA:   He never really went fishing, you know. Never once. His tackle box was full of chewing tobacco and all he ever did was drive out to the lake and sit in his car. Dawson told me. And Bennie at the bait shop, he told Dawson. They all laughed about it. And he'd come back from fishing and all he'd have to show for it was a . . . a whole pipe cleaner *family*—chickens, pigs, a dog with a bad leg—it was creepy strange. It made me sick to look at them and I hid his pipe cleaners a couple of times but he always had more somewhere.

JESSIE:  I thought it might be better for you after he died. You'd get interested in things. Breathe better. Change somehow.

MAMA:  Into what? The Queen? A clerk in a shoe store? Why should I? Because he said to? Because you said to? (*Jessie shakes her head.*) Well I wasn't here for his entertainment and I'm not here for yours either, Jessie. I don't know what I'm here for, but then I don't think about it. (*Realizing what all this means.*) But I bet you wouldn't be killing yourself if he were still alive. That's a fine thing to figure out, isn't it?

JESSIE (*filling the honey jar now*):  That's not true.

MAMA:  Oh no? Then what were you asking about him for? Why did you want to know if I loved him?

JESSIE:  I didn't think you did, that's all.

MAMA:  Fine then. You were right. Do you feel better now?

JESSIE (*cleaning the honey jar carefully*):  It feels good to be right about it.

MAMA:  It didn't matter whether I loved him. It didn't matter to me and it didn't matter to him. And it didn't mean we didn't get along. It wasn't important. We didn't talk about it. (*Sweeping the pots off the cabinet.*) Take all these pots out to the porch!

JESSIE:  What for?

MAMA:  Just leave me this one pan. (*She jerks the silverware drawer open.*) Get me one knife, one fork, one big spoon, and the can opener, and put them out where I can get them. (*Starts throwing knives and forks in one of the pans.*)

JESSIE:  Don't do that! I just straightened that drawer!

MAMA (*throwing the pan in the sink*):  And throw out all the plates and cups. I'll use paper. Loretta can have what she wants and Dawson can sell the rest.

JESSIE (*calmly*):  What are you doing?

MAMA:  I'm not going to cook. I never liked it, anyway. I like candy. Wrapped in plastic or coming in sacks. And tuna. I'll eat tuna, thank you.

JESSIE (*taking the pan out of the sink*):  What if you want to make apple butter? You can't make apple butter in that little pan. What if you leave carrots on cooking and burn up that pan?

MAMA:  I don't like carrots.

JESSIE:   What if the strawberries are good this year and you want to go picking with Agnes.

MAMA:   I'll tell her to bring a pan. You said you would do whatever I wanted! I don't want a bunch of pans cluttering up my cabinets I can't get down to, anyway. Throw them out. Every last one.

JESSIE *(gathering up the pots)*:   I'm putting them all back in. I'm not taking them to the porch. If you want them, they'll be here. You'll bend down and get them, like you got the one for the cocoa. And if somebody else comes over here to cook, they'll have something to cook in, and that's the end of it!

MAMA:   Who's going to come cook here?

JESSIE:   Agnes.

MAMA:   In my pots. Not on your life.

JESSIE:   There's no reason why the two of you couldn't just live here together. Be cheaper for both of you and somebody to talk to. And if the birds bothered you, well, one day when Agnes is out getting her hair done, you could take them all for a walk!

MAMA *(as Jessie straightens the silverware)*:   So that's why you're pestering me about Agnes. You think you can rest easy if you get me a new babysitter? Well, I don't want to live with Agnes. I barely want to talk with Agnes. She's just around. We go back, that's all. I'm not letting Agnes near this place. You don't get off as easy as that, child.

JESSIE:   O.K., then. It's just something to think about.

MAMA:   I don't like things to think about. I like things to go on.

JESSIE *(closing the silverware drawer)*:   I want to know what Daddy said to you the night he died. You came storming out of his room and said I could wait it out with him if I wanted to, but you were going to watch *Gunsmoke*. What did he say to you?

MAMA:   He didn't have *anything* to say to me, Jessie. That's why I left. He didn't say a thing. It was his last chance not to talk to me and he took full advantage of it.

JESSIE *(after a moment)*:   I'm sorry you didn't love him. Sorry for you, I mean. He seemed like a nice man.

MAMA *(as Jessie walks to the refrigerator)*:   Ready for your apple now?

JESSIE:   Soon as I'm through here. Mama.

MAMA:   You won't like the apple, either. It'll be just like the cocoa.

You never liked eating at all, did you? Any of it! What have you been living on all these years, toothpaste?

JESSIE (*as she starts to clean out the refrigerator*):  Now, you know the milkman comes on Wednesdays and Saturdays, and he leaves the order blank in an egg box, and you give the bills to Dawson once a month.

MAMA:  Do they still make that orangeade?

JESSIE:  It's not orangeade, it's just orange.

MAMA:  I'm going to get some. I thought they stopped making it. You just stopped ordering it.

JESSIE:  You should drink milk.

MAMA:  Not anymore, I'm not. That hot chocolate was the last. Hooray.

JESSIE (*getting the garbage can from under the sink*):  I told them to keep delivering a quart a week no matter what you said. I told them you'd run out of Cokes and you'd have to drink it. I told them I knew you wouldn't pour it on the ground . . .

MAMA (*finishing her sentence*):  And you told them you weren't going to be ordering anymore?

JESSIE:  I told them I was taking a little holiday and to look after you.

MAMA:  And they didn't think something was funny about that? You who doesn't go to the front steps? You, who only sees the driveway looking down from a stretcher passed out cold?

JESSIE (*enjoying this, but not laughing*):  They said it was about time, but why didn't I take you with me? And I said I didn't think you'd want to go, and they said. "Yeah, everybody's got their own idea of vacation."

MAMA:  I guess you think that's funny.

JESSIE (*pulling jars out of the refrigerator*):  You know there never was any reason to call the ambulance for me. All they ever did for me in the emergency room was let me wake up. I could've done that here. Now, I'll just call them out and you say yes or no. I know you like pickles. Ketchup?

MAMA:  Keep it.

JESSIE:  We've had this since last Fourth of July.

MAMA:  Keep the ketchup. Keep it all.

JESSIE:  Are you going to drink ketchup from the bottle or what? How can you want your food and not want your pots to cook it in? This stuff will all spoil in here, Mother.

MAMA:   Nothing I ever did was good enough for you and I want to know why.

JESSIE:   That's not true.

MAMA:   And I want to know why you've lived here this long feeling the way you do.

JESSIE:   You have no earthly idea how I feel.

MAMA:   Well, how could I? You're real far back there, Jessie.

JESSIE:   Back where?

MAMA:   What's it like over there, where you are? Do people always say the right thing or get whatever they want, or what?

JESSIE:   What are you talking about?

MAMA:   Why do you read the newspaper? Why don't you wear that sweater I made for you? Do you remember how I used to look, or am I just any old woman now? When you have a fit, do you see stars or what? How did you fall off the horse, really? Why did Cecil leave you? Where did you put my old glasses?

JESSIE *(stunned by Mama's intensity)*:   They're in the bottom drawer of your dresser in an old Milk of Magnesia box. Cecil left me because he made me choose between him and smoking.

MAMA:   Jessie, I know he wasn't that dumb.

JESSIE:   I never understood why he hated it so much when it's so good. Smoking is the only thing I know that's always just what you think it's going to be. Just like it was the last time, right there when you want it and real quiet.

MAMA:   Your fits made him sick and you know it.

JESSIE:   Say seizures, not fits. Seizures.

MAMA:   It's the same thing. A seizure in the hospital is a fit at home.

JESSIE:   They didn't bother him at all. Except he did feel responsible for it. It *was* his idea to go horseback riding that day. It was his idea I could do *anything* if I just made up my mind to. I fell off the horse because I didn't know how to hold on. Cecil left for pretty much the same reason.

MAMA:   He had a girl, Jessie. I walked right in on them in the toolshed.

JESSIE *(after a moment)*:   O.K. That's fair. (*Lighting another cigarette.*) Was she very pretty?

MAMA:   She was Agnes's girl, Carlene. Judge for yourself.

JESSIE *(as she walks to the living room)*:   I guess you and Agnes had a good talk about that, huh?

MAMA:   I never thought he was good enough for you. They moved here from Tennessee, you know.

JESSIE:   What are you talking about? You liked him better than I did. You flirted him out here to build your porch or I'd never even met him at all. You thought maybe he'd help you out around the place, come in and get some coffee and talk to you. God knows what you thought. All that curly hair.

MAMA:   He's the best carpenter I ever saw. That little house of yours will still be standing at the end of the world, Jessie.

JESSIE:   You didn't need a porch, Mama.

MAMA:   All right! I wanted you to have a husband.

JESSIE:   And I couldn't get one on my own, of course.

MAMA:   How were you going to get a husband never opening your mouth to a living soul?

JESSIE:   So I was quiet about it, so what?

MAMA:   So I should have let you just sit here? Sit like your daddy? Sit here?

JESSIE:   Maybe.

MAMA:   Well, I didn't think so.

JESSIE:   Well, what did you know?

MAMA:   I never said I knew much. How was I supposed to learn anything living out here? I didn't know enough to do half the things I did in my life. Things happen. You do what you can about them and you see what happens next. I married you off to the wrong man, I admit that. So I took you in when he left, I'm sorry.

JESSIE:   He wasn't the wrong man.

MAMA:   He didn't love you, Jessie, or he wouldn't have left.

JESSIE:   He wasn't the wrong man, Mama. I loved Cecil so much. And I tried to get more exercise and I tried to stay awake. I tried to learn to ride a horse. And I tried to stay outside with him, but he always knew I was trying, so it didn't work.

MAMA:   He was a selfish man. He told me once he hated to see people move into his houses after he built them. He knew they'd mess them up.

JESSIE:   I loved that bridge he built over the creek in back of the house. It didn't have to be anything special, a couple of boards would have been just fine, but he used that yellow pine and rubbed it so smooth . . .

MAMA:   He had responsibilities here. He had a wife and son here and he failed you.

JESSIE:   Or that baby bed he built for Ricky. I told him he didn't have to spend so much time on it, but he said it had to last, and the thing ended up weighing two hundred pounds and I couldn't move it. I said, "How long does a baby bed have to last, anyway?" But maybe he thought if it was strong enough, it might keep Ricky a baby.

MAMA:   Ricky is too much like Cecil.

JESSIE:   He is not. Ricky is as much like me as it's possible for any human to be. We even wear the same size pants. These are his, I think.

MAMA:   That's just the same size. That's not you're the same person.

JESSIE:   I see it on his face. I hear it when he talks. We look out at the world and we see the same thing: Not Fair. And the only difference between us is Ricky's out there trying to get even. And he knows not to trust anybody and he got it straight from me. And he knows not to try to get work, and guess where he got that. He walks around like there's loose boards in the floor, and you know who laid that floor, I did.

MAMA:   Ricky isn't through yet. You don't know how he'll turn out!

JESSIE (going back to the kitchen):   Yes I do and so did Cecil. Ricky is the two of us together for all time in too small a space. And we're tearing each other apart, like always, inside that boy, and if you don't see it, then you're just blind.

MAMA:   Give him time, Jess.

JESSIE:   Oh, he'll have plenty of that. Five years for forgery, ten years for armed assault . . .

MAMA (furious):   Stop that! (Then pleading.) Jessie, Cecil might be ready to try it again, honey, that happens sometimes. Go downtown. Find him. Talk to him. He didn't know what he had in you. Maybe he sees things different now, but you're not going to know that till you see him. Or call him up! Right now! He might be home.

JESSIE:   And say what? Nothing's changed, Cecil, I'd just like to look at you, if you don't mind? No. He loved me, Mama. He just didn't know how things fall down around me like they do. I think he did the right thing. He gave himself another chance, that's all. But I did beg him to take me with him. I did tell him I would leave Ricky and you and everything I loved out here if only he would take me with him, but he couldn't and I understood that. (*Pause.*) I wrote that note I showed you. I wrote it. Not Cecil. I said "I'm sorry, Jessie, I can't fix it all for you." I said I'd always love me, not Cecil. But that's how he felt.

MAMA:   Then he should've taken you with him!

JESSIE (*picking up the garbage bag she has filled*):   Mama, you don't pack your garbage when you move.

MAMA:   You will not call yourself garbage, Jessie.

JESSIE (*taking the bag to the big garbage can near the back door*):   Just a way of saying it, Mama. Thinking about my list, that's all. (*Opening the can, putting the garbage in, then securing the lid.*) Well, a little more than that. I was trying to say it's all right that Cecil left. It was . . . a relief in a way. I never was what he wanted to see, so it was better when he wasn't looking at me all the time.

MAMA:   I'll make your apple now.

JESSIE:   No thanks. You get the manicure stuff and I'll be right there.

*Jessie ties up the big garbage bag in the can and replaces the small garbage bag under the sink, all the time trying desperately to regain her calm. Mama watches, from a distance, her hand reaching unconsciously for the phone. Then she has a better idea. Or rather she thinks of the only other thing left and is willing to try it. Maybe she is even convinced it will work.*

MAMA:   Jessie, I think your daddy had little . . .

JESSIE (*interrupting her*):   Garbage night is Tuesday. Put it out as late as you can. The Davis's dogs get in it if you don't. (*Replacing the garbage bag in the can under the sink.*) And keep ordering the heavy black bags. It doesn't pay to buy the cheap ones. And I've got all the ties here with the hammers and all. Take them out of the box as soon as you open a new one and put them in this drawer. They'll get lost if you don't, and rubber bands or something else won't work.

MAMA:   I think your daddy had fits, too. I think he sat in his chair and had little fits. I read this a long time ago in a magazine, how little fits go, just little blackouts where maybe their eyes don't even close and people just call them "thinking spells."

JESSIE *(getting the slipcover out of the laundry basket)*:   I don't think you want this manicure we've been looking forward to. I washed this cover for the sofa, but it'll take both of us to get it back on.

MAMA:   I watched his eyes. I know that's what it was. The magazine said some people don't even know they've had one.

JESSIE:   Daddy would've known if he'd had fits, Mama.

MAMA:   The lady in this story had kept track of hers and she'd had eighty thousand of them in the last eleven years.

JESSIE:   Next time you wash this cover, it'll dry better if you put it on wet.

MAMA:   Jessie, listen to what I'm telling you. This lady had anywhere between five and five hundred fits a day and they lasted maybe fifteen seconds apiece, so that out of her life, she'd only lost about two weeks altogether, and she had a full-time secretary job and an IQ of 120.

JESSIE *(amused by Mama's approach)*:   You want to talk about the fits, is that it?

MAMA:   Yes. I do. I want to say . . .

JESSIE *(interrupting)*:   Most of the time I wouldn't even know I'd had one, except I wake up with different clothes on, feeling like I've been run over. Sometimes I feel my head start to turn around or hear myself scream. And sometimes there *is* this dizzy stupid feeling a little before it, but if the TV's on, well, it's easy to miss.

*As Jessie and Mama replace the slipcover on the sofa and the afghan on the chair, the physical struggle somehow mirrors the emotional one in the conversation.*

MAMA:   I can tell when you're about to have one. Your eyes get this big! But, Jessie, you haven't . . .

JESSIE *(taking charge of this)*:   What do they look like? The seizures.

MAMA *(reluctant)*:   Different each time, Jess.

JESSIE:   O.K. Pick one, then. A good one. I think I want to know now.

MAMA:   There's not much to tell. You just . . . crumple, in a heap, like a puppet and somebody cut the strings all at once, or like the firing squad in some Mexican movie, you just slide down the wall, you know. You don't know what happens? How can you not know what happens?

JESSIE:   I'm busy.

MAMA:   That's not funny.

JESSIE:   I'm not laughing. My head turns around and I fall down and then what?

MAMA:   Well, your chest squeezes in and out, and you sound like you're gagging, sucking air in and out like you can't breathe.

JESSIE:   Do it for me. Make the sound for me.

MAMA:   I will not. It's awful-sounding.

JESSIE:   Yeah. It felt like it might be. What's next?

MAMA:   Your mouth bites down and I have to get your tongue out of the way fast, so you don't bite yourself.

JESSIE:   Or you. I bite you, too, don't I?

MAMA:   You got me once real good. I had to get a tetanus! But I know what to watch for now. And then you turn blue and the jerks start up. Like I'm standing there poking you with a cattle prod or you're sticking your finger in a light socket as fast as you can . . .

JESSIE:   Foaming like a mad dog the whole time.

MAMA:   It's bubbling, Jess, not foam like the washer overflowed, for God's sake; it's bubbling like a baby spitting up. I go get a wet washcloth, that's all. And then the jerks slow down and you wet yourself and it's over. Two minutes tops.

JESSIE:   How do I get to bed?

MAMA:   How do you think?

JESSIE:   I'm too heavy for you now. How do you do it?

MAMA:   I call Dawson. But I get you cleaned up before he gets here and I make him leave before you wake up.

JESSIE:   You could just leave me on the floor.

MAMA:   I want you to wake up someplace nice, O.K.? (*Then making a real effort.*) But, Jessie, and this is the reason I even brought this up! You haven't had a seizure for a solid year. A whole year, do you realize that?

JESSIE:   Yeah, the phenobarb's about right now, I guess.

MAMA:   You bet it is. You might never have another one, ever! You might be through with it for all time!

JESSIE:   Could be.

MAMA:   You are. I know you are!

JESSIE:   I sure am feeling good. I really am. The double vision's gone and my gums aren't swelling. No rashes or anything. I'm feeling as good as I ever felt in my life. I'm even feeling like worrying or getting mad and I'm not afraid it will start a fit if I do, I just go ahead.

MAMA:   Of course you do! You can even scream at me, if you want to. I can take it. You don't have to act like you're just visiting here, Jessie. This is your house, too.

JESSIE:   The best part is, my memory's back.

MAMA:   Your memory's always been good. When couldn't you remember things? You're always reminding me what . . .

JESSIE:   Because I've made lists for everything. But now I remember what things mean on my lists. I see "dish towels," and I used to wonder whether I was supposed to wash them, buy them, or look for them because I wouldn't remember where I put them after I washed them, but now I know it means wrap them up, they're a present for Loretta's birthday.

MAMA *(finished with the sofa now):*   You used to go looking for your lists, too, I've noticed that. You always know where they are now! *(Then suddenly worried.)* Loretta's birthday isn't coming up, is it?

JESSIE:   I made a list of all the birthdays for you. I even put yours on it. *(A small smile.)* So you can call Loretta and remind her.

MAMA:   Let's take Loretta to Howard Johnson's and have those fried clams. I *know* you love that clam roll.

JESSIE *(slight pause):*   I won't be here, Mama.

MAMA:   What have we just been talking about? You'll be here. You're well, Jessie. You're starting all over. You said it yourself. You're remembering things and . . .

JESSIE:   I won't be here. If I'd ever had a year like this, to think straight and all, before now, I'd be gone already.

MAMA *(not pleading, commanding):*   No, Jessie.

JESSIE *(folding the rest of the laundry):*   Yes, Mama. Once I started remembering, I could see what it all added up to.

MAMA:   The fits are over!

JESSIE:   It's not the fits, Mama.

MAMA:   Then it's me for giving them to you, but I didn't do it!

JESSIE:   It's not the fits! You said it yourself, the medicine takes care of the fits.

MAMA *(interrupting)*:   Your daddy gave you those fits, Jessie. He passed it down to you like your green eyes, and your straight hair. It's not my fault!

JESSIE:   So what if he had little fits? It's not inherited. I fell off the horse. It was an accident.

MAMA:   The horse wasn't the first time, Jessie. You had a fit when you were five years old.

JESSIE:   I did not.

MAMA:   You did! You were eating a popsicle and down you went. He gave it to you. It's *his* fault, not mine.

JESSIE:   Well, you took your time telling me.

MAMA:   How do you tell that to a five-year-old?

JESSIE:   What did the doctor say?

MAMA:   He said kids have them all the time. He said there wasn't anything to do but wait for another one.

JESSIE:   But I didn't have another one.

*Now there is a real silence.*

JESSIE:   You mean to tell me I had fits all the time as a kid and you just told me I fell down or something and it wasn't till I had the fit when Cecil was looking that anybody bothered to find out what was the matter with me?

MAMA:   It wasn't *all the time*, Jessie. And they changed when you started to school. More like your daddy's. Oh, that was some swell time, sitting here with the two of you turning off and on like light bulbs some nights.

JESSIE:   How many fits did I have?

MAMA:   You never hurt yourself. I never let you out of my sight. I caught you every time.

JESSIE:   But you didn't tell anybody.

MAMA:   It was none of their business.

JESSIE:   You were ashamed.

MAMA:   I didn't want anybody to know. Least of all you.

JESSIE:   Least of all me. Oh, right. That was mine to know, Mama, not yours. Did Daddy know?

MAMA:   He thought you were . . . you fell down a lot. That's what he thought. You were careless. Or maybe he thought I beat you. I don't know what he thought. He didn't think about it.

JESSIE:   Because you didn't tell him!

MAMA:   If I told him about you, I'd have to tell him about him!

JESSIE:   I don't like this. I don't like this one bit.

MAMA:   I didn't think you'd like it. That's why I didn't tell you.

JESSIE:   If I'd known I was an epileptic, Mama, I wouldn't have ridden any horses.

MAMA:   Make you feel like a freak, is that what I should have done?

JESSIE:   Just get the manicure tray and sit down!

MAMA (*throwing it to the floor*):   I don't want a manicure!

JESSIE:   Doesn't look like you do, no.

MAMA:   Maybe I did drop you, you don't know.

JESSIE:   If you say you didn't, you didn't.

MAMA (*beginning to break down*):   Maybe I fed you the wrong thing. Maybe you had a fever sometime and I didn't know it soon enough. Maybe it's a punishment.

JESSIE:   For what?

MAMA:   I don't know. Because of how I felt about your father. Because I didn't want any more children. Because I smoked too much or didn't eat right when I was carrying you. It has to be something I did.

JESSIE:   It does not. It's just a sickness, not a curse. Epilepsy doesn't mean anything. It just is.

MAMA:   I'm not talking about the fits here, Jessie! I'm talking about this killing yourself. It has to be me that's the matter here. You wouldn't be doing this if it wasn't. I didn't tell you things or I married you off to the wrong man or I took you in and let your life get away from you or all of it put together. I don't know what I did, but I did it. I know. This is all my fault, Jessie, but I don't know what to do about it now!

JESSIE (*exasperated at having to say this again*):   It doesn't have anything to do with you!

MAMA:   Everything you do has to do with me, Jessie. You can't do *anything*, wash your face or cut your finger, without doing it to me. That's right! You might as well kill me as you, Jessie, it's the same thing. This has to do with me, Jessie.

JESSIE:   Then what if it does! What if it has everything to do with

you! What if you are all I have and you're not enough? What
if I could take all the rest of it if only I didn't have you here?
What if the only way I can get away from you for good is to
kill myself? What if it is? I can *still* do it!

MAMA *(in desperate tears)*:   Don't leave me, Jessie! *(Jessie stands for
a moment, then turns for the bedroom.)* No! *(She grabs Jessie's arm.)*

JESSIE *(carefully taking her arm away)*:   I have a box of things I want
people to have. I'm just going to go get it for you. You . . .
just rest a minute.

*Jessie is gone. Mama heads for the telephone, but she can't even
pick up the receiver this time and, instead, stoops to clean up the
bottles that have spilled out of the manicure tray.*

*Jessie returns, carrying a box that groceries were delivered in. It
probably says Hershey Kisses or Starkist Tuna. Mama is still down
on the floor cleaning up, hoping that maybe if she just makes it look
nice enough, Jessie will stay.*

MAMA:   Jessie, how can I live here without you? I need you!
You're supposed to tell me to stand up straight and say how
nice I look in my pink dress, and drink my milk. You're
supposed to go around and lock up so I know we're safe for
the night, and when I wake up, you're supposed to be out
there making the coffee and watching me get older every day,
and you're supposed to help me die when the time comes. I
can't do that by myself, Jessie. I'm not like you, Jessie. I hate
the quiet and I don't want to die and I don't want you to go,
Jessie. How can I . . . *(Has to stop a moment.)* How can I get
up every day knowing you had to kill yourself to make it stop
hurting and I was here all the time and I never even saw it.
And then you gave me this chance to make it better, convince
you to stay alive, and I couldn't do it. How can I live with
myself after this, Jessie?

JESSIE:   I only told you so I could explain it, so you wouldn't
blame yourself, so you wouldn't feel bad. There wasn't anything you could say to change my mind. I didn't want you to
save me. I just wanted you to know.

MAMA:   Stay with me just a little longer. Just a few more years. I
don't have that many more to go, Jessie. And as soon as I'm
dead, you can do whatever you want. Maybe with me gone,

you'll have all the quiet you want, right here in the house. And maybe one day you'll put in some begonias up the walk and get just the right rain for them all summer. And Ricky will be married by then and he'll bring your grandbabies over and you can sneak them a piece of candy when their daddy's not looking and then be real glad when they've gone home and left you to your quiet again.

JESSIE: Don't you see, Mama, everything I do winds up like this. How could I think you would understand? How could I think you would want a manicure? We could hold hands for an hour and then I could go shoot myself? I'm sorry about tonight, Mama, but it's exactly why I'm doing it.

MAMA: If you've got the guts to kill yourself, Jessie, you've got the guts to stay alive.

JESSIE: I know that. So it's really just a matter of where I'd rather be.

MAMA: Look, maybe I can't think of what you should do, but that doesn't mean there isn't something that would help. *You* find it. *You* think of it. You can keep trying. You can get brave and try some more. You don't have to give up!

JESSIE: I'm *not* giving up! This *is* the other thing I'm trying. And I'm sure there are some other things that might work, but *might* work isn't good enough anymore. I need something that *will* work. *This* will work. That's why I picked it.

MAMA: But something might happen. Something that could change everything. Who knows what it might be, but it might be worth waiting for! (*Jessie doesn't respond.*) Try it for two more weeks. We could have more talks like tonight.

JESSIE: No, Mama.

MAMA: I'll pay more attention to you. Tell the truth when you ask me. Let you have your say.

JESSIE: No, Mama! We wouldn't have more talks like tonight, because it's this next part that's made this last part so good, Mama. No, Mama. *This* is how I have my say. This is how I say what I thought about it *all* and I say no. To Dawson and Loretta and the Red Chinese and epilepsy and Ricky and Cecil and you. And me. And hope. I say no! (*Then going to Mama on the sofa.*) Just let me go easy, Mama.

MAMA: How can I let you go?

JESSIE:  You can because you have to. It's what you've always done.

MAMA:  You are my child!

JESSIE:  I am what became of your child. (*Mama cannot answer.*) I found an old baby picture of me. And it was somebody else, not me. It was somebody pink and fat who never heard of sick or lonely, somebody who cried and got fed, and reached up and got held and kicked but didn't hurt anybody, and slept whenever she wanted to, just by closing her eyes. Somebody who mainly just laid there and laughed at the colors waving around over her head and chewed on a polka-dot whale and woke up knowing some new trick nearly every day, and rolled over and drooled on the sheet and felt your hand pulling my quilt back up over me. That's who I started out and this is who is left. (*There is no self-pity here.*) That's what this is about. It's somebody I lost, all right, it's my own self. Who I never was. Or who I tried to be and never got there. Somebody I waited for who never came. And never will. So, see, it doesn't much matter what else happens in the world or in this house, even. I'm what was worth waiting for and I didn't make it. Me . . . who might have made a difference to me . . . I'm not going to show up, so there's no reason to stay, except to keep you company . . . not reason enough because I'm not . . . very good company. (*Pause.*) Am I?

MAMA (*knowing she must tell the truth*):  No. And neither am I.

JESSIE:  I had this strange little thought, well, maybe it's not so strange. Anyway, after Christmas, after I decided to do this, I would wonder, sometimes, what might keep me here, what might be worth staying for, and you know what it was? It was maybe if there was something I really liked, like maybe if I really liked rice pudding or cornflakes for breakfast or something, that might be enough.

MAMA:  Rice pudding is good.

JESSIE:  Not to me.

MAMA:  And you're not afraid?

JESSIE:  Afraid of what?

MAMA:  I'm afraid of it, for me, I mean. When my time comes. I know it's coming, but . . .

JESSIE:  You don't know when. Like in a scary movie.

MAMA:   Yeah, sneaking up on me like some killer on the loose, hiding out in the back yard just waiting for me to have my hands full someday and how am I supposed to protect myself anyhow when I don't know what he looks like and I don't know how he sounds coming up behind me like that or if it will hurt or take very long or what I don't get done before it happens.

JESSIE:   You've got plenty of time left.

MAMA:   I forget what for, right now.

JESSIE:   For whatever happens, I don't know. For the rest of your life. For Agnes burning down one more house or Dawson losing his hair or . . .

MAMA (*quickly*):   Jessie, I can't just sit here and say O.K., kill yourself if you want to.

JESSIE:   Sure you can. You just did. Say it again.

MAMA (*really startled*):   Jessie! (*Quiet horror.*) How dare you! (*Furious.*) How dare you! You think you can just leave whenever you want, like you're watching television here? No, you can't, Jessie. You make me feel like a fool for being alive, child, and you are so wrong! I like it here, and I will stay here until they make me go, until they drag me screaming and I mean screeching into my grave, and you're real smart to get away before then because, I mean, honey, you've never heard noise like that in your life. (*Jessie turns away.*) Who am I talking to? You're gone already, aren't you? I'm looking right through you! I can't stop you because you're already gone! I guess you think they'll all have to talk about you now! I guess you think this will really confuse them. Oh yes, ever since Christmas you've been laughing to yourself and thinking, "Boy, are they all in for a surprise." Well, nobody's going to be a bit surprised, sweetheart. This is just like you. Do it the hard way, that's my girl, all right. (*Jessie gets up and goes into the kitchen, but Mama follows her.*) You know who they're going to feel sorry for? Me! How about that! Not you, me! They're going to be *ashamed* of you. Yes. *Ashamed!* If somebody asks Dawson about it, he'll change the subject as fast as he can. He'll talk about how much he has to pay to park his car these days.

JESSIE:   Leave me alone.

MAMA:   It's the truth!

JESSIE:   I should've just left you a note!

MAMA (*screaming*):   Yes! (*Then suddenly understanding what she has said, nearly paralyzed by the thought of it, she turns slowly to face Jessie, nearly whispering.*) No. No. I . . . might not have thought of all the things you've said.

JESSIE:   It's O.K., Mama.

*Mama is nearly unconscious from the emotional devastation of these last few moments. She sits down at the kitchen table, hurt and angry and desperately afraid. But she looks almost numb. She is so far beyond what is known as pain that she is virtually unreachable and Jessie knows this, and talks quietly, watching for signs of recovery.*

JESSIE (*washes her hands in the sink*):   I remember you liked that preacher who did Daddy's, so if you want to ask him to do the service, that's O.K. with me.

MAMA (*not an answer, just a word*):   What.

JESSIE (*putting on hand lotion as she talks*):   And pick some songs you like or let Agnes pick, she'll know exactly which ones. Oh, and I had your dress cleaned that you wore to Daddy's. You looked real good in that.

MAMA:   I don't remember, hon.

JESSIE:   And it won't be so bad once your friends start coming to the funeral home. You'll probably see people you haven't seen for years, but I thought about what you should say to get you over that nervous part when they first come in.

MAMA (*simply repeating*):   Come in.

JESSIE:   Take them up to see their flowers, they'd like that. And when they say, "I'm so sorry, Thelma," you just say, "I appreciate your coming, Connie." And then ask how their garden was this summer or what they're doing for Thanksgiving or how their children . . .

MAMA:   I don't think I should ask about their children. I'll talk about what they have on, that's always good. And I'll have some crochet work with me.

JESSIE:   And Agnes will be there, so you might not have to talk at all.

MAMA:   Maybe if Connie Richards does come, I can get her to tell me where she gets that Irish yarn, she calls it. I know it doesn't come from Ireland. I think it just comes with a green wrapper.

JESSIE:   And be sure to invite enough people home afterward so you get enough food to feed them all and have some left for you. But don't let anybody take anything home, especially Loretta.

MAMA:   Loretta will get all the food set up, honey. It's only fair to let her have some macaroni or something.

JESSIE:   No, Mama. You have to be more selfish from now on. (*Sitting at the table with Mama.*) Now, somebody's bound to ask you why I did it and you just say you don't know. That you loved me and you know I loved you and we just sat around tonight like every other night of our lives, and then I came over and kissed you and said, "'Night, Mother," and you heard me close my bedroom door and the next thing you heard was the shot. And whatever reasons I had, well, you guess I just took them with me.

MAMA (*quietly*):   It was something personal.

JESSIE:   Good. That's good, Mama.

MAMA:   That's what I'll say, then.

JESSIE:   Personal. Yeah.

MAMA:   Is that what I tell Dawson and Loretta, too? We sat around, you kissed me, "'Night, Mother"? They'll want to know more, Jessie. They won't believe it.

JESSIE:   Well, then, tell them what we did. I filled up the candy jars. I cleaned out the refrigerator. We made some hot chocolate and put the cover back on the sofa. You had no idea. All right? I really think it's better that way. If they know we talked about it, they really won't understand how you let me go.

MAMA:   I guess not.

JESSIE:   It's private. Tonight is private, yours and mine, and I don't want anybody else to have any of it.

MAMA:   O.K., then.

JESSIE (*standing behind Mama now, holding her shoulders*):   Now, when you hear the shot, I don't want you to come in. First of all, you won't be able to get in by yourself, but I don't want you trying. Call Dawson, then call the police, and then call Agnes. And then you'll need something to do till somebody gets here, so wash the hot-chocolate pan. You wash that pan till you hear the doorbell ring and I don't care if it's an hour, you keep washing that pan.

MAMA:   I'll make my calls and then I'll just sit. I won't need something to do. What will the police say?

JESSIE:   They'll do that gunpowder test, I guess, and ask you what happened, and by that time, the ambulance will be here and they'll come in and get me and you know how that goes. You stay out here with Dawson and Loretta. You keep Dawson out here. I want the police in the room first, not Dawson, O.K.?

MAMA:   What if Dawson and Loretta want me to go home with them?

JESSIE *(returning to the living room)*:   That's up to you.

MAMA:   I think I'll stay here. All they've got is Sanka.

JESSIE:   Maybe Agnes could come stay with you for a few days.

MAMA *(standing up, looking into the living room)*:   I'd rather be by myself, I think. *(Walking toward the box Jessie brought in earlier.)* You want me to give people those things?

JESSIE *(they sit down on the sofa, Jessie holding the box on her lap)*: I want Loretta to have my little calculator. Dawson bought it for himself, you know, but then he saw one he liked better and he couldn't bring both of them home with Loretta counting every penny the way she does, so he gave the first one to me. Be funny for her to have it now, don't you think? And all my house slippers are in a sack for her in my closet. Tell her I know they'll fit and I've never worn any of them, and make sure Dawson hears you tell her that. I'm glad he loves Loretta so much, but I wish he knew not everybody has her size feet.

MAMA *(taking the calculator)*:   O.K.

JESSIE *(reaching into the box again)*:   This letter is for Dawson, but it's mostly about you, so read it if you want. There's a list of presents for you for at least twenty more Christmases and birthdays, so if you want anything special you better add it to this list before you give it to him. Or if you want to be surprised, just don't read that page. This Christmas, you're getting mostly stuff for the house, like a new rug in your bathroom and needlework, but next Christmas, you're really going to cost him next Christmas. I think you'll like it a lot and you'd never think of it.

MAMA:   And you think he'll go for it?

JESSIE:   I think he'll feel like a real jerk if he doesn't. Me telling him to, like this and all. Now, this number's where you call Cecil. I called it last week and he answered, so I know he still lives there.

MAMA:   What do you want me to tell him?

JESSIE:   Tell him we talked about him and I only had good things to say about him, but mainly tell him to find Ricky and tell him what I did, and tell Ricky you have something for him, out here, from me, and to come get it. (*Pulls a sack out of the box.*)

MAMA (*the sack feels empty*):   What is it?

JESSIE (*taking it off*):   My watch. (*Putting it in the sack and taking a ribbon out of the sack to tie around the top of it.*)

MAMA:   He'll sell it!

JESSIE:   That's the idea. I appreciate him not stealing it already. I'd like to buy him a good meal.

MAMA:   He'll buy dope with it!

JESSIE:   Well, then, I hope he gets some good dope with it, Mama. And the rest of this is for you. (*Handing Mama the box now. Mama picks up the things and looks at them.*)

MAMA (*surprised and pleased*):   When did you do all this? During my naps, I guess.

JESSIE:   I guess. I tried to be quiet about it. (*As Mama is puzzled by the presents.*) Those are just little presents. For whenever you need one. They're not bought presents, just things I thought you might like to look at, pictures or things you think you've lost. Things you didn't know you had, even. You'll see.

MAMA:   I'm not sure I want them. They'll make me think of you.

JESSIE:   No they won't. They're just things, like a free tube of toothpaste I found hanging on the door one day.

MAMA:   Oh. All right, then.

JESSIE:   Well, maybe there's one nice present in there somewhere. It's Granny's ring she gave me and I thought you might like to have it, but I didn't think you'd wear it if I gave it to you right now.

MAMA (*taking the box to a table nearby*):   No. Probably not. (*turning back to face her.*) I'm ready for my manicure, I guess. Want me to wash my hands again?

JESSIE (*standing up*):   It's time for me to go, Mama.

MAMA (*starting for her*):   No, Jessie, you've got all night!

JESSIE (*as Mama grabs her*):   No, Mama.

MAMA:  It's not even ten o'clock.

JESSIE *(very calm)*:  Let me go, Mama.

MAMA:  I can't. You can't go. You can't do this. You didn't say it would be so soon, Jessie. I'm scared. I love you.

JESSIE *(takes her hands away)*:  Let go of me, Mama. I've said everything I had to say.

MAMA *(standing still a minute)*:  You said you wanted to do my nails.

JESSIE *(taking a small step backward)*:  I can't. It's too late.

MAMA:  It's not too late!

JESSIE:  I don't want you to wake Dawson and Loretta when you call. I want them to still be up and dressed so they can get right over.

MAMA *(as Jessie backs up, Mama moves in on her, but carefully)*:  They wake up fast, Jessie, if they have to. They don't matter here, Jessie. You do. I do. We're not through yet. We've got a lot of things to take care of here. I don't know where my prescriptions are and you didn't tell me what to tell Dr. Davis when he calls or how much you want me to tell Ricky or who I call to rake the leaves or . . .

JESSIE:  Don't try and stop me, Mama, you can't do it.

MAMA *(grabbing her again, this time hard)*:  I can too! I'll stand in front of this hall and you can't get past me. *(They struggle.)* You'll have to knock me down to get away from me, Jessie. I'm not about to let you . . .

*Mama struggles with Jessie at the door and in the struggle Jessie gets away from her and——*

JESSIE *(almost a whisper)*:  'Night, Mother. *(She vanishes into her bedroom and we hear the door lock just as Mama gets to it.)*

MAMA *(screams)*:  Jessie! *(Pounding on the door.)* Jessie, you let me in there. Don't you do this, Jessie. I'm not going to stop screaming until you open this door, Jessie. Jessie! Jessie! What if I don't do any of the things you told me to do! I'll tell Cecil what a miserable man he was to make you feel the way he did and I'll give Ricky's watch to Dawson if I feel like it and the only way you can make sure I do what you want is you come out here and make me, Jessie! *(Pounding again.)* Jessie!

Stop this! I didn't know! I was here with you all the time. How could I know you were so alone?

*And Mama stops for a moment, breathless and frantic, putting her ear to the door, and when she doesn't hear anything, she stands up straight again and screams once more.*

Jessie! Please!

*And we hear the shot, and it sounds like an answer, it sounds like No.*
*Mama collapses against the door, tears streaming down her face, but not screaming anymore. In shock now.*

Jessie, Jessie, child . . . Forgive me. (*Pause.*) I thought you were mine.

*And she leaves the door and makes her way through the living room, around the furniture, as though she didn't know where it was, not knowing what to do. Finally, she goes to the stove in the kitchen and picks up the hot-chocolate pan and carries it with her to the telephone, and holds on to it while she dials the number. She looks down at the pan, holding it tight like her life depended on it. She hears Loretta answer.*

MAMA:   Loretta, let me talk to Dawson, honey.

# WRITING ABOUT LITERATURE

The premise of this book is that people make literature happen, that a story, poem, or play, comes alive through the imaginative collaboration of the author and his or her audience. A literary audience helps to shape the meaning and value of a work. In the genre introductions, we concentrated on reading as an active response to literature. Although reading is primary and indispensable, it is often only the beginning of a series of different kinds of responses, each of which enriches the quality of human thought and experience.

There are four basic ways to respond to literature. Two of them, reading and reflection, are private activities in which we keep our ideas and feelings to ourselves. Two other ways to respond to literature are social, for they involve sharing: one is by talking about literature, the other by writing about it. Both are self-expressive, and both can contribute greatly to the vitality and value of stories, poems, and plays. Writing about literature has two chief advantages over conversation, however: writing allows us to present ideas more clearly and sequentially than we can do when we talk about them, and it establishes a record of our thinking that we can refer to later on.

Writing as a way of responding to literature takes many forms. One of these uses the literary work as an occasion to explore personal ideas and feelings beyond the work itself. So Louis Simpson writes "Walt Whitman at Bear Mountain," which expresses his view of the outcome of Whitman's vision of America. Or someone else might write an essay about the connections between Young Goodman Brown and a neighbor, or himself or herself. A less personal and more intellectual variation of this approach relates a work to an author's life and times, or sees it as an instance of a political, moral, or artistic philosophy or condition. In all these examples, the literary subject is used instrumentally, as a means toward some other end.

A second way to respond focuses primarily on the work of literature itself, with the purpose of clarifying its vision and methods. Of the many ways to achieve this purpose, analysis of one work, or comparison and contrast with another, are especially useful approaches. Using comparison and contrast, you can clarify the vision and methods of two or more works by concentrating on their similarities and differences in relation to one idea: for example, the effects of new experience in Eudora Welty's "A Worn Path" and Toni Cade Bambara's "The Lesson," or the struggles between sons and mothers in Shakespeare's *Hamlet* and Ed Bullins's *A Son, Come Home*, or the significance of decision and action in T. S. Eliot's "The Love Song of J. Alfred Prufrock" and Robert Frost's "The Road Not Taken."

You can also compare and contrast matters of literary form, such as characterization, plot, point of view, and style, to illuminate the insights and artistry of literary works.

Of course, as a writer about literature, you may choose to concentrate exclusively on one work with the purpose of clarifying it. This common approach has the advantage of the close-up in photography and, if carried out with a clear focus, will bring out connections among many seemingly unrelated details, and establish the wholeness of a particular story, poem, or play. The example below shows one way to use this approach.

Whatever approach you decide on, however, writing about literature is a process involving prewriting, writing, revising, and rewriting.

For you as a writer, *prewriting* involves the steps successful writers have found helpful: reading, thinking, note-taking, and making preliminary decisions about subject, theme, and structure. Before writing a first draft, you should make lists of ideas and take notes from the text. Next, you should arrange these items logically. At this point, many writers construct a formal outline that divides a subject into parts, and breaks down each part into interrelated smaller parts. Whether you develop a plan from lists and notes, or use a formal outline, the prewriting stage is critical: it lets you gauge when the main idea is clear enough for you to begin writing a first draft, and it identifies the sections that need strengthening. For many people, prewriting is the stage when a main idea, thesis, or theme "clicks."

Suppose you have read "Young Goodman Brown" and are

asked to write an essay of about five pages. Scope and focus of your *subject* are crucial to success. You will guarantee yourself anguish if you write about Nathaniel Hawthorne's life and works, or even about the story as a whole. An entire book would be needed for the first, an essay of at least twenty pages for the second. On the other hand, if you limit your subject to a particular part or element of the story—perhaps a character or a technique of characterization, the role of the narrator, the setting of the story, the use of symbolism, or distinctive traits of style—you will have a good chance at success.

Suppose you choose the setting (the time, place, and atmosphere) of Hawthorne's story as your subject. Your next major task is to establish a *main idea, thesis,* or *theme.* To prove productive, a main idea should be supportable by examples and reasons, be honestly yours, and matter to you. An effective main idea, like a subject, must have manageable scope and focus. With the story's setting as your general subject, you need to ask yourself some hard questions. Why does setting seem important to you? Suppose your answer is that "setting influences the conduct and reputation of the main character." You must also ask yourself whether this idea is clear, supportable by evidence, and small enough to cover in a short paper.

You are now well on your way. You have trimmed down a general subject, "the setting of 'Young Goodman Brown,'" to a specific subject, "the influence of setting in 'Young Goodman Brown.'" You have also sharpened a general main idea, "setting is important in the story," into the specific, workable main idea, "setting influences the main character's behavior."

Because your thesis is clear, your *purpose* is now clear, too: you want to convince your readers that setting does, in fact, influence Goodman Brown's behavior. The rest of your work flows from this thesis and purpose. In order to convince other people that your idea about the setting has validity, you need to offer reasons that relate to each other and support the main idea of your paper. Now you go back to the notes you took in the prewriting stage, when you were looking for a subject, and check off ideas and quotations that relate to the influence of setting on Goodman Brown's behavior. After grouping these together and adding new ones that occur to you, you separate the leading ideas from the supporting ones.

Now suppose that you have come up with two strong ideas, and discovered that the rest are supporting evidence for these. Before outlining your argument, you will need to remember that *you* are the "speaker" of the essay, which means that you are observing the action from a particular perspective or point of view, just as storytellers, poets, and playwrights do. Because what Brown did on the night he ventured into the forest was the critical turning point in his life, you have a natural point of demarcation. His actions might fall into three categories, then: his behavior before, during, and after his night journey.

Having categorized your details and insights under each of these headings, you are ready to consider different options for your sequence. As one option, you may choose, for instance, to write your first draft in the conventional order of before, during, and after the night. Or, as a second option, you may prefer to follow the narrator's example by beginning with the night, bringing out details of Brown's past during the night's experience, and concluding with the aftermath, Brown's decline and death. Or, as a third option, you may decide to begin with the ending of the story, Brown's death, since the narrator himself is actually looking back on Brown's life. Suppose you choose the third option. Your ideas, when grouped, will look like this:

Thesis:   Setting influences Goodman Brown's behavior throughout the story.

I.   Setting influences Brown's behavior after his night journey.

II.   Setting influences his behavior before his night journey.

III.   Setting influences his behavior during his night journey.

Conclusion:   Setting influences Young Goodman Brown's behavior throughout the story.

*Writing,* your next step, should go fairly easily now, because you have a structure to follow. After introducing the story briefly and stating your main idea or thesis, you assert your first point and back it up with the evidence you have found to support it. Then you move on to the second and third points and do the same thing. In your conclusion, you restate your main idea in a stronger way, since now you have concrete evidence to rely on as you discuss the importance of the setting to the entire story.

When you have completed your first draft, you are ready for *revising and rewriting,* the editing stage of your work. To give your work the attention it deserves and get the most out of this stage, you should be very tough on yourself. After you read the first draft, correct errors, and expand or tighten where necessary, you may want to put the essay aside for a few days to gain the critical distance necessary for more objective evaluation. After you have returned to the draft and made further changes, you are ready to write and polish the second draft. After careful review of the second draft for clarity, usage, and mechanics, you may want to rewrite a third, perhaps even fourth, time until you are satisfied that you have really done your best.

But suppose that you have done your best and still want to do better. Ask questions. Try again. Writing is an ongoing creative venture of great value. By making new connections among ideas, it adds knowledge to the world. By sharing these new ideas with other people, writing strengthens the bonds of human understanding. Walt Whitman's "A Noiseless Patient Spider," our constant guide through this journey together, explores the challenge and value of the creative struggle as a search for relationships in a world in which it is easy to feel isolated yet surrounded. But just as the spider seeks to make connections, so the speaker recognizes that his inner self, his imagination, must keep on reaching out—

> Till the bridge you will need be formed, till the ductile anchor
>    hold,
> Till the gossamer thread you fling catch somewhere, O my soul.

# GLOSSARY OF
# LITERARY TERMS

**Abstract language:** Any language that employs intangible, nonspecific concepts. *Love, beauty,* and *truth* are abstractions. Abstract language is the opposite of concrete language.

**Absurdism:** A twentieth-century literary movement emphasizing the irrational elements in ordinary experience. The theater of the absurd is a type of drama associated with this movement. *Example:* Eugène Ionesco's *The Lesson.*

**Accent:** Stress or vocal emphasis in poetic rhythm. *Example:* In the word *accent,* the stress or accent falls on the first syllable.

**Allegory:** A narrative in which persons, objects, setting, or events represent general concepts, moral qualities, or other abstractions. Edmund Spenser's "The Faerie Queene" and John Bunyan's "Pilgrim's Progress" are notable complete allegories. Allegorical elements may be found in many stories, poems, and plays, however. Certain details of plot and character in Nathaniel Hawthorne's "Young Goodman Brown" suggest allegory to many readers.

**Alliteration:** The repetition of initial consonant sounds. *Example:*

> Five *m*iles *m*eandering with a *m*azy *m*otion.
> *Samuel Taylor Coleridge, "Kubla Khan"*

**Allusion:** A reference to other literature or to historical events. Louis Simpson's "Walt Whitman at Bear Mountain" and Allen Ginsberg's "A Supermarket in California" allude to Walt Whitman to comment on American vision and values.

**Ambiguity:** A condition of language that implies several meanings at once. In William Blake's poem "London," for example, the word *charter'd* modifies both the street and the river Thames. *Charter'd* may mean legally granted or deeded, or it may mean bought and sold. In the context of the poem, *charter'd* is ambiguous. Both its meanings pertain simultaneously, intensifying Blake's ironic critique of the quality of life in eighteenth-century London.

**Anapest/anapestic foot:** A common poetic foot of three syllables, the third of which is stressed. Because the unstressed syllables are followed by a stressed syllable, the anapest is called an ascending, or rising, foot. *Examples:*

| – – / | – – / | – – / |
|---|---|---|
| Jo-li-et | Mar-ti-nique | Ten-nes-see |

**Apostrophe:** A figure of speech in which absent, inanimate, or abstract things are addressed as though alive and present. *Example:*

> Western wind, when will thou blow,
> The small rain down can rain?
>
> Anonymous, **"Western Wind"**

**Approximate (slant) rhyme:** A type of rhyme in which the vowels and consonants of the rhyming words are similar, but not identical. *Example:*

> I heard a Fly buzz—when I died—
> The Stillness in the *Room*
> Was like the Stillness in the Air—
> Between the Heaves of *Storm*—
>
> Emily Dickinson,
> **"I heard a Fly buzz—when I died"**

**Ascending (rising) foot:** A poetic foot that begins with an unstressed syllable (or syllables) and concludes with a stressed syllable. Iambs and anapests are ascending, or rising, feet. *Examples:*

| – / | – – / |
|---|---|
| New York | Mar-ti-nique |

**Aside:** In drama, a brief remark that a character speaks directly to the audience. Asides are not heard by other characters. A small relative of the soliloquy, the aside enables Shakespeare to reveal Hamlet's thoughts as he converses with his hated uncle, Claudius (1.2.65): "A little more than kin, and less than kind!"

**Assonance:** The repetition of vowel sounds in words in which consonant sounds differ. *Example:*

> Thou still unravished bride of quietness,
> Thou foster child of silence and slow time,
> John Keats, **"Ode on a Grecian Urn"**

**Ballad:** A narrative poem originating in an oral folk tradition or, as a literary ballad, written in the manner of a folk ballad. Typical characteristics of ballads are reportorial style and refrains. *Examples:* "Western Wind" and "Edward."

**Ballad stanza:** A stanzaic pattern common to early folk ballads that employs iambic tetrameter in quatrains with an *abab* or *abcb* rhyme scheme. *Example:* "Western Wind."

**Blank verse:** Unrhymed iambic pentameter. *Example:* Hamlet's soliloquy in William Shakespeare's *Hamlet* (3.1.56–89): "To be, or not to be: that is the question."

**Cadence:** In free verse, an irregular rhythmic pattern created by the phrasing of ordinary speech. *Example:*

> Can your foreigner's nose / smell mullets /
> roasting in a glaze / of brown bean paste /
> and sprinkled with novas / of sea salt? //
> *Garrett Kaoru Hongo,* **"Who among You**
> **Knows the Essence of Garlic?"**

Some readers might find separate cadences in "in a glaze" and "with novas."

**Caesura:** A pause within a poetic line usually accomplished by punctuation or syntax. *Example:*

> So long as men can breathe, // or eyes can see,
> So long lives this, // and this gives life to thee.
> *William Shakespeare,* **Sonnet 18**

**Carpe diem:** A Latin phrase meaning "seize the day." *Carpe diem* poetry was common in pastoral poetry of the Renaissance, which used shepherds and shepherdesses as characters in love poems. *Examples:* Sir Walter Ralegh's "The Nymph's Reply to the Shepherd," Christopher Marlowe's "The Passionate Shepherd to His Love," John Donne's "The Bait," and Robert Herrick's "To the Virgins, to Make Much of Time."

**Catharsis:** Aristotle's word for emotional release in audiences at the conclusion of tragedies. As Aristotle said, tragedies evoke tragic emotions, most notably pity and fear. When Oedipus blinds himself in *Oedipus Rex*, the audience experiences a release of the tensions that the action has built.

**Chorus:** In drama, primarily in Greek tragedy, a group of actors speaking or chanting together, and often expressing the general society's views on the action. *Example:* Sophocles' *Oedipus Rex*. Modern scholars sometimes apply the term to a character who stands apart from the action and provides another, more general, perspective on the events. In this way, the narrator of William Faulkner's story "A Rose for Emily" could be said to be a chorus character speaking for the townspeople.

**Climax:** The moment of greatest intensity and conflict in the action of a story or play just before a reversal. *Example:* Sophocles' *Oedipus Rex,* Scene 4, the hero's interrogation of the Shepherd.

**Comedy:** A type of drama that emphasizes human foolishness rather than greatness and generally has a happy ending. *Example:* Anton Chekhov's *A Marriage Proposal.*

**Complication:** Also known as the *rising action,* the sequence of events that leads to the climax, dénouement, and resolution of dramatic or narrative action. The plague visiting Thebes, the riddle of the Sphinx, and other events leading up to Oedipus's recognition in *Oedipus Rex* are examples. The complication of Anton Chekhov's *A Marriage Proposal* is developed by the series of arguments among the suitor, his would-be fiancée, and her father regarding ownership of land.

**Conceit:** Originally meaning an idea or image, the literary conceit has come to mean a striking, elaborate, and extended analogy, metaphor, or simile. Petrarchan conceits, referring to the once-novel images employed by the Italian poet Petrarch in his love sonnets and adapted by English sonneteers and lyricists, often compare a lover's eyes to wells, for instance. See Shakespeare's parody, in Sonnet 130, of the Petrarchan conceits fashionable in his day. Metaphysical conceits are especially exaggerated, and usually formulated in an argument comparing a spiritual entity with an unconventionally related material one, as in John Donne's comparison of seduction and fishing in "The Bait."

**Concrete language:** Any language that appeals to the senses of sight, hearing, taste, smell, and touch by virtue of its physicality and specificity. *Stones, chairs,* and *hands* are concrete words. Concrete language is the opposite of abstract language.

**Concrete poetry:** Sometimes called *shaped poetry,* poetry whose visual design suggests a specific meaning. The shape of a poem may be nonobjective, as in poems whose words are organized into a nonobjective design; or the poem's shape may resemble an object of significance, as in George Herbert's "Easter Wings."

**Conflict:** Antagonism between characters, ideas, lines of action; between one character and the outside world; or between aspects of a character's nature. Thus, the introspective Hamlet experiences conflicts between his motivations for forbearance and revenge, and between his desire to live and to end his life.

**Connotation:** In language, the suggestions or associations generated by words. The antonym for connotation is denotation, or definition, which signifies literal meaning. Consider the different connotations of *hit, struck, slapped,* and *slugged.*

**Consonance:** The repetition of internal or final consonant sounds in a sequence of words whose vowel sounds differ. *Examples:*

> Rolled round in earth's diurnal course
> With rocks, and stones, and trees.
> > William Wordsworth,
> > *"A Slumber Did My Spirit Seal"*

Notice the s-consonance in "earth's" "course," and "rocks," and the z-consonance in "stones" and "trees."

**Context:** The environment surrounding a piece of literature, a character's action, or a word or words within a story, poem, or play. To say that "Young Goodman Brown" is set in Puritan New England, with its strong moral beliefs, provides cultural reasons for the hero's actions and reactions.

**Convention:** A habit, or custom, peculiar to a literary genre. The use of a chorus is conventional in classical Greek dramas such as *Oedipus Rex*; the use of soliloquies and asides is conventional in dramas of Elizabethan England.

**Couplet:** A two-line stanza, or two lines of poetry that summarize preceding lines, as in Shakespeare's sonnets or plays. *Example:*

> The play's the thing
> Wherein I'll catch the conscience of the King.
> > *"Hamlet,"* 2.2.595–596

**Dactyl/dactylic foot:** A metrical foot containing one initial stressed syllable followed by two unstressed syllables. Because the unstressed syllables follow the stressed syllable, the dactyl is called a descending, or falling, foot. *Examples:*

>  /  -  -          /  -  -
> Flo-ri-da      Is-tan-bul

**Denotation:** The literal, dictionary meaning of a word or words; thus, the opposite of connotation.

**Dénouement:** A French word meaning "unknotting" or "unravelling" often applied to plot, especially of a play. A dénouement sometimes involves a recognition or discovery, and usually includes a reversal of fortunes.

**Descending (falling) foot:** A poetic foot whose first syllable is stressed, and whose final syllable, or syllables, are unstressed. Trochees and dactyls are descending feet. *Examples:*

>  /  -            /  -  -
> Bos-ton      Mi-chi-gan

**Diction:** A writer's selection of words. A particular pattern or arrangement of words in prose sentences and paragraphs, or in poetic lines and stanzas, constitutes literary style.

**Dimeter:** A poetic line of two feet. The concluding lines of the ten stanzas in Dickey's "The Lifeguard" are dimeters. *Example:* "The moon / outside."

**Dramatic (tragic) irony:** Refers to a statement by a character expressing the opposite of what the audience knows lies ahead. The term may also refer to actions and situations. In John Millington Synge's *Riders to the Sea*, for example, it is dramatic irony that the rope Bartley uses as a bridle for the horses he is selling to support the family will probably lower his coffin into the ground.

**Dramatic monologue:** A type of poem spoken by a single person to a listener. Like the soliloquy in drama, the dramatic monologue reveals aspects of character and personality, as well as of situation and conflict. *Example:* Robert Browning's "My Last Duchess."

**Dramatic poetry:** A type of poetry that emphasizes character and conflict, normally through dialogue. *Examples:* Sophocles' *Oedipus Rex*, the ballad "Edward," William Shakespeare's *Hamlet*, and Langston Hughes's "Night Funeral in Harlem."

**End-rhyme:** A characteristic of stanzas by which the final syllables of two or more lines rhyme. *Example:*

> Two roads diverged in a yellow wood,
> And sorry I could not travel both
> And be one traveler, long I stood
> And looked down one as far as I could
> To where it bent in the undergrowth;
> *Robert Frost, **"The Road Not Taken"***

In this stanza, "wood," "stood," and "could" constitute the first (*a*) rhyme; "both" and "undergrowth," the second (*b*) rhyme.

**End-stopped line:** A poetic line whose conclusion coincides with a natural reading pause, usually at the end of a phrase or clause. The opposite of enjambment. *Example:*

> About suffering they *were never wrong,*
> The Old Masters: how well they understood
> Its human position; how it takes place
> *W. H. Auden, **"Musée des Beaux Arts"***

**Enjambment:** The continuation of a phrase beyond the end of a line of poetry. Also called a run-on line. *Example:*

> About suffering they were never wrong,
> The Old Masters: how well they *understood*
> *Its human position*; how it takes place
> W. H. Auden, *"Musée des Beaux Arts"*

**Epic:** A long narrative poem of substantial scope and elevated style, recounting the actions and fortunes of a hero and a nation or race. *Examples:* Homer's *Iliad* and *Odyssey*.

**Exact rhyme:** Sometimes called true rhyme or perfect rhyme, refers to lines whose end syllables exhibit vowel-sound duplication and consonant-sound near-duplication. *Example:*

> That's my last Duchess painted on the *wall*,
> Looking as if she were alive. I *call*
> That a piece of wonder, now . . .
> Robert Browning, *"My Last Duchess"*

**Exposition:** In drama, the presentation of background and other contextual information shedding light on the action.

**Expressionism:** A modern literary movement and style that seeks to objectify the state of mind of an author, or of characters, by exaggerating features of language, stage design and lighting, as well as by employing nonrealistic time sequences and symbolic characters. Paragraph 3 of the stage directions for Scene 1 of Tennessee Williams's *The Glass Menagerie* shows the influence of expressionism:

> The scene is memory and is therefore nonrealistic. Memory takes a lot of poetic license. It omits some details; others are exaggerated, according to the emotional value of the articles it touches, for memory is seated predominantly in the heart. The interior is therefore rather dim and poetic.

**Farce:** Sometimes called low comedy—as opposed to high comedy, a type of play with one-dimensional characters in ludicrous situations. The misunderstandings in Anton Chekhov's comedy *The Marriage Proposal* have farcical overtones.

**Figurative language:** Suggestive, rather than literal, language employing metaphor, simile, or other figures of speech. Poetry has much figurative language, but stories and plays employ it as well for specific effects. For example, in the character descriptions in *The Glass Menagerie*, Tennessee Williams uses figurative language to describe the effects of Laura's handicap:

> Stemming from this, Laura's separation increases till she is like a piece of her own glass collection, too exquisitely fragile to move from the shelf.

**Figure of speech:** A specific group of words that means something more or other than what it literally says. *Examples:* metaphor, simile, hyperbole, synecdoche.

**First-person narrator:** In a story told by an individual, the "I" who presents the characters and events. Montresor is the first-person narrator of Edgar Allan Poe's "The Cask of Amontillado." Tom in Tennessee Williams's *The Glass Menagerie* serves as a first-person narrator, a device highly unusual in drama. *See* Point of view.

**Foot (metrical foot):** In metrically regular poetry, a grouping of stressed and unstressed syllables usually occurring in one of these major patterns: iambic, trochaic, anapestic, dactylic, and spondaic. Unless a poem is written in free verse cadences, its basic unit of rhythm is the foot.

**Foreshadowing:** Words, gestures, and other actions that suggest future events or outcomes. In *Oedipus Rex*, the oracle's prophesy that Oedipus would kill his father and marry his mother foreshadows the terrible events to come.

**Free verse:** Poetry that establishes its own phrasal cadences—as opposed to poetry that follows traditional metrical patterns. Walt Whitman was an early practitioner of free verse. Much twentieth-century poetry, especially since William Carlos Williams, D. H. Lawrence, Ezra Pound, and H. D., has been written in free verse.

**Genre:** The types, kinds, or divisions of literature, such as fiction, poetry, and drama.

**Hubris:** The excessive pride that ancient Greeks considered a hero's greatest tragic flaw.

**Hyperbole:** A figure of speech employing gross overstatement or exaggeration to make a point.

**Iamb/iambic foot:** A metrical foot of two syllables, the second of which is stressed. Because the stressed syllable follows the unstressed one, the iamb is called an ascending, or rising, foot. *Examples:*

| $-$ / | $-$ / | $-$ / |
|---|---|---|
| New York | San Juan | Za-ire |

**Image:** A word or group of words evoking concrete visual, auditory, or tactile associations. *Examples:* the grandeur of God as "shook foil," and "ooze of oil / Crushed" in Gerard Manley Hopkins's "God's Grandeur," and the carriage ride from childhood to death described by Emily Dickinson in "Because I could not stop for Death."

**Incongruity:** The juxtaposition of two or more dissimilar ideas, objects, or tones. Paradoxes, hyperboles, metaphors, and similes are based on incongruity.

**Internal rhyme:** The repetition of vowel and consonant sound within lines. *Example:*

> The splendor *falls* on castle *walls*
> And snowy summits old in story;
> The long light *shakes* across the *lakes,*
> And the wild cataract leaps in glory
> *Alfred, Lord Tennyson,*
> ***"The Splendor Falls on Castle Walls"***

**Irony:** A mode of expression that intends the opposite of what it says by playing upon the different meanings of words and situations. The would-be lover's assertion in Andrew Marvell's "To His Coy Mistress" that "The grave's a fine and private place, / But none, I think, do there embrace" is an instance of verbal irony.

**Literature:** A deeply unified verbal event produced in the imagination and experienced through the collaboration of authors and readers, viewers, or listeners. Also, a collection of written works, usually imaginative, and highly valued by a culture.

**Lyric poetry:** A poetic genre, originally sung to the lyre, characterized by personal expressions of emotion. *Examples:* Elizabeth Barrett Browning's "If thou must love me, let it be for nought" and Matthew Arnold's "Dover Beach."

**Mataphor:** A figure of speech that compares two dissimilar entities directly, without using *like* or *as. Example:*

> The Sea of Faith
> Was once, too, at the full
> *Matthew Arnold,*
> ***"Dover Beach"***

The sea and faith are being compared; the sea is a metaphor for faith.

**Meter:** The recurrence in a poetic line of a regular rhythmic unit. In English, meter is usually determined by a regular pattern of stresses, or accents, within lines with a fairly common number of syllables. The most common meters in English poetry are iambic trimeter (three feet), tetrameter (four feet), and pentameter (five feet).

**Metonymy:** A figure of speech that refers to an idea, person, or object by a word or phrase naming something closely associated with it. *Example: The crown* for *king.*

**Monometer:** A poetic line of one metrical foot. The monometer is extremely rare.

**Myth:** A story believed by a culture, or cultural subgroup, purporting to explain the origins, meaning, or purposes of personal and social life, or other large questions. The myth of Oedipus and the Sphinx is the foundation of Sophocles' *Oedipus Rex.*

**Narrative poetry:** Poetry that tells a story or relates events. *Example:* Carolyn Forché's "The Colonel."

**Nonameter:** A poetic line of nine metrical feet. The nonameter is very rare.

**Objective observer:** A narrator who presents characters and reports events in a matter-of-fact, documentary style, without insight into the private thoughts and feelings of the characters.

**Octameter:** A poetic line of eight metrical feet. The octameter is rare.

**Octave:** An eight-line stanza, or rhymed unit within an Italian (Petrarchan) sonnet. *Examples:* the first stanza of William Butler Yeats's "The Second Coming" and the first eight lines of John Milton's sonnet "When I consider how my light is spent."

**Ode:** A lengthy lyric poem of praise. *Examples:* Percy Bysshe Shelley's "Ode to the West Wind" and John Keats's "Ode on a Grecian Urn" and "To Autumn."

**Off-rhyme (approximate or slant rhyme):** As opposed to exact rhyme, the near-agreement of vowels in rhyming words. *See* Approximate rhyme.

**Omniscient narrator:** A narrator who seems to know everything about events and characters, including private thoughts. Tolstoy's story "How Much Land Does a Man Need?" is told by an omniscient narrator.

**Onomatopoeia:** A use of words in which sounds suggest sense. Examples: *buzz, hiss, murmur.*

**Ottava rima:** An eight-line stanza, or octave, rhyming *abababcc. Example:* William Butler Yeats's "Sailing to Byzantium."

**Oxymoron:** A paradox containing two terms that in ordinary usage are contraries. *Examples: wise fool, deafening silence.*

**Paradox:** A statement that seems absurd or contradictory, but which conveys meaning. *Examples:*

> Take me to you, imprison me, for I,
> *Except you enthral me, never shall be free,*
> *Nor ever chaste, except you ravish me.*
> John Donne,
> ***"Batter my heart, three-person'd God"***

**Parody:** Broad satire achieved through exaggerated imitation of a character, an action, a style, or an entire literary work. Shakespeare's Sonnet 130 parodies excessive Petrarchan conceits.

**Pentameter:** A poetic line of five metrical feet. *Example:*

> With how / sad steps, / Oh Moon, / thou climb'st / the skies!
>
> *Sir Philip Sidney,* ***"With how sad steps . . ."***

**Persona:** The speaker or narrator, as distinguished from the author, of a literary work. The persona is the role or mask writers take on to achieve needed distance from, and control over, their material. Prufrock is the persona chosen by T. S. Eliot in "The Love Song of J. Alfred Prufrock."

**Personification:** The attribution of human qualities to an inanimate object or idea. *Example:*

> Because I could not stop for Death—
> He kindly stopped for me—
> The Carriage held but just Ourselves—
> And Immortality.
>
> *Emily Dickinson,*<br>***"Because I could not stop for Death"***

**Plot:** The sequence of events in a narrative or dramatic work, usually in a cause-and-effect relationship.

**Point of view:** The perspective, thus the degree of involvement, of the narrator, usually in fiction. The first-person point of view uses *I*, the second-person *you* (rare), and the third-person *he, she, it,* and *they.* Point of view may also be said to be limited or omniscient, subjective or objective, depending upon a writer's purposes and strategies. When considering a story's point of view, it is helpful to determine whether the narrator is reporting concurrently or retrospectively, is observing or participating in the action, and whether he or she is emotionally involved. Edgar Allan Poe's "The Cask of Amontillado" and James Joyce's "Araby" are told in the first-person subjective and limited point of view, since their narrators are very much involved in the action. William Faulkner's "A Rose for Emily" is told in the first-person objective point of view, since the "I" telling the story is relatively removed. Eudora Welty's "A Worn Path" is written in the third-person objective point of view, since the narrator observes what the character is doing, thinking, and feeling, but seems emotionally distant. Ralph Ellison's "King of the Bingo Game" is written in the third-person subjective point of view, since its "outside" narrator seems to know and feel the character's actions and reactions as intimately as if they were his own.

**Prosody:** The analysis of poetic sound and rhythm. Prosody has no relation to prose.

**Protagonist:** The main character in a literary work with a complete or suggested plot. Rose is the protagonist in "Miss Rosie," Brown in "Young Goodman Brown," and Nora in *A Doll's House.*

**Quatrain:** A four-line stanza. William Blake's "London" consists of four quatrains.

**Quintain:** A five-line stanza. The first and third stanzas of Robert Hayden's "Those Winter Sundays" are quintains; the second is a quatrain.

**Refrain:** In poetry, a word, phrase, or clause repeated at regular intervals for emphasis. In Alfred, Lord Tennyson's "The Splendor Falls," the refrain "Blow, bugle, blow, set the wild echoes flying / Blow, bugle; answer, echoes, dying, dying, dying!" is repeated with some variation at the end of each stanza.

**Rhyme:** The repetition of vowel or consonant sounds internally or finally in a line of poetry. In the first stanza of Robert Frost's "The Road Not Taken," "wood," "stood," and "could" rhyme; "both" and "undergrowth" do as well.

**Rhyme-scheme:** The predominant pattern established by end-rhymes in a stanza or poem. The rhyme-scheme of Robert Frost's "The Road Not Taken" is *abaab*.

**Rhythm:** The pattern of recurrent stresses and pauses in poems and poetic lines. The rhythm of Robert Frost's "The Road Not Taken" is iambic tetrameter.

**Run-on line:** Also known as enjambment, a line of poetry whose syntax and rhetorical meaning carry over into the following line, whether or not rhyme is employed at the end of a line. A run-on line is the opposite of an end-stopped one.

**Satire:** Literature that exposes human folly by evoking amusement, contempt, or scorn. Sir Walter Ralegh's "The Nymph's Reply to the Shepherd" is a satirical rejoinder to her aspiring lover.

**Scansion:** The process of identifying, or marking, a poem's rhythmic pattern of stressed and unstressed syllables. One common way to mark a line is to indicate a stressed syllable with a slant, an unstressed one with a dash. *Example:*

> - /   - /   - / - /
> A slumber did my spirit seal;
> - /   - /   -   /
> I had no human fears:
> —   /   - /   -   /   - /
> She seemed a thing that could not feel
> —   /   - /   -   /
> The touch of earthly years.

*William Wordsworth,*
***"A Slumber Did My Spirit Seal"***

Once the lines have been marked for their pattern of stresses, scansion provides a shorthand for indicating rhyme and meter. In each stanza, in their normal order, letters of the alphabet are applied to new end-rhymes. Numerical exponents are then placed right after and above the letters to signify the number of feet in each line. In the Wordsworth poem above, stanzas would be scanned as follows:

$$a^4 \ b^3 \ a^4 \ b^3$$

**Sestet:** A six-line stanza; or rhymed unit within a stanza, as in the Italian sonnet. All ten stanzas of James Dickey's "The Lifeguard" are sestets.

**Simile:** A verbal comparison using *like* or *as. Example:*

> What happens to a dream deferred?
>
> Does it dry up
> like a raisin in the sun?
> *Langston Hughes, "Harlem"*

**Slant rhyme (approximate or off-rhyme):** As opposed to exact rhyme, the variation of vowels in otherwise identical, or nearly identical, words. *See* Approximate rhyme.

**Soliloquy:** A speech made to oneself or to unseen listeners, out of hearing of other characters, thus a device employed to allow the audience insight into a character's private thoughts. *Example:* the initial soliloquy of *Hamlet* (1.2.129–159).

**Sonnet:** A poem of fourteen lines in one stanza, written in iambic pentameter, with an elaborate rhyme scheme. The English (Shakespearean) sonnet is a type of sonnet consisting of three quatrains and a couplet. The Petrarchan (Italian) sonnet is organized by an octave and a sestet; see John Milton's "When I consider how my light is spent."

**Spondee/spondaic foot:** In English, a rare poetic foot of two stressed syllables occurring often as a substitute foot within a line. Because no change in emphasis occurs—both syllables are stressed—the spondee is neither ascending, nor descending. *Examples:*

|  /    /  |   /    /   |   /    /  |
| Dix Hills | South Bend | Hong Kong |

Gwendolyn Brooks's "We Real Cool" contains many spondees.

**Stanza:** A group of poetic lines set off typographically as a unit. In traditional poetry, the rhyme scheme, rhythm, and meter of the first stanza usually establish a pattern that subsequent stanzas follow. In free verse poetry, the term *verse paragraph* is sometimes used instead of stanza, especially in poems that resemble prose in their visual design. *Examples:* Allen Ginsberg's "A Supermarket in California" and Carolyn Forché's "The Colonel."

**Stress (accent):** The vocal emphasis given to one syllable in relation to another. In traditional poetry, a pattern of stressed and unstressed syllables creates rhythm and meter.

**Structure:** The organizational pattern, or relation among the parts, of a piece of literature. The larger structure of a literary work is determined by its parts. Thus, the play *Hamlet* consists of five acts, the poem "Ode on a Grecian Urn" of five ten-line stanzas.

**Symbol:** A reference to a concrete image, object, character, pattern, or action whose associations evoke significant meanings beyond its literal meanings. An *archetype* or *archetypal symbol* is a symbol whose associations are said to be universal, that is, they extend beyond those of a particular society or culture. Thus, a cross, representing sacrifice and resurrection, or a dove, representing peace, are said to be archetypal symbols. Yeats's "Spiritus Mundi" and "rough beast" in "The Second Coming" are also archetypes.

**Synecdoche:** A figure of speech in which a part stands for a whole. *Example: Fifty winters passed him by,* meaning "fifty years."

**Syntax:** The grammatical structure of a sentence.

**Tercet:** A three-line stanza, as in Percy Bysshe Shelley's "Ode to the West Wind."

**Terza rima:** A poem of tercets with a specific, continous rhyme-scheme that interlaces new with established rhymes in all stanzas. Thus, the first tercet rhymes *aba,* the second *bcb,* the third *cdc,* the fourth, *ded,* and so on. *Example:* Percy Bysshe Shelley's "Ode to the West Wind."

**Tetrameter:** Any poetic line of four feet. *Example:*

> Two roads / diverged / in a yell / ow wood /
> *Robert Frost, "The Road Not Taken"*

This particular line is predominantly iambic tetrameter, with a substitute anapest in its third foot.

**Theme:** In literature generally, an idea that unites all parts of a work, or a motif that runs throughout the work. In an essay, theme is understood to mean the thesis or doctrine being argued.

**Tone:** The attitude taken by a writer toward subject matter and audience. For example, the tone of a work may be impassioned, playful, or matter-of-fact. Tone is distinct from atmosphere, which refers to the mood of a literary work.

**Tragedy:** In drama, a type of play representing serious, consequential actions that turn out disastrously for the hero. *Examples:* Sophocles' *Oedipus Rex* and William Shakespeare's *Hamlet.*

**Tragic flaw:** A weakness in a hero's character that precipitates the hero's downfall. Commonly, the weakness is an exaggeration of a positive or neutral character trait. Excessive pride, arrogance, rashness, uncontrollable anger, and paralysis of action are examples of common tragic flaws. The term is most often associated with classical Greek drama.

**Trimeter:** A poetic line of three feet. Emily Dickinson frequently alternates lines of tetrameter with lines of trimeter in her quatrains, as in

> Because / I could / not stop / for Death— / [tetrameter]
> He kind / ly stopped / for me— / [trimeter]
> The Car / riage held / but just / Our selves— / [tetrameter]
> And Im / morta / lity. // [trimeter]
> *Emily Dickinson,* **"Because I could not stop for Death"**

This form is also known as the hymn stanza.

**Trochee/trochaic foot:** A common metrical foot of two syllables, the first of which is stressed. Because the unstressed syllable follows the stressed one, the trochee is called a descending, or falling, foot. *Examples:*

$$/ \quad - \qquad / \quad -$$

King-ston    Tok-yo

**Villanelle:** A poem of nineteen lines and only two rhymes. The first line is repeated in lines 6, 12, 18; the third line is repeated in lines 9, 15, and 19. The villanelle has six stanzas, five of which have three lines, the sixth four lines. Usually the tercets rhyme *aba,* and the quatrain *abaa.* *Example:* Dylan Thomas's "Do Not Go Gentle into That Good Night."

**Voice:** A writer's characteristic manner and mode of expression, what we come to know as the unique qualities of subject, theme, style, and tone that distinguish the work of one writer from that of another.

**Acknowledgments** (*continued from p. ii*)

*Poems, 1965–1975* by Margaret Atwood. Copyright © 1976 by Margaret Atwood. Reprinted by permission of Houghton Mifflin Company. Canadian rights for "Book of Ancestors" and "Game after Supper" from *Selected Poems,* copyright © Margaret Atwood; reprinted by permission of Oxford University Press Canada.

**W. H. Auden.** "Musee des Beaux Arts" from *W. H. Auden: Collected Poems,* edited by Edward Mendelson. Copyright © 1940 and renewed in 1968 by W. H. Auden. Reprinted by permission of Random House, Inc. and Faber and Faber Ltd.

**Arcadii Averchenko.** "The Young Man Who Flew Past," from *A Treasury of Russian Literature.* Edited and translated by Bernard Guilbert Guerney. Copyright 1943, 1965 by Bernard Guilbert Guerney. Reprinted by permission of Vanguard Press, a division of Random House.

**Jimmy Santiago Baca.** "Cloudy Day" from *Immigrants in Our Own Land* by Jimmy Santiago Baca. Reprinted by permission of Louisiana State University Press. Copyright © 1979 by Jimmy Santiago Baca.

**Toni Cade Bambara.** "The Lesson" from *Gorilla, My Love* by Toni Cade Bambara. Copyright © 1972 by Toni Cade Bambara. Reprinted by permission of Random House, Inc.

**Donald Barthelme.** "The King of Jazz" from *Great Days* by Donald Barthelme. Copyright © 1977, 1979 by Donald Barthelme. Reprinted by permission of Farrar, Straus and Giroux, Inc.

**Ann Beattie.** "Tuesday Night" from *Secrets and Surprises* by Ann Beattie. Copyright © 1976, 1977, 1978 by Ann Beattie. Reprinted by permission of Random House, Inc.

**Elizabeth Bishop.** "In the Waiting Room" from *The Complete Poems, 1927–1979* by Elizabeth Bishop. Copyright © 1979, 1983 by Alice Helen Methfessel. Reprinted by permission of Farrar, Straus and Giroux, Inc.

**Robert Bly.** "For My Son, Noah, Ten Years Old" from *The Man in the Black Coat Turns.* Copyright © 1981 by Robert Bly. A Dial Press Book. Reprinted by permission of Doubleday, a division of Bantam Doubleday Dell Publishing Group, Inc.

**Gwendolyn Brooks.** "The Mother" and "We Real Cool" from *The World of Gwendolyn Brooks.* Copyright © 1959 by Gwendolyn Brooks. Reprinted by permission of Harper & Row, Publishers, Inc. and the author.

**Ed Bullins.** "A Son, Come Home" from *Five Plays by Ed Bullins,* copyright © 1969 by Ed Bullins. Reprinted by permission of Macmillan Publishing Company.

**Raymond Carver.** "The Third Thing That Killed My Father Off" from *Furious Seasons and Other Stories* by Raymond Carver. Copyright © 1977. Reprinted by permission of Capra Press.

**T. S. Eliot.** "The Love Song of J. Alfred Prufrock" from *Collected Poems, 1909–1962* by T. S. Eliot. Copyright © 1936 by Harcourt Brace Jovanovich, Inc., copyright © 1964, 1963 by T. S. Eliot. Reprinted by permission of the publisher. Canadians right to reprint granted by permission of Faber and Faber Ltd.

**Ralph Ellison.** "King of the Bingo Game." Reprinted by permission of the William Morris Agency on behalf of the author. Copyright 1944.

**James T. Farrell.** "The Benefits of American Life" from *The Short Stories of James T. Farrell.* Copyright 1937, 1964 by James T. Farrell. Reprinted by permission of the estate of James T. Farrell.

**William Faulkner.** "A Rose for Emily" from *Collected Stories of William Faulkner.* Copyright 1930, renewed 1958 by William Faulkner. Reprinted by permission of Random House, Inc.

**Carolyn Forché.** "The Colonel" from *The Country Between Us* by Carolyn Forché. Copyright © 1980 by Carolyn Forché. Reprinted by permission of Harper & Row, Publishers, Inc.

**Robert Frost.** "Birches" and "The Road Not Taken" from *The Poetry of Robert Frost*, edited by Edward Connery Lathem. Copyright © 1916, 1969 by Holt, Rinehart and Winston. Copyright © 1944 by Robert Frost. Reprinted by permission of Henry Holt and Company, Inc.

**Tess Gallagher.** "The Sky Behind It" from *Under Stars.* Copyright © 1978 by Tess Gallagher. Reprinted by permission of Graywolf Press.

**Gabriel Garcia Marquez.** "A Very Old Man with Enormous Wings" from *Collected Stories* by Gabriel Garcia Marquez, copyright © 1971. Reprinted by permission of Harper & Row, Publishers, Inc.

**Allen Ginsberg.** "A Supermarket in California" from *Collected Poems, 1947–1980* by Allen Ginsberg, copyright © 1955. Reprinted by permission of Harper & Row, Publishers, Inc.

**Susan Glaspell.** "Trifles" from *Plays* by Susan Glaspell. Copyright © 1951 by Walter H. Baker Company. "Trifles" is the sole property of the author and is fully protected under the copyright laws of the United States, the British Empire including the Dominion of Canada, and all other countries of the Copyright Union, and are subject to royalty. The play may not be acted by professionals or amateurs without formal permission in writing and the payment of royalty. All rights, including professional, amateur, stock, radio and television broadcasting, motion picture, recitation, lecturing, public reading and the rights of translation in foreign languages are reserved. All inquiries should be directed to Baker's Plays, 100 Chauncy Street, Boston, MA 02111.

**Nadine Gordimer.** "Town and Country Lovers" from *A Soldier's Embrace.* Copyright © 1975, 1977, 1980 by Nadine Gordimer. Originally published in *The New Yorker.* Reprinted by permission of Viking Penguin, a division of Penguin Books USA, Inc.

**H. D. (Hilda Doolittle).** "Oread" from *Collected Poems 1912–1944.* Copyright © 1982 by The Estate of Hilda Doolittle. Reprinted by permission of New Direction Publishing Corporation.

**Thomas Hardy.** "The Darkling Thrush" and "Neutral Tones" from *The Complete Poems of Thomas Hardy,* edited by James Gibson. Reprinted by permission of Macmillan (New York), 1978, and outside the U.S. by Macmillan Ltd. (London).

**Robert Hayden.** "Those Winter Sundays" from *Angle of Ascent: New and Selected Poems* by Robert Hayden. Copyright © 1966, 1970, 1972, 1975 by Robert Hayden. Reprinted by permission of Liveright Publishing Corporation.

**Seamus Heaney.** "Digging" from *Death of a Naturalist* and *Poems, 1965–1975* by Seamus Heaney, copyright © 1966, 1969, 1972, 1975, 1980. Reprinted by permission of Farrar, Straus and Giroux, Inc. and for Canadian rights by permission of Faber and Faber Ltd.

**Ernest Hemingway.** "A Clean, Well-Lighted Place" from *Winner Take Nothing.* Copyright © 1933 by Charles Scribner's Sons, renewal copyright © 1961 by Mary Hemingway. Reprinted with permission of Charles Scribner's Sons, an imprint of Macmillan Publishing Company.

**Garrett Kaoru Hongo.** "Who Among You Knows the Essence of Garlic?" from *Yellow Light.* Copyright © 1979 by Garrett Kaoru Hongo. Reprinted by permission of University Press of New England.

**Gerard Manley Hopkins.** "God's Grandeur" and "Pied Beauty" from *The Poems of Gerard Manley Hopkins,* 4th edition, edited by W. H. Gardner and N. H. Mackenzie. Published by arrangement with the Society of Jesus. Reprinted by permission of the Oxford University Press. These two poems by Gerard Manley Hopkins are public domain.

**Langston Hughes.** "Harlem" from *The Panther and the Lash,* by Langston Hughes, copyright © 1951. Reprinted by permission of Alfred A. Knopf. "Night Funeral in Harlem" by Langston Hughes, copyright © 1951. Copyright renewed 1979 by George Houston Bass. Reprinted by permission of Harold Ober Associates. "Thank you, M'am," copyright © 1958 by Langston Hughes, copyright renewed 1986 by George Houston Bass. Reprinted by permission of Harold Ober Associates, Inc.

**Ted Hughes.** "The Thought-Fox" from *New and Selected Poems* by Ted Hughes. Copyright © 1957 by Ted Hughes. Reprinted by permission of Harper & Row, Publishers, Inc.

**Henrik Ibsen.** "A Doll's House" translated by Otto Reinert. Copyright © 1977 by Otto Reinert. Reprinted by permission.

**David Ignatow.** "Did you know that hair is flying around in the universe?" Copyright © 1975 by David Ignatow. Reprinted from *New and Collected Poems, 1975–1985* by permission of University Press of New England.

**Eugene Ionesco.** "The Lesson" from *Four Plays* by Eugene Ionesco, translated by Donald M. Allen. Copyright © 1958 by Grove Press. Reprinted by permission of Grove Weideneld.

**Randall Jarrell.** "The Woman at the Washington Zoo" from *Selected Poems* by Randall Jarrell. Reprinted by permission of Mrs. Mary Jarrell.

**James Joyce.** "Araby" from *The Dubliners* by James Joyce. Copyright 1916 by B. W. Heubsch. Definitive text copyright © 1967 by the Estate of James Joyce. Reprinted by permission of Viking Penguin, a division of Penguin Books USA, Inc.

**Franz Kafka.** "The Judgement" from *The Metamorphosis, The Penal Colony, and Other Stories* translated by Willa and Edwin Muir. Copyright 1948 by Schocken Books, Inc. Copyright renewed 1975 by Schocken Books Inc. Reprinted by permission of Schocken Books, published by Pantheon Books, a division of Random House, Inc.

**Galway Kinnell.** "Vapor Trail Reflected in the Frog Pond" from *Body Rags* by Galway Kinnell, copyright © 1965, 1966, 1967. Reprinted by permission of Houghton Mifflin Company.

**Tommaso Landolfi.** "Wedding Night" from *Gogol's Wife and Other Stories,* translated by Raymond Rosenthal. Copyright © 1961, 1963 by New Directions Publishing Corporation. Reprinted by permission of New Directions Publishing Corporation.

**D. H. Lawrence.** "The Blind Man" from *The Complete Short Stories of D. H. Lawrence, Volume II.* Copyright 1933 by the Estate of D. H. Lawrence. Copyright renewed © 1961 by Angelo Ravagli and C. Montague Weekley, Executors of the Estate of Frieda Lawrence Ravagli. Reprinted by permission of Viking Penguin, a division of Penguin Books USA, Inc. "Kangaroo" from *The Complete Poems of D. H. Lawrence,* collected and edited by Vivian de Sola Pinto and F. Warren Roberts. Copyright © 1964, 1971 by Angelo Ravagli and C. M. Weekley, Executors of the Estate of Frieda Lawrence Ravagli. Reprinted by permission of Viking Penguin, a division of Penguin Books USA, Inc.

**Denise Levertov.** "The Dragonfly-Mother" from *Candles in Babylon.* Copyright © 1982 by Denise Levertov. Reprinted by permission of New Directions Publishing Corporation.

**Philip Levine.** "Starlight" from *Ashes* by Philip Levine, copyright © 1971, 1979. Originally published in the *Iowa Review.* Reprinted by permission of Atheneum Publishers, an imprint of Macmillan Publishing Company.

**Amy Lowell.** "The Taxi" from *The Complete Poetical Works of Amy Lowell* by Amy Lowell. Copyright © 1955 by Houghton Mifflin Company. Copyright renewed by Houghton Mifflin Co., Brinton P. Roberts, Esquire, and G. D'Andelot Belin, Esquire.

enue South, New York, NY 10016. No amateur performance of the play may be given without obtaining in advance the written permission of the Dramatists Play Service, Inc., and paying the requisite fee.

**Joyce Carol Oates.** "The Girl" from *The Goddess and Other Stories* by Joyce Carol Oates, copyright © 1966 by Joyce Carol Oates. Reprinted by permission of John Hawkins & Associates, Inc.

**Flannery O'Connor.** "A Temple of the Holy Ghost" from *A Good Man Is Hard to Find and Other Stories,* copyright © 1955 by Flannery O'Connor and renewed 1983 by Mrs. Regina O'Connor. Reprinted by permission of Harcourt Brace Jovanovich, Inc.

**Sharon Olds.** "The Victims" from *The Dead and the Living,* copyright © 1983 by Sharon Olds. Reprinted by permission of Alfred A. Knopf, Inc.

**Mary Oliver.** "Poem for My Father's Ghost" from *Twelve Moons* by Mary Oliver, copyright © 1976. Reprinted by permission of Little, Brown and Company.

**Tillie Olsen.** "I Stand Here Ironing" excerpted from the book *Tell Me a Riddle,* by Tillie Olsen, copyright 1956, 1957, 1960, 1961. Used by permission of Delacorte Press/Seymour Lawrence, a division of Bantam, Doubleday, Dell Publishing Group, Inc.

**Grace Paley.** "A Conversation with My Father" from *Enormous Changes at the Last Minute,* copyright © 1972, 1974 by Grace Paley. Reprinted by permission of Farrar, Straus and Giroux, Inc.

**Jayne Anne Philips.** "Cheers" from *Black Tickets,* copyright © 1979 by Jayne Anne Philips. Used by permission of Delacorte Press/Seymour Lawrence, a division of Bantam, Doubleday, Dell Publishing Group, Inc.

**Sylvia Plath.** "Mary's Song" by Sylvia Plath. Copyright © 1963 by Ted Hughes. "Morning Song" by Sylvia Plath. Copyright © 1961 by Ted Hughes. Reprinted from *The Collected Poems of Sylvia Plath,* edited by Ted Hughes. Permission granted by Harper & Row, Publishers, Inc., and Olwyn Hughes.

**Katherine Anne Porter.** "Rope" from *Flowering Judas and Other Stories,* copyright © 1930 and renewed in 1958 by Katherine Anne Porter. Reprinted by permission of Harcourt Brace Jovanovich, Inc.

**Ezra Pound.** "A Station in the Metro" and "The River Merchant's Wife: A Letter" from *Personae.* Copyright © 1926 by Ezra Pound. Reprinted by permission of New Directions Publishing Corporation.

**Adrienne Rich.** "Diving into the Wreck" from *The Fact of a Doorframe, Poems Selected and New, 1950–1984,* by Adrienne Rich, copyright © 1981, 1984. Copyright © 1975, 1978 by W. W. Norton & Company, Inc. Reprinted by permission of W. W. Norton & Company, Inc.

**Theodore Roethke.** "I Knew a Woman" from *The Collected Poems of Theodore Roethke.* Copyright © 1954 by Theodore Roethke. Reprinted by permission of Doubleday, a division of Bantam Doubleday Dell Publishing Group, Inc.

**Richard Wilbur.** "Love Calls Us to the Things of This World" from *Things of This World,* copyright © 1956 and renewed 1982 by Richard Wilbur. Reprinted by permission of Harcourt Brace Jovanovich, Inc.

**Tennessee Williams.** *The Glass Menagerie.* Copyright © 1945 by Tennessee Williams and Edwina D. Williams. Renewed in 1973 by Tennessee Williams. Reprinted by permission of Random House, Inc.

**William Carlos Williams.** "To Elsie" from *Collected Poems, Volume I, 1909–1939.* Copyright © 1938 by New Directions Publishing Corporation. Reprinted by permission of New Directions Publishing Corporation.

**James Wright.** "A Blessing" from *Collected Poems,* copyright © 1961. Reprinted by permission of University Press of New England.

**William Butler Yeats.** "The Second Coming" from *The Poems of W. B. Yeats: A New Edition.* Copyright © 1924 by Macmillan Publishing Company, and renewed 1952 by Bertha Georgie Yeats. "Sailing to Byzantium" from *The Poems of W. B. Yeats: A New Edition.* Copyright © 1928 by Macmillan Publishing Company, and renewed 1956 by Bertha Georgie Yeats.

**A. E. Housman.** "Loveliest of Trees, the Cherry Now" from *The Collected Poems of A. E. Housman.* Copyright © 1939, 1940, © 1965 by Holt, Rinehart and Winston. Copyright © 1967, 1968 by Robert E. Symons. Reprinted by permission of Henry Holt and Company, Inc.

# INDEX